I REMEMBER *Heaven* BEFORE EARTH

A Philosophical Memoir,
Volume One of *The Rapture Series.*

An Edgy Autobiography That Re-Explores History

The focus of my compounded stories is for everyone to examine ideologies. The premise is for readers to understand mysteries lost in time, but not forgotten by me.

Written by,
LORI "CLEOPATRA" VANDER ARK

© 2017 Lori Cleopatra Vander Ark
All rights reserved.

ISBN: 0615453074
ISBN 13: 9780615453071

of what the magnolia blossom symbolizes, opening up and spreading my petals. The secrets within me, the pages, the petals of my life blooms with truth as I reveal the camouflaged people within American society and government.

For historically correct stated origins, the late Claus Von Amsberg, the former Prince of the Netherlands is my biological father. I was adopted through Bethany Christian Services in the 1970's. My age is based upon American paperwork, in 1978 I made a decision at age eight years old to stay in America. Going back to the Netherlands would have seemed "foreign" to me. In my formative years I attended and graduated from Greenfield Elementary, and first grade at Hudsonville Christian Elementary in the old white school house. I attended and graduated from Jenison Christian Jr. High and in 1988 I graduated from Unity Christian High in Hudsonville, Michigan. Later I sold real estate in Michigan for many, many years as a licensed real estate sales agent and later real estate broker. I left the world of real estate with a perfect real estate record to begin writing books.

The big question: How did I arrive in America if I was not actually born in America? This is one memory I remember well during my childhood; Cindy Stob Vander Ark Honderd explained when I questioned a Netherlands Antilles souvenir plaque hanging on the wall and asked, "What is that?" Cindy my adopted mother explained to me she and my adopted father Chuck were detained for three weeks in a Florida jail after getting caught bringing me from the Dutch Caribbean islands to Florida during a cruise stop, during their planned and premediated vacation planned by the CIA. Premediated from the CIA staffed at a Netherlands hospital to the winter cruise to the Dutch Caribbean islands were I would be picked up and brought to America on a cruise ship. Cindy zoned out for a minute or two just staring at the wall decoration hanging on the wallpapered laundry room wall. Cindy began murmuring details of the past crimes that greatly contradict my beginning origins from Bethany Christian Services as she stared blankly ahead with empty emotions in her piercing pupils. Then Cindy remarks in her narcissistic sorrow "I did not know if we were ever going to get out of there, that was a really scary time. I thought my career and life were over and I would forever be stuck in a Florida jail cell." Cindy explained that the American Central Intelligence Agency funded the vacation. Which could account for all the CIA agents filtering in and out of my young life in Michigan and later my adulthood. Cindy also abducted "Lisa Pare" from Acapulco, Mexico in the late 1960's. Lisa grew up next to me during my very early years on Pinewood Street in Jenison, Michigan, Lamplight Estates. The Acapulco vacation was again paid and supported by the American CIA.

Lisa Pare Bankston is the biological daughter of Adolf Hitler and Ava Braun. Lisa joined and served in the U.S. Military and is a wonderful human being. A 1974 (Jenison) and 1976 (Hudsonville) photograph of Lisa and I at my birthday party in Michigan is shown on my Amazon author pages, along with a school photo of Lisa in 1982. Lisa Pare attended Jenison public schools; I attended the Dutch Christian Reformed schools. Lisa Pare Bankston still lives in West Michigan. Lisa Pare Bankston made a home on School Street in Hudsonville, Michigan near Unity Christian High.

After many years living in East Lansing/ Okemos Michigan, my husband, son and I decided to move south to Georgia in August 2014. We live forty- five minutes north of Atlanta in a mountainous neighborhood as I write volume one, third edition of my memoirs titled, I Remember Heaven Before Earth.

The very first house I lived in when arriving to Michigan was 2432 Pinewood Street in Jenison, Michigan in Lamplight Estates. My adopted father was an alcoholic and a builder by skilled trade. Cindy was a CIA sub-contractor willing to do any dirty work for the CIA as long as she was not criminally charged. I would learn that many CIA sub-contractors have economic hardships, lack of a steady income, or no income, and usually no college education. Therefore, the CIA can almost ensure a willingness for cooperation and loyalty for the many illegal and criminal CIA covert projects. Sometimes it is the money that motivates and attracts the CIA sub-contractor, but for Cindy it was not the money, it was the opportunity to commit crimes and get away with the crimes that made the jobs ideal in Cindy's mind and attitude. The safest place for a criminal, according to Cindy, is working for the CIA or FBI. Cindy was back then and may still be a serial kidnapper and killer affiliated with a huge and vast American human trafficking network funded and structured by the Central Intelligence Agency. One avenue of revenue in financial matters is the CIA and CIA sub-contractors making money in illegal ways. Such as in 1984 selling me on paper behind my back to wealthy Saudi Arabian men, clients of Warren Stob's California aerospace company buying luxury planes and girls with favorable pedigree papers. I was sold on paper behind my back in the summers of 1984 & 2001 according to Jean Stob of Grandville, Michigan recounting how they collected the money.

Michigan's Judge Miles handled all the fake/false Michigan birth certificates during the Nixon years. Ironically in Michigan on March 29, 2012 President Obama appoints Judge Mile's son to be the secret CIA group's leverage in Michigan overseeing courts and outcomes as the U.S. Attorney General for Michigan and Washington D.C., making sure the cards would always fall in their favor. The connection could explain why many people question President Obama's legitimately legal and very fake birth certificate, real or not real? In June of 2012 CIA John Brennan approached me in East Lansing, Michigan where I was living for twelve years of my adult years. During my life CIA General David Petraeus, Leon Panetta, and CIA John Brennan, FBI & attorney James Comey, and many other CIA agents would locate me and approach me both in Michigan and Georgia (USA). My memoir content explains why. I have not written every aspect of my lives lived. I have only selected a few highlights of my remarkable soul's journeys.

In 2012 I contacted the FBI about how organized crime was hustling money from allocated public school funds in Michigan and possibly elsewhere in America. I was the whistle-blower that also received an enormous amount of retaliation from the police and one school district in Michigan. The number one law firm to launder the illegally gained money is Alles Law Firm in Grand Rapids, Michigan. The estate planners create power of attorney paperwork over the set amount laundered. Once the illegal money is dispersed the Living Trust paperwork is dissolved, leaving no money trail to the well-educated attorneys at work for the dirty clients in such places but not limited to; Byron Center, Kentwood, and Grandville, Michigan.

However, the retaliation is not confined just to Michigan. In 2015 I passed the Georgia real estate exam and paid my license fee to the Georgia Real Estate Commission. Sadly in 2016 I received a denial for a Georgia real estate license. The 2016 letter from the Georgia board stated and I quote, "Your Georgia real estate salesperson license is denied because you exposed too much in Michigan."

Capturing the essence of the characters is so purposeful for a great story, the ever evolving and unfolding magnolia blossom effect in each of us.

The Rapture

Are the evangelicals and Calvinists of the common general public aware that the original Bible was not written in English? Are the Christians and non-Christians and people in general alike aware that there are possibly many word definitions per one word? On 10/24/2009 I was watching The History Channel on Satan Vs. God, that was the topic, the title of the show. I disagreed with some of the producers interpretations, just as you might as well. But one point I did agree with, a scholar who pointed out a very relevant fact that the word "rapture" is the English translation of a word written in the original text, and "rapture" was the closest, <u>not</u> <u>the</u> <u>exact</u> <u>meaning</u> from the ancient original ancient word, but rather the *closest* English translation of the ancient original word written in the Bible. The scholar being interviewed went onto say that the original word written when translated in that original language actually meant, "zap" or "zapped." I asked my husband, a dentist, and an evangelical Christian, whom believes nothing of what I write within these pages when it comes to any reference of Jesus, and his identity within these pages, I asked Ed this, "Honey, what does the word "rapture" mean, do you know?"

My husband, a dentist, an educated man by many standards, said, "Rapture means when we are taken up in the clouds to see Jesus, and the world is destroyed."

I responded back, "Rapture. What does the word "rapture" mean all by itself?"

Ed responded, "Total destruction of the world."

I asked, "How do you know this?"

Ed responded, "Bible studies, that is what the Bible teaches."

I responded back with an additional question, "The Bible teaches, or a minister teaches?'

"What? What do you mean? What are you talking about?" Ed inquired.

I responded to my husband, "According to The History Channel on T.V., a scholar stated that the word "rapture" actually means, "zap" or to be zapped. I am going to look up the word zap from The American Century Dictionary."

Ed responded aloofly, "O.k. look up the word zap, I know it will say total destruction. But go ahead look up the word."

I read aloud to my husband Ed, as I also first read the meaning of the word "zap." This is what was written in the American Century Dictionary:

Zap /zap/ Slang. V. (zapped, zap-ping) 1a. Kill; destroy; attack b. Hit hard 2. Move quickly 3. Cook or heat in a microwave oven 4. Change a television channel with a remote control --- interj. 5. Expressing the sound or impact of a bullet, ray gun, etc. or any sudden event.

I can guarantee that you will appreciate my story, no matter what race, religion, or culture you are, but you must learn English. My will and wish is for my memoirs and any manuscript to book to only be published in the English language "as the world becomes one."

I REMEMBER *Heaven* BEFORE EARTH

Written by,

Lori "Cleopatra" Vander Ark.

Table of Contents

Chapter one	Somewhere in the Deep South	1
Chapter two	A British Tutor	15
Chapter three	Magnolia Blossoms	27
Chapter four	The Magnolia Plantation	43
Chapter five	Lafayette Square	55
Chapter six	The Magnolia Tree	85
Chapter seven	Moon Jellyfish	103
Chapter eight	The Return of Bessy	149
Chapter nine	"Twelve"	179
Chapter ten	A Haze	251
Chapter eleven	Gods and Monsters	273
Chapter twelve	The Great Octopus.......*A Bully Union*	437
Chapter thirteen	Paper Dolls	507
Chapter fourteen	Tentacles	539
Chapter fifteen	Harvest Moon	617

Chapter sixteen	"Medium Coeli"................641	
Chapter seventeen	2012, The End of What?.............669	
Chapter eighteen	Moving To Georgia Again, August 2014.....717	

Reincarnation does exists, and my story, my memoir begins in the deep south, Georgia, during the outbreak of the civil war. I am a southern belle, a confederate daughter named Lilly, my father Morgan is a Rebel. My wealthy aristocratic father Morgan who loves me dearly hires a British tutor named Alan to shape and mold my mind, my father Morgan's wish is that I become a famous writer in his day. My British tutor changes my life forever, through his teachings during the 1860's, I blossom as a student of philosophy and English literature…….Tragically, it would be years later before this story could be told…..and so the secrets are finally written. The book begins and ends through the eyes of a child, as I lead you down the path of higher learning, first through the eyes of a Lilly narrating. This is my experience well told on a paper canvas. Painted for all to understand life, the stars, and planets, the matrix of God's design in our life stories as he combats evil. The grid of our natal blueprint astrology charts, the pull of God, and the pull of evil within the world. May you all become wise like the Magi in your understanding of the universe. Some of us are the teachers in life, some of us are the followers, some of us are learning, and in the end, you will all be surprised………...

   Greek; Apocalypse, "apokalypsis"; "lifting of the veil" or "revelation". A disclosure of something hidden from the majority of mankind.

Posted: Not A Through Street, when reading this book.

Author,
~Lori "Cleopatra" Vander Ark.

This story is revolutionary!

Somewhere in the Deep South
CHAPTER ONE

Like a masterpiece being painted on a canvas one stroke at a time, so opens each flower petal on a magnolia tree blossom late each spring, so luring is her scent to a passerby. In the south, I discovered my first love under a magnolia tree. I still miss Alan tutoring me on philosophy, law, astronomy and astrology, and literary art under the shade of that old magnolia tree in the south. Alan once explained to me in the sultry heat of a Georgia afternoon, as we both stared at each other, quenched of water, that despite the draught we feel physically, the mental exploration of taking a reader upon ones story that you read or that you write, is a journey nevertheless. A mental exploration felt, experienced, savored, and most of all, remembered. As if your words are forever etched upon a readers mind.

"The mental metamorphosis that a reader experiences is a far greater way to transform a person than any bloody ravishing brutal wars fought….." Alan preached on, "Lilly, real winning comes from within, that is your reward, as much as it is mine, you take the reader upon a ship, a journey, it is your mental direction of that ship that you control," Alan told me, taught me. Explaining on and on in the heat of those Georgia afternoons; literature, philosophy, this existence here on earth, as a writer you can make a journey, take us all with you, you as the ship captain"…….. I can still hear his refined English voice, his tone, "and I as your first mate, or when I read to you, you are my first mate. A reading adventure that changes us both, and where we end up, in the end, is part of my direction, or yours as the one in the nautical control room, or I in the nautical ship platform….Lilly." Alan spoke in such refined English at times I would just listen to how his syllables resonated with the buzz of those constant afternoon insects in the Georgia thicket, like before it rains…….. "The painting, take the reader into the painting, take the reader through the other side of this existence Lilly, of knowing and seeing, of simply just being. Come along Lilly, I am thirsty." Alan pointed and preached, I liked him. He had purpose, much purpose in my life……..

I was told by my father Morgan I was going to be a famous writer, that was in the 1860's. It would be another lifetime later that my famous collection of stories of all that I remember, would eventually culminate onto this paper canvas for God's astonishing reveal to all of mankind.

I do believe my soul first emerged on earth in the east during the time of the Pharaohs. My most fondest of memories stay harvested in my soul and take place in the south and therefore the story of my life in this storybook unfolds in the deep south, Georgia.

As I type my memoirs from Michigan so many years later after Alan has left my side, I do know that somewhere in the deep south there is a magnolia tree in full bloom as I write this story. It is a rare sight, even for local southerners, it is said that the bloom of a magnolia tree always comes later than most spring or summer blooms, "a late bloomer," the southern locals would comment. The wide, low branches can extend just as wide as the tree is tall, making for a perfect tree to climb when you're a young child growing up in the south. At dusk, a saucer magnolia tree can appear slightly sinister, a bit eerie, hiding the evening sunset by extending her ominous darkened tree limbs wide and tall. So real is that creepy feeling one can get while walking under a magnolia tree's heavy dark branches at night, somewhere on a grand southern estate.

As my pen touches the pages of this storybook that I am about to reveal on a paper canvas, boldly goes my mind, to a time and place before Broadway plays ever existed. Before major highways connected the states, well before modern technology took over our busy lives, lays buried in a restless grave, a sweet slice of American art that I am unearthing.

A drama far reaching…..etched in my mind's memories for years. I finally come to grips with the reality within me, in which to reveal my story as I stare out my basement windows to the cold snow piling up outside in the harsh Michigan landscape of the desolate north. It's as if I am getting buried alive in the north with each inch of accumulating snowfall that transcends on the frozen eye level tundra. I dust off the pages filed within my soul, and begin writing my untold ghost of a story of my experiences, so long ago, so many, many years ago. The rust colored Georgia soil kicking up a heap of copper dust behind a bustling team of horses in my mind…. of escaping, carrying me back to another time and place in American history, the life I once enjoyed and adored. I can feel the heat of the southern sun warming my back now. I can feel the stillness of humidity around me now, caught in the layers of trapped Confederate soldiers heavy in the thick air I breathe in, urging me to tell my story, so that they too can move on. I can hear the sound of the mandolin, the fiddle and banjo, the strings of the bass in the background, the tapping of African-Caribbean drumbeats growing stronger in my mind, faster, louder as I type my story. Taking me back in my mind, back in time to the southern sophisticated family that loved me so. My father Morgan who wanted the very best of everything for me, the black mamme we all called Bessy. And yes, Alan, my first true love, all have lived their lives in full so many years ago. I search for their long buried gravesites as I feel my soul escape, the limestone carved words probably have washed away by now, but oh, do I remember those sauntering days gone by in Georgia……….

I learned from Alan, my British born Philosophy and English literature tutor, that destiny refers to a predetermined course of events, like planet gazing astrologers believe in certain concepts of unfolding inevitable fateful events. Just like ancient Magi followed maps within the night sky during Biblical times. "The unchangeable philosophical doctrine that is manifested in the universe all around us." Spoke Alan boldly. It was a larger than life concept for me to comprehend in the 1860's at age twelve, and for those reading my memoirs for the first time, you will come to understand more about the planets and star constellations in our galaxy.

In the deep south where cotton is king and Rebel flags blow freely, fate, astrology, are rarely taught within a prominent philosophical doctrine of school subjects around these parts. Life is simple, complicated bully northerners could never rule over us, local order is how we kept our slaves from running away, our crops gathered and sold, our sense of a perfect system flowing along. Just to read and write at a young age like me, well if you could, you were a cut above the rest of the children. Lincoln's preaching political philosophy of bigger government, bigger ideals, bigger spending, and bigger consequences if we here in the south did not go along with "his bigger plan," was in my youthful mind, just dinner gossip in these parts. Federal government could never hold power over the south, the south was just too expansive for that kind of winning from the north.

My father Morgan tells us just about daily now, "I'll be damned if some northern teenage white boy twit soldier marches into my house and tells me how to live and conduct my business here in the south! My God, that is insane! His skin's no whiter than mine! You watch now, when the north comes hollering at my front door, ready to bust their business and bully values my way, you just watch! When push comes to shove, I'll give them young boys something real special to write home, complaining about to their mommas, they'll be hurtin for certain, alright, you just wait now ya hear. I'll show those boys home, don't yous worry. No filthy, young punk, don't know squat about anything, will ever take over this house. I don't even want them dead and buried on my property, containmentin' my soil! I'll burn each and every one of them. Theys ain't white people I want in mines race. I will. Ya hear?" My father Morgan wiped the sweat from his brow, removed his knee from resting on that fine dining chair, and stepped out of the room to get a sip of water. But I knew, I knew that was not the last of his speeches on the subject of war. Values. What's right in all.

We here in the household all murmured, "Yes, sir. We understand."

I would learn later on in the calm and soothing heat of the early afternoon hours from Alan, reading to me from many enduring and poetic Greek novels and plays under that old magnolia tree out back, that many Greek legends and tales teach the futility of trying to outmaneuver an inexorable fate that has been correctly predicted by the star constellations and planet arrangements in the heavens above us. My fate would be a difficult lesson, I would learn that those close to one, will become your greatest strength, or your fateful demise………

Today like yesterday, is particularly warm, I know that the hot steam of the long summer months are approaching. With little warning, so will the northern soldiers be arriving we fear here. Much news about the war from the north travels to our home almost daily now, it seems to be more than just a rumor us kids fear. My fragile mind loamed with imaginations of red tailed silver metal hats gleaming in the hot summer, marching towards me and my hidden homestead. Deep fears set in, my thoughts raced at times. Hoping that the war between the states would subside and simply just thunder, rain, and disappear as a storm cloud can, was a reality so unreal. I did not know my future. I could feel inside me a relinquished childhood, anxiety that my life was about to be changed forever, but I did not know exactly how, or when. I simply could sense future drama was near. The kind you can't change or run from.

My parents seem to be very distracted and irritated these days. I fear it has more to do with the approaching northerners than the heat and stickiness that the longer days bring us now. I have only heard of the northern soldiers destructive ways by other kids, and parents chit chatting around our long dining room table. I hear those northern soldiers burn houses and crops, and steal livestock to starve us southerners. I know that our house is just too beautiful for any Yankee from that Lincoln's army to ever think about raising a flamed touch to her. Our house stands tall and proud. Like a graceful Rebel flag blowing in the breeze on atop a mammoth bold mountain, so too is the sight of our southern mansion nestled deep within a thick garden of oak groves and magnolia trees decorated within the drips of invading Spanish moss and thick ivy. Our house seems to be a gathering place for many social parties here in the deep south. I can still smell the strong aroma of the walnut hardwoods as I enter that gracious home again to write. I know the undeniable beauty of our grand southern mansion would keep those Yankee fire torches from ever setting fire to her. I just know we'll be safe from those "Lincoln's men" by the sight of her sheer beauty…..that's what my Daddy calls the northern soldiers, "Lincoln's men."

My parents have imported British dressers, tables and armoires to furnish our magnificent halls and decadent spacious rooms. The velvet royal blue and gold yellow draperies look so regal against the lavish tapestries, painted woodworking and trim, and British paintings that adorn her tall walls. I like to touch the fancy paintings of the large British ships, restless waves of oceans yet unexplored in my mind's eye. Sometimes, when no one is looking……I take my fingernails and chip and chisel at some of the white and navy blue part of the waves that seem to protrude outward from the frame, as if those waves want me to touch them. I take the little paint chips and sneak them into the pocket of my skirt. Then I go upstairs and place the little paint chips into a porcelain saucer dish and close the lid. It appears to be just the right and perfect hiding spot, that fancy fragile dish that my father brought back from London, England, no one for years has noticed that I do this. Right next to the imported clock from Amsterdam that rests on my walnut dresser inlaid with marble. I have many little secrets I keep.

There are many cotton, tobacco, peanut and corn plantations around us within an hour or two buggy ride, many rolling green hillsides close by, but my daddy is not an owner of a plantation. We have a large yard and just as immense is the size and style of our southern mansion. My daddy located a section of rolling wooded hills just north of the bustling Atlanta streets before I was even born. He built our mansion here in the north section of Atlanta with bold alabaster columns and a two layer sweeping veranda in which to play and dream upon. Our homestead is located just north of the bustling town of Atlanta where he owns a store.

On hot southern nights, when the night air cannot seem to cool for comfort, I escape at the top veranda, and spread out my pillow and blanket for comfort. Somehow the summer night air seems to find a way to just stick to me anyway.

My Bessy always finds me out there in the dark hours of the wee morning, fussing at me to get back in bed before my parents see me out there…."yous get in here now child." Bessy would scold as she waved for me to get up.

My daddy Morgan sells, trades, and purchases just about everything at his store, located in the heart of that big gateway connected to the Atlantic sea called Atlanta. He was always meeting with local Georgia plantation owners at our home. Keeping Bessy mighty busy, fussing over all the company that would arrive at the front door unexpectedly, it is a good thing she has plenty of colored help. I call her Bessy, and that name just stuck, much better than her real name of Mabus.

My daddy seemed to like to collect and trade for profit just about anything those farmers and plantation owners brought to him. From slaves, to corn, to Georgia pine, cotton, peanuts, tobacco, sugar, and sometimes these strange people with strange sounding English voices would arrive to our home. They had the strangest hairstyles, and the fanciest of clothes, and would sell my daddy boxes of the richest, most colorful china sets I ever did lay my eyes on. Our house was a trading stop of sorts, always a new face at the door wanting to do business with my daddy. Most figured out or heard that they could find him at home, before they would be able to locate him at his large trading store in Atlanta, or at a Savannah shipyard, or the shipyard we owned in Charleston. I loved the trips to the seaport towns to visit our relatives and taste the strange salty sea as we all swam like little fishes splashing our tails along the sandy shoreline. I guess you could say, I've always been curious about what lived in the vast, deep, dark blue sea.

The summer of 1863 was approaching, ringing in the hot summer season were the sounds of locusts. Despite the war looming from the north, my daddy was never so busy with his booming trade business as he was now it seemed, he was importing and exporting so much these days, "a trading frenzy," he would call it. He even had plantation owners auctioning off slaves in our back barn in the late evening when most folks were fast asleep. At times I could hear the auctioneer, Mr. Tibbles, from my bedroom window late at night, after the day seemed just about over, his voice talking so fast, would just carry through the starry night sky above my window, "mesmerizing," was his voice. His voice would put me to sleep many of nights in the sultry south. Like how one lays on the sandy shores and listens to the resonating constant ocean waves of all that is familiar in one's world. Just peaceful, comforting I suppose.

There was not one thing that my father could not provide, negotiate, buy or trade…. if you just asked him. My father was a strapping young man in his late thirties. He had dark wavy brown hair, almost black in the winter it looked. He had large blue eyes, I think God gave him such large ocean blue eyes so that my daddy could recognize just about any opportunity or good deal that came his way. He has large rounded check bones chiseled on his face. Although his height nearly reached six foot tall, he seemed to lose a few inches from his shoulders in the way they always were leaning forward as I talked.

I am the oldest of four children. Like my father Morgan, I have big blue eyes, quite fitting for me as well. I am the most curious kid he ever did raise he'd tell me. My hair is reddish-blonde, just like my mother's hair. My mother Elizabeth likes to roll my hair up just about every other night in these big curlers. Bessy is our colored mamme. Just about everyone I know has a mamme. From what I can figure, a mamme is pretty necessary for both children and mothers. I do not know how I would dress myself, feed myself a hot meal, have clean linens on my bed, or have clean clothes to wear if it wasn't for my Bessy. When I grow up and marry in a few years' time, I plan on taking Bessy with me, like part of my wedding gift I suppose.

My daddy says those Lincoln men may threaten any chance of keeping my Bessy. I could not imagine life without her, she is part of our family, and I plan on keeping it that way forever. I love my Bessy, she can scold after me in a fussy tone of voice, but mostly she spends her day doting over my needs as a child, sometimes under her tired breath, complaining about her life. She forgets she's loved, at least by me, and most I know.

I often would wonder what life would be like in the north. No mammes, and enduring long cold blizzard type winters for months on end, aside from so much snow and no keeping slaves, how was life in the north so different than life in the south? And why does that Abraham Lincoln want us to let Bessy and all the other helpers go? And where would Bessy go? Why is that so important to those northern soldiers what we do within our daily lives here in the south anyway? Do the northerners secretly want to collect all our colored help to work on their farms, and cook and clean up after them all in their homes, but the north is too cheap to pay, so they are stealing our servants? Why must we change in the south? Why do some people from the north hate us so? We don't want to change our lifestyles, it's too good here, and doesn't need fixen. I would spend hours wondering about the north, the real reasons for the war between the states, and why should anyone make another change, if a person thinks life is grand, can't they just leave us alone? Instead of napping like my mamme Bessy thinks I do, I would spend my afternoons in my bedroom wondering with a beehive of curiosity stirring in my most curious of minds for a eleven year old…what is life like in the north? And my other question….what lies in the bed of the vast deep blue sea?

Tomorrow I am told we are making a trip to Charleston, a seaport southern town. My daddy says that we will all go, and Bessy and the other colored help will stay behind. It will take us three days to arrive there by horse and buggy. My daddy says we have many supplies to bring to our relatives in Charleston. I also think my daddy is hiding something, there is something he is not telling us, I can tell.

I dread the long buggy ride to Charleston, and Bessy I will miss. I look forward to swimming in the cool sea, and collecting shells along the shore for a necklace Bessy could later make for me.

"Yous need to clean up Lilly, dinner is servin' soon, and we's need to get the trunks packed and ready for yous trip to Charleston." Bessy called out to me as I sat on the arm of a big magnolia tree gracing our backyard.

I climbed down from the tree arm, and went skipping inside as told.

"Now yous go upstairs, I's be right there to clean yous up, oh, my's, we have a lot to do." Bessy said shaking her head and hands frantically. I think my parents put her in charge, then like to give her too many demands and chores, Bessy gets frantic at times, not knowing where to begin, and what should need finishing.

After dinner Bessy tucked me in my nice clean bedding. She asked the strangest thing of me right then and there……

"Now, when yous arrive in Charleston, yous need to bring me back seven jars of sea water, do ya here me's Lilly?" Bessy ordered of me.

"Seven jars of sea water, I's have packed seven empty canning jars in yous trunk, make sure yous scoop them all of salt water from the sea now, and bring them back to me. If yous parents ask what they are for, yous just say they are yours, do ya hear me young lady?" Bessy repeated.

"Yes, mam." I said. I was curious as to why Bessy needed seven jars of salt water, what was she going to make from salty sea water? Surely, not bread pudding, or cake, what was she up to this time? I wondered as I laid awake staring out my window. I thought to myself, Bessy has some strange customs that she took with her from Haiti, I wonder if this is all part of another strange undertaking of hers. She was the most superstitious, ritualistic person I knew, outside of the catholic priest that would visit us from time to time blessing our house on a religious basis now and then. Bessy seemed second in touch with the spiritual world that she says is all around us, we just don't know it, she tells me.

The ride to Charleston was long, as usual. I noticed Charleston was different this time around. There were strange men carrying long rifles and muskets in the streets, and standing by the docks now. They were loud, and eating bread with no plate or butter, just right out of their hand, carrying on right in the middle of the street. My cousins house faced the sea, their front door faced the wooden boardwalk that runs along the sea.

We could hardly get thru the street to my cousins house, with the loud and rude soldiers asking us questions that should not be of their concern. That was my first glimpse of the brazen Yankee soldier's way, the Yankee soldiers were all a bit like bulls attracted to the red south I do believe. My daddy looked annoyed, but did not appear frightened, and shaking inside the buggy as I was feeling mighty nervous at the new sights and sounds of foreigners in these parts.

Despite all my questions about the Yankee soldiers in Charleston, I kept my unanswered curious childish questions to myself. I wanted to remain strong for my daddy and family with this latest development I was witnessing first hand with my young impressions.

When we arrived at my cousin's sand colored washed stone colonial house at the sea, we were greeted upon our buggy pulling onto their homestead. The chickens and roasters squawked and scattered about, my cousins Mary and Adam came running to the buggy, waving and shouting with joy that we had finally arrived. Us kids all went in the backyard, we took our boots off and ran in the sloppy sand towards the waves approaching the sandy shore, we laughed the whole way down to the beach. My favorite vacations were at the sea, right here in Charleston with Mary and Adam.

My younger brother William played well with Adam, and my two younger sisters, Grace, Kate and I, played with Mary who was two years younger than me. The breeze off the sea was balmy. I could tell by the moisture in the breeze brushing fiercely against my cheek and locks of curls that a storm was brewing at sea, and like most summer visits to the seaport village, rain and winds would surely follow us this time as well.

That night I heard thunder crackling like bolts of fury, all night almost. I listened, unable to hardly breathe I was so scared. My cousins Mary and Adam, slept right through the long night storm I noticed.

Not I, nor Grace, Kate or little William could sleep through the noise in the sky, we all huddled together that particular night.

The next day, I awoke, apparently I had fallen asleep too after all that banging in the sky. After breakfast of grits and eggs, we ran to the seashore out front. The waves were crashing onto the wet shore very loudly, I looked up to see the sky, it's as if God was still angry, but we couldn't know why. The sudden storm was a secret crackling open in a wild fury that night. Behind the billowing clouds hid the light of the sun, yellow reflections against all those clouds told me the storm was over for now. Along the sand we walked, I had never seen so many dead sea creatures washed up to shore as I did that very morning. I saw starfish, and an assortment of tropical colorful fish. They were so beautiful and interesting to look at, I looked up for a moment and Mary was calling us all over to see a large brown mass, as we all approached, I smelled the worse smell of all.

"What is that?" I asked with disgust in my tone of voice.

Mary responded, "It's a dead octopus."

"An octopus?" Inquired one of the youngsters.

"Yes, an octopus, it's the largest one I've seen yet." Spoke Mary.

We all stood there for a while, taking sticks of wood, poking at the octopus, we even turned it over, as if we'd be disturbing a resting creature. Just then Adam called for us to head over to him, there was not one, but many jellyfishes washed up to their sandy shallow gravesite. We again took our sticks and poked at the jellyfish and sea creatures washed up to shore, to see if they all were really dead, we had a wide curiosity to see if anything was moving, twitching on shore, I suppose.

I looked out to the sea, I looked beyond the waves, and into the vast blue waters that mounted until breaking away, forming a smaller wave that pushed its way to the shoreline. I wondered what life was like for these sea creatures before the storm pulled them from out of their comfortable homes under the deep blue cascading world of theirs. What other creatures and secrets laid hidden from me under those crashing waves, would I ever find out someday?

My father Morgan had much carrying on about the family business in Charleston with my uncle George. My father was a more serious man at the table than my uncle George, more cautious and leery was my father with giving his input on business subjects discussed and debated while women were seated at the table.

After lunch my father and uncle went to visit the seaport shipyards that our family owned. That afternoon my mother Elizabeth and aunt Mary sat on the lawn facing the sea, sipping on iced tea, talking secretly, if us kids approached, my mom would wave us away. My aunt Mary just smiled with a welcoming nod. I told my mom I want to get my canning jars from out of the trunk to collect things on the beach.

Grace and Kate helped me carry the jars to the sandy beach. One by one, we scooped up the salty water filling the seven jars just like Bessy asked of me. The sun was making the dead sea life smell of something awful. I realized their life was cut short, and very suddenly at that. Like a lily flower in a field, so very unaware of being trampled to death. I set down the jars of sea water on the sandy shelf I made on the banks, and asked my sisters to take a stick and move the sea creatures back to the water where they belong. One by one, we pushed the dead sea life back into the ocean with the longest sticks we could find, little by little the jellyfish that had washed up to shore were scooted back into the blue sanctuary where they resided in the beginning, before the storm washed them to land.

The waves seem to carry the once lifeless sea creatures floating and moving back on into the deep waters of the sea where they belong. Even the big octopus looked alive with the motion of the sea waves under his body. The tide looked an unusual shade to us children, "red tide," my uncle called out as he telescoped the sea landscape before him……

Would a storm at sea ever again intercept with a sea creatures way of life? So I wondered in my young and curious of a mind for a child.

A British Tutor
CHAPTER TWO

That particular trip to Charleston had held many new surprises. My father seemed to be in deep concentration as he drove the horses down the winding dirt road back to Georgia. My jars of salt water splashed in the big trunk as our buggy rode on down the bumpy trail beneath us. We also had extra company with us. Uncle George and aunt Mary had twelve colored servants, all but two remained with them now. My daddy was having the ten servants of my uncle to travel home to Atlanta with us for safekeeping of sorts, one could say. As I looked behind the buggy, the servants seemed to appear to be a collection of items stuffed into a ladies handbag, one thing not matching the other, but somehow very needed to the owner of that handbag. I wondered if the four women ever had any children? Were any of them ever married? Bessy was young, but these coloreds look as if they have already lived their lives, full, or not so full lives, so I wondered quietly to myself about the hodgepodge mixture of folks behind us. I wore a blank stare back to them, wondering where this war would take us all? I stared back at their worn tired expressions staring back blankly at me from the buggy behind me, what were they thinking about?

My father made an announcement to me on the dusty trail ride back to bustling Atlanta. "I have something to tell you Lilly. Are you listening to me?" My father asked.

"Yes, I am listening to you." I responded.

"I have arranged for an arrival of a British tutor to stay with us for a few months."

My mother looked surprised, a restless jealous glance she wore, a spike of jealousy in her glare at me. I do not think my father even told my mother that news prior to his surprise announcement just now.

"You have?" Questioned my mother to my father as she grabbed the ribbon strings on her bonnet, clutching the ribbons tightly. She looked annoyed by my father's most recent bursting announcement.

My father turned to her and said to us all, "Lilly is going to be a famous writer." We all laughed and giggled in the back. I noticed my mother looked away, glaring into the clearing of the field alongside our buggy.

"Why must Lilly be a writer?" Grace spoke up.

"Well, your sister Lilly has quite the curious of minds, she likes to explore, and most of all, a writer is just about the most powerful position a women could hold in this world, besides marrying British royals or marrying a prosperous plantation owner! Lilly will be a powerful woman, plays will be written from her novels." Chimed my father. He then looked at my mother, and gleefully nudged her and said, "You just wait and see Elizabeth. Our daughter will be remembered, a real famous author from the south! England will come calling, wanting her to speak in front of those stuffy white hat intellectuals, you just wait and see. She'll write about love, this war all around us in the south, she'll comment on politics and government, I bet she has a powerful love story just brewing in her."

My mother looked jealous, as if my father Morgan somehow simply forgot about what important things she has to say, or could say. At times the tension was intense and uncomfortable between them, they looked great together, but there was some kinda bond missing, you couldn't see it, you could just sense it, when, well, he gave to me, or was proud of me. He always leaned forward when I talked. And with my mother

Elizabeth, he would always try to pacify her with his tone and attitude, no matter what she had to say. When I spoke it was like nectar towards a bird, it was somehow important what I had to say to him, and vice versa. My mother Elizabeth noticed this quality about us two. Although it was never brought out formally within a conversation, or dispute of hers on her mental list of jealousies ever spoken, the uncomfortable moments like this existed in my family due to my mother's jealousy of me.

I smiled at my daddy, "I am going to be a writer?" I was a bit surprised by his announcement too. His plan for my life. Every father seemingly has a plan for his children, a vision of the ideal future for them, I suppose.

"Not just any writer Lilly, you are going to be the best writer, the finest writer that my money can buy, and I got a lot of it to spend on you." Spoke my father boldly with confidence as he glanced at my mother, then into the woods trailing the landscape brush alongside of us, whipping the horses to move faster.

My brother William and two sisters giggled at my father's announcement. I was intrigued on how I would be this writer he thought I would become. "But what will I write about?" I inquired.

"There are plenty of things to write about in this world, you could write about the south, perhaps create a gothic novel from your sheer imagination, surprise us all Lilly." Spoke my father.

Just then I heard not one but several gun shots from the dust emerging from the woods. In the clearing that connected to the trail in front of us, ran out twelve Yankee soldiers, yelling fiercely at us to stop the buggy immediately. The horses went wild with anxiety, the horses letting out a sound of fear, us kids became instantly terrified too. Little William clutched my side, my two sisters startled with fear themselves, clutched each other tightly. What was going on? I wondered.

"Stop your horses. Stop!" More wild shots rang in the air as the smell of gun powder filled the air that afternoon. At first it appeared my father was going to outrun the Yankee commotion that seemed to just leap from the woods. Then he abruptly stopped the horses from going any further. One Yankee man grabbed the left horse's reins, as another soldier grabbed the reins of the horse on the right.

"Where do you think you're going?" Asked the bully leader of the brazen Yankee pack. I hated the sound of that Yankee soldiers voice, I hated the way he looked at my father. How would we be let go, and get back to our home in Atlanta? I wondered quietly.

"What are all these men and women doing traveling behind your wagon?" Asked the bully leader.

"We are headed back to our home." Responded my father with confidence.

"Where's your home?" Asked the inquisitive bully leader.

Just let us go, just let us go, I kept saying to myself quietly.

"Georgia." Responded my father firmly.

"Not with all these colored people you're not." Slurred the sweaty Yankee man at my father. His glassy blue eyes hid secrets, I could tell he was a no good man, just a bully up to know good, that stupid Yankee man.

No sooner were we to the South Carolina, Georgia border and we are now trapped in this hopeless hostage situation by no good Yankee men. When was this man going to let us continue on our path home? I wondered to myself.

The bully Yankee leader yelled for his men to release my uncle George's servants, yelling and screaming at his men to get the servants. I could not believe what I was witnessing. Those people belonged to my uncle George, not him, I could not believe he was just going to steal them from us, right here on a sunny summer afternoon, and my father just sat there doing nothing about the situation at hand, why? I wanted to give that Yankee man a piece of my mind! How dare he take from us!

I looked out the back of the buggy, where I sat so still, the men and women were mumbling to themselves. One Yankee soldier waved his rifle in the air for my uncle George's servants to "just get," he said. The men and women looked as confused about this new development as we were in the buggy. My eyes have never been so fixated with hate and anger as they were right then, no one takes from my family. I glared at those Yankee men helping my uncle's servants out of the buggy behind us.

"Get, get, go on now!" Shouted another soldier at the heap of muttering servants.

One soldier shouted, "Don't be like a swarm of cows not wanting to leave the burning barn, get on now! I said,"

"Go, get, scatter!" Spoke the glassy blue eyed Yankee leader, all sweaty, and stinky with an unshaven face.

The men and women servants of uncle George's finally turned and headed back the way we just came from, back into the heart of South Carolina, where would they go? Those Yankees chased our family servants off into an opening of nowhere, and those Yankees kept our uncle's horses and buggy.

After that showdown, the Yankee leader shot his rifle in the air, and slurred these last words, "You get on out of here too." He said to my father, and off we went, too stunned to utter a word to each other, we all longed to be finally home in Georgia. The next hours of silence melted with the heat of the day into the quietness of that still southern night sky above us all.

We finally stopped and built a campfire for dinner. My father tried to calm my hysterical mother, but to no avail, her bitterness turned into a snippy attitude towards us all for the duration of that long trip back to Atlanta. I could tell this war was changing her mood, her personality, she did not like the changes happening around her, neither did I. Like seeking shelter in a dark protective closet, we crossed into Georgia that night.

Bessy was waiting for us the next evening. Boy, was I glad to see her. Our homestead appeared the same, and for that I was thankful. The summer night was warm, the night air thick with secrets, it felt as if the locusts were talking amongst each other in a language all their own, if insects could chant? We were all just too tired, and too used to the sounds and ringing they made on a daily basis to realize anything was different here in the south.

Bessy unpacked our trunk the next day for us, she must have located the jars of sea water and put them in her room, I could find them nowhere. Oh, I must have left my hair brush in Charleston, it was not on my dressing table as usual I noticed as I walked into my bedroom that I missed so.

Weeks of normalcy passed, and then one day there was a knock at the front door. Bessy answered with us kids next to her apron strings peering with inquisition at the new arrival……at last, a British tutor had arrived for Lilly.

"Now get along kids, go get yous father Lilly, we's have company from England, go tell him now, run along kids." Spoke Bessy to us kids in the foyer of that magnificent mansion. Bessy had just brought in bread from the big oven of a fireplace next to the house. The oven fireplace she uses when the heat of the summer is too dangerous to bake inside our mansion.

Another colored servant arrived in the foyer to help with the handsome traveler's bags and trunk. I arrived back in the foyer with my father Morgan. My father reached his hand to greet the young handsome man at our house. My father always wore a smile, mostly, even when my mother did not. Her mood, he seemed to ignore, much like her at times, I suppose.

We all were smiling now, eager to see our new arrival from England, it was exciting to have a house guest. I believe it will lift the mood around these parts, the heavy spirit of this turbulent war that seemed to be aching at everyone's unnerving fabric these days. He seemed to be a welcoming ray of sunshine, amidst the storm we all felt inside.

"Well, hello, you must be hungry from your travels young man." Spoke my father, he was happy this young man was finally here, that's what I could gather from my father's enthusiasm of our new house guest.

"How long will you be staying with us?" I asked with sheer amazement at how much older he was, yet he seemed young too.

"Well young lady, I plan to stay just as long as your father needs me to stay. I am a recent graduate from Oxford University, and have yet to set up a teaching position for myself in England." Spoke the charming foreigner. I liked his accent, the way words flowed off his tongue in such a dignified manner. Me, I felt like biting my tongue just so I wouldn't sound young, or maybe not refined enough?

I just stared at the tutor my father hired for me, as my father and him carried on a clever conversation amongst themselves just off of the grand foyer. I wanted to sound smart too, and was purposely quiet, as to not say anything too childish, as I wanted to impress my new tutor who would be staying with us. I was only eleven, but I secretly desired to be fifteen as I stood real tall like in the foyer. I saw he was impressed with the size and grandeur of our home, I could tell that from how his eyes tried to engulf the sights all around him as he carried on with my father in the study next to the foyer. He even gave me a little glance. I noticed. I did want him for some reason…. to engulf me, right then, and there. Like how a frog goes after a bug, I've seen it. I don't know why, it was a silly fleeting wish, weird really. But nevertheless, I never felt drawn to someone like I was now, I was staring, I know. But the child in me couldn't let go of his sight, my eyes on him…..not quite yet. I felt like being bold. And then I felt nervous. I don't know why. But I suddenly realized what the emotion of "awkward" was or is. I liked him, but I did not like "awkward." I could feel my face get warm, without even placing my hand to my cheek.

I hugged the hall pillar as if to hide from my new found attraction towards my new literary tutor, I stared quietly and smartly into the study. Attraction is weird, I felt silly, and I wanted to instantly pretend I was older. I am not one to lie, but I did contemplate secretly, privately, as I hugged and danced in a circle around the pillar post in the foyer about strategies. I was beginning to develop strategies within my thoughts to myself. What do I do when he asks my age, my real age? I thought as I twirled in the foyer………Just then Bessy abruptly delivered a tray of food and a pitcher of tea to my father and my new tutor. As she brushed up against me, startling me out of my very pleasant dreamy thoughts.

The young man was not quite as tall as my father, but statuesque nevertheless.

His hair was almost black, his eyes brown, and I liked how he smiled and seemed to be impressed with my father. I wondered if he would be impressed with me during our lessons to be, or grow to be agitated with me the way my mother becomes with me, and passes me off to Bessy to watch over me and the other active children.

Bessy showed the excited foreigner to his room, us kids followed closely behind him in a trailing line. I wanted to reach out behind him and just touch his clothes. But I refrained from my bold curiosities. Us kids liked the excitement that the young man brought to our home.

"What's your name?" Asked Grace my sister.

"My name young lady? My name is Alan, Alan Hubbard."

"How long will you be staying with us Alan Hubbard?" Asked my other sister Kate.

"Well, a few months, I will be Lilly's English tutor." Spoke the refined traveler.

"Why does Lilly need an English tutor?" Asked Kate.

"Lilly is going to learn all about the English language, your father wants Lilly to be a fine writer, and a fine writer of literature she will become, plays and novels she will learn to write. I will teach her everything about fine writing." Responded Alan with great enthusiasm.

We all smiled at the English man as Bessy closed his door for him. "Now get along children, our guest needs to rest now." Bessy waved for us to go away from Alan's bedroom door, now closed.

The writing lessons with Alan were just about every morning, soon school would be starting, and our lessons would move to early evening. I learned so much about structuring my sentences, and creating conversations on paper. I began writing short stories with invented plots and invented endings, it was more fun tapping into my imagination than I had earlier anticipated from my father first announcing my literary lessons to the family. There were some weekends the family and Alan spent picnicking at the base of Stone Mountain. Us kids loved to climb the big boulder of a mountain, we could see for miles at the top. Bessy would gather stone fragments and put them into her apron pocket.

Summer blended with the warm breezes of September, and soon it was my birthday. I would be turning twelve tomorrow, Bessy was busy baking a white cake with her homemade white creamy frosting that she would swirl on the top and sides. I pulled out several small candles from the drawer in the dining room, counting out twelve candles. I then set the cream candles aside for tomorrow's family gathering.

The next morning before school I went to the barn out back. To my amazement, my father was talking with Bessy, or so it seemed. It was just him and Bessy in the horse stall alone. One colored help was sweeping the wood plank floor near where we kept piles of hay and Mr. Tibbles would stand. As I opened the closed barn door upon my entrance as I walked into the barn looking for some eggs to bring inside the colored barn help looked at me with astonishment in a protective gesture towards Bessy and my father being inappropriate, "What are yous doing here so early young miss?" He asked of me.

There was my father alone with Bessy in the barn stall, his shirt was off, and they both looked shocked to see me in the barn. Usually it was Bessy who would bring in the morning eggs for breakfast. Today, she was late, and I was up earlier than usual. I knew I saw something I was not supposed to ever see. I knew a secret that no one else knew in my family, and it was going to stay that way forever, so I had planned. My father never scrambled to get on his shirt in a modest gesture that morning as he stood in the stall, he just asked in a firm and commanding tone for me to leave and go inside the house, he held no shame of the moment. In fact, he sounded like he was scolding after me. I did nothing wrong.

That evening was my birthday party, Mr. Tibbles and his wife and kids were over. Bessy looked and acted the same, and everyone carried on as expected of each other. I was the only one who seemed to know what was written under the book cover of secrets during that gala held at our house that evening.

Just like every festive event held at our house, Christmas was soon around the corner too, and the words written of family secrets stayed sealed on a dusty shelf in my own world of relevancies and sealed secrets of the family, how my father Morgan was behind closed doors, so to speak.

I blew my candles out as I made a wish…..the cake glowed before me as my cheeks blushed a shade of pink from the surprise hug and kind gesture of birthday wishes from Alan and those around him, surrounding me. I knew I was becoming a young lady, and my father was proud of me. As a birthday gift my father gave me a gold blessed Virgin Mary pendant to wear around my neck.

Later that same evening Bessy pulled me aside in the kitchen prep area, and said the most startling statement I have ever heard from her, or about her life.

"Yous know Lilly, I's have a baby girl too, she's be about two years old now. I's could not help but think about the last two birthday's I have never seen of hers as when you blew out yous candles tonight."

The blood drained from my face, "You have a baby girl Bessy?"

"Yes, she's not live here, I's could not keep her Lilly, it would not have been right. She's live up in Tennessee on a plantation, and is being raised by a family up there, that is all I's know about her's now." Bessy held my hands tightly as she spoke to me about a shocking fact I never knew.

The only thing I could think to say to respond to Bessy was, "I never knew you were married before coming to work and live with us, you're so young Bessy."

Bessy responded, "I's never married Lilly, she's just couldn't live here. I's couldn't raise her as my own in this house, it's just the way things are in the south, do ya understand dear?"

But I did not understand Bessy's story fully. I could not comprehend giving birth to a baby girl, and not holding on to her and not raising her. I could never let go of what Bessy said to me the night of my twelfth birthday. I could never imagine the pain she must have felt in her heart as she spoke to me about such an adult matter. As I grew into a young lady, Bessy and I grew a bond of deep friendship. Bessy would always say to me under her breath, "I's do wish things could be different for mines life."

Bessy was a strong willed woman, she was young and full of life, and had a strong soul about her. Unlike the other coloreds that lived on our property, Bessy did not look like an overworked, tired mule. Nor did she carry on in slow motion movements when she swept the floors like some not so bright and cheery help. Bessy was hard working, young, and vibrant. I could recognize qualities within her that my father must have found attractive, needless to say, that is no excuse for his chosen behavior with her, I thought quietly, as Bessy swept the floors that evening.

Magnolia Blossoms
CHAPTER THREE

This Christmas season like most Christmas seasons were a time of friends and family gatherings at our home. Adam and Mary would be coming with uncle George and aunt Mary in a week. I helped Bessy before school with dressing up our mantels with Georgia pine tree branches. My father had a wagon full of these woodsy smelling decorations that he had gathered from a local plantation owner. Bessy and I tied red ribbons around the pine limbs. We sat and talked like best friends, as I was growing and developing, I also noticed a twinge of jealousy from Bessy these days. I detected her jealousy in her tone of voice at times. She seemed to think my life was a blessing, and hers was not, in her blatant opinion. Strange, when I was a child, I never felt she was jealous of my life, I was just a chore to her back then, not a teenage rival. Bessy was considered to be a "pretty black girl," a mixture of Hispanic and African she looked, she was nineteen now.

After school on the few warm afternoons left in the month of December 1863, Alan would read to me from his books of philosophy, books he brought with him from England. Under that old magnolia tree I learned about philosophy, and all sorts of sophisticated things not taught by my teachers at school. Alan seemed to teach that thoughts are most revered when insightful and independent notions are high on the level of genius. I absorbed each word, each sentence, each theory he spoke of each afternoon under that ol' magnolia tree. I had no idea how fun learning could be at age twelve. Listening to Alan was far more interesting than anything I was currently learning in school. Only sometimes would my mind drift frivolously in a way that might embarrass me if I actually acted upon my thoughts concerning Alan. Potent fantasies that seemed to be born from the very seeds of the words he would speak to me, from the words that would echo from his steady stable voice speaking to me under that old magnolia tree as he read words from imported English books with worn covers and pages alike. I loved Alan's English accent, and when he would complement me by saying to me when I would originate original thoughts and speak profound statements, "Brilliant Lilly, that is brilliant Lilly."

I seemed to be a natural student of the branch of knowledge devoted to the systematic examination of basic concepts such as truth, existence, reality, causality, and freedom, an ancient study, a school of thought called "philosophy."

I listened very closely to Alan as he spoke of symbolism, the power of mysticism. He explained Greek mythology as some of us were placed on earth with inherited gifts of insight, intuitive spiritual revelations to the rest of the world listening. He taught me about Greek gods and the role they played in the molding of a society.

"Symbolism is important, it is a powerful and useful tool in telling a story, evoking emotion, connection to the audience of readers. The placement of that symbolism, the timing, the reveal, it all matters." Spoke Alan with such enthusiasm.

As his thoughts and words carried on, I was thinking about seduction. It was a new word I had heard recently, explained to me by Alan. I felt connected to that word, like how the tight skin envelopes around an apple, I felt so close to the description of that new word. I was learning lots of words, new words each day. I was challenged by Alan to begin using all these new words into my sentences. The word seduction, I wanted to hide, and decide later, how I would unravel the use of that new word into a sentence for Alan. I was in a trance almost, my eyes would grow wide lately as I looked at Alan with pride and yearning. He liked to look into my eyes, I could feel such a connection, beyond just the pupil part of one's eye. We connected, it almost felt as if we were sedating one another with every new lesson. It felt like a waltz, Alan and I, where the music would take us, I did not know, or really care, just as long as the music kept playing. I felt more cautious with each sentence I spoke to Alan, as if I was crossing the bridge from childhood to becoming a young lady. If there is such a bridge, I was on it, I was not looking back towards being a child. I just kept moving forward so to speak.

I listened intently as his eyes held fire on what he taught. He opened old aged books on Egyptian beliefs of the afterlife, astrology, the connections between many religions. The importance of prophetic returning within those ancient religions, forecasting cataclysmic events through stars and planets and patterns in the sky. He claimed each and every one of us is a piece in God's puzzle. Alan had a way of invoking in me a wider curiosity about things in life as I knew it in the deep south. I knew he was a scholar, and I, was just a child about to transcend into the other side, heaven was there, I thought, in romance form, if I keep walking over that bridge to the other side. I was a young lady who absorbed wisdom from him like rain on the Georgia soil after many long dreadful draughts. I anticipated our lessons just like that too, like Georgia soil in the summer, yearning for the rain to come back to me. I was the soil, he was the rain, our time together that is, the anticipation of our lessons under this ol' magnolia tree. Then the reward of seeing each other would be like how the rain would touch the dry soil, finally upon me, that quenching in my mind. I could see, I could feel, to me he was that red apple in the garden, you know, that old Bible story. I wanted to be that to him, that red apple. I suppose in many ways it might seem a bit forbidden.

Alan explained to me that in ancient times, two thousand years ago and longer in counting, that the ancient astrologers were called "Magi" and the Magi were known as wise men, educated men of a family tradition in studying the night sky with revelations to reveal to the common person. And more importantly to reveal to kings and powerful rulers that would often hire the Magi to seek out information from the heavens that could assist kings of that era to make decisions of when to plant crops, when to go to war. When the planet Jupiter was on the horizon, also known back an ancient times, back then as the "kingmaker planet," which would denote the birth of a new ruler or king of that day. Alan explained that Jupiter to ancient astrologers is associated with thunder, power. To the Greeks of long ago, their god Zeus was associated with Jupiter the planet, the king of kings planet, was the planet theory in ancient times.

As we laid down to rest from reading and holding unto books we gazed upward to the bluest of skies. I could not see one planet or star formation that Alan was always talking about these days. But I had what some would call a recollection, an epiphany. A sudden realization that I have been under a beautiful tree like this before, with green grass all around us, just like this enjoyable moment.

"Do you remember heaven before earth Alan?" I asked exquisitely one afternoon.

Alan looked up from his book, paused in a moment of silence, and said this to me softly, sweetly, "I do remember the afterlife, before this life, before being born in England. I often have wondered in fear if something tragic would happen to me in this lifetime, as I recall of the afterlife. I do not think God was too happy with me for some unknown reason to me. I remember I was going to wed my dream girl, and then, I was informed by watching, that she was, or had a bigger part in creation and reproducing the inhabitants of earth than what I was prepared for, the wedding was called off. That was the last memory I had of the afterlife, well, the life before now."

"So you do remember heaven before earth?" I inquired.

Alan sighed, "I do remember."

"Do you feel a connection to the afterworld?" I asked.

Alan responded, "No, no, not really. Not in this life I live now. I do however, have a sinking feeling that something terrible will happen to me in this lifetime."

The warm afternoons of late fall gave way to a bitter cold wind. Christmas day finally arrived that year, Alan helped my father bring in our tall Christmas tree that particular Christmas day. I helped Bessy in the kitchen with making sugar cookies and hot apple cider to serve our guests later that afternoon. Adam and Mary were here to celebrate Christmas and decorate our tree with us all.

It was a happy time, one that I will always treasure. Odd, how when you're going from child to adult, everything is awakened in your world. All gazing eyes seem to be on you at this tender age, the attention is quite wonderful, everything is so promising to a twelve year old. You just want to bite into life itself, for the sheer intensity of tasting life on a grandeur scale than most at this exciting time, for all life has to offer you. Life moves slowly at twelve, but moments are more deeply absorbed at the ripe age of twelve. Your memory is good, and there is so much to take in, the sounds, the smells, each word of advice is like a sentence served on a silver platter, that's just how keen your memory and senses are at twelve. I can still smell the strong aroma of pine branches lost somewhere in my memory, even now, as I write this story. Like a dusty old file I can bring to the front of the drawer, blow the dust off and just open the pages……….and I am right there in Georgia again. I can hear the cackling of laughter in our grand living room during one of those southern gala's my parents would host. I liked those parties, it seemed to bring my parents together, in a happy way.

My father gave my mother several boxes to unwrap first. Each preciously wrapped box was topped by a large red ribbon, inside were the most beautiful dresses from England. All of us reached into the boxes to feel the fabric of such lavish and ornate dresses we ever did see or touch. My father did spoil my mother, she had everything she wanted, why she could be so snippy to us kids was something I never could figure out. Each of us kids, including Adam and Mary received candy and boxes of wooden toys and dolls handcrafted in England. In fact, all the boxes were stamped, "Made in England." Bessy received beautiful jeweled hair combs, I suppose she could wear it under the cloth she wrapped around her head. Why would my father give such a gift to Bessy? It would only stay hidden under her head wrap anyways. It was a very precious gift for colored help to receive, Bessy did like to comb our hair and pretty up us girls with fancy hairdos that she could create. Perhaps, it would be I that would actually wear such a fancy gift from England one of these fine days.

Bessy had a gift for me, wrapped in a brown bag box under the candle lit tree was a small box. Bessy said to me, "Goes get the box Lilly, I's make yous something special dear."

I opened the brown bag box, I thought it would be jewelry, and it was. Bessy had made me a necklace from the sea shells I brought back from Charleston.

Bessy helped put the necklace on me as Alan commented from under his sipping of hot cider, "How, very native."

My father and mother brought a small trunk out from a closet in the hall, they asked Alan to open the trunk, he seemed very surprised. As he opened it up he was amazed at the new wardrobe of trousers he received. Gone now could be those funny British knickers he wore every day. Finally he was going to look as if he really was going to belong in the south, dressing the way southern men really do dress in these parts.

My mother really did lay on her southern charm during the festive holiday parties, one after another. She hosted those parties with such refined grace. She glowed and charmed all that entered our galas with her warm, refined conversation at gatherings held at our house. My father must have met her at a southern party when he decided to court my mother, she must have charmed his socks off then. But as usual, she ultimately then retreated back into her shell, until the next party she would host.

That night I wore the sea shell necklace that Bessy had given to me for Christmas, I never dreamt such a disturbing dream as I did that night. I dreamt I was on a raft in the middle of the ocean, no family was around to help me to shore, and there I drifted until morning when I woke myself up. I was not wearing a dress in the dream, but pants like a boy, the sea was extra dark, not crystal blue like I remembered the sea to be in real life. Oddly enough, it was snowing in the middle of the ocean, like I have never even seen before.....suddenly I woke up. I had never been so relieved that a dream was just that, a dream. And I was back in the south. I felt transported. I did not want to fall asleep, back to sleep, or sleep tonight. I feared dreams all of a sudden, like never before. Strange.

I could never imagine living without my family. I loved my mother and father, I adored my brother and sisters, I even loved Bessy, and also knew I was beginning to bond with and love Alan my tutor. I took off that sea shell necklace, and tossed it into a drawer near my dresser table and mirror.

Two days later, I noticed the shells were missing, only the string remained coiled like a snake at the bottom of my empty dresser drawer.

January in Georgia can be very cold, sometimes we would huddle on the main floor and take turns putting firewood into the fireplace pit. It can be a fun time, but most of all, I hated the way my feet and toes would freeze up, making it painful to walk or do anything fun. I missed the warmth and gentle breeze of late fall under that old magnolia tree where my endless lessons of philosophy and writing could be taught. Outside, I loved how the smell of pine and oak leaves could awaken my senses as the chilly wind would bring such sweet breezes to my learning sessions with Alan. My imagination so alive and magical under that magnolia tree. Although today, like yesterday, our session would be inside next to the fireplace in the keeping room.

Despite Georgia's short winters I was having cabin fever and found it difficult to concentrate on my studies. Instead, I wanted to just ask questions of Alan, I wanted to know more about him and his life and family he left behind in England to pursue a way of life here in the south. He revealed to me that his first ambition was to sail the wide open seas, discovering new worlds, land, and customs, perhaps a business of exporting and importing, he said.

I could feel Alan looking at me more intensely during our lessons now, he would look at me longer than usual, I was flattered. I was also two inches taller than when we first met, and was becoming more filled out, even much to my pleasant surprise. My face was like a porcelain doll, my face features were perfectly portioned. I still had a splash of golden freckles across my nose, but hopefully they would disappear with maturity. If not, Bessy told me lemons take away freckles.

"You look like an imported English doll, like the kind your father has at his store in Atlanta." Alan would commonly remark to me during our lessons.

I did spend time wondering who would court me someday, and eventually be engaged to, and marry? When would this war between the states be all over? And just how long would Alan be staying with us, and of course, what I would ever write about? What would my famous novel be about? What subject? The premise?

Our home was a magical kind of mansion to be sort of locked in, during a cold storm. The wind would howl outside and rain would pound against her leaded glass. When the sun would eventually arrive to shine, the glass moldings within some windows would sparkle like the diamond encrusted waves atop the sea at Charleston. My home felt ornate in her cascading beauty and peaceful in safety within her tall armored detailed walls and crown molding.

One day Bessy and I were in the kitchen prep area talking, most of our meats were roasted in the basement quarters over a hot fire pit, next to where some of the colored house guests slept. Mostly our breads were baked on the main floor by Bessy in the kitchen prep area where I could usually locate Bessy sitting, busy preparing something wonderful. I wanted to learn all of her wonderful recipes, and be one to make my husband smile with joy that I was one that knew how to please his stomach, and his heart.

"Bessy, whatever did you do with those seven jars of sea water you had me bring back to you from Charleston?" I asked inquisitively as I kneaded bread dough with Bessy at the table with me. Bessy looked up, just glanced at me, then went back to kneading dough. "Bessy, I asked, what did you do with those jars of salt water from the sea, why did you need them?" I asked again.

Bessy took a deep sigh from within herself, and said this, "Someday yous will know what it is like to be me. What's it like to toil, and be someone's mamme. When that day happens for yous Lilly dear, maybe you'll stop asking me's about mines business."

"What do you mean?" I asked, confused as ever now. I stared at Bessy, her eyes beamed an intensity like no other, on fire, her eyes were today. Bessy's pupils took on an animalistic quality. Her pupils could change shape, molding to that of a cat. Bessy had something on her mind, something important, real deep in thought. Bessy seemed annoyed by me this moment, as if I was bugging her, taking her away from her deep thoughts.

"In Haiti mines mother was a voodoo high priestess, I's too can carry on her traditions ya' know." Spoke Bessy. She went on to tell me that a person who has a spell cast upon him or her has glassy eyes, "That's how yous can tell if someone is hexed." She went on to explain to me that burning candles on a full moon, then burying the candles the next day can ward off evil spells cast on one, and bring about new positive changes.

"Spells." I said with a totally blank expression on my face.

Bessy does spells? Bessy wards off spell sending and spell casting by burning candles, then burying the candle wax the next day? "Bessy, do you do spells and such on people?" I wanted to laugh out loud, it seemed silly, but I did not laugh. "Bessy, what is a priestess? A high priestess?"

Bessy remarked, "Oh, Lilly, there is so little I's should tell yous. Someday we's talk about my religion that involves the elements of this earth, when the time is right Lilly dear."

The rain pouring outside and the thunder and lightning crackling, somehow, took on an air of wicked enchantment all its own as we spoke further.

"I's think Alan has taken a liking to yous dear Lilly." Spoke Bessy, her eyes almost taken on an air of animalistic appearances, like a wild animal untamed almost.

I questioned further about her spell casting abilities that she proclaimed her mother Aunt Agnes had taught her many years ago when Bessy was just a small child in Haiti. But the time never did seem right lately for Bessy to tell me more about her mysterious ways behind closed doors that I so wanted to inquire about these days, I was a curious child. My bedroom windows faced the barn out back towards the old magnolia tree. I noticed as the early morning fog would fold away like a heavy curtain in the wee hours of the morning, I could hear the faint chanting of Bessy and Netty in the barn doing chores and such, the beat of a drum sounding reverberatingly hollow. Candles flickering against the dried out course barn walls echoed in my mind. Sometimes I could hear the faint chanting of the other coloreds joining Bessy and Netty, it sounded like singing and chanting played by voice and instruments, drumbeats and such. I peered out my bedroom window towards the barn where Mr. Tibbles would carry on with auctions. I miss falling asleep to the sound of his voice. I miss the old south, as I can see and hear her changing, life is different now, just not the same. Too much commotion, the peaceful sultry south was becoming a distant memory of times that once were, the turbulence and disturbances of disorder were more of the recurrent scenes and feelings lately, so it seemed. Bessy wasn't so loving, she was becoming slightly cold yet smothering, a combination she knew I did not like from her. I miss the old Bessy who held only joyful smiles for me.

By dawn, the fog lifted off the worn ground around back, the sun was bright, and my dreams turned into daylight thoughts, that was what I knew and could remember about my dreams soon faded, as day would break. Mysticism was blending with surrealism in my subconscious thoughts at night, the soft tapping of drums had faded in the night, as did my nightmares for the moment.

"Alan, would you like to take me and my sisters to town with you on that buggy?" I shouted to Alan as I ran down the winding path of a driveway holding my bonnet that very brisk and sunny southern morning.

Alan halted the horses from prancing any further. Then held my hand as he helped me onto the driver's seat of the buggy, his touch felt magical, as if electricity could run though his palms. I called for Grace and Kate to join our travels into town, as we sat for a quiet pace of a moment together. Alan brushed against my side as I settled on the seat next to him. "What do you think I will ever write about Alan? Do you ever wonder about what I will eventually put on paper as my artistic display for all of your long hours of tutoring me?"

"I bet you could buy a house with all the money my father has given you by now, or perhaps open your own import, export store." I said with bold confidence.

Alan just smiled back to me as I sat alongside him, he had a certain sparkle in his eyes. He gave me a little nudge on my side and said this, "You'll think of a story to write someday Lilly, when your writing skills join with your talent, a story will emerge from out of your mind, your heart. And when that day comes, the ink won't dry until you are finished with your novel, that's how inspiration works with talent Lilly."

"But when will that day come? When can I tell my father I have begun a novel, thanks to all the hours of tutoring from you?" I asked repeatedly with a smile as we took turns driving the team of horses to town, the orange Georgia soil created a cloud of copper dust behind us. I loved to sit up high on that buggy seat, he was my guide in life, and I was his confederate southern belle, the south our kingdom to keep, so I felt that day in my heart.

When we arrived in the bustling Atlanta square, we gasped in our buggy at what reality laid ahead of us. There were those Yankee soldiers and their horses gathering like a streamline along the posts of the stores, their horses drinking from our horse troughs. When we arrived to my father's store, we again gasped at the sight of the northern intruders. When would the confederates get rid of those Yankee soldiers? I wanted them out! I wanted them away from my father's store. I truly hated the sheer sight of them bully union soldiers on our soil.

We did not dare stop our horse and buggy and park. We kept riding down the middle of the street as if we did not belong in Atlanta, and were mere travelers from out of town only passing thru. Then we were abruptly stopped by a group of three Yankees. I motioned for my siblings to remain quiet with my gaze to them at the back of the buggy. Alan spoke for us when the officer in union clothes questioned us.

We were let go, this time. The feeling of pins and needles could not have been felt more than the horse buggy ride back to our homestead thirty minutes away, that late morning in the spring of 1864. Alan seemed distraught that he had brought us into a possible dangerous confrontation with soldiers from the north.

When we arrived back to the house, my little brother William and two younger sisters, Grace and Kate, ran inside the front door yelling that the Yankee soldiers had arrived to town. My father was not in town, he will be distressed to say the least when he arrives back home to Georgia. I felt unsafe, and on precariously shaky ground in my once pristine surroundings here in Georgia, devoid of Yankees. I knew the Yankees were going to encroach further into my world that I treasured with my family, I wanted them Yankees stopped immediately. I felt helpless, not big enough all of a sudden. I wanted to lean on Alan, I wanted to deluge my love on him, in exchange I would gather strength and protection from him.

As we both stood next to the horse and buggy in the barn, Alan began taking the halter off the two horses. Alan apologized over and over just how sorry he was for bringing us to town, he had no idea the Yankees had arrived overnight in Atlanta. Those damn Yankee's were like a blanket now covering the south, we wanted them out of our business, our livelihoods, but how could we buck them? I spoke softly and slowly with my questions in the barn to Alan, "Alan, when will the south over throw the north?" I inquired.

"I don't know Lilly, the north has industries, and steel factories, banking centrals, and they have the President of the federal government on their side, and all the money and wealth in the north to back the union troops and union generals. I am not sure if the south can ever shake the union troops off, keeping life as it is in the south. The life that you know and love could actually change someday, and soon I fear, I may have to return back to England." Spoke Alan.

"You know Alan, someday I will own industries, I'll build them here in the south, I'll show those ruthless Yankees who can conquer economically!" I spoke boldly with confidence, but inside I was crumbling. I did not want Alan to return back to England, or for my family's life to change here in the south.

"You're going to be a famous writer Lilly, that is your father's intentions for your future. I am here to ensure you learn all you need to learn concerning dramatic literature. You certainly have an abundance of ambition, Lilly, to also own factories and banks someday." Spoke Alan with a sparkle in his eyes.

Alan kept brushing the horses down, I wanted more of his attention, not just answers to my nagging questions that plagued my mind these days. I then reached to touch Alan's back, I wanted to know what my hand on his back felt like, curious I suppose.

Alan looked back to me along his side belt, and then kept brushing off the dusty, sweaty horses. "Alan, I know you must be much older than me, but I want you to know that our age in years does not affect what I think of you." I could not believe I uttered that sentence out loud to Alan. My private thoughts were now wrapping around in a spontaneous whimsical conversation with Alan in the barn that particular day.

At age twelve I was not so concerned with how he might be feeling towards me. I knew he thought highly of me as his student with aspiring literary talents, and that opinion was all that mattered to me in my young mind frame. "Alan I have something to tell you" ……a pause was in our conversation, I waited, and then said this to Alan, "I have a secret to tell you."

"A secret Lilly, what kind of secret do you wish to tell me?" Alan smiled down to me as he still kept brushing the horses side.

I reached to tell Alan a secret in his ear, and instead of whispering my thoughts, I kissed him on the lips, and to my surprise, I learned that day in the barn that kisses can last a long time. If you were to ask me today what love is like? What does love feel like? I would say that love feels like the shade of a magnolia tree. The rest of the world is sunny, perhaps hot from the days heat, but the cool shade a magnolia tree brings is a relief, separate from what others feel during the morning or afternoon. Under a magnolia tree the wind can blow a warm breeze on your cheek away from the blistering rays of the sunlight. The shadows of the tree branches bring comfort, the sweet aroma of the blossoms worth tasting and smelling. That's how I would best describe love to you, the love that Alan and I began to share and discover within each other's embrace that afternoon in the barn. What began as an innocent discovery in the barn, was just the onset of something far greater in intensity for us to both feel. Honestly, we were on the response side of traveling over the edge, right on into forbidden territory. Resting on the tip of curiosity laid the land of addiction, we could finally begin to see, taste it, feel it, a real addiction circulating, penetrating, beyond just a mutual desire of strong willed lovers. Which in and of itself, was like walking and treading in the Florida everglades, some things, well, seemed to be resting on the edge of dangerous that late morning in the barn.

I left the barn before anyone would come looking for me, those barn walls seemed to be collecting secrets in its rafters, I do believe. As I entered upon the worn green grass trail leading from the barn to the back kitchen door I noticed a flock of crows or ravens feasting on worms under our trees. The sudden slam of the barn door scattered the flock of black birds upwards in the hazy afternoon mid-heaven Georgia sky.

I could smell the melting lard and the zing of lemon as I approached the back door leading to the kitchen prep area. I knew by that smell Bessy was dipping candle strings in wax, or making soap, or perhaps both of those chores were going on all at once.

I felt like I needed a bath to immerse the guilty sins off from me, so near on this hot spring afternoon, somehow I did not feel hungry for lunch. Instead I felt a bit dizzy. I stated to Bessy I was not hungry, but rather began pumping water and carrying buckets of water to fill the tub. Bessy looked up for a long moment, gave me a stare down, but did not say anything to me. There were strings of light yellow candle wax dripping dry on the cords they hung from in the kitchen over a long grey tin as I best remember.

As I laid in the bath tub, I realized I had the power to seduce. It was something I never realized that I had at age twelve, but a quality nevertheless, that would stay with me for a very long time indeed. It almost felt as if Alan had waited longer for the kiss I gave him, then that moment in the barn that seemed more spontaneous, than "a romantic wait" for me.

But for Alan, it seemed to be a long awaited moment in the barn, a moment he seemed to contemplate on a more complicated level than I ever had imagined in my visions of him and I before today.

I would never tell my father about the long kiss I shared with Alan in the barn, for fear Alan would no longer be part of this household, and for some growing protective desire within my maze of curiosities about life and love, I could never let Alan go, never. Like a garden of hedges on a grand estate, so would I hide throughout the coming days, weeks, and months, my love affair with Alan within this household. I would weave through a maze of excuses of where I might be, as we both hid our new exploration of a novel still unwritten, but nevertheless explored, blossoming in my young exuberant easily excitable mind. Like a magnolia blossom opening up wide in late spring, so opened the petals of my heart that particular spring, deep…. in the mysterious enchanted south.

The Magnolia Plantation
CHAPTER FOUR

My love affair with Alan began to grow and flourish like roots taken hold underground. My mamme Bessy began to grow suspicious of where I might go and be all the time. Unlike being a child who played in her presence, I had a new found independence about me these days. Bessy was asking too many questions about Alan, and me, and where we might both be. She was catching on to the fact I was hiding my first love, my doting relationship with Alan. An apparent concealed salient passion we both were hiding. I began to feel as if Bessy was eavesdropping on me, as if that was her obsessed passion of knowing these days. Bessy appeared to me as if she was a trapped spider these days with beady eyes staring back towards me. She was too young to feel trapped as she was on our estate under my father's roof, she felt unloved, but I loved and needed her.

I received news from Bessy that we were all going to Louisiana, deep in bayou country to visit the Magnolia Plantation. The owner was a client of my fathers. My father had informed me that the plantation was a large planting style plantation. We would be bringing back some slaves, tobacco and cotton during this trip to Louisiana, all for his very prosperous exporting and importing trade business. The plantation master supervisor had ordered a large shipment of wheels, tools and nails from my father Morgan, all will be delivered next week to the Magnolia Plantation. Bessy was looking forward to this particular trip. Bessy had family members that worked as planters and house slaves on the Magnolia Plantation. It had been a long time since she had seen her mother known as "aunt Agnes" on the plantation, almost three years had passed since we all traveled there together.

My mother Elizabeth's family lives near Natchitoches, Louisiana. We would be staying with them on their large family estate. My mother's original name is "Eloise," my father had been calling her "Elizabeth" ever since they met at a dance on a plantation just outside of Atlanta, near Kennesaw Mountain. My mother's family is of French descent, her coloring of light hair and blue eyes appears English or Irish, but her face is elongated and very elegant in features. Her charm at socials and her rare beauty are her strong points, as are her refined manners from being brought up by a wealthy French elite family in Louisiana. Caring for us kids is something that she leaves to Bessy, yet some of the chores of cooking she does share with Bessy and the colored slaves on this estate. My mother Elizabeth does carry a deep resentment towards my father, or her move from Louisiana to Georgia when she was a young lady, something.

Late afternoon was blending with the sounds of evening birds in the trees, it appeared a storm was brewing in the skies above. "A heat storm," my father shouted upwards towards the sky looming dark above us as we gathered for a meal on our open lawn with a fine linen table set by Bessy and the others. Bessy's original name when she arrived in Charleston, was Mabus. I did not like her name, and I changed it to Bessy. She has been known as Bessy ever since in our home.

Tonight I laid awake just thinking about today's events, thinking about Alan, and how he can make me feel. A feeling I never knew I would experience with Alan when I first met him, you know, when I first laid eyes on him at our doorstep. And now I wondered how long we would be able to keep our love affair a secret from the rest of my family, and all those in-between people on our estate. As I laid awake with my bustling thoughts, the faint sound of drums began beating in the distant back barn.

I was too tired to get up and peer out my window to see if I could see any carrying on in the barn. The leaves began to rustle in the breeze and the air vibrated with the bellowing songs from bullfrogs and locusts….. and then just as I began to dose off….I heard faint chanting over the coos of an owl, and louder drumbeats. I got up to see if Bessy was in her bedroom. I knocked softly and peered into Bessy's bedroom, she was gone. Who could I ask as I inquired about the afterhours party in the back barn?

I went back to my room and put on a robe, then quietly crept down the winding staircase to the back door. Slowly I approached the barn and through a crack in the barn wall I listened to the strange chanting, there were flamed torches behind the barn and a ceremony of sorts. Maybe some slave died? I could not figure out why all the commotion so late at night. The men were dressed with black beads strung around their neck, and the women in white gowns. They seemed all so nocturnal, even with a full day's work earlier. Bessy had a special head ornament on and seemed to be the leader of the party. She looked as if in a trance as she held her arms upwards into the midnight sky above, as others danced around her. As strangely frightening as the scene grew, so did my curiosity grow of this party. The word Loa, was repeated over and over, hymns of sorts were sung addressing "Loa."

I knew I needed to get back to my room not to be seen by anyone. Like a curious wide eye cat lurking in the moonlit night, I crept back into the house. Am I the only one that notices these late night drum ceremonies?

The next day I asked Bessy, "Who or what is Loa?"

Bessy's eyes grew larger, more intense with prelude to my strange line up of questions for her.

"What prompted yous to ask such a question dear Lilly?" Responded Bessy, as she packed trunks of clothes and items for our travels to the Magnolia Plantation, packing almost in a frenzy, as she does every unexpected trip.

"I just wondered Bessy, I want to know more about what you do late night, can't I know?"

"Yous really shouldn't dear, yous really should mind yous own business Lilly dear." Remarked Bessy frantically.

"I want to know what you do behind the barn and why. It looks intriguing, the stuff you do behind the barn."

"Well dear, there is something yous can help me with. Yous see in Haiti mines mother was a voodoo high priestess, she would always involve a blood sacrifice during hers commencing with the dead, with hers persuasions to the spirit world to exert their influence in this world by hers commands. But I's do not need to make a blood sacrifice as long as I's have something personal and valued. Yous have a gold blessed Virgin Mary pendant around yous neck, yous can help, and be part of a 'wishing ceremony' by donating yous pendant. Trust me Lilly dears, I's will make sure the spirits keep those Yankee warriors from setting a torch to yous house when theys' be arriving at yous doorstep. And Lilly, I's keep yous and Alan together, yous will write beautiful books Lilly. Yous will be a famous writer someday, with Alan by yous side dear, yous always feel him breathe on you, next to you as you write. He's will be by yous side forever, trust me, I's can help Lilly dear. Yous look young and beautiful all your life, the belle of the ball always so young, I's make yous appear." Bessy spoke with a very convincing tone and reassured me she had special powers, a sort of connection to the other side, the spirit world, to make all wishes real and lasting my mamme explained.

"But why ask the spirit world of dead ancestors for help Bessy? What help can the dead offer? They are dead Bessy. And why do you need my gold pendent I received as a gift when I turned twelve last fall?" I inquired.

"Well dears, it's an offering to the spirit world for theirs help, yous need their help, yous don't know it, but yous do dear Lilly, to keep all things precious to yous." Spoke Bessy with persuading confidence.

I unlatched the gold blessed Virgin Mary pendant off my neck and handed Bessy my sacred and beloved necklace. "Please do not tell anyone what you might know about Alan and I, I do not want my father to send Alan back to England."

I spoke in a pleading tone as Bessy and I held that beloved pendant in my hand so tightly. Bessy squeezed my hand with reassurance that she indeed knew what she was doing, and for me to trust her. Just then her eyes turned strange, red, cat like pupils.

"Tonight, I's will ask Loa to keep yous and Alan in love, to keep this beautiful mansion yous call home, safe from the Yankees fire, yous be Alan's forever, and he forever be yous to keep." Bessy spoke with a graceful tone of confidence, of happiness in her voice, her eyes lit up with a twinge of jealousy though, almost like I just stared too close to a raging animal inside a closed barn stall, when she mentioned the words, Alan and I. But why would she be jealous? Maybe because she is not free to love, I thought. Bessy took six herbal plants, six beads, and six candles to the barn that afternoon, all in her preparation of her many drum séances in the wee hours behind the barn. "Tonight the moon is full." Bessy hissed as her eyes came to life in excitement.

I left the room in great confidence that eavesdropping overprotective lately Ms. Bessy had special powers to keep Alan forever mine. I strolled down the path leading from the back kitchen to the old magnolia tree out back to meet Alan for another lesson in English literature. But really I wanted to sit close enough to him, to smell him. I loved the scent of Alan, his skin smell was invigorating, reminding me of his kisses given yesterday. Today though Alan seemed serious during our lessons of learning. I began to feel serious too, not just a child anymore, but a young adult lady I was becoming in his presence, so I felt.

I stopped his serious lesson on English literature, and his lesson on the great writers of the past, and all they supposedly brought to the world of literature. I paused the sentence coming from Alan's mouth, and asked this, "What does it mean to want what you can't have?"

Alan responded, "What does it mean to want what you can't have, Lilly? Is this the question that needs to be answered right now, during our lesson today?"

"Yes. I want to know what it's like for you to want something you can't have Alan. What would that be like, Alan?"

Alan asked me this question, "Do you know what it is like to want something you cannot have in this world, this immediate world of yours?"

I began to stumble over my words and sentence compositions in my mind. I gathered the strength in this response to speak clearly, "I know what it must feel like to **want** to marry, but I cannot marry because I am too young for marriage. And I can't marry you because my father would feel his trust in you and I was dishonored, all this sneaking around throughout the day and evening."

I pause and then continue by saying to Alan, "Eventually he will catch us, he is a smart man, it is tough to keep secrets from him Alan."

Alan looked down with a sober expression on his face and said this reassuring response to my question, "Lilly, someday we will be together as often as we like. As you get older and I save for a place and land to call my own, I will send for you, and ask your father for your hand in marriage." With that response, Alan drew a fancy English ship with four sails in the dirt with his finger, next to a wide bridge, and said this, "Someday we will own shipyards, and businesses, be wealthy merchants and sail the open sea together. Our lives will not be governed by this household, or fear of your father." Spoke Alan solemnly to me. Alan went unto explain the significance of the bridge, what a bridge means, with his very polished philosophical flare of his, and formal English tone, he said this, "The nautical ship controls the platform, from the ships control room, a bridge simply means, from which the captain controls its course."

I side stepped his philosophical analogies for a brief moment, he was far more metaphoric in the way he taught and spoke than I was. I was bold, twelve, vivacious, and ready to learn, mostly to learn the answers to the questions that laid deep within my wandering of curiosities of sorts these days………. "You want to marry me Alan? Your love for me is that deep and penetrating?"

Alan did speak up to my most relevant of questions, I did take him off the course of philosophical wizardry that afternoon in Georgia. I was gaining insight into Alan's deepest of emotions, how he felt towards me, what could make this man tick, I wondered. What did our future hold I also contemplated in my penetrating young mind.

"Lilly there is no women who makes me feel as you make me feel, you are a young woman Lilly, not a child anymore, it must be love, it has to be love that I feel in my heart for you. Lilly are my greatest desire, my greatest literary sculpture that I control and mold together, all wrapped into this passion that grows deeper with each moment we are together. In my mind I see I am creating a sculpture of us, I am a fierce and powerful lion, you are on my back, I carry you away. A volcano erupts as society scatters from the impeding lava. There are times I feel I must be serious and control this fire of a love storm brewing in my heart for your young and tender touches. I feel I am losing control all the time, over this feeling inside for you." Alan looked so sober, a bit meek, with an intensity of love propelling his interest towards me, I could see it in his eyes.

"When will we be together all night in each other's arms, when?" I pleaded with unknown qualities unremarkable to me.

Just then Bessy stepped outside from the back door leading to the kitchen prep room, she wore a serious optical gaze towards us.

"Lilly, yous lesson will have to continue later. I's need yous to pick out yous dresses for tomorrows trip to Louisiana." Bessy wore a disapproving expression as she held the back door open for me to enter the back hall. Bessy looked about five to seven years older than me, but by far she acted more like an overprotective parent not wanting me to grow up and find myself. To stay within her reach forever, her control. At times I feared, I must be all she has in this lifetime of loathing her life, and loving me. An evident smothering concoction between what you want and cannot have, or secretly desire and want.

"When are we going to leave tomorrow?" I asked Bessy. I gazed towards the magnolia tree, my heart was still under the tree as I retreated inside for lunch. Bessy trimmed my long locks, and commented to me that she was going to make a doll for me to play with, Bessy sighed as she spoke.

"Yous need to be a child, yous too young to be in love Lilly." Bessy spoke in a prideful knowledgeable tone of voice as she combed my hair and snipped off four inches of my hair. "We's gonna leave at the crack of dawn Lilly, yous need to eat and rest now." Spoke Bessy in a domineering and firm tone.

My appetite was weak, yet my desires strong for Alan, it was difficult to eat lunch with so much yearning in my soul to be next to Alan, to be his, the way he is my teacher. I knew I was too young to marry him, I wanted to be all grown up and have my wishes taken seriously as adults have their wishes fulfilled, well, white adults have their wishes taken seriously.

The crack of dawn came early on that Wednesday morning. I woke to the sound of horses as the carriages were being latched onto several teams of hyper, jittery horses. We were headed to Louisiana this morning, we would be gone just over three weeks. My father Morgan will be letting William, Grace, Kate, Netty and Bessy, myself and my mother all off at my mother's family estate in Louisiana, near Derry, just outside of Natchitoches. He would then continue to the Magnolia Plantation to do his trading. Alan would be staying back in Georgia, where I wished to stay as well.

Along the way we saw cows roaming the countryside, no owners plantation even insight. My father said that the union soldiers of the north would burn crops, burn plantations and barns, then confiscate the cattle and horses all they could muster, and just let the rest of the cows and chickens and such wander.

"Why?" I asked. "Why do the Yankee men do that?" I asked along the way.

"They think they can bully and destroy our way of life here in the south, it's their way of breaking us down. But they ain't gonna break me, or you, or anyone we know Lilly. We are above those scare tactics of destroying our ways, what we value and know is the way Lilly." My father spoke with complete reassurance as we traveled through the unraveling destruction along the way to our Louisiana destination.

Some farmer homes and barns still had smoke rising from the smoldering ashes left behind from those Yankee torches, that was all that was left, large piles of ashes with smoke and boards barely making an outline of what once stood erected in its former place. I remember seeing grand plantations along this route to Louisiana before with young children waving to us from the front porches. And now the bare landscape yielded death, poverty, and unraveling destruction. There were even these young children with no boots on, just wearing one ragged clothing piece, hardly stitched together, they would come running up to our carriages begging for food, no mother or father around, just abandoned children left behind. My mother would just beg for my father to stop and feed the young starving children, he did not want to, I could not understand why? He just wanted to remain hardened in heart and mind to what our eyes bared witness to throughout our beloved south. He would drive that team of horses not wanting to see reality now, the changed south. I reached into a few burlap bags and quietly dropped apples, pears and whole potatoes from the back of the wagon towards the children running towards us.

The landscape of destruction eventually would catch up to him and became upsetting to my father. Like a swarm of unwanted flies at a picnic, my father could not shake off the approaching danger brought on by the northern states politics. Times were changing all around us, the south looked different now, there were even freed black slaves walking here and there as we traveled down our route further southwest into Alabama and Mississippi, right on into the Louisiana bayou country. Something I just never saw before in Georgia, was very prevalent alongside this country route.

As we rounded the bend to my mother's family estate, I noticed the white paint peeling off the slabs of wood. The cattle in the back field looked hungry, and my grandparents looked worn, older, I suppose. My mother commented to my father as we pulled into the winding path leading to the front veranda, "Boy, this war from the north is taken it's toil. My parents are giving all they can to support our confederate soldiers, all they can." She sighed.

My grandparents greeted us upon arrival, it looked as if half their help was gone. Things were different this trip around, life was changing all around us, so I was witnessing first hand, with my own young eyes.

I'll never forget the first time I saw my first alligator, I nearly jumped twelve feet back. My mother's family had ponds on their estate, "swamp lands" some would say littered their estate land. Like most aristocratic French in Louisiana, my mother's family had their wealth built by slaves clearing down acres of trees, upon thousands of acres for cotton fields to be planted, each cotton plant handpicked each season by the slaves they owned. If a slave escaped, he or she was hunted, sometimes all the way to Texas. Hunger, whippings, and shackling was a form of corporal punishment used for runaway slaves. I've seen my daddy use all three forms of punishment when a slave was returned back to him. Even Bessy once received a whipping from my father when she first arrived to our home and tried to run away, well before she fitted in with us all like she does now.

My father stayed the night with us all under my grandparents roof. My grandma doted on my father Morgan, and always made sure there was a staff of her finest servants waiting on him hand and foot. She had fresh squeezed lemon water, no sugar though this time around. Why? I wondered. Netty and Bessy slept in a back brick house slave quarter. Bessy sighed as she headed with Netty down a path leading to one of those brick houses out back, giving me a look of disgust. Bessy was not as enthusiastic about this trip as I appeared to be tonight. I do think she would like to see her mother, "aunt Agnes" tomorrow, it's been sometime. I always wondered what it would be like to not be raised by your own flesh and blood mother? I just couldn't imagine that horror, that disconnection with your mother and lost years never to be recovered.

I do realize that I am practically raised by Bessy, but that's different when you're a child, unable to touch and feel and see your mother when you want to, and where is Bessy's father? I never met him. The loud locusts and bullfrogs kept me up until midnight with my swirling thoughts, I had the strangest dreams that night. I saw bright twinkling lights of pink and yellow, shiny black covered sofas, and there was Alan, he was grown, like my father's age, and I was "twenty- something," Alan's hands were all over me in my dream. This time, he made me feel uncomfortable, there was this strange redheaded southern aristocratic man that looked just like Mr. Tibbles staring Alan down as Alan grabbed all over me, creating fear and tension within the room setting. The dream startled me so that I woke myself up in a panic ridden state.

Alan would never make me feel uncomfortable, but he did in my dream that night…how could that be? I wondered.

My father Morgan rose early as usual, he took Netty and Bessy with him down the road to the Magnolia Plantation, one parish over from us. Upon arriving he was greeted by union troops. To his surprise the supervisors house was burning and he learned the supervisor had been shot in his refusal to let union troops sleep there overnight. My father had supplies to deliver to a man no longer alive. He quickly turned his team of horses around. That was the last time we traveled to the Magnolia Plantation, that was the last time Bessy ever had hopes of seeing "aunt Agnes," her mother.

That afternoon my grandparents had a local four player band over a pig roast they hosted, it was typical 1830's banjo lyrics. The southern festive music took my mind off the news of the day, but Bessy seemed very disengaging to the day's festive events.

My mother begged for her parents to come back with us to Atlanta, they refused her request. My mother and father were not going to leave my grandparents on their estate with so much danger from the north just around the horseshoe bend. It was only a two day wait, and like an impending tornado approaching to touch down, the Yankee's arrived late one afternoon as we ate leftover ham by the table.

I will never forget that moment of real danger arriving in our families solitude of hearing wooden foreign soles on the front porch as we ate dinner around grandma's table. The five northern soldiers had planted themselves upon my grandparents soil. Fear of how our lives were going to change was just around the corner…….

Lafayette Square
CHAPTER FIVE

It did not take long for my father Morgan to reach for a rifle, we all knew the drill, and headed up the back servants staircase to the upper foyer loft area, away from the windows, away from any crossfire. We moved in silence, only my heartbeat could be heard above my grandparents deep sighs and breathing as we all held hands and crept quietly up those pine stairs to a safe resting place. My father Morgan and five male servants held rifles. Like a drill practiced and rehearsed in his mind only, my father aimed his rifle from an upstairs bedroom, with one shot fired, he shot and killed one Yankee down. As if very well anticipated, but never experienced before that day, out blasted from nowhere the foreign roaring thundering crackling of lightening hitting the side of my grandparents' home. Better described as the bombarding of ammunition splintering throughout that house. Like a haze of morning clouds over a pond, smoke began to rise upwards. I never forgot the strong stench of ammunition being fired, or the screams of my mother and younger siblings when my father made his way from a front bedroom into the upstairs parlor where we all waited for him and the others to be done with the musket battle scene. What did those Yankee men want from us? Why can't they just leave us alone? It is as if voodoo had messed with their senses as white men, I thought silently to myself.

My father clutched his leg, dragging his left leg he made his way into the upstairs parlor room where we all waited in anticipation for the smoke to clear. My father had a look of agony, blood swept over his beaded brow onto his thick dark wavy hair. My mother gasped and reached for him. My grandfather surprised us by getting up in his knelt position and taking the slumped rifle from my father's hand. "No granddaddy!" I called, "Stay here with us!" I called out in surprised horror. But he was too determined to not pitch into the battle and win our safety back. Shots were being fired from the lower level and upper level from the slaves trying to save our ground, shots were also being fired into my grandparents' home. The sound of crackling glass being exploded onto hardwoods made my dinner turn in my stomach. When was it going to end? My siblings were crying out, "Daddy, daddy's hurt!"

I knew my grandfather knew how to shoot a rifle, but I do not believe he has ever aimed to kill another human being before. There was no time for practice drills, this was a matter of life or death for us all. It was less than five minutes, we all heard granddad give a loud yelp, the sound of shattered glass accompanied his cry. My father dragging his own body along the rug that connected to the bedroom where my granddad laid moaning, made his way ever so quickly. Like a snake weaving back into the tumbleweed, so moved my father. He grabbed the rifle back from my granddad and fired the last rounds heard. In the brief solitude of silence of the moment my father yelled, "It's over, it's over," brought only a momentary relief for my family of peace. For what we soon gathered and saw in the next room can only be described as unanticipated horror. Granddad was bleeding from his heart, and dying. My mother and one slave brought my granddad onto a bed close by, and laid him out. There was not much we could do to save him, it was only a matter of time before his eyes would close shut.

My brave grandmother made her way down the back staircase. The slaves on the main floor scolded her to go back upstairs, I could hear them. Grandma refused, she went directly to the front door and ordered for the five dead union soldiers to be brought back to the back pond beyond the first cotton field. She ordered for Bessy and Netty to pump buckets of water from out back and scrub the front porch clean. "I don't want a drip of that Yankee blood left on my front porch!" She ordered in a rage. Then she turned to the black slave men pealing the union soldiers off the front porch unto a wagon, and said this, "You make sure the alligators eat well tonight, do ya hear me!" I was in shock over what changes within our lives had transpired in a matter of one hour's time. Grandma was bitterly angry, and for some reason could not go to tend to my dying grandpa's side, it is if she was ready to fight and not in a mood to grieve. My mother was crying uncontrollably as she tied my father's leg in linens ripped from the bed. She was washing my father's wound as he laid in agony for her to take the bullet out of his wounded leg. It was a sight I wish I had not witnessed, but nevertheless, absorbed in the collection of all my childhood memories.

For as long as I can remember my father always walked with a cane after that dramatic scene still being played out in my mind today as I stare at the springy bloom of that ol' magnolia blossom tree. My father Morgan had promised our family "No white man would ever change us." He lied to us. And there was plenty of evidence that he had lied to us. My granddad was brought to be buried under a willow tree that very same night that he met his tragic ending. It would be too dangerous for us to stay in Louisiana, the large gathering of union soldiers at the Magnolia Plantation would soon find out of the lost men. My grandma put several slaves in a carriage with her, ordered Daniel a confidant of a slave that helped fight against the Yankee five to be now in charge of her cotton plantation until she or my father Morgan arrived back. She ordered that her house be boarded up for now, until further orders be given. She packed along with a few of her prized belongings, jewelry and such, a bottle of rose perfume. Her European French wedding china she left behind for when she arrived back to her Louisiana plantation. She made her way to Atlanta with us that very early morning of the next dawn.

Bessy looked distraught and tired, quite frankly we all felt worn like birds who had flown too far from the nest, unable to fully rest, we just wanted to be back home in Georgia. My father said we were going to take a different route home this time. The large exotic leaves sounded like duck feathers flapping in the wind alongside of us as our carriage headed northeast to Georgia. The frogs, insects, and general nature of the trees and woods seemed to be larger in Louisiana. Mysterious how the black slaves on a few plantations left would stare right through us as we passed on by them slowly. As I looked behind me towards the end of yet another tiring day traveled, I saw a golden copper canvas with the silhouette of wild willow trees framed against a sadden artist's canvas. As the horses moved us closer to home, I saw peaks and valleys covered in charred remains where land owners had once abundantly prospered this time of year. The signs of the union soldiers devastation cascaded the southern terrains before us, we felt our sorrow deepen. Famine was quite evident on this route back as well, this was a different road than we had taken into bayou country, sadly, not better, but worse were the signs of the war torn south. The smell of rotten dead cattle carried through the hot days heat into our open carriage as yet another reminder of the brutality of how the north wanted to change our lives in the south. I held my arm over my mouth and nose during parts of the trip back home in my attempts to escape reality all around us now.

The remaining slaves in the fields out yonder held a mysterious connection to each other, that the ordinary person could not see with their naked eyes, but I could see. I could see the hidden mysteries in their eyes, the anger, the bitter rage held against the white owners, the voodoo cast spells upon the south for all that the slaves had lost in their extended past, their extended stay in the south. I hugged my father tight as we crossed into Georgia, that was the last road trip we would take as a family, it was late June 1864. When we arrived near our street, the horses gasped in their tired anticipation of awaiting water in the cool shade of the barn, confederate soldiers we also passed along the way home. My father offered the soldiers guns, and wheels, and tobacco, ham, all we had on the carriage to give our beloved confederates, and boy did we need our men of the south.

The next morning I woke early to find a surprise of a situation, my father was severely drunk on imported British whiskey. He seemed barely alive as he laid on the living room sofa. He could hardly move, but I could make out his words, slowly he uttered one sentence, slowly he began to speak to me. His eyes glassed over and red, hardly an eyelid open, just a wince of a glance he gave me as I approached him on the desolate sofa. He just did not have his confidence as I so remembered. He kept murmuring, "The damn Yankees, and Lincoln's unnerving Emancipation Proclamation, was goina kill us all, we'd all be poor by the time this war is done." I did not like how he appeared beaten in spirit and in body, not the strong and confident man I knew and loved. He was becoming a man I did not know or recognize since our return from Louisiana. I reminded my father Morgan, "Yes we can win, it may take some time to throw off the northern armies, but we will win to keep our lives just the way they are, it takes time daddy. Don't lose hope, that's what the north wants, don't lose hope daddy."

On June 27, 1864, from Marietta, Georgia to Kennesaw Mountain, a huge battle broke out while we were in Louisiana. Confederate commander Joseph E. Johnston won the bloody battle for our side. Thanks to the strength of over a hundred thousand Tennessee confederates, and with help by our men of Georgia, we won the battle of Kennesaw Mountain, but not without bloody consequences and losses of life in the low thousands. Bloodshed was rampaging throughout our beloved south, all around us were men carrying riffles and muskets, cannons being dragged behind soldiers marching down the copper dusted streets. The sounds and smell of war were distinct that year of 1864. I was really just a child absorbing adult conflicts, just trying to make sense of it all.

Although slavery was illegal when the colony of Georgia was first founded, slave labor was a well-established trade in other American colonies back in the 1700's. Settlers were confronted back then in the 1700's as we are now with the competing Carolinians producing cash crops with slave labor that would significantly undersell commodities produced in Georgia by freedmen. South Carolina planters provided the first slaves that arrived in Georgia. Economic pressure forced us to have and own slave labor, I do not think the north realizes the economics of why we need slave labor here in Georgia. People need to realize that high labor prices paid will cause an economic collapse. Maybe the freed slaves would work at reasonably low prices? I thought. My father would often say at the table, "Too many Chiefs, and not enough Indians will be an economic disaster. You just watch."

The storm clouds began brewing a typical summer heat storm here in Atlanta, with the clambering of loud crackling throughout the southern sky. Soon the strong rains will be blowing through Atlanta. I ran upstairs to shut the windows. My grandma left out her expensive rose perfume on her table dresser, I gave the yellow puff handle a squeeze. As I looked at my reflection in the dresser mirror, I saw Bessy staring back at me. "Don't get into yous granny's things now Lilly dear," Bessy scolded after me.

Bessy was noticing how I was developing into a young woman. She was watching me like a hawk, she would circle me, stare me down, and always want to know what I was up to these days. She'd glance at my chest, wonder with her eyes at how I was becoming shapely now, and just how far Alan and I were expressing our love towards each other. Bessy was already a young woman, but no first love for her. I too would be a young woman soon, but I had love, I had a future with a man. Bessy did not care for my new found independence on life, my well educated view of the world forming as she stayed mostly in the kitchen prep area or sweeping floors. You could see a dramatic change in attitude from Bessy towards me these days, an attitude towards me for how sophisticated my words were sounding, how complete my sentences sounded and were heard by all in my presence. But there was more to it than that, Bessy was beginning to have layers of attitude towards me, in my ability to be able to love and be loved by a man. Which was beginning to undue Bessy's generally positive upbeat attitude in the house now. Bessy would stare me down, I sensed jealousy as she doted upon me. A direct tension felt within the air as she fused over me now.

I was becoming a reminder to Bessy these days of all the wonderful things she would be starved of in this lifetime, like falling in love, and marrying your true love. Bessy had a good life with us, much better than a cotton picker on a plantation. But Bessy, she felt thirsty for something, hungry, deprived of things in life she realized I would obtain all too easily, and yet all within her grasp, but not her future. It was all to be my future, and my dreams realized, within her world too. All the while mind you, Bessy would only appear to be a shadow in the background of my very fruitful existence. This bothered Bessy, way more than I could comprehend at this young and tender age of trying to understand coloreds. They say that there is a very thin line between love and hate, Bessy was beginning to walk on a balance beam like a gymnast taking careful strides. You could just see it in her eyes these days as she carried on with her duties caring for me, cleaning for me, washing my linens, brushing my hair, cooking my meals. Bessy was always muttering under her breath now days as she scrubbed dishes, or while she fussed after me, muttering about how she wished for her life to be, and how I just did not understand. As if I was ignorant to the world. But I beg to differ, I am very well educated for a child or an adult standard in Georgia. I would remind Bessy of that fact. Bessy would get quiet, and just stare me down. We had differences of opinions about matters as I was suddenly becoming a woman and emerging into wearing more grown up lady clothes.

It was almost time for my lesson with Alan. Today he promised we would be studying English plays, symbolism, and the historical role of theater in English society. He also spoke of how the Greeks and Romans of ancient times believed that "higher deities could be born on earth and take on a human identity. Often kings anointed on earth, believed their role began before their earthly reign, their earthly anointment. Gods and monsters." Alan explained all this by the kitchen table as I pulled up a chair. Bessy listened in at times, Alan just ignored her. But I could most definitely feel her presence in the room, even if Bessy remained quiet as she did, just listening in and tending to her chores around the house.

I responded to Alan's rehearsal of what we would be learning in today's lesson by saying, "I want to be the reincarnation and embodiment of wisdom on earth."

Alan just smiled and asked. "Where did that come from Lilly?"

I replied as I shrugged my shoulders, "I don't know, it just seems to be a subject on my mind these days. I don't know why. But I want to be known for my wisdom, I want more wisdom. And then I'll write a famous novel about wisdom. You mentioned I need a good introduction, a good premise and storyline, the plot, the climax, and an ending that will surmount and surpass that last great book ever written."

Alan just stared at me for a moment, amazed that despite my endless afternoons of falling in love with him, staying up at night in a trance of fantasies as he laid in another room, I was actually, surprisingly, able to retain and regurgitate such knowledge back to him at this moment, my teacher.

Alan seemed the same as I remembered him from before we left for bayou country. Strange how one can stay away from a passionate love interest, and the moment you see one another, you just get this stomach jumping feeling instantly. Like the surge of fierce lightning brought on by the sheer sight of the person you want, love and desire. The reaction I have for Alan is like that description, the reaction that goes on inside of me is excitedly intoxicating, he seems to control the core of my essence. An overpowering tingly feeling I begin to feel in my lower extremities, it just hits me, this strange feeling every time I am in the room with Alan, like right now. I want to reach and touch his head, running my fingers through his shiny thick dark brown hair. Touch his arm, and stroke him lightly. I secretly possess inside, or rather he possesses in me such a powerful reaction to him. Yet, all must be kept hidden from the rest of the household, especially my father resting in the next room.

My younger siblings, Bessy, and my mother were upstairs when Alan and I sat at the kitchen prep table to quietly conduct our teacher student session that particular afternoon. Alan began reading some play which had a tragic ending, a love story peril could best describe the theme of the play he read so fervently to me from his heart of emotions. Which at times, his emotions when he read was like an untamed wild white water journey, a real Lewis and Clark adventure ride were his emotions when he read to me. It was as if he was in the story, the rising action, the plot, the climax. Then suddenly there I was in his last gasp of air, on the page with him, not missing a paddle stroke of his epic adventure on turbulent water, as if I always was with him, from the beginning of the story. At first, just hiding behind a word, lost in a paragraph, just looking to provoke, incite his next raging high water, dancing or rolling onto the next page. Just before he slipped his finger around the corner, to see where I had gone. I was listening, but my mind drifted in fantasies about my place within the story. I wanted to be every character, every dazzling woman, say every funny line. I wanted to make him cry for the first time between us, and keep his attention for the duration of the novel. But I wasn't. I was just behind the words of his emotions as he read. When he looked up from the table, there I was again, with him all the way. He just could not see me, I wore different clothes, I spoke in a foreign language, drank, and laughed with him as if I never left Georgia this afternoon as he embarked on a rollercoaster of a ride with his intense emotions of feeling, teaching, and experiencing through a story. I was there for him. I was in every line.

My mind began dancing with images as he read on, my eyes glassed over during the sad parts he read aloud. But really, I wanted to take advantage of the quietness of the house during this particular tutoring lesson. I reached for Alan's hand, for him to put down the book he was reading from with such keen emotion. I began a slow descent to kiss Alan, in a raw, bold, sensual, earthy, unusual way, I, as his student, gained his attention that moment in the kitchen like never before. I wore a royal blue linen dress, a dress imported from France. Alan whispered in my ear, he referred to me as, "**his blue star**."

"Brilliant Lilly.....just brilliant" ......spoke the perfect pronunciation of Alan's very refined English grammar to me as he put down the book he was reading from, as his interests began to angle towards me, and rightly so. He then leaned over the wooden table towards me, softly speaking these words again, "Brilliant Lilly..... just brilliant." This time he whispered those words in my ear as I began to lay back against the worn sawn wooden table. I stared at the book cover for a moment, then kissed Alan again and again. In a unique way, I began exploring different ways of kissing Alan. Kissing Alan in different sections, privately seducing him with each kiss imprinted upon his skin and exploration discovered.

The smell of freshly made bread resting well on the antique style wooden table still fills my mind's memories today. The rain poured down that early afternoon in Georgia, one window had undoubtedly been left open from before the onset of this thunderstorm. Like never before did the rain pour down, spilling against and into the kitchen like a million beads of onlookers pressing their essence up against the glass, as if to get closer to us, as if trying to reach in and feel our passion. The thunderstorm scared me, but in Alan's arms, I felt reassured somehow, and resumed expressing my love on him. The rain poured down and into the kitchen as if yearning to be part of the air of that steamy afternoon session, into our sensual gardening of plucking a rose. The rain touched the windows in earnest to feel, taste, and touch our sensuous experiences at bay. I would never thirst or hunger again I thought as I laid back further on the table. It was a dinner party I would never forget, the breaking of bread with Alan at the kitchen table. I was like a fragile magnolia flower in full bloom. Blooming like the end of a five day peak in late spring, that is how Alan must have thought of me as his eyes glazed downward upon my body resting against his on that raw wooden table, then gazing back up to my face. His stance of emotion seemed to brim, the ambiance of the kitchen was that of a combination of rose petals in the capering air, humidity building up, and that of rain pouring down as if trying to reach into the room through the windows. To simply feel and touch what we could experience on the table, on that rainy, steamy smoldering afternoon in Georgia. The aroma lingered in the air of bread warming in the kitchen, one could taste and smell in the air so thick of fragrant passion. Our sensory of touch and smell that afternoon in the south was so vividly awakening to us both. Drunk on what the other could provide for relief of our hunger and thirst that day in the kitchen.

My head dizzy from the onset of strange and unusual emotions first felt within me. The vibrations of what I could feel from simply his touch, his movement, in and around. I could though, still clearly see with my naked eyes how overwhelming our love grew that afternoon in the deep south for Alan. How abundantly impaired by an intensity of emotion that we both could feel as I looked into Alan's glassy dazed over scoping eye span covering my semi-nude appearance against worn sawn wood before him as the addiction mounted, escalated. It was such intense pleasure, an army could not keep us apart. In my mind, I begged of God for no one to walk in and interrupt us.

My gentle touch on his arm must have been like an intense bolt of lightning felt for Alan. A raging atmospheric electricity pressure that only we could seemingly feel together with our touches, our sensory of love to experience. As I recall those days gone by, my mind races back to that time and place in my private history. It was an experience to savor, remembering his touch, of yearning for more, for the first time ever in that particular lifetime.

Our passion was our secretly shared ingredient of what would become a well-worn addiction of seeing and experiencing all at once, the anticipations were just as good as the reveal and final count of knowing each other privately. Certainly not an easy habit to break, or one you would want to break free from with your own vision and soul. How would we keep this love affair secret? Surely until I am at least seventeen, I thought. The war had no direct effect on our love, but danger could be sensed in our everyday lives now, and knowingly so, would encounter this household at any time.

During a long era in history, at a time in the late 1800's when showing ones ankles to a man was considered risqué, well, I seemed to be way ahead of the times. I was twelve but looked fifteen, as bold as I was revealing, so was the knowledge Alan had about a woman's body for a twenty-three year old gentlemen. I knew only about seduction and what I thought he wanted. Alan could have written the book on how to make love to a woman, how to prepare the pot, when to increase the heat and pressure in his controls, making me feel as if I always wanted more, and then weak again from well received satisfaction. Why he just knew or read so much about that foreign subject of sex was not the question, when we could be together again to feed my addiction was always the real intensity that rested on my mind. If love was ever to be classified as a true addiction, then ours would probably have a lasting effect in this lifetime and the afterlife. Powerful connections tied us together, a bond so real of the truest love that death could not separate, the boundaries of heaven nor hell could keep us apart. And still the thunder loamed in anger above us, shaking our house to the rafters, to the foundation. We waited for a moment longer, and then began kissing and holding onto our secret addiction of the others touch. Holding and cuddling as we devoured each other's unique scent, as we both felt the electricity storm pass over us, again and again that late sultry afternoon as we laid in each other's arms. I felt as if my very skin was emitting rawness and heat from my secret desires for Alan, no longer oppressed, sweltering was the pink shade of my petals. Alan described the way I looked, when it was all said and done in that kitchen, well, he whispered in my ear, "It appears… like pink frosting on a special occasion, the resolution we feel of this moment."

I spoke up first, "Alan, when you were touching me I could vividly see another time period."

Alan inquired as he buttoned up his shirt, "What time period would that be Lilly?"

I responded promptly, "Long ago."

There was a pause in our conversation as we smartly finished dressing each other as quickly as we could. Then I continued by adding in these details, "My name was not Lilly back then, long ago. There were many sandstone buildings, a desert, desert paths and vegetation not of this world we know here in the south. You had other ladies in the room with us. Your hair was blonde curls, you looked Roman and younger than me, powerful. I was at least ten years older and wore a black wig. Under my black wig I had red dyed locks of hair wrapped in a loosely worn bun on the top of my head. I lost a war against you, your Roman army……. the women in the room wanted me dead, they poisoned me when you left the room. You said something just before you left the room, I think you even knew those women would poison me! You leaned over on the bed as your blonde curls brushed up against my cheek and you said something awful about my future, my kingdom I once ruled over, and what you had ordered done."

Alan stopped me there and inquired, "Did we have a child together?"

I gasped and replied, "Yes! Yes! That was the reason for the war. You had a war career for Rome. You whispered in my ear on my death bed in your chambers, "Marc Antony is dead and buried under the temple of David near your not so loyal castle servants."

I felt anger. I felt rage and passion bubbling up inside me as I screamed softly speaking intensely "Alan, you cared more about your war career than you did about me and our son. My Jewish castle servants raised my youngest son, our child, they told everyone he was the son of God. I was dead. I died. I remember spitting or choking and then escaping Rome on a one horse chariot back to my castle….it was Egypt…wasn't it Alan?....I believe. My hair was soaked in sweat as I neared the city gates. The city was ablaze with fire torches and frantic people, chaos filled the streets of the city, uncertainty. The night was dark. I knew I was doomed. I could hear the Romans behind me." I point to Alan.

"You….you were going to kill me to prove your allegiance, your pledge to Rome and all that Rome stood for in those days, why? Why Alan?"

I was or just had experienced such raw emotions so intense, that even I, at that moment did not like myself, or what I was feeling.

Alan just paused, refrained from commenting in the strangest of conversations for a moment as he gathered his thoughts clearly and then said this to my red and perspiring face, "Those were different times. Roman leaders were godlike, revered as gods on earth, holy deities Lilly.… I had to do what was right for Rome."

I jumped up and said to Alan, "So you could see, you could see into the past, when you were touching me, did you see me or another?"

Alan looked as if the blood had drained from his face as he said slowly as if too shocked to say too much more, "I saw you. It was you."

I stared at him. He stared at me. And then I broke the silence with my inquisitiveness and asked Alan this, "Did we Alan, long ago, in ancient times, did we contribute, our lives that is, our son we had together….. did we contribute to creating a religion, and the Jewish people in that time period, some of those Jewish people were all too eager to create their version of royalty on earth? Those Jewish castle servants were always idolizing me. I remember, and the more you touch me, the more I can remember. Those Jewish women wanted royalty for themselves, they even began wearing wigs like I had been wearing."

Alan looked at me very intensely and stated very matter of fact, "I changed my name back then, after the war with Egypt and you. I changed my name to Caesar Augustus."

I gave a look of bewilderment and asked Alan, "But why?"

And then the kitchen door opened, it was Bessy. That ancient chapter now etched in my young mind closed very abruptly before the ink, the blood could dry as the kitchen door opened right then and there, I was back to the year 1864. I was a woman, a royal woman from the east now trapped in the body of a twelve year old, that is how I felt now. Alan made me feel now. My chest was not even fully developed in this lifetime, just like the rest of me. However, I began to see, I knew now of the taste of that Biblical apple, that forbidden fruit. And Alan? I noticed he smelled of forbidden fruit as we both exited the kitchen prep room where freshly baked bread still laid out on the wooden table now behind us.

That particular full afternoon was one I would miss that evening and in the days to come. I only wondered before what it had meant to be a lady in love, now I knew I experienced something we both controlled in each other, very powerful emotions and physical responses to one another. In the hidden aspects of the nights and weeks to come, I wanted to touch, reminisce, take my hand and brush a stroke against my skin as I reminisced about every distinguishing feature of his that was so different than mine…...

From out of nowhere, and to everyone's surprise, uncle George and my cousins Mary and Adam were knocking on that grand antebellum entrance door of ours. Goods from uncle George were brought in for safe keeping. Boxes of English china and fancy tea sets, English linens, colorful items from the Caribbean, cans of sugar, all lined against our formal dining room wall.

"We need to export some sugar cane and cans of tobacco before those Yankee's take over our Savannah port, do you hear me Morgan?" Uncle George spoke in a loud voice, a voice commanding attention to my drunk father still resting on the sofa half asleep. My father still resting on the living room sofa, suddenly sat up when my uncle George entered the room surprising all of us.

"I can't believe the danger those damn Yankees are causing our families. I just can't get over how they have the indecency to come down here and boss us around, grown white men, telling us what we can and can't do in our business. I just don't know when they will go back north." Spoke my uncle George.

"We just gotta kill them all, one by one, they won't retreat back, they are a swarm of bees as busy into destroying our lives here in the south as I ever did see. I can't believe a white man telling me to let a slave go, and why would a white man fight for the life of a colored's freedom, makes no sense to me either." Chimed in my father, now sober of the whiskey he drank so freely of earlier in the day.

"We have got to get to Savannah and ship out these goods before those Yankee soldiers confiscate our wealth in this shipment. We gotta get these items out immediately, I've already been prepaid to do so. You ain't in any shape to carry on to Savannah. I am going to leave Adam and Mary here, and maybe Bessy, or Alan can drive one team of horses behind my carriage." Announced my uncle George to my father.

"Bessy can ride with you, and Alan and Lilly will ride behind in a carriage. Lilly knows how to aim a gun, and I'll make sure she has a rifle by her side. She can hold her own pretty good now, I've seen her practice shooting on old mister Benfield's plantation grounds." Spoke my father in a proud tone of voice.

"Let's eat. Bessy and Elizabeth, are you ready for us to sit at the table now? You've got two hungry grown men needing a hot meal and some of that warm baked bread I've been smelling all afternoon." My father spoke with a smile and a twinkle in his eyes. He was happy to see his brother George. We all were happy to see uncle George and my cousins, Adam and Mary. Somehow there was strength in being near family during these unsettling, restless times in the south.

Like all road trips, this one to Savannah is like navigating through unchartered waters, everything should be expected, nothing should be taken for granted. My father packed a rifle next to me, with plenty of ready to reach ammunition by my side. I did not know when I would need to use it, but I knew that time would come, in a very unexpectedly way, that time would come I feared. I felt like a child absorbing life's experiences, but my parents and Alan and the others all seemed to view me as a young adult.

My father Morgan was so against the north coming to his south, his territory, where his family had resided since the American Revolution against the British for freedom. Many of our ancestors had lost their life in Savannah during the American revolt against British rule almost a hundred years ago. Telling him what he could or could not do with his properties by fellow Americans really drove a stake through his heart at times. The looming battle was driving him mad inside, that at times I feared he simply had bad judgment in his continued business of exporting and importing during war times, especially his slave trade auctions. I felt the impending danger of the road trip I was about to embark on with Alan. My father Morgan was so bullheaded now days, more than ever stubborn not to change. He was not going to be stopped by Lincoln in some Emancipation Proclamation to free all our southern black slaves. The slaves are the labor for the southern plantations and the help we needed as well, nothing or no one could ever change his mind, he was never going to become an abolisher of slavery. My father grew more bitter as he grew worn and tired from his injured leg.

"The problem in the south is not the black slave help, hell, we need the slaves, the problem in the south is the north, they gotta go." He'd say over and over, as if words could really push those Yankees back north.

My father was donating all he could, over half his profits these days went to the confederate forces to make the north retreat back. General Robert E. Lee, a confederate top general and a top graduate of West Point had some success in the east, but lost so much ground at Gettysburg in Pennsylvania and the battle of Cheat Mountain in Virginia. General Lee was a commander known for his success in trench digging, so I am told. My father Morgan said often, "I would rather give what I have left to the confederate forces, before those Lincoln men take what I got left anyway. They're damn near killing me."

Would the south win at last? At least maybe we could keep some slaves, I thought. We needed their labor for the plantations and businesses to profit well in the south. The confederate win at the battle of Kennesaw Mountain gave us some much needed solitude of hope inside. But we needed more victories to push the north away.

It was my understanding that my father had donated so much to the confederate forces that General Robert E. Lee himself was coming for dinner someday soon. I should hope not to miss that opportunity to spy on such a dinner guest, what an honor it would be to be in his presence, to have him in our home for dinner. But before such important guests would be arriving, we needed to head to Macon, Georgia, to a cotton plantation to drop off large boxes of English imported china to a wealthy family in Macon.

The early morning haze as we left Atlanta implemented the heat and humidity we would encounter throughout that day and the next. I felt like a wilted daisy in the days long heat before we even left Atlanta. The atmospheric moisture was melting me under my layers of dress as I sat next to Alan in the buggy. I longed to locate a stream of water or lake to swim in along the way to Macon. I just desired to not feel like a wilted daisy in the heat under my dress, as I do now.

We stayed in Macon that night at the most gracious antebellum plantation mansion, with the most enormous grand ballroom I ever did lay eyes on. Alan and I stayed in separate rooms at the plantation mansion. I closed my eyes that night and dreamt of being married to Alan, carrying on like married couples do at a fancy ballroom dance. I dreamt in wonderment of other gracious couples accepting Alan and I as a married couple, not an odd pair couple, of a tutor and a young student. But a real married couple, living on a plantation, Alan would work to oversee the wealthy plantation, and I would write gothic epic novels from our upstairs bedroom draped in flowing draperies and large open air windows like so long ago. I would become a famous writer in the south, in our world together. My mind was full of expanding fantasies of how I wished things could be, but nevertheless could not be. I enjoyed how the passion was so awakening in my young vibrant world, the world of Alan and I. It was Alan that seemed to set the sun, and I that seemed to light up the night sky above us, that's how our world felt and seemed to us both, secretly of course.

The next morning I woke tired from our travels, and perhaps unrested from my night of ballroom dancing, the music I felt last night in my room, kept me awake most of the night. I pulled out a new dress and began waltzing across the planks of the polished Georgia pine, someday we'll dance together, for all to see……..

I met Alan at the large table for breakfast, I could tell in his eyes he had longed for me that same evening of last night, the way I had longed for him too. Perhaps when we reach Savannah, away from the watchful eye of uncle George, is when we can pretend to be at a ballroom dance, or at least pretend to be married in secret.

Alan loaded the china cargo off the carriage and lifted up boxes of tobacco unto the back of the carriage. Uncle George collected the money in gold, and shortly we found ourselves traveling yet down another barren terrain route to Savannah. There were open fields of hollow valleys and one old oak tree every so often on a slight hill of sorts. I wondered with the obvious overgrowth of brush on the cleared fields, who before had cleared the fields before slaves could do such work for us, or was it always slaves that worked that overgrown field at one time? Now just an abandoned grassland of weeds and brush. Soon we rounded a corner that led to a waterfall pouring into a swimming hole. "Can we stop to go swimming," I shouted up ahead to uncle George.

He just kept driving his team of horses ignoring my question, then uncle George abruptly halted his horses, "Woa, woa." Said uncle George sitting next to Bessy.

I ran into the water, then stopped at my knees. I looked around for snakes, then called for the others to join me. Bessy sat under a tree as

Alan and I swam in the cool pool of fresh water. She stared as we swam close together, laughing, and enjoying the cool moment. Uncle George took a nap on the wagon, his hat tilted forward, he saw nothing of the touching and feeling that went on under the water. Bessy closed her eyes but never let herself sleep fully, it was not her nature to ever dose off in my company, especially now that she had the worries of Alan and I to tend to in her watchful care.

After an hour of wading in water, Alan and I let the rays of the sun dry off our clothes that we still wore. We were damp dry by the time we headed down the winding road lined of oak trees as we headed further southeast to Savannah, our destination. After about two hours on our route I shouted and pointed ahead, under an old oak tree laid dead, over ten confederate soldiers. My uncle George commanded his horses to stop, we stopped. Uncle George asked that we stay in our carriage as he would check to see how long those solders had been dead. "Shisshh," he said. " I don't want those Yankees to hear us now, I don't know if they are still around this place, ya hear."

Silence laid on us like an evening sky hiding our fears that late afternoon as our carriages stopped abruptly as we unmasked the devastation upon which we so unexpectedly discovered that hot afternoon. I wanted to relinquish what I had just engulfed into my memory, child or adult now, I wanted peace. The shipyard Port of Savannah was still a ways off. I wondered if we would reach a battle by nightfall, or tomorrow be caught in this civil war crossfire? We traveled through the humidity lined air, that thick early evening air felt as if the souls of our deceased confederates were following us back to southern civilization, back to laughter and whiskey found in that port city. It was as if the souls were trapped in the immensely humid air all around us, as if we could feel their emotions as we breathed in the heavy air. Although every once in a while I felt a chill among the heated climate. The ambiance of the paranormal gave way to a discussion between Alan and I about Bessy practicing voodoo behind our barn late in the night on full moons. Alan responded by telling me that native religions are just hocus pocus, and not to be feared or intrigued by the lure of any magic practiced by

Bessy. "It's not magic Alan, it's a real religion practiced by Bessy and the other coloreds. Bessy says it's real, and it works to call upon deceased souls and to give offerings in manipulating the deceased ancestors to help you get your way in this lifetime, like with love, or like with ending slavery for example in Bessy's situation. I think Bessy is jealous that we are in love, she feels so unloved, so she tells me."

I went onto explain to Alan about last summer when Bessy asked me to take home seven jars of sea water from Charleston. "Bessy never would tell me what the seven jars are for when I probed her for answers. But she did slip out a bit of knowledge as to maybe why she needed the salt water last year. Bessy told me she knew I wanted to be a famous writer, just as my father wants me to be as well. Bessy told me that she could assist in my dream of writing, but she never elaborated on the subject of the seven jars. I do keep asking though."

"Don't bother with Bessy, she is just a house slave Lilly." Spoke Alan.

"You know Alan, Bessy tells me someday she'll live a life like a white woman. Living on a large farm, with hundreds of cows, like a real wealthy land owner."

Alan laughed.

I responded, "I am telling you the truth, she told me that Alan!"

"Well, if she offers a sacrifice fit for a mad king, maybe Lincoln's commander Sherman will give her the life she has always dreamt about, in her dances beyond the barn." Alan went onto say this, "Well, regardless of a free life, the south has crops to grow back, the war is monumental in economic disaster for the south, do you think Bessy is to blame? Do you really think Bessy's barn fire pit rants and raves nonsense is to blame for the south now in a losing position, losing ground? The union troops are everywhere in the south." Spoke Alan in a very logical tone.

I responded to Alan, "I want to own industries, banking centrals, a large empire right here in the south."

"Well Lilly, you have many aspirations." Alan spoke in a patronizing tone of voice now.

"I have plenty to say to the north, I will address the north on many issues. I will write my words to the north in my books, my books will be studied and read in northern schools someday Alan. I do have ideas how to create a better world around us, without all this bloodshed over disagreeing opinions and values. I agree with my father, we can't have too many Chiefs and not enough Indians, it will never work in economics." I said.

Alan smiled and looked ahead as he said, "Brilliant Lilly, just brilliant Lilly."

When we neared the city of Savannah it was the evening of the next day, the gaslight lantern cobblestone streets echoed music being played on the patio restaurants. I could hear the bass and the fiddle playing a popular French melody, "Tipsy Gypsy" as we entered the streets. The billowy clouds had passed into the dusk of the mysterious evening sky upon us. I did not feel as if we traveled alone on our carriage ride into Savannah. I felt the souls of our confederates in the air all around us, caught between the humidity and the heavens above, like an army protecting us as we traveled further into the heat of the city gala before us now.

We passed the Georgia Auction House, where we would go with uncle George tomorrow for the slave auction. There was a shipment of the west Indies slaves that had arrived to Savannah that we were having auctioned off tomorrow. My uncle George had over twenty men and over ten woman and children to auction off tomorrow, just in from the west Indies. The slaves will not draw as big of a crowd due to their lack of our language and lack of usable skills. But I reckon, they will all make could planters somewhere. On average, a healthy Negro man with skills of carpentry and the field can be a prize earnings of about fifteen hundred dollars. However these Negros that uncle George has brought in from overseas, won't sell for more than six or nine hundred dollars. But nevertheless, still good income for our family business.

The gas lit flames illuminated an eerie atmosphere along the streets as the winds picked up off the coast nearby. I knew by the smell of salt water in the air there was a storm brewing at sea somewhere. I was very familiar with how the air feels and smells before the dangerous winds surprise us all. Yet, the enchanted music played on into the howling night winds above us, as if to keep all things festive at the moment. We had a home in Savannah, next to Mr. Butlers brownstone. The home was three stories, Alan and I would be sleeping on separate floors.

The next day we headed to the Georgia Auction House. When we arrived, there were local plantation owners, as well as families from Florida, all checking out our slaves for sale. The white men would point at the Negros teeth in the plantation owners attempt to inspect the Negros teeth. There were two women holding infant babies in their arms, as the fathers were unable to speak English to ask a ticket payer inspecting his family to buy them all together in a wrapped deal. Just as the plantation owners would select which men and women and children they would want to purchase, so would the slaves in previous auctions urge a specific white man to buy him and his family. As if each involved in this process, including the slaves for sale had a voice in where they might want to live and work. The slaves in the past that could speak English always would brag to a specific white patron that they liked, "I's can do carpentry, field planting, I's am a prime rice planter, I do's brick laying for yous, my wife is good with I's baking sir, mines kids no trouble either, they's work too." But not these coloreds just brought in for this particular auction, they were right off the boat.

The wind blew the auction house doors shut with a force. The wind's fury could be heard blowing through the flanked boards, the rain pounded harder, more fierce. I thought the roof was going to blow off before the auction could even get under way. This was Alan's first slave auction ever attended, he seemed in awe at the whole process, how Bessy and the others actually ended up on an estate such as ours. Alan remained quiet most of the afternoon at the auction house. Some slaves appeared sad, withdrawn, others tried to keep up in earnest with the rapid pace of the auctioneer and what the auctioneer was saying to the crowd about them.

Some slaves would step off the auctioning block without caring to cast even a glance at their new owners who held their fate in their hands. Some Negros would smile and give a wince at the white patron who just bid on them. I do not know what it was like to be auctioned off like Bessy had been years ago, but I do know this, she has a good life with us, she is like family, she is dear to me. Unlike a field planter, Bessy's duties revolve in the shade and comfort of our home, Bessy has a life better than most slaves, I do believe.

I suppose I can't see her point in her complaining about her life, as she will carry on now and then under her breath as she fusses over me. Some slaves save up enough money to purchase their freedom. I've seen it before where a black man pretends to be lame in one foot so that he is not auctioned at top bid, later in the year after acting lame in one foot, the cleaver Negro buys himself his freedom for only about six or seven hundred dollars saved up, sometimes even paying less than that amount for his own purchased new freedom. But he still can't own land here in the south, well he might buy land, but it would be confiscated later, that's a sure bet.

We had arrived late to the auction that day. But needless to say it was a successful afternoon for our family. Uncle George gave Alan one hundred dollars for his time in traveling to Savannah, dropping off goods, and seeing to it that I return safely to Atlanta. Alan and I strolled the cobblestone sidewalks, some sidewalks still were made of lumber, and damp from the down pouring of rain earlier. We came across a jeweler in town who had ornate wedding bands displayed. Alan asked if I wanted to go inside. With my heart racing, Alan held the door for me as we entered the store. I felt uncomfortable as the jewelry store owner asked how he could help us. Laying on top of draped green velvet laid a pair of gold wedding bands with tiny rubies and diamonds decorating the top of the female band, it was a fancy set of engagement rings. I remained quiet in Alan's negotiating for the set of rings. The Jeweler would not let the pair of rings go for any less than twenty-five dollars. Alan handed the man across the counter the money, then Alan tried the ring on my finger and a ring on his finger. Alan asked the man, "How much to size the rings sir?"

The robust man replied back, "I can do the sizing for free, it will only take a day or so, how long are you staying in Savannah?"

"Well at least another day or so sir." Replied Alan.

"Well then, I'll have them both ready for ya all by three o'clock tomorrow afternoon….how's that for you folks?"

Alan nodded at the man in agreement, then handed over the two rings for sizing.

A bell jingled as we left the store. "Alan, what are you doing buying two gold wedding bands, it's too early Alan, it's too early to marry, we need to wait at least a few more years until I reach seventeen."

Meanwhile, Bessy was making dinner for us back at the brownstone. I blushed and smiled as we walked through the front door. Bessy shuffled us into the formal dining room where our hot meal was awaiting us. "Yous two look as if yous keeping a secret from me. I's know all. Yous can't keep yous secret from me, I's know yous in love with each others."

Bessy went unto say, "I's make sure the time is right for yous to be together, yous know, like married couples, I's am working on something special for yous."

"You are working on something very special for us, like what Bessy, are you knitting a quilt?" I asked after taking a sip of her chicken soup.

"A quilt dear? No's I's be working on something real special for yous. A love story yous will write about, a famous love story Lilly dear, a love story that goes on like oceans of time, oceans of time Lilly, yous and Alan." Spoke Bessy almost overjoyed this evening as I sipped on more soup she had made.

I smiled at Alan sitting across from me, simply not even adhering to what Bessy had to say, like most always, he could care less what she had to say. This evening was no different in his non-support of Bessy and what she had to say. Bessy seemed to know that fact all too well about how Alan perceived her. We finished the homemade chicken soup and fresh rye bread, delicious as always. I knew I would be taking Bessy with me someday when I married Alan. I hope there would not be any future conflict between my adoration for Bessy my mamme, and Alan my true love. Bessy noticed too how Alan would clearly look away when she spoke to us. Alan would act distracted when she spoke to me, at times he would just flat out cut her off upon mid-sentence. Then begin his own topic of conversation with me as I sat opposite of him by the dining room table. He just did not respect Bessy, or think highly of Bessy, or perhaps did not like her illiterate sounding words, or just how she pronounced her words. I understood Bessy perfectly, she made sense to me, but some folks just saw her as less, less than a perfect human being. Bessy loved me, she knew I accepted her and loved her, more than most whites would. But she was like a mother to me, more so than my own white mother. Bessy was losing control over the one thing that she lived for, we bonded like a real mother daughter relationship. Bessy was losing control over controlling me as I headed down an unmovable passage of falling deeply in love with Alan. Whom someday Alan would be a mighty powerful man right here in the south, having control of land, me, our children, and servants if we are allowed. And Bessy would always be serving soup and sweeping floors, just being Bessy, my mamme, just older with each passing year I suppose. In which Bessy unavoidably tossed away her own youthfulness and impossible dreams to fulfill for the simple sake of not being born with the right skin color. Sure, I noticed her skin color, but I accepted Bessy for who she was to me, just like a daughter loves a caring mother in the way Bessy dotes on me as her child. Undoubtedly, Bessy did loathe seeing me in love, it wasn't a reward for her, just a reward for Alan and I.

The next day we took a walk to the jeweler in town, the rings were a perfect fit now. Alan thanked the man repeatedly, then Alan placed the rings in his upper shirt pocket. We stopped for something sweet, but ended up eating crab cakes at a popular restaurant in town. We then strolled down to the corner of Abercorn and Charleston, I could hear a waterfall, "Let's follow the sound of the waterfall," I said to Alan. It was the sound of the water flowing from the black cast iron three tiered fountain at Lafayette Square.

"Let's walk over here, shall we?" Spoke up Alan.

The Spanish moss dripped down upon us like a wild garden for lovers, drizzled over the overgrown willow and oak tree branches, the Spanish moss hung, hiding the fountain at Lafayette Square from a distance. The closer we came to the fountain, the closer Alan walked next to me holding my hand in the disguising of our affection within the ruffle of my puffed purple full skirt that I wore that day. The birds sang over the three tiered fountain's waterfall splashing sound, it felt like a promise was going to be made to me that day……and a revelation of Alan's love for me *was* made as we sat and talked for hours until dusk. My blonde curls frizzed in the southern moisture trapped in the Savannah air off the sea in that garden island of ours, we sat for hours. Sneaking soft caresses from one another in private.

"You look like an angel," spoke Alan softly in his usual steady voice of his as he laid back, resting his head in his folded palms looking up above to the green canopy shielding the hot sun of that afternoon. Alan went on to promise this bewildering statement to me on that hot and sticky afternoon in Savannah, "If anything should happen to you Lilly, I will place a death wish on Bessy and condemn all of that dreaded bloody native Haiti, the place she comes from. I will Lilly, with every ounce of my soul, condemn Bessy and Haiti. She is very jealous of our love, she is not free to marry, she is owned by your father to watch over you Lilly. Bessy resents that fact everyday she sees you and I together, Lilly. I know you confide with her like she is your best friend, but you must understand she is jealous, and jealousy can lead to danger, you must keep our engagement a secret. You must not tell that drum beating, doll weaving, animal torturer, house slave, nanny of yours, Bessy, nothing of our engagement, you must hide this ring." Spoke Alan as he went onto say this……..

"We are a reminder of what she does not have, or ever will have, Bessy is young and remorseful. Bessy is very, very contentious towards you having happiness in life, and not her, deep down she desires to be you, I fear. Bessy's mind is not brilliant and original like yours. Bessy is not free to love, she is locked with invisible bars within your fathers household. You and I will write a famous love story someday and she knows it, and between the pages, gain notoriety for our writing style, hiding between the lines of that great love story will drip our seduction secretly. Hiding behind vowels and nouns, bridges and metaphors, behind the prolific words we will run naked and free, expressing our love as we best know how for centuries to come. We will carry on like lovers do, like the invisible yet real heat of this sultry Savannah afternoon felt here today, we will be felt but not seen in people's minds. People will read the sensual sentences of our books to be, but they will not be able to see with the naked eye of this hot and damp vapor we feel so trapped in freely, like the ghost casting of the atmospheric moisture called humidity we won't be found. We will hid this visual passion from our readers eyes. Yet tempt them into a viewing of a reality most know nothing about, just like our long engagement…..we will create a new heaven and a new earth, we will stay forever together this time." Spoke Alan so convincingly, so prophetically.

"We must wait until the time is right Lilly for a reveal within the pages of our novels to be. You must keep all we share today in this garden of ours from Bessy's prying ears a secret, and all that we know of our secret for now." Spoke Alan firmly.

I did not respond to Alan's statement **"to be aware"** of Bessy's jealous nature. I really wondered what exactly Alan saw that I could not see in Bessy. I just was oblivious to dangerous natured individuals, especially close females imposing as close confidants who could keep the lid on my secrets tightly shut, I suppose.

My creamy ivory skin must have resembled an ivory rose with dew stuck to its petals on that sultry damp afternoon in Lafayette Square. I held the gold band that sparkled with rubies and diamonds like something discovered from a pirates quest of treasures until I feared my palm's perspiration would cause the ring to slip out of my hand. I slipped the ring on my necklace and hid my secret within my dress, it was perfect. The wait to marry Alan would be years I feared, but a wait we would both contend with during our long engagement ahead of us.

As I clutch the side of my left cheek today, I can still remember Alan brushing my cheek with his hand in Lafayette Square. His skin felt so different than the feminine softness of my cheek. I can hear the low soft hush of his English accent as he would often say when we were together, "Brilliant Lilly, just brilliant Lilly." He was so different than my exuberant vivacious character, but that is what I admired about Alan.

His extensive knowledge of the English literature was what I respected him for, and what I loved about Alan, how he made me feel so grown up, like a woman so perfectly suited for him.

Someday I had hoped, as Alan had envisioned too, as well, sailing above the wild dashing of the ocean waves, unto a journey far removed from ordinary society. A journey guided only by the twinkling shine of the stars, traveling through the dark and jealous moonlight, we would travel onward to a place to call our own. A resting spot into the hidden mist of spellbound love and find our place among the stars. A place we would revere as our heaven, our place, where natural springs burst and are abundant, a place where the earth touches the sky.

Alan would have said then, as he would probably comment now, "A *spring* is a time of renewal, a time of new growth and regeneration." Alan had this uncanny way of looking at life, a word, or common phase. "Our love affair, would become a metempsychosis experience, lasting through the ages, through the pages, for generations, that's how love works in the universe, in great English gothic novels and Greek and Egyptian mythology."

Alan drew in the Georgia red soil, a bull with horns, an eagle, a lion, and an angel, he explained their relevancy in detail to me about a love saga that was difficult for me to fathom. Alan just kept on explaining the story to me, the meaning of those four symbols.

I had little meaning of many of the words Alan spoke of when I was twelve, but I believed in my heart our literary accomplishments would become revolutionary as Alan had so fervently pointed out to me.

Alan would always address the most unusual of meanings within words, or about words. He resisted with his mind all that could be described in a conventional way, he looked behind the first description of just about every word he would express. Alan was like a god of literature and philosophy to me, giving me the insight into the unconventional descriptions, insight into portals of wisdom and knowledge beyond my years of just about everything he touched upon or read aloud. He was uncommon in his thinking, a genuine original, as if he was close to the source of something spiritual. The core of something profound he could always seemingly touch upon somehow……..that's how I was taught by him, inspired by him.

"Someday Lilly you will have wings, and teach me all you know." Alan said as he closed yet another book in my presence. As I gasped, my eyes twinkled a hue of silvery blue, I had no idea what he was referencing within his play of words. I felt one prevalent factor, something lovers cannot control, as if I was on a collision course of experiencing love at a very young conjunction of meeting my soul mate.

The Magnolia Tree
CHAPTER SIX

It was a late morning during in the summer of 1864 in Atlanta, Georgia. A sultry heat seemed to rise from the ground, not unusual late in the summer like it is now. The tree leaves vibrated and rustled in the wind as fall was approaching, so would Indian summer soon be upon us. I heard a loud banging on the front door, more like a clambering of something hard hitting the front door of our Atlanta estate. I heard the scuffling of wooden sole boots on our front veranda, the low murmuring of foreign sounding voices carried in and upward through the upper windows, I remember it as if it were yesterday. Something's in life, one always remembers, those pivotal days or situations where your life dramatically changes for better or worse, and life is simply never the same. I can still see just how my cream bedroom drapes blew in the late summer sounds and breezes, flowing creamy silky panels as a humidity storm was brewing in the sky above. A downpour of rain mixed with dread was about to hit our home, I just was not aware of how hard. I heard distant Yankee voices at our door. I remember what I wore that day, and how my hair was braided. I remember how it felt when my heart sank into my stomach, and a nervous pulse began a beat that was uncontrollable to stop. Like an untamed African-Caribbean style drumming as I heard so many nights in the past from behind the barn of Bessy's echo of days gone by.

I laid looking at the lavender painted walls and cream taffeta puffed drapes in my room on the second story floor, I sat frozen in fear. I heard a jar fall out, down, in my closet. It startled me so, I went to open my closet and rolling on the floor was a jar, not just any jar, but a jar filled with large enormous Georgia field spiders. Were they dead or alive? I was curious and opened the jar and jumped. BOOM, BOOM, went a loud thud at our front door. As I dropped the jar, it smashed on the hardwoods. Doom. I was not sure if I should wake my brother and two sisters for fear they would confront the danger in our house. A fleeting thought of what should I do now, how should we all escape the danger? Grab my siblings and run out the back door? My childhood fears conjured in my mind were met with a harsh reality in my home that fateful day in August 1864. Like watching a tornado in the distance come closer, so was the storm about to hit our household like a northern harsh storm breeze so out of control, our front door busted wide open. Fear set in…….real fear…..beyond yelling or screaming fear. Fear that made me silent and my heart pound loud within my small frame.

The Yankees were burning barns and crops in the south, causing a huge food shortage in the south, all to just prove that we can't own slaves. I think there is some kind of misunderstanding, we needed Bessy, and Bessy needed us. It was the story all through the south. But our story, and our lives were about to change forever. Bessy answered to the loud commotion in the front foyer, and in marched those Yankee soldiers, further intruding upon our beloved dwelling. They smelled of something awful, imported Yankee filth upon our gleaming hardwoods.

The northern foreign soldiers began their intrusion into our home by first sitting at our long dining room table. I loathed those men from that very rude and intrusive moment on. The men were smelly and tired looking, their faces covered with marks of dirt and dried blood scabs. The intruders pounded their hands on the table demanding Bessy and Netty serve them bread immediately.

One colored who walked in on all the commotion so unexpectedly was ordered to kill chickens out back, and serve them all a hot meal. "We are famished" the soldiers said as they eyed our house furnishings, including Bessy. I could not believe what I heard from the top of the staircase, just then, one Yankee soldier began walking up the steps! The creaking steps instilled this awful dread, fear of the worst kind inside of me, I felt doomed. Just then the Yankee turned back down the staircase towards the others. I ran to get my brother William and gathered him up in my arms as I ran to get my sisters. My mother and father were in town, yet had not arrived back home yet. These bully guests, could care less whether or not my parents were home or not. The joy of being a child blossoming into a young lady drained from my heart with the foreign occupation within our home of those Yankee soldiers that fateful dreaded late day in August of 1864.

I remember peering down from the atop the staircase banister looking down at those gruff union soldiers. Some still gathered in talk in our large foyer area, yet some shouting at our dinner table. Their skin was not a shade whiter than mine, or my fathers, or anyone in our family. I could not understand it either, how a white man could barge into another man's house, and bully him into believing he was right, correct, or justified in his attitude towards us here in the south. My father Morgan was right, it made no logical sense, none. I just did not understand this northern philosophy of intrusion and war over how we conducted our business here in the south. Not many white folks could rightly understand that bully brazen attitude from another white, how can they all act this way towards us? Deep down, I just think those northerners want what is ours.

My family and I were now forced to all sleep in one room. The Lincoln's men took over our mansion like an Inn owned by them. My father had the deed to our house, built and paid for our southern mansion with his money. There was no property sale, or signing off on our deed to our house, we were just doomed. Doomed because of a war that had gone way too far. Our situation was unfair, unjust. Un-constitutional in how the union soldiers treated us with theft and bully tactics. And I know if we all were anywhere near a southern courthouse, these Yankee men would of been tried and hung in the same afternoon. But this situation, this war so out of control, and had no system of justice for how these men took and treated us. Bessy and Netty had to cater to them, cooking for them, polishing their dirty smelly boots. I just stood back and watched my world stop.

Even Alan had to sleep in our room, all of us crammed into one room each night. There was not one evening that I did not go to bed hungry, all of us were hungry. For now it seemed my romance with Alan was put on hold. I had felt guilty for the secrets I kept hidden from the rest of my family concerning Alan and I. But I also needed and treasured him. I was not sure when life would improve around these parts. With the development of no privacy now, I was back to just being a kid again, just an ordinary child in a pretty lilac colored dress.

I no longer felt "grown up," as I did on the lap of Alan as we role played in secrecy. There was limited role playing, hardly any secrecy, our world we had secretly created for ourselves in private had faded for now, taken for now. It was as if we had never kissed at all. It was like having a lit torch placed in my garden hedges, and all I could do now is just step back and watch my love affair with Alan go up in flames, like one of those bon fires out back, behind the barn. It was becoming increasingly more difficult to locate a place to give a kiss in private, to dream of our future, and just be. I missed my many afternoon escapes with Alan.

I wondered when the confederates would gather and come rescue us? The south was drowning in saturated imbued bloodshed. You could feel the heated doom of this war, it was all around us now. I just kept wondering as I gasped in horror….. when would we get our home back? Our lives back? When would these damn Yankees just leave us be? Perhaps Alan was right, the side with the most money always wins, the side with the most powerful connections always wins a war, that damn bully north.

I noticed now that my father was in no shape to put up a fight against the Yankee soldiers, and outnumbered, my father's spirit began to crumble further, so I noticed. Was I the only one left strong in this household? I wondered quietly to myself. I still had fight left in me. I sat in quiet desperation for others in the household to feel as I do right now. The north is wrong. This is wrong!

This is our house, our land. Land owned by father! The enemy was not an Indian, or someone from a different country, or someone of lighter skin than us. The enemy was a white man, a bully white man that took over everything of ours from a brainwashed voodoo driven northern government. It was just mass confusion how another white could treat us here in our home. Without telling us, I saw my dad was a changed man now that the Yankees had occupied the south.

The saddest part of the Lincoln mens' arriving was their demand that we immediately let our slave servants go at once. Some of the older slaves out back did not want to go, even Netty asked the Yankee soldiers if she could stay and be the cook for the troops and stay with the family. But Bessy was different, more strong minded than Netty I suppose. Bessy decided this was her opportunity to be free without having to pay a large amount for her freedom. Contradictory to popular belief of customs here in the south, there was no money exchanged, just the wave of a Yankee soldier asking her to go, "Get, go on now, pack your bags."

I could never leave a child I had raised. But Bessy inside was more selfish than she portrayed in her earlier devotion to me and my siblings. Some mothers are selfish deep down, some mammes are too I learned very abruptly that day in August 1864. One just doesn't know it until time displays an opportunity, such as the one I was witnessing with mine own eyes.

Bessy gathered some of her belongings upstairs and carried down a suitcase of sorts. I remember so vividly how angry my father was at Bessy for thinking she could just take her clothes in his suitcase. Just up and pack "his property" with her and simply walk out the front door. He called her a thief and a trader, a heated argument broke out between them, him yelling at her mostly. My father was adamant he was not going to take too kindly to Bessy walking out on the family household never to be seen or heard of again. The Yankee soldiers escorted Ms.

Bessy outside and there she walked down our pathway leading away from our home, not even looking back at us, not even once. I called for her, "Bessy, Bessy we need you, come back Bessy, come back, we need you, don't leave us!" I pleaded as I ran from the veranda. Bessy kept looking forward, not once did she turn her head back to reply to my pleadings. I ran after Bessy before she reached the end of the dusty trail, tears dripping from my young doll like face. I grabbed a hold of her hand, begging for her to stop, like a young child I grabbed ahold of her hand with all my body weight as if to swing or anchor on her arm and stop her from running away. "Please don't go Bessy, life will not be better for you if you leave. Your life is good here, Netty is going to stay, please stay too." I pleaded.

Bessy kept looking ahead, down the road, and said this as she shook her arm free from me, "Someday I's will be white like yous Lilly, I's be a real equal to ya'll, do yous hear me Lilly dear? We's be equal someday I's said. I's be born in a family that's has lots of land and cows, somewhere in the north. I's be white like yous someday Lilly. I's want mines freedom Lilly, nows is the time. Yous remember this Lilly, when yous and Alan are reading love poetry under that ol' magnolia tree out yonder, yous remember that I's will create in yous a great love story Lilly. Many family members theys come back like characters for your novel Lilly, a real famous novel. Yous goinna remembers alls yours love, alls yours memories come back to yous Lilly. I dig up some real fine memories from your past, yous be famous, just like Morgan wants for his beloved Lilly. Yous trust me Lilly. Yous remember me toos, and all I do's for yous family now."

Bessy continued to try and plead for me to let go of her apron. But I couldn't seem to obey her at that moment. Bessy untied her apron strings and allowed for me to cry and beg as I held the fabric and smells of days gone by in my hands. My mind can still smell the lingering of charred logs from the fireplace pit from her baking.

I looked up with red swollen eyes as my father yelled profanities in the backdrop of my once beloved life. Bessy spoke her last words to me before her departure.

"Yous remember mine eyes Lilly, yous knows me when yous see me again Lilly." Bessy's eyes at times seemed ablaze, like a ram ready to charge on, she had fire in her eyes. A real electrical charge radiated from out of her eyes at times. As if her eyes could go from an animal to a person, or from a person to a untamed ram glaring back at me, ready to charge onto me in full animal aggression.

"Yous forgive me's Lilly for leaving now, I's must be going, I's have many things to do with mines life Lilly dear. Someday Lilly yous write and write like there is no tomorrow, yous absorb the sea around you and write all you remember, until the sea is gone. Dis white, dis black will all pass, trust me Lilly, I's know whats I'm doing." Bessy stopped walking and turned to me and said this, "Someday I put my snake hat on, like the one I wore behind the barns yous see me in from time to time. I's going to open those seven sealed jars of salt water from Charleston yous brought me, and I's pour it out, yous be a famous writer Lilly when I's do, yous be able to taste the sea, soak up that old sea, and write yous a tale. A real famous tale about all that swims in dis sea, washes up to shore. Writing about the afterlife and what exists beyond what most common folks knows is true, the underworld and heaven, yous write about philosophy. Yous write about mines life and yours, yous write a love story like yous always wanted to do withs Alan by your side. Yous forgive me's now though, I's must be going, yous know I's love you child, like mines own, like a childs I's cannot hold and call mines own."

I responded, "I hate the northern soldiers, I hate them for what they have done to my family, they are bullies! Don't leave us, we need you." As I screamed the words, "hate the northern soldiers," Bessy lifted her chin, tilted her head back and laughed. Bessy had an unusual smile on her face as she left, I never heard her cackle and laugh like that before. I could obviously feel in the air, the thick humidity all around us that we were experiencing such different of emotions. I was heartbroken and scared, Bessy was not.

Bessy looked down at me still pleading with her. I knew it was time to let her hand go this time, but it was hard to let go of the one who had taken care of me all my life. As long as I could remember, Bessy was always there for me.

Time passed slowly after Bessy left our household. I longed for secret moments with Alan. I longed for Bessy's return to our home to care for me. I had so much to confide in with her, often like best friends we'd talk alone on nights I could not seem to fall asleep. I was just an awkward lonely teenager now, love and friendship seemed to have vanished from my young, fresh world here in the south.

That night I could not sleep, the rest of my family lay like hostages on the floor and beds in the room, but me. I began strolling towards the awakening fervent light of the moon's vibrating rays by one of the bedroom's tall windows. I reached my hand out to touch the white illuminating moonlight stirring into my room. Very quiet, mesmerizing moonlight tonight, I thought to myself. No drum beats stirring in the background tonight, just quiet moonlight all around me now.

The moon must be just about full right now, typically on a night like this I would hear Bessy and the other coloreds in the barn or behind the barn. Chanting and dancing with fire and drums on a full moon night like this one. But tonight the evening air was still with a moon so full, without Bessy, tonight was disturbingly quiet I thought to myself. Where is Bessy sleeping tonight? I wondered, where was Bessy going to live? I hated the north. And knew I would never visit such a place of Lincoln's men. I could not even muster an army in my house to get the bully's off our land here in the south. I clutched the doll that Bessy made for me, the golden hair doll was made from my own hair that Bessy had cut, and was all I had at this moment to connect me to Bessy. The moon full, my emotions savored my lost childhood. Such radiating moonlight upon me and my doll. I was just a kid caught up in too many adult situations, I thought. I was too young to be old, and not old enough to be taken seriously by the union soldiers occupying our house if indeed I did shout, "Get out you damn Yankees! And stay out!" No one would have taken me seriously and obeyed me. I just stood in my house, wide awake for some unknown reason, just standing. Saturated in the fervent moonlight now simply blissfully unaware of the hidden dangers that laid ahead in my future.

I looked at my father Morgan, he was too young to live his life like a beaten man now. It was difficult for me to grasp why he seemed to have lost his zeal to win this war against the north. He promised me that the northern soldiers occupying the south, our house, would never break him. But he lied, as I looked across the crowded room, I saw my father as a broken spirited man, a man who lost hope of ever getting rid of the northern bullies. How could he **not** put up a fight against these bully northern soldiers changing our lives here in the south? The damn Yankees occupying our home like drunken pirates lost at sea they did, they did not build or own this house, it is our house. White men bullying us, it was surreal, this disagreement just can't be I thought. I was angry at the north, angry at my father too, and why wouldn't Alan put up a fight like a real man would? Alan seemed to only jump as high as my father would ask of him, I suppose. Why can't Alan play the role of Romeo moving in a way that could spellbound love towards me right now, I was hypnotized. A drunk love as I floated in my mind of memories past and gone for now.

I then heard a voice in the moonlight, felt something, a sick resonating feeling that Bessy had been killed. I could not sleep a wink that night. Restless…. my head ached. It felt as if I was running, and running, and tripped, in the woods, over something, and then, just now my head inside my skull. Like never before extreme pain felt, my head on the side is aching beyond belief. Finally daylight broke………..

I achieved to live yet another day, and the pain was no longer. I felt empty, as if I had lost something within me, and I was not going to get it back. Just a bizarre empty feeling inside. I suppose this war was really taking a toll on me, in my brain, or something?

That afternoon I spotted Alan near the barn feeding the chickens, I decided to approach him. Maybe we can have some alone time?

Alan had a certain twinkle in his eyes as he looked back over his shoulder noticing me approaching him by the barn. Alan spoke up first, "You know Lilly I have been giving a lot of thought to what you disclosed to me about seeing a life you lived, we lived, in a different time period than this one. I am more curious than ever Lilly, I want to hear more about your memories and all. What else do you remember Lilly?"

"I had children, more than just one son. My oldest son I conceived was from a different father than my youngest son. My oldest, his father rather pushed himself on me when I was about nineteen or so, that's how the relationship with his father began and ended." I said as I motioned for Alan to join me under the shade of the ol' magnolia tree.

Alan looked serious as he asked me this next question, "Do you think Lilly that one of these Lincolns' men is Marc Antony looking to take you away from me?"

I was shocked and horrified at that claim by Alan, that odd and inappropriate inquisitiveness by him. And then Alan went further with his claims towards me, more accusing this time around as Alan said, "I saw you kiss one of those Lincoln's men Lilly… Right on the lips."

I clutched my bonnet strings and defensibly spoke up and said to Alan, "You are dreaming things! You had a bad dream and are now accusing me of unthinkable acts Alan!"

Alan looked sad and sober, serious, and commented to me as he said, "Maybe I dream with my eyes wide open."

I inquired, "Can we change the subject Alan? This conversation is going nowhere."

Alan responded, "Yes, we can change the topic of conversation. Tell me more about what you remember from a past life Lilly."

I begin talking as I gave an up and down once over with my eyes towards Alan. "I had children, more than just one son. My oldest son I conceived with Marc Antony when he rather pushed himself on me. Marc Antony wanted the riches of the kingdom I ruled over, Egypt. Marc Antony had a futuristic power play plan to control the water from the Nile River and create a large territory of land for himself and our children we had together."

Alan inquires further concerning mysteries from the past, "Why did Marc Antony use you for the riches of Egypt? That sounds selfish and conceited of him. Not a true love story that history has always narrated to us listening ears Lilly."

I remark back to Alan, "He was vain, Marc Antony was a smug arrogant. War was always on his agenda and in our future together, building a mighty empire. Gaining land for himself and later his war campaigns incorporated the idea of building an empire with his children he had with me."

As I pause for just a second, Alan speaks up and remarks rather coolly, "You had talks with me about building a large empire by joining Egypt with Rome."

I graciously respond to Alan's accusations as my young mind tries to make sense of all the nightmares in my head. In a moderately warm tone of voice I respond to Alan by saying, "I know. My oldest son possessed a strong distrust for Jewish servants. I had a dream last night my oldest son from ancient days gone by raged a war against all Jews. He burned them alive, he starved them. He carried out his untamed anger in my dream for the lost war against Rome and the kingdom he ultimately lost too, so long ago during Biblical times. My dreams allow for me to see into the past and into the future. I too Alan dream with my eyes wide open."

I stare at Alan, Alan stares at me then I begin talking again, "In my dreams my oldest son is warning me to be very careful to whom I place my trust. Then he comments to me in my dreams, "Mom, you almost got away, you almost escaped.""

Alan inquires, "You had a plan to escape if the war with Rome, with me did not end in the favor of Egypt, the victory for Egypt?" There was a long pause as we both immersed ourselves with painful memories from the dreaded dark past that loomed in our relationship.

"Yes, there was going to be a cover-up. Someone, a woman was going to die in place of me. I was going to be joined with my children and Marc Antony in a foreign place. However I did not escape once I returned to Egypt after leaving your chambers. There were too many Roman soldiers waiting in Egypt and I did not know in which direction to turn on the dusty trails from the direction of Rome to Egypt. I went back to the only place I know, or should I say knew. I was killed in Egypt and buried in a temple tomb that is now submerged underwater, twenty leagues under the salty sea along with all my ancient secrets."

Alan asks, "How do you know Lilly? How do you really know that you were killed by Roman soldiers and placed into a temple tomb that is now under the sea?"

I respond to Alan in a serious tone, "I was not killed by a multitude of Roman soldiers, I was killed by you. I still can taste the gurgling salt water when you first kissed me Alan. Can I just tell my story Alan, or should I call you Octavia?"

Alan looks up from the ground where his eyes met mine and coolly remarks, "Lilly, you have always had a lot of secrets, both in this lifetime of ours and also during Biblical times. I could not trust you or your loyalty towards me. I understood my war position with Rome, at times I could not understand you and where your loyalties laid."

Alan took a late blooming magnolia flower and placed the flower in my hand. "Let's go find the others, the day is too young for us to feel this much dread."

It was an early afternoon in September 1864, I was back being just a kid again, playing with William, Grace, and Kate in the backyard. We were sitting on a thick curving long hanging magnolia tree branch, laughing and carrying on the way kids do at that age. I announced to everyone that I was going to climb to the top of the tree. The others cheered me on with their open mouth expressions of awe at my daring feats of skill as I climbed upward, above them. My wooden sole boots slipped slightly as my soles embraced the magnolia tree bark expressively smooth ridges. I knew I had the strength to make it to the top, my stomach turned upside down as the faces of my brother and sisters appeared smaller from atop the massive mountain of branches I was climbing upon. I stood on the tallest branch of the tree, I raised my hand in a victorious pose. My siblings beneath me cheered. I felt a rush of dizziness transcend from my head to my body in an entirely strange way. I took a deep gasp of fresh air. I then made my way down the tree, ever so carefully.

It was different climbing up the tree, then making my way down the tree, I felt queasy, and my boots felt slippery on the bottom like they do at times climbing the stone embankment of Stone Mountain here in Georgia. It was like balancing on ice all of a sudden way up at the top. I knew I needed to get down.

I held more weight in my arms this time, I thought, trying to use my arms as my strength in holding my weight as I made my way down. Maybe I was too old for this kinda thing now? I felt clumsy and unskilled climbing down the tree. Like a sleek sheet of ice underneath my foot, I then felt an invisible push out of nowhere. As quickly as my boot slipped, I fell backward hitting my head hard on a thick tree limb at the top. From what I recall, it was a short way down. I had been perched up high in that old magnolia tree, as I fell to my tragedy. I specifically could see the defined shadow of Bessy, like a ghost staring stoically at me from the back window of the kitchen prep area. Her ghost reflection held no expression on her face as I fell, and kept falling, until I hit the hard ground with a thump.

I could hear the blood hurling screams of William, Grace and Kate as I hit the ground hard, I could hear a big "thump" when I hit the dirt floor beneath the tree. My head and back ached, the sting could not be calmed, I could not seem to get up, I lost my breath. The next thing I remember is my hand reaching in my mind to get back to that scene under the old magnolia tree, but I couldn't get back to calm the hysteria surrounding my laying still body. My vision became like a tunnel, my eyesight under the magnolia tree became bleak, then diminished.

Alan was above my face trying to talk to me, but I could not seem to communicate back to him, as much as I desired to do so, I couldn't seem to speak. He kept rocking me in place, sobbing, as my lifeless body was then carried in the house by my father. I held no expression on my face after a few hours or so, my father Morgan laid me on my bed, he closed my eyes for me that night. I could hear the whaling cries of my mother going crazy. I could hear and feel the weeping hysteria of my grandmother. Moreover, I could distinctively taste the most despicable taste when I had hit the dirt pavement below……I tasted salt, salty water from the sea like at Charleston.

The next day, Alan, with my brother William and two sisters, Kate and Grace, gathered lilacs and placed the fragrant lilacs under the magnolia tree, in the very spot of dirt I had come to rest against after my long fall.

The next scene that I can remember so well, even to this day, I find myself at the sandy shores of Charleston, next to the wooden boardwalk, dressed in my Sunday best. My Sunday shiny boots are on, the boots Bessy had polished so well just weeks before my fall. I am splashing in the waves crashing unto shore, like a bold warrior taking on the crashing waves I jump and skip. I appear to have my hair in curls, and my fanciest bow in my hair.

My golden long locks of curls blowing in the dusk of the southern breeze off the ocean. I could not figure out where Adam and Mary were? And why my brother and sisters were not with me as I played in my white dress all alone along the sandy shoreline. I seemed mesmerized by the diamond encrusted waves, it reminded me of the sunlight filtering through the leaded glass that adorned our mansion windows. Where was everyone?

I kept remembering back to that conversation I had with Bessy on our way to that Magnolia Plantation in Louisiana, she said this to me, "Within voodoo, there are no accidents, nothing and no event has a life of its own. Voodoo means in translation, yous two, yous too. The universe is all one. Each thing effects something else. We's are not separate, this black and white war, we's all serve as parts of one. What I's mean dear Lilly, what yous do unto another, yous do unto yourself, because yous are the other, voodoo, means view yous, view your spirit. What you kill, you can become. We's are mirrors of each other's souls. I's be white, or yous are black, it does not matter, we's are all one. There's a sacred cycle between the living and the dead. I's know how to end my misery as a slave girl, and the misery of other slaves. I's need that gold pendant around your neck, trust me Lilly, I's will make sure that your home is saved from those Yankee's fire torches, trust me Lilly dear. I's will keep Alan and yous in love forever, a beautiful and moving love story to make yous famous together, in each other's arms."

But this felt more like an accident, was it? Was I some kind of voodoo sacrifice in this unexpected fall? Why can't I go back to the tree and climb down and be with my beloved family and Alan? Why did I see the shadowy reflection of Bessy staring blankly, stoically, through the glass of the kitchen prep room as I felt myself fall from so high up from the wee branches of that ol' magnolia tree? The same tree I fell in love under, where I would listen endlessly to Alan. Now, the last thing I can remember, which was the last thing I remember before my head ached so, and my back was so stiff with pain I could not get up, was the magnolia flower in my hand. I had that flower in my hand as I climbed. I just couldn't catch my breath again. I couldn't breathe, or move.

I reflect back to a distant conversation I had with Bessy, she told me this, "If yous are going to know what it's like to walk in another's shoes, yous will be born again, then yous see and feel the other person's life Lilly."

Why was I dressed in my Sunday best on the beach alone? Why did I seemingly not care that my boots were on as I splashed and jumped over the waves crashing onto the sandy shoreline here in Charleston? Where was Alan, weren't we supposed to marry someday, as soon as I turned seventeen? I do not want to sail this journey before me…….. alone. I want to wait for Alan to join me here on the beach. I don't want to swim alone, be alone.

With the balmy southern breeze off the sea, brought on the vibrant unusual sweet aroma of lilacs in the air. The sun was setting behind the curvature of the earth. The colors above me looked like a kaleidoscope, the kind I could play with, the shifting patterns of light blue and peach graced the skies before me over the deep blue mounds of moving sea. I felt drawn to the warm, radiant God like rays revolving in succession from the sun, just drawn to the beautiful light before me. I felt a wave of my miserable physical pain gone, and began feeling no need to question or concern myself with any earthy matter, was all somehow beginning to shift, disappearing from my mind. Just like how the sea began pulling the earthly sand at shore beneath its waves……I began to move forward into time and space, into a new realm of understanding the universe, far removed from Alan, and my father Morgan, or my families teachings. I began to go home, so it seemed.

My eyes began to open to the secrets of the vast sea as my soul began a new voyage. I was discarding the old, and embracing the new, as others had before me, as I headed down an immutable new course of existence……. I could feel a connection to every living thing around me. From the birds singing to me, to the fish in the deep blue sea, it all connected, and felt connected. I could feel inside of others, I could feel Bessy's remorse, her jealousy stung me. I could feel Alan's passion towards me. I could feel what it was like to be auctioned off and separated from my mother. I simply could feel and taste through another, for what seemed like an eternity, to a distant faint memory of the afterlife I had experienced. I felt washed in human understanding, an awareness of walking in everyone's shoes around me. I felt the strength of angels around me as they carried me upwards, they radiated love, a powerful love.

I remember these great souls, angels, powerful heavenly beings who gave me great love, by standing next to them, one could feel a surge of their love, encouragement, and confidence, by their overwhelming commandingly intense presence I felt empowered. God was like that too, in his presence, it was bright, his energy powerful, yet dormant mostly on earth, not seen, and not felt as much as he had envisioned for earth since the beginning of time.

On occasion, my thoughts would drift in wonderment about those I had left behind in the south………left on that grand southern estate in Georgia in the late 1800's. Memories, teachings, and experiences forever stored in my mind, but why stored to remember?

I had been told by my mother Elizabeth and my dear aunt Mary that when I reached into my twenties I would know what living was all about, that life would peek for me in my twenties. I would be married to a handsome wealthy merchant or plantation owner, have children on my lap, and still have the beauty and grace to be the belle of the ball for community dances and socials. I could stay up late sipping on imported beverages, and have as many mammes as I so desired to help me with my home and children, so they would tell me on occasion. I could still hear the banjo, fiddle, and bass music strumming in the background of that party I once attended in Savannah as a child.

I would never know twenty-something, I would never marry my first love Alan.

Like entering an unknown yet familiar passage, my existence did not feel like the end of something. The passage was not a neutral reality either, it was like entering a book that also had no sign posted, "not a thru street."

I would remember all I could about all I learned from all my teachers, and tutors. About all the various subjects that I was asked to learn, did learn, and most of all, I remembered the subjects I wanted to learn. The subjects my rebel father Morgan wanted me to learn and treasure. As he put it, "That's the most powerful position for a woman to have in the world Lilly, a famous writer you will be someday."

I would remember all I could from Alan's teachings of literary art and philosophy under that old magnolia tree, all that he taught me in the 1860's, when I was young and he was young within that lifetime once lived. I would remember he would always stress the importance of original thought and symbolism within my writings, to circulate in-depth knowledge within each word, each cord, each phase, each paragraph. Teaching me how to take the reader onto a voyage, enabling them to touch and feel the ship around them as the story, wasn't just a story, it was a profound journey. An everlasting adventure of knowing, experiencing, and forever seeing through the eyes and senses of the main characters of that dinner party at sea, "the book." The Ark."

I recall during our lessons, Alan would take objects in the air and hold them up for me to describe during a lesson, such as an apple. To not describe the apple as simply red, shiny, or round, but to give potent abstract meanings within my descriptions. I would say abstractly, "Polished rounded crimson, devolved like the earth, against the pear in a crystal encrusted prism bowl, resting on a wooden table."

"That's it Lilly, that's it!" Alan would remark with positive tone and enthusiasm.

Like a fine tuned thinker he would make me describe the ordinary in original ways. Alan told me that would set my platform as an original author someday.

Somewhere in the deep south are the names of my family members craved on limestone, under a weeping willow tree? Or a magnolia tree? I don't know exactly where, but in my heart, I still feel as if I am there. Connected like a rainbow to that time and place in the deep south, Georgia. A southern heaven, a place I feel at home, just like in the real heaven.

Moon Jellyfish

1970's

CHAPTER SEVEN

The Calvinists of the world will think this novel series is "an antinomy," meaning a "philosophical paradoxical result: a contradictory and illogical conclusion produced by two apparently correct and reasonable statements or facts."

(Definition by Microsoft Windows dictionary)

Antinomy; A contradiction between two apparently equally valid principles. I Remember Heaven Before Earth. However, the home at 2432 Pinewood Street in Lamplight Estates in Jenison, Michigan is where my hell begins. That was the first of several homes Cindy and Chuck, my newly adopted parents would move me and their problems. Forever trailing, if not leading my hellish life on earth was the American Central Intelligence Agency.

I don't understand God, his plan, or what is going on, but I kept trusting God, and remained part of his reveal, his puzzle piece. My umbilical cord remained attached to heaven, and at times I always felt like I was floating through my life in the north, not really sinking into the bottom of that north sea existence, never really experiencing life, the way everybody else would carry on, and really enjoy every experience. I just did not enjoy every experience in my life so far. I felt, well, just sort of here, there, existing, just breathing in and out, observing life around me. My roots of enjoying life, never really solidified, yet, I suppose. Aloof in really enjoying life I suppose on earth. Would it always be that way for me? Well, I did not know. Nothing about how people were living made sense, it appeared everything was so very contradictory to what they verbally were saying, a real political mentality.

I had a witty bubbly personality, and therefore I was accepted, but I never felt like I really fit into civilization on earth, the way it was here in the north. I wanted to know and experience life, but at times, I felt more attached to heaven, than earth, or drawn in and out of different lifetimes, from my past…..a zoning out.

These people here in west Michigan only wanted to hear the familiar. Like how a person might get caught up into a certain style of hairdo, clothing, and music beat and rhythm, what made them feel a certain way, was comfortable. And comfortable, is where these "moon jellyfish" wanted to stay. Breathing in actual air, and stepping out on land, to see more, have more, from the oxygen provided by their surroundings here in the bottom of nowhere, just wasn't something they wanted to try on an individual level or as a group society challenge. But how would I get them to try? I need them to see how they are living, treating all people, not just the ones they consider saved and perfect (in their social grasp of filed conclusions). I was going to take a philosophical kaleidoscope and make them all see at once, how would I do that?

As I would recall many years later in this lifetime of becoming a transplant within the north, a territory that was once dreaded in thought and reason from the woven treads of my memories past and my past families spilled blood, I do remember, I remember vividly the colors of heaven. The feeling one had when in heaven, the love, the empowerment, the connection to the angels. A place I know as home in the afterlife, a real universe and place above and beyond earth. I also recall agreeing to travel down to the playing field, a place called earth. I was told by God that a life path was already paved and in place, I just had to agree to be the soul that would occupy the body of the young baby that was going to be born, and begin a new kind of revolution on earth. One that I would be directed in how to win, as I went along. I would not win in an earthly way against the evil, it was just to rampant. Along with the necessity of Jews wanting to belong to Jews, and protestants wanting to belong to their faith. Each group knew and needed strength in numbers. Belonging feels better than not belonging. True. Very true, but at some point within your group's existence, you need to ask as a group and an individual, what are we belonging to? What am I belonging to? That is the premise, the basic core concept, the seed to which you understand your life on earth.

Throughout my life on earth it was agreed upon, told to me prior to coming to earth that I would be connected to the heavens through a channel, revelations would be made to me about my life and what I was to reveal to others. In such a way that the people on earth would understand and benefit greatly. Mind you, there are more times when the heavens just keep that pipe line closed, walk away, and I know washed their hands of what they knew, but did not stop in my life. Many times.

The north sea was a sleepy Dutch Christian Reformed community very unaware of their actions, as if covered with the depths of the ocean's deep sea, and for good reason. Very unaware of what was about to emerge in this lifetime, what I would be lifting up in my work on earth, a rare treasure? A rare art? Certainly not expected.

I would encounter the far reaching tentacles of what I would term in this life lived thus far, as a large sea bottom feeding creature, the largest octopus in the sea, the Dutch Calvinist society within.........It appeared to be alive and very busy, a bustling octopus creature in the north sea, Michigan.

This book series is a liberation, part of my mission in dispelling what some perceive as a correct path, sadly, is not. Shocking may be the religious truths housed in history from ancient Roman Caesar days, when the Pharaohs and Caesars were viewed to be God-like, leaders of earth.

Revered by some historians and commoners as God in a human form on earth. Representing the powers in heaven while they ruled on earth. Both the ancient commoner viewed their role that way, as did the Caesars and the line of Pharaohs themselves. Kings today are not viewed in that same light. They are viewed as a lineage of earthly royalty. But 2000 years ago, that was a different time, different philosophical and religious beliefs shaped and molded the perceptions. Today as one looks back, things are different, viewed differently. For reasons of that ever evolving prism that shapes and molds what is accepted and what is discarded as myth, folklore, or simply not applying to our modern day and age, our times now. Social evolution structure works that way, whether for good or bad, it will always be that way.

I always thought to myself growing up that famous people actually had it worse than non-famous people. Why? Because the really famous were locked in, trapped by cameras and media, unable to just back out of their driveway and come and go as they please, less freedom than the norm. Always being watched and followed, scrutinized for everything, every subject, for ordering dessert and gaining a pound or ten, or fifty. Freedom is important, to everyone I am sure.

As seductive and private as my story would be read and reviewed on a paper canvas, so opposite would become the resounding definite drumbeats of a new society painted upon the skies canvas, God's canvas, not Bessy's will or spell.

The famous British music storyteller Sting once said that artists can live such philandering of lives, often lost in drugs and alcohol, not exactly good role models for good behavior. Yet for some reason seem to tap into something purely profound as they perform their music, as if they have a connection to the core, something spiritual, close to God, next to something important. I can only repeat for memory what Sting had said as he tried to explain in detail "about faith" to a small bar crowd listening in Atlanta to his acoustical style music played on a quiet stage. He explained the lyrics he had written about a song entitled, "If I Ever Lose My Faith In You," from his 1993 album, Ten Summoner's Tale.

As a child I too saw life through an artist's prism of viewing the spectrum of my own life, and how my life was woven into other people's interactions, and vice versa, differently than most, as you will read. I liked British Sting's ability to dare to express, whether his speech on faith was relevant to traditional views of faith, or what faith is supposed to be about in one's heart or the role faith plays in society. Musicians, like all artists, have a need to express, and are adamant that they do express themselves. Whereas, the majority of the inhabitants of the world, especially places where the Dutch Christian Reformed Calvinists reside, place very little value on self-expression, originality, or uniqueness in views. In fact, little expression, is actually admired among them, originality is shunned.

Acceptance is not what I have to say to them, or about their values. Unless of course, it is expressing one of their socially accepted values, well, then do it mildly, meekly, and all will admire you, well, some might still gossip.

Somehow I felt more connected to the comedians who said a raw joke about the truth, about any subject, and then everyone really understood. Whether they laughed or not. Or how a musician dared to dress in his or her own style, create their own music, sing and express the way they want, and give the message of the song in exactly their own unique style of saying and wording whatever it is they wanted to say. I just instantly connected to the original artist package category verses what the Calvinists were suggesting as what is acceptable expression. I always wanted to ask the Dutch Calvinists as a whole, do you really think 2000 years ago that Jesus was accepted by the Jews? Or the Romans? He was a rebel, he constantly criticized the Jewish faith. Or was it just the authors in the Bible that projected in words that Jesus did not agree with anything current? Think about. But no one does dare to criticize within the Calvinists subculture, unless it is about an outsider of their faith, and then it is sticks and stones, until the rebel leaves. I once asked several people, such as my Calvinists brother Ric, "Do you think there will be Jews in heaven?" He responded by saying "No. Because the Jews have rejected Jesus, and do not believe he is God's son who died on a cross for our sins. Jews are unsaved. They will not enter heaven."

I inquired further, probing, "But, how would you know?"

He responded, "Because the Bible states that Lori." Then he glared at me, as if his eyes had the power to crunch and stomp me upon a glance only.

I wanted to say as my response, "Jesus for a fact never signed his speeches, or wrote a single Bible verse, let alone a chapter in the Bible, so how could you be so correct without factual proof Ric?" But Ric Vander Ark, or any Calvinists for that matter, would not accept any notion outside what is comfortable in their mind, in the sense of what they were taught to believe. And if what they were taught to believe is the general norm, the accepted status quo, well then, it therefore is correct? Not necessarily so, what if ones memory of history is different than what is presented on historical paper? What if. What if I remember Biblical times and things that were left out of the Bible? What if my memory is overwhelmingly stronger than the current conformity by the masses within this lifetime? Let me place this reality into perspective for you; the very first person to announce to a bunch of nonbelievers that the world is actually round verses the world being flat was laughed at, ridiculed and labeled crazy by the status quo of the time period. Most of you now believe the world is round or flat? Not much light was shed on the truth during the dark ages, Christianity and Catholicism are living in the dark ages today. That truth being said, I do not promote or recommend another religion.

I would best describe my memoir collection as rare coins of extraordinary value to humankind. I have an uncanny portal to past lives lived. Including my life once lived over 2000 years ago during Biblical times. During ancient times the Romans and those who lived were able to write history remembered. The dead never wrote history or recorded actual dates of occurrences such as death and birth dates. Only the living has ever held that privilege. Jesus never authored any of the published chapters in the Bible. Yet Christians and Catholics alike will always be willing to remark what Jesus would or would not do. Acceptance of certain translations of beliefs is the glue to hold organized religion together. In the end Jesus would not be holding together any religion on earth.

God expected from me to change the Calvinists, to change the world's view of their current religion. But I would learn lesson, after lesson, after lesson, from them the Calvinists, those moon jellyfish in fact wanted me changed. And quite honestly, it was their metamorphosis' of my life, my existence, that actually took place, not the other way around as I was instructed and told by God that would occur. If you are confused right now, well, at times I was confused too. As you will all read about in the proceeding chapters. It truly was the other way around, the Calvinists changed my life, it was an astonishing set of events, circumstances, throughout the course of the first forty plus years of my life, they changed me.

I knew the truth. The truth about religion, Jesus, Mary, the Jews, the servants, and what religion has integrated as "the truth to be remembered." I knew the truth even as a child in the 1970's surrounded by a world of delusionists. I knew the truth, and I was not going to be their painted impression. I am God's original. The world will be reborn in the truth. A mothers truth, a saga of over two thousand years.

I seemed to connect to music. I like music for the simple universal fact that a song, music, is orthodox and pure in your personal translation. Religion seemed only be translated in one vision to the Calvinists, their vision. So therefore music became like an island for me as I listened. I had connected to British Sting in this lifetime in his attempt to describe his faith in the 1990's. As often times on legal forms when asked what his religion was, he would write out, "devote musician," as all listened in the audience that night so closely to what he had to say about faith, you could hear a pin drop. Sting stated that people **do require** faith, faith in something, as he went onto explaining about faith. I could easily have created a conversation with the musical genius Sting, during, or after the pub style concert.

I would have said, "I know what you mean, concerning your brief, but profound message on faith, I do understand what you had explained on stage to the audience listening so intently to your words and music, others do get 'it' too. People do understand the message of faith, of believing in something unforeseen and positive in direction."

I hope when you open the pages of this book tomorrow, or next year, you can still hear the music of my original cord written, a rainbow bridge to the other side of you, to hear that musical cord still playing years from now as you read my books and the rain stops from the other side.

I would have also have told Sting this, "I believe that God reaches all people, that is how God works. Religion creates boundaries, strict guidelines, but the essence of God reaches all people, that is how God wants to work, to be everywhere, to everyone, all at once. A God with no boundaries, that is how God works." Artists in similar fashion work with no boundaries and/or club membership to one particular organized group. Organized religion wants everyone to be the same, but be so careful of what you are being like, or becoming the same as. That would be my message, if I wrote a song.

An artist can reach people of all ages, colors, and backgrounds. An artist can touch the hearts of royalty with a song or painting, yet profoundly move and inspire hope in a person's soul resting on the edge of homelessness as well.

A well written message in a book can also cross the divides of continents, and bring something to all who read and listen, just as God works in his ability to connect. A prolific songwriter, artist, or novelist with a touching and profound message that moves, can seemingly radiate a solar connection to people, within ones soul. In a mysterious way an artist will tap into a faith far reaching than a conventional club membership style faith, which, its essence was not created and ever devised to become universal by its definite guidelines, restriction style conversion techniques, rules governed by a particular society. But an artist works so differently, God-like in a far reaching and penetrating way, mysterious, with a message not contained and housed within the boundaries of an earthly made structure, or a societal invisible fence. Faith in God, is in one's heart, not a location housed with bricks and mortar created by man which decomposes with time. Faith is not an earthy address locale.

Religious practices are manmade securities, real hick-ups to what God is and wants of you. Religion adopted God. God is not owned by religions. Remember that fact when you worship.

The word "believe" has many definitions, some people are yet once again unaware that many words have various interrelated or quite astoundingly different meanings housed within the same word and the word's definition(s). To believe, for me means to have trust and faith, to be confident that somebody or something is worthwhile or effective. Thus, "I believe in my deity, I believe in God."

A musician, novelist or artist has an ability to translate to the world. They are the "revealist" in society, that is their gift or specialty to offer all this world has to offer, with their reveal. I do understand Sting with his message during that acoustical storytelling, others understand his message too. God does believe in free will. Everyone has a natal astrological blueprint design, yet you will still have your free will to make decisions.

The word "Messiah" means savior or liberator: "Somebody regarded as or claiming to be a savior or a liberator of a country, people, or the world." (quote from Microsoft Windows dictionary.)

Liberated means: 1) Released from social constraints: Freed from traditional socially imposed constraints, such as those arising from sexual or ageist stereotyping. 2) Released from the enemy: Freed from enemy control. (quote from Microsoft Windows dictionary.)

The word apocalypse according to Microsoft Windows dictionary has two very different meanings, the first means "total destruction;" the destruction or devastation of something. The second meaning of the word apocalypse means, "revelation of future;" a revelation made concerning the future. I would be the later, meaning my book, my story, has a prolific reveal to society as a whole through my book series. More than a healer, I would become a reformer of society on a macro level. On a micro level I would make others aware of their daily deeds as the veil is lifted in a unique reveal. The earth will shake, an amazing sequence of eclipses will occur. Eclipses to astrologers means a time of sudden change and reveals, an emerging truth from the heavens to earth.

Like an absorbent obedient flower I would gather and endure the acts of society and the Christians, endure and absorb on my petals throughout the first part of my forty plus year lifetime. Then unfold like a late blooming magnolia flower at the beginning of the second forty year span of my lifetime, like a rainbow around the world, amazing colors will be seen in the heavens.

Faith in God, a higher deity than myself, guided by the channels of heaven, I would begin my reign of correcting earths civilization through my books, lift boundaries formed by societies, subcultures and religions alike. As a true *rebel* philosopher of this age, paint a canvas for God, one page at a time, as God uses my life, my words, his message will be told without the confines built by man and societies alike. Profound and original, would be my innate selections.

Rebel as defined by Microsoft Windows Dictionary as in the first meaning 1] "A Rebel is somebody unconventional, somebody who rejects the codes and conventions of society."

To write is to reveal, to read is to travel through a passage into an opening of understanding, a radiant light. By opening this book you have become an explorer of a rare kind, you dare to tread were most angels dare not walk, my life's journey thus far, now written upon these pages. "Shine on, shine on….." Alan would probably have said to me as I write and paint the pages on a glowing and vibrant canvas. "Shine on dear Lilly, it's brilliant" …….

I was told it would be a dangerous journey to undertake, this lifetime of mine in the north, that's what I was told in heaven, I do remember heaven before coming to earth. Nevertheless one that I would rather travel on into, the uncharted dangerous waters of the raging north sea. Rather than watch from a distance the downward spiraling of souls in this lifetime of what society, politics, and religion had evolved into, a civilization drowning in a flood, lost in their directions by leaders and standards, their progression built on a unsafe foundation for their civilization to continue. This book series might feel like a volcano exploding from underneath, to some. Exploding wisdom within the sheets, the white sheets, the white pages you hold.

Before accepting the journey of this life to live it was reminded to me numerous times that it would be a life of feeling as if I would be drowning rather than floating or walking like a lamb on solid ground.

The subculture I was about to enter would be the "example subculture" to explain why society and religions need to wake up, fold in their ways, and begin a new path in the light of God's way.

I was told my life would be a huge impact on earth, I was part of something very special from the heavens to earth. I would pave a path of understanding for God in you, in how mysterious God can be in one's life. I was told that at first people would not believe, or be dumbfounded to say the least, I would be ridiculed, shunned, tortured, and laid to rest in a grave dug by the Calvinists by age forty. I was told if I made it to forty, then I had already lived the portion of my life of enduring for God's message. God would then begin to push the petals of my life outward to the world, and begin his very unique reveal to a society of followers, a civilization that always viewed themselves as superior, the ones that have been awaiting for a return of Jesus' message on earth.

I would come face to face with a religious society misrepresenting Jesus and God, and would see mounting evil energy spreading like a rapid fire within this religious sector, the Calvinists. The only light, would be within my soul to guide me as my umbilical cord to heaven remained attached. At times I could feel myself wear and get weary, as if I had a faint dimmer of light at most.

The Mayans predicted their own fate, their own end by mapping and charting the stars in the galaxy, the cycle of the moon and sun was very important to the Mayan star gazing priests of long ago. Basically they carried on traditions of that of ancient wise men of long ago, the Magi. A highly complex solar system of knowledge of that time, as it is now.

The Mayans believed that a new civilization would manifest great harmony and compassion to all humankind. They were so precise in their cosmic calculations, they even predicted when this new era, The Golden Age, the walk thru the passage of, "The Sacred Hall Of Mirrors" would begin, the date, December 21, 2012.

My story reads like a continuing memoir as I brush off the collected dust particles which had been resting on a shelf within my soul for some time...................

I was adopted on March 26, 1970, I was only three weeks old. I know this because that is what Cindy told me as I grew. There is of course a reason why a child is given up for adoption, and always a reason why a child is later adopted.

It was explained to me that my birth parents were high school sweethearts, young in age. As for the adopted mother-to-be of me, who would apply for adopting a baby girl, as was her request. Well, usually a mother, a parent, or a couple adopts because they are unable to conceive a child of their own. That is probably the most persistent factor, the driving force, that primitive need to have a child, or children, for a couple to create a completed family. However, I would learn over the years that is not why I was adopted by Cindy and Charles Vander Ark. I would learn it was Cindy who wanted a baby girl, and the devastating secret of why she wanted a baby girl, and liked to foster girls from Bethany Christian Services with the aided assistance in her paperwork and career for the American Central Intelligence Agency, the top secret projects. The classified files. The hidden from society files that if went public would shut down the Central Intelligence Agency, the C.I.A.

Anything Cindy wanted was indeed possible through government, high government. Cindy was a C.I.A. sub-contractor, a career that began for her in the 1960's when she began abducting babies for the C.I.A. Why babies you ask? Well, that's what the C.I.A. project called for back then, Cindy was willing as long as she was not criminally charged. Committing a crime, many crimes, and never being criminally charged was her libido in life, the C.I.A. nailed it! The C.I.A. offered protection from any criminal charges to the C.I.A. sub-contractors. If the American government needed a task done that involved crime, the C.I.A. would call upon ordinary people to commit the crime. Many of these people would not even have a college degree or any special training. If a degree or identification was or would be needed the C.I.A. would create and print the authentically illegal paperwork to appear as legal as needed. Cindy explained everything to me beginning in the 1970's. Cindy bragged and relished in her crime sprees for the C.I.A. The types of crimes the

C.I.A. sub-contractors do? Anything illegal such as but not limited to; baby abductions, murders, kidnappings. The huge problem of the C.I.A. having staffed nurses stealing babies out of hospitals everywhere around the world was such a problem that baby ankle security bracelets were introduced and produced, an alarm would sound off if a baby was carried too close to a hospital door.

As the 1960's and 1970's rolled around so did the development of new C.I.A. directors and confidential C.I.A. projects go underway. The C.I.A. had moved away from the German directors, to more mainstream American directors with very devious ideas for their confidential careers. Including the testing of certain races of people to see if indeed there are natural born traits within each race of people. Genetics, and the scientific breakthroughs in studies thereof were very big federally funded and important projects during the 1960's and 1970's for the American C.I.A. Essentially the brain of evidence in criminal cases that arrived onto the court scene of the conventionally accepted field of the 1980's DNA testing. The infancy of DNA testing however was unsettling and bizarre science testing conducted during the 1960-1970's, with some of the C.I.A's side projects.

Cindy was a natural at going along with the taboo for high American government. Her part was providing the infant babies and toddlers for the testing. The government would provide the lifelong testing and surveillance of the subjects (the person), you know, the science part of the American government projects. No family would be looking for the babies that were given up by their biological mother and father. Bethany Christian Services kept the paperwork and files of the babies. Some babies and toddlers, so I was told by family members and the 5'8 C.I.A. David Petraeus, would in fact not make it, not live. And no one would be looking for a baby that was given up at birth, so I was told and reminded.

On cue Cindy would and could display many names and phone numbers that would give her a great rating as a Christian, and what it means to be a Christian among them, her friends, associates, and business partners all alike. If you disagree with Cindy, her ways, her attitude, well, you are done. Your goose is cooked in her mind, although you may not know it, oh, it is.

I can only wonder if my adopted father Charles drank to dilute his discovery of what Cindy was all about during their marriage. There is always a reason someone becomes an alcoholic. Dilute reality? Escapism? He always disagreed with Cindy. "Disagreements" was very much a part of their everyday marriage.

As unusual and sadistic as Cindy would be as my mother, an adult female. I knew at a very young age, I inherently knew she was doing bad things to me as a young child. I instinctively knew who and what she was, which was far different than who I was inside. I could see the evil of the darkest realm within Cindy, but quite honestly, I was too afraid of her to speak up. Which was one of her tools, in how she got away with murder, or any act. After all, life is just a play, and it was just "an act."

Cindy and her CIA friends, both male and females, had an annoying need to see and feel me, an unusual sexual appetite for a mother, or for any person to have towards a child. For me to discuss my experiences growing up would be for me to face my reality in Cindy's household, what I represented to her, it was not a reality left fond in my mind. It was a constant battle for her to get her way with me, to see, to touch, to bully me, and hurt me. As a right she thought she had in her control of me. And demonstrating her authority and power over my body, my mind, my zero rights, and power to keep me quiet for instilling a dreadful fear of what she was, or could be at any minute during my childhood. As I grew older, Cindy became like a tennis player, on one court she wanted to make money off me in any career I would have. Then on the other court, she had a need to "just end" my memory as her witness, paint that sunset scene, in any way she thought she could end me.

Cindy informed me, warned me that if I ever had a bank account the CIA would steal my money. Cindy warned me that if I ever grew up and went through the process of purchasing real estate the CIA would break my nose. She reminded me daily that I had no rights, no legal rights. Part of me feared her, part of me wanted to run from her and have rights, rights that other people have and exercised. Cindy did not lie to my face. Cindy had absolutely told me the truth of my various fates, all came true, just as she had warned me.

I am sure you are wondering who was Cindy's very first victim? Her very first murder victim was her two-year old brother David. Cindy electrocuted her two year old brother by having him chew on an electrical cord as she placed his hand on metal stretching his arm to a metal register when her mother was away from the home. Cindy told me that her younger brother received all the love and attention, everything her parents could afford went to David and not Cindy. She explained that the look on her mother's face was a great satisfaction and that her mother became Judge and Jury and beat Cindy behind closed doors for the murder. Cindy explained to me that taking something dear from someone is worth all the beatings in the world. The beatings did little to change Cindy's course in life, she would indeed become the world's greatest camouflaged serial killer. The murder of her brother David made headlines in The Grand Rapid's Press. Cindy developed a criminal appetite to get ahold of and beat females younger and smaller than her, a mental tick she herself could not explain. Why the need to beat and torture is not something Cindy could explain about herself. If anyone talked about Cindy's crimes, Cindy would aggressively call the victim crazy and heavily medicate the victim senseless. Cindy would always reign supreme among the Dutch Calvinist of west Michigan that valued her church going attitude and attendance, their same mannerisms and style of dress and hair. On the outside shell of what Cindy was and is allowed her the perfect escape from her sins. Cindy appeared as flawlessly the same as all the other Calvinists on what they value most, to be like them.

I had a strong will to defend myself against all things I do not want to go along with in Cindy's community. Raising a baby girl that had an inherently strong will was not what Cindy bargained for with her God, or Bethany Christian Services. Cindy would go ballistic on me if I used the word "no" towards her. Well, others would also see that telling Cindy "no" made her go ballistic. She would become very jealous of me which would add another layer of horror to my life.

Children that come from heaven instinctively know what is bad and good in their surroundings, what does not feel correct. I believe the term or phrase is "having a conscious." I came into the world with a sense of knowing of the other side. Cindy wanting to examine me all the time, look at me inappropriately was not a fascination I could understand completely. The harassment would become a battle to just grow up and not get harassed by her and her powerful high government CIA associates. One CIA official that would visit our house on Pinewood Street in Jenison, Michigan was CIA David Petraeus. My first impression of him before I was even old enough to attend kindergarten was that he looked and acted like Mr. Rogers from Mr. Roger's Neighborhood. My impression of him when he would visit Atlanta's The Gold Club remained the same, he looks and acts just like Mr. Rogers from Mr. Roger's Neighborhood, and he likes children. General David Petraeus said to me at The Gold Club, "I had feelings for you when you were young." I do not believe that he could ever pass a lie detector test if he answered no when asked if he ever really made that statement to my face at The Gold Club in the early 1990's. My ultimate impression of him? Whomever placed him in such a position of power in America should be fired.

I learned at a very young age about the social conditioning that Cindy was programming in my young and very impressionable mind. What Cindy seemingly was preparing me for in life, what role she was projecting and what role she would want others to believe of me. To see me as a whore in this lifetime. As a child Cindy's role looked as if she would appear like a saint embedded in the social glue work of Bible study meetings, church, and the Calvinists community at large. She would project me as a problem child in her control over her secrets, and her personal American government's secret projects. Image was her propelled propaganda. How she made others look whom did not agree with her was her internalized war in the Calvinist's community of west Michigan. Cindy is a very good warrior, but God is not her commander.

Cindy would use manipulations, such as taking away birthday cakes, gifts never bought, or a party I would rather not have anyways. I hated her constant demands and demoralizing ways with my life. I hated how

I was to go without basic human rights during the entire duration of my childhood, all because Cindy was in control of my childhood.

Cindy was regarded and embedded into that community as a saint, and I would be regarded as a problem if I spoke up about my clear disgust for her, "the propaganda saint." She would regard me as a whore, a mental case, a rebellious daughter, an uncontrollable child with a strong will, that was her campaign methods laid out in her mental map, before I even arrived to that house on Pinewood in Lamplight estates in Jenison on March 26, 1970. Cindy had her strategies, before I could even speak. I lost my virginity at a very early age, not from a male, but from Cindy. When Cindy was questioned by the pediatrician, she had every excuse in the book, but the truth. But no one could believe such a story, because that is not normal acceptable mother behavior. Therefore much of what I said concerning Cindy would be regarded as "fictitious" by the Dutch Calvinists. I think readers alike believe what they want, that is just how a readers mind functions. There are many situations that have happened within my own life that I would be the first to admit, if it had not happened to me, I would not believe it. Some events whether public or privately occurring, are just too astonishing for a person to comprehend, why is that? Why is the bizarre so unbelievable? I would learn from experience and from enduring the crimes that the CIA would capitalize on the fact that the bizarreness within crimes would lend doubt that the crime actual took place by utilizing the unthinkable, the bizarre within the CIA's crimes towards me and other victims of the CIA.

I was born with natural blue eyes, fair skin, reddish-blonde hair, a porcelain doll face, weighing at birth 7 pounds, 7 ½ ounces. In an era of underlining racial unrest, both in the north and south, most would comment that I have an upper hand in the world I was being born into. That is if you judged a person's surroundings and appearances, by all *outside* appearances of the home, schools and community I was about to enter into….. "An easy life ahead of her," some would have commented.

But I did not have an upper hand. All appearances would be deceiving to those who peered into that house on Pinewood Street, located within Lamplight Estates in Jenison, Michigan. I would face many harsh unthinkable realities in this journey living among the warped Christians like Cindy.

For me in the early 1970's I was just a baby absorbing my new world. Even if I wanted to go back, I couldn't.

I would describe my newly adopted parents, Charles and Cindy as a couple in disaccord. Their marriage was like tea served without sugar or cookies. When you entered the home and began interacting with the both of them, you sensed that they interacted with you, but not with each other in meaningful thought and conversation, something was missing in their marriage.

I realized at an early age that I had a voice that mattered not at all to Cindy. I was just a child. In her view children do not have rights, the voice of a child entering into an adoption agency does not have the ability to speak for oneself, babies going out for adoption also have no voice, no say, no way to protect themselves, Cindy knew that fact well. Cindy and the CIA capitalized on that fact, as did the American government.

It is ultimately up to the social worker to decide which family, which couple has a solid marriage, no drinking, or alcoholism, no mental disorders noted on the interviews and psychological testing. Correct? You would think so, but Bethany Christian Services was a large, lucrative, and privately run Dutch Christian Reformed adoption agency with their own agenda, and due process. It was white crime within a church run adoption agency what occurred to me being adopted out to the woman who applied for me, Cindy. I was just a baby. Like the girls that Cindy had fostered before me during the 1960's, before adopting me as an infant, there was a long established human trafficking of young baby girls and children going out to predators in the community, just like Cindy. Which is information that Cindy provided to me about the human trafficking organization in her proud, boastful power schemes, she bragged to me. Cindy would take, rob, and brag. She was that comfortable in her surroundings and who she had influenced.

Charles would play the role of my father in this lifetime, but really it was I, his mother from 2000 years ago, coming to save him from

Cindy's destruction. I too, would be caught up in surviving and just trying to live, coping with Cindy behind closed doors. Cindy was born on a full moon night, on no other than on a Friday the thirteenth in December during the 1930's in America. Her parents Martin and Teresa Stob decided to name their daughter "Cindy" which means moon, for she was born on a full moon on Friday the thirteenth in December.

This next part of my memoirs is to reveal, reveal my life in Michigan in hopes that lawmakers and law enforcers will also read this book and realize a list of both state and federal laws to mandate to Bethany Christian Services to ensure that no one should endure the hardships that I so unfairly experienced at the hands of others, both from the predators and those in positions of power and authority ,within that closed door community. As well as a way to encourage the enforcement of the new laws created to protect, in the future.

I would never bond on an emotional level with Cindy, she would not want to take me shopping for new clothes, or out for lunch, ever, like a normal mother. Instead she would reveal to me what she could get away with, by appearances only. The important reflections desired and judged within the Dutch Christian Reformed society, known as "the Calvinists." Cindy began this overpowering domination in my most earliest years to make me out to be a whore.

I was the whore in the photo, before I even knew what a whore was, or before the photo was even photographed, that is how the painting began, and would end. Cindy was the accepted by society, "saint." A saint of a woman that had adopted me. A real savior Cindy was, a real messiah. It was a theory that Cindy believed in and therefore she could project her truths to all for the first forty years of my life. The moon jellyfish people would gravitate towards "the saint Cindy." Her saintly persona she could role play day in and day out. As if acting was really her calling in life and my role was to simply observe and then wake-up, or die. Whichever would come first, by her means, a sunset was her creation on the canvas next. How close I came to defying her, in her powerful demise of a will, for a mother, or caretaker, was harsh. Deciding who lives, and who dies, was a roll she wanted, the steps Cindy began, would lead her right down that winding path, right to that unthinkable threshold, beyond the taboo. Beyond "the ordinary evil," such evil that is best termed as uncomprensive. Dealing with Cindy on a day to day basis and learning what she was all about was like a psychological tango, the dimensions of her evil, that when I finally kicked my shoes off, it was more than my feet that ached. I was exhausted, mentally, emotionally, the essence of my soul hurt. When I slept at night I would wake tired in the morning. I was on edge comprehending as a child how to psychologically process and deal with murderess adult Cindy.

Charles and Cindy were like the wrong furniture in a room, and that is immutably how I remember them during my early years in their house as I peered out of my crib into my new world, way back when.

Charles was a short rugged man, a builder by trade, and Cindy was a housewife by choice, her choice of course, but she was more of an actress by role. Charles Vander Ark, the man I would come to know as my father on earth in this lifetime was warm hearted, generous to a fault, who dearly wanted me to have everything wonderful in this world. Even more was his wish for me to have everything, which was more than what he wished for Cindy, which again caused unavoidable problems for me. He had an explosive temper, which my mother always seemed to know how to trigger in his presence, typically before major holidays, or before, during, or after dinner. Existence in the house was like walking on egg shells, easily explosive. It's like when in weather you have a cold front meeting a warm front, a tornado is likely, my life was like that too, with them. When they joined in a room, so I observed, I would want to just go for shelter in another room. I would always wonder, even to this day, just as you reading this probably have wondered too; why did Bethany Christian Adoption Agency decide to allow these parents to adopt me? My adopted father was an alcoholic and a builder by skilled trade. Cindy was a housewife by all appearances and a CIA sub-contractor committing crimes for the American government. Why was I adopted into that household? I too will always wonder.

Cindy was accustomed to getting her way. Not that she grew up in a household with a mother or father who gave into her demands, rants and rages. Quite the opposite, Cindy grew up in a household where the parents thought little of the girls in the world, and viewed boys, men as superior and a blessing from God.

Therefore her brothers would get the new clothes, the store bought outfits, the college education funds, whatever the boys wanted or needed. Cindy grew up knowing she was not getting her way and set forth her driving mission in life to get her way at any cost to others. Her quest of how to manipulate to be cunning in disguise, so much so, as she embarked upon her adult life of getting whatever she wanted, and from whom she wanted. The word "no," would receive a not so warm reception in Cindy's ear or presence. The word "no" could and would make her grow cooler in a room, cold, icy, as if the carpet froze over like a January pond freeze.

Yet Cindy could remain quiet, aloof, then get up and slam kitchen cupboards in her silent hell of hearing the word "no." You would wonder what you had done other that just saying no? Or Cindy might launch a raid attack of a person's character. She would twist and dilute the truth so that in the end, you were supposed to apologize to her for saying "no." Or so it seemed as one observed in her anger that they must have done something wrong, because of how Cindy was acting like the victim again. At times her anger was loud and fierce, at other times she attacked. Her evil was to dilute the truth, especially if you began viewing or judging her as a bad person or Christian.

My father Charles would rarely give into her ballistic behavior and rarely apologize…...for saying "no." During the standoff Cindy would often call the minister in her tyrant childish tactics of complaining to the church minister that she is married to an unbearable non-God fearing man who drinks. I often wonder if Cindy was the one that actually introduced my father to drinking Vodka and orange juice so that Cindy could be viewed and recognized in the Calvinist community as the Christian church lady married to her problematic alcoholic husband Chuck. We were all required by Cindy to go to church twice on Sunday, each Sunday, not a Sunday missed. Cindy wanted Chuck's mind fuzzy, not clear, not a good witness as she went about her business. The truth was never discovered of what caused their many fights in the house. Cindy's behavioral issues were not being addressed. The ministers always forgot to preach about Cindy, clue us in to not be evil. Cindy's behavioral issues were being ignored because she was married to an alcoholic. And therefore no one on the outside of that marriage was even paying attention to all the crimes of theft and kidnapping and disappearances Cindy was committing. It was always someone else's fault, someone else had the behavioral problem. And if you did not agree with her on that sharply delusional point, well, I fear for you. My three brothers began fearing for my safety, for what Cindy would claim as, "sassy." The fights Cindy imposed on my dad at such a young age I can still feel that tension if I reflect back to one of their many, many fights. Sometimes the drama would escalate to Cindy grabbing me and driving me to uncle Warren and aunt Jean's house for a few hours so that in the silence left in an empty house might just encourage my father to think about saying "yes," and then apologize for saying "no" upon the arrival and return of Cindy, when she decides to return. Cindy had a broad range of tactics used in her adult life to get her way, all stemming from a childhood that never seemed to focus on her, revolve around her wishes and what she wanted in life. Cindy was acting out what she was inside, a murderer, and all the abuse from her Judge and Jury mother Teresa made her even more volatile to be around.

Even as a young child I had so much insight into Cindy. Yet for the most part, I would try and avoid her, yet wonder what I was missing in my childhood. There was a lonely void. I would come to learn years later that "wanting" a mother does not mean I will have a mother. I would learn a very poignant, painfully truthful lesson in this lifetime, my journey, which is "wanting something" or "wishing" to have this or that, is simply put, "a wish." Wanting a mother, or a loving family would be a wish, a goal, but not all wishes are to come true. The other delicate balance within this premise of my life is to help you the reader see and understand the truth, without delusion. See how something can be created within a family, a networked community, and the destructive anger of a person or group. Which in and of itself was just now, a very profound philosophical statement for me to make, to write, to paint in your mind.

Cindy was not a warm mother or wife, but she seemed to be friendly enough to those she wanted to influence within that tightly woven fabric of the Dutch society, Cindy was the wool within the fabric. I came to know that society as a great octopus that seemingly had its tentacles on everything influential, as Cindy was also aware of this well-known fact as I was growing up. Cindy was surprisingly polite and friendly to those only chosen by her, or she desired to befriend, or wanted to be accepted by within the tight-knit community of that octopus in the sea. Cindy knew the attorneys in the historic district of Grandville, Michigan, the bottom feeders that took over the stone and granite old State bank building on the corner of the edge of Chicago Drive and Wilson.

Cindy's campaign wasn't to be noticed, Cindy was great at building up alliances in that region of west Michigan, and that made her believable in what she was doing to my life. Cindy was the complete opposite of Charles, if it is true that opposites attract then the laws of attraction were at play when they met and married. They actually met in church, Plymouth Heights Christian Reformed Church. Cindy really was "the church lady," even in her high school, that renowned religious high school of Grand Rapids Christian High. Cindy understood the large Calvinist community in west Michigan, that understanding broadened her horizons and consequently her camouflage. When detectives on television mention that sadistic serial killers are as beige as beige can be, I think to myself, that is exactly Cindy.

People embraced her shallow appearances as the true light of Christian values and morals, as something more solid, something noteworthy…..than what Cindy was making me out to be….a whore….a whore not to be believed. I had no idea what a whore was growing up, I only knew it was what Cindy thought I would become, so I was reminded on a daily basis, by Cindy. One day I was bold, and asked Cindy, "What is this whore that you think I will become, what does that mean, whore someday?"

Cindy looked at me as if she wanted to hit me for asking, for mentioning what she calls me, Cindy pauses, and looks me straight in the face…..and says…. "A whore is what you will become, you have a will of your own, you are too strong headed, just like your aunt Carol. You will be a whore just like her."

I looked bewildered, I needed to know more, "Aunt Carol is a whore?"

And then Cindy slapped me, almost broke my nose. I just asked a question. The questions promptly and very rudely, abruptly came to a halt in Cindy's presence.

Cindy was a demanding and selfish woman a daily bleak darkness in that marriage and household. Cindy found arguing to get her way was a far better road to take than not getting her way and just accept the word "no." Needless to say, it was a loud marriage between the both of them. My mother Cindy's nagging verses an intelligent debate with my father was her ploy in the fact she was the victim. Too stupid to debate Cindy just keep nagging, and she suddenly was just an annoying victim. I can tell you though, it was never that easy of an act for me to believe of her. Yet would inevitably turn into a loud fight with my father's explosive temper getting the best of him. He wouldn't hit her, he just would not give into her annoying victim nag act, and so their fights would last quite a while. He discovered what she was inside and thought he could change her. Cindy however possessed an evil within her that would not compromise, she had to win, that was her will, her battle.

Charles might have been fooled in the beginning of what she projected in church, but then something happened, and her demons were revealed. Drinking was what he began to do before and after their fighting escapades. So I witnessed growing up in the harsh northern landscape of that loveless marriage. She told me that a good cold shoulder can give a woman want she wants, that was the advice she gave me in how to act towards a man. Even then I knew it wasn't true, or any advice she gave me. I knew any advice from Cindy was to make me stumble, purposely. I would teach myself to walk and think in this lifetime.

Cindy would not verbally argue, or spell out a good convincing argument. Rather, her intelligence was to convince through her disguise of being a suburban nagging housewife. She would slam kitchen cupboards, cry on her cue, and demand, demand, demand. It was the worse display of making a man happy that I ever did see or witness. But I realized, life as she knew it, was not about marrying to make the man happy, it was her ticket to financial freedom, and doing what she wanted with her life. But she was always missing the point of what a woman's role is in a husband's life. But she did not care to listen to me, it was "all about Cindy," and her immediate gratification of whatever the hell she wanted. Cindy is from the underworld, she is not from heaven.

My parents endless war saga would cause me to fear marriage, a phobia I held onto deep into my adult life.

Cindy's life path in numerology is six. Which means like it or not, she would receive much cooperation and responsibility during her lifetime. I have witnessed her life, and she has. It is as if she is a monster and has some sort of "out of this world" protection from never getting caught.

My relationship with Cindy, my newly named adopted mother would be one of psychological warfare, a warfare my father Charles Vander Ark would become exhausted in battle and drink to dilute his reality of what he had married. In the end, I would finish the fight for God in the psychological warfare battled with Cindy. What God reveals about Cindy and her followers in the Calvinistic society would shock the world, just as I was shocked. Cindy was very embedded within the Dutch Christian Reformed society, very woven into what that society believes. The Calvinists, the community, they all "praise her." Cindy was so community career minded as if to weave herself within the mostly honest, warm, and good hearted religious sector of west Michigan like lamb's wool on an expensive sweater that you must have, so was Cindy's career that would continue throughout her entire lifetime. But how the Dutch Calvinists judge a person would be their own demise.

Cindy would gain followers in her stronghold within Calvinism from weak hearted followers of God. Such followers that skimmed the surface of Christianity and knowing God, even many ministers, who truly do not know the real God and his ways. People, many, many people, like the thick skin on top of pudding being made in a pan, they keep skimming the surface and never really pay attention to their actions. My reveal, my message from God would be as if I had so dared to go into the kitchen and scuffled what the Calvinist society was brewing on the oven stovetop. To stop and think, even question Cindy, or other prominent leaders and ministers within the religious sect, a real cult in Michigan, in itself would be frowned upon, only skimming is accepted. Oh no, I am going to stir that pot and make the world stop and think about the Calvinists who keep giving themselves rounds and rounds of ovations.

What the Calvinists were not realizing about their very orderly, very measured in worth accountability of measuring the values of God in their existence according to the local leaders interpretation, was in fact a formula so misinterpreted and mishandled. I can only come to one conclusion and say that the Calvinists were acting so similar in nature to the Jews and Jewish Pharisees of 2000 years ago. So exacting in values and measuring a person's worth and acceptance within their religious sector, that in fact, their way of measuring a person's worth would blindside their intelligence of who and what God is, and the role I was playing in their lives. I was viewed as watching on the sidelines, not really playing, but that is o.k.

What matters most to religious ministers, Popes, and religious leaders alike is that you follow their interpretation of the scriptures. Yet God does not want religious leaders to drive a nail into interpretations that divide.

Think of yourself as a cocoon, the words on the pages, my life story that I will lay before you will warm that cocoon into a metamorphosis. Towards the end of my book series, each of you will have your own stage of when you transformed, you will begin to feel a restlessness, you'll feel movement within your wings, and you will transform into a butterfly. Some readers sooner than others, but all of you who read will feel this transformation from within your soul, as in the end, as in the middle, I will bring you to a cloud. A cloud can be described as, "A visible body of very fine water droplets." Clouds are billowy water absorbing fluff from the earth and water of the earth, correct? We all can agree on that notion, concept of truth in description, right?

I have an inherent gift to see the world around me through a unique prism which is around me now, I would best describe the Dutch Christian Reformed suburbs of Grand Rapids, Michigan like a place in the sea, "a society in the north sea." A part of the sea where moon jellyfish seem to gather and live on the bottom of the sandy sea floor bed. SeaWorld stated on a poster that a moon jellyfish has only two stages of life. One stage of a moon jellyfishes life is one of drifting, wandering aimlessly through the vast blue underworld of the sea, just searching, exploring. The other stage of life that a moon jellyfish will experience is to lay on the bottom of the ocean reproducing, creating little pods, and basically staying put for a period of time during the stage of reproduction. It seemed that I was placed in the part of the ocean with a huge community of sea bottom dwelling moon jellyfish. Like the moon jellyfish, an octopus also lives primarily on the bottom of the sea, hardly seen were the far reaching tentacles of the Dutch society within the bluest of waters so deep and hidden with a large head and jelly bottom.

The reproducing seabed of a community seemed to stretch across and over the western hemisphere of Michigan. The closed door society that stayed attached to everything they wanted to control was like an octopus with sticky powerful tentacles that could close in on anything it choose to attach to on the seafloor. If an octopus feels as if it needs to defend itself, it will squirt a red substance, not blood, but a red substance in its attempt to get away. To create a cloud of red enveloping around itself and in the waters as it dashes and disappears from the danger it perceives as imposing.

I am sure if someone from land was to peer into the moon jellyfishes community bowl, here in the bottom of nowhere, one would say the life of a moon jellyfish "appears" as transparent in meaningless value as their seemingly see through selves, with not much apparent substance. But everyone and everything living or passed on, has meaning to God. One from land would not recognize the value these "moon jellyfish" bring to the planet, but they do have great meaning for my story. From all outside appearances the religious west Michigan community appears harmless, meaningless to a stand-by. But oh no, that is only the projection west Michigan wants to create to the outsiders, and has very successfully done so. They would carry on with their life and business of breeding pods and pods in great numbers. Despite the rest of the world, the "moon jellies," as I like to refer to them, carried on in their underwater paradise with great importance and pride. They were as blissfully oblivious to your way of life elsewhere in the big wide world, as you might not value their small ant size existence in the north sea, they hardly bothered each other, or stirred the water, so it had seemed.

I suppose that was how groups of sea life saw one another as well, each fish, each sea creature to be, was only concerned about their survival, and their underwater "group" survival. And for a moon jellyfish there was safety and security in numbers of the same kind.

Like a person drifting aimlessly on a raft in the middle of a storm at sea, with little help or guidance to stay afloat, far from one's adoring family ties, so too would be this lonely beginning I would feel as a child. My biggest surprise when I was young; I was a Yankee. I would now grow up knowing that I was far away from my roots, the Georgia family I once had was a distant reminder to everything I did not have now in the north. Now a Yankee, that would be always an underlining dislike, a dissonant fact of mine now still to this day.

I would learn with a fierce reality like a dark looming cloud around me that northern attitudes, culture, and the general way northerners treated one another on a day to day level was a world far, far removed, and far away from my past, my beloved young life once lived. Bessy might have enjoyed pointing out to me with a smirk on her face while I lived on northern soil now, "that's just how life is dear."

I would learn in this lifetime how the defining codes and practices observed within this Dutch Calvinistic subculture in the north define the perceived notion of who enters the gates of heaven and who does not, by their standards judged of you. A culture held together like the wrappings on a gift box.

Believe it or not, "Cindy," my newly adopted mother had a dream three months before Bethany Christian Services of Grand Rapids called her to announce the possibility of a baby girl arriving, as per my mother Cindy's written application request. Her dream? She had a dream she was going to adopt a daughter, that daughter would be "Cleopatra," not just a name to what she should call me, or want to name me, but the actual long ago Cleopatra is what that dream told her.

Cindy went onto say the dream was very real, strikingly riveting in vividness that she could not let go of the "realness" of that vivid dream. As if God himself really had relayed that dream, that information to her in a dream.

When my newly adopted father, a local builder, "Charles Vander Ark" held me, he said to my mother Cindy, I think we have the soul of a southerner, we should give her a southern sounding name. I was a mere three and a half weeks old when I became known as "Lori Sue" on a cold winters day in late March, 1970.

As much to my dislike that I was not ever reunited with my father Morgan, and mother Elizabeth, my mamme Bessy, my little brother William, or sisters Grace and Kate on our southern estate somewhere in the deep south, and should I never forget my beloved first love, Alan Hubbard in the 1860's, there was joy in being young and alive. Despite now living in the north with all these Yankees I had once despised with a vengeance for changing my life in the south during the civil war era. I was young, and with youth comes vibrancy, laughter in one's soul, a need to explore and find ones way in life. No matter where one is placed in the world when young, no matter how harsh the realities around a youths beginning are, there is joy in simply being young and alive.

When I began to speak my northern family began taping my voice. They found it so odd and amusing that a two and then would be three year old would speak with long drawn out vowels when no one else in the family spoke that way.

They laughed and were amused. I felt I was just lost in a world I did not know or recognize. I would tell my mother Cindy that I miss my black mamme and would like a "black aunt Jemmia mamme" someday as I pointed to the syrup bottle on the table next to the stack of pancakes. Somehow that bottle reminded me of a comforting life once enjoyed. I would stare at that brown lady figure syrup bottle, just stare, I thought if I stared long enough at the bottle she might begin to talk to me, comfort me, take care of me. Oh, how each day at breakfast I would stare and hope towards that brown glass syrup bottle, just curious I suppose, could a bottle really come to life? I did need Bessy, so I thought. Every young child needs a Bessy, not a cold white mother uninterested in my comfort, mad she has to prepare meals for me, take care of my needs, which was a nuisance to Cindy. Cindy was always disgruntled about something, always, if the morning or day or evening did not involve revolving around herself, her world, she snapped and hissed. Cindy wore an angry cold stare and scowl on her face inside the home, her tiny black dot size pupils held no emotion. Unless the doorbell rang and it was someone important from "the outside" of my existence. My childhood was like an eighteen year jail sentence and no one ever bothered to tell me what I was in for, my crime? What did I do? Cindy ran the prison and saw me as her prisoner with no rights. A child prisoner.

If I talked about what went on behind those prison walls, I knew people at church or in the community would say, "You are not locked in a prison Lori, there are no metal bars on the windows, what a silly thing to say about your mother, she adopted you, be grateful, she sings in the church choir, and is a lovely lady, we know her very well." I would often wonder why I could not have the mother that Cindy seemed to be at church? I got the flip side of some awful coin toss, just about every day when around Cindy.

I was informed by my newly adopted parents Cindy and Charles Vander Ark that I was adopted through a Dutch Christian Reformed adoption agency in Grand Rapids, Michigan. I was told that my real mother was young and in her freshmen year of college when she learned she was pregnant with me and decided to give me up for adoption. I was told my mother was of German and Dutch origins and lived in Muskegon, Michigan. I was informed that my biological mother gave birth to me in Grand Rapids, Michigan, almost an hour and a half from Muskegon. I would notice there was no scrutiny of the household I was placed in for adoption. I was left for endless hours during the day by Cindy while my father Chuck was at work on construction jobsites. In order for me to get daily necessary water I would open the bathroom lower vanity drawer in the upstairs bathroom near my bedroom and step up and climb the bathroom vanity to the counter top and then sit and lean on the counter top with my head in the bathroom sink to get water to quench my thirst. I remember it hurt to climb up on that vanity and required a lot of strength. I must have been very young, but I do not know the exact age. If I fell down the large staircase from upstairs I would lay on the base of the stairs for hours staring up at my surroundings that seemed so empty to me no matter how much furniture or toys filled the rooms. Cindy and the family I was placed in had fully demonstrated to me what the word "facade" meant before I had even heard the word pronounced and had the word formally introduced to my vocabulary. I noticed my newly adopted parents would fight before, during, and after dinner and any major holiday. I would wonder why they were so unhappy and angry. I would often wonder why Bethany Christian Services never came by to check on me and why the adoption agency thought that it would be o.k. for me to live here on Pinewood Street in this household, with this family. The ones that would come by and check on me on Pinewood Street were CIA agents. CIA David Petraeus was a revolving fixture going through the front and side door at the house on Pinewood. CIA David Petraeus told me once as he bent his back to become eye level with me, that the U.S. government was very interested in my adoption file and all the secrets that file contained. He told me that my mother Cindy played a vital role for the CIA. I would grow up to be able to recognize other facades in how the CIA would create facades like movie props, using people and companies to create one picture believed, as behind the scenes another reality was taking place. I would be able to clearly detect what a person or company projects as the truth or motto and how to begin getting to the truth and get to the criminals. The truth lost in the layers of truth behind the facade I so recognized in others now and I had not even entered the young grade of kindergarten. I would also learn how expendable the U.S. government viewed a person's life who dared to expose the truth. Especially if the U.S. government viewed the truth as damaging to the USA's image projected democracy motto, then the U.S. government would damage the person telling the truth.

I had three brothers growing up in Michigan, not natural blood related brothers, just three brothers, Ric, Dave and Mike. Ric always was building model airplanes in his bedroom down the hall from mine. Ric had a huge collection of model airplanes. If you walked near his bedroom you could smell the glue soaking in sunlight as the model airplanes dried on his desk by the window. Ric carefully painted each one in his collection, great pride he took in the design and finished product. He once told me he was going to build an airplane and fly far away from Michigan. Later when he graduated from Unity Christian High only three years after I arrived in the home on Pinewood, Ric joined the U.S. Airforce in Colorado. His hopes of becoming an Airforce pilot diminished when he could not pass the eyesight test. Ric had glasses, thick glasses, as did Dave and Mike, all due to poor nutrition by Cindy who could care less about taking care of children, even if the children were her own biological children. Wild animals possessed better mothering skills instinctively towards their young than Cindy, I observed it with my own eyes on one of those National Geographic T.V. specials that aired once. I always wished angels would lift me up and carry me away from the homes we lived in during the 1970's and 1980's. The new construction homes my dad built were nice, but the household, the inside was scary and dangerous with Cindy. Her very unpredictable personality, her turbulent emotions were like a high stakes game of roulette, off the busy Vegas strip in a dimly lit room, where that ball landed might just be the end of you. Ric never moved back to Michigan, not even near Michigan. I learned to like the outdoors in Michigan, even if it was raining or snowing, or the temperature was only ten degrees or colder. I would build an igloo out of snow or shovel off the snow piled high on our backyard swimming pool frozen by winter and ice skate endlessly for hours. In the warmer months I would ride my bike, roller skate outdoors, swim in the backyard pool, make friends in the neighborhood.

My oldest brother Ric could usually be found tinkering with his model airplanes down the hall. Ric could shut his door and dream about an aerial escape plan, or go hang out at a buddy's house since he did not much care for Dave and Mike. My other two brothers were both brothers and friends to each other and shared a bedroom together next to mine in the home on Pinewood Street. My brothers Dave and Mike have the same reading and writing skill level. They are forever stuck developmentally in the year they witnessed too much. I am convinced by them that a person has to be in the right frame of mind so to speak, to even desire to grow up and learn and become educated. Like a wooly mammoth frozen in an iceberg for seemingly all eternity. Traumatically stuck in a dirt embankment attached to an unexplored mountain, with so many years of passing time their developing minds lay frozen at the time of serious crimes they witnessed or endured. It is as if my brothers could not progress forward developmentally in school that particular year, that season. As if their speech and writing and reading level froze during the grade level at the time they witnessed horrifying crimes at home. Events that were too horrifying for their young and developing minds to process at that time. Traumatic events and crimes that shook the core of them. Crimes that took place in that home on Pinewood before I was even brought to Pinewood Street in Lamplight Estates in Jenison, Michigan. Mike had said to me in the 1970's, "Because mom and dad went to jail after the Caribbean cruise, mom does not dare to steal anymore babies for the CIA, I think it's done. I think you are the last one. There were so many babies coming and going out of this house, it was so sad what happened to them. You are lucky to be alive."

How did I feel? I felt lucky to just be alive.

What was the awful illegal CIA projects funded, fully supported and documented by the American Central Intelligence Agency that I mentioned briefly earlier? Cribs. During the 1960's and 1970's infant security alarm ankle bracelets did not exist on newborn babies born in hospitals. The CIA staffed nurses within hospitals all around the world according to Cindy. The CIA was conducting experiments on babies in cribs. What type of experiments? Measuring heads. Cindy explained to me that there is a connection between the size of a newborn's head and their ability to exercise a need to survive and their need to locate food and water to survive, as well as intelligence of the newborn. Heredity traits in various races of babies is what the CIA was studying and still studies. According to many sources within the CIA, the babies with larger heads made attempts to move and escape the crib searching for food and water to live. Once a baby made attempts to locate food or water the baby was rewarded with food and water. The babies with smaller heads and from certain races that did not display any overtly outstanding movement to locate food and water to survive in the crib, died on Pinewood Street in the bedroom Cindy housed me in during the early 1970's. Where are the babies? The dead babies are in blocks of residential or commercial cement, according to Cindy and other CIA agent informants. Sound's strange and illegal of the CIA? It was. All of the CIA's experiments conducted back then or now are filed under top secret classified information so the CIA can never be criminally prosecuted through the American judicial system of courts and jails. However, there is no rule of law that if one survives such an experiment by the CIA that one is forbidden to write about the experiment, correct? I am not obligated to keep my mouth shut.

My advice to the American people? Demand democracy prevails and have a governing agency expose each and every covert project of the CIA's that took place or is taking place currently on American soil. Audit with multiple accounting devices and agencies each and every person and or company that I mention within the pages here. The reason the secret projects are labeled top secret or confidential is so that the trusting American people do not actually know what the CIA is up to. Closed files, classified files remain quiet. Therefore the big budget that goes to the U.S. Department of Justice to pay for the secret projects is not in the hands of democracy and control by the people of America to stop and criticize the CIA for how the CIA spends their time, which has very little to do with security or protection of any kind. The only individuals that are receiving protection are the ones stamping "confidential and classified" on file after file, covert project after project. Because of the great confidence the CIA has built as an American military based intelligence company that they are an agency that advises the U.S. Presidents and protects Americans, my battle would always sound like a song that never could make it on the radio. That was the CIA's plan all along toward the general population of people that would give the CIA the control needed to slither under leaves undetected since the 1950's. The larger the government, the less power to the people, an ideology that has been occurring since the 1950's in America. The larger the government budgets, the less power and control the people have to stop anything from occurring by their created government.

Cindy explained that the CIA was after purebred Germans, comparing the survival tactics and rates to other races of newborn babies. Cindy also explained how my neighbor and childhood friend on Pinewood Street, Lisa Pare came to America in the late 1960's. I would also learn from Cindy that I was not actually born in America either. The next big question in your mind; How did I arrive in America if I was not actually born in America? This is one memory I remember well during my childhood; Cindy explained to me when I questioned a Netherlands Antilles souvenir plaque hanging on the wall and I asked, "What is that?" Cindy my adopted mother explained to me that she and my adopted father Chuck spent three weeks in a Florida jail after getting caught bringing me from the Dutch Caribbean Islands to Florida during a cruise stop, during a planned and premediated vacation. Cindy zoned out for a minute or two just staring at the orange, royal blue and black wall decoration hanging on the wallpapered laundry room wall and murmured as her pupils almost disappeared into tiny pin like black dots as she stared in stark horror blankly ahead with emptiness in her eyes as she said, "I did not know if we were ever going to get out of there, that was a really scary time. I thought my career and life was over and I would forever be stuck in a Florida jail cell." Cindy explained that the American Central Intelligence Agency funded the vacation. Which could account for all the CIA agents filtering in and out of my young life in Michigan and later my adulthood. Cindy abducted "Lisa Pare" from Acapulco, Mexico in the late 1960's during a Mexican vacation. Lisa grew up next to me during my very early years in Jenison, Michigan. The Acapulco vacation was again paid and supported by the American CIA.

Lisa Pare Bankston is the biological daughter of Adolf Hitler and Ava Braun. Lisa later joined and served in the U.S. Military and is a wonderful human being. A 1974 (Jenison) and 1976 (Hudsonville) photograph of Lisa and I at my birthday party in Michigan is shown on my Amazon author pages, along with a school photo of Lisa in 1982. Lisa Pare attended Jenison Public Schools. I attended the Dutch Christian Reformed Schools. In 1974-1975 we moved from Pinewood Street in Jenison to Crestview Lane in Georgetown Forest in Hudsonville, Michigan. I attended Hudsonville Christian Elementary for kindergarten and the old white school house for first grade. Then we moved to Curwood Street in Lamplight Estates in Jenison, Michigan where I attended and graduated from Greenfield Christian Elementary. Then I attended and graduated from Jenison Christian Jr. High, the rumor is the C.I.A. had the building torn down, and therefore the school is gone and off the map in Jenison. I attended and graduated from Unity Christian High School in Hudsonville, Michigan in 1988. Lisa Pare Bankston still lives in west Michigan, she is now married and has two children. Lisa Pare Bankston made a home on School Street in Hudsonville, Michigan near Unity Christian High in a very conservative, no crime area, surrounded by peaceful authentic Dutch people.

I remember I had once asked Lisa when we both were younger, "What do you know about your real parents?" Lisa informed me that she knew only a few things. She knew that her biological mother was too old to care for her and that is why she was giving up for adoption. Lisa also was given information that her parents originated out of Poland, and that was about all she knew.

It was Cindy who informed me that Adolf Hitler and Ava Braun were Lisa's real parents. In the 1970's I did not know who Adolf Hitler or Ava Braun were. It was not until I read the book Ann Frank's Diary that I even knew who Adolf Hitler was, other than a name. The Dutch in west Michigan never bring him up in conversation like the rest of the world and media does from time to time. I visited in 1988 the old attic above the clock shop in or near Amsterdam after studying history in high school at Unity that I actually learned who Adolf Hitler and Ava Braun were in history. The Dutch clock shop was still there in 1988. I remember being 122 pounds and only 5'3 tall and I still considered the narrow attic stairs as difficult to ascend. When I got to the attic I looked at the space above the clock shop which was wood planks and very small, very crowded at one time. I peered out the window that brought in so much light. I could clearly see all of the cobblestone streets on both side of the water canal. I could clearly see every village style Bavarian looking brick two-story building. How many other Jews were hiding out in the upstairs attic spaces of all those buildings? I do not know if we will ever know. One thing is for sure, the Jews that were protected by the Dutch never received a thank-you from the Simon Wiesenthal Foundation and Holocaust Museum. Maybe it is a hereditary trait of Jewish people not to be grateful to others. Jewish people always seem to complain to others, but not show and verbalize gratitude. Gratitude is not seemingly innately natural to them, so I observed. Perhaps observation is seemingly innately a natural DNA trait of mine?

Michigan's Judge Miles legitimatized the false and freshly printed Michigan birth certificates during the Nixon years. Ironically in Michigan on March 29, 2012 President Obama appointed Judge Mile's son to be the secret CIA group's leverage in Michigan overseeing courts and outcomes as the U.S. Attorney General for Michigan and Washington D.C, making sure the cards would always fall in their favor. The connection could explain why many people question President Obama's legitimately legal and possibly very fake birth certificate, real or not real? In June of 2012 CIA John Brennan approached me in East Lansing, Michigan where I was living for twelve of my adult years. During my life CIA General David Petraeus, Leon Panetta, and CIA John Brennan, FBI & attorney James Comey, and many others working for the CIA such as Bob Baer and many other agents would locate me and approach me both in Michigan and Georgia (USA). My memoir explains why.

My speech dialect in the north was not improving as I grew and developed into a vivacious young girl. My southern draw of my vowels and words were not shedding with age as the Yankee doctors had once promised to my mother Cindy. When my age approached five, kindergarten would be starting soon. The night before kindergarten my mother sat me at the kitchen table with a sheet of paper that listed all the things I was already supposed to know upon entering kindergarten. I had no idea what the alphabet was, but seemingly was getting yelled at by Cindy for not knowing. Everything on the list that I was supposed to know upon entering kindergarten, I did not have a clue about. What would my frantic mother do? I was like a jellyfish out of water in my new inhabitants, and every time I opened my mouth to utter another sentence, my Yankee family laughed and sneered. They were at their wits ends to make me sound "normal" in the north, somehow "normal" like them. School would become a problem in the sense I had a father who worked all the time, and a mother, Cindy, who could care less if I could read or write, or was intelligent in the eyes of the world. That was not why she adopted me. Becoming aware of why she adopted me was an invisible truth I wore. I knew at an early age that crying never helped, there was no one around in the house, but me. I knew something was off, something was not right in my childhood but I did not know the word or term "neglect," that word had not reached my verbal or writing skills yet when I was young. When my father left for work, a construction job site, Cindy left shortly thereafter, and would leave me alone. Which was a constant battle, verbal fights of my father towards Cindy's mothering skills, and lack thereof. Cindy would cry, because he yelled at her, she never could seem to get in line with being a good parent. She liked the title of housewife, stay at home mom, but she was not a mother that cared, or was there, or worked. She came and went as she pleased and created excuses to her friends and business associates of sorts, I can only assume, that she had hired a babysitter to watch me. But there was no one that I could see, and so I began talking to the angels. Sometimes just connecting in my mind, via that pipeline to heaven, that umbilical cord which connected me from out of my prison hell.

Books, learning, a great life, a wonderful future, was the world outside my existence, I was on my own in that department. If I could not have a question of mine answered in the classroom, the chances of me learning an answer was very short lived about a subject, so I learned answers by observing.

School in west Michigan in the area I lived in primarily was a strong protestant faith run area, known to the world as, "the protestant elite." "The Calvinists," which all belonged to that community from what I could observe. From the fine public schools, to the outstanding parochial schools, to the policing systems, and the community pillars within the Dutch community, to all the churches, banks, one law office in Grandville on the corner of Wilson and Chicago Drive in a granite building, to general stores in town, those tentacles grew, and grew, large and round, was that close knit community. Very powerful and proud they were and are today.

All of my formative school years were spent in the Dutch Christian Reformed Schools during the school year from 8am to 3pm. You might think of a "Christian run school" as a small unit. But nothing could be said of the like about the Christian schools in Jenison, Hudsonville, Bryon Center, and Grandville, Michigan, all the way to Calvin College in the big city of Grand Rapids thirty minutes away from the sleepy suburbs where I grew up as a child in Jenison and Hudsonville.

I think I had close to thirty kids in my kindergarten class. And there were at least two to three kindergarten classes during each school year. The school was large and modern, the playground and landscaped grounds were large and impressive too, not just from a child's perspective. The Christian schools were then, and still are a great pride within the Dutch Christian Reformed community, from the many elementary schools, to Calvin Christian High, South Christian High, to the school I graduated from, Unity Christian High in Hudsonville, Michigan with just over two hundred kids in my graduating class. Built next to the rich farmlands in the north called muck fields. Quaint Dutch built white colonials that lined the quiet streets with manicured lawns with grass that never made it above two and a quarter inches tall. The Dutch would measure with their eyes and scrutinize those who did not value the shine of their windows. Each spring the bright orange and yellow tulips would pop out of the ground opening their petals so wide until the wavering tulips long green stems leaned forward and fell after the many rainstorms we all would encounter each spring. We all knew then that warm weather had finally arrived, soon the Tulip Time Parade would begin. A parade in Holland I would participated in as a cheerleader turned flag girl each spring.

As I recall looking back there would be maybe three or five of us kids gathered in the teachers aid room at any given time, all of the speech instructors fervently working on our various speech challenges. My aunt Jean Stob was one such speech therapist at Greenfield Christian Elementary. Most of the few kids there in the room with me had stuttering issues with their speech. As if the words they spoke were stuck and could only partially be spoken at a time. I can still hear those few stuttering children's mouths speaking. I can still feel their frustration for being different than the other kids in class, for simply how they pronounced their words slightly differently than the general norm.

The "speech nannies" as I liked to refer to the speech therapists, simply embarrassed me with taking me out of regular class, to endure their very prompt slapping and clapping motions with their hands to indicate to me, a signal of theirs when I was supposed to stop saying a word, or stop drawing out a vowel sound. I had to almost learn all of my vowel pronunciations from scratch, derived from square one from out of their northern handbook on how to speak impressively. Despite my foreign southern drawl speech impediment, I was a particular bright child, by the startling insightful statements that I would make to adults, "from just out of the blue." They would look at me in shock and bewilderment from an insightful profound comment I might make from time to time during my youth. That remarkable, where did that come from gaze towards me for my out of the blue wisdom. The adults would glare, smile, and size me up, a child, with scholar wisdom at times.

Sometimes insightful wisdom that seemed to be beyond my years, and beyond the reach of many adults around me that would startle some adults, make them squint their eyes at me in their haughty northern sneers and say as they looked me up and down, "You think you're smart for a child do yeh?"

I was peculiar in that sense of my childhood, startling statements of wisdom would emerge from me, from just out of the blue. It occurred to me that adults always seemed puzzled as to how I could say such insightful, philosophically independent comments and original opinions about worldly topics.

While I was in elementary school during the daytime Cindy entered nursing school. When one is a child it is simple to remember odd things adults say, but difficult to understand and fathom what adults mean by what they say at times. For instance, one day Cindy was in the kitchen after a day in nursing school, Cindy remarked that she was learning about all kinds of drugs that could silently kill someone. I remember getting chills when Cindy said that statement and saying that word "kill" while at the kitchen sink at that house we lived in on Curwood Drive in Lamplight Estates. I could not understand why she would make such an awful statement, or why she would even think such an awful thing to say. Not understanding that statement Cindy made to me would not erase the memory of Cindy making that statement to me, that's how it is when you're a child, one might remember what was said by an adult, but not understand the meaning behind the words, the statement.

One day I walked into my new home my dad had just built in Lamplight Estates on Curwood Drive. Cindy looked panicky and exhausted, as if she had no sleep lately. The year was around 1977, I was around seven years old. I immediately just marched to my room to escape the fight scene. I could hear through the walls Cindy blurted out to my dad, "We just moved here from Georgetown Forest, we can't move again!"

Then I could hear footsteps coming down the hallway towards my bedroom door. I knew my bedroom door was about to be busted wide open by Cindy as I quietly played with my Barbie dolls on the carpet floor in my butterfly pastel wallpapered new bedroom on Curwood Drive. What Cindy is about to inform me of in her rants and rages I had already heard quietly and politely bits and pieces of from our Dutch neighbors Den Hartighs whom were fresh off the boat from the Netherlands, as was the very thin Dutch lady who lived alone next to Cheryl Poskey's house. The very thin Dutch lady always traveled alone and stayed only a few weeks each year, she would always stare at me while I played ourside.

Just as expected, Cindy came in my bedroom to see me as she said sadly, "Your real parents want you back, the Dutch international detectives have been in touch with our lawyers at Visser & Bolhouse. That Dutch lady that moved in the cul-de-sac has been gathering school photos of you from school and information about you from the neighbors Den Haritighs. That Dutch lady who goes by the name Mrs. Van Houten is really Princess Margaret from the Netherlands. What I can gather from neighborhood sources she is your biological mother or knows your biological mother very well and that is why she is collecting photos and information on you. Your parents want you back. You better decide if you want to go back. Bethany Christian Services is getting nervous, this is not a good situation."

I paused from playing with my Barbie dolls in my bedroom and looked up stunned at the latest from Cindy. I inquired, "I thought you said my real mother was an unwed freshman in college when she gave birth to me?" I felt horrified that Cindy would even say anything different than what I knew to be the truth, which is what she had told me since I was a toddler. What is this now? My biological family does not even speak the only language I know, English. I could not mentally process this new information Cindy was giving me about my birth origins, the information conflicted with an earlier story Cindy had told me about my birth origins. I was attached to my friends, I was attached to my Barbie dolls, I was attached to the community where I live. I was attached to my bedroom and my things, all that was normal and familiar to me. I pondered to myself, would I have to give up my bike, and roller skates, my dog Benji, and my toys, and friends, and school, and learn a new language? That would be weird. I don't understand why this is going on in my life.

Cindy remarked, "What are you talking about?"

I responded back to Cindy, "You just said that my parents wanted me back. You used the term parents as if they are married."

Cindy's sadness evaporated in an instant as she simultaneously turned angry and overwhelmed all at once as she exploded in my doorway, "Don't you be smart with me lady Jane! The lawyer bill is going to cost this family a fortune! We may have to sell this house! I am going to have that CIA pay this bill if it is the last thing I do before I leave! The CIA will pay! I am not going back to jail, back to being detained in Florida and lose it all!"

I looked up at Cindy and asked, "You're going to leave?"

Cindy took a deep breath and remarks with a relieved expression worn as she glances out my bedroom window from where she is standing, "I am thinking about it."

Cindy and Chuck got the best lawyers in town, Visser & Bolhouse. Cindy and Chuck's finances were dramatically drained, and I was ordered to say I wanted to stay in America and not move. Very honestly, I was very freaked out when I was faced with losing my friends and all that I knew as my world. I should have said "Yes I would go," but I was too scared of change, even if the change of circumstances would have been positive. I was scared of change, the unknown. I was also scared of Cindy.

If I did respond with saying "Yes I would like to go back and live with my real parents." I next could see a scene of Cindy driving me to a dense cornfield and putting my dad's hunting gun next to my head where no witnesses would see my trauma or crime of Cindy's undoing. I would be dead with black crows pecking at my lifeless body that never reached the intended destination. Saying that I wanted to stay, was safe, or so I thought.

I just moved forward, but things at home were getting really bad. I felt as though any decision would have been the wrong decision with no happy outcome. I liked school and my friends at school and in my neighborhood though.

One day my elementary teacher met with my adopted parents one evening during parent teacher conferences, meetings in the fourth and fifth grade, urging my parents to move me up a grade or two. Relaying to my parents I was not being intellectually challenged enough. My father wanted me to move up in the grade system taking the teachers advice for fear I might become bored and lose interest in school. My mother argued that she just wanted me "to fit in" and stay with kids my own age. Cindy's philosophy has always been the importance of "fitting into this world around us." "Blending and fitting in is better than sticking out like a sore thumb," Cindy would say often.

During my school years in the Christian school system, over thirteen years' worth in west Michigan, we were taught that if it was not in the Bible it simply must not be true. I always found it odd in a factual sense that Jesus never wrote any of the chapters in the Bible, others wrote of him. But he never wrote a single chapter or verse, yet "Jesus said this, or Jesus said that," was law in west Michigan. As you can see it was a dangerous place to grow up, if indeed you were an independent thinker like myself, attached to an umbilical cord to heaven, unlike most of them. As I would turn on the television set or read a Kid's Discovery magazine or National Geographic magazine and saw dinosaur fossils printed, and pictures of prehistoric life, and large animals far different than what is on earth today, I would then take the magazines to class and show my teachers. Do you know what their response was?

"That does not exist, nor has it ever existed, it has never been printed or written about in the Bible, that is propaganda from worldly scientists that view God's world differently than us." I would always hear a twist or turn of that same response from any Christian school teacher. They would scowl at me, frown, and wonder about my faith in God for even being curious about anything not printed or written about in the Bible, that history book of God's in their minds. I knew at a young age if I had a question maybe I better stay quiet or else face being pushed out or ridiculed by the Christian teachers and students alike. I made sure to dress like the other kids, wear my hair like them, talk like them, laugh like them, and only talk about subject matter that was appropriate for that society. It was my "survival guide" at school to stop asking so many questions and to stop bringing in worldly magazines. Do you know what happened next? I became very popular, I was voted most friendly, most humorous, and voted vice-president of student counsel, I became like them, and for a short while, I experienced "acceptance by the Calvinists." Wonderful if I remained reserved on the outside, but inside, I was a rebel philosopher caged.

My survival guide at home was ask for nothing and avoid erratic, unpredictable and explosive Cindy. Childhood was learning how to become accepted among the Christian society subculture that I lived in, and simply endure, observe, and experience. There would be a time for revelation, but I also needed to survive within that subculture to tell my story.

As simple as a moon jellyfish can look and move about his business for years, simply minding his or her own business in his or her mindless, pointless existence, there comes a time, when a moon jellyfish can give quite a sting. When opposition meets confrontation within the moon jellyfishes world if they discover you are an outsider, or disagree with them, about anything. As much as I felt out of place in my new world located in the north sea (west Michigan), there was a reason my philosophical mind and absorbing true nature was placed here in the north. Eventually though, I would intercept with life underwater here, and discover the burning sting that a moon jellyfish can deliver without warning to me, an outsider like myself. No one reading this book for the first time would understand firsthand the far reaching tentacles of the octopus, the Dutch society within. The octopus would go to extremes in covering up the dust of crimes committed on the seabed. Perhaps my story will encourage these moon jellyfish to simply lift off the bottom of the ocean floor and begin their very possible second stage of existence. Which is to float aimlessly, just searching and exploring the vast sea underworld of theirs in their quest to discover a wider world around them. Traveling the ocean current….lifting up off the seafloor and simply seeing.

I inherently knew the analog of my life would be revolutionary. I would reach and touch many with my life story someday. A story I really did not want to tell, a story I would keep to myself for a long time. Yet, deep down, I always knew my life would be an original cord in a song, a true original in every sense of the word….that was God's astrological design.

Alan would probably say to me now as he looks over the bridge, across the rainbow of existence from this life to another, "Shine on dear Lilly, shine on…….you will be brilliant, your life story needs to be told and resonated by many."

The Return of Bessy
CHAPTER EIGHT

In psychology class one will learn that the emotion of hate and the emotion of love are closely connected. In the sense those two deep emotions are derived from the same part of the brain that gives off a particular associated chemical release, sort of an adrenalin. I could only reflect now and wonder what Bessy must have felt towards me in my previous life lived. My short, young, beloved life hardly experienced or lived, and now, impossibly far out of my reach of returning to under that old magnolia tree in Georgia. I wonder in this lifetime, how many jars of salt water would be opened? What had Bessy done? Did her jealousy consume her reasoning with me? Would I ever see my family members of my past in this lifetime? Let alone, ever come face to face with Bessy in this new life journey? Which I have embarked upon in agreement with God and the heavenly angels. I had so many questions to ask of Bessy and all that I am now assuming she took part in, "wishing and chanting" so many, many, years ago in the deep south behind that old barn. Had Bessy truly wanted the very best for me, like I was her child she had raised as if her own? But she also had a deep layer of sinister jealousy towards me and the life I lived in the 1860's? As I recall so many years later as I peer out of my Michigan window, here in the north, in the middle of nowhere……..as if I am left to be lost at sea for what feels like an eternity. I feel as if I am watching my life, my lost in time opportunities disappear with each snowflake here in the north as I continue to write my memoirs. I can't see what God has planned for my life, I just keep on marching, and marching, typing, and typing…….

I would learn the far reaching consequences of Bessy's jealousy during this lifetime. I would learn just how deep her jealousy must have been for me during the 1860's, towards the end of being twelve years old. Just as her intentions of taking my beloved life lived as Lilly in the south, causing me to ironically slip from that ol' magnolia tree where I fell in love. Could jealousy really be a driving factor in one person wanting to push another person out of their life? Could jealousy truly cloud a person's sensibility towards another? My life would become a journey, an endless march into searching for those answers that plagued my curiosity within my soul about my past.

If you were to ask me to describe the north, the State of Michigan, a place I would grow up in the 1970's and 1980's, and technically would always be required to mark as my birthplace, my place of origin now in this lifetime, I would tell you Michigan has beautiful pristine waters. The clearest blue waters, as if the glaciers had just melted in this lifetime, cold and clear are the large bodies of water known as "the big lakes." In the spring and fall, the air outside smells like a wet oak leaf, a soggy and damp pile of wet, rotten, layered oak leaves. The musty still stench of oak leaves piled on each other, a graveyard of wet oak leaves, is a very prevalent smell in Michigan during the spring and fall months. The state abounds in dense uninhabited woods, surrounded by ponds, bogs, lakes and rivers. Despite the pure pristine waters and greenest grass, despite the natural beauty in Michigan, I felt a disconnection in the north. I had a longing for my southern roots and my once southern existence in the 1860's. The culture of the north is far different than in the south. In the south one says "hello" and makes conversation with just about anybody. But in the north, conversation is only regarded as useful to those you know. Family is not so important here in the north from what I can observe, and the people are rude, domineering, and think only of themselves, not of you, even most of one's family is regarded as strangers, at least that is what I observed in the north. I do long for a normal, stable childhood, wishing upon the stars tonight, just like last night…….

Summertime is a revered time in Michigan, with minor humidity in the air, many people come to Michigan from Florida and other places to vacation, getting away from other states that have hot and humid summers. The quaint early 1900's period portraiture towns in Michigan are full of county fairs and festivals celebrating tulips, cherries, apples, folk art, folk music, just about everything in Michigan has a summer festival attached to a celebration each week or each weekend during the late spring through early fall. There truly is no better place to visit in the summer time, than Michigan. The summers always involve live music in the city squares or county fairs, parks, and lakefront stages. Plenty of cotton candy, Michigan brewed German root beer, and rides and games for the kids. Everybody appears to smile more in the summertime in Michigan. For some, the summers in Michigan are so wonderful, it is what keeps a middle class family desiring to live here all year around. It really can be the splendid storybook time of year that pulls people together and keeps people bonded together, tolerating the treacherous long snowy winters which arrive shortly after the kids trick or treat from house to house in late October. As the once colorful autumn leaves of warm Indian summer blow the now crisp dried leaves onto the cold ground, for now, the summer paradise is gone as Thanksgiving and Christmas yield a few nice memories before the long artic winds blow a blizzard of snow and ice our way. We can only hope, that the long winter months will feel like weeks, but honestly, it never is that way.

I first met Carmen my best friend in elementary school. She was not the most popular student at school. In fact most people did not know why they did not accept her, but the other kids seem to just let Carmen be, as if she had an invisible plague attached to her. She was quiet and a bit unassuming. Carmen had long straight dark brown hair, and dark, wide, large, almost bug eyes. She has a huge nose and mouth features too. Her nostrils are wide at the opening, her nose is wide and big, and her mouth displayed the largest mouth and set of lips of any child or adult I had ever seen in the north. Kids would describe her face as, "over featured," in school. Carmen very much looks like a Dutch Jew, not like a typical Dutch with classic Dutch features and coloring. My adopted father Chuck Vander Ark was a Dutch Jew and I trusted him. Perhaps I gravitated towards Carmen because she looked trustworthy with the imprinting that had taken place early on in my childhood. Carmen's skin was pale white, she was slightly overweight in elementary school, but would blossom with age and would begin to apply makeup as she entered junior high.

Carmen's body was shaped like an African-American, her face resembled a black mamme, but she was white, and born into a Dutch family, so of course she was not black or of African descent. In the 1980's when Oprah Winfrey began her "Oprah Show," I thought if you took Oprah, put her on Slim Fast shakes for ninety days, maybe one hundred and twenty days, bleached Oprah's skin, you'd have Carmen. And Carmen loved to ask questions, get down to the knitty gritty….. "Show me the sex baby! Let's get down to the sensationalism baby! Here is the stage baby!!! Carmen's personality was very different than a typical Dutch Calvinist.

Whereas I often forget to ask all those important questions, the opposite could have been said about Carmen's personality. I was bubbly and witty, and I just like to make people feel at ease, and feel accepted, no matter what their flaws might entail. But Carmen liked to search layer after layer within a person, very serious. Carmen always looked as if she had another question resting on the horizon, and she did. All the while she remained a polite book cover, just going along with the system. For me, I was quiet too, I was constantly questioning "the systems" and wondering why everything was so very contradictory. Like how the Christians worshipped. They were and still are so very adamant that their way is the way to heaven. Demanding, preaching you must believe every single word and verse of the Bible. However the Christian Calvinist treated the Bible verses as sections they alone can deem important or relevant to them in their personal lives. And like fishing, they would keep what was important, and ignore the rest of what the Bible had to say. It was so very contradictory.

Carmen's family owned lots of farming land, half a river, and one of the largest dairy farms in western Michigan. All that would impress most Dutch people in west Michigan who heavily worship wealth and deem wealth as a sign that God favors one, but for some reason or another Carmen was not accepted in school. Not by the cool kids at least, not really by anyone. I felt a little sorry for her.

I invited Carmen to my ten year old slumber birthday party, she accepted, I suppose in her attempt to become popular, to join the ranks as one of the popular girls. Carmen seemed reluctant to talk in a social gathering situation. She sat right next to me as all the girls sat in a circle watching me open my birthday gifts. Carmen gave me a blank journal style notebook and a bottle of "rose milk lotion."

Carmen felt only comfortable next to me, she seemed familiar, and I to her. Carmen seemed to open up easily with words to me, but very shy and standoffish to the other girls at my party whom were all exuberant in laughter, and not timid with playing song melodies on our piano that evening. Carmen was not silly in nature, she was rather stoic, a practical sort, she reminded me of an adult in a child's body, she seemed beyond her years. Me? I felt much younger than her, at least by five years, but I wasn't, in fact, I am one year older than her, you would never believe it though.

When the time came to open gifts, and opening Carmen's gift to me, she said, "Yous don't have to like the gift, my mother had these items in the house, and we did not have time to shop, I thought yous might like them though."

"Yes, I like them very much. My mother never buys lotion for me, the rose milk smells very nice. I like creative writing which we are learning in school. I like my gifts very much Carmen." I spoke with reassurance as I thanked Carmen for the lotion and journals.

"I know yous like to write." Responded Carmen, as she looked right through me with her penetrating big brownish-green eyes as we both sat Indian style in my living room, everyone in a circle.

As the other girls carried on with laughter and talking to one another, I stared at Carmen, as she looked through me, as if she saw inside me, my soul, as if Carmen could see and know things about me inside that another could not.

It was not a uncomfortable feeling I felt at that moment, but rather a deep bond that went beyond this lifetime. We really seemed to know each other, especially Carmen really seemed to recognize me, or know me from the past. Carmen seemed ahead of me in connecting all the dots, in my past, or our past lives. She was wiser, and beyond her years, I could feel that or sense that by how Carmen stared at me.

I was in wonderment at her statement, then I asked Carmen, "You know I like to write Carmen? How would you know I like to write?" I asked bewildered.

"I don't know how I's know that, I's just know yous do." Said Carmen as she shrugged her shoulders in her response, her big greenish-brown eyes stared right through me, searching, not trying to connect her soul searching to Lori, but trying to reach me in my past, somehow, inside, Carmen just stared right through me. I don't know how else to explain the feeling I experienced right then and there, as did Carmen feel and sense. I stared at Carmen. The other girls carried on in laughter around us, but I just stared at Carmen for a minute as if to push "pause." Just then my father Chuck walked in with two pizza's he had just picked up, he walked inside the house with a smile as he laid the pizzas down on the kitchen table. My mother forgot to bake dinner and there was a brief exchange of harsh words spoken under my father's breath as he laid down the hot pizzas on the table passing by the kitchen. He mumbled a few gruff words about my mother's lack of preparation for my big turning ten birthday party. I could only hope it would not turn into a full scale argument like most nights between my father and mother. My stomach briefly turned a notch in awful anticipation of a heated argument between those two. As much as I was aware of my parents strong dislike for each other, I wanted to present a picture that all is well, and I have a happy family life. Even if it was just a twenty- four hour projection for the other girls at my slumber party. It surely was like walking on egg shells. For the blessed moment a heated argument remained dormant.

I think I received maybe two to four birthday cakes ever on my birthday. Most of my father's side and my mother's side of the family lived close by, yet never did my mother Cindy ask any relatives, cousins, or even my two sets of grandparents over for my birthday party as most mothers would do. Probably because Cindy never threw many birthday parties for me. It was always what I could do for Cindy, she instilled those conditioned thoughts into me and my brothers at a very young age, it was her social conditioning of us in our childhood. Although at the time, I did not know I was being "socially conditioned," only Cindy knew what she was doing. I never knew differently, it just was my reality, as long as I let her control my reality, it would never change.

What I would tap into later on in my life was the age old concepts of my past studies such as; Philosophy, which is the examination of basic concepts such as truth, existence, reality, causality, and freedom, all of which was a school of thought particularly dangerous to what Cindy and the religious community around me were trying desperately to keep me from. It is as if Cindy and others like Cindy were aware that indeed I was from heaven.

Despite my turbulent relationship with Cindy, my so called named "mother," on paper documents, I did find a friendship with Carmen, a bond. I seemingly could make friends with just about anybody. Except bond with Cindy my named mother in my life, we were like water and oil, a match that could never bond, but why? Why can't Cindy be a normal, caring mother? Why did Cindy always make the most unusual remarks to me growing up? Very, very sexually inappropriate remarks about her body, her genitals, and remarks about how I looked. Cindy was always trying to mold me into a whore, demoralize me, she saw me not as a daughter, but an object she owned and controlled, to gain from, or secretly murder? Cindy would go to extremes to embed herself into the Calvinist society around us. Cindy created this persona that she is a victim within my father's alcoholism, and she was also a saint, that is her victim-saint dual portrait she painted. We must all believe Cindy, so I was <u>conditioned</u> to believe, before I could think for myself, before I had a resurrection of all I know. Before I was given the tools to paint.

I later would be talked about in such a demoralizing way by Cindy, that people at Hillcrest Christian Reformed Church in Hudsonville, just were not buying Cindy's saga, tales, and drama of her being the victim-saint in her marriage and her role as a mother. Cindy then demanded we change churches as a family. We were always changing churches, on account of Cindy, the matriarch in the family, in her search of a congregation that would not ask questions to her, or of her. Cindy was determined to reign as queen of the Dutch Christian Reformed society, it was her very attainable platform mission in life, making my father look like he was bad or had a problem, or was the problem, or I had problems. Or I was mentally instable, I was fat, or I had an unruly personality. Cindy tried just about everything and anything that gave Cindy a platform in which she could gain a spotlight of sympathizers and believers. Some people really bought into her drama propaganda……but why?

I would for the most part put my family turbulences behind me when I closed the garage door and headed for the bus stop. School was at least my world, not Cindy's destruction of my world. School was a safe island, in school I had hope. I could learn and dream and not hear that I was a waste of a person, or an adoption. I was stuck in Cindy's drama outside of the hours of 8:30am to 3:15pm, for now. I muttered softly, "I will make it to eighteen and leave her control and demise of my young life, what is left of it anyways." I said often to myself with an exhausted sigh as I headed to the bus stop each morning. I learned mental armor was the best way of not letting her beat me down emotionally, or control me psychologically, the best I could. The toll surely did wear on me, and sometimes I just snipped back, and gave her a piece of my mind, what I thought of her, as a person, as a wife to my adopted father, as a woman what I thought of her cold chilly mother ways. There were times I decided it was better to get slapped by her, Cindy, than to keep my mouth shut about the horrible person she was. Oh, I would learn to keep my mouth shut when around Cindy.

I raised myself the best I knew how, without even knowing I was raising myself on my own. I just knew I did not have a helpful kind mother to guide me along. Only a mother who ridiculed me, demoralized me, and took out her frustrations of her failing marriage on me.

As well as her bizarre interests in looking or touching me sexually, and flying into rages when she could not own me, or I would not allow her to do as she pleased. The word "no," I said often to Cindy. I wanted to change Cindy. However, strong-willed Cindy was set in her course to change me. It was a battle of wills, I was just the child. Cindy was determined to crush my self-importance or any healthy self-image I might still have left in me, before I graduated. Break me psychologically to then gain control of my life, and not hear "no," from me or anyone with a strong will. Cindy was like a social tornado, if you spoke the word "no" to her, you might not know she was a social tornado in your life, but behind your back……she was, she'd plot and plunder, you had no chance. So I have discovered. Cindy was that same way with my adopted father Charles. He gave up trying to change Cindy and drank to dilute his own reality, purposely. If he divorced her in the 1970's or 1980's a Judge in those days would have believed Cindy. Why? The divorce laws in those days favored given the wife everything, plus some. He was an alcoholic, not stupid, he knew he'd lose sight of me, and I would end up dead one day from shooting off my mouth in a verbal defense battle with Cindy. I learned early on I could debate, and make her think. Which ironically as you might also guess, would just infuriated Cindy, my intelligence. Believe it or not, my intelligent scope of what she was enraged her.

My dad just drank, and gave up, he was losing strength against ever changing Cindy, but I would not give up. Eventually I would turn eighteen, graduate from high school, move out, but not give up. My dad was losing hope, he saw himself as just a paycheck to her, with no real hope. Drinking sadly was his escapism from his reality of what he had married. Cindy appeared to be winning the race, she was a cunning and devious warrior in that marriage, in my life, and that community. I would often wonder if Cindy had not poured the first alcoholic drink for my dad and got him hooked. He was the alcoholic, and she was perceived as not having the problem, or not having anything wrong with her.

Needless to say, I did not have a normal mother- daughter relationship, it was her ownership over me and my future, my life. I was on my own in developing into a nice, charming and beautiful young lady. My teenage years were of instincts and observing others on how to become a woman, one of trial and error.

I would look to magazines to give me idea's how to wear my hair, and grasp unto the outside world for guidance on the matter of style and beauty tips. Sometimes Carmen would apply makeup on me, style my hair. When I would look into the mirror when she finished "beautifying" me, I shockingly knew she did not want boys to admire me. Carmen liked me to focus on just being her friend and not fly away with a crush on some teenage boy that would come between our new friendship, like a black mamme, a jealous one.

I would seemingly be the one that was going to bring Carmen into the group of popular girls. Later in life Carmen would become a professional cosmetologist, you would never have known that fact by seeing how she preferred for me to look, how she would do my hair and make-up at her house. It was a joke. She loved to overfeed me with the richest sweets and pastries and vitamin D milk. Carmen would always remind me that I did not have to marry, that marriage is not a necessity. Carmen made it clear she wanted me single, for as long as she could. She most definitely did not want me falling in love, she did not want to hear about any crush I might have on a teenage boy. As if it would break her black mamme heart if I changed my stupid hairstyle she gave me, make-up, lost weight, and moved away from her, and her beady black mamme eyes. She was a spider, but needless to say, she loved to dote on me, she catered to me. It was twisted devotion, she truly loved me, but then also could not stand the sight of any boy next to me, especially any boy that resembled…..Alan, from the 1860's era in time. Carmen's eyes naturally, innately, without any kind of formal training in such, had eyes of that of a watch dog on me, from whom I talked with, laughed with, sat next to.

But nevertheless, past life friendships, relationships and such, when you meet up in this lifetime, on this big ball of a playing field, well, let me tell you, past life connections are always stronger of a bonding feeling, than conversing or relating to someone for the first time. The real first lifetime connections always rate second in natural bonding, that instant connection one can feel and have with another they decide must be a friend from a previous lifetime is a stronger connection than first time friendships.

My mother Cindy was controlling of what she wanted me to become in her world. Carmen also had controlling dimensions within herself towards me. Like a grip of a domineering underpaid nanny has on a child left in her care, yet her personality was far better than any words spoken by Cindy to me.

In the presiding junior high years people would say to me, "Why do you even bother to talk with Carmen? She lives on a farm and smells like pigs, we hear her aunt sacrifices cats on their land." Laughter would follow their teasing statements of inquiring why I would even speak to Carmen.

I remember vividly during one of those fifteen minute morning breaks between classes, I saw Carmen by herself leaning her back against the hall heater. How she could handle the raging heat from the boiling green painted hot metal? I still do not know to this day. But she is instantly, always, attracted to heat, and elements of fire.

Carmen would stare out the green metal school door window, or she would just look ahead into the blank space of the hall, seemingly o.k. with being so alone in school, with no one to talk with. I felt a bit of empathy for Carmen, after all, no one should be alone in school, not with the abundance of all these kids to be friends with. I approached her by that green boiler heat vent against the school wall. My heart and friendship always went out to all people at school. I was later voted most friendly and most humorous in school by my classmates, I think because of my friendliness, and adopting school as my choice to be, verses home. I remember one of our very first conversations by the green boiler heat vent…

"So how are you Carmen? What are you doing?" I asked with a cheery smile.

"I'm fine, what are yous doing here?" Carmen asked bewildered as to why I would approach her at school, when other kids would not.

"Well, it's break time." I said. Carmen seemed a bit surprised that I would talk with her, that I even bothered to approach her by the hall wall heater where she often placed her hands behind her back, flat against the hot green metal, the metal matched little speckles in her eyes. Then within one year Carmen began wearing brown eye contacts.

Still she looked in features like a black girl, yet Carmen was white. I always kept that comment to myself.

"So do you like living on a farm?" I asked.

"We's do live on a farm, I's prefer to live in the suburbs like yous." Carmen was always putting "s" on the back of you's, we's, and I's, and other words. Her mother spoke that way too, so I learned later. I think her mother's family was from Kentucky or someplace south of Michigan.

"I think that would be pretty neat to live on a farm. Do you have your own horse?" That's what I remember about our friendship, what I asked, some of my very first questions, I still remember. Why? Maybe, because I always asked such few questions of Carmen. Anyways, I remember how our friendship first began to sprout, it was always easy to talk with Carmen. She was always telling me something revealing about what I might like, know, or want, or simply just a fact about me, before I even would tell her myself, or know myself. Odd how she just simply knew things about me. It was always easy to be with Carmen, in her company, because I never had to explain myself or what I like. I visited her farm many times in the coming months and years. Odd how she would open up to me but not with other kids at school, odd, even more odd, but odd in a good way is how she seemed to know things about myself, things I never told her, ever. Do you know how it is when you're comfortable with someone's company? When you do not have to talk excessively, just being in each other's presence was a bonding experience, comfortable. A friendship between us grew as we entered grade after grade. Carmen became my best friend, we were locker partners from ninth grade thru high school graduation, our senior year at Unity Christian High in Hudsonville, Michigan.

The other girls at school began thinking more highly of Carmen with each passing year, as I brought her into the group of popular girls. The popular girls from Jenison Christian Junior High; Kim, Lynda, Heather, Jane, myself, there were a few others too, we then joined with the popular girls from Hudsonville Christian Junior High, Marla and Cheri. We all hung out during our breaks from classes and ate our lunches all together. What did we have that other girls in high school did not have, well, I don't know either, but we had something, we were all "in," and so was Carmen now.

Carmen invited me to sleep over on a Friday night, the next day we went horseback riding on her horse. I got bucked off, and Carmen laughed uncontrollably. The next week at school I asked Carmen, "Where is my hair brush? Have you seen my hairbrush, I think I left it at your home Carmen, last weekend?"

The whole week went by, maybe even two weeks. Then I was back at Carmen's house, "There is my brush!" Resting on the bathroom countertop was my turquoise hairbrush!

Carmen looked at me with reserved emotion, her spider eyes just stared at me as I responded in such a naïve exuberance as I reached for my lost hairbrush. Carmen held up the brush, "Oh, this brush? My aunt Annabelle had this brush, she wanted it for some reason." Carmen says this to me as she chillingly picks up my brush in a casual gesture, as if to say with her passive so reserved for a child expressions always, "this brush?" My hair was gone, my hair cleaned out of my brush, but at least I had my favorite hairbrush back……right? So I thought at that moment in time of finally locating what was lost for two weeks. Rumors stirred around junior high school that her aunt Annabelle had pulled out the potions and spells that week on me.

I remember having vivid and startling dreams growing up, dreams that would wake me up in the wee hours of the night, unable to fall back to sleep. I must have yawned many of times during school from the sheer lack of a full nights rest. I remember from the age of about eight years old telling my father that in my dreams I have thick long black hair. So hot does my hair get a want to shave off my hair for relief of the heat caused by my thick dark long hair as I ride in my chariot. My face looked the same in my dreams with a few differences. I still had my white porcelain skin, and a distinctive European nose, a Ptolemy appearing nose some would comment later in life. My eyes were dark and sunken in more on my face during my dreams, but during the day my eyes were light blue and not so sunken in with my appearance. I would wake up in a sweat, so real was the dream, my gold-blonde thin curls of hair would perspire. Oddly enough, as if hot like the mane of hair I possessed in my dreams. I would talk about a chariot ride back to a city in the dead of night, feeling doomed as I approached the firelight glowing within the walls of that city of a lost major battle. Romans at my city gate, Romans behind me, I was trapped, and then wake up to just escape the entrenching Romans. I would wake up each night before I approached the city with this overwhelming feeling of loss and dread. During the day, I had stomach aches, as if the stress from the vivid, horrifying, very fast pace war dreams were seemingly the cause of added anxiety growing up. My father Chuck, slang for Charles, gave me the nickname, "Cleopatra." He told me he too thought he came from a line of Pharaohs, and it is the Ptolemy family that comes back to me in my dreams to warn me of something. He said that in his dreams he is like King Tut, a boy king, who had a powerful curse placed on anyone who opened his tomb. He said this over and over from about the ages that I was nine to about fourteen, these dreams he was having, it would cause him to drink? Perhaps drinking because he lived with my mother, and drinking helped him deal with Cindy, creating a fuzzy and bearable reality of what Cindy was behind closed doors.

Distorting his reality was more pleasurable than facing Cindy sober I suppose. But I saw how alcoholism took over control of him and his life, and gave Cindy control over what she wanted to paint as a picture of him. I knew at a young age I wanted to stay in control. Staying in control is what I needed to have when dealing with Cindy, to always be on alert, it was like walking on egg shells inside the home, not a comfortable childhood or adolescence. A war.

Among the other factors in my father's life, my mother's focused on herself and money. Then the crucially devastating high mortgage interest rates from 1979 to 1982, which destroyed many residential construction careers, including my father's building career. Probably all caused a ripple effect that led him to want to consume Vodka on a daily basis now. Vodka and orange juice was his choice of drink.

In the summer of 1980, my father volunteered his building services for a summer in New Mexico for about seven to ten weeks. At the end of August my mom and I took an Amtrak train ride from New Mexico to Michigan. My father drove home three weeks later in September of 1980. I heard him talking to my mother in the kitchen late September, about how this Indian medicine man, a Shaman approached him while he was building a Sunday school building for a church in Shiprock, New Mexico. The building project was sponsored by the local church there, my father donated his time, his labor, and taught the skills of building to the young local Indian men in the community for the summer of 1980 in exchange for groceries and a home to stay in while the work took place. The Indian medicine man Shaman took my father to a body of water, a lake, and placed tea leaves? Bay leaves? Some type of leaves on my father's back, he then proceeded to tell my father as the medicine man began having visions, "Someday…"

I was ten years old when I overheard that conversation my father told my mother at our house that my father had built on Curwood Drive in Jenison, Lamplight estates. My father said the Indian medicine man, a Shaman, was very convincing and was just adamant in what he prophesied to my father. I clearly remember my father telling my mother about that Indian medicine man, and my mother saying how stupid that sounded, and that cannot be true. Odd I suppose, but what did that Indian medicine man see in his visions, of the future? That I also see in my visions channeled from heaven of a world transforming, and prophecies being fulfilled.

Throughout my life, whether in Michigan or elsewhere, I would hear a constant, bewildering statement made to my face, as individuals would look hard and deep into my soul and say this, "If you had black hair you would be Cleopatra." They would say that statement in a sober and very deliberant tone of voice as they stared right thru my apparent blue eyes. What did these individuals see within me? Were they enemies from a previous life lived? From a war once fought and lost? Were these enemies coming back as my confidants? Or just Romans? A loathed group of enemies that recognized me in this lifetime, even though my eyes are blue and hair is auburn red? If someone touches my arm, or I touch their arm, I can tell you about that person. Sometimes I get flashbacks of that persons previous life with me, the role they played. Others have this ability too, I'm not alone.

Carmen also would comment to me out of the blue one day as we were watching television, as she handed me the remote from her T.V., "If you had black hair, you would be Cleopatra," She again stared thru to my soul, as if not seeing Lori, but reaching deeper within my soul to something else she could see within me, some history in the past, we had shared, as if she was searching for answers, about the past, a past life. Carmen, looked "panicky" to say the least, as if she fears I am Cleopatra, and she is doomed if I am, because she knows I know of a truth. A truth hidden, stolen from me, 2000 years ago, about my son. Carmen would look agitated as if nervous that the truth will be exposed if we continue as friends and I will tell her, with knowledge I was born with about who I believe she is. As if "I caught her, the Jewish nanny who stole my beloved son."

Odd, when Carmen said that to me, I had been having a series of dreams again, I lived in a sandstone building. I had lots of Jewish looking servants and maid servants. Carmen was Jewish in my dream………..

Carmen (Mary) was one of my newer servant ladies, introduced by her mother, who, her mother had been a servant of mine as well. Carmen thus became the nanny to my son, my youngest son I had at one time in history been honing in on to become king someday. The one in line who would be the crowned king of a vast empire I was building by connecting to Rome, in my dreams. Carmen was not nanny to my oldest sons who at that point in time did not need a nanny anymore. My oldest sons I had with Marc Antony did not trust the Jewish castle servants with secrets. My oldest sons believed the Jewish castle servants eavesdropped too much and were a security threat to the kingdom of Egypt, the kingdom I ruled over.

In my dreams I call Carmen, Mary. I see in my dreams how she grew a special bond with my youngest son, she was a Jewish slave girl in Egypt, in my castle. I was very focused on acquiring more land at that particular phase in my reign, she took over in the role of motherhood. You have heard that notion, a cliché, "Be weary of the hand that rocks the cradle?"

I planned an escape route for my children if I lost a major war against Rome, the plan was devised if we lost a major battle of that time in building a larger dynasty. If I lost the war in my dream, an escape plan after the war would come into play to save my children from Roman forces seizing and killing my children. Prior to going into battle, any battle, birth certificates were forged, always. Documents naming Mary as my youngest son's mother, who was then Jewish nurse and high ranking servant of mine to my youngest son, which was Carmen, Carmen is Mary. But there was more going on behind my back as I was often gone from my castle. Something between the Jewish servants, a plan of their own, to elevate one of their own? A plot? From servant to royalty status? Behind my back? The Romans were involved, such as Roman spies or bribes given to the Jewish castle servants? In my dreams it is as if my mind wants to see what is going on behind my back. There is a plan of theirs, a scheming plan, above or beside what my orders are and were at the time if I was to lose that major battle between Octavia and Marcus Agrippa, that the Roman forces….. Mary left with another Jewish servant. Did I fake my death over two thousand years ago? But then later, really die from the hands of a female in Octavia's concubine? Or from Octavia himself?

Later after the lost war, my death, Mary and my son, and the other Jewish servant had to travel back to Egypt later for a census, I was dead by then. A Roman demanded census by Octavia, also known as Caesar Augustus after the battle he won against me and my mate Marc Antony. My son, a royal, would be raised as a Jew now that I had lost the war and was dead. Mary was aware of the planet Jupiter over his birthplace at the time of his birth. I was aware as well that he would be a young crowned king of my dynasty, as all royals such as myself had a proper education in the study of planets and the interpretation from the heavens to earth. But Carmen, Mary, had her own scheme of rising from a slave position, to be like me? Or in her delusions supported by her mother and aunt, had a plan to elevate the status of Jews in Egypt? Whom at the time were castle servants of mine. The Jews were slaves in Egypt, many of them were at least. I believe I must have trusted the wrong people to watch over my son. I did. I placed too much trust in Mary and her family. Why? Because they always appeared so faithful to me, and I was good to them, they lived in my castle, ate of my food, and had a very good life. Why would I think I could not trust them? Or why would I think they would ever go against me? It made no logical sense, unless it had to do with creating the Jews to be seen as more than what they were at that time in Egypt, over 2000 years ago under Pharaoh rule and domain?

The Romans hired revered astrologers known as the wise men, Magi, of the day to locate through the stars and planets, a mapping system in those days, to locate a boy that would be king someday and follow the planet Jupiter as it moved in the sky over a period of a few years? "The Jupiter affect," Jupiter to ancients meant a leader, a king has been born on earth. "An anointing sign by the heavens." Roman leaders located their rising rivals by mapping planets such as Jupiter and Leo within the constellation of stars and planets.

It was a mapping and tracking device to locate potential powerful rivals to a thrown. When the wise men hired by Roman leaders located the boy king undercover, my biological son, they gave gifts to Mary, to befriend her perhaps, to get closer to the boy king? The Romans remained on his back for the rest of his life, I think Mary had a big mouth, unable to hold my precious secret in exchange for money and gifts? Or she and her mother and aunt had stolen a legend to hold and have, and boast about? The Roman empire and local Jews outside of Mary and Joseph's circle must have feared the Romans discovering the truth, which was a lie of a Jew, and were on my child's back for the rest of his life, the Romans eventually stoned my son, they crucified him? Mary came up with a solution to what the wise men astrologers had discovered? Stating that he was a king of the Jews, just as she was Jewish, was that her plan all along? Even prior to me going off to a major battle? The last battle. The big battle where I lost everything.

And through the puzzle pieces laid out by God, perhaps that was his plan as well for my son? I was only trying to cover-up his identity with forged birth certificates, if I lost a war against Rome. Mary, my trusted servant would cover-up his birth to protect his identity, his royal line. My youngest son would always respond to the Roman soldiers that questioned who in fact his true biological father was, the soldiers that traveled with Octavia to my castle steps, my son would say, "No one comes to the father accept through me." My youngest would never give up who his biological father was, which was heavily rumored to be Octavia. And then I woke up.

I wonder in my awakened hours if Mary had fled with my youngest son **before** even learning that Marc Antony and I lost against the Romans? She was young, a slave girl, and very bonded in a motherly way to the boy king, my son. I wonder if history will be re-written based on the knowledge I bring to the table with my memoirs, my memories of my past life? As the Christians would say, "If it is not written within the pages of the Bible, it cannot be true."

I would say in my response, "There are no record of dinosaurs that had ever lived on earth according to the Bible, yet science and discoveries has proven that what is not in the Bible, still might have, and very well did exist on earth at one time."

As you well know, "the unknown" is labeled "evil," or "not of God," "not of God's history, and therefore does not matter." The unknown can somehow create such hype within one's mind, or church, or place of worship, or community, it therefore is disregarded and receives a less than favorable response. "The unknown," "The unknown history," "The undiscovered history," has never been given a positive approach or connotation, ever.

After the war, Egypt became a providence of Rome, the line of Pharaohs was over…..at least that is what I can remember in my dreams. But my sons importance was not overlooked in the constellations, his location was astrologically graphed and mapped, from his natal chart origins to where he might be located? His future impact and magnitude graphed by the Magi, would be on his immediate lifetime and the future of his legacy as a king, a ruler….strongly denoted with Jupiter the "king planet on his horizon line." I can only read scriptures now, and say, oh my Lord, is that what happened to my son after I lost the war against the Roman forces and died? Written by historians of the day, hired by powerful Rome, based on what was occurring, what was kept secret from the historians because of the birth certificates forged. But the birth certificates were forged <u>prior</u> to me going into battle, as I remember. I can only wonder if Mary his nanny and her Jewish male counterpart had motives that were unknown to me at the time…..2000 years ago. Perhaps they were not to be trusted servants? Perhaps in their selfishness, greed, or overcoming slave status in Egypt, well then, they saw opportunity of their own will? The astrological plan of God took place, fate? Was Mary jealous of the powerful empire I was building with my soul mate and leading man Marc Antony? As I rolled the dice against Octavia.

Did Mary give my locations and strategies away to Rome? Did she secretly want to take the thrown, my son, my thrown in Egypt because she had her eye on my leading man, Marc Antony? Or another blonde soldier who liked to visit me from Rome….Octavia? Did Mary have an undercurrent devised plan to take my ruling place in my empire I was building?

My youngest son born of a Roman father, Octavia. The Roman leader whom was younger than me and who was always jealous of Caesar, jealous of his power he had over me. Caesar who was my first male alliance with Rome, my first trophy of a proven alliance. Why would I ever go against Rome? I had spent a lifetime seducing Rome's most powerful, why would I go against Rome in the end?

Why? I'll tell you why, Octavia wanted my other older children I had with Marc Antony killed, and that spawned a war, the big war to keep and hold on to all my children, and my empire. An affair will be revealed, and perhaps it was Marc Antony that <u>knew</u> Octavia and I had been involved prior to a war beginning in the desert? Perhaps at the end of this book you will understand love, loyalty, and God's plan for your lives, mostly you will just say, "Oh, my God, Lori, this is all just about reincarnation, and your very devoted mothers love of a son, of what a real mother would do, which would be to take the cross or persecution in place of a son." Perhaps you are right.

There was one person who knew how my mind worked, Mary. She knew my plans, she bathed in my conquering power and glory and all I would share with her, that trusted young Jewish servant, she knew too much? And also wanted so much of my glory, my men I seduced, my royal title? I can only look back and relapse what had gone so terribly wrong…..Mary was not loyal to me, but loyal in her quest for all I had won over and possessed? Mary saw me as gold? As her opportunity? Mary was a castle servant who did not know her place, an obsessed servant of my life in a past life……who adored blonde haired men from Rome at my castle doorsteps? Mary wanted to rise in ranks as a slave girl, she wanted to rise in legend, power, and what I was in Egypt, Cleopatra.

My youngest son was of Roman descent, fathered by Octavia, a secret that could destroy Octavia's plan of becoming Rome's most powerful leader. Octavia was growing in popularity in Rome, as I was loathed in Rome. Eventually Octavia would have to make a decision, would it be the right decision? Or one he would later regret, and then locate his heir, our son, after I had been murdered? And my children with Marc Antony, were murdered? Octavia would have to locate the boy king to save his position with Rome.

My son must have secretly always known he was a king to be, a Pharaoh to be crowned, an anointed one of both the Roman Empire and the Egyptian dynasty. A master plan of joining is what I had envisioned, but I also was not willing to have my other older children killed, as Octavia demanded, children I had with Marc Antony. My son who escaped with his nanny Mary later would have to live in hiding of those facts. He must have inherited a reforming mind such as mine, he must have loathed the Roman dominate control, he probably was just as outspoken as I had been in my war campaigns. He must have saw my bloodshed of controlling and gaining territory of the day as both dangerous and not the way he would gain influence, in his world. Children often learn from the mistakes of their parents, children often see life differently than how a parent would want them to view life. Children have their own agenda, their own processed perception on life…..their own view of how things really are. They learn through the mistakes of their parents and the immediate world around them, children just do. Was my oldest son crucified, and then loathed and cursed the Jews? Would he rise up and exact his revenge on Jews? With war? Old fashion, traditional war?

I remember in 1984, I was fourteen then, Carmen and I sat next to each other in science class, our friendship was blossoming in 1984. Carmen looked at me, in one of those deep probing stares, as if to talk to me now, in the present, yet reach deeper to something in the past, before our lives lived on earth? During this era in time, she kept staring at me and saying, "I know you are Cleopatra, just say it, admit it."

I giggled, I felt uncomfortable about my memories, which I was not sharing with Carmen, nor my dreams of what I remember of 2000 years ago. I was keeping my mouth sealed, the dreams were so very startlingly to me, haunting, and weird, and not in the present day sense. If I wanted to stay popular, well-liked by my classmates, I had to remain quiet about my weird dreams, and Carmen's probing as if a detective interrogating me, Cleopatra. As she was afraid that I would expose her, the former Jewish nanny. Carmen had fear in her eyes that was now emerging 2000 years later, fear in her eyes that history would be told in the true light of the rightful mother of that son she claimed was hers. I would deny, being Cleopatra, it would have ended our friendship. I just kept insisting to Carmen's probing, "I'm not Cleopatra."

Carmen would respond as she stared deep into my eyes and point at me, "If you had black hair you would be Cleopatra!"……. Carmen would end with a rant, "I know you are Cleopatra, you have two lines on your forehead, you are just pretending to be my friend, and when you are no longer my friend…."

I responded, "What? I do not have two lines on my forehead."

Carmen kept insisting in 1984, "You have two wrinkles forming, two lines that look like the number two, Roman numeral two. I can see them before you can see them forming, you will have those two wrinkles, you're really not my friend. You are two faced, I know you are……you are just pretending to be my friend. Your mother Cindy told me to tell you that when those two parallel lines between your brow are visible a horrific act will occur by the CIA.

I went home that night and studied my face for hours in 1984, I was fourteen years old. I had no wrinkles at age fourteen, I had no idea what she was talking about. Until the summer of 2001, I was thirty-one years old, I moved up north to Petoskey, and Carmen said to me in August 2001, "I see your two lines, you are two-faced, you are not my friend, we are no longer friends, I know you are going to tell the world…"

Could that theory taught in psychology class about the derivative emotion of love, and the thin line of emotion between love and hate be so closely connected, really be true?

And what I experience so freakishly in this lifetime be a batch of leftovers of a black magic dance of Bessy's from the 1860's in the deep south, so far away from here in time and place and origin?

In this lifetime I appear to be full of zest with a driving need to conquer, spill over the truth bucket, and bring awareness to the world of a better way to live. I have this fire, this ambition to conquer evil and spill over the truth. Sometime between the years 1977 and 1982 a new boy arrived to Jenison, Michigan during the summer months. Often I would ride my bike through Lamplight Estates with Lisa Pare. The new boy in town, the much older by at least six years was Adam Duritz. Adam Duritz during the summertime would often spot me and stop me right near my school bus stop. The years were 1977, 1978, 1979, I was seven, eight, and nine years old. I could tell by his height he was much older and he had under arm hair. Adam Duritz looked too big to ride a ten speed bike, he was much bigger and older than the other normal kids playing outside in the neighborhood. Adam was a stranger to that neighborhood and up to no good, even as I child that was something I picked up on right away. The Adam Duritz who would later become the lead singer of the band The Counting Crows. I was nine years old and he was fifteen. Often I would ride my bike around Lamplight Estates, riding my bike with Lisa Pare, swim in her pool or she would swim in my pool. Often times riding my bike home from Lisa Pare's house I would be stopped by a big kid on a ten speed bike, that big kid was Adam Duritz. He would like to stop and talk with me, he explained that our parents knew each other. I was a bit bewildered as to what he was talking about, I had never seen him before.

Cindy would always be talking about everything a young girl fears, <u>everything</u>. Often at the table on Curwood Drive while my father was away Cindy would clip out of local newspapers including The Grand Rapids Press anything morbid in printed news concerning young girls. Such as a two year old kept in a closet within the girl's parents house for six years on the NW side of Grand Rapids. Reading the horrific details of how the girl lived in a closet and the emaciated description of the girl when the girl was found would light up Cindy's eyes as she read and relished the horrors the little girl lived through. Cindy's mood turned to elated as she read any news article about child abuse and the scene and situation published within the newspaper. As Cindy sat on the sofa and clipped away at The Grand Rapids Press I stared in fear of Cindy's jubilant mood. I stood and absorbed the horrific details that Cindy said out loud in my presence as a child as she read the news article. Details such as, the girl was found in her own feces in a closet off the kitchen for six years with little food, only enough food to sustain life to receive abuse by her tormenters. Once rescued the girl could not speak in full sentences or know how to eat with utensils. Her development was severely stunted. Cindy kept a scape book of newspaper clippings of trauma, abuse, death of young children in the Grand Rapids area. Cindy would often comment that such an abused child would become so abnormal in this world that someone should end the life. I watched Cindy's eyes as the wheels would turn in her mind. I stood in fear of Cindy's jubilant mood. The very first Grand Rapids Press newspaper clipping in Cindy's horror scape book is that of her two year old brother David that was murdered by Cindy when Cindy had David her younger brother chew on an electrical cord while child Cindy stretched his arm as far as possible to then place his tiny hand on a metal register while her mother was gone buying family groceries. Cindy would love to talk about young girls getting raped and relish in the details of the horror. Cindy and her friends considered the sensationalism of the horror those young girls must have gone through as meaningful and interesting topics to discuss at the table. Cindy would relish in the power tactics that the perpetrators would use upon the helpless naïve or trapped young girls. Cindy's eyes would light up on dark subject matters and become over joyed with enthusiasm. I knew Cindy was a monster, and not a mom. Cindy went on one day talking about how a twelve year old girl in Grand Rapids was raped by her stepdad on the kitchen floor as her mother held down the helpless girl. I avoided the kitchen as much as possible in the preceding years ahead of me while in the care of Calvinist Cindy.

As you can guess, as a young girl I would always keep my distance from Cindy in the household. I would easily be described as aloof around Cindy. I created an invisible safety net around me as I would drown out any mother-daughter relationship tie with Cindy. Cindy was always trying to enter that safety net of my making. I would always try and not be in the same room as Cindy growing up. It was not until the 1970's decade was over and I grew into a young lady that I learned the meanings, the word definitions to the words Cindy would use at the dinner table during the 1970's. To this day I hate sitting at the dinner table, unless I go out to eat. Sometimes as much as I want to change mental conditioning of phobias instilled into me by Cindy and her CIA associates, I simply cannot. I feel as though I have avoidance issues lodged inside my brain that are too stuck inside my brain to leave my mind, too embedded into my fears and phobias to even know where to begin to change. After all my fears have kept me relatively safe, recognizing monsters and knowing how to deal safely with monsters such as Cindy. So why again would I want my childhood fears to escape the safety of my mind, the mind that I trust.

One day I walked in my house and Adam Duritz's mother was sitting at the dining room table at our house on Curwood Drive, Lamplight Estates. I stared at her, she smiled and stared at me. She wore an experienced adult expression that said she knew a lot about me. Cindy introduced the lady at the table as Mrs. Duritz.

Mrs. Duritz stated that she had a daughter about my age that she would bring by some time for me to meet. Mrs. Duritz sitting at the dining room table asked if she could touch my hair. I said "That would be o.k." As she touched my hair, I knew instantly who she was in a previous lifetime lived. Mrs. Duritz locked eyes with me, me just a child. Mrs. Durtiz affirmed what she suspected all along, who I was in a previous lifetime lived. She then commented, "I like your hair. I bet when you turn sixteen you'll change the color, I bet you just hate your hair color."

I stared at Mrs. Duritz and answered the remark silently, I do hate my hair color, I would like to change my hair color.

I looked at Mrs. Duritz, a full grown adult as I felt so helpless, I instantly felt victimized in her presence. There she was, standing in front of me after all these years, over 2000 years, there was the aunt of my son's nanny from way back when. At one time she lived in my castle in Egypt. She was there, she knew everything, way back when in my sandstone castle when she was a high ranking Jewish castle servant of mine. Mrs. Duritz looked at me in a shocked dead lock stare as she then just realized as she touched my hair who I am inside, my soul, and our history together. Mrs. Duritz's eyes spoke to me, yes, Lori also knows who I am too. Without verbalizing history, we both knew right then and there, the whole course of Egypt had changed because of her and the other high ranking Jewish castle servants, and I am alive, which means I can talk now.

My youngest son I had with Octavia later became the Biblical Jesus. My youngest son was later named Jesus by Jewish Mary. My youngest son named Jesus by the Jews was also the soul of my adopted father Charles Vander Ark. Jesus was an outsider to the Jewish religion 2000 years ago during Biblical days. As an outsider Jesus saw from the outside within the Jewish camps and cities, he was inside looking out so to speak. Jesus knew through observing as a child between the ages of one and six living in Egypt that war was never the answer. War caused devastations and emotional wounds that could never be healed on an earthly plain. Jesus saw and experienced everything he had lost because of war. Jesus lost his true biological mother, the kingdom I ruled over and the kingdom he called his home. Everything lost could never be regained, losses to many to list, all caused by war.

Later that summer, I believe was the summer of 1979 I did meet Mrs. Duritz's daughter, she brought her daughter over to our house. Mrs. Duritz commented to us both as she looked at me, "It's hard to believe you are both the same age, Lori is so much taller and bigger." I always thought that I was large and tall for my age because I wanted to escape my childhood. When I realized that being a teenager was just as scary around Cindy and her CIA associates, I stopped growing by age twelve and have remained five foot three ever since.

One day like many days during the summer months off from school Carmen Haverdink called and invited me to her farm on Filmore Street. The bike ride was about three miles but I was no stranger to riding my bike. My selected choice of freedom, I knew when the wind first brushed against my hair and blew my hair back I was free. One day on the way home, back to my house on Curwood in Lamplight Estates I road along on a sandy dirt long driveway or road of sorts, I passed by an old small ranch style house on my way back to my subdivision. This was my normal travel route as I rode my bike to and from Carmen's house. Later a local real estate developer removed that small old ranch house and paved the dirt alleyway style road and built larger homes that fit into the landscape of the other Lamplight Estates newer and larger homes. Anyways, on that particular summer day in 1979 a little girl came running out to me as I neared the connection where the sandy road connected to a row of white and black stumps that blocked and backed up to a cul-de-sac that connected to the street of Lamplight Estates near Curwood Drive. The little girl came running towards me on my bike, begging and convincing me to just stop and play with her. Let me clarify, the little girl was not Adam Duritz's sister. We played in her yard for a while, her older sisters came out and she asked her older sisters if I could spend the night. I was taken aback that she wanted me to spend the night, we had just met, but she was so insistent. At the time I had no idea at age nine that I was being set up for being molested at her house that night in her home. In hindsight I realize now that someone had set her up to invite me over. At the time I did not know bad things were going to happen to me. My parents were fighting more than ever, day and night fighting, so I accepted the invitation and told her I would go home and ask my mom if I could sleep over at her house. I remember going home and pointing down the street to the end of the cul-de-sac where the long dirt alleyway road connected to the old small ranch house that bordered Lamplight Estates, our neighborhood. Cindy seemed slightly hesitant and then said o.k. I could stay at the strangers house. In hindsight as a parent myself now, I do think it is or was odd that Cindy never asked to meet the girl's parents or see exactly where I would be staying the night. However at the time in 1979, I simply packed my overnight bag and rode my bike back to her house just down the paved road where the cul-de-sac met the sandy long alleyway. I remember her parents were not home, she had a babysitter that offered me cherry Kool-Aid late in the afternoon. I drank the glass of cherry Kool-Aid and then passed out. I woke up in the middle of the night it was completely dark outside. I felt scared and sore in places I just knew I was not supposed to ordinarily be sore. Barefoot, I slipped on my flip-flops and walked across the sandy light colored hardwoods with my overnight bag in my hand. I walked to my bike and in the wee hours of the night or wee morning of the next day I headed up the sandy driveway to the paved street on my bike. I remember how sore I was to sit on my bike seat and how odd it was to ride my bike in the middle of the night. Lamplight Estates was so quiet and dark, the moonlight and light from the stars above seemed to create just enough light for me to ride my bike home to Curwood Drive.

Adam Duritz came over with his mother that same week. Adam and I were outside talking on a landscape mound in our fenced backyard facing Hager Park. He approached me and kept trying to hold onto me, hug me. I remember feeling uncomfortable. Kids just don't hang and hug on other kids. Then Adam asked me if I feel sore down there. I felt uncomfortable that he knew I felt sore in my private parts. Then he asked if I had been raped. I did not even know what the word "rape" or "raped" even meant in 1979. In the back of my mind I wondered if he was talking about or referring to something that might have happened in that old small ranch house. I do not even know what happened to me. Then Adam Duritz comments, "There sure are a lot of German looking girls around here, I have never seen so many blonde hair, blue eyed girls in my life. Where I come from you just do not see this many German looking girls. I am in heaven. I am going to have sex with as many as I can while we are here in town."

At age nine, I did not even know what the words "sex" and "rape" meant. Adam wanted me to touch him, right then and there in my backyard. I just wanted to stay a child and was shocked and bewildered by most of what he had to say and do to me that day, that summer day in Michigan in 1979.

Then on another occasion as I rode my bike through my neighborhood Adam stopped me again on my bike, he was on his ten speed bike as he approached me. He wore his hair as if he had straightened his curly dark hair like a worn disguise, his hair looked crimped and frizzy. This time I talked verses looking at him in bewilderment in the middle of the street, this time I asked him questions. I inquired to Adam Duritz, "I have never seen you in my neighborhood before this summer, where are you from?"

Adam informed me that he was from Maryland.

I asked, "Where is Maryland?"

Adam went on to inform me that Maryland is on the east coast. I inquired, "But why would you be here in Michigan if you are from the east coast?"

Adam informed me that the CIA moved his family here. He also stated that what happened to me at the ranch house over there was filmed by the CIA. He told me that the CIA was going to connect him to Hollywood and make him a famous musician for going along with orders from some military CIA guy named David.

About ten to fourteen years later Adam Duritz emerged as the lead singer of his own rock band called The Counting Crows. In the early 1990's I would be living in Atlanta, Georgia and be working at The Gold Club. Adam approached me years later in the 1990's at The Gold Club and groped me on more than one occasion. He asked me in 1991-1992, "Do or did you have a Jewish father? And are you originally from Michigan? Then Adam informed me that the CIA told him he could locate me at The Gold Club. He informed me in 1991 that the CIA was taking my lineage chart and photographs of me and selling me behind my back. I did not believe Adam Duritz at the time because I simply did not want to believe that was going on behind my back. I wanted to believe I could create a normal life out of my shattered by Cindy life. Shattered by Cindy and all her disgusting CIA associates that have way too much ink drying on their hands like bloody fingerprints from that almighty "classified" red ink stamp. Cindy and her CIA associates were always trying to tip life upside down in their constant unwavering reminding me that my life is U.S. property, I knew to stay away from Cindy and her associates. However, I could stop the behavior of Cindy and her CIA associates and all the CIA sub-contractor's behavior towards me. I would dare to guess that millions were made off me behind my back based on sources informing me, and I would also dare to estimate that millions were paid out over the years in elaborate schemes towards me. Harassment from Cindy and her behind the scenes CIA was almost an everyday occurrence in my life, even to this day now. What U.S. agency or department actually polices the CIA? Answer: The CIA is not policed.

Later on Adam Duritz's mother Mrs. Duritz would locate me married in East Lansing, Michigan and would approach me and talk with me as I walked my dog George in my thirties. Mrs. Duritz would locate me working out at the East Lansing, Michigan YMCA. She would stare and see me with my child Eddie and my husband Ed. She had a longing or sadness in her eyes, grey streaked through her black course hair and heaviness through her hips. Mrs. Duritz had once told me at my kitchen dining room table on Curwood in Jenison, Michigan, "I know your lineage is royalty, I have your lineage chart in my home, my son Adam wanted to marry you once, but you were too young."

"Twelve"
CHAPTER NINE

They say when you are twelve all gazing eyes are on you. It is a magical time when the world holds much promise for one's youth and future. When you're twelve you look through a prism to the outward world within yours. The sparkly glass cone resembles the diamonds in one's eyes when you're twelve, that's how the world looks from the view from the eyes of a twelve year old. It's a time when going from a child to an adult is approaching, every day holds a brilliant cup of promise and hope. It's easy to be optimistic when you're twelve, one has the whole world ahead of you, no adult mistakes made, just simple choices to make, and a world to explore further. You have a youths body to hold the energy to explore, travel, and exist with ease. When you're twelve going on thirteen, I suppose it's easy for an adult female to be jealous, like Bessy had been of my life many decades ago in the south. This lifetime would also impose other jealous females upon my exuberant, vivacious, and very stunning self. Like in the south, so many years ago once lived, I too in this lifetime looked fifteen, when I was really only twelve. It would be later I would mask my beauty as a survival technique, strange, but true.

When you're twelve, advice given is like having words and information served on a silver platter. When you're twelve your mind absorbs the world around oneself, as if to taste a bite of life itself in the rawest, realest way, everything is real and so alive. At age twelve, your mind learns with impressions, and sounds, and keen awareness about what is really going on in the world around you, not just what adults want you to believe. When you're twelve you live in the moment but are detached from the adult world that seems to govern all children, and purposely so is one detached from the adult world of mistakes and regrets, when you're twelve. By age twelve I was aware there were adult U.S. government spies all around my neighborhood. I would learn they could crush my knees, beat me to the point of needing surgery for repairs of the damage of deep bruising tissue damage. But I never knew why this was happening to me, there seemingly was no cause. A doctor who examined my broken knees said to me in his exam room, that I had perhaps made a military man jealous. Someone about thirty-five years old to my age of twelve. The military man was seeking my medical records is what was spoken to my mother Cindy. Many horrific scenes made no sense to me. In my mind I thought it was just a bad evil voodoo spell from Bessy.

At a ripe age of twelve, or perhaps even by the tender age of eight, I knew that if I was going to ever grow up and have a successful marriage and family life, I would have to be the opposite of Cindy my adopted mother. Cindy my named mother on paper would do just about anything to get her way, except honest hard work to gain her way in this journey called life. She would nag, nag some more, grow hostile and aloof towards my father, then go into bitter violent fits of raging aggression when hearing the word "no." Cindy would slam kitchen cabinet doors, she would drive off in her car in a chaotic stance. Anything but simply working hard for anything she wanted in life. Cindy wandered between displaying aggressive behavior and that of passive-aggressive behavior. She lacked working roots, that driving stick to it mentality of hard working wholesome values, referred to as integrity. Cindy often would sleep in, well past 10am. She would often go off like a malfunctioning firework throughout the day as she demanded to get her way with money, *her* life, *her* children, *her* time, *her* schedule, and the most petty of decisions to be rendered involving what *she* wanted to do in life, with *her* life, that day, today, any day, every day. Cindy was "neglectful," that is the term used today. But not a term common in the 1970's and 1980's. Cindy would drive away for hours, even the whole day while I might be playing in the yard or basement. Never to say a word of where she was going, simply, she would disappear for the day or morning or afternoon. It might seem odd to you. It certainly seems like odd very unacceptable behavior now that I am an adult and would never consider Cindy's behavior as the right behavior as a mother myself. However, in my childhood daytime or even nighttime absences of Cindy were very common occurrences within my childhood home. Honestly, I never complained or begged Cindy to stay around the house, "Don't go mom" or "Do not leave me mom" was never uttered from my mouth. No Cindy around was much better than Cindy around causing harm and chaos towards me.

At around age eleven or twelve I posted at a local D & W grocery store in Jenison, the town I lived in, I placed a notice on a white paper plate announcing babysitting services with cut and pull tabs cut into the white paper plate with my phone number. I began receiving babysitting jobs on Saturday nights and during the summer months. The money earned I would save and then ride my bike for miles and miles down the hill to Meijers in Jenison to buy my own school clothes. I could select what I wanted to wear and not have to bother unpleasant Cindy, my mom. I then learned of gymnastics teachers needed for community gymnastics during the summer, I also taught gymnastics through community education. I very much liked being independent, self-reliant, it made me feel grown-up. I liked my childhood with acceptation to Cindy and the unpleasantness she could bring to any occasion or day for that matter.

I knew at a young age I wanted to work hard, get up early always, have a career, present myself in a very polished way, and never ask or nag a man or woman for anything. Especially my future husband, whomever he might be someday, out there in that vast blue sea of opportunities unexplored. Cindy would say of the men she brought to the house, that "he wants to marry you." Back in 1978, I did not know what and why a mother would say that to me. I knew I was just a child and only adults marry. Adam Duritz and his mother came to pay a visit to me in Jenison, Michigan. Cindy explained that Adam wanted to marry me.

Cindy would often speak with improper grammar. Her knowledge seemed to be so limited of the English language. Each sentence Cindy spoke or wrote was a fragmented sentence, her mind like spokes on a roulette ring, her mind was not a full circle of and in itself. But inside she was a smooth engineered criminal. Often she would use the wrong verbiages in a sentence, also so poorly constructed. Linguistically speaking, Cindy lacked refinement, as did the sound and tone of her voice. Which sounded as if she was chiseling away at the English language one sentence at a time. Rather than speaking a formal word or smooth sentence in full. Her tone was gruff, not like a fine tuned string instrument, but rather very surly. Cindy could act confused at times, and then people felt sorry for her, sorry for her mind, or something. But people were so far off base, as to the core of what Cindy was all about.

Despite the headache I would encounter as I listened to her talk in her surly Yankee tone, there was something very masterminding diabolical lodged within her intelligence, attached to her core personality. Cindy certainly did not sound intelligent in her dialect, or even well educated, but there was something behind, within, something sinisterly very intelligent about her aura that I realized even as a child. When she did sing in choir, she would just try to be loud and heard by all, rather than singing a fine harmony of a tune. Cindy's camouflage was just that, to be well disguised, her intentions were disguised, her real actions were very well disguised. That was her plan. At times in my life I felt like I was pointing at something in a bucket, and everyone was peering into a bucket, saw nothing, and just dismissed me as crazy. That is how well she was disguised. That was her plan, or perhaps the American Central Intelligence's plan? Perhaps laid out on some shiny cherry table in Washington D.C., and we were just mere puppets in the suburb's moose trap existence called Lamplight Estates. When I would ask questions about why this or that is happening to me, Cindy would explain. She informed me "That the U.S. government is testing out experiments on children of particular genetic backgrounds for a CIA lifelong study project. When the CIA is done studying you and your life, the CIA will have you killed. We know your background is heavy with Germans. Some of the children from the experiments did not make it, I do not know if you'll make it."

I gasped, then inquired with chills, "Where are these children that did not make it?"

Cindy replied cautiously… "They are buried under cement."

"Where under cement?" I asked.

Cindy answered, "I do not know. That's not my department or my care."

I was always afraid of her, Cindy. And it is as if when I speak with her, she only gives me more reasons to be afraid of her. That is exactly how I remember my childhood with Cindy. Asking questions to Cindy was mentally painful.

Looking back to 1980 and the preceding years that Cindy was a licensed nurse employed at Blodgett Hospital in Grand Rapids, Michigan brings chills. Cindy would finish a night shift and complain that her female boss was suspicious Cindy was murdering patients at night, during the graveyard shift. During the daytime I noticed Cindy would become almost trance like as she would often relish in reliving other people's horrors, especially helpless people Cindy would gravitate towards, but not in a helpful way, in a way she could control, and very easily. Getting away with crimes behind doors and walls is what Cindy likes to do. Anyone really close to Cindy learns that fact, then the relationship, the situation, becomes like one back paddling up a river to get away from Cindy, the best one can. The Calvinist community would aid and abed with superficially accepting anyone that spoke of Jesus the way they believed, it was code. Cindy was in, and so became a very undetected serial killer living in west Michigan, Cindy. I observed first hand that superficially accepting anyone is dangerous.

Cindy smelled of something awful as I remember growing up in her household, she never woke up and showered in the beginning of her day, or later in the day, she claimed to shower at work only. She wore the same outfit over and over, she refused to do laundry on a regular basis for the household. She did not dress smart. But that was her plan. In her mind, that was smart. As for my clothes, she could care less if I had a clean outfit, because she could care less. She would simply put my dirty clothes back in my dresser drawers, dirty socks and all, verses having a laundry hamper in my room or anywhere in the house. A laundry hamper never existed growing up. Cindy refused to teach me how to do laundry even though we had a washer and dryer on the main floor! She never applied cosmetics, or perfume, or showed any desire to be feminine after she said her marriage vows many, many years ago to my adopted father Charles. She never fussed over my appearance either. I was on my own in learning how to become a young woman and entice a mate, a future husband. She, Cindy, never seemed thrilled about being a woman, or a mother, or a wife. Because that was never her goal, her intentions. She spent her entire existence while being my mother, as I knew her growing up under her roof as if she was not happy with her part in a play she had been cast in, caught in, in a fateful karma kinda way. As if Cindy had long stemming regrets about her part in this theater called "everyday life," and everyone around her was to be blamed by her, for her unhappiness. As if she did not hold any responsibility to anything, anybody, or any ill word or action performed by her leading role as "Cindy." She never owned her own actions, so it appeared behind the scenes, and everyone in society was to be influenced by whatever opinion she held. My father and I were treated as regrets, that's how I remember age twelve in 1982 in Michigan. As I remember my childhood being raised in a household of mostly absent Cindy.

My father, a strong Leo personality of sorts, would argue with my mother Cindy about the fact she would take off shopping, go out for lunch, play tennis, and simply not watch me, or do any housework. Just as my father would roar, Cindy had a solution, as selfish and shallow as it appears on paper, it was completely wrong of her to do. Cindy always had a very selfish solution in response to my father's point of view, his argument towards her, rather than do just anything that my father asked or required of her during the day. She either shrugged off my dad's advice like litter tossed quickly into the trash, or she put up a fight to remind him that she is in control of her day and her ways, as she pleased. She was an adult by your standards, although, by what I witnessed, she was like a child younger than me with her rants and rages, her selfishness. She literally had, and still displays frequently adult temper tantrums beyond belief.

Looking back over the years I think I was five when Cindy solved my father's nagging request for a clean house. I moved up in the world, from a child she did not know what to do with in raising me, to then becoming her personal housekeeper. Dusting and polishing furniture, vacuuming, washing floors, I actually started vacuuming for Cindy before I could even see over the vacuum handle. I did all her housecleaning. As she played tennis, she had her lunch socials with the Dutch Calvinists, in her attempts to rule "as the saint," I was the child housekeeper.

When my father learned of her neglecting motherhood, he would go into a rage as well, usually accompanied by, or fueled by alcohol. Cindy would threaten to leave my father, divorce him, reminding him that she would take the house and me, as per what most divorce Judges would sanction in that era. The wife in the early 1980's would get everything back then, which only sunk my father into a deeper alcoholic stage of escaping co-existence with Cindy. Which appeared to be or was his only immediate retreat from his reality created by an overly zealous selfish woman, Cindy. I knew by watching her, if I wanted to be happy in a marriage, I would have to be the complete opposite of her in every way, shape and form. And then hope the man I would marry would not take advantage of me, for being so good. Needless to say, I did not have a female role model growing up. I desperately leaned on Carmen to teach me hairstyles and makeup application, I certainly would come to say in Carmen, I saw a mother I did not have at the time growing up in Michigan. Although in Carmen, I also located a very jealous female, called "a best friend."

My mother Cindy was a bitter and violent woman, often times she would black out and not remember hitting me, **not** due to any alcohol consumption, but her sheer revolving twirling memory of sorts. Cindy's mind was like a busy roulette table, constantly moving, no one knew which emotion the ball would land on, including Cindy. Even as a toddler Cindy would leave me behind in a cold car during the winter for hours, or the heat of the summer months, as she shopped in the grocery store. My life was also her gamble. That was her way of "taking me along," as per my father's request to have me shop with her. Cindy had her own agenda, her own strong willed mind, and behind her thoughts never was I in her best interest, nor was my father. Cindy treated my father as just a means of obtaining quick money, to grasp what she wanted in her immediate world. She would bark towards me, "If you ever want to get what you want in life, you'd better marry a rich man Lori!"

I would always disagree with her wildly shallow statements on life, and remind her, "I am going to college, and I'll have a career."

Cindy would bark back, "Oh, aren't you a smart one, lady Jane!"

Cindy and I, we never saw eye to eye on any subject, there was no warmth in her tone of voice towards me. There was no drifting apart as mother and daughter either, there just was never a caring developed bond formed. Cindy had an insanely curious sexual appetite, and I was afraid of her, and her roulette table spinning in her mind, what would she make me do next? I am the whore, Cindy is the saint. And Jesus was a drunk, an alcoholic. Just ask Cindy, she is the know it all in west Michigan amongst the Calvinists community at large. Cindy knows everything. And what Cindy does not know, well, just ask C.I.A. agent John Brennan and the other CIA agents, they know everything. And they all know that I know that fact about them. Which bothers them.

Cindy will admit to this day that she would leave me in the car, or the crib when I was a baby and a toddler, for hours, as she did her shopping in the 1970's. Only to **remind** me that back in the 1970's there were no state or federal laws banning such neglectful acts on children as there are now days. Cindy feels no guilt, has no guilt, has no regrets, other than I am still alive to talk about my childhood. And very capable and able as an adult to diminish her propaganda of what she wants others to believe of her in the Dutch, very religious community. The community that is still waiting for Jesus to come back. But just like the Bible states, "Jesus will come in like a thief in the night." Well, he did. Jesus stole me. My father Charles Vander Ark was the boy king from 2000 years ago.

I recall Cindy telling me herself that at times she did not feed me for three days or so when I was a toddler, "But there was no law on how often a toddler needed to be fed." Later Cindy also commented…. "All my children lost a pound or two after they were born before the first doctor's appointment." Cindy would shriek, "Kids lose and gain weight all the time."

Food, meals, when you could obtain food, you would want to overeat, not knowing when your next meal would come from. Meals were very inconsistent during the day, as were Cindy's moods. Odd. Because my father's income could support three square meals. But Cindy did not care because meal planning or preparation cut into her day, her schedule. Don't ever forget that fact! It's all about Cindy. All about the moon.

I remember spending the days alone often, I was my own babysitter growing up. I still remember those earlier days too young to reach for water and open the refrigerator, too young to even know why I felt so alone, I was just alone. I knew something was "off" throughout the morning and afternoon. I was very young, and alone. I would just wander the house hungry. When I finally received a meal or piece of food, overeating was, or became a habit, if I could, to simply feel full for once. I ate rapidly, devouring down as much food as possible in one sitting, not knowing when I would get my next meal. My lips were chapped always, I was consistently feeling dehydrated. I was bathed, maybe once a week, sometimes less. After all, taking care of a young child was work, and work of any kind was not what selfish Cindy wanted to partake in during "her day, her schedule." She had the conviction that Jesus wipes away the sins of his followers. Like a clean slate board each morning she would begin yet another day with seemingly no accountability, no guilt, no conscious for her actions or lack of actions. Not really caring who Cindy caused pain and misery in a direct or indirect way. It simply was not a recognizable concern of hers, her sins were taken away with Jesus, her sins no longer were her concern, or ever were her concern. And if you were to this day, "to remind her of her sins," she would be the first to remind *you* of Jesus and the cross, and forgiveness by Jesus. But Cindy still does not believe in angels. Cindy only believes what suits her, what pertains to her solution of "no guilt."

I would often just be baffled about Cindy's soul, her core being, Cindy attended church twice on Sunday. It was a big deal, a great value of Cindy's that she and the whole family make it on time to Hillcrest Christian Reformed Church in Hudsonville, Michigan. The church was large, the people so friendly and seemed so good. But one question still rests on my mind's memory, why can't God penetrate through Cindy's soul? Why is God not reaching Cindy's core? She displayed no signs of love to anyone in the family, we just existed in her world. Cindy was more about how people perceived her than she was concerned for us. Cindy gave 10% of my dad's income to the church, yet cared nothing about saving a penny for my college education that I wanted so badly. Cindy made sure there was going to be no college for any of us, but why? Why is it that Cindy had no desire and wish that I or my brothers became college educated? Why did she not want us to grow into adults and become adult members of the Calvinists society? Answer: Cindy projected propaganda of what she wanted others to believe of her and us. Cindy desperately sought out acceptance within the Calvinistic society, and so did her siblings, uncle Harvey and aunt Audrey, and uncle Warren and aunt Jean as the most important objective of their life, but why?

I liked it when Cindy & Charles my adopted mom and dad would invite church people over after Sunday morning church service, or during the week. I remember my mouth dropping in surprise at just how nice Cindy could make her voice sound, and how caring she was of me for that one hour, maybe hour and a half if I was lucky. I would sit and smile and wish for those people to never leave our coffee hour, it was the best part of my week! Sunday after church.

Cindy hated it when I would give her advice, let alone philosophical advice as I grew from a child into a preteen, after all I was just twelve years old. I did suggest that if she wanted to change her life she should have a career and earn her own money to spend the way she wanted to verses looking to others for handouts, or what she wanted me to become or marry. She did go back to college in 1980 to receive a two-year nursing degree. Cindy worked a few years, then quit, she really hated to work, especially to work hard for anything. Cindy roamed from hospital to doctor office jobs to nursing home jobs, she began to get fired from each job for mysteries death during her shifts.

Outwardly Cindy despised any advice I gave her. Cindy called me a "wise cracking young lady Jane." I was detached from her situation, her life, and therefore **could see** clearly how she should and could change to have a better marriage and life. Cindy wanted nothing to do with an examining microscope on her mothering, or being a wife, or her "Christian interpretation." She had all the snap, crackle, pop, kind of answers to dish out, yet she always seemed to be miserable and resentful. I would ask her, "Do you think Jesus will forgive you, always, even for how you treat dad and I?"

Cindy would answer back, "Jesus always forgives us of our sins if we go to him in prayer, if you trust and believe in him that he died on the cross for your sins." Although she attended church twice each Sunday, she never knew much more than the forgiveness knowledge of the Christian faith, perhaps, that was the most vital Bible knowledge that concerned her ways, her life, her outlook, her society.

Cindy needed forgiveness from God through Jesus, the blood of the lamb, as I witnessed growing up. And so Cindy felt deeply about all the minister said and preached to her, she always received Jesus' daily forgiveness, although mainly she seemed obliviously to what her daily sins were. She never cared about my father's opinion of her, nor did Cindy care about what my opinion is of her. Why? I can only conclude that my father and I were her targets of hate and regrets, the community was where she needed to influence her opinion of me, and of him. And most of all…..that everyone in church thought highly of her, Cindy. That was her game, her aim, her strategy, her role……Cindy deserves an award. An Oscar.

Cindy hated being a mother, it was a responsibility not worth undertaking in her book. Needless to say, I raised myself the best a child knows how. I also began babysitting jobs on Saturday nights and during the long summer breaks. I was somewhere between a child and an adult. I was large for twelve, tall too for twelve. I rode my bike everywhere, it was my vehicle of transportation when I was young. I would save my money to buy school clothes, then ride my bike to a store in town. My father would say, "Save your money. I'll give your mom money to buy new school clothes for you."

Cindy despised shopping for school clothes for me, to spend money on me was a chore not worth doing in her book. Anything involving a need of a child such as my needs, was not what she wanted to be doing with her precious adult life. My father would make her lay out the items from the shopping bags that she brought home to see if she really did use the money to buy school clothes for me. I can still see those tags on the clothes resting in a cluttered piled mess on the round dining room table as my father examined the receipts with intense care like airport security examining someone's belongings to see if Cindy actually purchased clothes for me or for her.

Cindy would yell at me all the way to the mall and all the way home about having to take me shopping. She was just furious to spend money on me that my dad gave her. I would sink in my seat, cringe at the whole unsatisfying experience of shopping as well. If I lifted an item I liked off the clothes rack to show her, Cindy would shout in the young misses department, loud and rude, like most damn Yankee's screech when disapproving of something, as she stood right next to me, "THAT'S TOO EXPENSIVE!" That rude and embarrassing statement by Cindy would echo as all standing within one hundred feet looked our way.

We never shopped anywhere outside of a JC Penny or Meijer's store. I would think to myself, I can't wait to grow up and shop anywhere I like. I noticed when I was twelve I was beginning to blossom into a young teenage girl. Clothes would fit me differently now, nothing seemed to fit right, be right, or hang on me right like when I was just a child. My mother noticed too, she was not happy that I was "developing curves." She would go into fits of rage that I was developing, or not fitting into my childhood clothes from last year. Cindy was mad I was going from a child to a young adult. Not that she would miss me when I grew up and left home. But odd as it was, she was angry I was something she was not. Or perhaps mad because the American CIA was still following me everywhere, and now she could not get rid of the project she joined. Keep in mind, I never agreed to join any project of the government's doing, or anyone's doing.

Cindy after a while began torture. The more I grew and developed, the more she beat me, she would snap and go ballistic. It's like she made bad choices in life, and if she was mean to me, it made her feel better somehow, about her choices. Weird. Cindy demoralized me behind my father's back when he was away from the house. Cindy refused to even shop at JC Penny or Meijers and brought home used, consignment shop bra's, used bathing suits, used clothes for me to wear from Goodwill or Salvation Army stores as I began to show curves in my twelve year old outline. If I complained, she would slap me and emotionally and psychologically throw darts and arrows. I felt confused, I just did not understand Cindy. There was the Cindy that the church and community knew, and then there was the Cindy that my father and I feared. Keep in mind, she had the financial means to shop anywhere for me. However, humiliation was a route she preferred to take with me. Not only did I long for my past life, my past parents, I longed to be grown up and live in a world not governed by her sadistic mothering and CIA friends. My father learned he could not change Cindy, and thus escaped by drinking. I can only imagine that he saw drinking as a cure, to escape his reality co-existing with Cindy.

I escaped by daydreaming, dreams of going to college, having a life far and away from her grasp of trying to destroy my youth, and the life I still had in me, what was left of me anyways. She was becoming increasingly jealous of me developing into a young lady, I hardly dared to be around her, she was always snipping at me about one thing or another, or beating out her frustrations on me. I most definitely felt I was in the middle of a war and Cindy was the opposition. I was seen as the opposition to Cindy if I did not go along with what she wanted of me.

I began at age twelve going through a series of CAT scans at the hospital in Grand Rapids. I was suffering from intense head pain, I had dizzy spells, and often blacked out. When I stood up I felt so dizzy I would have to lay back down. Cindy was determined to barge into that hospital and convince the no good stupid nurses that her daughter must be checked for a brain tumor. After all, Cindy was the caring mother of me, right?

So on went these exams, CAT scans, where the nurse sticks you in a tube, you get rolled in, a series of x-ray photographs are taken of your brain. I wanted to raise my hand and say to the nurse and doctor, "I think my head hurts because of my mother Cindy's severe beatings on me." But I couldn't tell the truth, and off we went from neurologists after neurologists. Cindy complained that her daughter was having severe headaches and she was just concerned it wasn't something else, like a brain tumor. Cindy played the role of "concerned mother." It was like "take ten" "wrap it up" for all those hospital professionals to document that she was a concerned parent. I remember being twelve and staring right at the doctors all dressed in white, the nurses, the medical x-rays of the inside of my head, and wondering too, had they applied for their role too? It all seemed so surreal. Then on the way home, driving home, I would just stare straight ahead out the car dashboard like looking out towards a flat world ahead of me. We were different here in west Michigan than the rest of the world, our world here really is flat.

I was always wondering as I sat slumped in the front seat of the car, if Cindy was trying to hustle fear into me? Or just trying to take my wits about me out, part of my soul? Leave my body on earth, release back into the sky my soul, by her criminal mothering towards me. But on the books, the record, she was so crafty combined with intimidating, she would never get caught, and she knew that about her powers. "Oprah's Law" would never apply to her, or Oprah. In fact, Oprah once stated on her show that she knew she wanted to move out of Mississippi when the white police never even cared to investigate the smothering death of her newborn baby. The whites in charge of the county finances just did not care enough about the black part of town to waste the resources in solving and fighting crime like they would for the white part of town. Like blacks did not matter in Mississippi in the part of town she came from anyways, that was a pivotal point Oprah went on to say in why she wanted to leave Mississippi and head for a new life in Chicago.

And then of course, well, I did not see this one coming either......

One day, she really let her rage extend into dangerous uncharted territory, perturbed that I was developing into a beautiful lady, Cindy went ballistic one late morning, exploding into a jealous rage after seeing me in a bathing suit? Or was it my father's comment he made while seeing me in a bathing suit? Only Cindy would really know what set her off. Her mind and moods were very unpredictable like a roulette ball, which mood, which personality, which compartment, no one really knew in the horrifying intensity of Cindy's revolving mind where that ball would land, in the end, on the roulette table.

Cindy took her adult strength of her arms, hands and fists, and pounded on my young and tender developing chest. She was very intent on destroying my essence. I think I even blacked out from the sheer surprise attack from Cindy that morning. I went into shock, physically and mentally. I went into shock as she hit my head and chest, it was a grenade of anger towards me, and I was getting attacked, going down. They say for every one rat you see, there are fifty you don't see. That could best describe what my mother Cindy saw as her legal right to treat me any which way she wanted behind closed doors, inside that closed door community of west Michigan, Babylon.

From Bethany Christian Services, Cindy only requested females, young girls she would foster. Cindy even bragged about her perilous of ways to me. She could say anything, after all who would believe an orphan? Cindy fostered almost one hundred young girls in the 1960's, all under the age of three, and before I was even born. Cindy bragged at how easy it was for her to go undetected, even among the highest most well educated at Bethany, those with master's degree in psychology! Cindy knew her drill of being a Christian living among the Calvinists. And Cindy was correct. Who would believe me? And if they did, what would be my fate in Cindy's eyes? I can tell you. Death. Cindy made that clear. And yes, I was afraid of her.

I was always being hit or kicked by Cindy. She was mad about her failing marriage, and I was perhaps the most available source to vent her frustration in her mind. I was a prisoner without rights I was. Yet the Calvinist society could never seem to see beyond the perception Cindy seemed to excel at so well. If they could not see the real Cindy, chances of me trying to explain the real Cindy wouldn't go too far in the avenue of justice in Ottawa County. Cindy was a saint, and I was "a problem." I was not a problem to myself, or a problem in my life. I was someone that Cindy could beat up on, and scream at me, like I was her problem. Cindy has many problems within herself, raging problems. I do realize I just happened to be in her presence, in her home so she blamed me for just about everything, because she could. I was just a mental and physical source for Cindy to express her anger. But I am not the problem. I would remain emotionally detached in an attempt to save my mind and emotions from being destroyed, I looked at the Dutch subculture in west Michigan in a very elusive way. Perplexed in my outlook at how two sided this society was and still is today. A society that totally lacks real human substance of warmth, what we are is not someone's punching bag, or a puppet perception world, I am so much more, and so are you.

My aunt Carol on Cindy's side said the same of my grandmother raising her, grandmother Theresa, Cindy's mother. Cindy's mother raised her boys very differently than her two girls. The boys received college educations, new clothes, praise, the best of the best. The girls would be looked upon as a burden their entire childhood. My aunt Carol would say she was always treated like the outsider. Aunt Carol was hooked on drugs by age thirteen, in and out of behavioral intuitions for describing her childhood to her teachers.

I think abuse can catch up to a person's mind, and make them go mad inside, make them act out, take drugs, the list goes on and on. Everyone looks at the "crazy person" as "the lonely person," as the source of craziness, unacceptable, unwanted behavior in society. But what about the behavior that drove that person off the mental cliff? The root of most mental disorders can be located in a person's childhood, how a person is treated by another, I am just sure of it. Often times more often than not that is where the perpetrator resided too, in the childhood of the person society wants to toss out or disregard.

I do see that is how the world operates, very superficial to not look deeper into the sources. The reflection on the water is what most trained eyes see, not trained or desiring to see the depths of the ocean and what lays on the bottom of that watery domain. I think love and safety are key components in a person's mental stability verses prescribed pills that do not address the source of the problem to begin with, Cindy. What pill can I take to make Cindy stop acting the way she does towards me? What pill can I take to make the CIA stop stalking and harassing me? What pill can I take to make the CIA stop committing criminal acts against me? Anyone? Anyone? Can anyone answer that question for me? Like an alcoholic, what drives a person to drink? What is the source? The problem? Everybody just looks at the alcohol in the glass and who is drinking the beer, or wine, or vodka as the problem, the source of the alcoholism. But I am telling you the truth, Cindy's lack of decent human kindness, along with a whole train of other situations she dishes and shovels towards innocent people who cannot escape her treatment is what could drive anyone to drink.

On October 28, 1982 at age twelve I had my first surgery due to the damage caused by Cindy's hands. "Medical records in hospitals last forever!!!" Was and is Cindy's resounding greatest complaint screamed at me of her concern spoken out loud the morning prior to my surgery taken place. She repeated that over and over as she slammed kitchen cupboard doors in one of her many hissy fits. I begged for what seemed like weeks or months to have relief from the cysts forming under my young and tender developing nipples from a severe beating by Cindy. The bruises were barely going away, my skin was a shade of purple. The surgery took place late in October of 1982, but the beating happened in late August of that same year (1982) after Cindy saw me in a two piece bathing suit. Cindy was probably jealous of how I looked in a bathing suit, or any comments made about my developing young body at the tender and ripe age of twelve as if I looked like I was going on fifteen.

Cindy and her brothers had a different take on it than me. They had a defensively acute shortage of any tolerance to anyone that spoke ill of Cindy during this entire saga. A newspaper reporter could have written an article about how I was beaten to a pulp that then required surgery, and Cindy and her beloved brothers would have read it, remained emotionally intact with a edge of hate towards me, the victim. Values I learned from observing them and the Calvinists just like them, were distorted values, not of heaven. Shocking values they had towards me. But not to them, it was a combination of protecting their perception of west Michigan. Victims are not wanted.

To Cindy and her brothers the bruises were seen as the problem, the cysts to remove under the skin from the severe beating was seen as the problem. Me complaining about the pain, was the problem. I tossed and turned each night, not knowing which way to escape the pain on my chest region. It felt like a hot sunburn with lumps, day and night, after about thirty days of pain, she finally took me to see a doctor, then a surgeon. His name was Dr. Lovell of Grand Rapids. My hospital patient No. was 82-12602. My surgery to remove the painful cysts was on October 28, 1982 at Blodgett Memorial Medical Center, which is now part of Spectrum Health.

Yet, Cindy was the real problem, but not enough people would agree. The verdict was not just out, oh no, I was a problem for talking about their society, for remarking and noticing of the Calvinists in a not so pristine light. To them in Babylon, I was the problem.

Mending a public relations possible nightmare was their distress in the middle of nowhere to most people living in America. But to the Calvinists, this was their pristine world, their projection of that world they created so perfectly from hating any report that tainted what the world thought of them was a black spot against perfection. Which would become my distress, for being "their black spot," I suppose. Victims, true victims are shunned in west Michigan. Cindy's emotional outbursts of crying in public or a Bible study because she is married to an alcoholic, is not shunned.

Gambling was not seen as gambling in Cindy's roulette ball trigger of a mind, she was too good at propaganda of what she was, "the church lady." Whom she was seen as doing no wrong in the Calvinists' community. Such as character witnesses from Cindy's minister and church affiliates, Bible study fellowship fellows, and the choir group, the volleyball group, the tennis group, were outstanding character witnesses that Cindy housed like chips to be played and raised at the poker table if need be. I was keenly aware of her hand, and my hand at age twelve at the poker table. I was smart enough to know her hand, the cards and chips she could play, I was not in a winning position. If I wanted to drive away, well, I couldn't. I did not even have a driver's license. I knew I could be beat anytime, that's according to Cindy, and I knew it was true. Believe it or not, silence over the matter saved me from being murdered by her before I graduated from high school, I know that fact, and so does Cindy.

Dr. Lovell at Blodgett Memorial Medical Center pulled me aside in October of 1982, sat me on a hospital bed just before performing the surgery. Dr. Lovell opened my gown in the front and made me look down at my bruised breasts, they were covered in the deepest blackest and bluest circle imprints with faded blue around those bruises. I looked away. He grabbed my chin and made me look down at my chest and repeated the same unremitting question over and over, "Who did this to you?" "Who did this to you?" He was so serious in tone. I was so embarrassed and kept looking away, the doctor took my chin and made me look down again. "I can put them in jail." Dr. Lovell said.

I thought silently, if you put Cindy in jail, I would be dead before her jail sentence ever began. In my book, Cindy held the power. I was going to survive and not talk. Not tell on her. Him even asking me was like treading on thin ice in the hospital room. I was not about to join him on that thin ice arena. No sir. I'll stay over here, was my stance. I stayed quiet. I remained on the sidelines of my fate, thank-you very much.

I then started to laugh from the seriousness of the moment, a seriousness I was not willing to face. A topic of questioning I did not want to be involved with any longer. A flash of Cindy's rage of me telling the doctor who had done this to me, a flash of her rage in my mind, kept me quiet. Dr. Lovell went onto comment, "I have never seen a female as young as twelve with cysts forming under the breasts from a severe beating like this. The last woman I operated on to remove cysts like this was a thirty- five year old woman who received an extreme beating from a jealous boyfriend. He's in jail now, I can put the person who did this to you in jail, just give me the name of the person who did this to you."

My answer was only silence, only silence. I could not tell this doctor "My mother did this to me," and ever expect to see the light of dawn again. Let alone reach the blessed age of eighteen and finally be freed of Cindy's governorship over my life, or what was left of my life. If I ever make it to eighteen, so I thought and wondered, and still wished. I had a strong will to live, and knew to keep silent was to live.

What the freedom of eighteen would feel and taste like….. If I ever make it safely into my adulthood I thought with my chin down, then my life would be my own. Just as the doctor was persistent with his questioning of who had done this to me, I also learned there is survival in keeping secrets. I was smart. I will never forget the unending burning sensation of walking around for weeks with a severely painfully injured beaten chest for a month and a half. I will always remember how strong I was to survive each and every day under Cindy's roof. It was a boot camp, a war, it was not heaven in her presence. I was aware at age twelve of the unexpected sting that a moon jellyfish can deliver so poignantly.

Throughout all my misery, Carmen was there for me. Like a best friend she would listen to my hardships as tears would swell up in my eyes, listening so intently of all that I would encounter and endure throughout my childhood in the north. At times it appeared that Carmen's eyes would tear up a bit too, and at other times almost bask and revel in each word I would utter to her in shock and dismay. As if my life was a soap opera and I was her favorite drama character to watch.

I think my mother had a pocket full of excuses to the doctors and nurses as to why I ended up on the Blodgett Memorial Hospital operating table on October 28, 1982 with a severely beaten chest. She told my dad that some kid at school beat me on the schoolyard. Yet another person that questioned Cindy, well, Cindy answered by saying that a kid down the street beat me with a baseball bat. She had every excuse under the sun, but the truth to tell. She even claimed the American CIA did strange things to me, drugged me unconscious, that she could not control or stop, because they were to powerful. The church believed whatever she said.

One thing remains very consistent………..Cindy never did try and locate "that boy" who supposedly harmed me, I wonder why? Nor did she cry or fret that her daughter was harmed. She did not even care. She never went to the police and made a report. The doctor called the police. It is a question the church should ask Cindy. On Cindy's astrology chart, she has the planet Mars in her first house. Established and revered astrologers as well as books of "Astrology For Dummies" will explain to you that typically the planet Mars is always in the first house of the twelve zodiac houses of an athlete, how interesting. The planets in their naturally ruled house, such as Mars naturally rules the first house, which makes that planet even more powerful for that person if placed within the first house category. Enabling the person with the most powerful aspects and energies of Mars. And the planet "Jupiter" is always in the first house of a politician, king or queen, or a world leader, or someone who has something important to say to the world, expansive in theme and or message.

Despite how Cindy treated me inwardly, outwardly she projected quite a different perception of the truth to the sleepy Dutch Christian Reformed society. To that great octopus in the sea which has far reaching tentacles, power she wanted, power she could obtain. Cindy and Charles attended church twice each and every Sunday, even on family vacations we always located a church to attend. I am sure that part of their resume in adopting me from Bethany Christian Services served me well in my childhood experiences rendered.

While residing in Jenison and Hudsonville, the sleepy Christian communities just outside of Grand Rapids, Michigan, we attended Hillcrest Christian Reformed Church in Hudsonville while growing up. A fine church that had no idea of the actual horror that laid behind the facade of Cindy. The church would never have a need to learn, after all Cindy was not insanely jealous of the church, or its members. She needed the church, she needed the church's approval, there was acceptance in approval, there was powerful influence to gain with the church members as her friends. My father on the other hand seemed to care less and less about "church acceptance" as he grew older. He seemed more influenced by the idea of escapism, escaping with alcohol in his attempts to create a vague cloud over his reality of who he had married. They say in psychology class, that one seems to marry a woman like their mother. But my father's mother whose name is Kate, she was a gracious and beautiful wife and mother, unselfish and very caring towards her family. My father's parents were happily married, my grandmother Kate made my grandfather Charles senior and all their five children happy, no divorcees on the Vander Ark side, not one. My adopted mothers side, Cindy's side flourished in divorce statistics. Cindy's maiden name is Stob, a Scottish sir name, people from Great Britian also have the highest divorce and crime rates of any predominantly white country, how interesting. My adopted father Charles went into the marriage with Cindy blindsided. Just assuming all women are just like his mother Kate, perfect. Cindy had no warning label on her. Nor would she ever give off any steam to indicate she was not perfect, not during courtship.

I can only guess, assume, that my adopted father Charles assumed that all woman would be polished and warm like my grandmother, his mother Kate. And therefore he was very unaware that woman are different, or could be different. There are good women and some women that a man looking for happiness in adulthood should never even ask out on a first date. My father was only nineteen when he married, hardly old enough to experience that not all women are or want to be perfect and bring a man happiness, such as his mother Kate had brought his father. My dad had a great childhood, a wonderful family and doting perfect parents. He assumed all woman were just like Kate, his birth mother, and the mother who raised him.

For my father, well, drinking became his escape from his marriage to a very violent and selfish woman, Cindy. She truly is a delusion of light, just as her name means "moon." Cindy was and is not a source of light, just a reflection.

It was as if Cindy drew pleasure from demeaning me. She loved to make me look ugly, she threw fits if I tried to bath or shower, was it all about control? Was it a sadistic addiction of hers as a parent to deny me love, positive direction in life? A sadistic addiction of Cindy's to make people think I was crazy, or sick? Was my body reacting to not being able to take anymore abuse from her? Was my mind beginning to develop an overload of abuse from Cindy? Cindy adopted me, she was out to be the saint, and I was just an orphan child, one she saw as a whore? Control of perception, to make others believe that anything negative of me, seemingly made her shine? I was submerged into a religious subculture that valued appearances and expected order, your reflection to judge, that tangible reflection. The only thing I could see clearly, or wanted to judge was a person's aura and the deep layers of their soul. I liked to get right to the heart of a person.

I noticed in Cindy she was very well received in the Christian community, "one of them," she truly belonged. Why? Why can't they see through her façade? Because she would repeat "that phrase," "I believe in Jesus." Then everyone just assumed she was a Christian, a non-selfish, caring individual? Unbelievably superficial was the acceptance status quo. It was the very shallow Christian communities rules and regulations that determined membership into their Calvinist Club. Nostradamus predicted in the year 2012 that the John Calvin followers would lose followers, and the faith of John Calvin, the religious sect of the Calvinists would be severely examined as a religion and be no more. I can only scratch my head and say, did Nostradamus see my life story getting published near 2011 -2012 of my life and horrors of my experiences in a John Calvin community?

I do not know the future of Calvinism, would this love story read, "Calvinism, A Love Story, 2012." A great movie title for my philosophical memoirs? What would John Calvin yell out and call me, if he could? "A whore?"

Cindy would often say, "I always thought you'd make an excellent lawyer, you shouldn't become one though they live unhappy lives ya know. But I got this feeling you might marry one someday. By the way,

I found your journals, no one really cares what you have to say. You will never become a writer, just give up that imaginative daydreaming of yours, there is no money in it…..telling the truth about me." Cindy barked in a sober voice so matter of fact she spoke to me, as if she could control my dreams, my future, my education, and crush my hopes of growing up and escaping her grasp of what is left of my soul. What did she see in me? A bright mind to destroy the hopes of? A sharp and analytical mind to damper and cool? She did see me as a child to stomp on, not a person to influence with a fake persona presented as Cindy so carefully projected to the outside world, the Dutch community around us. Cindy knew I did not buy or believe what she was projecting to the outside community, and in her mind, there was one solution for me.

I noticed the ones that Cindy really could influence in the Dutch society were the ones who seemed to skim the surface of understanding God and religion. People easily influenced by their own devastating and shallow standards of simply not questioning much of anything within that Dutch bubble of a community that they all belonged in and wanted to be included in, just for the simple sake of belonging and conforming on the outside. The pudding top skimmers, loved and accepted Cindy, they fed off each other in acceptance. No matter if their ways of persona was a cover to conceal their real identities. People easily influenced because the wheel of the systematically moving religious wheel, was a wheel spoke worth clinging onto. A safe feeling of belonging, a place for many not questioning Cindy. I noticed many of the woman all had similar characteristics in their outward lens to be seen by all. Many ladies have the same "gosh, darn it," quirky attitude about politics, and that "gosh darn it," hand moving gestures, like that Sarah Palin lady. The same empty expressions worn on their faces, although they seemingly looked so smart and sassy in glasses. Stylish, similar and causal and conservative two piece matching outfits, those matchy, matchy outfits from the local conservative everything is a great deal sale, double decker Grandville mall. Each and every Sunday the woman would clip out those 20% off sale coupons, as if it was their religion of choice. The church women topped off the conservative persona with those short rolled curled hairstyles and discussed this and that female hairdresser, prices, deals, and husbands and all. Sales, good deals, church socials, Bible studies, and who knows who in that bubble, are important aspects when deciding to relocate to the bottom of nowhere called Grandville, Michigan.

I knew it was a religious society I was not going to grow into with time. I was not going to worship a false persona, or have others demand that of me. I believe in what is real, and what I know. Technically, logically, objectively, rationally, believing as such. I knew it was all about fitting in to their community, Cindy's community within this Dutch Christian Reformed bubble. With hardly anything to do with exploring the dimensions of God and gaining wisdom outside of a Bible study, which was what I was on a quest to do. I was an adventuresome spirit, a pioneer brought into that Dutch religious bubble that wanted to dig a hole and bury me the moment I began becoming very outspoken within their religion and life. I was viewed as rebellious, a real live rebel.

Cindy had made it clear to me at a very early age that she would never pay for my wedding someday, nor should she or would she pay for my college education. Those were two means for me "to get ahead in life," a bridge, a rainbow to a better life with her not in the driver's seat of controlling my life. Cindy was not going to pay for that ladder, that bridge to my happiness and watch my happiness transpire away from her reality, her controls. I was determined to have hope, a brighter future than my everyday real life in Michigan. Cindy never expected me to go to college someday, she feared the law, and knew how to win.

Looking back, I can see how she wanted me to remain stupid and single. Why? So she could control and manipulate what others in the community thought of me. Which ironically was also Carmen's plan and motivations.

The summer of 1984 was approaching, I was fourteen years old, vivacious, yet awkward. I was flown to Thousand Oaks, California the summer my oldest divorced brother Ric married his second wife Lori Kay. Cindy had many problems, and many plans. I stayed in Thousand Oaks, California with my aunt Jean and uncle Warren Stob the summer of 1984. My uncle Warren is Cindy's brother they are very close. He is always manipulated by his sister Cindy's problems and general whinny attitude. Their relationship is a resentment of my aunt Jean. Uncle Warren was the vice president of a successful aerospace company in California. The American CIA were his lunch companions and the U.S. government was one of his many clients. He also had many wealthy Saudi Arabian clients purchasing luxury airplanes. One day I was just sitting in the main floor guest bedroom where I stayed. My aunt and uncle were in the kitchen were having a very heated argument. I can only best describe the information I heard from them as so alarming, it was hard to mentally digest their words into my memory, as I stood up and then listened by my closed door. Horrific. Uncle Warren was mad, just furious that the Saudi men from his latest Saudi Arabian trip would not purchase me, not sign the paperwork that the Central Intelligence Agency presented to his wealthy Saudi men clients, and he could not figure out why. He went back to Saudi Arabia many times that summer of 1984, with no luck in what the American CIA and Cindy wanted. A sale of me, to stop the questions coming out of the Ottawa County police department during the years of 1982-1984.

Later my aunt Jean Stob whom now resides back in Grandville, Michigan informed me during a bridal shower that I was sold on paper behind my back in 1984 and 2001 by her husband and the CIA. My aunt Jean informed me that uncle Warren Stob was fired from the Thousand Oaks, California vice president position when the aerospace company learned of his side deals of me to wealthy Saudi clients that were purchasing luxury airplanes from Warren Stob and paying up front for a girl with favorable pedigree papers. My aunt Jean Stob explained that no criminal charges were filed against Warren Stob and his sister Cindy because the CIA was involved with the transactions. She went on to explain to me that his California lawyer collected the money. Some of the money was given to their son in law to purchase Hudsonville Bowling Lanes, uncle Warren mostly placed his money in stocks. She informed me that often times the CIA will take a lump sum of money, open a Living Trust estate account. Then give handouts to ordinary citizens who did the work for the CIA (better known as CIA subcontractors). Once the money is dispersed the Living Trust account is dissolved by the attorneys. Aunt Jean Stob explained in 2001 to my face that she feels a war is going to break out with all of the tangled webs the CIA was weaving by collecting the money upfront before the deal actual is sealed in the middle east with a vast CIA human trafficking ring located in the states.

By age fourteen in September of 1984, my mother thought she "had enough of him," my father that is, can you believe it? "She," had enough of, "him." Yes, Cindy filed for legal separation from my father Charles Vander Ark. Cindy convinced even manipulated the Dutch Christian Reformed Church into sanctioning an approval for the divorce separation, due to my father's drinking problem. She got the house and me, all thanks in part to the court systems of the early 1980's favoring the mothers rights, and not considering the father's rights. I never saw my father after they separated in September 1984. I was too young to drive a car and was too young to understand divorcing parents. I never asked about seeing my father much, or the subject of my father, due in part to the extremities of my mother's convulsing violent rages towards me if I asked about him. As I grew from fourteen on into sixteen I would have bruises covering my calves and legs, primarily from running away from her screaming at me. Cindy raising her arms and fists was a sight to run from as she would chase me through the house. My bruises on my calves and legs were from bumping into furniture as I ran away from her. Most of the time it was not anything I ever did, it was that I walked into the kitchen while she was having what I term as her "dark moments." Cindy would live in the darkest corners of her mind, most of the time while in the house.

I learned in a "oh, by the way" tone of voice of Cindy's after dinner while watching television, that in March of 1986, my father finally divorced Cindy. She had filed for separation in September 1984, gave my father "a list of changes" he must and shall make before he could return to the home he bought. If not, she would divorce him. After about two years in 1986 I think my father had enough of Cindy and her rules, her values, her morals, coupled with the lack of love, and ever proving in or out of court just how evil Cindy really is and was, and could be behind closed doors, in the notorious closed door society of those Calvinists and Catholics alike, and shoved the divorce papers to her to sign.

I was not void of what Cindy wanted to change, Cindy would also write down a list of ten items on how she wanted me "to improve." I kept thinking to myself, why not just love your child Cindy? Why not just love your husband you married Cindy? Love is a more difficult subject for Cindy to explore. By asking everyone else to change, life is easier for Cindy in how she operates. The energy around Cindy, her aura, her core, is the opposite of God's energy. Keep in mind, Cindy expects God and Jesus to love her unconditionally. That is just how her world works, her minister reminds her of how wonderful that mere yet profound concept is from Roman days gone by when the Jews created a religion from my long ago son, who plays the role of father in this lifetime, Chuck Vander Ark.

Cindy was fired from Blodgett Hospital in 1985. I was fifteen years old. Cindy informed me as she mumbled and complained that the head nurse, a female, believed Cindy was murdering patients during Cindy's shifts at the hospital and the head nurse had gone to the Grand Rapid's police. There was not enough substantial evidence against Cindy, and therefore, sadly, no arrest. Cindy would never be able to get another hospital job in Michigan, ever. That lady boss of Cindy's would make sure of that, to warn other hospitals not to hire Cindy. The best Cindy could do now was to locate a receptionist position at a doctor's office, very low paying position for a nurse.

Oddly enough, strange and more disturbing news filtered into the fish tank one day in late June 1986. My grandparents, Cindy's parents Martin and Teresa Stob pushed open our front door as I was on the phone one summers afternoon, I was just sixteen. "Your father is dead. He was found dead at his home in Grand Rapids, the police are there now, your mom discovered him dead this afternoon after dropping off his accumulated mail she had been receiving." Spoke my mother's parents to me.

I was in shock. I dropped the phone. And then was not in shock. I knew this whole divorce situation would only bring more bad news, nothing good was coming out of any decision involving Cindy. Then I went back into shock, just not believing that my father which I am forbidden to see was actually, really deceased, and I would never see him again. Not even when I turned eighteen, would I ever be able to reach him by car, for he was now dead.

"My mom dropped off his mail?" I asked my grandparents, Cindy's parents. "My mom always mails his mail directly to his house that we receive here, she sends his mail off in a big yellow envelope to him…….. she found him dead?" I asked again and again. I must have sounded rude just repeating the same question and statement over and over to Cindy's parents, my grandparents….. "She brought his mail to him?" "Why?" I asked again. That alone made no logical sense in her behavior. For two years now, every two weeks or so, Cindy would stuff his bills in a big yellow envelope and send it off to his house in Grand Rapids.

Something smelled "fishy" about the situation like the oddness of wandering around an empty house all alone feeling hungry and thirsty as I would often feel as a young toddler growing up under Cindy's roof, this too felt "off," "odd." I could not quite place my finger on what made the story odd, or what was causing an odd feeling to reverberate throughout my body, but something was odd….. "off" about the whole situation. It's like with any other situation with Cindy involving my dad, or involving me. Cindy always, inevitably, crosses the line, somehow, someway, in some crafty devised plan, or a sporadic plan of her devious mind. I just know by the way my gut is speaking to me, she crossed the line, again. But I can't prove it. Just like always. Cindy wanted him dead. And then suddenly God answered her prayers? And he is dead suddenly? She crossed the line with her powers of what she thinks she can control in this lifetime of hers, mine, his, anybody's life, she just does.

I did not have the whole puzzle in front of me when everything seemed to be happening at once in my young and tender life? Or perhaps pieces of Cindy's story I would hear next, had the pieces, but I was too young to put together such a diabolical puzzle of a criminal mastermind puzzle? It was all so complicated, and I was too young, and most of all, I wished dearly for a normal life, so much so, I would ignore the pieces of the puzzle, as the pieces were being placed into the puzzle. Or perhaps at the age of fifty-two my father really had died in his sleep of chronic lung disease? He did smoke and drink, can that cause a person to lay down in ones sleep and never wake up again? I learned later his alcohol level was very minute, very trace. Had the police and the rookie coroner who had only just begun a few months before, forgotten to seriously question the resentful, bitter woman, who hated my father? Cindy.

I lived in a puppet world of Cindy's, the police were puppets too, it was a real "Mr. Rogers Neighborhood." Cindy literally convinced the Grand Rapids police detective that my father was an abusive alcoholic. There was no autopsy. There was no investigation. "Nor would there ever be an autopsy." Stated Cindy later that night.

I can only imagine that her powerful church role, choir singer role, pillar of the community stance, well, just for one night her no encore of a role received acclaim by the detective who arrived on the scene of my father's death. Odd. No one even bothered to take me to talk to the police, or go to his house where the police were deciding whether or not to waste their man power, Grand Rapid's tax payer dollars on spending any time or energy on a crime scene possibility? Or the motive of Cindy? Hate. Another motive of Cindy; the very Christian Calvinist community were not accepting the newly divorced Cindy into their church socials, like they once did when poor ol' Cindy was married to an alcoholic.

"Acceptance" into that Calvinists community is Cindy's trigger point. We all have what makes us tick, that drive, that libido. Whereas "acceptance" is not so important to you or I, potentially? Probably? But to Cindy influence over another, influence over her Roman empire community and acceptance, well, that was her libido, what made her tick. Which was what made her desire to have a career out of always fitting in, or staying in so important, not a spotlight that something is not right with Cindy. Being divorced was not a good spotlight for Cindy.

I will always have those nagging questions of doubt in my mind, those chilling, absurdly annoying questions penetrating subconsciously. Always wondering if Cindy did in my dad? Yet, I was sixteen, and I did not want to face another harsh reality that my mother had done my father in, murdered him. I did not ask for this life, in the sense of enduring without a family, or love, or comfort. It appeared that every page I turned of this life I was adopted into became more shocking, more horrifying. I was not sure how much more I could even process mentally. I just want to believe my life is normal, or at least on some level of normalcy like all the other kids that go to Unity Christian High.

My mother stayed out late the day I received the news my father was dead via news from her parents. I went to bed long before she arrived home that night. I had a babysitting job the next day, a three mile bike ride in the morning.

The day of my babysitting job, I arrived back home by 5pm, Cindy was in the kitchen, in a manic state. Almost "elated," very hyper, her eyes appeared wildly wired as if getting ready for a party or celebration gathering, but there was not a real party. Her happy attitude in combination with her elated mood, made my stomach turn. I felt nauseous making small talk with this over happy, zealous woman. The next thing Cindy said sent a shock wave throughout me, to the point my arm hair stood on end. "I am happy Chuck is dead, I can get on with my life now, that chapter is done in my life." Cindy said with a smile and crazed look in her eyes.

I paused in shock of her statement, then responded to Cindy in a soft, slow, almost hushed stable tone of voice as I gathered emotional strength from within me, "You were divorced from dad, what do you mean **that chapter** is now over?" I was sincerely bewildered as to how this women thought, baffled, just baffled, and feeling sick in anticipation at what awful thing this women Cindy would say next to my wounded heart.

"Well…..I just felt that this tight knit Christian community did not accept me, I felt shunned in a way, being a divorcee and all. I want you to join me in telling our neighbors that Chuck is dead." Cindy spoke proudly as if she was an actress giving her Oscar acceptance speech, addressing crowds of onlookers, not just speaking to single me standing at the top of the basement staircase.

"What?" I asked.

"Yes, I think our neighbors need to know." Cindy acted like she just finished campaigning and was running late for her acceptance speech of winning and grabbing onto a real gold trophy as she ran around the kitchen drying off her hands on a kitchen towel. She just kept smiling. Cindy was hyper and happy.

"What? What for?" I asked again.

"Now don't you be funny, you come with me, our neighbors have no idea that Chuck is gone." Cindy said firmly with an irritated tinge of anger as if she was going to punish me if I did not go with her knocking on the doors in the neighborhood to announce that my father is dead.

We went door to door, everyone just stared blankly ahead as they held open their front door. Smells of their dinner simmering in the background, as my mother rattled on how Chuck is gone, "He's dead." "He's dead." Within days neighbors were bringing over meals wrapped in baskets, as if to console Cindy in her time of need. But Cindy never cried, she smiled crazy like, and was so happy.

It was so warped. How you think a person acts when another dies, well, Cindy had a whole new twist on how to act or react.

Within weeks the overwhelmingly deceptive Cindy joined a small group at Hillcrest Church called the "grieving widows group." They actually welcomed her in, as is the Christian way, I suppose. One would notice that she is the only one smiling in all of the group photographs, taken from places they would go to as a group, a support group of sorts for those grieving the loss of their spouse. If Cindy was not already joined in the church choir, or the bells on Tuesday nights, and seen so publicly at every Bible study offered at church, she probably would not have been so widely accepted at the Hillcrest church widows group. Cindy was Oprah with her success on moving on after a loss. My eyes were open to her deceptive ways, she was out to fool the community into believing she had a heart of heaven, and that Jesus loves her for her serious involvement in the church and the community. I would learn throughout my lifetime of many Christians who follow in the traditional recipe of Cindy. Doing and acting of what is outwardly expected of them, going to church, singing in choir, belonging to a Bible study. But in their hearts, those same people were and are "selfish and uncaring," which literally means Un-Christian, just like Cindy. However, let me be very clear, Cindy was fake, but she wholeheartedly believed anything taught in the CRC churches. Cindy believed and probably still believes everything about forgiveness and how Jesus died on the cross so that she could be forgiven in this lifetime, all her sins forgiven. Cindy believed and/or believes wholeheartedly without a doubt the CRC's recipe to go to heaven in the afterlife and be accepted by them while on earth. Cindy is a true believer in every sense of the word, she is not a fake believer.

One night only weeks after my father's funeral. Cindy explained over dinner one night that some people were coming up to her and asking if she, "Had done in Chuck," killed him. That was her dinner conversation she made to me just weeks after my dad died. I did not ask who in the community? I did not respond, I only absorbed. It was a topic of horror, and certainly not an area I wanted to accept as reality, that my mother murdered my father. Secretly, I always wondered who were these people? After all, only my father and I ever knew the real side of Cindy, the other side of Cindy, so I had thought, up until this dinner conversation that sprouted out of the thin air.

Cindy had such a façade of sorts, almost political was her driving force in joining the church choir, getting involved with the tight knit Hudsonville Dutch Christian Reformed Church of Hillcrest. It was quite a campaign she had going. Always arriving to church on time and never ever accepting a seat in the back row, no sir! Cindy had everyone fooled in the community, most everyone. Who were these "other people" that would question Cindy, people mentioned in the community, she had stated in her non-benign dinner conversation with me. But what were their names? Where did they live? And most plaguing of all the questions….on what level could they know Cindy to have asked her such a deliberate question? Had she revealed, accidentally of course, another side, her real side, to members of this prominent group of a social elite Christian sect? I wondered many questions, but feared the answers most of all, I just remained silent. I was rational of the very fear of Cindy that she could input upon another, and anymore upsetting news that would make my stomach ache, was not news I was ready to hear. Cindy had a way of instilling fear in me, that if I talked about her evils, extreme pain would come my way. Then, the next step, was her next formula, strategy, Cindy would paint this rosy glow delusion for the world, that I am mental case, a problem child. Cindy was her own defense attorney, out to always purposely make me go crazy or be classified as crazy, and then not believed. And quite honestly, I do not like or respect her, I do act different around her, she annoys me and is very condescending towards me. Her behavior wears on me mentally and emotionally, and that is what she wants, her goal, if she can just get near me. Cindy always acting in a dignified way somehow, superior adult Cindy, which made me always resent her. How others in the community that appeared in such patronizing and contradictory manners towards others. Cindy is the model for evil. You would never believe me, and that is how perfectly evil she is, so undetected. "Under the radar," would be the legal literal term. I saw with my own eyes, I witnessed my whole life thus far in how Cindy needed the Dutch Calvinist community like a snake uses its tail to mimic a worm to lure victims, very predatory in camouflage was Cindy. Cindy was very aware of what she is and what she needs, like a soldier in camouflage.

Cindy had even convinced the minister of Hillcrest Christian Reformed Church that Chuck did not deserve a proper church funeral, that the funeral would be held at the Cook Funeral home in Jenison, not in a church. I would learn and witness that he was not Cindy enough to even deserve a proper church funeral. As a child I felt helpless in how Cindy and her CIA associates treated him, and treated me. As a mother of him 2000 years ago, I felt like a failure now. The whole purpose of me looking down from heaven into this lifetime was to save him, somehow protect him. It was always him and I that would stick together against Cindy and the CIA.

My father is dead, and Cindy still is getting her way, she convinced his entire family that he was bad, and drinking was his sin, and may God have mercy on his sinful soul as Cindy announced we would not being seeing him in heaven. It was scary how such an evil woman controlled the living in the audience at his funeral, her ex-husband of three months.

Despite Cindy's gossip of how awful my dad was when alive, many attended the funeral and the visitation of my father, people that knew him. People who had done business with him sent large ornate flower arrangements, many, more than any other funeral I had ever attended. I remember the large amount of flowers, and plant arrangements sent, very large elaborate flower assortments mounted everywhere in the front of the funeral home. The casket was a closed casket, you could not see him. For Cindy had found him very decomposed at his house. "Bloated with black skin," is what she kept saying to others in her carrying on with morbid detail conversations that just lit her up as if she had waited and waited, and then this day finally came, to finally speak and gossip at Chuck's funeral. I think she was more elated with his funeral than when she had married him. Cindy beamed of that of an exuberant bride, happy her groom was dead kind of day. It was creepy, I stayed away from her, I avoided her. I must have appeared aloof when in the presence of Cindy. She was like sandpaper against a raw open heart. Asking Cindy questions, any questions about his death was emotionally painful.

By my mother's description of my dad, you just would not have expected so many flowers to be sent in his name and in his honor. Many from old business associates, people in the building and construction fields, and people in the community, family members too. I thought to myself then, as I do now, boy, my father would have appreciated all those cheery flowers arrangements to be sent directly to his house in Grand Rapids during his despairing last years alone, separated in Grand Rapids as a broken man. When at least he would have been alive to enjoy the flowers. He would have loved to see the brightness those flower arrangements brought to the room, the splendor those many flower arrangements brought could have possibly lightened his spirits within his darkened world he was shoved into by my mother Cindy. It almost seemed to me that the flowers had been sent too late.

My father had died a broken man. They say that who you marry can make all the difference in the world to the outcome of your life, your happiness in this world and such. I know this fact straight on; If my father had married a better woman, a caring and warm woman, a professional and hard working woman, he would still be alive, he'd be healthy and happy, I am sure of it. It is 2010 when I began my memoir collection, he'd be about 77 years old as I complete my first memoir edition. Obviously there was not a smoking gun in Cindy's hand, but I was there during that entire last fourteen years of a marriage saga played out, she had killed him. In her heart she wanted him dead. In her selfish focus of herself she wanted him dead. In her hate of him, she wanted him dead. If he, or you, or me, became worthless in her eyes, she had a vendetta. Growing up, if he despised her as well, she would turn the sword on him. Cindy would say that it was Chuck that had spiraled out of control in the last years because he drank and smoked tobacco. Plus take in consideration of the high real estate interest rates of 18% and 20% on home loans, all sabotaged his building career and home sales from 1979 to 1982. Cindy needed to call him a failure so she could be the saint to be believed among those Calvinists. I viewed her differently than the Calvinists, and therefore Cindy and I did not get along. I thought the Calvinists were foolish and superficial. Generally speaking the Dutch people were good, the religion was almost a deterrent to the good people the Dutch are by nature.

But ask this question, what was Cindy's excuse for spiraling out of control throughout my entire life? She did not smoke, drink, party, take drugs, she was as sober as the night was dark. I saw her as a failure. A sinful soul. As I closed my eyes and then looked up at the funeral home situation, I could not help feeling dizzy. I could hear her loud cackling in the distant room, and her loud statements carried in the room. Degrading my father's life by saying, "It's just best he is dead," to all those that wanted to hear her talk in their circles. I wanted to shout and point at the people in the funeral home: "Who would want to listen to Cindy?" "Why do you always listen to Cindy?"

I wanted to scream, "Is this a standing ovation for Cindy being a victim?" Why would anyone in their right mind gather around her? Listening to her cackling hen mouth and stupidest church lady act ever? But they do. They just do. People from the church, her Bible shit circle friends, the entire side of her family the Stobs, they did everything but congratulate Cindy with a certificate of authenticity for being the perfect victim within the marriage she had with my dad. Cindy was a hen, is a hen, and everyone wanted to just adore her, feathers and all. She was one of them, cackling hen types, so happy Jesus died so she could have everlasting life. It was so warped. I felt helpless, in helping the helpless, my dad. How do you change a person? How do you change a community? No one made Cindy accountable for how she treated my dad during their marriage, let alone when she was separated and briefly divorced from him.

As you can gather, Cindy made sure I was not allowed to talk, speak, or fathom giving a speech at his funeral. Cindy is in control. She knew that there would be too much power in my words, shedding a new light on familiar subject matter of Cindy.

Cindy smiled and greeted the funeral guests with perfect prideful ease as if being on that show The Love Boat. According to Cindy who convinced the minister, they both agreed like bias voting members of that elite in an old Roman Senate against anything non-Roman, that indeed Chuck would not have a church funeral, he wasn't good enough, he wasn't Cindy enough. He wasn't Roman enough for the Calvinists community at large.

During my parents legal separation saga in my young world induced by Cindy, we had started to see a family counselor, Dr. Terri Ann Rosander was her name. She was a round, short, pudgy Jewish woman with piercing pupils in her eyes. She had a gentle voice, and was a good listener. Dr. Terri Ann seemed very detached from the Dutch Christian Reformed bubble, even though her office was located right next to Calvin College. Dr. Terri Ann, the family therapist was detached mentally, socially, emotionally from the Dutch Christian octopus tentacles, I liked that about Dr. Terri Ann. I found that fact interesting about her, fascinating, how she could have a counseling office right next to Calvin College, and could care less about the Calvinists, refreshing. She went on to describe my mother Cindy as sadistic, I remember having to ask Dr. Terri Ann what that word meant, sadistic. Dr. Terri Ann in 1986 went on to say she wondered if my mother had done my father in. Dr. Terri Ann pointed out that perhaps because of the nice suburbs my mother lives in and the bad and poor neighborhood my father was found dead in, which was a house in a bad area of Grand Rapids, that perhaps the cops were too naïve to even question a college graduate such as my mother Cindy. After all, Jenison, Michigan was a good Christian community, with a low crime rate. Criminals just don't seem to come from those parts of town. Dr. Terri Ann asked me if I thought my mother had done in my father? I responded, "I don't want to even think about that."

"Someday when you're ready you will think about it Lori." Dr. Terri Ann said with confidence. Dr. Terri Ann took my arm, and brushed her hand over my left arm resting on an arm chair in her comfortable office, and said this, "Every time you see me you look pale and have a greenish skin tone, do not drink from open containers of milk or pop in your refrigerator."

"Why? What are you talking about?" I asked.

"I have diagnosed your mother Cindy with Munchausen by Proxy Syndrome, a rare mental condition that most police know nothing about, let alone can pronounce. Munchausen is when a mother purposely makes a child sick in order to gain attention from others, to point attention to a child, to make a child dependent upon that parent in order to recover the child from a sickness. To make the child dependent as that child grows independent or shows relative signs of independency......A classic occupation for someone with Munchausen by Proxy is nursing, your mom is a nurse. Also classic is the reason a person develops this mental case, she is classic, both her parents doted and favored her brothers growing up and ignored her, so she feels. Your grandmother blames Cindy for an uncle of yours dying at age two while in Cindy's care, 'David, was his name.' Then Cindy marries and feels neglected in her marriage in her adulthood. Often your mother deliberately has made you sick, she admitted this in my office. In this case she is trying to convince others that you have a mental problem, you have social problems, something is wrong with you, or tries to convince me that you hate men because of your father being an alcoholic. In an exuberant campaign of propaganda by Cindy, all this exacerbated effort on her part to take the focus off from her. You have never mentioned you hate men or your father. You are popular in school, and very involved with social activities within your school. You are optimistic and full of life, you have a boyfriend. Munchausen by Proxy is a relatively uncommon condition. It is also hard to prove and gather evidence on. Your very best decision you can make is to leave at eighteen, go to college and create your own world, separate from the world your mother Cindy is creating for you here in Michigan. As you grow into adulthood and marry and have children, I predict Cindy will grow dangerously jealous of your life then. Especially if you are happily married with a wonderful family life, having something she does not have, may give her intent to sabotage your relationships. Especially the relationships she grows envious of, just keep to yourself growing up." Dr. Terri Ann said with serious tone.

Dr. Terri Ann went on to say this, "I also fear your mother might have multiple personalities, also a very rare condition."

I asked, "Why would you say that?"

"Well Lori, every time I see your mother, speak about a topic of concern, bring up a subject, the next week she does not remember what we even talked about from the previous week. We can never make any progress on a subject or issue because she does not remember one week to the next. Something is not connecting in her brain, in her memory of events. She operates in a very disconnected reality, disassociates." Said Dr. Terri Ann Rosander.

A chill ran down my spine at the realization that others also could see into my world at home, a private embossing hell for such a proud person such as myself with a mother such as Cindy. Where is normalcy? Where is it?

A reality I was not creating for myself, but a reality to avoid open liquid containers, a situation of survival within Cindy's world for me. Living with the enemy. I was trying to just keep my head above water, and Dr. Terri Ann could see me treading for my life. I wanted out of the north sea and the moon jellyfish community I was placed into. I was tired of always looking over my shoulder from Cindy, sleeping with one eye open, and not feeling safe, I felt exhausted.

The nice thing about my life, I suppose, was Carmen was always there for me, always willing to listen to my terrible situations, my plight in this lifetime. The many unhappy family situations and arguments I had with my mother Cindy. I felt like a plague covered my life, like a hex of sorts I would tell Carmen. She would respond, "That's silly, a hex, really Lori, that's foolish talk. Why would you even say such a thing?" Carmen would inquire from under her bewitching concerned smile and warm brownish-green eyes. That would not be the only time I would ever bring up the fact I believed my life had been hexed while speaking with Carmen.

I did seem to have a great school life from 8:30am to 3:15pm, I worked a part time job in the evenings, and was busy with school events with friends. By age seventeen I could drive, I did not pass drivers education at age sixteen and therefore it was not until seventeen that I received a drivers permit. I inherited my father's life insurance policy, it was not much, but it paid for my first car, a used, but sporty black Mustang. The small life insurance money would help out with going on to college, and having a college degree someday, so I hoped. The State of Michigan also began sending a monthly check of five hundred dollars from my dad's social security benefits, which began when I was sixteen and a half and continued until I was eighteen. My mother remained bitter and disturbed that my father had changed his will just three months before he passed away, without even notifying her that he had done so behind her back. She was also frustrated that the government would not give her a monthly social security benefits check, like I was receiving, because she had been divorced, not married at the time of his death. Cindy apparently did not know those relative facts before, and now resented me more than ever, and all that I inherited, although a small portion it was. Cindy was always arguing her point that she had been married to my father for twenty-seven years and that she should receive some financial benefits through the State of Michigan or his will. My father had his debts when he died though. And when the phone would ring at our house, asking for money due to the person on the other end of the line, my mother very promptly and loudly would say, "Chuck is dead, and we were divorced at the time of his death! I am not responsible for his debts! Don't call here!"

Disturbing for me was the demand of hers from Visser & Bolhouse attorneys to be placed on my bank account, the same bank account that had my father's life insurance benefits. That same checking account would also hold the monthly social security benefits checks that I received monthly. Monthly five hundred dollar checks until I turned eighteen, not much, her attorneys got Cindy her way, as always.

I stated over and over, "I don't want you on my accounts." Cindy's eyes grew furious in rage and full blown resentment, almost fiery red at times as she grinded her teeth down when responding to my unlikely response to her "banking demands," of placing her name on my bank accounts.

Like venom she would shriek and spit in her attempts in her force feeding vocally, "It's the law. I am your mother! I have a legal right to be on those accounts! I spoke with the law office of Don Visser & Rick Bolhouse in Grandville, that Rick he told me I have a legal right as your parent and legal guardian to be on your bank accounts, you are only sixteen lady Jane."

Growing up I would often wonder why Cindy had not named me Jane instead of Lori, after all, she loved to address me as, "Lady Jane!!"

More disturbing was not the fact that I did not consult with an attorney over adding her name to my bank accounts. Rather she just added herself, without my permission, there, appearing like a nightmare was her name on my two accounts when I next went inside the bank the next day. Never is there much of a compromise or discussion with Cindy. It was her way, or there would be a disruption by her, on her end, and then she would bully her way to the finish line. Mostly, usually, using or quoting Mr. Rick Bolhouse or Mr. Don Visser in Grandville the legally powerful attorneys in town located in the metropolitan area of historic Grandville.

Every month I would balance my checkbook, but my checking and savings account monthly statements were not matching in correlation to my checking and savings memo book that I kept in my purse. I would sit by the dinner table while she fussed in the kitchen which was open to the table area, for hours, as I was obviously baffled as to why the bank was subtracting money out of my account, checks were then bouncing that

I would write. Yet, I thought the money was there to cover the checks I wrote? I had checks bouncing left and right and I could not seem to understand why? Cindy never spoke up in the kitchen this whole time for hours that I am bewildered and wondering why I cannot balance my checkbook. I finally questioned her if she knew anything about my accounts and money missing? Cindy admitted to taking money, lots of money, but this whole time I am frantic at the table trying to balance my checkbook, she just ignores my scene of distress for hours. Cindy was not going to speak up from her constant need for dishonesty, what she could get away with? What she could take and not tell me? Inform me of? What kind of bond is created when a mother steals from a child, pulling money from behind my back? Then on top of it all, from the tender age of sixteen I was charged room and board fees weekly from Cindy, meal fees, toiletry fees for shampoo and toilet paper she would buy for me at the grocery store. I was writing her weekly checks, including paying $125.00 per month for health insurance premiums. The only thing Cindy paid for was a life insurance policy on me, I was sixteen and healthy! Her life insurance policies on me lasted year after year! Cindy had Hillcrest Church pay half of my high school tuition, I paid the other half. She wanted no financial responsibilities for me, only benefits she would accept.

At age sixteen in 1986 I received my social security number. Now I could work legally outside of babysitting, and that is exactly what I did. My first legal job I held at age sixteen was at Russ' Restaurant in Grandville, Michigan. I was the salad girl making salads in the back, in the kitchen area. Hudsonville is known as the salad bowl capital of the world, Dutch people love gourmet salads. I earned $4.35 per hour, slightly over minimum wage at that time. I worked two or three evenings a week all the while attending Unity Christian High and maintaining a 3.22 grade point average and never doing any homework, I had no time for homework in high school. I liked to work and I liked being independent from Cindy's control of my life. Later I also became a hostess at Mike's Restaurant in Hudsonville, Michigan where I met Jamie Smith. I liked to work and be out of the house, away from erratic and criminal Cindy.

I had issue after issue with Cindy, my checkbook and bank statements were never, ever an exact match in Cindy's household, why? Because Cindy was going directly to the bank to withdraw money from my accounts, behind my back, not telling me, or asking me. Cindy had this inherent "taking" nature, Cindy would not stop. Control is her libido, along with the Calvinists' acceptance. I did not accept Cindy, nor did I want her to control my life. Therefore we got along splendidly? Not exactly.

I had to pay my car insurance, fuel for my car and all repairs while still in High School. Pay for all my clothes. If we went out for dinner, I had to pick up the tab. I had cost her nothing from ages sixteen to eighteen, she even **made** money raising me during my high school years.

Cindy would comment to me in the years of 1986 to 1989, that with my figure, and if I dyed my hair, I could earn a lot of money.

"What?" I asked. I had no idea what she was talking about. But in the years to come, I would soon learn about life and reality. I was young, naïve, and hardly known to the world that Cindy and her friend best buddy, I swear they are gay, Ms. Kim Livermore, were about to introduce me into. A world, I had no idea even existed. A world of dancing, but not with ballerina shoes on.

I was so ready to get out into the world and begin a world that was not governed by Cindy, her gay friends, her CIA friends, or her Bible shit friends. I could not wait until I turned eighteen and was old enough, legally old enough, to say….. "Stop Cindy, you don't own me!" But every child wants a mother, and so my visions of marrying, having a family of my own, marrying a man, were put on the back burner. Visions of my happiness, how I envisioned happiness for myself, appeared more like melted marshmallows, the froth resonating on the cup of life. I was convinced at times by Cindy's enduring programing of my mind, that I did not even own the ingredients of my life.

She was a chilling mother to have to say the least, but she was the only mother I knew. The mother-daughter relationship lacked real caring and nurturing on Cindy's part, on the foundation that Cindy built, right from the beginning of this nightmare Cindy was driving. I always felt as if kidnapped and raised by her, right from the very beginning, raised by my kidnapper. My life lacked many things that could have been offered but were not.

When my father had passed away in the summer of 1986 Cindy also made us kids, that would be my older brothers, Ric, Dave, and Mike, clean out my father's house after my father had been found dead, and had been dead for quite some time before Cindy found him ironically dead in his bed. When we arrived to my father's former house there were flies everywhere on the windows. Some flies found dead by the front door, piled up on a stack of ruffled newspapers gathering on the front porch. I'll never forget the sound of those buzzing flies around the inside of the window frames on the main floor. It was as if they were so busy, real busy bodies, and I felt frozen in time for a moment, unable to move or go inside. My mother Cindy yelled at me to "Keep moving, get, go ahead, get in there now! Don't be funny lady Jane."

I thought about her words, "don't be funny" (?). I was not being funny. I just did not want to go inside, those flies were irritating me, their fanatic buzzing I could not stand. Cindy's demanding busy body tone in her surly Yankee voice simply held not a stitch of the emotions I felt inside me. Cindy had the worst concept of word meanings, like so many Christians in that Calvinist subculture. The English language was not of importance to them, nor was knowing what words really mean. What remained important was just the Biblical reference of Jesus Christ, and his instant forgiveness act was of greatest importance to her and her subculture she controlled. Jesus was a quick fix antidote to the Calvinist and Catholic lifestyle choices, nothing else mattered, just instant forgiveness, via the grapevine forgiveness act of Jesus, so some Roman wrote 2000 years ago.

My emotional state felt fragile. I did not feel tough. Life is a war, amidst Cindy.

I felt my emotions at that very moment were felt like an exasperated mule, tired and hopeless, as my owner Cindy kept cracking a whip with her very demanding tone and words spoken to me on that porch. As Cindy forged ahead with her cracking ill manners as a guardian of me, a caretaker of the worst kind. The accumulation of emotions of that afternoon would once again be filed somewhere in a mental folder, lost in that abyss of a place referred to as my mind's cabinet. I would always know that pushing and pushing the bad memories with ill-fated emotions towards the abyss of my mind would be a reaction of mine in my coping of situations within this Dutch subculture of Grand Rapids, Michigan. What I did not realize at the time was that those filed folders I tossed into my mental abyss on a regular basis would circulate, cumulate, and wash up to shore like a lost treasure of gold someday as I would reveal why and how a person could have a mental break down. "The washing up to shore," would happen much, much later. Although at the time, I thought I was coping, forgetting how Cindy was as a parent towards me.

It was July in Michigan, the summer of 1986, I was sixteen. As I recall, the heat was unbearable as were Cindy's demands that we all clean the fly infested windows, and go through my father's stuff. I kept saying, "No, no, I don't want to clean his house. You go sort all this stuff and clean the windows." I pleaded to no avail. The smell of rotted dead father staunchly smothering in the trapped vapor air of that house as we entered, combined with the staunch smell of ammonia in the Windex was too much to breathe in emotionally. I begged to wait in the car. I just kept begging for air, I needed emotionally fresh air. I needed physically fresh air immediately. But I was not going to get either that afternoon under Cindy's tyrannical authority. Cindy was going to have her demanded way again, she was like a reckless driver in the seat of parenthood. I just did not want to be in that house, breathing any longer. It was such a powerful remainder of how my life seemed to be turning out thus far. I just could not bear to be in that dramatic climatic argument that Cindy kept forcing upon me, "Clean! Clean! Lady Jane, don't be smart, don't be funny with me!" Spoke the voice of the chilling woman I was legally bound to call mother.

With a heavy heart and slow motion movements I started over by an open window by my father's desk. This old, worn antique roller style top drawer on the desk, which was open, seemed like a starting point. On the top shelf inside the roller accordion drawer was a proudly displayed homemade arts and crafts style Father's Day gift I gave to my father when I was in seventh grade. On a small wooden block of wood

I had glued navy floral fabric on the wood. The fabric print had small pink flowers against navy, I took a school picture of me from seventh grade junior high school and cut the photograph into an oval shape. I then took some fancy border trim and cut and glued a framed picture of me onto the fabric. I then wrote in marker on paper also glued to the block of wood, "I love you Dad." I can only imagine now, as I did then, as I stood by his former desk what he must have felt when he read that block of wood in his unfamiliar house, located in a bad section of Grand Rapids.

His house was old, it looked as if it was under a multitude of remodeling projects, although it also looked as if the funds ran dry before any project could officially be completed. Everything was in such disarray, filthy dirty, old, with a sofa, desk, and bed to make up his furniture collection, that is what he had left after the divorce. I hated my mother. It probably was not the first moment that I looked at her with contempt and resentment. I despised her from the beginning. She was a demanding, selfish, bullish creature of a woman who only thought of herself and her gains, the older I became, the more I noticed. She had no warmth, no sense of caring for another. Including love or kindness for her natural children, and me, and obviously not for her deceased ex-husband. There she stood pointing at us from her commando spot in the living room. Only Cindy's orchestrated cleaning duties could be heard, snapping her fingers in a hiss if we stopped cleaning or sorting or packing. To this day I hate the smell of ammonia in Windex. Especially in hot humid trapped air kind of places such as a two-way foyer. The smell makes me feel as if my dad just died and the emotions are resurfacing, regurgitating of what I was never ready to face at age sixteen, his absence always now from my life from now on during this journey called life. I do miss having a fierce father figure, Cindy always has to win, she would kill a dog of mine if she felt I held onto the dog too tightly, or kissed on the dog with affection. And then she'd kick me, just because she could and therefore she would. No one looks, there is no video, and no cop would ever dare question the damn good ol' church lady, Cindy.

My mother divorcing my father, giving him nothing, was Cindy's push off the edge of giving him no will to live or get better, which is her way with people. People can lose their will to live if pushed far enough so Carmen told me that night on the phone. I think I agree, but for some reason, I do have this fire in my belly and I can't stand to lose a fight, a war, a battle with evil. I just can't give up in life, it is not in my astrological configuration, or my will.

As if that summer day in 1986 was not traumatic enough for a sixteen year old. Cindy stops at the two week just dug gravesite of my father while we were in Grand Rapids. My brother Ric and I step out and walk in a wandering sort of way through the Chapel Hill cemetery. The sunlight was bright, it was supposed to be a sunny, beautiful summer afternoon, and in someone else's world, perhaps it was. We walked and walked, and towards the back of the cemetery we located a freshly dug grave, the manicured thick sod of the green grass was torn up in a rectangular outlined shape. There was no grave marker. But my mother convinced us in her excited manic tone of excitement felt only on her side, "This is it, This is it! This is where Chuck is buried." Then Cindy pulls out her camera from her purse, her smile manic, her eyes lit, and states to my brother Ric and I, "Sit. Sit on the grave, I want to take your picture."

I looked startled and dazed by the entire afternoon sequence of events and requests of Cindy thus far. I had this to say back to her in my firm tone of voice, "I do not want my picture taken. I do not want to step on my father's gravesite." I just kept shaking my head in a firm gesture of "no." My strong will made Cindy furious, like kerosene onto an already excitable lit fire. Cindy fumed and frowned, as always, when I spoke the word "no."

My brother Ric chimed in and said, "Yeah, mom, we are not up for photos right now, maybe you can put down the camera, that's not a good idea right now mom."

"Just kneel down, Sit. Sit. I want to take your pictures next to the grave, just do it, com' on now, kneel down I want to take a picture, don't be funny now!" Her words were very firm and excited in tone, demonically excited were her eyes and high decibel Midwest squelching tone of this moment. Void of warmth, comforting, and connecting to us. We wanted nothing but to just be alone in silence. Cindy was not going to let up in her excitement of that insane moment. We had to do as she asked, or she would continue to insist and rudely request, as if just pounding further, then get very angry if we just kept on refusing. I, nor my brother were up for dealing with my mother's anger at us at this point in the long already so emotionally tiresome day. We just could not take any more of her attitude today. So we gave in, knelt down on that loose brown dirt that framed my father's final resting spot, and had to hear her scold and fuss at us in her Midwest church woman twang…….. "Smile. Smile….. Lori, now don't be funny! Smile for me."

I sighed, rolled my eyes, then looked at my brother Ric obeying her commands to smile as well, and responded beat emotionally to her request. Physically now drained of energy to put up a debate of whether this is a good time or not to be snapping photos and muttered, "Please just take the photograph mother, I want to go, I do not want to be resting on dad's gravesite." I said in a tired voice, despicably disgusted with Cindy and exhausted with her as well. Just unable to grasp why my life has had so many sad twists and turns as I stared at the camera lens she held in her quivering excited hand as she snapped away. And why was she smiling? Why did she look so manic in her squinting eyes?

Weeks and months passed, almost a year to the date of when my father was found dead in his Grand Rapids home located in a bad area of town by Cindy when my aunts and uncles on the Vander Ark side kept calling my mom's condo. They wanted to discuss with my mother about putting a headstone on my father's gravesite. Cindy responded very mad, irritated that anyone, including his family would even stop and think about him after he died. "No, I am not going to contribute for some fancy expensive headstone," Cindy snapped firmly back into the phone receiver. Cindy was in a bad mood the rest of that evening. I, at times had to pop Advil to just release the pain her voice and harsh words would cause my brain from her staunch Yankee twang and non-loving approach to just about everything and anything that was not around her church functions.

I learned later that my aunts and uncles on the Vander Ark side paid for a gravestone marker, a bronze plaque. Cindy paid not a penny in contributions nor did she care to be there when the plaque was placed on the ground. But one thing is for sure, she kept attending the Hillcrest CRC widows club (for the outsiders; CRC means, Christian Reformed Church). Cindy joined the "grieving widows club," week after week. I just wondered, what do the real widows think of Cindy? She has not one emotion in her heart that they all feel, and *grieve* in their despair of losing a spouse. What could she possibly have in common with them as they sip on coffee and talk in a small group?

Perhaps Cindy's very unpleasant demeanor was the reason why she could not hold a steady job, her brazen Yankee attitude and demeanor in the medical field. But ever since she became licensed in 1980 as a nurse she would constantly be fired or asked to resign from her various nursing positions. But why? I can only speculate, and shiver at the thought of being a patient under her watchful care. I feel sorry for those unfortunate people, saddened for their unfortunate set of circumstances, events, to then be placed under her nursing care in a hospital. Did they ever die a mysterious death like my young dad at age fifty-two? Signed, Just wondering.

Cindy is not caring, she is anything but a caring woman, nurse, mother, or wife to someone. I often wonder if I was the detective called to my dad's house, I would certainly want to sleuth around and speak with Cindy's previous administrators in the medical field. For they might be able to shed light on what she is like around helpless patients.

Any type of music from the 1980's, I just can't listen to, it makes me nauseous at the memory of my home life back then in Jenison, Michigan. Amazing how music can evoke such emotion of sadness in a person. I would often wonder, why, if my mother attends church religiously, has joined the choir, sings the loudest in church, rings bells for the church, why is she so un-Godlike when she spends so much time in church religiously? Why can't Christian music or the minister's sermons penetrate her heart and soul? Why are the sermons not reaching her, molding her, why is God not radiating from her soul, her aura? The minister at Hillcrest Church was an outstanding minister, but why were the messages of God not reaching her like they should? Perhaps she had created too many worries, and not enough space in her mind to absorb profound thoughts? I think many questions need to be asked of Cindy, many, many, direct questions preferably in a high police elite situation or FBI setting. Or was the FBI business partners with Cindy and her CIA friends? Then nothing would be solved in the realm of corruption and politics. Or from a documentary film maker's approach, probing and very public could be the interview. I wish I could step on stage and take away the props that Cindy puts on stage, the music, the black curtain and have Cindy stand alone, just as she pushes upon others.

The visits, or should I say "therapy sessions," with Dr. Terri Ann continued on into my senior year at Unity Christian High. From the age of about twelve to the age of seventeen I was experiencing more intense, desperately severe stomach aches. I went to my doctor in Grandville complaining of constant stomach pains. As it turned out the lining in my stomach had mysteriously dissolved, "disappeared," was the exact medical term the doctor used of my diagnosis. I was prescribed medication, pills, to rebuild the lining in my weak stomach. I still have a weak stomach to this day. I think there was reason to fear Cindy was poisoning me, proof was starting to surface with symptoms in 1986. I remember going to the doctor before and complaining of severe stomach aches. He had asked then, "When do you feel these severe stomach aches?"

I responded, "After I eat dinner, after a few mouthfuls, I have to walk cramped over in pain to the sofa almost immediately after consumption. The pain is so intense I cannot even stretch to stand up. I lay cramped for hours, and just end up going to bed, I can't walk straight. I do not feel dizzy, I feel the sharpest pain in my stomach and intestinal area."

In the back of my mind, I would try to connect the dots. I refused gravy these days at the dinner table. I refused any dish that Cindy was not also putting on her plate as well, or placing on her plate first, advice given also by Dr. Terri Ann.

Dr. Terri Ann was trying to make me aware of something my young sixteen year old mind wanted to desperately reject as a possibility and reality. Dr. Terri Ann made it very point blank clear to me that she fears Cindy had murdered in her past and I need to be very aware of Cindy's capabilities to make her murders looks accidental, with not a trace of evidence. I can still hear Dr. Terri Ann's words in my head, "And the Grand Rapids police detective is too proud to admit a possible mistake and retrace his steps in determining whether he had an actual crime scene when he located your dad. Statistics show that the first person on the scene of a dead person is also a very good lead as to who the killer is. Often when a spouse or ex-spouse is the first one on the scene, as well as the last one to see the person, it is that person who is the killer, the guilty one, that's what statistics reveal."

Dr. Terri Ann went on to inform me of yet other realities I was not mentally ready to accept as real warnings. If I did not believe it, it would not happen, it was not true, I thought. This is the warning and information our family therapist gave me: "Your mother would babysit her younger brother David. One day your grandmother Theresa came home and David, who would be your uncle David, was not alive. Your mother Cindy reveled in your grandmothers tears and desperate expression of the loss of David. The loss of David gave Cindy a very deep seated power trigger that Cindy learned at a very young age. Cindy explained to me in confidential, that David was your grandmother Theresa's favorite. David had been the first born male into the family, your mother the oldest and a girl, felt overlooked in worth. Your mother confided in me, and I can only best determine that from a very young age Cindy learned not an important lesson of watching a child better, but she learned the power of the feeling of taking away, the power of murder. Cindy possesses and acquired a power to take, a power murder brought Cindy. Cindy never shed a tear. Cindy never felt any remorse over David's death of chewing a cord and touching metal that caused his electrocution while in Cindy's care, while Cindy watched. Cindy gloats in how stupid the Calvinists are and how naïve and shallow their rules to belonging actually are, she is proud, undeniably proud, of things she can get away with. Your mother needs the Calvinists community, she needs the Calvinist lawyers and Calvinist police, it fits into her plan very well Lori. Do you understand? You need to move Lori, far away from here. I went to the police, and the police informed me that a crime has not taken place. You must move away when you are able to. You must. Far away from Cindy and her Bethany Christian Services adoption friends, her church friends." Spoke Dr. Terri Ann in harsh warnings of my future and what she knew Cindy was all about.

I remember Cindy telling me while she was in nursing school in the late 1970's, an odd comment she made to me, "You know that under the sink, basic cleaning chemicals can cause a person to die. I learned that in nursing school today." Cindy said that to me as she stood in the kitchen as I removed the dishes from the dinner table one evening.

Cindy never had anything warm and interesting to say to me like a normal mother daughter conversation, everything she said had an element of morbid attached to the topic. Cindy was very sexually inappropriate, especially for a mother to say to a daughter, and do to a daughter and insist. Cindy would read through the newspaper and mention upon weird and horrid events written up in the newspaper. Cindy was deeply fascinated with morbid gruesome acts upon another was such an interest to her. "Fascinating," she would explain as her eyes lit up over the topics raised by her as she read of some gruesome act of torture in the newspaper. She loved to watch old fashioned bloody Spanish bull coliseum style showdowns. She even became a surgical nurse, handing instruments to surgeons as they cut open people. She liked victims, helplessness, and she was the sadist, the dictator, the one in charge. If you talked about what she had done, she reveled in her glory to cover-up, dilute what occurred, and pull the wool over societies eyes. Essentially, that was her trigger of glory within her massively destructive brain. She would rant and rave about the bloody scene of the day, her eyes would tweak with a mesmerizing haze of lit up scariness, hospital gloom scenes. Cindy would tell of the gruesome hospital stories, often at the dinner table. She would cut and clip out newspaper stories as hobbies, such as of a girl found at age six living in a closet for six years, forced in a closet to live on the northwest side of Grand Rapids for years, found not able to talk, or walk. Almost infant like with a studded growth, mentally and physically. You can see that Cindy was not a shoulder to lean on, but a polarizing force to grow away from during my childhood. Her interests, her comments, make me shudder to this day. Cindy looked at me during most of my childhood and adolescence like a sunset she could paint and fade away under an ocean wave if she and the Central Intelligence Agency wanted to that day. It was eerie how she looked at me, it made me want to run. Love and comfort, was distant. Love, tender moments, and comfort was just a fantasy of mine.

If you asked Cindy the same question seven times, you would **not** get the same answer seven times. Rather, strangely, you would hear or see written, more than likely seven **different** answers that you might believe. Or at least a continuous spin on her answers, until you believed one, and the police left her alone then. And no one ever makes Cindy accountable, she is a very networked Christian. So forgiven by her religion, the Calvinists, instant forgiveness by the blood of Jesus, was indeed their motto lived. It is as if the Calvinist religion is in fact her liberator, her messiah, her Jesus, the exact faith that she needs.

Cindy is perfectly positioned within the social glue work of the Dutch community and Dutch Christian Reformed Church at large, the great octopus. Although, if ever interrogated or even slightly questioned, Cindy has a mind that seemed to have more "skips" than a warped record on an old fashioned record player. Her mind would just skip and change answers, continuously. Oddly, the family just felt sorry for her, the church too. Because of who she is, a major player with the Calvinists society and her church. Cindy is very well respected by other very integrated and networked Christians as a clone of them. She remains in the bubble unscathed, and very undetected, just like them. Everything, and everybody, it is all so pristine, or so projected that way. Christianity has become a perfect faith, a perfect religion, a perfect path in life, if you are a criminal or a truly perfect person, it does not matter, no one can tell the difference. It's like peas are to carrots, they go together perfectly on a plate, and everybody serves them.

I remember back to another odd scene in my childhood. I was five years old, we lived in a nice new construction house on Crestlane Drive in Georgetown Forest Estates, it was around 1975 or so.

Cindy was a stay at home mother, but rarely was at home. However would leave me at home, alone, all the time. Cindy once again left me alone, which was not odd or unusual, but when Cindy walked through the door late one morning and came home again she had a little blonde haired boy with her. Cindy led the little boy into the bathroom and stated to me he had to go to the bathroom. I stood in the bathroom just wondering how and why my mother Cindy had this little boy all of a sudden at our house. She held his "private part" as he went to the bathroom. He had trouble standing and understanding the concept of "going the bathroom" as if he was not potty trained yet. I noticed he wore diapers, he must have not been more than two years old. He cried, and cried out for his mother, but where was his mother? I kept asking Cindy that question too, it must have annoyed her as she snapped back at me to go downstairs. Cindy stated that she found this little boy wandering in our neighborhood lost, and she found him. Cindy the saint, had found him. The boy stayed with us that morning and afternoon, maybe a total of five hours or so. I was told to go downstairs or to my bedroom during that time he was at our house on Crestlane. It stands out as an odd memory that my mother suddenly shows up with this little boy at our house. At first I believed Cindy's story, of him being lost and all, but then when I look back, it was odd. My mother Cindy then leaves the house and says she will be back to look for his mother. I stayed back at our house alone, which was not odd. Cindy took the little boy and left again. But what Cindy said when she returned always struck me as "odd"……"off." Cindy said that she drove the little boy back to his house, and when she pulled into his driveway his mother came out screaming and yelling at her (Cindy).

"The little boy's mother threatened to call the police, she was so mad at me!" Said panicky Cindy. Cindy remained back at our house, starring out the big kitchen bay window which faced the road in front, she was on alert, and in fear.

I asked later, "I thought you said he was lost mom?" "How did you know where he lived?"

Cindy responded, "Oh, just hush, shut your mouth…you just go to your room lady Jane. I saw him in his front yard I suppose, I did not know that was <u>his</u> front yard, I thought he really was lost, now go to your room you are such a smart alec." Cindy was always sending me to my room for asking too many questions concerning her behavior. Sending me to my room was her way of getting rid of me and my questions of her. Asking Cindy one question, just one right question, sent her over the edge causing her temperament to set off like malfunctioning fireworks exploding on the home front. Cindy answered always, "That Jesus forgives her," "Jesus died for her sins on a cross."

"Jesus" lives in a faraway galaxy, so she assumes, like most Christians just like her, hiding this, that, or another daily crime, sin or ill action towards another, for Cindy. Therefore Cindy does not need to have a conscious, she and others like her within that community have figured out, because Jesus takes away their sins and crimes instantly, "instant forgiveness," preaches the CRC ministers, the Catholics, and all ministers. Zero accountability for their sins. "Jesus" dying on the cross for their sins and transgressions is a great concept for criminals, can you see why? Can you see my point about the evolution of Christianity? My life is a testament of what these monster Christians are capable of, they do not apologize for their wrongs towards another, they simply keep sinning, there is no end in sight, for Jesus forgives. Therefore these Christians have no developed conscious. Non-accountability is the emphasized resounding shallow echo within churches and its members alike.

From a legal standpoint, Jesus never wrote his own autobiography. Nor did he sign his names to the Biblical ancient scrolls and what was written of his life and words later, Jesus never signed one page in the Bible. Not one chapter in the Bible did Jesus write or paraphrase. Prophets were the authors of Jesus words. Writers, mostly Roman historians. Has anyone considered how out of context a person's words can become when a story is written by another? It happens daily in this world. Historians in those days were also governed by Rome in harsh authority matters, history was written as a ruling governing leader wanted history told and written. Has anyone in Christianity or the Catholic faith considered those very poignant thoughts as you live your life caught in a system of non-accountability that you keep agreeing to? I am a voice of reason. I am a voice for accountability within these religious subcultures.

Back to my teenage memoirs, the 1980's………..

When prom season rolled around my mother refused to take prom pictures of me with my date, beginning at age fourteen through my senior prom. When my date arrived, my mother would storm off in her car, slamming her car door, screaming at me that I look like a slut. Odd no one else thought so, needless to say, proms made her go into wild erratic rages. To this day, I have not one prom photo she ever took, none exist. I have no photos of me in my teenage years taken by Cindy.

When my date and I would arrive at his house, his parents would both come outside and take a multitude of photographs, my date's parents always seemed so nice and polite, excited for us both. My date's mother would complement me, his father would snap photos, they always showed so much enthusiasm over prom night photos. I remember after the photos were taken and I was not required to smile anymore at a flashing light, I remember feeling…..something is odd, something is off, in my home life. My home was different than his, I would think to myself. Prom photograph time always made me feel as if I had something missing in my home life, there was an empty feeling inside of me behind what the camera could capture. I would feel this pain inside as his parents would snap photo after photo, asking us to smile big. I felt the imprint of sadness almost, inside me, an emptiness as the camera flashed on in the late afternoon sunlight. I just did not have a joyous home, it was just Cindy and me.

With senior prom time, also came the vibrant smell of cherry blossoms covering lower Michigan. The State of Michigan glowed a cotton candy pink color in the spring. I always felt I was looking outward, towards something, in which to hope upon in my surroundings…… where was Alan? When would he return?

The opening of the cherry blossom flower signaled to us seniors that graduation was just around the corner, a new opening, a fresh sign of improvements for my life. I would love to just sit under a blooming cherry blossom tree resting my back against the bark of the tree. A canopy of pink above me, watching the wind carry the blossoms off the tree branches so delicately, each small fragile petal floating down into the green grass in numbers.

Soon after graduating from Unity Christian High in the early part of June 1988, Carmen and I headed off to the Netherlands together, sponsored by the Dutch International Society. Sort of an exchange student experience offered in Grand Rapids, Michigan. For high school graduation, like many other special events celebrated, Carmen gave me a hard cover journal, the pages blank inside. I think I had received about seven of these hard cover style journals from Carmen thus far. She told me she had a feeling someday I would become a famous writer, she said that again to me at graduation time. Only Carmen and my high school literature teacher, Mr. Joel Brouwer shared that resounding hometown opinion of me.

I remember leaving my boyfriend for the first time as we boarded a bus to the airport, I missed him. I missed McDonalds, I missed the summer at Holland beach in Michigan. I pretty much spent six weeks missing America and everything offered so conveniently in the States. Sure we traveled abroad, it was a cultural adventure, we saw castles, and Anne Frank's attic where she wrote her diary during world war II as she hid with her family from the German Nazis in a closet size room above the bustling clock shop. Believe it or not, the clock shop is still there, ticking little clocks and grandfather clocks offered for sale as if there never was a war, or Jews hiding with the help of the Dutch from the contemptuous Nazis occupation of Holland. We even walked through Amsterdam's red light district during the day. Women standing in department style glass windows, it was strange and alarming to say the least. The Dutch civilization in the Netherlands, was about free speech, tolerances of all people and races. Carmen and I would watch television in the Netherlands, the Dutch tolerated "full nudity," in commercials. Such as a commercial about shampoo or body wash being advertised and promoted, and then the next scene of the woman in the shower nude, or a nude woman running down the beach. Carmen and I looked at each other and would remark what does nudity have to do with the commercial and advertising a shampoo? I said, "I don't know, it's weird, how very different the Dutch people are here in the Netherlands than at home in Michigan."

The Dutch people sell marijuana at bars in Amsterdam. "That would never happen in Michigan." I said to Carmen.

Carmen went on to inform me that John Calvin reformed a group of Dutch people and moved them to west Michigan because the Dutch were acting too badly in the Netherlands.

I responded by saying….. "Oh. Really? So now, the new Dutch residing in west Michigan, transported by John Calvin, are the new and improved Dutch?" I remarked to Carmen.

Carmen replied, "Yup. These Dutch have no censorship. They are out of control with values and morals."

One day while strolling through a quant village in the Netherlands Carmen and I stopped at a Dutch bakery to compare authentic Dutch pastries to Dutch pastries we had tasted in Hudsonville, Michigan. The Dutch pastries taste exactly the same. What was startling is what was said to us from the young girl behind the counter helping us select a pastry. The eighteen year old Dutch girl said to me as she nodded her head to the right, which would be my left towards Carmen and remarked to me a warning about Carmen. This is what the Dutch girl said to me very directly, giving me a direct warning about Carmen, "You look Dutch, she does not. You may be friends now but eventually you will grow apart. Dutch people are a certain way and others want in our country and want what they think we will give or provide to them. But they are not Dutch, eventually the non-Dutch show their true selves and a clash will happen, it's inevitable."

Then Carmen spoke up, not to ever be too silent when defending herself, "I have a Dutch last name."

The bakery girl spoke firmly back to Carmen, "It does not matter."

Carmen spoke up again, "My last name is Haverdink. Hers is Vander Ark. We are both Dutch, we live in west Michigan, but our ancestors are from the Netherlands."

The Dutch bakery girl shock her head as she deposited our money into the cash register, "No you are both not Dutch. Someday you will have a rift and then you will understand your friend is not Dutch as she claims she is, and then you will understand my point, my warning about her." And then the bakery girl our age proceeded to help the next guest in line.

Carmen and I paid for our pastries and just as soon as we stepped out of that bakery, Carmen fumed, "Was that not rude of that girl to say that right to our face? I can't believe she said that to us. I am mad."

As I ate my pastry puff outside with Carmen I commented to Carmen, "What does a Dutch girl look like compared to you? You have a Dutch last name." I tried to calm Carmen down. Despite my nonchalant who cares attitude at that moment, I knew that Dutch bakery girl would always remain in Carmen's bucket list of people she hates.

Before the age of five and entering kindergarten not many questions were answered when I had a question, so I learned by observing. I had to admit I had no idea what that bakery girl was referring to, Carmen is a fine person. Carmen has dark hair, exotic features on her face, dark eyes naturally that her green contacts hide. I refer to her colored contacts as "oh, you got your fake eyes in today."

I had heard a saying before, "Birds of the same color flock together." Maybe that is what the bakery girl meant? People that look Dutch should stay together? Maybe it is so much more than that though. I had observed growing up that true authentic Dutch transplants were the most honest, the most hardworking, the most meek and sincere people in west Michigan. They had the cleanest house windows and perfectly maintained lawns and gardens. Many were farmers or would at least grow their own vegetables. They lived very conservatively in comparison to their income level. Most had no home or business mortgages or car loans. Every business started small and grew without bank help or bank interference. The authentic Dutch had a meticulous way of doing everything, from humble jobs or chores such as cleaning all the way to structured rigorous business positions, everything was done with competence and on schedule. The Dutch utilize their time well with a sense of pride and with little supervision needed. Which can explain their hard-wired DNA to not gravitate towards promoting and supporting large government and large government wasteful spending that the Dutch do not need. The authentic Dutch waste nor want, they ask for nothing, and do all they can for themselves and others. The Dutch in the Netherlands were the same as many Dutch families in west Michigan, almost exactly the same. I could easily see why other races of people would gravitate, migrate towards the Dutch and want what the Dutch have. However, the Dutch have what they have, what they have built for themselves based on Dutch DNA hard-wired into them which produces so much of what they have earned, reaped in rewards. I have never, ever in my life met an authentic Dutch on welfare or have asked the government for any hand-out, that would be inconceivable in the Dutch mind. Hitler and the Nazi's did not kill the Dutch based on what the Dutch were, the qualities to build a successful and sustaining society. However, the Dutch do not like war or Nazis. The Dutch have never started a war in history. The Dutch are peaceful humans by nature. I think it is difficult for the Dutch to understand countries or peoples that gravitate towards fighting, quarrels, and bloodshed as a means to win. The Dutch do not like bloodshed as a means to make a winning point or to win. The Dutch believe that being industrious and not lazy or full of excuses is how to live a good life. One thing about the Dutch is they believe what they believe and no convincing argument would ever pull them away from their hard-wired peaceful mentality, that's just how the Dutch are, their DNA dictates their behavior. If the Dutch faced a problem they would solve it without war, and ask no one to solve their problems for them.

The largest residential home in America was built and owned by a Dutch man, Cornelius Vander Bilt, The Biltmore Estate in Asheville, North Carolina. The largest home and estate in America was built without loans and debts, unlike how the American government functions in ideologies.

Sometimes I do wonder why the mass media does not comment on human DNA in relation to human behavior the way the media and internet will list DNA qualities of behavior within dogs and what to expect from each breed. Why are scientists politically restrained, socially restrained, culturally restrained from observing human behavior and DNA studies, to then report the findings to the mass media? What group of people would ban the study by starting fires, jumping on cars, looting stores and destroying property after property until the city looked unsafe because it is unsafe? The test group? DNA is related to behavior in all species. However, I did not always believe that, until one day I woke up and started observing. Then I realized through observations, I was the one being tested by the CIA.

In west Michigan growing up I would hear a term from Cindy and many others referring to people that looked too dark to be authentic Dutch as "dark Dutch," I am not talking about candy bars and sweets. I am referring to a term Cindy would say when talking about two of her brothers that looked so dark in features, hair, face, eyes, you could not even hardly believe they were related to the other three in the family that had blue eyes and blonde hair. Many other people in west Michigan would also comment when a person possesses a Dutch last name but does not appear to look Dutch because their hair, face, eyes were very dark, that person was termed a dark Dutch. Trust me though, Cindy's two brothers with dark hair, dark eyes, dark features were far better in morals than Cindy and her blonde haired, blue eyed brother Warren Stob. I would describe Cindy and Warren as evil with a dark soul.

I would notice the dark Dutch. My neighbors on Curwood in Lamplight Estates were referred to as dark Dutch. Their last name was Den Hartigh, a very Dutch last name, they wore wooden shoes doing lawn work. They came from the Netherlands and the parents preferred to speak in Dutch. Lisa Pare though maybe they were Italian. I think now as an adult and know more about the world they were Moroccan, they looked identical to people from Morocco or maybe Iraq. The Den Hartigh family were wonderful neighbors, I have not one bad thing to say about them.

My years at Unity Christian High and all my formative schooling in west Michigan were only around Dutch and German heritage children. In the history of Unity Christian High I do not believe there ever was any ethnic races other than Dutch or German or both. I realized that part of my formative years was a bit sheltering, I realized I lived in a bubble community. Crime did not exist in Unity Christian High or any of the Christian high schools in west Michigan. I always assumed there was no crime because we grew up Christian, we all had Christian values, so we were taught. However, when I look back to my childhood, I would ask myself, why would Cindy commit so many crimes? Cindy loved to drive around the country side, the rural areas above Grand Rapids and locate old homes that appeared vacant, lived in, but the people were not home. Then she would enter the home and snatch up any antique she could lift and stick in the trunk of her car. I would wonder as a child and later wonder as an adult, Cindy lived among the Calvinists and was one of them, a Christian, why would Cindy always commit crimes? Crimes I would never commit. If we went to a restaurant she would begin putting silverware from the table in her purse towards the end of the meal, and then scan the table for any other nick knacks she could take and hide, steal. Cindy's father Martin Stob is Scottish. Cindy's mother Teresa Vander Molen Stob is half Dutch, and Sicilian. Cindy's parents are from Chicago.

I lived in a bubble community growing up, and then for me to experience the world outside the bubble is when I began to notice differences in a dramatic way in how people other than Dutch and German operate under stress, from economic stress, to school stress, to work stress, relationship stress, I observed others were more prone to criminal acts than the Dutch and German people. I know it sounds politically incorrect. Yet if you turn on the T.V. and watch the news being reported about crimes or simply tune out T.V. and observe the world around you, there is something connected, attached, built-in, hard-wired into people's DNA that we cannot see with the naked eye that makes us human and different. Different in the reality of how both an American Pit-Bull and a Golden Retriever are dogs, but their DNA will exhibit different behavior, innately, naturally under stressful circumstances, or possibly any situation outside of receiving. You know; eating, drinking, and petting from their owner. I have heard randomly, periodically from time to time on the nightly news case after case from time to time how an American Pit-Bull got loose and attacked furiously a child or adult to death. Never has a Golden Retriever murdered a human in history. Beware of all dogs or some dogs? Based on knowledge? Based on experience?

While Carmen and I were in the Netherlands during the summer of 1988 we went to parties that the Dutch families would host. All the teenagers and young adults would gather from the small village at these parties, to see real live Americans, so many that attended the parties were not Dutch looking though. Over fourth of July, I remember asking my host family, "Hey, where are the fireworks being shot off tonight"? I was serious. They laughed. Everything American was missing, I just wanted to get back to the States.

They wanted their picture taken with us, it was quite a treat we learned to have Americans visiting their remote lost in time villages. We stayed with a nice host family. The house was attached to the barn and the grandma's portion of the house, which was an apartment size house attached to the other side of the house we stayed in. The grandmother was a chain smoker, I think that was when I began smoking, just one afternoon as she sat alone by her kitchen table, shut off from the rest of the family. I felt sorry for her. Her English was not so good, the conversations were limited, but I think she appreciated the company. She remarked in broken English, "You look just like the queen of the Netherlands, Queen Beatrix."

Carmen and I rode our bikes everywhere, even to the discothèques. I asked Carmen, "Why are you dating Doug now, verses Randy?"

"Why would you ask that question, Lori?" Carmen asked.

I responded, "Well, Randy thought the world of you, he put you on a pedestal. Why would you break up with Randy to begin dating Doug?"

Carmen paused, and looked at me, "I wish I could put Randy in a jar, and pull him out later, just in case it does not work out with Doug. Doug uses credit cards, he is more sophisticated than Randy. Don't get me wrong, I love Randy. I wish I could put him in a jar and take him out when I need him, or want him. But Doug has more business sense, he is an entrepreneur type. In fact, when he went to Cedar Point this summer he had his photo taken on "Fortune magazine," he is a real Donald Trump kind of guy image, that's his ambition in life, that's the kind of guy I am looking for Lori. Someday you'll meet a guy and have to decide what your values are, life is about making the right business choices for yourself Lori. Not some fantasy pursuit of philosophical nonsense. You are too dreamy at times, you're going to end up marrying some kind of artsy loser guy if you do not watch it! I do not want to live on Harold Street in Jenison Michigan, behind Sunset Manor, and just be average like what Randy would provide. I want a man who can provide well for me, the way I want to be provided for, you'll grow up someday and understand. Life is a process of recognizing opportunities. You do Lori, have a head for business, you're ambitious and bright, but don't let your artsy side take over and spend your days hanging out with artsy loser types. Stick with your sharp analytical mind, just be ambitious. Life is about business, you'll see what I am talking about someday."

Carmen always had such a philosophical spin on materialism. She explained to me that life is about attaining wealth. " I had no idea." I responded.

Carmen laughed as if remarking with her laughter how ridiculous I am, and said, "Lori, having money and a nice house is power, after all what else is there?"

I remarked, "Carmen, I do not see money and a nice house as the base of power."

Carmen completely disagreed and said, "Someday you will understand love and power, Lori." Carmen said soberly, then laughed.

I respond, "I think having people listen to me is power, not being silent or not being silenced is power Carmen."

I do like Carmen for who she is. I like her practical, stable approach to people, conversations, groups, she is so grounded in her speech and comments. She never acts odd or off, she is very, very dependable in a solid personality kind of approach to life. Never does she have "this bottled high energy," like I do in some social situations. Carmen is a Virgo, and is detailed in what it means to be stable, she is like a grounding rock. As sometimes my mind will just float, she likes to stop the daydreaming and make me very practical and have me concentrate on the here and now. She could make me feel grounded simply by the sound of her voice, so earthy.

Carmen often will crack up and say, "Lori, you say what other people think, and that makes you very funny, I can't believe you just say whatever is on your mind Lori. Most people just don't say those kind of weird things that you think of, your angle, your approach to how you see things is very unique."

While in the Netherlands I brought up another off the wall topic with Carmen. I brought up an unusual topic of conversation to Carmen one night. I could talk about just about everything and anything with Carmen, she liked that about me.

"You know Carmen, I remember life before I was born," I said one day in our shared bedroom as we sat and spoke near a window in the Netherlands at our Dutch sponsor's home.

Carmen responded back, "I read a book recently titled, **Children Of The Light**, gathered collections and cases of near death experiences of children. Such as a child having surgery then dying for a moment and coming back to life to talk about their experiences. Lori you mentioned the light, a radiant light, you have to read this book, when we get back to the States. I'll lend you the book to read, you just have to read it, it sounds like what you are describing to me."

"Carmen, I remember before I was born on earth, not dying and then remembering an afterlife. I remember the angels telling me my life on earth was going to be difficult, they were not even sure if I would live very long. The angels had their doubts whether or not I would be able to endure my life and make it."

Carmen just stared at me.

As Carmen grew into adulthood, she dropped adding "s" onto her words, a childish language habit I suppose. Or perhaps just speech impediment from another long ago life lived of hers. Perhaps the other teenagers teasing her made an impression for her to change. Carmen was able to break free from adding "s" to the end of her words as she grew into her late teenage years. Like the way my southern drawl turned into a real Midwest accent as I entered puberty.

I went on to respond to Carmen, "I do not remember dying for twenty minutes then awakened from a surgery sleep. I remember my life before I was even born, I remember life before I was a baby on earth. I know I will go back to the radiant loving and empowering group of people in heaven when I die on earth, it is where I was made and belong. It does not matter that a Christian memorizes and truly believes in a Bible verse recipe for entering heaven, rehearsing over and over a belief that Jesus died on the cross for their sins, or if a person goes to church or does not go to church. Those are relevant to society in how to judge a person, but that is not what God values, that's not how he judges, or sees as important to him. Christians have a quirky way of perceiving God, forgiveness, the afterlife and heaven, they memorize certain Bible verses in order so that therefore they can always ask God through Jesus for forgiveness of their daily sins so that they can enter heaven when they pass. You can go directly to God, you do not have to always go through Jesus when praying to God. Heaven was where my soul was created, shaped and molded. Heaven is where I belong, where I come from.

Carmen just stared at me. I broke the silence by adding, "Jesus never created a religion because he wanted to create a new religion. He criticized the Jewish religion, he was a critic of the Jewish religion. I see myself as a critic of the Dutch Christian Reformed religion."

Carmen just stared at me. I went on to say, "I am attached to heaven while on earth, and then I'll go back when my life is done. Going to heaven is not just believing that Jesus died for your sins, then you enter through an actual gate. I think the Christians of today have so focused on just a fire prevention method of interpreting their own religious beliefs of a possible afterlife in hell and thus have sized their belief system to fit their needs for the life they live here on earth. Like some ten step program that makes sense. Most Christian religions have become a narrow way of thinking. God has a different lens when looking through to people, the world. His lens is very different than most people can comprehend. Most

Christian devotional or inspirational books just offer this 'fuzzy feel good narrow interpretation' of the scriptures that we read in school." I spoke with conviction.

Carmen responded, "But that is what the Bible says, if you believe in the Lord Jesus as your Savior, then you will be saved. Murderers, robbers, and the gravest of sinners will be saved if they ask for repentance through Jesus Christ. How can you NOT believe that fact Lori? Christianity is based on that Biblical fact Lori! That is what we have been taught in school and church and home. Lori, I worry about your soul. You seem to know or believe something that is different than what we are taught." Carmen looked worried, she really looked alarmed and concerned all at once for me.

I responded, "I know the afterlife has to do with a person's soul, their essence, it is more than just a focus on just a brief passage in the Bible to memorize as such. Why has the rest of the Bible not been focused on, examined? The study of the Bible by Christians seems to be like an uneven mattress being worn, the other side, the other chapters and verses need to be explored and worn out by Christianity as well. I know the Dutch Christian Reformers view heaven as a large and wonderful event of a blonde haired, blued eyed protestant reunion coming together for an afterlife of an everlasting reunion. A church service with the best minister, the best choir to be heard. They believe God judges a person on how they are within a community such as Grand Rapids, Michigan. How many times they have gone to church. As if God is a school teacher holding up a who's who of charts to examine on how the outside world views them. God sees right through to a person's light within their heart. Who is the closest to that core of what God is, determines value and placement. If I never have attended church, or never go back to church, it has no relevancy to God, it may have relevancy to the church or church going societies. It does have relevancy to the individual for learning or acceptance purposes within that particular subculture. What does the Bible have to say about those who harm children? That they would be better off being thrown into the deepest part of the sea with an anchor around them than face the wrath of God. Why can't Christians focus on their essence, their souls, how they treat people, children, and animals?

Verses this instant forgiveness status quo they believe they have received and achieved for memorizing a Bible verse? The perception given to the world around the Calvinists is a far greater joy to them as is their central focus of their lives than how they behave behind closed doors."

Carmen just stared at me.

I remarked poignantly, "I am a critic Carmen."

Carmen responded, "Oh, Lori, I worry about you. You have got to start reading the Bible more, join a Bible study Lori, when we get back home, promise me." Spoke Carmen with her brownish-green eyes illuminating warmth for her cause she felt deep in her soul for me.

I responded, "I remember heaven before coming to earth. I remember having a choice whether or not to stay in heaven or take this life path that was already carved out for someone. I took this life path, just as God asked of me to do.

I remember heaven, and the doubts the angels had, they told me before I was even born it would be a difficult life, many hardships. The angels wondered if I would even make it, they were worried before I even was born."

Carmen just stared at me then said, "Just stop this nonsense talk Lori."

I further remarked, "Baptism, the debate whether baptism should be at infancy or young adult. It does not matter. The concept of water and the blessing, the symbolism, is not relevant to the point of believing or arguing that a child or an adult non-baptized will not go to heaven is false and absurd. The debate, the divide between many religions on symbolism, which symbol is correct is again not important to God. Catholics believe that Jesus should be symbolically left on the cross, stating in their symbolism to remember his sufferings, his death.

Protestant Christians have symbolically placed Jesus off the cross, an empty cross, stating on their walls and Bibles printed that Jesus has died and risen, and has taken their sins away, washed away. Outward symbolism matters not to God, not to the extent that organized religions have placed value on. God is not owned by religions. Religions do not own him, they have adopted the concept of God, molded and shaped him into their ideal for that generation, for that subculture. But they do not really know God, his energy, his realism, his message, his light, his energy, what he can do for this world. What he has done within this world is positive, it's what unites. Calvinism, Catholicism, organized religions, they mean to unite, but often divide, and keep dividing, so many sectors, and branches off the interpretation of Jesus alone. You would think there was in Jesus' day, many, not just one Jesus, think about how many followers of Jesus' teachings there are and have been, yet they all believe so differently. To the point of arguing and dividing among themselves, and forming pods of new seeding clones of their interpretation rendered."

Carmen slowly and seriously remarked, "You need help. Maybe a mental ward."

I responded with a smart smirk and quick wit, "Now Carmen, don't go nailing me to a cross. Or should I call you Mary?"

At times Carmen was my dearest confident, and other times she reminded me of a jealous black mamme lurking in a web spun in the corner. Peering out like a spider sticking onto her web as I developed and blossomed into a young woman before her. Afraid I might leave her watchful beady eyes someday was the look she gave me these days. Furious I might fall in love with a man and not confide with her anymore. Carmen was always commenting these days how independent I had become. She seemed to be between a cross of envy and a cross of a 'home body,' someone who doesn't dare explore the world and jealous of those who are explorers of the world. I predict that in a month or two when I leave for California Baptist College in August of 1988, that Carmen would soon settle down and marry someone before I even graduate from college. I could see that she would become a sea dwelling moon jellyfish, always to remain resisting that very real possibility, the second stage of her existence, which was to lift off the bottom of the sea floor and drift aimlessly into the wide blue sea around her, just exploring and seeing.

When I was not discussing the Dutch Christian Reformed religion with Carmen, Carmen would often say to me, "You are so mesmerizing, you have a unique perspective on things."

I once said to her, "I want to be a great spiritual leader, I want the world to wake up, philosophize with me. You Carmen, you could never be a leader, you want to be accepted too much. And therefore see life in the direction of the status quo, even if the status quo is wrong. I am more like my son of 2000 years ago, in this lifetime. But deep down I know you envy me, who I am, just as you did 2000 years ago in Egypt."

Carmen's reaction to my statement about her not being a leader? And her envying me from 2000 years ago? It was as if the bombs dropped over Normandy, as I looked at her, and she glared at me like a bull ready to charge the target full speed ahead. The silence was unnerving. The air grew cold…..I looked at Carmen, stared her back in the eyes, and said, "Yeah. Ms. Jewish Mary……you know what? I think you did an awful job as an adopted mother of my youngest son. The prized son I had with Octavia."

Carmen froze in instant hate towards me, her eyes glared fixated at me, she did not mutter or say a word back. She just looked at me with deep seated hate, I resented her, she resented me. It was her trigger point. I located that mental set off within Carmen about past events, as I assumed who I knew her to be in a previous lifetime. Carmen deep down wants to be me, a leader who is heard. But she lacks wisdom and believes leadership is somehow located on the outside of a person, or on the outside of a deed or action. Carmen desires in her core, her soul to be a leader, a philosopher, and always knew she somehow could not, or was not anointed by the heavens perhaps? I don't know, but she gave me a look to kill, as if she could have killed me right then and there, for blowing history in her face. I never brought up that subject again, ever. I know there are others just like her, by that statement, I mean there were other Jews in her group, her family way back when, that did me wrong. They feared or fear I would emerge in this lifetime with the truth to tell, Bessy had feared too. When I decided to legally come forward and tell of my past life and change my middle name to "Cleopatra," Carmen flipped out with a group of others just like her that did not want the truth to emerge. They wanted nothing to change in this lifetime. The Dutch Christian Reformers wanted no criticism, just like the Jewish Pharisees hated Jesus criticizing their

Jewish religion and ways 2000 years ago and were happy to see Jesus silenced forever.

Philosophy, literature, and leadership, I believe is what Carmen inspires secretly to be, and sees that in me? As one becomes friends over a long time you learn each other's trigger points, you just do, it's inevitable, for better, or for worse.

For me now though, I had dreams, I was going to begin the stage of life I had been anticipating for so long, to just explore further and learn about the world, that big open sea around me. I was eighteen now, I had survived Cindy's governorship over my life, so I had assumed. I had simply survived with a resilience of spirit. I Learned to stay quiet in that closed door society. I am tired though. It felt good to clearly just exhale and inhale from out of Cindy's grasp, from not sleeping under her roof and her rules. It felt good to <u>not</u> have to write a check for room and board this week, or any bill Cindy made me pay. Come to think of it, the only bill Cindy would pay concerning me and expenses of me was a yearly Life Insurance policy.

As I fell asleep in the Netherlands it felt good to anticipate a life never to be lived under Cindy's roof, rants and sudden rages experienced under her roof, ever again. It felt good to just live, to be alive, to be eighteen. I had made it to eighteen, for that fact, I thanked God that night in prayer as I fell asleep in the Netherlands. I would often wonder to myself in private thoughts, was my life's so unfortunate of events and catastrophes a result of voodoo residue from Bessy? Whom was Mary 2000 years ago, who really is Carmen. Or is this life path paved before me and behind me, a difficult journey of colliding and collaging fate of the most unusual artistic compositions God has formulated?

At times it certainly felt perhaps that the sinister side of voodoo was clashing with inevitable astrological events blueprinted within my life's path. Despite my heavy curiosities looming in my mind of the unexplored world, I began to drift off in thought yet again, again, and begin to slumber into a deep sleep that night in the Netherlands.

I dreamt that night that I was twelve again, wandering through a field of magnolia trees, under a tree I located a glass prism. I picked up the glass prism and saw dimensions of colorful lighted angles symbolizing my life……I was twelve, I wore a blue satin long flowing dress with blue sheer layers. A man, very distinguished, salt and pepper hair was holding onto me, not letting go of me. I remember how he smelled, like something erotic and sensual, of the islands, like coconut rum, something erotic, as if Atlantis was in his pocket, I was the sea, it was completely engulfing eroticism of the addicting kind.

I saw life through a glass prism that night asleep, just as I was supposed to see life. As if I had derailed and now was back on course once again, directed by this most alive and vivid epiphany awakening within my mind, while asleep. Life sparkled as I looked outward, as did my eyes at age twelve. It's like advice is served on a silver platter when you're twelve, life slows down and one absorbs what life is really all about, when you're twelve. You see the world differently when you are twelve, you are detached from adult mistakes and adult regrets when you're twelve. The world is real and alive, full of promise and hope. You learn through impressions, and sounds, your memory is keen at twelve. One absorbs philosophical thought more rapidly at twelve. You don't have many misconceptions at age twelve. You see the rawness, the realness in people, places and things. You can't tell a lie to a twelve year old, they see right through you at age twelve. You remember history, one's historical past in faraway places and times when you are twelve. "Medium Coeli," which is Latin for "middle of the heavens."

A Haze
CHAPTER TEN

Carmen really did display an exemplary level of devotion as my best friend during my junior high and high school years, as I was her friend, she was always beside me. Carmen was always there listening to my private hell of a life under Cindy's roof, as I smiled to everyone else on the outside. She knew both my happy and bubbly side, and the dark side of my home life.

When we returned from the Netherlands we also were turning the pages of what we were to become in this lifetime. Time moved slowly in the past with each passing year as we had anticipated our teenage finality to be, senior graduation from Unity Christian High. The summer of 1988 which followed our senior year graduation moved in adult time now. Suddenly a fast forwarding succession of sequences, life had become now. Life had instigated into a fast pace now, and many important decisions made in our senior year were beginning to transpire before our eyes, whether or not we liked it or not. I would be leaving Michigan soon my high school boyfriend. In the middle of what seemed like the best days of summer and kissing him behind the tall windy grass in the sand dunes along the sandy shoreline of Holland beach in Michigan, was now all rapidly closing in on a decision I had made earlier in the school year. In a week I would be flying to Los Angeles to attend my freshman year of college at California Baptist College located in Riverside, California. I would not miss the long cold winters of Michigan. But I did wonder about my boyfriend, if I had made the correct decision to move on into my college years. Leaving him behind in the middle of what was rising into what appeared to become a steamy next chapter of my life to explore. I had wondered if I had made the right decision to attend college in such a foreign place such as California. A culture so different than the one I seemed to grow accustomed to, the west Michigan Calvinists' culture was like the slow growth of annoying stubborn moss under a tree bed tainting the healthy tree. I assumed any culture would be better than the Calvinists. So I had hoped as I headed to the airport to board that plane for sunny and progressive California.

I choose California for the sheer understanding that people in California are independent thinkers, that sounded wonderful to me. The Calvinists around here were hardly, if any, independent of social normalcy. I knew one thing was for sure, my life appeared to be my own now. Not part of Cindy's control of torture and secrets within the closed door society of west Michigan.

I felt positive that I could now finally navigate through the waters on my own, aboard my own vessel in life, my life. I said goodbye to my high school boyfriend. He did not look as well with my distance to be as my expression had gleamed that afternoon in anticipation of a life far and away from the Dutch Calvinist suffocation of me.

When I look back through the pages of my life, I still do wonder if I had made the correct decision to attend that small parochial college in Riverside, California called California Baptist College. I was told during the application process less than a year before attending that particular college, "that Baptists are much like the Dutch Christian Reformers." I attended the protestant based college with reserves and regrets. I wanted desperately to use my college fund for a public college. But Cindy insisted I must attend a small parochial college or she would not allow my funds released out of my bank account, excuse me, "our bank account."

When at California Baptist College I must have stood out with my wholesome appeal, natural Midwest girl next door looks, long curly blonde hair and blue eyes, and happy smile. I looked like a combination of the Dove soap girl and Marilyn Monroe, well, at least that is what people told me. Most kids on campus had been sent there by overzealous and religious parents looking to change their rebellious son or daughter into an obeying student of God, structured within society. The parents intent was for their kid to not remain a disruptive member of society, I suppose was the basis of their parents decision rendered. There was one large dormitory for the girls, and one large dormitory for the boys. The campus looked Spanish in architectural details and materials. Many halls and buildings were closed though, not in apparent use. Hoarded junk seemingly piled up in the non-occupied rooms and buildings. Perhaps at one time there was a larger class size in attendance at this college, maybe in the 1950's or so.

I had applied for three colleges in California, Pepperdine in Malibu and another protestant college in Santa Barbara, California, called Westmont, all three colleges had accepted me. Because California Baptist was less tuition and less room and board costs, I thus had decided on California Baptist College. I thought the money reserved for my college education in my account would go farther, last longer. Cindy and her buddy Kim Livermore were very insistent that California Baptist College would be a good school because of its small size, reminding me often "You won't just be a number, you'll be a name." They both commented that a small school would be a school I could not get lost in, I would be able to locate my classes. I would not just be a number, people would know me by name.

There were many kids there from around the world on scholarship, simply because they were foreign, or fit into a minority class, they were given full ride scholarships. I talked with such students, they laughed and explained to me in their broken English at how easy it was to get a college education in America. I responded back truly offended, I said in proper American English slang, "You gotta be kidding right?"

I would often ask the foreign students, "But where are you going to go when you are finished with college life in America? When you are holding onto your college degree, where are you going to work and establish yourself?"

"Back home, maybe I'll stay, if I like America enough. America is very different." They would explain to me.

I was shocked, I was amazed and simultaneously horrified at how the educational system had created such a wheel in place, for foreigners to use America. I only hoped my college money in my savings account back in Michigan would last the next four years of my life on campus. But with my greedy mother Cindy, I doubt my college dream of graduating would come to fruition. But I had hope, maybe I'll become a resident of California and possibly get in State tuition rates. Yeah, that's what I'll do. There is always hope. Apply for something called "a grant," whatever that is.

It was quickly determined in the first week of college, like a pecking order in action, who the popular kids at this college would be, who was going to be part of that revered "popular group." There was a tall Hispanic girl with a strong personality that acted as if she was picking team players for her social click of sorts, her name was "Rachael." She was an angry, feisty, tall, dark haired, dark skinned Mexican girl, she loved listening to the heavy metal band "Metallica."

Rachael's parents sent her there to straighten her values and morals out. There were many kids just like her, attending college not on their decision based selection. Rather CBC was their parents decision rendered or demanded, as a last hope of the parents to turn the lives of their child around. Rachael also happened to be on the same floor in my dormitory, just down the hall from me. I was not drawn to this particular loud, wise cracking group of hodgepodge misfits. I was searching for my own, people like me, artists and writers and philosophers. But I was not going to locate that group here at California Baptist College. I felt lonely and disappointed in my college decision, right from the very beginning.

I did sign up for Philosophy 101. I liked the teacher, I forget his name, but I remember his teachings that semester. The first day of class he stated that he was going to teach us students "**how to think**, **not what to think**." To me, my stomach turned, the hair on my arm stood up, the concept sounded religiously dangerous to teach such a notion at California Baptist College, I was interested. He went on to say that all our lives we have been told what to think, but he was going to teach us <u>how</u> to think. He kept repeating that phase throughout my freshman year at college….."yeah," I thought.

I decided to major in journalism. I thought maybe I would begin a career after college as a reporter or anchor woman, and in the wee hours, or after work I would write novels, squeeze in the time for my passion, maybe a screenplay or two. The other kids at school laughed and sneered at what I thought. I saw them as degenerates, just as their parents probably thought of them as well and had no patience any longer to house them. As much as I did not want to become part of the popular group, I was dragged in somehow, chosen I suppose. But most of these kids only had something vitally missing in their minds, like lost causes of sorts. Many of the Baptist kids just passing through a college system that I just so happened to stumble across in my attempts to make something bright of myself. These popular college kids had a dangerous element to their aura, some of them that is. I was a bit naive, I sensed a bad aura at California Baptist College, from the kids, their socialization of religion. I was unaware of all the dangers lurking around me.

Hispanic Rachael from Modesto, California was always inviting me to come to this or that party. Rachael seemed more concerned about escaping her parents grasp on her life or mind than creating a bright future for herself. It was a mental, invisible grasp they must have had on her, but a tight hold nevertheless. Rachael was angry inside. Rachael was stuck in a stage of rebellion and anger at her parents. Rather than a fire in the belly kind of push needed to succeed, a drive to move forward with creating a brighter future for herself. She was mentally stuck in neutral, do you know that type? Too angry at something to be something, so she remains a loser. An angry loser at best, maybe something worse.

Southern California offered many dance clubs, it all seemed fun and liberating. No school dances though, just dance clubs to visit on the weekends in Riverside, just like the high school I attended in Michigan no school dances allowed. It all was mostly harmless weekend fun, but as oblivious as I was to the mental grasp Rachael was trying to escape in her mind from her parents domination of her life and choices handed down upon her, the demons stayed lodged in her head. Simply unable to escape, have you ever met a person like this before?

I was naive to the oblivious friendly trust that I so wrongly placed with Rachael in believing we could be friends, or that she could be anyone's friend.

Late in the autumn of 1988, during an accepted invitation to accompany Rachael to Modesto California for the Thanksgiving holiday long weekend, Rachael took me to a party in Modesto. A reunion of sorts, mingling with her old friends, her old gang of sorts. The same group of friends her parents had instructed Rachael to stay away from, as per was her parents intentions by sending Rachael to a conservative Baptist college in southern California, to rid Rachael of these ill-considered friends of hers. I am not sure when Rachael planned such a destructive organized act on me, or when she had deceivably decided to orchestrate such a sin, but she did. Like a spider Rachael weaved a web of deception around the woven fabric of trust and friendship, and California Baptist College.

I spent the Thanksgiving Day weekend with her and her family in Modesto, California. On the third and last night spent in northern California, Rachael stated to her mother that we would be out late, "not to wait up for us."

Rachael took me to a friend's house, a party was going on when we arrived. Rachael took me into the bathroom at the house party and introduced me to white lines of powder drawn on the lemon yellow bathroom countertop. She took a wide striped straw that had been cut down to size, and snorted up the white powder. She tilted her head back, her eyes watered a bit as her eyes turned slightly red around the pupil frames. Rachael gave a yelp, shouted "alright." Then stuck her head down in the sink to get a gulp of cool water as she threw her head back in one fluid motion.

Rachael moved her thick haystack black mane of hair around, then over her shoulder, and motioned for me to take the straw from her hand. I stated to Rachael, "No. Why would I want to do that?" I gave her a bewildered look, like no thank-you, ma'am.

Rachael responded with shaking that half sized down straw and said firmly, "Take it, take this Lori, it will make you feel good. I promise you." I felt curious now, what did she mean? So I did bend down over the counter and began snorting up the white powder, it burned my nostrils a bit, then I abruptly stopped just as quickly as I had begun snorting up the mysterious white powder on the counter.

Rachael insisted, "Just do it Lori, snort it up quickly, it goes better if you snort it up quickly, hurry, someone is going to know what we are up to and want in this bathroom."

I did then, just snort it up quickly as Rachael had suggested to me. I did feel better, my mood seemed lighter, happier. She was right, I did feel better inside, all of a sudden.

Rachael did seem to be in a hurry at the first party, just as we had only just begun to enjoy the party and conversations she was now urging me to accompany her to another party. When we arrived at the next party, it was dark, evening had quickly set in. We walked up the drive to the big old 1940's style two-story house. There were many cars in the driveway. I was surprised when entering into the living room area that only a handful of people were sitting in the darkened quarters sipping on their beer mugs and red plastic beverage cups. Rachael and I went in and sat down. She made quiet chit chat with the owner of the house who kept gazing at me, contemplative in nature. My mood was that of being on cloud nine, as I approached a sofa and sat next to very standoffish people next to me. As I tried to make conversation, I got the impression these shy people were just having a beer on a sofa and they did not know me personally and were already involved in engaging conversation prior to my arrival, so I assumed by observation of the room. They had nothing to say to me, they just kept glancing at the owner of the house sitting next to Rachael, whom remained unusually quiet. The mood or atmosphere in the room made one want to blurt out, "O.k., what's going on?" But I remained silent too.

I asked where his bathroom might be, I needed to use the bathroom. Everyone on the sofa looked at one another. Another glance came from another on a chair. I thought quietly and looked around the room with a glance of, "o.k., what's up?" What's odd about the question of "where is your bathroom?" I thought.

The owner then motioned for me to go upstairs, he had a bathroom up there that I could use. That statement was made shortly after Rachael had just suggested to me, "Lori, why don't you go upstairs and use the bathroom."

I got up from the sofa and headed up the staircase which leaned against a dark paneled wall. The hallway upstairs was dark wood, paneled in that dark seventies style paneling. I located what I assumed was the bathroom door and turned on the light. I gasped at what I saw next. There were well over five, maybe even eight men in their twenties or so, crammed into the one bathroom, like sardines with their pants pulled down. As if in a male sickening group anticipating my arrival to that bathroom. I quickly turned the light back off and then stepped backwards into the hallway. As I reached for the hallway entrance to retreat the same way I had entered down, I was then intercepted by two tall men before I could make it to the staircase. Bullish men who pushed me back into the bathroom by the mirror over the bathroom vanity by the door. I gasped, I froze. It was not a scene I had anticipated or ever thought would happen to me tonight or any night. The bathroom light was on again, the rest of the upstairs seemed dark as a dungeon.

I looked up in the mirror before me, I turned to leave again, exiting quickly, but the group was aggressive. I was scared and feeling intimidated. My pants were already pulled down by a clambering of male hands acting like ruthless teenage boys. I looked at the fogged up mirror in my horrifying shock, my head felt hazy like the foggy hazed mirror in front of me.

Before I could even finish thinking to myself about the beer I drank earlier, if that was causing, making me so slow in my responses to defend myself? Before I could even count the number of beers I drank on one hand, or how many men were in front of me and alongside of me, grabbing. Or faintly remembering back to that white powder I never should have ingested into my nostrils earlier, my sweater of a shirt was raised up by several hands working in succession in the same team goal of sorts, to get me naked. Some men held onto my hips, as others tried their male desperations on a young freshman girl, me. I was still in my virgin stages, other than my mother being inappropriate to me when I was under the age of ten, and something Cindy and her friend planned when I was nine or ten, other than that, those incidents, I was still a virgin. I surely thought as I looked around the bathroom, even if they try to have sex with me, it won't work. They will never be physically able to enter me I thought as I struggled from all the grabbing, the quest to defy the physical odds.

I said in a drunken eighteen year old voice, scared out of my mind, almost blackening out from the sheer element of the situation to come, I said this to the group of naked men I did not know, "O.k., so you saw me naked, can I get dressed now." I hoped it was all about maybe, perhaps, just seeing me naked, that girl next door kind of curiosity of theirs, and then this clambering of sorts will of those men would not stop.

As I again tried to gain my clothes back on my body, clothes that were no longer seemingly even owned by me anymore as the men gathered frantically just to own and touch. I made a firm statement they must stop, not a question I was given them. I went to pull my jeans up as many hands firmly pushed my pants off.

I reached to pull my sweater down, my bra nowhere even on me now, broken or lost, tossed? I could not tell. I screamed for Rachael, it must have been thirty minutes I was in that bathroom screaming for her, standing and screaming. One man fighting another man for his turn, scrambling men, pulling. I was outnumbered in this battle which I had lost before knowing I was going to be at war tonight. I screamed, standing in defiance as these men took turns, some holding my hips, I just kept screaming in pain. It was unbearable pain.

Some men grabbing and squeezing what they could reach, it was like a shark feeding frenzy of sorts, as I refused to lay down and be dragged into deeper waters. They raped me standing, one or two guys held onto me as I tried to get away still standing, while I refused to lay down. I knew instantly, repeatedly, sex was not a pleasurable act. I did not like sex, sex was not for me. It was in the bottom ten of my favorite things to do or endure. I just kept standing there unable to move from the number of controlling hands on my body. I could not make out which hands belonged to which man. I thought about kicking the guy raping me, or hitting the hands covering and grabbing my chest. I was scared to get violent with the group of unknown men for fear they would gang up and not only rape me as they were obviously doing to my virgin body. But afraid if I introduced violence to them, to this already dangerous position I am in now, placed in against my will. That indeed they would turn more mean and more violent as if introducing the element of gruesome hate and it would be bestowed upon me as well. I had to play nice at this point. As if my need to survive was kicking in, I had to play nice. I kept thinking in that cloud of massive fear and confusion of how this could possibly have happened to me? How did I get in this situation in the bathroom here? I do not even know these guys. This uncontrollable situation for such an in control kind of girl that I am. I don't know these men, Rachael does. These men I thought, they acted like Cindy would act as a man, if she was a man. There are demons inside Rachael to set this act up.

I remember a warning that public school teacher Diane Umstead, my apparent biological mother of Dexter, Michigan gave me about Greg her husband, or a live in boyfriend of hers, the guy she shacks up with in Dexter, Michigan. It is as if her prediction of the summer of 1989 came true a year before I even met her, of what would happen to me in college. She warned me that the Central Intelligence Agency that her husband belonged to were planning a series of rape attacks on me. Her words haunted me in 1989 as I looked back to 1988. When I look back to 1989 which was the year I met her, my biological mother at Bethany Christian Services whom looks nothing like me, a year before the 1988 rapes, her words haunted me. I filed what she said as "odd" and "off" and why would she say that to me? Weird. Diane Marie at the adoption agency in Grand Rapids, Michigan said strange remark after strange remark to me. Diane explained that Greg was a registered sex offender with the State of Michigan, however, the American Central Intelligence Agency provided him many names and social security numbers to be who they needed him to be for their secret government projects. I remember glancing at Diane's teeth the very first time we met while sitting on the sofa at Bethany Christian Services Adoption Agency. One tooth of Diane's the front was not perfectly straight in Diane's mouth. I had a memory flashback to when I was fourteen, somewhere in that age frame when I had my braces pulled off after two years of being on. It felt so good to have my braces off. My orthodontist was Dr. DeVries in Jenison, Michigan. Everyone noticed how perfectly straight my teeth were. Then I had to go see Dr. DeVries for a post dental appointment now that my braces were off. During that post dental appointment he said, "O.k., you're going to feel a little pressure now," pressure = pain. Dr. DeVries took an instrument and twisted one tooth in the front of my mouth as I squirmed in my seat trying not to scream at age fourteen. Then move forward a few years; That same tooth that Diane Marie has not aligned in her smile. I am just left staring in shock at that same tooth location as she talks to me at Bethany Christian Services. It was not until much later that I had cosmetic dental repair to have that one and only tooth shaved down and cosmetically filled and shaped to be perfect again, perfect like when I was fourteen again.

Diane Marie bragged on and on about Greg, and how Greg would pay-off and intimidate any attorney I might hire if I tried to sue for any wrongs done to me. Diane Marie Bomers Umstead explained that the CIA would have me raped to test my ability to remember. Diane explained that intelligence is also linked to one's ability to remember and the CIA had many testing projects lined up for me in the CIA's lifelong comparison of German children to other races of children. Diane Marie's voice, her handwriting, her bone structure, physical appearance and personality was so different than mine, so I had observed. I felt zero connection to her. I felt as if the adoption agency had introduced me to a complete stranger, rather than a person long lost in my past. The adoption social worker even remarked in encouragement of manners to draw any warmth out of Diane Marie at that moment and commented to Diane Marie, "Well, you can hug her now."

Back to the memories in California....

After about thirty minutes, maybe forty-five minutes, I don't know, it is difficult to tell time when you are drunk, high on a white substance. Unable to physically move to even reach for a clock, or a door, or my clothes, a phone nowhere in sight, to move from the sheer amount of men preventing me to move away.

One of the men who had stopped me in the hallway earlier, a ring leader, pulled me into a vacated bedroom. Pulling me from the men clambering around me in that bathroom. I remember "commotion," then men pushing and arguing. He then blocked the bedroom door with a chair and a dresser. Then forced me to lean over a chair, he repeatedly raped me, in yet another painful way. This lasted an hour or so it seemed, he raped me in every way possible, there was nothing he held back. I did not know sex was a painful thing, I had no idea about force, and destructiveness from a man. That was the first time I looked to men as a bit scary, I viewed Christianity as a scary society, a cover for criminals, even if they were far or I was far away from the Calvinism society in Michigan.

Finally Rachael knocked on the door, shouting his name. Was I too exhausted to scream anymore, or to frightened of this man doing these atrocities to me to stand on my own? It felt like a haze, like a vague obscuring act of violence that they did not see or feel as painful or violent, or even wrong.

Then, just then, Rachael and the other men pushed down the door, loosened bolts, and shoved aside the dresser in the doorway. The thirty something year old man kept on raping me, as if his private torture of me was now a show he himself could not stop. Rachael tried to push him off me, pulling and pulling, off my back, away from me as I laid draped over a chair. Rachael yelled at him to stop, she knew his name. At that point, I also realized her diabolical connection to that whole haze of a college experience. It was Thanksgiving weekend, 1988, Modesto California, I was eighteen. I think the raping fiasco had continued another twenty minutes while Rachael now clearly saw it had gone too far, I was bleeding. Blood trickled down the inside of my legs, it was going to take an army to get that man to stop. I know in my heart, the homeowner did not know me, I had never been to his house before in northern California. I did not know not one of those men either in Modesto, I only knew Rachael. I knew somehow she was the instigator, the planner, perhaps she wanted me to endure some ritualistic sadistic college hazing that she had construed in her demented mind with her old associates, her old gang. I also knew I would never drink or party on white powder anytime soon. I would also not go to a party unless I knew the person hosting the party. I knew I never wanted to experience sex again. And I also knew that Rachael was not my friend, she had been just an enemy lurking closely to me, pretending to be a friend of sorts, a confidant, to then plan a destructive event in my life.

I remember when we returned to her parent's house, when I thought she was resting in bed, I crept out of the bed and snuck into the kitchen to locate a phone. I called my boyfriend back home looking for a safe mental resting spot on which to lay, I told him of the horrors of that night, it must have been 5am Michigan time. I heard quietness on the other end of the receiver, I then heard him crying on the other end of the receiver, and then he just hung up. I was wired from all the substances and shocking events of that evening, I could not fall asleep. I had my eyes open to once again, very shocking behavior from one person to another. I never expected to ever have such a college experience to tell, after all, I was attending California Baptist College. A place where values are taught of a higher standard, right? The girl I shared a dorm room with at California Baptist moved out, to another dorm room, another floor. I would then know exactly what Diane Marie was warning me about when it came to CIA Greg, her registered sex offender husband from Dexter, Michigan.

How did I cope with the Modesto, California massive rape of me? I mostly stayed in my room. I went to class, I ate breakfast and lunch with my meal pass, then went back to my dorm room after classes to be alone.

One night I was awoken by a tall dark haired man in my room. His skin was light colored, he was not Mexican or ethnic. As I awoke I asked him what he was doing in my dorm room. Men are not allowed in the female dormitory, there was only one female dormitory. "How did you get in my room?" I asked. "Who let you up the stairs?" He punched my face. He did not talk. He let me know not to ask questions and to fear him, scare me into silence. That man also turned on the light in my dorm room. I do not know why he turned on the light, the bright light, I was able to get a good look at him, as perhaps he was able to get a good look at me.

After about a week I kept experiencing uncontrollable bleeding from my rectum as I went to the bathroom. A girl on my floor drove me to the hospital in Riverside.

I checked into the emergency room and had to lay down on the table, no drugs to calm the physical pain as I screamed, as one nurse held me down and another put a camera scope up me to see what was causing the uncontrollable bleeding from a place I would rather not say.

The female who put the scope up me said to the male nurse "She's been raped anally, she is torn tremendously." The two medical people gave me suppositories to stop the irritation for weeks to come as I healed internally. Was the hospital experience worse than getting raped in the first place at my dorm in the spring of 1989? That is always a rape victim's dilemma I suppose, and now I know myself personally of the pain involved. The hospital experience was just as bad, really. I thought to myself on the way home to campus, if that ever should happen again to me, I honestly do not think I would go to the hospital. I think I would remain quiet then to re-experience any pain of the trauma.

I mostly stayed in my college dorm room and studied in my room, then would go to bed, skip dinner, and stare at the ceiling until I fell asleep. I could not wait for the school year to end of my first year at California Baptist College. I would hear girls running down the hall, having fun, bonding as friends, and I would just stare at my ceiling scared out of my mind of making friends at California Baptist College……understandably so. I told Carmen about the rape experience, she told me that if she was a guy, she could never marry a girl who had been raped. I learned to keep my mouth shut about such experiences if I ever wanted to meet "Mr. Right" and move along with my life in the direction of marriage and family and happiness, well the pursuit of those wonderful dreams.

I got a job as a hostess at a restaurant that bordered California Baptist College. I could walk there from the school campus, I needed the extra money. My mother had called and announced that my money was almost gone in both my accounts. Where it had evaporated to that spring of 1989, only Cindy really knows. Cindy mentioned something that again resonated within me as "odd," "off." Cindy informed me that the CIA was going to send a man up to my dorm room in the spring of 1989.

It was not until about twenty, twenty-one years later did I see one man who raped me in Modesto, California. Out of all the places. He looked about my age, he was backed into a parking space at the back part of the parking lot at Bennett Woods Elementary school in Okemos, Michigan where my son Eddie was attending school. Diane Marie had told me that the Central Intelligence Agency would be sending men that had raped me in my past and place them in a setting near me, in strange and unusual ways, to see if I could remember. And to shake me up mentally and emotionally. More testing? Odd. Why? Why CIA? Then one day, later in my thirties while Eddie was still attending Bennett Woods Elementary, Diane Marie came to my house in East Lansing, Michigan to bring Christmas gifts. Diane Marie really did it up, she must have spent well over two hundred dollars on gifts for me. Ed my husband asked if we were ever going to meet her husband Greg.

Diane Marie had a strange look on her face as if she was weirded out by the question asked towards her. Ed asked if Diane had any photos of Greg her husband, and she mentioned "One, one photo when the kids were young."

I stared at the photo Diane Marie showed from within her wallet. My mouth went dry, my heart skipped a beat or three, or ten, as I held my wits. The man in the photo was the man that broke my nose and raped me in my college dorm room, not the rapist from Modesto, California, the dorm room rapist.

I felt sick to my stomach. Back to 1989 in Riverside California…..

I knew I did not want to spend another year at California Baptist College. I was not sure if I even wanted to attend college anymore. Therefore I never yelled at my mother Cindy for blowing my college funds behind my back in Michigan.

As much as I thought I had entered upon a new chapter of my life, a chapter I owned, I directed, peaceful, my life felt bombarded. College life seemed to become such a loathing disappointment. It was a birthday party with no balloons, gifts, or friends to sing happy birthday to me. I thought most of my high school teachers back in Michigan taught me more about what I know today than the majority of the teachers here, not all professors, but most. For the most part, the vast majority of teachers lacked key ingredients at California Baptist College, inspiration and knowledge of subjects that mattered most to me.

I would stare at my dorm ceiling alone, the light yellow painted block walls were cold, not just perceived as cold, they were cold to the touch. I would huddle in my comforter and love what that blanket could do for me. I wanted to be a writer, perhaps write a song, or screenplay, or novel, or interesting article in a newspaper. I liked to stay huddled in my comforter and just dream, dream while still awake in the darkness of my dorm room. I always believed writers to preserve their thoughts, experiences, creativity, and most importantly their faith in print. We all have a story to tell for others to receive encouragement, inspiration, education, entertainment, and more. Writing is a way for an author and the readers to connect with each other over a message. If a book's message is strong enough and is shared by many, it can create change. I wanted to embark upon a ship with other writers, "I'm ready, I'm ready," I thought. I wanted out of California Baptist College, but they had my money for the school year, no refunds.

Lurking around the corner was "spring break 1989." Fast approaching a time of wild fun for college people alike. But I thought I would just stay in my dorm and enjoy the quietness of no stomping and running and the shrill laughter on that 3rd floor, for at least a week. I desired the comfort of quietness, it was my peace. But the other girls on that floor convinced me to go with them to Rosita Beach, Mexico for spring break 1989. I knew Rachael would be going, she would be the loudest and drunkest person at each of the party clubs we'd go to, I could avoid her and her entangled ways, so I thought. Rachael was like an enemy from a past life coming back to haunt and torture me, she looked at me that way, I could see it now. I reluctantly agreed to pack a duffle bag and ride along in the packed caravan of cars headed south to the border, the other girls convinced me.

I had money with me, in my purse from my after school job of being a hostess and waiting tables. I gave money for the hotel room, it seemed half the college was there in Baja. You could walk from your hotel room to most of the outside bars, one after another bar or club, many had outside dance floors too. The resort town had deep fried fish tacos, two tacos for a dollar. It was a normal kind of college spring break in many ways. Lots of staying up late night dancing and partying in the clubs along the ocean seaside resort town that seemed to have awaited our business that we brought to that area along the ocean.

On the second or third night in Mexico we noticed more and more kids we all recognized from school were arriving. One night Rachael and I began talking, she seemed friendly enough in conversation, I was now talking to her only to appeal this pecking order of sorts, and she was the alpha male, so to speak. So therefore, to make my trip comfortable, I responded to her while she talked with me in the hotel room as I got ready for another night of partying. All of us girls piled into a car and headed to another hotel to pick up two guys from our college that were also in Mexico for spring break. Rachael and another girl asked me to get out of the car and "go get the two guys." Rachael gave me the room number and said they were going to ride with us or follow us to the club. The guys I knew from college, it did not seem odd or strange at all, her request to go knock on their hotel door.

I jumped out, naïve in being helpful and went to the second story door to knock. They both answered the door and said they were not ready to go yet but would be ready in a minute. They asked me to come in, one guy was engaged to a girl and was always seen on campus with his girlfriend, they headed a Bible study class together on campus. I did not appear apprehensive, because I wasn't. The other guy, his name or nickname was "Kiwi," he was a tall, friendly sort of fellow, a goofy guy from New Zeeland that everyone on campus talked with, laughed with, very friendly and outgoing. I went in and sat down on the end of the bed as they directed for me to wait, then I looked at them both by the door. I noticed one guy move the slide of the metal rope across the top of the interior of the hotel door. The other guy turned out the lights as they approached me sitting in the dark of the foreign hotel room, on the end of the bed.

"What are you guys doing?" I asked in a startled voice.

"Just calm down, calm down, we are not going to hurt you." Spoke the words of Kiwi.

"Calm down? I want to go, everyone is waiting on us in the car, you're supposed to follow us, we're goinna miss the party." I said firmly as I pleaded out of this uncomfortable situation. What appeared innocent, then turned into a uncomfortable turn of events, a horror, my horror that is.

Both of the men were on me, Kiwi was holding down my shoulders kissing on my face. The other man had his pants off and was pulling my skirt up, he was the first to rape me in that hotel room. I could not stop him from what happened next, I kicked, and kicked. Kiwi jumped up and held my knees down and open on the bed as I tried to push that scoundrel off from me. Kiwi then took the position of that once Christian man. I just could not believe their actions towards me, the sadistic system of these Christian believers, they could get away with murder here! I wondered where the girls were that were supposedly in the car, we were going to a party and where were they? It was a knock that never was heard on the door during my ordeal.

I thought as I pleaded in vain to break away from their impending hands and body movements. I tried to verbally reason with Kiwi, he had an easy going stable personality. I could convince him to stop, "just stop" I pleaded in earnest, "I won't say a word to anyone, I won't go to the police, this is not a good idea to do this to me, I could get pregnant!" I pleaded and cried.

They just both told me to "shut-up, and stop crying." As if they were scolding me!

I then heard a knock at the door, more like a fervent pounding.

"Go away, go away, we'll catch up to you later!" Kiwi and that punk of a Christian example said in unison to the intrusive pounding into their sinful deeds saved by a thinly sliced metal door, hiding what they were doing to me as Kiwi covered my mouth tightly.

I kept pleading with Kiwi, "I have a boyfriend, I have a boyfriend, don't do this to me."

Within fifteen minutes I realized the hell was over, there was not going to be a winning of an argument, or a plea that would work, my rational argument mattered none at this point anymore. My terror was all over and I was free to get up and walk out. Kiwi drove me to the club where he assumed the others might be, in one of the string of clubs along that strip. Was I to call the police? Mexican police? That sounded scary as well. I do not even speak Spanish.

I realized what those two men must have thought that night as they both smiled, they looked as if they had been forgiven in their minds before the act even began. A void of conscious was prevalent, from my mother Cindy in my childhood located in the wholesome Midwest, to faraway places like this in Mexico. As if forgiveness by Jesus was instant coffee to them, instant forgiveness of ones deeds is what was the resounding and very prevailing philosophy of then, as it is now as I write my memoirs, as it was also growing up..........

"Just believe in Jesus, and you will be forgiven." The prevailing and overwhelming message radiating through the churches. It was unheard of to not believe in Jesus's forgiveness, and not have God's forgiveness rendered upon any action. To ever bring up the idea that Jesus wants you to be accountable for your actions was a very unacceptable theory within Christianity. Judgment of sins against another was lost in the back of a fairytale, not reality to these Christians all alike.

I thought the worst is behind me. I had hope. I was positive. I am grateful I did not get pregnant from their mistakes south of the border. But like an inward growing flower, eventually I would be summoned to begin my outward push to the sun and begin writing down my philosophical memoirs.

I joined the group of girls at the outside dance club, one girl asked me "What took you so long to arrive to the club?"

I responded with just a smile and resilience of spirit, "Oh, I don't know." I was not going to be dragged down by those men, not have fun, I was going to forget those two men won. I would create my own reality of that event I thought, and pretend as if nothing took place. Yes, I would act as if I was not filing that tragedy in my mind, it never happened. I was going to throw that memory file collected towards the back of my mind like an unwanted slide show card. As if one can really edit the bad memories. However, at age nineteen like any year in my life, it seemed like a positive plan.

I hated college in California, I hated spring break 1989. I thought the people attending school there walked vicariously through life like God was on their side, they could do no wrongs collected as sins in God's tracking system. Forgiveness mattered most to them. Church was an alibi for their character witnesses, for the Christians, no one would believe they committed any crimes on or off campus. All because of the notion they attended church and were white collar people, they looked wholesome and good.

Going to church was the norm, the status quo. Belonging to Christianity was a ticket to forgiveness for any acts committed today, or yesterday, or in the future, in their eyes. Delusional as a way to keep Christianity afloat for future generations to come, for the fairytale of Christianity to never have an ending.

Committing crimes, going to church, asking for "Jesus' forgiveness" and staying very tight knit within their Christian society like a school of fish, alike in species was their prescribed therapy of a religion that their preaching ministers processed. Their philosophical belief so practiced and revered, no matter where I traveled and lived.

Me? My perception of California? I hated the loneliness of California. I felt so sad there, it was instant. As soon as I landed on that ground called California, it was as if you could feel sadness blowing through the dry heat breeze, the air.

The people were superficial, not one person shared a meaningful conversation with me during those two semesters at California Baptist College, or outside of the college. To be a writer you need to be real, to capture what is. It was a society I wanted nothing to do with, lacking in depths in what I need in people, the realness to be felt in their hearts. They did not even appear to be happy or sad, they just existed on a superficial plane of existence. Revolving in a cycle, a system, not even knowing why?

That spring of 1989 towards the end of the semester I had a very real and vivid dream. I heard the strumming of a fiddle being played in the background, and banjo and bass, cords of southern mountain style music, real old fashioned style southern music. Sounding so familiar though, it looked familiar somehow in my dream, the land I was being carried to…

The next day I stepped out of my college dorm. In that dry dusty hardened ground I drew a ship with sails in the ground, signaling Alan to return to the ship control room. I needed him.

To die is to break through to the other side, to feel inside another, to feel their pain as you have bestowed unfortunate events upon them during your lifetime and their lifetime lived on this earth. To live is too feel you have a sense of God, to believe and understand…..to stay connected to the other side, heaven, while on earth, as one enters the sacred hall of mirrors into the reflection of your personal soul. Your cocoon to butterfly process can happen, your radiance can blossom.

Many people define God's location by bricks, mortar and church addresses. Or point to the clouds for that fairytale ending, but he seeps through all and is very expansive by nature….. "God works in mysterious ways," is what is written in the Bible.

As much as so many people can be monsters that I encountered and will countlessly encounter during my lifetime, so opposite can be described of others along my journey.

Gods and Monsters
CHAPTER ELEVEN

I was nineteen when I finished my first and only year at California Baptist College in Riverside, California, for those two semesters to be done was a chapter closed in my life. I returned to Michigan and decided to accept an offer to go to a rock concert in Detroit with Robin, a school acquaintance from Unity Christian High located in Hudsonville, Michigan. Bruce Springsteen was playing in Detroit, "The Born In The USA tour." Robin had won free tickets from being the tenth caller on the radio. We took a shuttle bus from Grand Rapids to Detroit with the radio station crew, and a few other lucky winners.

It was a packed concert in a large amphitheater in Detroit. Robin and I stood separate from the others that had tickets for the various winning seats, everybody who had winning tickets had seats in different rows. During the concert I felt the eyes of someone staring at me, as if trying to draw my attention to the left side, and back one row. He had green eyes, a slightly Jewish looking nose, brown hair, not dark silky hair, just brown, medium brown hair. He was not your typical Dutch or German looking guy that I see so much of in Michigan. He was about 5'9, maybe 5'10, he had a stocky, husky build, muscular arms, and very warm penetrating green eyes that would not let go of me. He hardly watched the concert I observed as I tossed my head back to keep feeling his warm stare upon me. As our eyes began locking, I thought to myself, I know this man, from a previous life lived….but what life? And what role did he play? He is just more than some man staring at me, this is just not any acquiesce acquaintance type of moment, it just wasn't. He was someone in my past, a past life lived, but who is he inside? I wondered.

If you were to hand me a blank canvas and have me paint a portrait of my dream man, to paint a description of the ideal man, I would say six foot, two hundred pounds, dark brown silky hair. The kind of silky dark hair that falls just right and shines after a shower and hair tossed dry from a towel. Sensitive to only me inside his soul. Someone I deeply bond with on the ever elusive yet magnetic sensuous balancing of the male, female, dualities of making me feel like a woman. I desire strong chemistry felt between me and a man, and that magnetic connection was most obviously taking place, in the oddest of places. Detroit. In a large amphitheater with millions of people, it felt as if it was just us, in relative importance of this moment…….

Medium complexion, yet not tan, broad shoulders, strong knees and leg muscles…..

Well, for a moment you can wipe that "ideal" description of my dream man I always wanted and had envisioned coming into my life. This man staring at me was not my completely in full drawn description of what I thought I would want in this lifetime lived. He was though, very, very mesmerizing in his stare towards me. Which was very luring in itself, his warm penetrating green eyes. It was as if he was saying with his eyes, I am going to give you all you want in this lifetime, I will be your protector. How can a look do that? I don't know how to explain it, that promise just penetrated from his eyes so real of the biggest kind of love ever towards me. His stare at me was how he saw me not as just any nineteen year old, but he wanted to put down a sword and walk across enemy lines and seduce me gently yet bravely in the desert…….could he be Octavia? I did not feel from his stare that he was Marc Antony, as I remember Marc Antony 2000 years ago. This man, he seemed focused, and focused on me. What is going on with my life? Sometimes I want to faint, I feel dizzy at what I can see in others, the past life regression stuff.

I wore a navy blue and green plaid one piece dress, a short dress, no nylons, and slightly flat grey shoes, which I had slipped on before leaving the house. My hair was bobbed in curls like a Marilyn Monroe style hairdo, reddish-blonde in color. I weighed 122 pounds, I was 5'4. I naturally have strong developed legs and had been jogging as a sport for a year. I was curvy and soft, yet tone in my legs, and nineteen, and well…… very developed. This man I had staring at me, he wanted me in a previous lifetime as well, he saw right through me. He wanted me to accompany him back to Rome, and leave Marc Antony behind. For me to come back with him, Octavia….. after I lost a battle, against him? This man staring at me was with a date, not very attractive, maybe just a friend who was a girl he happened to take to the concert? He stared at me during the entire concert. Every time I looked back at him over my left shoulder, his warm green eyes kept penetrating through me. As if he wanted me to feel his love, his admiration through his eyes somehow.

Nearing the end of the concert, I saw him stopping for a moment in his staring and not wanting to lose sight of me. As if he put down his scepter and crossed over a dry, dusty desert cement foundation beneath his boots to finally reach me in this lifetime. As he slowly and deliberately wrote down a message and his name and phone number. The message read, "You are my blue star." He walked slowly towards me, never looking down or away. His gaze to my blue eyes was fixated, very non-wavering, and yet probingly warm. He did not want to open his mouth and shout over the loud music. He slowly passed the note to me as if to give me a slow pause about that moment in time. As he was handing me the note, slowly our hands touched slightly. I could feel the masculine touch of his skin touch the soft lily white skin of my hand.

The lighting in the amphitheater in Detroit was dark, and my senses perked up, I smelled a warrior. I saw brown leather strapped to a shiny silver iron plate on his chest and shoulders. His Roman red feather hat resting on his arm as he handed me the note, his hair was ringlets of blonde curls for a moment. When he walked away slowly, he was wearing jeans and boots, and smelled nothing of a warrior, his hair was back to being medium brown. We had exchanged phone numbers, and more than that, we discovered something in who we were in a previous life lived. He said something to me as he tipped his neck slightly and leaned forward, he took a whiff of my perfume of 1989. A well-worn collaboration of expensive Poison perfume and Liz Claiborne perfume, and then he whispered….. "You smell like sex and candy."

I pulled the lollipop out of my mouth and said with a witty smirk, "In heaven there is no candy. I want all I can get in this lifetime." Then I smiled at him. He looked very mesmerized, contemplating in nature as he searched with a glance downward at me, as if to remember my response always. He smiled back.

My mind raced back in time too….had Octavia falling in love with me 2000 years ago when I was a warrior queen in a previous life lived? Is that the memory that surfaced just then, but how could that story be? Did this man want me to accompany him back to Rome after a lost battle? Was my last child I bore 2000 years ago, his child? Our child? From an affair of me conquering all I could in the only world I knew back then…..2000 years ago….seemingly surfacing now in this lifetime? I felt faint for a moment, almost delirious. I can only scratch my head and wonder……..what a life, and what a memory which just surfaced as we touched ever so slightly. Nevertheless a serious past life regression emerged, just then. I felt anger and passion, dread, a combustion of a past life regression flooded my mind and reverberated throughout my body.

Why do I feel I am always meeting people from past lives lived? But not one person is a double of the other, this is such an original drama. I felt like a brick hit me over the head, and I was waking up from a dream….but my visions are real, and so is my life, so are my memories, my history remembered.

He called my mom's condo in Jenison, Michigan where I resided the summer of 1989. I did not know he had called while I was away at Holland beach. However, I learned he was trying to communicate again, my mother Cindy went ballistic when he sent a letter to me, via her condo mailbox. She, Cindy, wrote him back after a phone call she received from him, and she told him off in a letter back to him, never did she want him to call or pursue me, her young daughter, her only daughter in which she wanted to control. She asked his age, then she told him off more. I remember the number, the age she said he was, which really was not his age. And now in 2009, I understand the numerology of his message when I was nineteen…...." 3+5 =8." The message was intended for me to understand later in this life passage if he could not become my husband, if he could not marry me and crown me queen in this lifetime. Why does it take me so long to understand the coded messages? I was almost forty when I understand his secret encoded message, and how he would communicate with me in the future with encoded messages, word plays, strange usages of words and phrases spoken. Earth was a learning playing field……

At times though, the heavens tell me things too, I channel the heavens. Yet unforeseen sometimes the angels just close the passage, close the tunnel of higher information off, and I can't receive information on what is going on in the heavens, or what is going to occur next on earth, in my life. I know what I know and that is all the angels in heaven will allow for me to see into the future. It is as if the angels close the lid over the tunnel and just walk away at times, sometimes for long periods of time. I am not a predictor of future events by my own free will or a skilled talent as a psychic to hire for a party. I only know what the heavens channel to me in their unpredicted fashion, not verbally heard, just information passes from above like a beam of light through me. Like how information is transmitted within a computer system to the computer screen, not actually seen, the information just appears.

He is Octavia, the man I met at the rock concert, and in a previous lifetime I lost a war to his Roman armies. In this lifetime, he comes back full force and lives as Alan. I do understand, it took me the longest time ever to put together that numerology of "3+5 =8." Power. Infinity. The number eight.

In a previous life lived I had naturally black hair, ironically though, my face looked the same, very European in white skin and shape, my nose looked similar 2000 years ago. My eyes in Egypt were more sunken in, not as they are now, as I recall what I looked like in my dreams. I have blue eyes and light eyebrows now, but back then my eyes were dark and I had dark eyebrows and lashes. I remember exactly how I looked based on the many dreams and nightmares I have had growing up in Michigan. In Egypt I would use henna to dye my hair red, then I would wrap my hair in a bun under a black cropped wig. Only my lovers knew what color my hair was under the wig. I would only take my wig off in private for my lovers to then pull down the bun atop my head and let my red locks unfold onto my shoulders. I think this man at the rock concert knew that in a previous life lived. That 2000 years ago I used henna, a natural red dye. But my people I governed over in Egypt 2000 years ago did not know me as my lovers did in private. I wore a black wig, a large ornate headdress. Who were the men I seduced back then, 2000 years ago? Only the most powerful men of that time, other than seducing for more power and to create alliances for my kingdom I remained celibate for my country I ruled over. Celibacy was my secret I pass on into this lifetime on how a woman keeps her power, it is a powerful tool. Why? I believe an orgasm releases power and therefore I would contain my power. It is an ancient secret I still believe holds truth and value, even today. Seduction is enticing, but sex is a far different category and knowledge, and an orgasm, the climax, is a release of built up power. Are you aware of this, how a woman can be so powerful? Or how a man can control a woman? It never was or ever will be through the mind.

I never spoke to Octavia in Michigan. A friend of mine, his name is Jamie asked me if I wanted to go down to Atlanta, Georgia, to move to Atlanta in 1989. I had no furniture to sell, just clothes to pack and a used black Mustang car I owned to get down south. Jamie and I took turns driving Labor Day weekend 1989. I had hundred dollars in my purse, Jamie had his dad's credit card.

I remember the drive down south to Georgia as we drove through the green rolling hills of Kentucky. I began to smell a familiar scent woven within the familiar southern heavy humid air I once knew so well, the greenness and the warmth in the scent so familiar. How could a scent carry such memories back to me? I don't know. I can't explain every mystery I experience. I felt as if we were driving to a place I had seen before, been before, I was going back in time to a familiar setting, in the south. This was not an adventure of exploring a new place to live, a new start in unfamiliar territory, not at all. I was driving back to something, some place I knew well. My senses perked up at the sights and scenery all around as we zoomed in my car through the large landscape of the south. As we drove further south, deeper into the south I had this overwhelming sensation come over me that I had once long ago been on a horse and carriage, along this once dirt road now paved in asphalt. The vast green terrain through Tennessee and the rocky Appalachians trail welded a wealth of traveling memories, how could this be? I thought silently as I peered in wonderment out the passenger side window. What was I getting close to in my past? More flooded memories of a past, a lover, and an aristocratic family in an antebellum mansion came into focus as we drove right on past a sign written boldly, "Welcome to Georgia."

The orange clay soil along the car, the rocky hills at the tip of northern Georgia, made me feel like I was close to something I once knew and loved. I was really close to where my past was now confronting my present life's direction. I was close…to my life…..the life I loved….. the life I once was in, in a different time period. As if I held a treasure map and I was almost to my pot of gold, buried in the past, here, somewhere, and close. I rolled down the window further to investigate what was supposed to be my first time in the south, Georgia. I kept breathing in that familiar air, the humidity was actually a transfusion of refreshing air into my body, one that I welcomed. I felt anew, I literary felt reborn. I felt dizzy at the collision of realizing that I instantly felt as if I was born in Georgia as just then my past life in Michigan felt more like a distant memory as we crossed into Georgia. But I somehow had these past delusional memories of growing up in the north during the 1970's and 1980's, it was an odd combination, and a reality my mind could not shake off. The memories of the 1970's and 1980's, growing up in Michigan were real memories like a haunting, some still too harsh for words and far too disturbing to write about. But what I see, feel, and I am experiencing right now, this is where I am from suddenly, this is where my family is from, my roots I loved so dearly. I felt as if a flash of a loving family I adored, and my black mamme just surfaced. I quickly began turning the pages to see where they might be in my story, my life, my mind. And then the pages just ran blank, no more pictures in my mind to zoom in on, focus, find, locate, I am almost there......

Darkness began setting in the south, the landscape grew dark, I remember these southern evenings from before, but how? And how the air grows a chill as if coldness seeps into the black night, trapped within the lingering balmy wind and humidity, there is a chill, so familiar is this night I thought. I remember lots of nights like this in my past, from a past life, old southern music began to play in my head. And then I zoned back to the present, from an apparent past life regression. The pause button stopped being pushed and I was brought up to speed...so to speak, in this lifetime, 1989. I was nineteen as we traveled further into the deep south, further into Georgia. I was a young adult, not a child anymore.

Jamie's dad was a business pilot for Joe Rogers who owned all the Waffle Houses in the south. We moved into his father's house in Marietta, Georgia. I quickly found a job at Winston's Pub to create an income for us, less the dependency that a lack of money can bring a person. Never did I think I would cross paths with the acquaintance I had so briefly encountered at that rock concert in Detroit, ever, really. I never really gave it a second thought that the CIA would be waiting for me in Georgia ready to resume stalking me and recording my life in Georgia. I had no idea how structured and immense the CIA was and is at age nineteen. I had no idea of the dangers ahead of me now that Cindy was not part of my life. With Cindy in Michigan I thought danger would never enter my life again. Have you ever had a time where someone terrible exits your life and you just assume life will now be easy sailing for here on out? Well, that is how I felt in 1989 leaving

Michigan and leaving Cindy. I had no idea when I left Michigan and the CIA with their scattered and structured bizarre and harmful CIA classified top secret criminal projects in Michigan that I would actually be bombarded in Georgia by CIA agents providing me with such shocking inside information about the CIA. Cindy had packed me a pair of high heels, pink lipstick and pink lip gloss, and said directly to my face as I left Michigan and her household, "Don't you ever get drunk. Let the men get drunk."

Honestly, I had no idea what she was talking about, really.

I got a job working at Winston's Pub as a waitress in the autumn of 1989. I served English beer, fish and chips, chili and burgers. There was a girl there by the name of Sophie. She was the head server and had been at that pub since the grand opening a few years back. Sophie had regular costumers that liked to sit in her section to chat with her during the routine process of eating a hot meal of burgers and drenching the taste buds of old familiar beer. But a problem was brewing now, some of her "regular" customers, families, couples, etc. were now wanting to sit and dine in my section, liking my bubbly fun personality over dinner and drinks too.

I could hardly keep up with the fast pace of restaurant bar business. My section was overwhelmingly full of people who wanted to talk with me, laugh with me, order more beers and burgers and desserts from my section. By the spring of 1990 Sophie complained to the owner that I was taking her regular customers away from her causing her to lose big tips, her income, whatever. I did enjoy that English bar atmosphere. I made great money in a wholesome way, and had my days free to read and study philosophy and literature on my own, and scribble down my stories. I only worked five hours a night, four nights a week.

Autumn is my favorite in Georgia. I especially like the month of October, it is like having Michigan's Indian summer all season long in Georgia. I love how the fall leaves blow on the ground, yet the weather is warm like a late summer day in Michigan with a slight chill in the air at night. October and November in Georgia is a wonderful blend of summer and fall weather, full of hearty woodsy scents, all month long.

I took some modeling headshots and several modeling photo sheets to Take One in October of 1989, a modeling and talent agency in Atlanta, Georgia. The photo modeling/talent sheets had been photographed in Beverly Hills while I was attending California Baptist College in Riverside. The modeling jobs along with waiting tables at Winston's Pub was how I was saving money to get an apartment and furniture of my own, and eventually a house, I thought. I want to own my own house, free and clear, a real Georgia mansion with a plantation style veranda perhaps. I want to feel as I did back in the 1860's, if I could only go back. I'll know it when I see it, and walk into that house! I thought.

In 1989 in Georgia I was bubbly, young, I lost a lot of weight, maybe twenty pounds, weighing 116 pounds from my weight fluctuation days of 142 pounds in high school. My hair was ringlets of long pure spun blonde curls, blue eyes, my natural Bavarian looking face with creamy ivory complexion seemed welcome in these parts. The local southerners seemed to take pretty well to me, I loved southern cultural, how everybody just seemed to start up a conversation with you no matter if they knew you or not. My personality was very much innately just like this southern warm hospitable culture I thought. I never really felt like a northerner, ever, really. I can honestly say, I really never felt like a damn Yankee, really.

And certainly I did not see myself like one of those many ignorant John Calvin Calvinist cardboard cut- out papier-mâché wanna be's either. I wasn't sure if I was one of those good ol' Southern Baptist types. But I was southern inside. I was back in the south, this is where I belonged. It was just instantaneous for me, that feeling of "at last, the meaning of my life's direction, my life's roots," so to speak, was resonating in my soul. I belonged here, these people accepted me as part of the south, and I did feel like I was part of the south, not in a prejudice way, just in a southern rootsy kind of way.

Jamie (James Smith) worked for his dad and planned on staying with his dad just living off his father's wealth until that gig of Jamie's was worn out like an old t-shirt he would wear. Eventually Sophie at

Winston's Pub convinced the owner Bob to let me go, out of sheer spite and jealousy on her part, like how a jealous child acts when someone plays with their toys. I would learn that jealousy from others would become like a plague upon my life. Although at this young point in my new existence, well, I just did not know how prevalent that theory would become, or should I say, unfold.

During the early 1990's I wanted the Dove soap or Milk companies, or McDonalds or Coke-Cola companies to call on my Atlanta agent, maybe Estee Lauder or Chanel. But it was usually always Playboy executives calling from Chicago down to Atlanta, they would call Atlanta model and talent agencies always in search of the upcoming Bavarian-American girl next door. I guess I had to travel all the way from Michigan, the heart of the Midwest is full of Bavarian transplants, to then be discovered in Atlanta at age nineteen-twenty, ironic, it really is, so I thought.

One day in late spring of 1991 my agent from Take One Agency of Atlanta sent me to Stone Mountain, Georgia to meet a photographer for an Atlanta Magazine, featuring a story about how "the girl next door" was discovered in Atlanta, Georgia. I wore a green and plaid light wool short skirt which happened to be the trendy rage of the day, a dark green pullover snug sweater tank with a high collar and long sleeves, and thick tight style long trouser socks that covered my calves and knees, only revealing my strong suntanned thighs. I wore these funky pantheism black shiny short leather boots. I wore a layer or two of Coco Chanel perfume, mixed with a dash of patchouli mint oil that I sprayed on as I ran to my car, I was running a few minutes late.

My hairstyle and color transcended in 1990 from blonde bombshell to an earthly rare auburn red with warm highlights. A hairstyle recommendation from a Jewish guy friend of mine named Steve Sczczupak. He recommended I should dye my hair auburn red verses wearing my "Heidi blonde ringlets," as he described my current hairdo that he thought needed changing. My hair was auburn red today from a henna dye, a local Atlanta salon in Virginia Highlands actually would advise their clients to use henna when dying their hair a deep auburn color. Henna red natural dye is better than chemical dyes, henna red lasts longer, does not fade so quickly like an ordinary red dye. Ironically I remember 2000 years ago using the same exact concoction of henna on my hair.

Now, oddly enough, it seemed all the rage in Atlanta during the early 1990's to have auburn red hair, I don't know why. My hairdresser Burt said that many girls and wives would come into Van Michael hair salon in Buckhead requesting to have "Auburn red hair like this girl that dances at The Gold Club." Commenting that their husbands and boyfriends would talk about this girl at the dinner table or the bedroom, sometimes even on dates, and backyard B.B.Q's when tipsy.

I would just say to Burt…. "Oh, eh, uh, that's an interesting story, gossip, Burt about housewives, your clients and all…. But I naturally do have red hair…reddish-blonde, but I just like it a shade deeper, more of an auburn base, then maybe some highlights, it brings out my blue eyes. Or I like to wear my hair blonde, fully blonde." So I would comment back to Burt. I was friends with Amy who worked at Van Michaels,' she invited me once to a lake party of Van and Michael who are brothers. The hosts and their wives poured peach liqueur over the watermelon and fruit at the lake party. Everyone there had no false pretenses about who I was or who I wasn't, not like the Calvinists of west Michigan who hold judgment on occupations and appearances with so many hang ups. The south was different, southern culture had manners and accepted people. The southern people like to have fun and get to know people, they hate facades. Calvinists relish facades as realism of sorts. The north and south really are two strikingly very different cultures in America.

Today as I drove along, dazed, listening to the radio. Just thinking how I was looking forward to being interviewed, but really had no idea what I would say for the interview, or what I might be asked…….

It was a warm day in late spring of 1991, I was twenty-one, as I remember well.

I pulled up to the base of Stone Mountain and walked around the Whistle Stop café (which is no longer there by the way), and under a blooming magnolia tree in late spring, stood a familiar looking man. I gave him a puzzled look as I approached him under the tree. He looked late twenties, he had medium brown hair, a bit darker now was his hair, warm intense green eyes that felt like green love glue sticking upon me. His gaze towards me as he watched me come closer to the tree was warm and intense. He was about 5'9 or 5'10, stocky build, strong shoulders and arms you could see, even though his tweed suit coat covered his arms, I could see how strong he was. He just stared at me, fixated on me as I approached him……. "I know you. I know you." I said with a sparkle in my eyes.

I joked with a smile and a twinkle in my eyes over the obvious chemistry, and being in the south and all….. "I know you." I said again with a smile….as I approached the gentlemen residing his composure under that old magnolia tree in full bloom at the base of Stone Mountain. He had a book, as if he was going to read a book to me. I looked at him and said in a raw, earthy, sensual way…… "Are we going to get to know each other today? I need a real comfort specialist…ya' know."

The dark haired gentlemen flipped to the back of the book. I then commented in a flirty tone….. "What do you have planned? What are you doing?" I smiled. He smiled back as he flipped over the last page. And there stuck, taped to the last page was a gold wedding band with diamonds and rubies……just like the ring from the 1860's.

"I want to take you across the street, to that old plantation style mansion, upstairs, I have an area prepared for us." Spoke this dark haired gentlemen.

"Well, I just don't know, I just don't know…..I am only twenty-one, I have just begun to really live my life." I gasped. "Or did you just want to play doctor? Did you want me to pretend to have a heart attack, so you can unbutton my shirt right now?"

He laughed. I smiled.

The smell of pink magnolia blossoms in full bloom loamed overhead. A few fragile pink petals fell upon us like rose petals dusting the ground of a wedding set in heaven……and then he spoke again…..

We sat and made cauterization banter and light humor in our dialogue. I just couldn't believe this moment. It was 1991? Over a hundred years had passed since we last sat in this same place and looked at each other, just like this.

I asked, "Who are you? Who really are you?" He took his right hand and drew a British ship with four sails in the dusty copper Georgia soil. He then glanced at me with his green eyes from under his stern expression while drawing a rainbow next in the Georgia soil.

I commented…..and smiled…. "How about just two sails on the ship? That would be plenty."

"Two sails? That would be a sailboat, Lilly. We want us a **Big British Ship** my dear." Spoke the dark haired man with such distinction and enthusiasm in his voice.

"You're….Alan"………I said. Amazed at this meeting, this conjunction within my young mind of needing and yearning for an education in philosophy, foreign languages, English literature and American law. To be part of myth and legend, it was not just a fantasy, this was real. "I do want to be a writer, that has always been my passion, my driving desire in this lifetime, not pretty photos taken of me or serving beer at a pub. Alan you've been here all along, I met you in Detroit at that Bruce Springsteen rock concert…..almost two years ago." I said with enthusiasm and disbelief of this conjunction, our meeting again.

"Just a philosophy romance writer…. Lilly?" He asked.

And then I began asking questions of him……

"What is it that you do in Atlanta? What brings you here, how did you find me?" I asked a multitude of questions in sequence, inquisitively as my blue eyes began to illuminate an interest in how original this life of mine was beginning to bloom here in Georgia.

"I am a philosophy professor at Emory University, I have been teaching there for five years now, I'm thirty-one years old. I'm from Detroit, that's where my family lives, I have family in Chicago too…."

I intercepted, he paused, as I asked, "Are you acting?"

"At times I can act, but I am not acting now." He smiled and commented with a wink in his green eyes.

Then the dark haired gentlemen began to speak again, Alan began speaking to me, "I saw your name in a magazine it was written as your real name, Lori Vander Ark, so I hired a detective out of Michigan and Chicago to locate you. The detective gave me your agents phone number at Take One, here in Atlanta. I really had no idea that we would meet again, here in the south, Georgia. I thought the detective agency out of Grand Rapids would lead me to Michigan. I thought that was where you still were, maybe living with your mom. Believe me, I am just as surprised we are back in the south, together again." Alan said to me.

Alan spoke up again, "Your hair was blonde in the Playboy pictorial, but now it is auburn red, I like it auburn color like it is now. Maybe you could create a fictitious name, like a pen name or something with your hair this color. Everyone has a pen name."

I laughed, smiled, "Pen name?"

"You look sophisticated, yet very girl next door with the auburn color hair. If this is to become our greatest love affair, a real adventure in the making, I am by some standards of the definition, a real Playboy, a real Casanova, your Casanova. Your pen name can be, Ms. Jones. You look like a Ms. Jones. Ms. Jones…..would you like to accompany me in the next chapter of our life adventure on planet earth?" Alan held out his arm, his elbow for me to grab for us to make like a pretzel twist of a bonding companionship moment. I laughed nervously as I engulfed every inch of him with my eyes, secretly wondering to myself, who is this guy really? What is his agenda with me?

Alan's warm eyes were like love glue, like I had never felt before, or could ever feel that kind of intense caring ever, from anyone. I always look in a person's eyes and know what they think of me, or want from me, or what their overall general intentions are in life, for my life. His eyes were pure love towards me…..like a spring melting in my direction, felt and so remembered.

"You are from Detroit? Really? Between you and I, you look like a celebrity, are you? Are you on T.V.?" I asked, as Alan laughed. "I know you are not really a journalist. You really like to discover talent? Make people famous, that's your hobby, that's what you like to do when not teaching philosophy in the sultry south, isn't it?" I was the first one to break the ice with some real probing conversation topics.

I began talking, "My father's side of the family lives in Detroit and Grand Rapids, he's passed away now though. He always thought I would become famous, have a real famous love story he once told me. But what I really want is just a normal life. I want to know what it is like to just be normal, I am in search of what normal is. I have an overbearing not so nice mother in Michigan. If she was nicer, or helped me out in life, or really cared about me, I probably would still be in Michigan. But Cindy is all about herself, it is up to me to pay my rent, car payments, meals, tuition if I want to go back to college, etc. You know Cindy had me paying rent at her condo when I was still in high school. If I am going to continue to pay rent then it might as well be for my own place, less her rules and insane behavior towards me. Therefore I am trying to strike out on my own in life, make something of myself, stay positive I suppose. I like Georgia so far, the weather is great, the people are so friendly. The southern culture is so nonjudgmental in how a person looks or talks, or what church a person belongs to or does not belong to, ya' know. I love all the outside patio style restaurants, don't you? I love eating meals outside in warm weather or in the winter the Atlanta restaurants will just turn up tall heaters outside on the patios, it's so romantic with strings of lights decorating the patios and all." I spoke so much, still smiling in amazement that Alan is really here, back in my life.

"Your mother is something else, she said if I came near her condo she would teach me who has power……has she ever hit you? She talked in a severely threatening tone of voice. I got chills down my back just listening to her voice. Is she like a brut, bully man or something towards you?" Alan asked with a puzzled look, a concerned look for me.

"She is not so nice, but if you are a high ranking very networked Dutch Christian Reformed elitist from Grand Rapids, Michigan…..a Calvinist. Well then, you would probably comment about her that she is a fine, outstanding Christian woman, for that is the façade she will paint to those in that tight-knit Calvinist community that have opinions of her that matter most. My opinion of her does not matter. She wants me destroyed, my hopes, wishes, and bright future, done away with. She is insanely jealous of me I suppose, the less positive stuff I tell her, the better off I am, really." I commented to Alan.

He looked concerned, but relieved that he had found me at last.

Alan took my hand and guided me to sit down under the old magnolia tree, we both laid down resting ourselves on our supporting elbows as we talked that early afternoon in Georgia. The pink and fragrant magnolia blossoms covered our afternoon of ease just listening to each other talk. As an umbrella of pink flowers hovered above us, the warm sultry breeze blew petals onto us, and around us. Something about looking up though, to the ominous dark tree limbs that afternoon sent a sheer momentary anxiety shooting throughout my body as I looked upward to the haunting dark tree limbs against the cloudy sky. I then refocused my attention on Alan's steady voice, and all he had to say to me. He wore tan pants, and a London Fog style tweed suit coat and a white shirt, brown leather shoes, the kind a chic, hip kind of professor would wear. I loved the warmth of his green eyes penetrating through me, around me, he radiated love through his eyes. He spelled, "we have a history together," with his intense glassed over gazing of me.

"We are finally brought back together in another life, this life" …..I said slowly. "You know Alan, I've had dreams about you, I feel you speak to me, even before today." I spoke up in amazement, wondering how this could really all be true.

"I know. I am here to teach you, our relationship is one of a kind, not everyone who has been reincarnated is able to locate that soul from the past, like you and I, like now, here." With those words he caressed over my hand, and turned over my hands to see my inner palms, "I am this inner line of influence in your life, I am with you, even when you cannot hear my voice. I will always be with you Lilly, always, for at least fifty years"…. he rubbed his hand over mine and said this, "I will help you judge your enemies someday, you do not know it now, but I am going to teach you about psychological warfare, philosophical mind daggers, vast winning without bloodshed. I am a mental warrior here to help you win. Sometimes I come to you in your dreams. I am your teacher. I have a powerful mind and I will show you how your fierce mind will make your enemies shutter at the truth on paper before the metempsychosis can occur for them here on earth. We are part of God's puzzle, heaven's design, for his story to be told on earth. The forces of heaven and the underworld are joining together for the big battle, the real battle that will take place. It is a battle for a new philosophical foundation of many truths. You are going to lay down those truths with what is lodged inside of you. Your truths. God sent me to you, in another life I was sent as well to teach you, ours is a journey to explain to the world what evil energy really is. Evil is not just one defined being, such as "the devil." Alan said.

Odd how it is as if we just met, yet we just haven't met here for the first time, I thought as I gazed at him. He had so much to tell me, he acted as if our conversations were limited in time. I am twenty-one and he is thirty-one, we have plenty of time to communicate and spend time talking, I thought.

"Alan we have a connection that is unique and beyond what some will know as normal, this past life stuff, past life on earth, it is like our own secret isn't it?" I asked.

Alan kept rubbing my hand and said this, "I am a connection to the other side, I am here to help you. We together are going to open the door on many truths that have stayed lodged in history far too long." Alan seemed so serious at that moment. I still wore a smile as I listened on and on that balmy spring day in Georgia. I thought we'd have so much time together, we're both young.

Alan looked up to the magnolia tree, a pink petal fell on his shoulder as he noticed, he said this to me, "Love is like that."

"Like what?" I asked.

"Love is like a flower in full bloom, like the bloom of a magnolia tree. The blossoms are radiant and are constant throughout the life of a tree," He said.

Alan spoke on, " Love is like the constant renewal force of an annual bloom, some trees bloom early, some trees bloom later than others. God is like a magnolia tree, when you least expect anything, he reminds you somehow that all people can bloom." Alan said as his eyes twinkled.

Alan then said this after the two hour reunion on that sultry balmy late spring day in 1991 under that Stone Mountain magnolia tree in full bloom, "I would love to take you some place, and have a meal."

Responding to Alan's suggestion, I agreed. Alan said this to me, "I know of a casual German restaurant and bakery deli here in Stone Mountain near an old civil war cemetery."

I responded, "I can take us there, ride with me and show me the way." Still dumbfounded that Alan found me here in this lifetime, and Georgia of all places. Back here in Georgia together again, we then headed for my car.

We drove less than a mile, then the storm clouds began to roll in overhead. The sky grew dark as we entered the deli and asked for outside patio seating. The lunch customers had left, it was a quiet time of the day for the deli in the late afternoon hour. I did notice across the street, an old civil war cemetery. I mentioned to Alan, "Look over there, we knew each other before those cemetery headstones were carved in limestone. We knew each other when those soldiers were alive."

The bakery smelled of freshly baked loaves of bread warming in the main entrance hall leading to the back patio which had little string lights glowing overhead and candles set on the tables. Alan reached into his pocket and lit the candle resting in the jar at our white linen table, it was a pink candle. The rest of the tables all had ivory candles lit and glowing and flickering as we entered. "What are you up to Alan, is this synchronicity? How did you know to select this German bakery with muffins and fresh delicacies?" I asked Alan.

Alan ordered some blueberry pastries and English tea for us to share. The waitress left us alone for a moment. Alan responded, "I know you like the fresh aroma of homemade bread, this bakery and deli is the closest to Stone Mountain where I arranged for us to have a table after all this time."

I leaned over to kiss him, to be bold, to be the first to break the trance we both were feeling at that moment. The thunder crackled in from the east overhead, within minutes the beads of rain began pouring onto the plastic tent covered above us, like large balls of hail it poured. The risk of lightning seemed like approaching danger from the loaming low storm clouds in the sky above us. The immensity of danger combined with the strong element of love was real and well anticipated. I felt baptized in love as I stood up and moved to sit on Alan's lap. He acted as if he could not move out of his chair, so therefore I moved towards him. I straddled his lap gently and rested myself gently on his lap.

I looked him straight in his glassed over warm green eyes, and I said this, as I clutched his face in my palms, "We will write that gothic love novel, we will in this lifetime of ours." I touched his ear lobe and began kissing the sides of his neck, starting from his hair line down to his white starched collar. Alan reached around my waist and then dropped his hands lower, inching, moving my body closer on his lap towards his belt. He pulled me even closer and closer unto him. He reached under my plaid wool short skirt and felt my cold cheeks as he squeezed me closer on him. Brushing his hands along both sides of my upper topmost thigh region and then smoothly dragging the palms of his hands down over my long trouser style tights covering my knees and calves. Then he began hugging me and giving me a warm embrace as the beads of rain continued to drum fervently above us, like an annoying percussion instrument.....just drumming down rain beads. The sexual chemistry was so intense with Alan, like no one before him....but why? I thought to myself quietly, why is touching Alan so much more intense than any other guy I have ever kissed before? Why was there so much electricity between us, simply just sitting on his lap.

I took a small portion of warm bread from the table and placed it in his mouth. I watched him chew and swallow hard before me, close to me I stared at his eyes. I then took a warm soft piece and placed another in his mouth, this time I began kissing him slowly, biting on the bread that protruded from his lips gripping the end bread piece. My heart was racing. I felt his heart beating faster each time he pulled me closer to kiss him again and again between the pieces of warm bread falling out, or swallowing hard between our passionate kisses. I loved how inside we felt we wanted to go so fast, embracing quickly with what we felt towards each other, that escalating "next climatic emotion." But we actually moved much slower and gentler on that chair we shared together in semiprivate seclusion of knowing and anticipating from one another.

A waiter stepped out from the kitchen abruptly, surprisingly so, and set down a pot of tea and more freshly baked pastries. The waiter seemed nervous upon walking up to us while I sat in Alan's lap. We stopped kissing for a moment to look up, laughing a bit from nervousness. Then we ordered dinner while I sat in his lap. We then resumed feeding each other warm bread, as he, then I, pulled another bread piece from the basket on the table. The flame on the pink candle flickered in our moment of a passionate reunion.

Our passionate kisses wrapped in trying to engulf the warm bread, sneak in a kiss, an embrace, to just touch his lips against mine one more time. Tasting the aroma of freshly baked bread, taking us back to another time and place in American history that we once shared in each other's arms on a wooden antique table. I loved how his palms felt against my skin. I loved the masculine of him and he loved exploring the feminine of me. The civil war soldiers from across the street in their resting grave must have received an eye full of passion, of reuniting, the duality between a man and a woman is a powerful antidote, even for the dead watching us, I suppose.

We shared a yin, yang moment in that German deli, and there would be many more to share in Virginia Highlands at his house in the upcoming months and years.

We did separate at the table to snack on our dinner, we talked about a lot of things. I said to him, your last name…..is that a Jewish last name? He answered "yes," and explained that his mother is Irish and his father is Jewish.

"Well are you Jewish, do you practice Judaism?" I asked.

Alan responded……. "Sometimes…….in September…..the High Holidays."

"You know…..Lori……. is that the name that you would like me to call you?" Asked Alan.

"Yes, call me Lori." I responded….. "It means crowned one."

"Lori, let me explain to you firmly, life is not about making a grand entrance, or a great introduction, or seducing to get your way in life. Life and relationships **are not** all about seduction. Love is life long, often two entangled souls always come back in a similar situation. It is true, without speaking a syllable you seem to spell sex, cast an enticing story to the world in all the known human dialects known to man or woman. We have what some would call here in this establishment as a real Mars conjunct Venus connection. You could write a book on how to entice a man, how a woman should walk, talk, dress, and present herself. I think you are incredibly sexy, but you **should not** exploit yourself. Life is not all about seduction, it's about finding true love and holding onto that love." Alan said firmly, soberly he stared at me, as his warm green eyes gave me a look, like a look he could give no other woman.

I changed the subject of conversation by saying this, "I want to learn from you, like you once taught me in the 1860's under an old magnolia tree. I want to be a writer, maybe even a famous writer. Let's write a love story together, the most famous love story ever."

"O.k. Lori, let's begin here…." Alan said, as he began holding up objects for me to describe on the spot. Alan held up a silver spoon, then a creamy German pastry, then an empty plate, and a glass half full. Each time Alan held up an object I would have to quickly describe the object an a abstract, original, and detailed way, or face his criticism of the lame description I gave.

"I need everything you can possibly teach me in this lifetime…..we will run naked behind each word, freely expressing our emotions with each phrase, every dialect known to man or woman. We will Alan, I promise you, write the greatest love tale of all times, revolutionary will be our love between the words, the cords, and white sheets……" I said as I gave Alan a kiss.

Then I spoke up again…. "Our love story has just begun, but when it is written down in a novel, it will last forever, even after we grow old and die. Our story will live on, last on and on, like a fire burning like hot lava upon a lake that never ceases." Just then a crack in the plastic awning spilled fresh water from the sky, and in poured my raw emotions for this man as well, my greatest teacher and love, Alan. He had returned, and I had returned to him. We took turns feeding each other another loaf of bread that the owner brought over to us. I stuffed Alan's mouth, and he stuffed my mouth until I felt a chokepoint, like a narrow shallow sea corridor….that's how I would best describe my expression at that exact moment, I as the student, I was learning.

Alan said this at the table……..."When you yearn, and wish, and most of all have faith and believe……..your love does return, your teacher is here…….Lilly."

My emotions all of a sudden felt less sanctioned. My mind was open to learn and experience life from him, all of him. I remarked to Alan…."I didn't know you were…ready…..to…"

"Passion works that way…..like a thief Lilly upon your palate, you had no idea."

Alan and I began a serious courtship beginning in the spring of 1991. I was twenty-something, twenty-one, the belle of the ball, this would last for years. Like a long extended engagement from Lafayette Square our relationship blossomed again here in the sauntering south. The air felt damp from our passion towards each other. I did have my apartment in Lithia Springs, Georgia, located at The Waterford Place Apartments, just thirty minutes from downtown Atlanta. Alan's house was in the trendy and up and coming Virginia Highlands area, just fifteen minutes from Emory University. I liked going to his house in town, there was always much to do and see together on Peachtree street that ran through Buckhead. I liked strolling through Piedmont Park hand and hand, just talking about every spectrum of subjects possible under the rainbow. The big world around us, no subject, like no leaf left unturned was our conversational palate. I even introduced Alan to smoking his first hit of marijuana in Piedmont Park, during one of many allowed smoking days of "weed in the park." The police officers would stroll the boundaries of the park, reminding folks to stay inside the sidewalk lines. I loved to loosen Alan's collar in life and show him how to relax as he taught me everything about independent thinking and philosophy, I in turn taught him as well. Sometimes we would stay at my apartment, which was considered rural, country area. I liked the woods behind my apartment, how on warm sultry days in Georgia, and **there are many**, the sun would bake against the Georgia pine. I love the smell of greenness, woodsy, hearty pine scents to surround me.

One day at Alan's place he said this as he opened a book, "You know Lori, I have a painting to show you, it's of the Hopi Indians. Your novel, that book that is lodged inside of you, represents a harvest, like corn of plenty does to an Indian, a life staple on many standards, by many cultures. What you reveal brings oneness, what you reveal is that heaven is not based on what most in your culture believe it is based on. I can't tell you what that is, you are going to figure that one out on your own." Spoke Alan one late afternoon in his house just after a stroll in Piedmont Park.

I asked Alan that night, "What did you mean in that message at the rock concert, you are my blue star?"

Alan cleared his throat as he rested on his sofa then responded, "The first time we were together, *our first time* you wore a royal blue dress, you don't remember? I remember…..your name was similar to Lori…… Ms. Lilly."

"Alan was our first time here in the south during the civil war era, or was our first time two thousand years ago? Because when you touch me, when I put my head on your chest, I have flashbacks to Rome, and Marc Antony is sending spies to eavesdrop on us. It makes me nervous. My mother Cindy and her friend Kim Livermore are planning on visiting me. If she or both of them see me in love they both will create trouble for us, so I fear."

"What do you mean?" Asked Alan.

"When you touch me, when we're together, I have flashbacks of living in Egypt and you have blonde curly hair. You were younger than me, you wore Roman warrior clothes and you would come to my castle steps. I seduced you or you seduced me, I think I got pregnant, I gave birth to a son, he was my youngest son in that lifetime just over 2000 years ago."

Alan's face went white, the blood drained from his face as I spoke those words. He then responded, "I still have nightmares of a large bull head with horns, an eagle flying over top while I hold a bloody sword, I am haunted by a lion with an angel from being a Roman war general. I had to make a decision back then, I was in a crisis. I had to decide between my loyalty to Rome, or you. I choose Rome, I was young, I made a decision that haunts my dreams to this day. You lost a battle, you lost everything, it had to do with me and my decision I made prior to a war, it was an awful choice in my dreams. I was torn between you and Rome….in my dreams. It is not a dream or life I want to go back to, let's not talk about it, let's only talk about now, or the 1860's." Spoke Alan soberly.

"Don't want to go back to? Maybe I don't want to go back to reminiscing about the 1860's when I fell out of a magnolia tree and my life was cut short from marrying you!" I said. There was definitely an unfinished residue of emotions between us, and tapping into our memories was like opening a jar of which I was not sure I could handle the emotion that emerged with the memory, the jar. Sometimes I found smoking pot was a way to explore an emotion, a way of vegetating onto a plane of existence that I thought I could handle with Alan.

I spoke up, "I do remember the conflict I had with Rome, and all Rome wanted to control of Egypt. Rome wanted me and my youngest son. Not my other four children I had with Marc Antony. I do remember Octavia. Rome would have killed my other four children if I agreed to join you in Rome and not fight for what I believe in! Marc Antony and I raged war against Rome and you, I had to in order to keep my family together, and in the end I lost it all, I lost my children, my kingdom, my life. Rome…. you Octavia, you lost too. It was a lifetime that must have appeared glamorous to my servants despite my sleepless nights, legendary. But I ended up with nothing of what I dedicated my life for, what I fought so hard for, I did not win……….or keep my children together, my kingdom, and my mission of creating a utopian world.

I had plans to take down Rome, and you, for trying to make me make such a dreadful decision about my children. I had made the correct decision and went to war against you and Rome to preserve my family and kingdom in Egypt. Yet I did not win the war. After I lost, after I lost so much and I died, you searched for our son? Through a Roman census, in attempts to salvage something, salvage our love?...... Lives did not end well in that era." I said as I looked through to the depths of his soul as he sat on the sofa.

Alan made a profound statement, which inherently I have always known to be true as well, but most Christians would disagree whole heartedly. Alan said this, "Just because it is not written in the new or old testament of the Bible, does not mean it did not happen in history 2000 years ago."

"I agree with you Alan. Just as someday I may write my memoirs, what I leave out of the memoirs, does not mean it did not happen to me, or did not take place. It just means that I did not write it in my novel." I said.

"Precisely! Perhaps there will be stories left unsaid. I believe much was left out of the Bible, but that does not mean it did not happen in history. It just means it was not written about in a collection of dead sea scrolls found later." Spoke up Alan.

"Here, I'm finished with this bong, here it's your turn." I said as I packed more freshly grounded red bud marijuana into the filter screen, then passed the black plastic bong to Alan. "Do you think Alan, when we went to Little Five Points and selected off a shelf of bongs, which one to purchase? And the storeowner replied to my question of, "Why can a store sell bongs, but not legally sell pot? How can that be?"

And the storeowner replied, "Well that's simple, because bongs are not illegal to sell, pot is illegal to sell."

"Do you think that is a typical philosophical point, selecting what is, and what is not? Is that not what you have been teaching me to look at? What is relevant, and what is not? What is similar and what is not?" I asked.

"To have an edge, you need to learn how to think, not what to think, you are right that is the fundamentals of philosophy. If we exist, what is this existence called?" Responded Alan.

"That reminds me of another story. How can Christian adults and children have a near death experience. Claim to have gone to heaven for a moment, see Jesus and know it is Jesus by his markings on his body from the cross he died on 2000 years ago, and then also believe and claim that God heals all wounds in heaven but the wounds of Jesus." I remarked.

Alan responded, "Heals everyone else but Jesus? What do you mean?"

"Stories I read about near death experiences by Christians, they claim to have seen Jesus with markings on his hands and feet from the cross. Yet God healed or heals everyone else that enters heaven. No glasses to wear any longer, no scars for anyone else, no diseases or imperfections for everyone else in heaven. It does not make logical rational sense that God would not heal his son upon Jesus entering heaven, when in fact everyone else is healed upon entering heaven." I answered.

Alan responded, "Good point. You are going to be my favorite student in philosophy. Maybe the Christians want to convince others that are not of their faith that indeed Jesus is in heaven and does exist, and just added him in their real life drama of dying and going to heaven."

Often, on weekends, at night, Alan and I would smoke from my bong on my coffee table, my friend and buddy that I also met in 1990, Steve Szczupak, a Jewish friend of mine born in Poland in 1968, would join us. His parents are Jacob and Lucy Szczupak. Steve would often accompany us to play pool at The Famous Pub in the North Druid Hills area.

Steve always would supply Alan and I with the best marijuana. Steve had an interesting family, a close and very down to earth family. His uncle was a Rabbi, yet his uncle's daughter became a lesbian. Steve's family was maybe a typical Jewish family, maybe not? I went to many family socials he invited me to, his family was a bit dysfunctional, yet very down to earth and real. His aunt Marsha liked to talk with me, listening as if I always had something very interesting and profound to say in her presence. I remember his aunt Marsha and the Rabbi had two dishwashers, and two sets of dishes, one for meats and one for dairy. I said to Steve, "What does your aunt Marsha think about your family <u>not</u> having two dishwashers like her household does?"

Steve's response, "They think we are not as good as them, the more extreme they are in interpretation of the Torah, the less a light shines on us." Steve went onto say this, "There are many Jews here in the North Druid Hills area that also have two dishwashers, separating and symbolizing God's order to eat dairy separate from consumption of kosher meats."

I asked Steve once while playing pool at The Famous Pub, "What is antisemitism? You keep talking about how countries and groups of people hate the Jews and that is why your parents decided to flee Poland to get away from hate. Is that what antisemitism is about, hating the Jews?"

Steve responded stoned and serious, " Lori, antisemitism is hostility towards another person or persons for not being the status quo of that country or region."

I inquired further to Steve, more in-depth, "Please explain more."

Steve sighs and says, "Antisemitism is what the Jews have been fighting since the origins of the Jews in Israel. Antisemitism is hostility, prejudice, discrimination against Jews."

I inquire, "Can Jews hold hostility, prejudice and discrimination against non-Jews?"

Steve remarks in a condescending tone to me, "Non-Jews Lori, don't you mean Gentiles?"

I remark back, "Yes."

Steve sighs again and acts as if he is the frustrated underpaid teacher and I am the student as he remarks, "Well they can I suppose, but don't."

I remark while playing pool and taking my shot, "Can a Jew marry a non-Jew, a Gentile, and then be accepted in the Jewish culture, in the synagogue, in the Jewish network of landing a great job with NBC or it's affiliates?" I laugh and take another drink of my spiked cranberry juice as I await with curiosity at Steve's response to my lengthy question.

Steve acts sober and says rather firmly, "No. Jews marry Jews, that's the core of our survival. Look at royalty lines, royalty marry royalty, keep it all in the family, no one says anything about that, they're all inbred, look at prince Charles. But everyone is so quick to judge the Jews."

I remark keeping the glass close to my lips to conceal my smirk, "Steve, is that what happened to you?"

Steve remarks as he takes his turn, "What?"

I respond by elaborating, "Well if I have to be Jewish for a Jewish man to marry me that would be prejudice of the Jewish man and his Jewish faith not to marry me because I am not Jewish."

Steve responds with anger in his voice, "No it's not prejudice! That's the Jewish religion, that's what our parents expect of their children. If Jews did not marry other Jews we would be like everyone else and not Jewish, we'd all be Gentiles. We have to preserve our roots, our heritage."

I pause.

Steve asks, "What, what are you thinking?"

I respond, "I am thinking you just described the roots of hostility to me."

Steve responds a bit agitated, "What? I'm not hostile. I'm friends with everyone in this bar. It's your personality that does not always blend so well with others. Me, I'm friendly, easy going. I know how to make friends easier than you. You clam up on people."

I respond back to Steve, "No, you are Jewish and prejudice against people that are not Jewish."

Steve responds in a harsh tone, "Great, now look what you have done!"

I look at Steve directly and ask him, "What? What did I do?"

Steve responds in an acquisitive tone and gestures, "I was stoned, having a good time and you pulled me out of my good mood. I have no more pot left thanks in part to me sharing with you. Thanks a lot, this is my day off! I was just trying to enjoy myself and you go and ruin my good time."

I laughed. Then I remark, "Steve do you ever get the feeling that thousands of years of inbreeding within the Jewish religion was not such a good result when it comes to your short fuse, your temper, the littlest thing you do not agree with will set you off."

Steve stormed off like a quiet explosive. It did not help his mood that I won the pool game too.

One time Steve picked me up from the airport around Christmas time, and before driving me back to my apartment in Lithia Springs he brought me to his uncles house, the Rabbi, for a Hanukkah party. The table was filled with festive Tupperware and china from the 1970's era, orange and green china bowls filled with homemade fish balls and horseradish sauce, soup with chicken balls, brownies, etc. Downstairs we could hear his cousins laughing and playing Hanukkah games with a top looking device of sorts. We joined his cousins downstairs. It was the early 1990's that Steve and I became friends. There was at least laughter and happiness in Steve's family, and I longed to have a family connection which I felt I was missing within my life.

One thing I remember about Steve, he would always have pot, the best in town. He was nicknamed "Pig Pin" at The Famous Pub on North Druid Hills, where we often would play pool there together. Steve was always walking around with a cloud of smoke from being stoned all the time, he was a popular guy in town. He told me his name in Polish meant. "Pike….like a fish….a scavenger fish….that eats on the bottom." Odd how names can mean something. He also stated that his mother Lucy went to a psychic, that psychic stated to Lucy that she would have a very famous son someday. Interesting Tale.

But Alan was my true love, my heartthrob. Alan owned my heart, my soul, he controlled me in a way a man could. Alan was the only man I desired to really be with in an intimate way. One weekend evening Alan was over, it was just a typical weekend, like the one before, or the one after, it was always heaven when Alan touched me, was around me. I once asked Alan as we touched on the subject of religion, "Why do you think you are Jewish and I am not? Why did God plant this relationship this way, I am not Jewish, you are, and we're so in love." Alan would often just repeat my questions before answering as if to digest the question before he answered me. Then often he would act as if I rephrased a question to change the question to my advantage when I had not.

Alan responded, "What you are asking me, why you are not Jewish, or why we are not the same religion?"

I said to Alan, "Yes, why did God make you Jewish and make me a non-Jew who grew up Dutch Christian Reformed, a Calvinist. You like to refer to me as a W.A.S.P. a White Anglo-Saxon Protestant. But why do so many believe my religion is better than yours? That is what the Dutch believe, if you're not Dutch, you're not much. They all believe that in west Michigan, Alan, they will mock you for your nose, mock anything that is different than them. If a person stands up for another, they gang up on that person. Hostility spreads quickly in west Michigan, they are numerous in hating what is different. They keep breeding and breeding pods and pods of themselves, exact clones of prejudice hate. Peace is among them. Peace in their world for being like them, if you are. But peace could never be worldwide with a philosophy such as theirs, ever. Yet ironically enough, they have this great faith that Jesus will return and create peace worldwide, but what if they crucify him again? That one and only Jew that they supposedly worship in their history books? You and I know, he, Jesus was really from the Ptolemy dynasty, and will return to build the Ptolemy dynasty, that was or is his purpose on returning to earth."

Alan responded, "Do you really think God went through the effort of creating me, my father, to just have then instantly condemned us to hell because we do not wear crosses around our neck, go to a protestant church, celebrate Christmas, and believe the Jesus story like them? Jesus never liberated the Jews. It is a fact."

I responded, "The Christians believe that there will be no Jews in heaven because Jews do not believe in Jesus, and Christians believe the Jews had Jesus crucified. The Jews believe that Romans had Jesus crucified. Have you ever asked a Christian if Jews will be in heaven? Do it sometime, ask them that question. Ask <u>thousands</u> of them. They will think you are nuts, a real nutcase if you do not believe just as them and their ministers. One must believe exactly like them or you are an outsider, an outcast of their society.

Alan responded, "You, or those Calvinists, actually believe that God is so stupid that he had me born on this earth, had me raised as a Jew, only to say that route of believing and worshiping is wrong? And God made a mistake by having my background, my ancestry, my religion wrong, all along, a religion created by God? Do Christians believe God was out to condemn me and my family from the start? And when I die and transcend into a new world, a heavenly realm will not accept me because God purposely placed me in a Jewish home, only to condemn me later after I die? I believe God has more intelligence to just assume God misplaces people, to give them a route, a religion that is wrong from the very beginning of that person's life, to only condemn them when they die. Perhaps each person has their own journey, their own destination of locating God within their life. Perhaps religion, no matter what the religion basis is as a foundation, is that persons personal path to God. How can one religion say their path is better than another route to getting in touch with God in their life? They are not God."

"God never created religion Alan. I do not think you are stupid." I said in response to his preaching.

"Very keen. At times I will make statements and I am looking to see how good of a philosopher you actually are." Spoke Alan so eloquently.

I chimed in, "So what you believe is that Christ is not the only way to God? But the Bible says Christ is the way. If you believe in him you are saved. Every Christian that I have asked, 'do you think there will be Jews in heaven?' Have stated the Bible says that Jews are not going to heaven. But I know from philosophy, how you make me think Alan, it does not say Jews will not be in heaven. Rather the Roman historian of ancient times wrote if you believe in Jesus you will have everlasting life. One thing is for sure, the Bible does not have a sentence that specifically states that there will be no Jews in heaven if they do not believe in Jesus. It only states if you believe in Jesus you will be given everlasting life."

"And remember Jesus never wrote any chapters of the Bible." Alan chimed in.

"Good point. But one that will anger many Christians if you bring that fact up. Christianity is not about facts from the author, Christ. Christianity is based on ancient authors, not Christ. What has become a trend, a status quo, gains momentum, and becomes Christian law." I stated very matter of fact.

Alan nodded and responded, "If you eat an apple a day, you'll keep the doctor away. If you do not eat an apple a day, that does not mean you still can't keep a doctor away? If you take the bridge you'll get to the other side, the bridge is the means to the other side. But if you take a boat you will also get to the other side. If you take a helicopter you will also get to the other side. Do you understand Lori, for Christians, Christ's mere existence upon this world, believing he lived and died just so that the Christians can go through the pearly gates, is the way, in their philosophy of repelling off Judgment upon their souls and the flames of hell. But for other religions, Christ existence is not the way, but there are similarities, parallels within many religions. Most Christians are selfish and uncaring, which actually means 'Un-Christian.' Most Christians believe that 'perception' is belief in God, 'acquiring knowledge of Jesus Christ' is their antidote for going to a better place after we leave this world. It is a very toxic ingredient to have the wrong perception of God. 'Perception,' can be a power additive for disaster. Someday when the world knows what Christians have done to you, as you so often say you are going to write a book and expose Christianity at its fundamental core level. Well, than 'perception' will again be the reigning chief ingredient of the Calvinists in Grand Rapids as their defense of anything you allege. They will say in their defense, 'we mow are lawns, we have white collar lives, we have families that adore us, we own homes, we go to church,' and they will say a whole lot about anyone who does not fit into their mold of a society they created." Alan spoke like a real stuffy professor.

He went on to say with his refined distinct voice of reason, "Outsiders will not be taken seriously enough to ever really be thought of as Christians themselves, by them. The Calvinists are just a society, a bubble, and you could never burst that bubble, really Lori. You do have profound statements to reform their ways, but to their criminal minds, they as a whole have the world fooled. The Calvinists have created a perception, a religious propaganda, a great defense for most. Guaranteed, cops go after blacks, not white Dutch people who hide crimes within their pristine of appearances of perfect neighborhoods. Religion is a study of appearance to most Christians who want to be accepted by other Christians. If you wear tight jeans, too much make-up, talk too loud, even laugh too loud……..

The Calvinists will think you are not one of them, and therefore, you are not a Christian, and by far, you are *not* fitting in, you are not as good as them in their social glue to really stick to them. Really the Calvinists should examine the definition and parameters of "sociology" and realize their actions coincide more closely with studying society, than studying and examining God and his truth in their lives. Society loves to take God and warp him into a shape they understand."

"Let's just take another bong hit and see where that leads us." I responded.

After getting high with Alan, often we'd watch old re-runs of I Love Lucy or The Andy Griffith Show, it was always non-stop hilarious when we were high and watching television. Then we'd move into my bathroom, I would prepare a large bubble bath for us. We'd sit in the large Jacuzzi tub I had in my bathroom, light candles around the tub and take turns bathing each other before going to bed. We'd sleep for a few hours, then wake up in the middle of the night. Just in the light of the moonlight I could see Alan beginning "to prepare" to make love to me by how he began caressing me in his curiosity in the middle of the night. He knew everything about preparing the dish, the flower, well before entering me. Which so happens to be the key ingredient to great love making, when to add or increase pressure upon areas of my body. What to do next on, in, or around my body which appeared like a ripe magnolia blossom in full bloom to him, like when we first met. Alan was always in control in this department, of making me feel as if I always wanted more, and then weak again and again. Sometimes we'd talk about reincarnation in the bedroom. Alan was convinced he was Sir Isaac Newton in a former life, and I was his royal mistress in England, I was married to a king he claimed. "In England, we'd have to sneak around in the darkness just like this evening." He remarked.

He would say pretty convincing memories, that would make me analyze just how many times we had actually made love together during our lifetimes.

At times when he touched me and hold down my hands above my head, I would have flashbacks to Rome, and decisions that were of the heart, and difficult for me to make. As if my hair would sweat at times, and I would see he was a powerful enemy ruler from my past, one that I both loathed and loved……thousands of years ago in a different time period.

Alan knew exactly how to arouse my body's response before entering to give me a final release of the electricity build- up between and in us, which became his control of choice, in and out of the bedroom.

Sometimes I would whisper to him afterwards…… "Brilliant Alan, that was brilliant." I was never sure if it was me that evoked the stimulation of our love making, or Alan, it just was. How he knew so much about a woman's body is beyond my comprehension. He must have just been born with an aptitude of how to make love to a woman. Perhaps books on how to make love to a woman? He did once make this comment to me in bed, "Most men are created equal, but not all women are created equal, most women cannot feel love making like you are able to feel and enjoy with me." I always was puzzled to what he meant, but sometimes I fail at asking appropriate questions in the bedroom.

Alan said to me as he held his arms loosely around me in bed, "When you write that great novel, the one I know you will write, never write the word 'sex,' never use any explicit words. Describe all you can in original thought, uniquely, our love affair, our experiences, let's always promise to be originals, devoted originals, to each other. Just like so many people take the Bible word for word, Jews believe that the Bible, the Torah was written figuratively with symbols and verses that are representational……I want this novel you write to be the same, allegorically written in description. If you are going to teach the world to become thinkers, philosophers of how to think like us, not what to think, then take my advice."

"Why do you think the man's part is so much bigger than the woman's part during the Shakespeare in the bedroom?" I asked during what I would term as "just a lesson."

Alan remarked, "Like when I stroke your leg, your upper thigh, like this, this position I take with you, as I do this……it lets you know who is in charge, it is my way of subduing you mentally and physically, it also shows me that I am in charge. You are very dependent that I produce pleasing pleasure. But for now, your senses are perked on being intimidated by having this part of me, this big part of me, roll back and forth against your exterior body. I am going to stand up and roll my part over your stomach, and grab what you use to nurture me, and totally let you begin to see, touch and experience being subdued by how large a man's part is in your life, so large. It is a caveman's theory why all men have such large parts, it is to subdue woman. The professor, the scholar in me, well, knows all, and what to do with it. I like to enter, then step back from the first page, and then do this aroused rolling pin over the bread of your thigh like this…….I am making you nervous, yet you are visibly excited, and very much want me to complete the chapter, and by your physical anticipation shown, soon. But in a seducing gesture, I want to make your mind and body submissive to me. And that is my rolling pin technique, just like over your bread, it is so important. Every man I have talked with ignores this basic step in seduction and subduing a woman. Rushing any pleasure is like a meal eaten too quickly. Moments like this should not be devoured too quickly either. I like to move the part of your flower bud that touches me. I like to pinch and slide it further into me, crashing into me. Then push and move it higher and pin you down like this. That's what I call this added technique of control of subduing you, you need this. This crashing feeling, repeated, crashing erotic pleasure….Crashing on to me like this as I move this rose bud part resting here of you on me, even further down, so all of you, this part into me, you go crashing, you have no control. I have full control of this extreme pleasure, you will become dependent upon me, the climax I deliver is just too good. I will make you addicted to me."

"What?" I asked...... "Crash into you? Crash onto you like an orgasm wave of pleasure you control?" I smiled with only slight bewilderment, then a gasp, yelp, and intense controlled pleasure began to occur at the control center of Alan's domain. He was inside the book, between the pages, holding onto my trigger button. Just as I could not stand the electric motion of all he controlled, every eight thousand nerve ending outside and inside me began to feel intensity beyond comprehension of extreme sexual control, how an orgasm should feel. As a direct control of sexual electricity he gave to me. He took his finger and pushed my raw pink flower bud up and then pushed his finger down on my bud, moving a sensitive point up and away. With no friction, no rhythm, just sheer pressure of a controlling nature with his finger pushing my pleasure point. Inside of me was sheer heightened stimulation of a rare kind, then he applied friction, friction I could not run or move away from. Pleasure I could never deliver upon or inside myself, never focus on the way he could, from him to me, a blended erotic feeling of within me and what showed.

"What are you doing?" I cried out.

"Concentrate." Alan gasped as he began breathing heavy as he talked on.....

"Concentrate on all the nerve endings that are already awaken inside this climatic ending inside you. Your trigger point, the eight thousand nerve endings I awoke, is my control, not part of what you can wish or direct for your ending. The pressure I place down on the outside lets your body and mind know that I direct your climax and mine as well. I am in control of your body and mind right now, again." Alan said in full control of the situation at hand.

Alan continued talking and explaining in the bedroom......"Then I will move this trigger point down again, making you crash into me..... like this, then I'll slide your engorged pink bud upwards and hold it down with my finger, creating a push button effect. The drama of both extremes, along with your nerve endings awakened inside this story book of ours......is you learning just how powerful in a good seduction way, I am, because, this is how I control you. This is how a man excites a woman, and learns, you learned.....didn't you? Yes. This is how a man really controls his woman, it never was through a woman's mind."

"Oh, my God, that was so good. I love being in control of my life. Then you were for a moment, this intense hour, in control of my mind and body, and then you talked during, explaining, communicating….. which made my mind and physiologically speaking as well….I had to just then concentrate on your "big masculine part" that big potent teaching device being inside, scoping, building pressure. As your hand, your finger, like pinched in a downward motion, then moved my exterior part upwards…which felt uncomfortable, and then you pushed and mushed my poor little bud down….and then kept repeating those two stages during, that was so Garden of Eden controlling….was I the apple?" I asked.

"I liked the control….climax….and control." I remarked as I huddled under my cotton filled comforter. The moments with Alan were so intense, hours conjoined days, wee hours of the morning filled our schedules. My relationship with Alan was as if crossing over a bridge, then looking over my shoulder and seeing that bridge collapse. I was a different woman inside for all I experienced and learned, by simply being with Alan.

"What I do….the sensual pleasures…..it is so forbidden….to be able to talk and experience this kind of life on earth…..there is a forbidden feel…..the novel still unwritten….that is the apple." Alan said. Then he remarked with a smile, "Did you like the squeezing at the end?……"

Alan went onto to whisper…..

"I like to not announce when the climax is in the nightly plot for me, just like tonight's story. I like to begin a squeezing, tapping motion on the sides of what you term, is your trigger point. I see it as a flower bud from my position. I like to talk and communicate verbally, explaining what I am doing, just like you. What you ask for me, communication during, yet with an added twist, I like to touch your body with a motion to communicate, reverberate that in a subtle way. Pay attention to every little thing I do to you. Just like I listen to you, you never announce verbally, you always grab my wrist and squeeze. When you just can't possibly feel anymore levels of intensity the climax is here. That's how we bond, with each story within each chapter of our book. I like it too. This is very intense for me too. I am very experienced. But this is very intense for me too." Alan said with such potent poetic tone in his very relaxed voice this evening.

Afterwards, in the end of such a story book experience we would often gather a comforter or sheet around ourselves and sit out on my back deck of the porch. None of the neighbors were awake, just us talking in the moonlight about abstract realities, life, politics. We'd talk and discuss Christians in west Michigan and how they act….We'd joke at 4am or so, joke about a show we liked to watch, The Kids In The Hall, or Saturday Night Live show takes about the church lady. Laughing about the dual realities of Christians, the life they live in public, which is the life they present, "**the perception given to the public.**" The terrible judgmental superfluous perceptions of Christians we'd joke and laugh, share stories, how a Christian judges another person or other Christians living within their community. Or how the Calvinists judge and view "the big strange outside world." The outside world represents the big wide world outside their bubble. Which of course, the Calvinists hope the big imposing world, never of course, imposes upon them. Alan would mock the Midwest accents, joke at their fakeness in how they would talk. Imitate how Midwest people cackle to one another and socialize on such a superficial level….imitate what they'd think of us, if they saw us.

We'd laugh loudly together, and reach for another bong hit or two. One night Alan said to me, "I understand you now, when I am stoned, I understand you, as a person…. I get you now, how you think, how your mind works inside, your thought patterns, you are my blue star, you may not realize it, but you are…...

"Shissssh. You'll make up the neighbors. I can't have cops knocking at my apartment door at 4am, it smells like pot." I said as I busted out laughing.

"We need another Pot In The Park day at Piedmont….that's our problem….that's the problem with the world…..everybody's mind is moving too fast, they cannot fathom solutions without a slowdown." I remarked.

I agreed with Alan, my abstract way of looking at life, and how I would describe how people relate to one another on a satirical level. Perhaps someday all societies will take a day or two to slow down from the pace of life. Just reflect and absorb life at a slower pace and momentum, a time of reflection. Verses a decision to live life in a hurried systematic flaw of not noticing their lives, or God trying to reach into their lives by examining life as they live it, and know it.

Life is meant to be experienced and explored, we both had that same subscription in a shared philosophy.

I had many blank journals given to me by Carmen in the past, I was always writing these days on the blank notebooks she had given to me. Explaining abstractly about society, and the way people communicate with one another.

I was meeting a lot of politicians and celebrities at The Gold Club where I worked in the early 1990's. Following the politicians and celebrities were always FBI and CIA in the club. One such politician I met in VIP at The Gold Club was the young Ted Cruz who would later become a Texas Senator and future Presidential hopeful for the Republican party. While I danced for him he informed me that he was on a hunt to marry a German woman, only a German would do. What was my impression of him? His face had strange facial features, scary almost, like a characterized head gone wrong with exaggerated features. He felt compelled to inform me that he was very well connected to the CIA. I just assumed most politicians told me that to sound powerful, especially as they climb that political ladder of sorts to higher power, higher government. What was my impression of Ted Cruz? I thought he was empty, shallow, not a man of substance, not a man who knew how to get things done for the greater good of the American people, or any people for that matter. The good politicians get things done that benefit. The bad politicians waste air and money.

"Narrow perceptions lead to cancerous encoding. Dangerous mass processing of information." Alan said in regards to the unwritten encoding within a society that can destroy itself without outside help.

Alan went onto describe the differences between Judaism and Christianity in relation to "misinterpretations." "In Judaism, we are taught to read the Torah, which is the old testament. The Rabbi does not spend thirty minutes in his personal translation of a verse or verses of the old testament that he just read. It is up to the reader, the listener, to translate in a personal growth relationship with God. Not for a doctrine created, and then another doctrine added in translation like the protestants and catholic faiths insist upon doing to their religion. Through mass personal and scholarly and language translations, the truth can be lost. The premise. The point….. To keep faith and the word of God pure, one must not continuously interpret to a large or small audience………God's message needs to be personal, not doctrine, rules, regulations, to then be selfishly translated by zealous ministers and religious leaders all alike. Scriptures are your personal connection to God, not a mass following of a religious leaders personal interpretation to be seen and viewed as 'the almighty translation from the divine.' Which can dangerously become a misinterpretation on various scales within various different congregations. Just another boundary defining definition that becomes a clause within a subculture that does not connect all people like God so intends and wishes. When you hear a song being played in the car, do you turn and interpret that song's meaning to those listening to that song? No. You listen. And to each person that song meaning is personal." Alan said.

As you the reader will understand the music of this book, in the end. That is the intention of God's word, not one million plus arguing translations of what God meant in the scriptures, or more personally, what God meant by my life read and revealed to you. Your opinion matters. Prophets and crusaders of the past were tortured for divine opinions. And yet, the same Biblical prophets, command us to believe what they write or else? Why? Or is that just a Roman Catholic Pope or minister's translation, for their motivation over your life and mind?

Here is my question to the Roman Catholic Pope, "If your catholic faith is so powerful, the correct road or else I parish for all eternity, then why are there so many archbishops that are some of the most high ranking in the catholic faith, and believe it is o.k. to molest children?" Religion is not the way, the path, or the plank! Wisdom and a connection to the divine is the path. Catholics believe it is more important to cover up a crime or a molestation, than to address the crime. The crimes taint the church. The United States Government, Hollywood, and many religions work that same way. One has to step back and analyze, is it the system that is wrong? Or the people within the system? Find out.

I said to Alan……..."Organized religions for the most part are religious subcultures that miss the mark, they could not ever create harmony, balance and peace within civilization, because of their foundation to have translators. Which turns into misinterpretations and peer pressure to believe one way only or be condemned, and/or thrown out of the community, society."

"Just look at history, read all you can about history, and wars in history and why the wars were started, it had to do with hate, intolerance, or power struggles, or a misunderstanding." Spoke Alan in his dramatic quest to enlighten my opening of learning every angle of that prism of understanding that stayed lodged within his great scope of knowing so much. I stayed rested on his upper legs, as I appeared open to all he could possibly teach me about the laws of physics concerning our universe on that steamy hot afternoon in Georgia.

I do not believe earthquakes happen in Georgia, but it felt like Cindy and her friend Kim Livermore, certainly wanted to shake it up some…….

One day in 1992 I received a call from Cindy. She was aware I was working at The Gold Club a few nights a week. She knew of the money I was making and the nice luxury apartment I could afford. Cindy was always giving me a sob story of sorts that would enable her to have me send her money or come home for a vacation and give her money.

I lived many states away from her, a whole world away by living in the south. And still Cindy would employ this psychological mind control of trying to own me and all that I could financially produce. As much as I liked my life in Georgia, away from her and her demands, she always found a way to call, complain, basically manipulate me in her attempts to gain my money that I earned. Quite possibly try to ruin my life in any which way she could. In 1992 I went back to college, worked nights and saw Alan mostly on the weekends. Now I learned that Cindy wanted to "visit me" in Georgia. What I was unprepared for, Cindy had plans to actually move into my apartment and live off me, for a longer time than just a vacation.

Instead of <u>asking</u> if she could live with me, and then hear a response of "no," from me. Cindy plots and schemes behind my back. Then announces that she is going to drive down and visit me. She ended up staying close to a year, all of which she premeditated.

The next day I told Alan of my mother's intention to visit me in Georgia.

"I hope that is all she intends to do….visit. Then she can leave." Spoke up Alan.

My life in the 1990's was like a song being sung under the branches of a tree, not heard by the rest of the forest. I knew my mother Cindy was not a normal mother. She was not a caring mother whatsoever, yet she was the only mother that claimed to be my mother. If I talked about Cindy to others, I might appear to be wrapped up in a non-normal life, **which** ironically, I was wrapped into a non- normal life. As much as I wanted to have a normal life, a normal mother, I just was not going to get that wish, not this time around in this lifetime lived. I longed so much for a mom and a dad.

I wanted to regress backwards and relive a happy home life in west Michigan. I still wanted a happy childhood in exchange for the childhood home life memories I seemingly had stuck inside my mind and emotions. How would I get these terrible memories and emptiness out of me, I wondered. Realizing that going back to one's own childhood to have all that might have been missing is not possible and that moving on with my life was the only option available, I moved forward with slipping on those high heels, the spiked five inch slippers that were not made out of glass. I experienced very abruptly from Cindy that wanting something is motivation in how to make money. The emotion and drive of want or wanting something is how I would carve out a good living in the early 1990's, making others want.

I loved Alan, but did not want to marry him because I literary still had so many bad flashbacks of my parents saga, horrors of their married life. I liked my life. Just the way it was, with Alan in my life. I am twenty three now, life is good. I did not want to change any element about my life. Alan would argue to me that it was my mother who controls my life. Not marrying him, was not avoiding the issue of control, which he claimed was my mother who destroyed me in her unusual light of always making me look like a whore, and she was the saint. I needed the money I produced at The Gold Club. Cindy liked the money I produced, and she liked to control what she could in just about every situation that involved money. Despite knowing all this, I knew I needed to let go of the fear of being controlled. What I would learn in the preceding years was that my fears and phobias would destroy wonderful chances in love. Cindy must have known that too in her tactics, along with Kim Livermore, her partner in crime when disturbing my life.

Cindy never paid for lunch, dinner, or any meal, it was always me. There never were shopping trips, it was what I could provide to her, give her, buy her. I knew she made me feel empty, but at the time I did not coin it as "demoralizing," it was just my reality. One thing was for sure, Cindy would not want me to quit The Gold Club, under any circumstances. She never helped me find another job either. I felt so young when I looked in the mirror, yet when I looked closely, inside, that is, I felt old. As if I was passing up the best years of my life. I wanted to locate "normal." What normal is and was. Not Cindy and her Central Intelligence friends and associates trampling over my young life like a pack of ol' wild west buffalos.

Cindy was always trying to make me feel as if my life and what I do with my life, I somehow owed her, because she is Cindy, my adopted mother. As if I should be honoring her, jumping as high as she wants, when she wants. As much as I would laugh about comedy shows that depicted fake housewives, and made fun of the Midwest, such as The Kids In The Hall. For some reason unknown to me, I could not erase this need that I am always supposed to please Cindy and do what Cindy wants with my life. It was a warped mental grasp Cindy embedded into my brain from the beginning of her adoption of me in the 1970's. At Christmas and her birthday, it was always what I could buy her, give her. That was life, that was my reality. I did not even at the time think it was odd that I never received birthday gifts, or a birthday cake from Cindy past the age of ten. Some people commented over the years it was weird or odd. But for me, it was my life, my reality, that was all I knew, so how could I compare a different realty? I was a fish who knew the sea, not how to swim on the land?

I did not deep down know a feeling other than empty, that was just how Cindy conditioned me since infancy. As if my emptiness would go away if I gave more to Cindy, and just kept ignored my own needs, so I was conditioned by Cindy. My father, a Leo, would roll over in his grave today if he read this book, in shock, that I actually would dare to say or write something negative about Cindy. Yet very truthful would be the spotlight I shed on Cindy and not care of a backlash within the Calvinistic society she knitted herself into, controlled, embedded into like wool on a sweater. Cindy went to church twice on Sunday, she joined Bible studies and religious charities. Made people that went against her wishes she would point out to be bad, a whore for me, and a drunk for my dad. The truth is, I did work at The Gold Club, which first was my idea, then I was stuck there because of some mind control Cindy had that The Gold Club is where I should be making lots of money. The truth is my dad was an alcoholic, but deep down Cindy did not care, my father's downfall with vodka in his glass daily gave Cindy purpose in being right, correct. To have the church and minister on her side, real power to her, in her world. Cindy would be perceived as the saint as she created other perceptions of others such as myself. I was mad I fit into the role of a whore as an adult, when as a child I thought I would own my adult years, I was mistaken.

I remember distinctively there are mirrors everywhere in The Gold Club. I remember standing, dancing nude, it is called a "table dance." I'd dance an arm's length away, nude, the men are not allowed to touch, nor are we allowed to touch the men. The men would just stare at me quietly and slip money in my garter as I did this Betty Bop sway dance. I remember looking at myself in the mirror wondering how I could just take my clothes off in front of a stranger? Not just once, but over and over throughout the night. I never even paused for a moment. How did I get this way I wondered? So jaded? Am I too young or too old not to blush? This is not normal how I am making a living, but why am I not grabbing my clothes on and running to the dressing room? I just stared at the mirror and the salt and pepper gentlemen in front of me…… the music overhead, around me. I glanced at him, looked at myself in the mirror.….and just stood there and wondered, this euphony tangle……I had an epiphany.……about my world….about this….and that……. Wondering that very profound question myself. The music blaring off the rafters, the sounds of wine glasses clinging………over the sound of Steve the D.J. announcing that I am next on stage………..In my mind I was silently searching for answers myself, just as you might search for answers, as I danced and swayed to the song playing at The Gold Club. Looking back into time, how did I get this jaded, how is it I am not modest anymore? Built-in modesty <u>did</u> once exist in me, it did. I would once fight to keep my modesty with Cindy, it would be a heated argument, one that I would not want to lose. Arguments over issues, resulting in me resenting Cindy and her ways. And then one day I looked in the mirror, I was not the innocent child with a rebellious Cindy being an awful mother. The tables had turned, at what point I cannot remember. I stared at myself in the glow of colored lights bouncing off the mirror, I looked and smelled like a whore. I realized I could not push against the glass of that Gold Club mirror and simply step back into Jenison, Michigan and resume my childhood as being innocent. I was seemingly the progressive rebel in the mirror, a whore, and Cindy was the saint. It's as if I had given my blank canvas and paint supplies away as I could care less how the picture was painted of me now. I didn't care. I was there to make more than minimum wage while a college student, and modesty was not even a topic to argue about with me anymore, I had a car payment, rent to pay, adult bills to pay now.

 I remember at the house on Curwood Drive in Jenson, getting ready for church one Sunday morning. My mother Cindy brought me a slip, a bra and underwear to put on in the bathroom after my shower. I must have been around eleven, maybe twelve. She then ordered for me to go to my bedroom to put on my Sunday dress in my bedroom. I just froze in fear of leaving the privacy of the bathroom. My bedroom was on the other side of the house. I could hear my two brothers and father talking and sitting around the kitchen table. I would have to walk past them to get to my bedroom down the hallway. My mother Cindy refused to bring me my Sunday dress which was located in my bedroom, on the other side of the house.

I clearly remember my fear and dread of walking past them in just a slip and bra that my mother was demanding would be my only garments to travel to my room to then locate my Sunday dress for church in my bedroom. I argued fiercely and pleaded with Cindy in my horror "to please get my dress for me and bring it here!!" It was a heated argument I had with her, I was in tears, I felt sick, I felt a rush of heat come over me, I was so modest…..then…..back then. Cindy was ready and threatening to slap me if I did not do as she had asked. Cindy was not a kind woman who cared about my feelings. I just as her daughter could not see her point of view. Cindy was mad and grabbed my arm and flung me so fast out of the bathroom to bully me and show me who is boss of my emotions. I felt crushed inside, just humiliated.

The more she refused to bring my church dress to me from my bedroom, the more I blushed and felt sick to my stomach. It was such a thing that I did not want to do, to walk past my two brothers and dad in just a slip and bra. I could clearly hear they were still at the kitchen table. I thought I was going to vomit, I felt panicky and scared. Cindy kept snarling towards me "To not be funny and march down to your bedroom to get my dress on down there, they are just you brothers and father, so what!" Cindy said in an angry demanding tone as she grunted her teeth at me. She grabbed my arm hard and pulled me out of the bathroom as I stood in tears. Cindy told me "To stop being funny, snap out of this mood, and go get my dress."

I still remember the horror of not having my privacy. I walked very quietly and quickly as I passed the dining room table. I saw in my peripheral vision, my brother and father stopped talking and watched me go past. I blushed and felt a deeper humiliation. I just kept staring ahead, down the hallway. Cindy did not care about my feelings as a child, a young teenager. Cindy had no compassion for my feelings. None. I was a rag doll that needed a beating in her eyes and her CIA associates to just listen to her. I just wanted a compassionate mother who cared about my feelings of modesty. It was Rome in her world, under her roof, and I did not like to bow to her commands. I wanted to fight for my modesty, my rights as a child, almost a teenager. She, Cindy, would not allow for my rights, my modesty to even be considered as "important." I felt so crushed then, but now, I am an adult who can make logical choices, so why do I not care about my modesty anymore? I don't understand.

My life was a tennis match of no victory, it was a continual match served of either humiliation or the wrath of Cindy. Which included a physical beating by her with an emotional roller coaster attached to her rage. In 1993 I was considered an adult, but in her eyes, Cindy that is, I was still her child to control. But I am an adult now!

I recalled that scene from my childhood as I stared in the mirror with the swirling colored lights of The Gold Club. The black club lights made my teeth glow white, my smile sincere, my skimpy tan lines glowed white. I remembered growing up Cindy would demand I get undressed in public places verses finding a place to put my bathing suit on. She loved to take away my sense of privacy that I relished back then, that once cherished privacy. Aunt Jean was that same way towards me, when Cindy was around, it wasn't just Cindy, it wasn't. Getting undressed in public as a child felt humiliating and demoralizing. Sometimes Cindy and aunt Jean Stob would have me stand up in the trunk of the car with the trunk hood up and demand I get undressed as they inspected my private parts before I entered puberty. Why I could not have privacy growing up, and now as an adult, I am stronger and wiser, right?

I was meeting just about every professional athlete, famous music band members, many celebrities at The Gold Club in the early 1990's. I even met British Simon Cowell at The Gold Club before he sky rocketed to fame and fortune as a Judge of a famous televised talent show. I table danced for him on the main floor arena by his table. In a serious and deeply contemplative tone and look Simon Cowell said to me as the song ended as did the table dance, "You are going to get raped." I was maybe twenty-two, twenty-three, I gave him a look without speaking words as if to respond, no I am not. Simon Cowell answered my look, my expression, and remarked again in a serious slow and steady voice of reason as he slipped money into my garter, "You cannot possibly think you are not going to be raped by how you look, how you move and dance naked, you just can't think you will not be raped."

I clipped on my skimpy thong bathing suit outfit and vocally remarked back to Simon Cowell, "No I am not." After all, I am in control, I thought.

Simon Cowell looked at me with an utterly shocked expression as if I am the most ignorant or stupidest person on the planet. As if I just don't get it, understand.

I had never had any patron ever say that I was going to get raped, ever. One thing is for sure, that famous Judge to be never said I was fat, ugly or too angelic, too innocent to be working at The Gold Club.

Many local Atlanta male news anchors were filtering into VIP at The Gold Club. Male anchors from The Weather Channel, CNN, Wolf Blitzer was a regular fixture in VIP. I would gather information while dancing as to why The Gold Club was so important to the CIA, you know, for the CIA's business, finances, systems and all. Alles Law Firm in Grand Rapids, Michigan and Visser & Bolhouse estate planners would play a key role in behind the scenes estate planning in the legal world of Living Trusts with illegally gained money. I would learn so much about what authority could care less about and always wonder why. Once a determined amount was placed into a Living Trust, people were paid out money, then the Living Trust would be dissolved. It apparently was the easiest and safest way from the CIA to launder money with every day folks willing to take a slight risk. Some folks well educated like the estate planning attorneys and some folks with no college education at all, just needing extra money, big lump sums of extra money like Kent Cement Companies in Byron Center, Michigan to just stay afloat in rocky financial times. With every hair toss, with every swaying beat to music in five inch heels I would learn and learn and gather and gather and then write down details in my journals Carmen gave me. Later those journals would be stolen out of 405 Discovery Drive in Wayland, Michigan in 1998 by someone very elite and well connected to Hollywood, the CIA. A CIA agent by a made up name of Sharon would refer to those journals as "the princess diaries" to my face in 1998 across from me at my dining room table in rural Wayland. Sharon knows CIA John Brennan and CIA David Petraeus very well, along with many Hollywood stars and agents, and The Gold Club owner Steve Kaplan.

I would beg, plead, and argue for privacy growing up, it was a cause worth fighting for, I reminisced in profound thoughts as I looked in the mirrors with swirling, twirling colorful lights. I wanted someone to now answer for me, my question again: How did I get this way? When? What was the pivotal turning point of modesty to stripper? I am sure the CIA has that very intelligent answer to my profound question inside a folder in Washington D.C. stamped in red ink, "classified information." And all the stuffy white haired men, whimsical and creepy CIA General David Petraeus, bald and creepy CIA John Brennan and FBI and attorney James Comey would all agree in sound unison like a jury of many in complete power that classified information is just that, closed to the public for viewing. What next? Then they would gang up Washington D.C. style to start a war. A literal premediated war with terrorist players in places, cities and regions most Americans cannot even pronounce, remote foreign places the CIA and FBI know well, very well. They would devise strategies so that the created enemy would have weapons provided through American sources, guns and machinery traced back to America, but not to them and their classified meetings and conversations. The criminals both in charge in the CIA and FBI would align with hostile forces overseas to build an alliance that the CIA and FBI is very needed in these troubling times. All in the fight, the war effort in why they are important in the budget and billions spent at The U.S. Department of Justice on all their activities and secret projects that are not spotlighted by the media. The poignant point: All past, current, and future secret projects can stay protected, closed, all information the CIA and FBI want to keep secret about on American soil, Mike Rogers is one of them that knows how an octopus can get away. All classified information remains as important and not checked by the trusting American people, not prosecuted by Americans if Americans are busy in fear. As the instigators to war and wars all escape justice and jail time to continue what they like to do most in secret. They will enlist and send men off to die in war for democracy to rid any curiosity by the public into what is actually going on with democracy within political control and not our control. I can only imagine if I wrote down such truth on paper that Cindy and the CIA would see to it that I am medicated. And if they ever really get caught, caught as in arrested and jailed for their huge criminal undertakings towards the very trusting American people, the very first thing they will ask the arresting officer, "Is Lori on her medication?".... " Damn it, someone get Lori medicated! Lori is running her mouth again about our classified activities! Someone needs to shut her up for good! For security reasons Lori needs to be silenced!"

Silenced for whose security? Let me ask you the reader a question to ponder. What becomes of a nation that remains foolish and in debt? I know the answer to that question, do you know the correct answer to that question?

During the early 1990's at The Gold Club CIA John Brennan might have had one to many when he babbled on and on in VIP. about the problems the current CIA faced. Such as sustaining as a valid and important needed department in times when congress was questioning the CIA's demand budget as relevant in tough economic times facing America. John Brennan went on to confess problems facing the current and future existence of the CIA at a time when congress wanted to eliminate a huge portion within America's budget for the CIA. John Brennan explained a plan, a mastermind plan at that to create a disaster on American soil where the CIA could then be seen as needed once again. He went on to say, "Don't worry honey, not an actual full blown attack where an enemy or hostile country to the U.S. goes to war with the U.S. in a full blown war bombarding America, just an attack, one attack." John explained the CIA would then kill the enemy, become the hero once again and be back on the requested budget amount with no further probing by congress into the relevancy of the CIA ever again. When I gave a look of horror to his statement to me John Brennan moved forward brushing up against my left shoulder with his chin and whispered in a raspy drunk voice to me, "I like to mess with people's security, my job offers me plenty of opportunity to do so, don't ever repeat anything to anyone." John Brennan whispered that statement and confession of problems and solutions as I danced naked in front of him in the early 1990's.

In June of 2012 I placed my son Eddie at the MAC daycare to have a few moments of rest in the sunshine. I was laying out by the MAC, known as the Michigan Athletic Club in East Lansing, Michigan near Michigan State University. John Brennan had stalked me there like many other places. John Brennan approached me by the MAC pool on a warm and sunny day in June of 2012 in Michigan. He proudly informed me as he spread suntan oil on himself that 9/11 guaranteed the future existence of the CIA. He informed me that democrat CIA agents selected the foreign attack during a republican presidency and if on 9/11 2001 there was a democrat President the attack on the twin towers never would have occurred. He went on to inform me that the Michigan school district that funneled the most money to the CIA to then provide Yemen a hefty bundle was also able to select the target II in America. The mastermind to 9/11 was the CIA, the terrorist were merely a tool in the process of the CIA asserting their value within congress's budget. The twin towers in New York was actually selected by a lesbian running one of Michigan's school districts that hates the duality between a man and a woman, all according to John Brennan in June of 2012. In numerology II stands for the symbol of the duality between a man and a woman, the sexual duality between a man and a woman. John Brennan also stated that I pissed off a lot of CIA agents when I requested in a letter to the FBI in Lansing to investigate why there are so many, well over fifteen hundred elementary children that enrolled in Okemos school district during a ten year period and then their parents pulled them out of the district never to re-enroll the young children again. John Brennan warned me that David Petraeus wants to jail me as a means to shut me up if I don't watch it and stop writing to the FBI to investigate school closings and failing school systems in Michigan. John Brennan warned me numerous times to stay away from the FBI or I would face dire circumstances if I suggested to any authority to audit allocated school funds in Michigan. John Brennan informed me that the State of Michigan does not want to audit school district funds and the State of Michigan would produce accounting paperwork to suggest I am a liar that created hype over nothing substantial. John Brennan suggested the CIA would work behind the scenes in the judicial system in Michigan and I would end up in jail or dead like a star on a wall as a warning for me to shut my mouth, dead by food poisoning in my cell and my son would grow up without a mother.

On the forefront of belief the CIA has creatively developed a notion they are providing well needed and intelligent advice to American Presidents and providing national security to all Americans, that is the forefront created and devised well by the CIA through the years. However, the forefront is just a front to hide what actually goes on behind the façade that the CIA has created. Behind the scenes, the CIA is very busy, and very involved with a multitude of very illegal secret projects, all of which are very dangerously stamped with red ink markings of "classified." After 9/11 the CIA was needed, revered as the foreign intelligence source to once again depend upon in troubling times. 9/11 was a huge benefit to the CIA. Soon the CIA would go after Ben Laden the person the media dubbed the mastermind to 9/11. The media created the narrative and we all followed.

John Brennan had informed me at The Gold Club in the 1990's that a target, not a full blown war against America on American shores, just a target on American soil would be attacked by a foreigner, a foreign enemy would be the tool the CIA used. Utilized for the survival of the CIA to stay amplified verses diminished in the budget set by congress. John Brennan was very correct when confessing in the 1990's at The Gold Club that the CIA would only need to attack once on American soil, not multitudes of times, just once. Demonstrating the need to be needed by the American people and the budget proposal voted on by congress. Just like a mental disease called Munchausen by Proxy Syndrome, the CIA would once again shake off the dust, come to the rescue and be needed.

John Brennan was not the only CIA to get drunk at The Gold Club and unwind and disclose CIA secrets to me while I was on the job in high heels dancing nude using a chemical warfare called "Coco Chanel." CIA David Petraeus echoed what John Brennan had informed me of at The Gold Club. The intelligence gathering did not take me long to realize those two shared the same CIA philosophies of CIA survival tactics. Both had told me of their foreign resources as those two CIA agents flexed their powerful positions within American government. CIA David Petraeus informed me that the CIA has always had a human trafficking system in place and that The Gold Club was part of the system and for me to be careful not to ever accept a date from a patron within that place. He explained that the CIA has staffed hospital pharmacists that provide knock out drugs to transport the women to places in the Middle East where blonde haired, blue eyed German looking girls are in high demand. Currently one such pharmacist that illegally provides hospital drugs to the CIA is Jody Lee Smith (male) who lives at 28 Aaron Lane in Cartersville, Georgia, Rowland Springs Estates. Mr. Smith works currently at Floyd Medical as the manager of the hospital pharmacy. According to CIA sources Jody Lee (male) & Heather Smith received their 8100 square foot house with high end finishes from a man working as a front man for the CIA. Jody Lee Smith & his wife Heather Smith received their 8100 square foot house for the low amount of $187,000 through the CIA in exchange for pharmaceutical services to be provided to the CIA when needed.

Both John Brennan and David Petraeus informed me on separate occasions, separate table dances, and on separate nights in the early 1990's at The Gold Club that the CIA launders money into night clubs, real estate companies, cement companies and a whole host of other places. Illegal money derived from the CIA's human trafficking and drug profits alone. Both men also informed me that human traffickers connected to the CIA will pay police to pull over a girl that has been selected by a buyer, boldly bragging in their expression of their power, that is just how easy a disappearance can happen.

I inquired, "Where are all the women?" Both Brennan and Petraeus informed me the Middle East if the transaction goes smoothly or as anticipated or if the woman or child proves to be too difficult and the drugs and brainwashing do not work they end up on a mountainous terrain dropped off by a helicopter or lay resting on the bottom of a bog in Michigan.

I inquired further, "What if the remains are located and the body and crime is traced back to the CIA?"

Bogs are not searched, and the woods along a mountain side can be burned if searchers get near the evidence. That is what Brennan and Petraeus told me, that is the information I gathered from them about their CIA organization. My conclusion? Putting the CIA in charge of national security and advising the U.S. Presidents on presidential actions is like placing a group of thieves next to an open vault of billions.

Down the row in VIP in the early 1990's at The Gold Club would often sit attorney James Comey who later became the FBI director selected by future President Obama to run the FBI. James Comey's eyes were blood shot, every tiny vein red in his drunken eyes resting on pillows of swollen flesh. James Comey informed me that the CIA would select people and persons to join political races and inevitably end up on the ballot in every facet.

My thoughts as I danced and swayed? Is that even true democracy when the CIA is enabling certain people and peoples to get on an election ballot? What are your thoughts?

James Comey very drunk staying up too late looked as if he had difficulty locating enough space for his legs and bent knees sitting on a tall bar stool in the very crowded VIP at The Gold Club against the mirror backdrop as I unraveled truth after <u>truth</u> in him. As if the bottom layer of most men is to say the truth, as if they <u>want</u> to tell the truth, especially when drunk. James Comey informed me that when the CIA abducts a girl the FBI will never be allowed to locate that kidnapped girl or child. However, if an average joe criminal abducts a child or woman the FBI is free to locate the missing person.

Then we began discussing politics again and the CIA's meddling with American and foreign election ballots. James Comey explained to me that the CIA has created a totalitarian government out of democracy propaganda tactics. He explained to me that my brother Dave (Dave Vander Ark) received a broken jaw that was then wired shut in 1984 for my brother's knowledge of sales to Saudi. James Comey explained why the CIA placed their political puppets on ballots. The CIA fast at work from every level within America's judicial system, even presidential elections. Elected pawns of the CIA and what the CIA needs done from directional views to courtroom favors. Then James Comey pointed out at The Gold Club in Atlanta, Georgia, a small feeble man with funky black Doc Martin shoes on his feet getting a table dance. "Take that man over there, the CIA is going to see that he is on the ballot for Judge for the 55th District Court in Mason, Michigan to oversee State of Michigan court cases and proceedings in a rural county of Michigan to silence people in a certain school district. One goal of the CIA's is to abolish Due Process and create a judicial dictatorship to handle cases." The young blonde girl that table danced for future Judge Thomas Boyd was never seen again after that particular night shift.

On another night in VIP at The Gold Club in Atlanta, Georgia James Comey pointed out Dick DeVos the businessman from Michigan. Attorney James Comey explained that Dick DeVos was very well connected to the CIA and that is why he comes to the CIA club. A guy sitting with James Comey remarks, "Amway is a front company with fictitious earning reports."

James Comey slouches and smirks in his response to that man's comment about Amway. James Comey informed me about Dick DeVos's very lucrative sex trafficking and human trafficking business with the CIA. James Comey informed me that the CIA would like to place Dick DeVos on an election ballot to further the interest of the CIA and what the CIA would be able to do power wise with little or no interference from any policing authorities and no scandals reported to the media. What type of girl does Dick DeVos like? From what I observed, very, very, very young types, school girl types, girls with fake I.D.'s that danced under age at The Gold Club were his type, or the CIA's type.

    I decided when the song ended with James Comey I would get dressed and walk past the semi-private VIP room where Dick DeVos was located. As I walked near the entrance to the VIP room Dick DeVos's eyes grew big and waved me into the room to sit down. The two CIA agents, regulars at The Gold Club looked alarmed, worried to say the least. I remember my first impression of Dick DeVos. He was tall, dark and not handsome. He has a Dutch last name and does not look Dutch at all. He would best be described as a tall dark Dutch, not one facial feature resembled Dutch, and he was so dark. He explained to me an hour after the cork blew off the champagne bottle in VIP that the Lebanese were starting Charter schools in Michigan as a way to launder money and a way to receive more and more allocated school funds from the American government. Then later I asked to see a picture of his wife, she looked fifty percent Jewish and fifty percent German. She did not look Dutch at all. I had a hard time believing he was Dutch. Nevertheless I am in the room to make money and ask questions to rest my curiosity of this man supposedly from west Michigan, my old turf, a place I know well. Dick DeVos had a few cocktails and was clearly relaxed with telling me about his business dealings with clubs and the CIA. I was maybe 122 pounds, around twenty-two or twenty-three years old, breast implants, tan lines with a tan that matched in color to my copper long hair with highlights. I wore a skimpy sky blue sequence thong of a stripper outfit on my body some of the time that we talked. I wore glitzy rhinestone jewelry that glowed white with my smile and white five inch heels. I had no wedding band because I was authentically single. I know that a female cop or female FBI agent could never have duplicated my look, my demeanor and have been me. I simply was always in the right places at the right time to receive information worthy to have supplied the authorities. However, I was there for money and curiosity which made me authentically real in all the situations at The Gold Club. It would not be until later that I felt I knew too much and had to tell someone, some authority. What I would shockingly learn though, is that authority really does not want to know any of what I have written here. This information matters little to authority, then I realized I was just a girl, a dancer, who learned too much.

Recalling back to the early 1990's; At some point a light when on in Dick DeVos's head as he so much wanted to sober up by what he had shared with a stripper stranger. He looked at me and asked me for my phone number. I gave him my phone number so he knew I was sincere in sitting next to him and all he shared with me about his shady dealings with earning income. I never saw that very young under age girl again, she never worked another shift at The Gold Club again, she simply disappeared. Then I had a scary situation happen to me about three days after meeting Dick DeVos. I was headed out to work the night shift at The Gold Club, as I backed out and then put my car in drive I stop abruptly as I notice a car right in front of me blocking the go lane. The man jumps out of his freshly parked car and states through my car window that he is lost and wants me to put my window down and help him, he's lost. His eyes were bugged out, the male stranger appeared frantic and crazed. I thought very quickly, no I am not going to put my window down or get out of my car. I drove around him and headed to my next shift at The Gold Club. If someone is lost, needs a map, go to a gas station, I thought as I drove to work that night. That was before GPS systems, that was the early 1990's, and I knew danger when I saw danger, most of the time that is.

I once table danced in the early 1990's for future U.S. President Barack Obama. I would describe him as very quiet. He appeared to be slightly uncomfortable in a high class white strip club surrounded by a lot of white men with a lot of money. Usually never did I ever see a black man in The Gold Club as a patron unless they were Emmett Smith or another athletic superstar.

CIA agent Bob Baer was a regular at The Gold Club, rarely if ever did he sit up top in V.I.P. on the second story loft of sorts. Bob Baer could usually always be found at a high top on the main floor center arena. Bob Baer liked both table dances and conversation. I would not describe him as intelligent even though he works for an intelligence gathering agency, the CIA. Do you know of that old cliché, it takes intelligence to recognize intelligence? O.k., well God must have short changed Bob in that category, but never the less he was hired to work for the CIA. Bob Baer informed me of the CIA's involvement with drugging and shipping girls overseas from small airports to never be heard of again by their families. Bob Baer also informed me of the CIA having many staffed pharmacists worldwide to provide drugs for transporting women, children and babies. Bob Baer was very aware of the criminal activities of the CIA as he warned me and other girls around him at the high top bar table of the CIA's devious tactics. However, he was never bold enough to stand up to his boss and stop the sex trafficking and human trafficking done by the CIA utilizing strip clubs to collect the demand and supply for wealthy clients waiting in the Middle East. Bob Baer informed me that sex trafficking and human trafficking can bring in a billion dollar surplus with worldwide covert operations. However, Bob Baer always acted like ten dollars was a lot of money to give for a table dance.

I see the click, click, flip of a slide show, just certain scenes of my childhood, as I realize the next man I am now dancing for is Adam Duritz. He whispers his question, "Is or was your adopted father Jewish? Are you originally from Michigan?"

I answered back, "Yes." And kept dancing until I heard the song end. Then he began groping me all over, all at once suddenly groping me and pulling me near him as I clipped my skimpy outfit back on me.

Adam Duritz asked me, "Can you sing?"

I laughed and said "No."

Adam Duritz then said, "I had to fly here and see for myself. I remember you before you even had pubic hair. Now you're all grown up, a young lady now. I want you. You're afraid of me, that's why you're shaking." He said calmly and deliberately……As he touched my arm and hugged on me. I began seeing scenes of world war II. As long as he held onto me, the scenes would continue. Then he leaned over and spoke sternly into my ear and said, "Don't be afraid of who I am. I know you can see."

I continued to dance…..then my mind flashed back to my childhood in Jenison, Michigan……..

As a ten year old you only absorb scenes, events, feelings, faces, etc. Kinda like now, I thought. Even though I am considered a grown young adult now. When you are a child one does not see from an adult perspective or know all the adult terms for your body and facts, or what sex is at age eight, nine, or ten. So what I could absorb emotionally and mentally about that scene before I was a teenager…I remember him touching me when I was eight? Nine? Ten? I remember seeing very vivid world war II scenes when he held on to me back then in my childhood, as now.

What ever happened to that teenage boy? There he was, just one day walked into The Gold Club and reminded me what happened, 1980, 1981? 1979? 1978?

The music blared at The Gold Club, the songs the D.J. played changed in rhythm and tune like the men I would dance for as I hopped from table to table. The twirling vibrant lights, above and around…….I would dance nude publicly as often silently I would become my own personal inner therapist trying to answer my own questions about my life in the 1990's……..as I danced………..in wonderment, how did I get this way? Jaded, bustling sexuality.

I admit Cindy was relentless, she thought I deserved no privacy when undressing. I was a person who had no valid point or feelings to consider as I grew up in her household. I remember another humiliating experience at the hands of Cindy, I was fifteen perhaps. I was at the community neighborhood pool in Jenison when Cindy had her condo. I was standing next to a girl in the neighborhood, Amy, who is about my age, she attended Jenison High. My mother sat in a chair next to her mother, "Mrs. B." My mother Cindy reaches between my legs, touching me inappropriately and grabs onto a white string, and pulls, pulls as a bully, Cindy says, "Your bathing suit has a string hanging down."

It was not a string, it was my Tampon. I squirmed and pulled back from the uncomfortable feeling of humiliation and said, "Don't do that!" The lady sitting next to Cindy, Mrs. B., just remained silent and shocked by Cindy's action towards me. I was humiliated having my private area touched and grabbed by Cindy in public, demoralized, horrified once again by Cindy. She had this processed delusional way of thinking of herself, that boundaries mean nothing, I am sure the CIA taught her that rule of business. Cindy is the mother, the ruler, and in her mind can touch, grab and humiliate me because she is in control of owning me. The community structure of west Michigan, and Michigan in general, hate victims, they consider the victim, the mess. When Cindy returned back home that afternoon to our condo, she stated that Mrs. B. would not speak to her all afternoon after Cindy had pulled my string on my bathing suit.

I looked at Cindy and remarked, "You and I and Mrs. B. know it was not a string from my bathing suit, it was my Tampon. You like to humiliate me as a child under the age of eighteen. You also like to humiliate me as a young woman nearing eighteen, that is how your power and control work Cindy."

Cindy mustered up fits of rage if I closed the bathroom door, locked the bathroom door, and or bedroom door growing up. I know I was born with a built-in sense of modesty, I was. But as I looked at myself totally naked in the mirrors at The Gold Club, dancing for a stranger or a patron I knew, I was trying to make sense of it all. The club had at least three hundred patrons packed into the nightclub each night, I felt not one piece of modesty, not a shred of modesty was left in me when I had reached twenty, I was now twenty-three.

I remember fighting and arguing for privacy growing up, and now, I saw no boundaries that Cindy had not crossed. In my opinion Cindy had the shallow people in God fooled, but not me, no matter if you viewed, tasted, or smelled me as a whore, I really am not a whore. It was not God-like, my career back then, it was warped. I could have all the privacy I wanted as an adult now, but I could care less now that I am twenty-something. Why? Why? Why? I kept asking myself in my emotionally aloof silence of trying to understand myself as the music blared on at The Gold Club in Atlanta, Georgia…….

I will never forget how white Alan's face went when he first met Cindy. He turned to me when in private, and stated, "Cindy is a monster, you do not know it, but she is……..Cindy is also very aware of what she is, and of those around her that want to blow her cover on earth. Monsters sense their opposition, and inflict upon the ones of God, the want to win on earth."

"What? Like a demon?" I asked.

He then went on to say this, "I find it alarming that the Dutch Calvinistic subculture that claims to know God on a better level than Jews, Muslims, and any other religion, cannot see through Cindy. I believe your dad saw through her after the honeymoon, and might have picked up his choice of "escapism of Cindy" soon after marrying her, alcohol."

I agreed with Alan on that subject.

Alan liked to stay up late at night and watch T.V., he'd watch Saturday Night Live and laugh and comment to me, "Your mother Cindy is the church lady, I swear Saturday Night Live knew of Cindy when creating the church lady character on SNL."

I agreed with Alan on that subject.

I would often watch a show in the afternoon called, "Kids In The Hall," I think it was on the comedy channel. The show painstakingly reminded me so much of those housewives and families sitting by a dinner table in western Michigan, how they act towards one another, fake almost, it was all about perception. I knew I would never become one of them, and why. I just can't be two-faced, or to pretend to live in some abstract conforming system of dysfunctional pillars in society created to make people feel that if you belong....You must act like us....the Christians. It is that way with any religion or political party. Live their life in a subculture world, with boundaries and dimensions created by them. Why do none of those Christians ever talk about heaven? They have never been there, that is why, they have the wrong path, I know it. On earth, this life, what matters is conformity, not the truth to them. Then supposedly life, your life, is worthwhile to Christianity, to Judaism, to Hinduism, Muslim, to Islam....the list of conformities goes on and on for the sake of religion.....at the end of conforming is it heaven? No. And in heaven, ya'll, there is no religion.

The communication to belong or else is both verbal and a physical backlash from the Calvinists with an unwritten motto, "you act just like us, and it does not matter what your intentions are, motives and such," "the goal is to just fit in," "to just conform." That is how west Michigan thinks and personifies the great profile of Christianity as a lumped together whole. There is a pattern within all religions and government alike, the more people conform, the less questions are asked of the leaders. Conformity to beliefs of what is preached is what leaders need in order to maintain control over the flock, the audience, the citizens.

Alan had many comments to make to me, unlike a student in his class, at times when I look back in hindsight, I failed to have raised my hand in class or the bedroom. Someday I will raise my hand and ask more questions. Such as when he said this startlingly statement to me one day, "On your astrology chart I examined yesterday your fortune is made in literature, it has to do with the sign of Aquarius which means radical, futuristic. Uranus is the planet that governs that particular sign, in ancient astrology Saturn was the planetary ruler. The Age of Aquarius is a good, well needed mixture of both characteristics of those planetary influences. The Age of Aquarius is upon us now in these times, The Age we have entered as a world."

I asked, "What? Explain what are you talking about?"

"The lens effect. The government lens effect. You have major psychological warfare with Cindy and a harsh society in your future. I read that on your digitally graphed astrology blueprint of your future on my software program at home." Alan said such interesting things to me, I wish I had paid more attention, asked more questions of him. He was such a source of knowledge.

Alan motioned and spoke up "Here. Let me snap some casual photos of you for safe keeping of what I am talking about, and compare it to your high school days when you looked like a young Queen Beatrix."

"Let's go to Savannah, it's St. Patrick's Day tomorrow. We can drive tonight, it's only four, maybe six hours away. The city square fountains, all twenty-four of them will have green water sprouting from them when we arrive." I suggested as I got up from the floor.

"Now? Let's go now? I have to pack." Remarked Alan putting away his camera.

"I have some extra shirts of yours, like that pink and tan striped shirt, t-shirts, let's go, we can pack here, what I have of yours." I said with convincing enthusiasm. I then ran my fingers through his hair.

"Now? You really want to go now?" He asked again.

"Yes, let's go. I'll even pack that green dress you bought me. The Moon River Brewing Company is having a Irish Red Killian's Beer St. Patrick's Day contest for the best looking redhead, I'm going to enter. Let's go and party and have some fun!" I said as I got up from the sofa to head into my closet to pack a suitcase full.

We did drive to Savannah that night. I put in old fashioned tapes and CD's of the 1800's era with melodies played from a mandolin and banjo to set the mood. The bed and breakfast we had hoped to stay at was full, due to the big St. Patrick's Day celebration lasting all week long, so we stayed at a hotel right in Savannah. The next morning we took a horse and buggy ride through the city. We had the driver stop at Lafayette Square.

I just stared and listened to the water fountain, the water was green. I could hear the water fountain flowing from the carriage. Alan helped me down like the perfect gentlemen that he was and we walked to the center of the square. The trees and bushes looked overgrown. As we neared the water fountain sounds I felt almost sad to go back to Lafayette Square for some reason. As if stepping closer to a life I loved and lost, closer to a life I wanted to hold onto but lost, had no control over keeping, I felt dread honestly. My life during the 1860's flashed before me again, and again, I had lost so much, yet recovered Alan in this new life.

Alan took my hand and guided me to the sparkling green water. He got down on one knee and asked, stated rather to me, "Won't you marry me Lori? Because if you don't I'm going to date other women."

I did not respond.

Alan then stood in front of me, pressed against me this time and said to me as he whispered firmly in my ear holding my hand as I leaned forward on him; "Marry me Lori."

I looked down to the ground and spoke against Alan's shoulder, "I think I will always push pause when a relationship gets to this point. You know I do not want to marry and have the life my adopted parents had when I was growing up in Michigan."

Alan then took green fountain water and splashed my arm, "May you always regret saying no." He was mad at me. It was Saint Patrick's Day in Savannah, Georgia, we were at Lafayette Square. But I was hurt by the words of his proposal. That was not a romantic proposal, it was blackmail.

That night I put on that green sexy tailored dress he had bought me months ago to wear on a date of ours to The Black Horse Tavern in Virginia Highlands near his home. Tonight I would not be wearing the dress over a romantic dinner and wine for a table for two. Instead, I was out to win a contest for fun. I love St. Patrick's Day for the sheer excitement of the celebration, the partying of the street crowds, the bars. In Atlanta it is always a big celebration too.

I did win the contest that night at The Moon River Brewing Co., it was announced just after 11pm that evening. Afterwards we walked back to the hotel room as I counted my money earnings along the way. Alan was mad though, he hated the guys drunk on the street carrying on and congratulating me. That evening, back at our hotel room, as much as Alan loved me, I saw a different side to him. As he made love to me, he just squeezed me, squeezing parts of me, squeezing me hard. It was as if he loved me, and also had an addiction he also wanted to break free from that night. Yet was physically, visibly and emotionally very unsure he could break free from loving me….and that made him mad, so it appeared to me.

I never accepted that blackmail of a marriage proposal by Alan. There would be other romantic moments, and after all, I am twenty-something, under twenty-five!

Sometimes my life was not full of Alan, sometimes I would take off with my friend Steve, sort of like a best friend, buddy kind of guy. Especially when Alan became controlling of my life. I would want to just run and free myself of any physical, emotional or mental control Alan had over me, or wanted over me, or was seemingly mad about loving me. It is terrible to be on the receiving end of a man who is mad he is in love with me.

Sometimes I needed a weekend away from Alan. I recall now, when my friend Steve was over at my apartment back then in the 1990's with friends like Sandra Dee. Steve and I would take bong hit after bong hit, maybe eight bong hits in a row. We'd look at each other and say to each other after the first draw of smoke, then the second, and the third, "I still feel the same…..do you?" He'd ask.

I'd say, "Yeah, I still feel the same, I don't feel stoned yet," and I'd reach for a fourth, fifth, until I felt high. Steve would finally say, "Poke me with a fork, I'm baked." Everyone would laugh, but it really took us longer to get high, to get stoned than everybody else at my gatherings.

I say it like it is folks. I think Steve and I naturally saw things oddly, originally, different. He was not such a romantic interest of mine, he was more like a best friend type. He was not a pushy older man trying to make me his wife. We took life on a slow calendar basis, our schedules in our minds our wheels just turned slower than most, naturally.

The one thing I did notice about Jewish people while living in Atlanta, which I did like, if you ever entered into a conversation with one of them, the sky was never the limit on subjects or boundaries to discuss. Life, love, sex, politics, religion, the world, or any irrelevant obscure subject that might come up in the conversation, could come up in conversation.

Opposite of great conversationalists are the Dutch Christian Reformed people, "the stoic Calvinists of West Michigan." If you go beyond asking how they are doing or feeling within the boundaries of a conversation, or how was their weekend? Or go beyond and above making polite talk about "accepted family questions" or "accepted work related" questions, the Calvinists would look at each other in unison, stop dead in their tracks, and say or whisper to each other. Even slightly kick the other's foot under the table and say or give a look with their eyes, "code blue, free thinker on board." Then of course ostracize you in public if they could, any independent thinker was always ostracized. As I remember growing up around them, I often thought quietly, if Jesus was here, living among the Calvinists, they would have ostracized him, for as we all know, he was an independent thinker, once on Time magazine for being "a rebel." A rebel for thinking outside the box of the religion he was placed into, an outsider to Judaism and how Jews thought. Jesus noticed the flaws of that religion that so contradicted the elements of heaven, what the religions noted as the path to God.

For example, my high school friends, especially Cheri Berens Hulst of Hudsonville, would kick Carmen's ankles under the table at a restaurant if I ever said anything "odd," or "different."

Cheri Berens Hulst would laugh in that "gosh darn it attitude," cackle like a hen in a barnyard, and say as she would nod and twitch her neck in a pecking way, "Gosh, Lori, we can't believe you just said that at the table." As Cheri would also nudge Carmen under the table. Carmen would always just laugh, sigh, and kick Cheri back under the table as I responded. I was aware that I thought outside of what I was taught growing up in Hudsonville and Jenison, Michigan, which bothered the Calvinists.

Often I found myself in the 1990's in a bit of a trance with flooded memories of my childhood, flooded memories of past lives emerging. And then suddenly, the crickets chirp, the smell of Midwest muck fields would seemingly stench up the summer air. Sights of rows of gold corn filled the here and now, and I was just back to the present day. I am wholesome, naïve, and just shocked at the dualities of others within the Christian Dutch community subculture of west Michigan. In Atlanta I could tell just about anyone or anybody that I am a dancer. No one cares. No one Judges. But here in the Midwest, there are two worlds, the world you show the world, and the world behind closed doors. Cindy and the Calvinists taught me the reality of duality well, I understood it at least.

When I would travel back to Michigan to visit when Carmen and I were alone, Carmen loved all I said about life, people, and the fakeness the Calvinists seem to transcend to others. Just like the Kids In The Hall comedy hour, Carmen would laugh at my jokes. Carmen would say, "That's so funny Lori, you just say things like you see it, but some people do enjoy having two worlds. That's just how Hudsonville operates, they can't be honest about being fake."

With me, how it works, I like to get to know the person, the person you are inside. I have a knack for reading auras and then gathering information. There must be something very pristine about my aura too.

Like an aura of a holy catholic priest, people seemingly love to confess information that is bottled up inside them, like confession time. I could care less about the outside daily façade you present to the community you want to belong to, or strive to belong to. What matters is what is real inside you, the nitty gritty of inside your soul that makes you, you. Not outside conformities meant to fool others. Belonging is an important need, it just is, I understand. When in Rome, act like a Roman, or dare not to…….. My role is not about a voting contest, or being political correct. I am "politically truthful," in both religion and politics, well, just about every category, really. A person's base, their foundation of their belief systems, their wisdom, is their substance, and so are their sins for the most part.

"You need to become famous, you need to step out in public. You need to not fear the public eye and criticism of the media." Said Alan as he sat back on my sofa sipping on a cocktail.

"I want to be normal. Not famous." I said from the kitchen. "Not everyone needs to be famous to be heard. I just want to be normal." I said.

Alan responded to my statement shaking his head, "Normal? You are afraid you will not be normal if you step out and allow for me to make you famous? The CIA owns Hollywood. Come on…..let's go have sex in some Savannah or Charleston cemetery….be the talk of every tabloid!"

"No." I said.

"You'll enjoy it." Alan remarked as he sipped on his beverage and swirled his ice, before taking a big gulp backwards, as he tilted his chin, that chin I just love to kiss.

"I wouldn't love what was written of us in the tabloids." I said soberly.

"The Sex. The sex you would love, in the middle of the afternoon. Our audience of onlookers some dead, some alive might like it too, a real love story in sultry Savannah. Let's give the world a real love story, sometime when I'm not too old or not too young Lori." Spoke Alan, a bit too relaxed on the sofa.

"I had a very unusual upbringing, a very unusual mother, I want to experience what is normal in life. Being famous is not normal. I deserve to know what normal is, and then when I am forty I will tell of Cleopatra, and the virgin Mary, the Jewish slave girl whose family worked for the Ptolemy dynasty. My life working at The Gold Club, perhaps is not a normal occupation, but I will have normal someday. I'm going to locate normal, and have it. I am in search of normal, in conjunction with being heard." I spoke with direction and purpose.

Alan responded, "You need a voice. If you are famous, people will listen to you, read your memoirs, someday you will have regrets. I hope I can convince you of the importance of being famous, verses having you not understand. When you are famous you have a protective invisible shield, you just do, you'll get favors when you need a favor."

"What? What are you saying Alan?" I asked just baffled at why he could not seem to understand me.

"Look, God wants you to have a voice, be famous, and you want to wallow in this normalcy debate, it is fruitless, you'll see." Said Alan.

Alan and I had so much to discuss about being two-faced, mocking people who are two-faced, and discuss why society is two-faced. Like a spin off to another topic, like a D.J. spinning music into our conversations, Alan and I talked about everything under the sun.

I said to Alan as he touched on the subject of marriage, possibly a wedding in Savannah, Georgia…. "Ideally I would want to rent out the Disney castle suite for a week, and spend my whole honeymoon park hopping at the different theme parks…..what do you think Alan?"

"I was thinking maybe the Caribbean….something tropical." Alan remarked as he looked me up and down.

I reached to put in some music, before slow dancing in front of Alan…..

"Fragile by Sting," shouted Alan.

"Shisssssh…..be quiet….." I said as I began taking my blouse off.

"Just unbutton the front….but keep the blouse on….just like that….. right there….that's perfect….If I had a professional camera in my car,

I'd say lay down, hold that pose, right there next to the fireplace……" Spoke Alan.

"Caribbean get-a-way? I have coconut rum and pineapple juice in the refrigerator, I can make you a drink, less the airplane ride and airport delays. After two drinks you'll feel like you're by the ocean, and oh look, there I am, or here I am." I laughed holding up a glass. Then I said with a smile…. "It's like the beach along Lake Michigan, like northern Michigan." I laughed as he began loosening his blanket in front of me as we laid on a comforter by my fireplace. "I love this song….."

"You know Lori, astrology has already set our design, who you are, who I am." Spoke Alan soberly outside, the starry night sky above us….. as he headed outside to get stoned, wrapped in a comforter.

Sometimes Alan and I would eat a big bowl of Captain Crunch cereal, naked and wrapped in loose blankets, as each of us slurped up little orange squares from a giant vegetable bowl {well, I slurped a little}. As we both sat outside in the last few hours of the wee evening. Then eventually we'd go back inside as the night gave signs of daylight approaching us, still naked, wrapped in our comforters, we'd head for the bedroom. I had a waterbed, I'd turn the heat up and we'd fall asleep naked in each other's arms for a few more hours. That was exactly how Alan liked to spend his weekends with me. I could have spent a lifetime on that same channel…… never considering picking up the remote to change the channel, ever.

We'd drive to Stone Mountain often on Sundays, sometimes we'd travel an hour and a half north, to Helen Georgia. Hike down to waterfalls, play cards, "Gin," on a picnic table overlooking the huge northern Georgia mountains that cannot be seen visibly from Atlanta. We'd love to hike on the trails, go white water rafting, ride horses, and eat meals by the various picnic tables, or an outside patio restaurant along a river in Helen, Georgia. The town reminded me so much of Petoskey, Michigan just placed in the mountains. We enjoyed the great climate in Georgia, and the opportunity to spend so much time in the great outdoors.

"There is so much to do in Georgia! One activity after another, with no schedule planner just time and us together, Alan." I exclaimed.

Sometimes after Alan's classes taught at Emory, on a night I was not working at "The Beer Mug" on Peachtree Road, which was just another sports pub of beer and burgers like Winston's Pub, or working at The Gold Club. I would drive to Emory and wait in the grassy lawn for his classes to end, just lay down and doze off a bit. Sometimes I would be tired during the day. Tired from the long hours and doing a themed act on stage. Like rolling out of a rug next to two Roman pillars, pull off my black bobbed wig and having a man take the stack of auburn curls folded and rolled in a bun off the top of my head releasing my long auburn locks as I paraded an act on stage doing my Cleopatra act, or green sequence tale mermaid act. (More stories later, maybe after a drink?)

Mostly though, I liked to spend time with Alan, that's how I liked to spend my days and evenings. We'd often hike up Stone Mountain, our shirts sticky from the humidity and exercise of the late afternoon walk up the side of Stone Mountain. At the top we'd look out to the city of Atlanta seen in the far distance. Then find a quiet place to talk, usually under a tree just around the bend. Alan even carved a heart with our names on it…….it is probably still carved on a Georgia pine tree atop Stone Mountain. Carved in the Georgia pine….."Love Forever….. Alan and Lori." Guarded by a park ranger I am sure.

Alan would explain Greek and Egyptian mythology to me, and give a shot at being my dream interpreter while we sat and talked atop Stone Mountain…..Perched on edge of the biggest love affair ever, drunk on what the other could provide for relief. That's how our love affair was with each other in the sauntering south. I miss those late afternoon hikes…..with Alan. He once read to me on top of Stone Mountain, two poems by Homer's near contemporary Hesiod, the Theogony and the **Works and Days**. Alan would often read from astrology books atop Stone Mountain, trying to fervently help me understand the universe beyond my daily existence of what I could see when I stared upwards to the clouds. Always trying to get me to understand the relevancy of how the ever changing movements of the planets and star constellations were stationed in our galaxy. Drawing out graphs in the Georgia dirt in his great hope of teaching me of his vast knowledge of astronomy and astrology. He often would comment that he, in relation to my astrological chart was the planet Saturn, the great teacher.

Some astrology books I read on my own, the description of fate that Saturn delivers can be so unpleasant, a nickname of Saturn is "Satan," the fate can be that unpleasant. The sign of Capricorn, the goat, is governed by Saturn, the elements of the teacher, responsibility, go farther, jump higher, and restriction, are all associated with the planet Saturn in the computer grid, the matrix, that giant computer program in the universe. Saturn "gels together," solidifies and condenses.

Which ironically, I do have on the seventh house cusp of open enemies and partnerships, Saturn in Taurus. Which is the type of guy I attract, and supposedly need, one who can handle responsibility, discipline, someone who is practical, generous in love and sweets.

"Especially prominent is Saturn connected in analogy to the planet Saturn is U.S. government, the pentagon." I commented to Alan. "I read that in an astrology book. Do you think that is true Alan?"

He just looked at me, then rolled over and said, "Men who stare at Capricorn to stop marital warfare." Alan starts laughing uncontrollably.

"What's so funny Alan? I am not a goat! Stop laughing, what is so funny Alan?" I inquired.

"Stop laughing Alan……"

Alan was born in May, May 6th to be exact, and is a Taurus, which also is on my line of open enemies and partnerships. He stated that he would have a profound effect on my life…..that I need him, and he needs me.

He never explained how, or why, yet his transformation of my view of the indigent childhood upbringing by Cindy opened my mind to realizing that sometimes the most unconventional of stories, the story you do not want to tell, can have the loudest resounding beat, the last word.

Alan went onto to say this obscure bit of information as we sat atop Stone Mountain, "I read your astrology chart, you have a major psychological battle that is brewing against you now, a warfare you must win. You must understand all that philosophy can teach you, all that I can teach now in your life. You must understand to recognize what is different to actually know what is different. You must thus know, so you can understand, so you can make correct choices with your life. To recognize evil, to recognize good, to recognize what is different, so that your psychological warfare will have a firm foundation, not to be tipped over and toppled by what others want you to believe. You need to be a warrior. A mentally strong warrior. I am not sure what this warfare will entail, but the odds are against you, and it involves large groups of people, perhaps societies of people? You must win this psychological battle, or you will lose so much. It is the battle of all battles! You will change the world with this battle, you don't know it, but you will." Spoke Alan in a convincing tone of voice.

As much as I wanted to understand more from Alan, I also remained positive about my life. And at times would not question what Alan said to me. I simply disregarded his statements of what I should be doing, as unheeded warnings. I did not want danger in my life, and so I ignored certain subjects that did not pertain to what I wanted to hear or discuss at that moment in time.

I mentioned to Alan, "You know Emory University is in the top ten of private universities, what made you decide to apply for a professorship at such a ridged institution of learning? You don't seem so ridged and formal to me."

Alan's response, "Well Lori, I entered law school at Emory, that is how I first was introduced to the university. After two semesters of law I decided that teaching was really what I wanted to do. Perhaps writing on the side, become an author….write a well told unique love story, is that not your intention in this lifetime as well with this relationship? To accumulate all we know and have experienced and spread it on a paper canvas."

The evening deep blue sky began showing signs of stars, the moon was full. A harvest full moon night as we gazed upward.

"I do like your expressions and how you verbally put things into perspective for me to understand. I love when you read to me about mythology. I love when you explain meanings of words, and spill knowledge on to my young and exuberant mind. I love how our intellect meets in the middle, how our bodies react to each other in a bold way, and our lives are sidereal. I like how our words and mind intermingle on a surreal, supramolecular plane. I agree, I believe that it takes intelligence to recognize intelligence." I said to Alan.

On the walk down from Stone Mountain the reflecting moonlight off the white washed mammoth stones that covered Stone Mountain guided our pathway downward, steeply to the base of that large rock of a Mountain.

We walked hand and hand back to our initial meeting grounds under a magnolia tree. I laid down on the grass below and pulled Alan on top of me. It felt good to be covered with the weight of his body, the heaviness of his love I could feel on top of me. I loved how his body felt, the smell of his skin, even if it had a slight odor from hiking, it was him, everything about Alan felt reassuring to me, comfortable. As each of us explored more and more of each other under that old magnolia tree Alan spoke this to me as he held my face in his hands, "Just embrace my love Lori." He looked through to my soul, just wondering why I could not leap off the rock of singlehood and become his wife. That next step seemed too big of a leap for me inside. If I liked this part of knowing Alan, why change anything? What if marriage does not turn out to be the best destination, the next great chapter, the next course that would be best for us? For me? How does one **really** know? I knew we had entered the land of addiction with each other. The land of passion is where I wanted to stay with Alan, not move from, on into unfamiliar territory.

When back at Alan's house in Virginia Highlands we showered separately. The bathroom smelled of fragrant cherry and almond scents, of cloves, and mint and lavender. I layered on a fresh green leaf lotion to couple the other scents of what I smelled of, it was a basket of earthy woodsy scents with a splash of Coco Chanel perfume. I put on a black and tan pinstriped shirt which I located from out of Alan's closet, and buttoned up slightly after my shower. Alan pointed out how my wetness clung to the bottom of the shirt a little. Alan knelt down with a tan beige towel covering himself as he made sweet homemade kettle popcorn in his fireplace before taking his turn in the shower. Alan knew I enjoyed the sweets of sugar and honey during love making, even spices would arouse me.

I laid on the white suede rug compressed of woven square pieces of fabric, like white leather of a velvety surfaced Wall Street floor after a long and prosperous day on the floor of the New York Stock Exchange. The room was filled with light yellow amber lighting from the flickering flames of candles in gold jars. My hair slightly damp underneath from my shower. I waited for Alan to return back from the bathroom as I had my head prompted up on a feather pillow. When he walked in by the roaring fire he had made minutes earlier he said this to me as he knelt down and I loosened his towel, as I laid on the rug next to the fireplace flames….."That was always my favorite Playboy photo of you, this time you're more undressed, I like it. Buying that magic carpet ride rug goes beautifully with my furnishings, I know you are more than an object of desire next to my fireplace, you are my greatest adventure ever, my greatest love……"

Alan knelt down beside me and removed the towel covering his body. His skin was still freshly damp from his shower. He smelled of Aveda soaps that I bought for him at Van Michael's salon in Buckhead.

I love the combination of clean, fresh, with a dash of a woodsy scent, whether on him or me. I could visibly see his growing anticipation of this evening of seeing me next to his stone fireplace as he walked before me. He pulled out two pink ribbons from a bag, and stated to me, "I want you to know everything about your life and what the CIA is setting up in your life." Alan whispered that most unusual of a statement to me as he began tying the pink ribbons around my thighs. I was baffled, but trusting, a song played on his stereo in the background….. Alan whispered softly, "Do you believe in magic?"

"When all of the classified files reaches worldwide destinations you'll remember this moment, the pink ribbons is the code, the clue that the media is about to begin broadcasting the relevant classified information of the CIA for the world to know the truth about so many forbidden and criminal secret projects." Spoke Alan in a hushed tone of voice to me.

I laugh from being a bit stoned as I inquired with a joking tone to my speech, "Alan, will there be war and rumors of war? In the end? Rampant floods and fires like the Book of Revelation prophesied so many thousands of years ago? Is this the end? Alan why do our lives always come together during Biblical times? Or should I call you Octavia? Caesar Augustus?"

Alan looked serious and spoke with confidence as he spoke orders to me with his body pressed against my body, "When you do publish your memoirs you must never reveal my true identity, my true name. I need to remain invisible. Invisible like God within society, invisible within any story you write down on paper. Do you understand Lori?"

I know you as the reader want to know what happened next……I do recall what I said, and what occurred next as that song played softly by the roar of the fire flames. I do know this, we both had plenty of green weed ambition in that love making that early evening back from Stone Mountain as I said this in response to Alan as he finished relaxing me, and then himself…..'Brilliant Alan, just brilliant, someday we will make a movie together, this love story of ours, it will be printed in a book, maybe a video, and hot off the press people will want to reach in like rain beads against a window for a chance like this, you and us…... when we step out together in public, it will rain like hail, our energy together." I kissed Alan on his neck, that part of him he likes being kissed on. Then moving southward sucking tighter I moved upwards then downwards in my attempts to keep the evening on a page with the words written somewhere as "forever."

"Brilliant Lilly…..just brilliant….but really dear….what I want is for you to marry me Lori." Spoke Alan very seriously. My body laid exposed with only the sheer material of my pinstripe shirt to cover my silk tan, nude body. My hair auburn, blending with my caramel toned tanned body beneath his body and dark hair exposed. I was twenty three now. The fiery flames roared heat upon our skin and love expressing, my head rested on a pillow, as I looked upward to Alan. I would best describe the next two hours as, "***closed caption with pink ribbons.***"

Alan whispered…. "I love the black hair….against the spiced praline….this is my favorite…..how I disappear inside and within….how I control you….and me…..like in this intense moment shared between us. When I touch you I am controlling myself."

I turned my face towards the crackling sparks of the fire that seemed to jump and crackle towards our every movement in a punishing heat. It was perfect. I wanted to think of anything but marriage. A union I wanted to put off as long as possible. I wanted to breath in life, and love Alan. I wanted to freely love Alan, yet own my own existence. Flashes of my parents fighting all the time sparked, the turmoil of the word marriage stopped my heart beating in a very bad way. I just wanted our love affair and all that I was feeling to simply and purely continue "as is." Alan kept pushing my button, nowhere written was the word pause on that button.

I accepted Alan for all that he was, or was not. I knew he liked to take me to certain massage parlors, spas, whatever you want to call them. For some women, for some girlfriends it would have been a situation of intense jealousy. But for me, it was just part of Alan, and what he wanted at that moment, a relief. A need to be pampered, a need to feel as if he was back in Rome with a title. It simply became part of our relationship, a need of his, to be touched and caressed in public settings, yet privately have his immediate needs met then and there. Often by one or two girls who worshipped his private temple after a massage like priests preparing holy water, at least that is how it appeared.

Alan once commented to me… "I want to make you my wife. I also want to have a concubine. We'll have rules, legal rules. Such as they cannot be disrespectful of you. I mostly want them to be what you do not have to do. Such as kneel and take turns, each one of them. You can sit next to me. You can be dressed or undressed. But I have this need to be like this lion of the jungle, and the woman kneel and take turns making me feel like a king of the jungle. You are the queen, you never need to feel as if on the same level of them, well, unless you want to participate. You will always be queen, do you understand?"

I responded, "What if one falls in love with you and poisons me? Then what?"

Alan and I spent many weekends in the quaint and trendy pubs and patio style restaurants in Buckhead and Midtown Atlanta just listening to acoustical style music, sipping on a selection of imported beers, and listening to other musicians and their storytelling in the evenings….how they arrived at the lyrics in their songwriting. The story behind the song always intrigued Alan and I. We especially liked to have dinner and a beer at The Dark Horse Tavern near his house.

Honestly, there are too many great taverns in Atlanta to mention them all, mostly Irish and English style pubs with a wide range of very trendy and fun restaurants and acoustical music places to sip on a beverage and just sit back and listen to music, listen to a person's story with an acoustical blend of harmony in the room. Sometimes well-known bands and singers we'd sit and listen to, sometimes, just a local singer on the brink of becoming big in the music business. I was meeting more and more musicians, of all places, The Gold Club. Many, many well-known bands, singers, and some bands and singers on the brink of musical stardom. For some reason, I was also starting to get asked out, by a few……

Sometimes after lunch on a day Alan was off from his teaching schedule at Emory, we'd love to get "his and her massages" in the afternoon hour from many of the various high end Swedish upscale spa salons. Sometimes he'd pay the massage girls extra, even at the usual places, the highest end spas.

He never failed to ask politely and pay generously ahead of time before entering upon the massage tables. I'd lay on my stomach wrapped in a heated blanket after our massages, just a few feet away on my massage table I'd watch Alan, as candles flickered and ocean music roared like waves crashing onto a shoreline in the room. Watching Alan close his eyes as two girls finished his massage. I would watch the profile of Alan as my face rested against my folded arms, as he rested his back against the white sheet table fully exposed in the room. His body covered in a slight glistening of lotions and oils evenly applied to his body in the amber toned lighting of the room. The candles burning an earthy woodsy aroma in the room like some kind of Indian ceremony of candles and incense.

I would just watch with my eyes wide open, curious I suppose. I would watch the massage technicians take turns, each of the two girls rubbing oils and pulling upwards on Alan, each girl reaching for more of Alan to touch in her hand of "his exposed masculinity" as he laid resting on his back, fully nude. Alan had a mass of dark course hair, he'd be covered, slippery and messy from the two girls touching "his favorite part" with various oils and techniques. Sometimes towards the end of the massage, as Alan would give a motioning signal by raising his hand up slightly as he stayed resting on his back the girls would move to block my view towards the end of "the act" with their backs turned, obstruct my view. Each girl taking turns wiping and cleaning his holy water before they moved a heated blanket over him. Often the girls would smirk or smile slightly at me as they left the room and closed the door behind themselves. I would then wait for Alan to get up and get dressed, before I got dressed.

I was content in just the massage part of being pampered, what makes me tic? Just being spoiled and feeling loved, comfort and love, great conversation, anyone who knows me well, knows that reality. I never got jealous. Some might say, "Well, that's because it's less work for you to do Lori, you're lazy, you hate messes, that's why you never cared if and when he ever pulled his remains of the day out when in public or private places." Maybe there is some truth to those comments made, maybe just a little truth. Alan always made me feel like a queen and everyone else was just an act he could pay, or seduce instantly. Like some magical twinkle eye power of his. I don't know how to explain it, it is just a man, woman thing, when you are us I suppose. I always felt pampered, but he was king….we had a courtship some might say, an unusual relationship and terms….something's were not discussed with Alan. Sometimes I felt like I was being followed……..from government looking men I danced for at The Gold Club.

When we'd arrive back to Alan's house, often, not always though, he'd lay me against a comforter on top of a white rug he bought from me.

We'd lay near his rustic old fireplace. Alan's house was old, with hardwood flooring and tall coved archways and tall ceilings, white painted walls. He'd put on some music which seemed to echo off the walls like a small amphitheater. It was his platform in the living room, "we're on stage," he'd say. We'd get undressed, I'd lay back, he'd take his palms, the fatty part of his palms and push open my lips. Kind of like a kiss, but with more fierce intensity, and with more pleasing pressure. He'd open my mouth, my flower in full bloom, my outer lips he'd push away and then up a bit to expose my tongue, very ready and ripe for him to kiss, kind of like a nose, a button nose. He would keep pressure on my outer lips by framing them hard against his palms, and pull up in a tight grip, and then hold my lips open, tightly. Firmly he'd take his tongue and push down hard on my tongue, or was it my nose? He'd begin licking softly on either side of my tongue, and then begin to take his tongue and push the center of the apple down hard as he reverently licked until my tree, my body, my legs began to shake. I'd have to push away his head, gripping his checks of his face to just stop the fervent licking motions that would cause my body to shake. His face I would grab and hold from the sheer intensity of his movements. His tongue still sticking out as if he wanted to give me more intensity until I was raw at that moment…….from the kiss. The kiss that brought so much pleasure and relaxation.

Sometimes I'd get an added surprise, and he'd enter me full force, as if he only needed a few hours to recharge his batteries. The love we shared together was real, the sex, the love making was an expression of who we were as a couple. I always knew my place, and he always wore a regal crown in my presence…....that is how to treat a man, really. It was a wonderful tango, our relationship. Sometimes he was a little bossy, but that was the Taurus in him. That raging bull personality, like an open enemy that would want to charge and take me on. But deep down, we were mirrors of each other's souls, alike, yet different somehow.

Many days on warm Georgia afternoons we'd like to eat Greek pizza at the Mellow Mushroom pizza place, we love feta cheese and spinach, sharing a meal as hip metro music of that era played in the background. Or travel to eat the best bread sticks and cream soda in town at Moe's

Pizza. I liked wearing my hair up during the hot and humid months in Georgia, otherwise I would have a hairdo of frizz from the natural wave in my hair melting in the hot days heat and moisture in the southern air. We always talked about a wide range of subjects, it was never, "Hi honey, how was your day?"

One day, when we were alone again, I asked Alan, "Do you remember heaven before earth? Before this lifetime, what do you remember?"

"But be specific, what exactly do you remember?" I asked.

His knowledge at times was more than what I could take, but I was always up for trying to absorb his wisdom he held.

Sometimes in the afternoon I'd wear a baseball cap, no make-up, and jean shorts, just look as if to be one of the guys for a day or evening and we'd go to a late night Braves baseball game. Drink beer and make a mess under our feet with peanut shells, sometimes stoned, sometimes "just because" we felt like being messy. Sometimes we'd watch the game, sometimes we'd be lost in our own philosophical discussions. People around us on the bleacher style seats would look down and demand from us…. "Shisssh….shisssh."

Alan and I would talk about God, the devil, who really is the devil? According to Alan the professor, the devil was an angel in heaven at one time, then God kicked him out, and he became a "fallen angel," thus termed, "the devil," by society and religions alike. But the question still remains, Alan and I agreed on this one……what made the devil become a fallen angel? Christianity also teaches that the devil is a "fallen angel," once housed in heaven….then kicked out by God. If of course, you believe in the story….about the devil…..history recorded…….

"That is a good, relevant question Lori, what made 'the devil' a fallen angel from heaven, become a non-housed angel of heaven by God? Condemned by all eternity, by religions, by society and future societies to come?"……. Asked Alan.

He then went on to say this profound statement of a question…….

"No one has brought up that very poignant question until now…..what made the devil lose his place in heaven? What upset God so much that he kicked the devil out of heaven labeling him 'Lucifer'? Later to be termed 'the devil,' scorned by religion and society for what seems like an eternity?"

Alan and I just looked at each other....buzzed slightly on warm, cheap stadium beer.... That is a good question I thought to myself, Christians never talk about it, do Jews? I wondered.

I asked Alan, "Do you **really** remember life before being born on earth?"

Alan responded by saying, "Yes, I do remember life before my life here."

"Alan do you think that I think outside of the box?" I asked.

"Do I think that you think outside of the box?" Alan just repeated the question it seemed without answering me directly.

"Yes, I do think you are an original, you most definitely think outside of the box." Alan said.

I asked Alan, "So Christians and Jews believe that the devil is a fallen angel, correct? But what is his role in religion? Is he evil like society through the ages have depleted him to be?"

Just then the crowd of people around us said....."Shisssh.....we can't hear who is up to bat.....shisssh!"

I continued in a lower tone of voice, and whispered.... "What was **his role** in heaven?" I asked Alan the professor.

Alan responded, "The devil as religious historians and theologians alike would probably agree or know was a prosecutor for God. After God judged a person's soul, a person's worth upon entering heaven, the devil was **thee absolute prosecutor for God**. God is the Judge. The devil is God's prosecutor that punishes the evildoers." Alan explained all this in his slurred voice, his green eyes radiating a touch of lighted hue.

"Punishments?" I asked Alan.

Alan stared straight through me as if for a moment he sobered up to say this to me, "The devil <u>had</u> a place in heaven, then he decided to do something? Or something happened? Which undoubtedly..... caused him to become a fallen angel? This is unknown to humankind why the devil became a fallen angel, led astray, a battle raged on. He was kicked out of God's house and giving his own portal, his own gate, his own place in the universe, "the underworld." Where the evil are housed and await to be punished. The condemned people are sent there, away from the radiance of heaven, sent there by God to be punished. It is a topic many people rarely if at all even discuss you know…..I wonder why that is Lilly?....Or should I call you Carolyn? Or Lori?……..It really is Cleopatra…..isn't it?" Alan smirked a serious glow in his eyes, his green eyes warm and radiating a wild penetrating love towards me…..

"But Alan, the devil knows both right and wrong, and every evil manipulation known…..the devil is evil, more so than not." I proclaimed. I protested.

Alan began slurring now on his speech and words a bit more as he began reaching for another sip of warm, cheap beer from his stadium cup. His chin under the beer cup, his face hiding under his baseball cap. As he spoke that last statement to me, this strange occurrence happened that night in the Braves stadium in Atlanta…..true story….the overhead huge lighting system dimmed that evening, then got suddenly brighter. Odd, just as he made that comment to me. True story…..it was 1993? 1994? The Atlanta Braves baseball team began having a winning season after that, a winning streak, going on to play in the World Series after Alan and I had that very profound conversation in the bleachers. Some would say that we "had hit on a truth that seemed buried in existence, a real home run"…… I kept scratching my head there for a moment, who tempted who? I knew I would be driving us home tonight….Alan had too much to drink again.

The next morning Alan woke up earlier than me this time. When I approached the kitchen table there was a box, the medium size box was wrapped up beautifully. "What is this Alan, is this for me I am assuming?" I inquired with a smile as I held the box with my hands.

"Yes, go ahead and open the box……" Spoke Alan sipping on gourmet hazelnut coffee.

"What is it?" I asked.

"Go ahead, it is something you like to wear when we travel in my car." Alan responded.

Alan drove a black Mazda convertible. I hated it when he had the top down because my hair would be a tousled mess by the time we arrived anywhere. I opened the box and discovered a new head scarf and wide rimmed sunglasses.

"You know Alan the last time I rode with you and we were talking in your car, as you drove, I swallowed a dragon fly. I could not spit it out, I literally swallowed a huge fly because your top was down. Now my hair can stay in place, and my eyes are protected from flying bugs, objects, insects and such, thank-you. But we can't talk while your top is down." I said with a smile.

"I have a surprise for you tonight, later this afternoon we are going to drive to Athens, Georgia. There is a band playing, The Black Crows, we have front row seats, a table in the bar. You're going to like this surprise." Alan said.

Later that afternoon I put the hot pink and black patterned scarf around my head and big wide rimmed sunglasses on as we headed down the Atlanta highway out of the city to Athens, Georgia. I wore black knit stocking pants, black cowboy boots, and a funky hip shirt.

Underneath, I had a surprise for Alan later, green satin and lace lingerie, his favorite colors of lingerie for me to have on under my clothes were or are, polo green jade or deep slate blue, or black lace.

As we arrived in Athens we did some sightseeing and had a late lunch at a favorite hang-out in Athens. I unbuttoned my shirt at the top, one button, and said to Alan as he sat across from me, "Don't ya just wish you could touch and feel lace?" I said that as our sandwiches arrived at the table.

Alan always would give me this look at times, as I stared him down, as if he could not move from out of his chair in public places. As if I could make him stuck in life, stuck in his chair, or at the table when we'd eat lunch or dinner together. It was kind of a fun game I would play with him, whether wrong or right. I liked to put a spin on things…..he was a big fish…..and I had fun reeling in that rod….I just did.

When you are in your early twenties, life is told from that perspective, how I saw life, how I see life around me, and how life was for me. The choices I made in my twenties, some would term it as "fate," but we all have choices to make. Sometimes I would stare off in a daydreaming kind of way…..just lost in my own philosophical dreamland as Alan spoke to me, or the music played in the backdrop of my life.

When we arrived at the college bar, the house was packed. The Black Crows were playing that evening and the people seemed excited around us. You could just feel the excitement in the air. We ordered drinks, it was nice to see Alan could get up and walk from that previous table we sat by for over an hour. It did take him at least forty five minutes before he felt comfortable standing up in public to leave the restaurant. He whispered in my ear as the crowd gathered and said I was like an addiction, and if there ever was an antibiotic drug created, he would be immune to the pills.

"You have such an amusing sense of humor, Alan." I said with a slight beer buzz, as the band was getting ready to play on stage before us.

The drummer began to warm up before the night's performance…….

"I have a surprise for you, just listen Lori." Alan said as we cuddled in that cozy bar in Athens.

The band leader, the main singer from The Black Crows made an announcement that evening. He cleared his throat slightly, and looked down towards our table, the singer had a twinkle in his eye and said this….. "The next song I would like to dedicate is from Alan to Lori, and someday I will officially place this dedication on my next album edition, if Alan and Lori ever write that love story of theirs on paper that is. I'll cover the album with jewelry, jewels and such."

His acoustical guitar began strumming the cords of, She Talks To Angels……

"This song is dedicated from Alan to Lori."

I looked at Alan with a surprise, my eyes beamed, what a nice surprise…..the singer on stage began singing…… "She talks to Angels." It goes something like this, from what I can remember….. "Never mention the word addiction, in certain company. She paints her eyes as black as night now. She pulls those shades down tight. She gives a smile when the pain comes. The pain gonna' make everything alright. Says she talks to angels. They call her out by her name. Oh, yeah, she talks to angels. Says they call her out by her name. She don't know no lovers. None that I've ever seen. And to her that means nothing. But to me it means everything….." Alan kissed me on that line. I did feel a bit guilty, inside that is, as he kissed me passionately at the table during his surprise dedication gift in Athens, Georgia that early sultry evening in a crowded smoky bar room.

"That was a nice surprise Alan. Do you really think that The Black Crows are going to ever dedicate that song to us?" I asked with a smile.

Alan responded, "I think there will be many songs dedicated to our love story still untold and unwritten. I think many artists and musicians alike will come forward with a song dedication, and make more songs and dedications public….we could call it Music Festival Loripolosa. Alan gave out a slight bellow of a laugh when I added, "Someday there will be a walk of fame, like in Hollywood, but in downtown Atlanta, or the walk around Stone Mountain, for authors and music writers who learn and express knowledge in cadence like us."

Alan grabbed my head, placed his hands around my cheeks and kissed my forehead as he said this to me, "We will write that book, it will be a seductive Bible, a source for all to understand the great mysteries, to validate reincarnation. To shed light on old subjects, new and refreshingly told philosophies to make this world better, we will. We will write that gothic novel together and change the world. We'll start a revolution, I see you blooming as my student, we'll help others express themselves too."

I inquired to Alan, "Bloom. To help others like the bloom of a magnolia flower?"

Alan paused, and looked down at me and commented, "Yeah, to help others bloom like you."

"Why do you say that Alan?" I asked.

"Because of who you and I are…..that's why Cleopatra, that's why." Alan slurred his words a bit……..

On the way home, Alan put in a musical CD, a British band, the song entitled, "Missionary Man." Alan looked at me as he popped in the CD, and said, "Alan says."

I laughed, "You say? Is this a game of Simon says? Alan says? You always say that to me, you really should get that posted on a vanity plate, then I'll play….. "You're so Vain……you probably think this book is about you, don't you…."

I laughed, Alan smiled as we sped towards the glow of nightlife, the lights of Atlanta, and then we pulled over alongside the road.

"You know what your name means, your last name?" Alan asked.

"Tell me." I responded.

"Vander Ark, it means "From out of the Ark of the covenant." Covenant theologies believe also that Calvinism philosophy believe that views of all history are under the aspect of God's covenants. Supposedly, the ark of the covenant was where God manifested his presence on earth. The Ark was also the Israelites means of relating to God. Some Jews believe that the messiah who will usher in the new messianic era of a utopian age will come from the ark of the covenant. Did you know that fact?" Alan said to me as I slid down in the seat.

"Where is The Ark from? Where did it originate from?" I asked.

"Some believe near Babylon, as the Jewish race exited Egypt with Moses. Many are still looking for the Ark." Alan said.

"The Ark and its sanctuary were considered the beauty of Israel." Alan commented as his eyes gleamed in the car dash light….. "paradise."

I listened intently as I would in absorbing Alan's knowledge.

Alan whispered in my ear, "The Ark was God's throne in his dwelling place in the tabernacle. Most people associate the ark of the covenant with judgment and wrath, and rightly so. The day is coming when God will judge the secrets of people's hearts. You have a seductive side Lori, but your life is God's reveal. Your life is a veil, tell the world all you know about all you experience and from whom."

"What?" I asked as I kissed his lips.

"I had a dream last night. Your dad that passed away, does he look like Bob Dylan?" Asked Alan.

"Who is Bob Dylan?" I inquired as I kept Alan's seat warm in the front seat.

"Did your dad who passed away when you were sixteen, kind of look like George Clooney if you were to add a classic Jewish hook nose and Jewish shaped lips?"

"I don't know, maybe, a little, why do you ask?" I inquired.

"I had a dream last night, he reached out to me with a message, he said, her life is behind a veil." Spoke Alan, as I interrupted.....

"Who is he?" I inquired, bewildered.

"He....your dad.... was referring to you in the dream. Did you, I don't know what made me feel or think this during the dream.....but did some guy propose to you at The Gold Club? I saw you in a white veil, covered in gold adornment, but I could not see what was behind you? I saw a man, I thought he was your father, that said to me, about you, that your life was 'behind a veil.' There was some guy behind you, in the dream." Alan said as he best could describe his recent dream.

I laughed, then kissed Alan some more. "I once, recently, had a notion about wanting to be in a milk advertisement with George Clooney."

"What? You don't watch that E.R. show do you?" Inquired Alan.

"No, no, I hate bloody scenes and stress. I've never had an interest to watch the show because of the blood and anxiety of what the show is about. I thought.....though.... he looked handsome in previews on television, that's all." I responded as I kissed Alan.

"He has never been to that Gold Club has he? I know a lot of celebrities like hanging out there." Alan inquired a bit mad all of a sudden.

"No, I never, ever, saw him at The Gold Club, ever. Really." Then I kissed Alan's cheek.

I added, "I once had a notion to have George Clooney dressed as Superman as I stood in front of him with just my Calvin Klein jeans on, topless, as George Clooney covers with his arm, my breasts in a hug position from behind. I think the way my body is built, and the sex appeal of what milk can do in building a strong and curvy body would actually sell a lot of milk for the American Dairy Association. George could of course be holding a milk jug with one hand. Or maybe he could be dressed as Superman, I am wearing just my Calvin Klein jeans and beige suede cowboy boots. I sit on him, with my back against the camera shot, I'm topless, drinking milk from a milk cartoon, and George Clooney looks at me, as he holds, hides my chest a little from public view of the camera shot, then I drink milk and look at the camera. We'd sell millions of gallons of milk…..Look What Milk Can Do……that's the new motto, logo, what have you. Everyone will go out and buy and drink milk. It will be an American Dairy Association craze of sorts."

"Breasts? He'd hold your breasts?" Inquired Alan.

"Yeah. Chest area from behind with his arm. For commercial use only of course Alan." I said as I demonstrated for Alan using one arm….. "Like this….George Clooney could have one arm around my chest and the other arm holding up a milk cartoon with one of those famous white milk mustaches as he stands behind me." I said as I leaned forward on Alan, topless in the front seat.

"Was that a fantasy of yours? To be with George Clooney with just jeans on, topless, him feeling you with his arm?" Inquired the slightly perturbed Alan.

"No. It was just an advertising idea. An ad idea Alan. Nothing comes between me and my milk but George Clooney." I comment and laugh hysterically.

Or, go with the original line, "Milk it does the body good. Look what Milk can do for you!…….. It would be a great campaign idea, a funny line in an ad, that's all, media, marketing, in such. I think I could have a knack for advertising. A real job, ya' know. I want a normal career someday." I commented.

"That's your normal career adjustment?" Inquired Alan.

"Yeah, I sent the ad idea to The American Dairy Association last week."

"You did? Have they responded?" Inquired Alan.

"Well, no, but I forgot to include a picture of myself." I said with a smile.

"I am sure that is the delay in their response to your brilliant ad idea that you thought of while you were stoned. I am sure of it." Barked Alan in a serious tone as he adjusted his steering wheel height.

Alan seemed mad, his jealous side of his personality comes out when you least expect it to. What may appear to be simple conversation can turn to instant heated animosity like how a new stove reacts, he just overheats on certain subjects, even comical subjects he can overheat. But Alan was out to burn me, always have the last word in edge wise when he gets perturbed as he is now.

"Come on, let's finish. I can see you're still in the mood." I insisted. I then stated dramatically…… "I need you Alan…..oh, Rhett…….when will this war be over?"

Alan blurts out…….

"No. No. That's o.k., I'm lactose intolerant. I'm just not in the mood I suppose. You come from the land of plenty, you made your point. Just get off from me now. That's no way to treat a man, making me think that you are thinking about George Clooney while we are together and my dick is hard." Stated the now sulking and angry Alan, who always, always retreats to insulting me when he is angry in a jealous way.

I went on to say this to my sweetheart, "We really are soul mates, our downfall? We are both bossy towards each other." Then I mumbled….. "And let's not forget the very double standards of Alan, he gets jealous when you least expect tension, he can fume." I remarked with the top down, the crickets chirping in the fields around us as we drove back to Atlanta. I just love southern balmy night air, it is so romantic, it's peaceful and calming, yet excitedly electric in a sexual chemistry kind of way for me, the south, the sauntering south.

Alan had a wall of a music collection in his living room, CD's from a variety of musical artists. He especially liked Sting, he'd play that song "Fragile," over and over. Alan also had a whole category of southern bluegrass music, mandolin and banjo music CD's. Often he would play that music taking us back to the 1800's. He'd light candles on his back deck, drape white bed sheets from the roof of his covered deck so his neighbors would not know what we were up to behind the sheets. He'd lay a fluffy down comforter on a table on his patio. Alan slowly and gently would seduce me into his vast knowledge of subjects I was just a student in, a lover of the arts and harmonic rhythms. A lover of all he would do to me while I laid back on that fluffy goose down comforter. Alan and I would talk for hours about what we could remember about our past lives once lived…..A child, our child kidnapped from my dynasty by a Jewish slave girl, we'd talk about if that happened today, that child of ours, our prized son, he would have been placed on the back of a milk carton.

I knew when he touched me, it often flooded memories of the past, 2000 years ago. I wondered now if this would become our best life ever as my eyes glassed over, tucked away in his embrace, mesmerized in his moments of deep love making towards me. Another moment shared in private….another moment I was made to feel weak…...by him, again and again. I remember the song that played in the background that evening on his deck patio. The song "Fragile" by the musician Sting was playing in the background, Alan loved that song. He'd play it as he had me undressed on his back patio table. I might have looked fragile, venerable when undressed, exposed, ready for Alan. But when I looked into Alan's eyes, his soul, it was him that was so fragile, I thought to myself in quiet as the locust chirped and hummed a tune as they watched us.

Alan whispered words of love to me that night while I laid on my back totally exposed, as he laid along side of me resting on his right elbow, our shadows reflecting larger than life on the sheets all around us.

Alan said this, "Someday I'll propose marriage to you in Savannah, Georgia. The day I give you a gold band with diamonds and rubies is the day we'll get married in Savannah, I won't lose you this time. I'll have a Judge or lawyer at a bed and breakfast Inn and we'll be hitched, as simple as that Lori. But I need to know that you love me, not question or doubt how deep your love for me is, now and forever. The ring I had taped to the last chapter of the book I held at the base of Stone Mountain….I still have it…..I'm saving it for you."

When I looked into his eyes I could see that love was something he could feel deeper than me, but I was confused as to how he could feel more than me? I just did not understand, or feel the emotions in life that he could feel. I wanted to feel more, like him. I wondered when I would feel emotions like him in love.

Alan had plenty to teach me in this lifetime. Sometimes after his classes at Emory I would wait for him down the hallway. I remember looking up to the wall of photos taken in the early 1900's, searching for a man on the wall that looked like Alan back then. Originally, Emory College was founded in 1836 in a small Georgia town called Oxford. The Methodist Episcopalian Church first founded the university. The Atlanta based Coca-Cola Company donated family fortunes to expand and build Emory University in Atlanta, in Dekalb County, the North Druid Hills area. As my eyes spanned over the black and white antique photos my eyes rested on a picture....but just then Alan emerged from his classroom.

The Alan I knew in the 1860's, graduated from Oxford University in England. All the small synergy of synchronized existences, all seemed connected in this lifetime of mine. Strange coincidences. Oddities, as I would often refer to coincidentally occurring in my life.

Odd, how everything has a tie, a connection to the past somehow and comes out in the unraveling of life as I know it to be. The Alan in the 1860's that I remember was almost six foot, dark shiny hair that fell just right. Medium complexion, broad shoulders, a strong build. His eyes might have been blue or brown, warm eyes like the Alan I know. I wonder if I looked the same? I wonder if Alan would ever take me to Savannah, Georgia and propose marriage to me at Lafayette Square in this lifetime with a ring in hand?.....That question was on my mind these days. I had made some homemade bread that I placed within a picnic basket of roast beef sandwiches, Alan's favorite. I actually bought a bread book and was always making homemade bread for Alan and I to share over a meal. Today we were going back to Stone Mountain, he was going to teach me symbolism and discuss the importance of a good premise in literature. How to build a climax worth having a reader hold on to tightly, like a rare piece of art....He was a god of philosophy and

English literature to me, and by far a man worth focusing all my attention on these days.

My mind flashed to two nights ago, a stage show I did, and well, had performed that stage skit in the last month. A show that was creating buzz, men were circulating into The Gold Club. I knew it would make Alan mad if he knew I was performing that act I did in private for him, well, for a large audience of men slipping big bills into my garter. The Gold Club in Atlanta was owned by two attorneys when I first began. I was known for wearing shell pink satin costumes, sometimes light blue which matched my eyes, or white to glow on stage. We were asked to do these "stage shows," the props, the club would build or obtain from a local movie stage company in town. I will tell you later about the Roman pillars and "the rug" the bouncers would carry upon the stage at a later date…..Alan just emerged from his classroom.

Alan took my hand and led me into his now empty classroom. He moved a few thick books towards the edge of his desk then took a pile of books and stacked three books as a cushion for my head rest. He took off his belt and blindfolded me with his tie. Alan asked me to lay back, he then undressed me slightly. I was exposed, just as he wanted me to be. He had me rest my head on a stack of books and pulled my hips down to the edge of the wooden desk as he squeezed my cheeks deeply. I pulled out roast beef on homemade bread that I baked, we each took a bite, then I rested our sandwiches down on the desk. I could not convince him to just have a picnic upon the desk.

My legs rested off the table, my knees bent, he began to undress himself. He took my hand and let me feel him undress. I could feel his stomach was bare and I could hear him unzip his pants, and feel he was almost naked. I could feel his anticipation of the sensual moment at hand. I laid on my back, my knees slightly apart resting my calves off the edge of his wooden desk. Alan pulled out two pink ribbons. Alan then took an apple from his desk drawer. He then placed the apple on my navel, with the resting apple on my stomach, I asked, "What are you doing Alan?"

As I laid on my back, a bit uncomfortable. I felt something sticky on my stomach as he swirled honey against my suntanned midriff. I heard him open a squeaky top drawer in his desk, as I peeked out from under the tie, I could see he pulled out a kitchen knife.

"I am putting honey on you, and slicing this apple." Alan announced boldly, proudly. My legs were tied apart with pink ribbons....I felt like a sensual sacrifice in the middle of the late afternoon.

I could see Alan as I peeked out from under the silk tie wrapped loosely around my head. Alan began slicing an apple with a knife over my body that he pulled out from his desk. The apple slices which began to fall slowly on my navel began sticking to the swirled pool of honey like a sticky sweet pond.

Alan began speaking in a fierce tone of voice, it made me shutter a bit from surprise. The words spoken of Alan were firm and direct as I laid rested and helpless on stacked books and a wooden table desk next to a green chalk board....I'll never forget what he wrote on the board next, ever..... it was a quote from a famous sea explorer that once sailed the ocean upon a ship. Then Alan underlined a sentence under the sea quote he had written, the line; Lori you are the embodiment of wisdom on earth.

"What is this about Alan?" I asked as I peeked from under his silk tie wrapped around my head, covering slightly my eyelids. I waited for him to respond. He kept pouring more honey on my body and his "favorite part." Alan kept slicing the apple until most slices were resting on or around my navel.

Alan responded, "This is September, your ribbons are slightly undressed, it is the High Holiday season, the most celebrated and important of Jewish holidays of the year…the celebration of Rosh Hashanah and Yom Kippur. Do you want me to untie these pink ribbons? You have a choice to make now." Asked Alan.

"No," I said, "I want to go through this phase of my life, of learning all you can teach me. Someday I will write this experience down on a paper canvas. A mental documentary film painted with words and descriptions, all will see the candle light and fall through. We will all become, if you could imagine, one in understanding of this moment…..Alan."

Alan began speaking above me, "The celebration of a great mystery, the ram's horn, this emphasizes the special relationship between God and humanity. Our dependence upon God as our creator and sustainer, and God's dependence upon us as ones who make His presence known and felt in His world. Rosh Hashanah is the anniversary of the creation of Adam and Eve, the first man and woman, and their first actions towards the realization of mankind's role."

I remarked with a smirk….. "Like a skeleton from my past?"

"But I am not Eve," I felt nervous, "I am like….I am like the forbidden apple…don't bite me! I am not the woman who told you to eat of the forbidden fruit, I am not Eve!"……. "Alan, I am polished crimson red, devolved like the earth, resting against the green pear on a crystal prism encrusted bowl, resting on a wooden table!" I said quickly and poetically as I squirmed a bit under the pressure Alan was adding to me.

Alan began using sticky honey as he dipped the apple slices on my pressure points. Sandwiching my pressure points with sticky honey and cold slices of apples just sliced freshly with a knife he held upwards in front of me…."This is so odd Alan!" Alan then rolled open the drawer, putting the knife down inside his hidden wooden compartment. Alan looked at me with intensely warm green eyes, he looked fierce, his eyes almost ready to cry. He began speaking slowly……..

"Just say love…..and stop saying life is all about the introduction, the seduction, the experiences in life, Lori, life is not a staged act! My feelings for you are real! You need to feel what love is like! You need to feel as I do at this moment!" Alan spoke and lectured to my helpless body seriously as he moved, he stayed focused on his point, very non-wavering. Like a stubborn ram staged in a stance for a battle he was just determined to win as he took his stand in front of me. His stance inside of me was felt and remembered, always….it was almost a reversal of roles in the end, him trying to teach me about love and feelings and yearning. I was stoic in the love department, in my heart and my observations of what was going on, he was like a young school boy in love for the first time. Not wanting to let go of me, his object of desire that he could not control or contain…..or was I describing him….not in control? Not able to contain?

The pressure he stroked on my body was layers of intensity of a rare kind. The buildup of pressuring pleasure was like the peak of building, escalating Georgia humidity in late summer, then the thunderstorm of pleasure he controlled…. rolled in….and onward. His smooth and unanticipated application of all the details he seemingly knew so much about. He never grew tired of "preparing the pot," stroking the intimate layers of the petals of the magnolia blossom bud, cautiously, delicately. At times he would stand and enter only half way, it was his way of letting me know he is ready, then he would begin to "prepare the pot" more and more with ointments.

To make sure the electricity he was feeling was also a spine tingling adventure for my senses as well. Determined to seduce me, before pushing onward, giving me more than I could handle. Or seemingly underestimate during the heat of our private moments while held in each other's arms.

"Today you are going to learn a lesson, this time you will see the world as I see my world. Just…..say love! Now! Say you love me, just say it Lori!" Alan said as he began another lecture while deep inside me, he acted angry about the subject of love.

"This time I am in full control Lori, you are not getting away….." Alan said as he began another lecture holding my palms against his as he pressed my hands against the wooden desk surface in a tight grip. His fists in a locked position with my hands helpless, rested, gripped within the circumference of his hands above my head. I am unable to move, hardly able to squirm in this position that he held me in, I felt locked in the situation, the moment…..Kind of like heaven, but I began to sweat more with each intense movement from Alan. My arousal grew and felt intense, as were Alan's eyes, scoping and telling me all he could see, and I could only feel in his control.

I responded directly to Alan as I stared through to his deepest points within his eyes, "Love is a journey Alan…..not a destination on top of this desk, your lecturing desk. I know what you are up to, I see it in your eyes, you want to get me pregnant and trap me into marriage because I am not going willingly to the altar. I'm not ready for that next stage in our relationship yet." I said as I stared through his penetrating, almost angry green eyes fixated on me. "Love is a journey Alan, not a destination as you seem to think it is, or want me to believe it is, and marriage is not a destination of which I want to journey to quite yet." I said, this time firmly and slowly speaking back to him.

Alan spoke fiercely to me as I rested on the wooden, "You will see my point! You will in this lifetime! I do remember, my memory spans generations, just like yours dear Cleopatra. Every time I touch you, I know who you are, don't deny the truth of our history!" Alan spoke with such intensity like a raging bull before me. I knew I could not get pregnant, it was the wrong time of the month. I do understand his message of "becoming Jewish by injection," that particular afternoon. As Alan termed that afternoon rendezvous on his desk top with pink ribbons tied around my ankles to the base of his desk. It was September.

I felt stuck, like I could not move off the wooden desk table. He had me there, pinned down with his body in me and my hands wrapped in his sweaty palms as he squeezed my hands in his, harder and tighter together against that wooden desk…."say love….stop acting like it is all about seduction, stop saying you will marry me later!" Alan kept saying firmly…. "Marc Antony will be a lost ship at sea if you ever come in contact with him in this lifetime. He will never love you like I love you, I will have you understand my point of reference when you grow up."

Then he wrapped me, engulfing me in his arms, his tears began to flow down his face onto my face. He was still inside of me, he just kept clutching unto me, crying, unable to stop hugging and embracing my back for support. Holding as much as my body that he could hold all at once, it felt like a crush. Like he was trying to crush me.

"Is this about making me Jewish?" I remarked in the silence of that classroom.

I never did forget my first lesson of Rosh Hashanah, "Alan's style" at Emory University, Adam and Eve all. I could never order apple dippers in the future at McDonalds without smiling and thinking about becoming Jewish by injection on a desk at Emory University, as I swirled honey and caramel with apple slices, really. Alan's techniques in making me realize who he is, or was, was extraordinary at times. Philosophy was a field I knew well, in the arena of wisdom, I knew Alan, I knew his games, and all whom I had fiercely promised before this lifetime.

When he touched me, I did see a Roman warrior, with curly blonde ringlets at times. When he touched me did he see dark black roots on an ancient warrior queen thirsty for more power and knowledge. A woman who sees literature as the way to dominate the world.... Imaginative, creative writing....recognized artistic value....the body of written works of the English language. I was a distinct combination of rare wisdom, intelligence, beauty, creativity, originality……..

"Please do not try and be funny, I need you serious at times." Alan said unwavering.

We drove to Stone Mountain, the song, "Missionary Man," happened to be playing on the radio, ironically enough as we drove down the road that afternoon of Alan teaching me all he could, about every subject he knew.….he was extraordinary in his methods……very unique in getting across his points.

Alan read to me again under that magnolia tree at Stone Mountain near the old Whistle Stop café. I would listen to all the Shakespeare plays and Tennessee Williams plays he'd read endlessly. As if reading plays was far more enjoyment than watching television. He'd get lost in worded plots, as though he could not find his way out of a book.

At times I was his dose of reality to pull him through to the end. I really was, as he tried to find his way through the rising action, the plot, the climax, the ending…..and then I looked up from resting on the grass at the base of Stone Mountain and said, "I do love you Octavia, like no other, I love you with all my heart, soul, and body. I really do. Marc Antony has nothing on you."

Alan looked at me with an inquisitive scowl, "Has nothing on me? You've met Marc Antony?"

I reply, "Yes. Once when I was young at my dad's second cousin's house in Caledonia. He was visiting my dad's cousin, it was winter and he asked me to take my snowmobile across the pond, a dare of sorts. I believe he became a CIA agent, that's what somebody told me anyways. I don't think he even lives in Michigan anymore."

Alan inquired, "He? And how old were you?"

I replied, "About seven, maybe eight. It was 1977 or 1978. He is older by at least ten or fifteen years. He is tall, well built, muscular, dark brownish black hair. He said to me, 'Cleopatra when you get older we are having sex.'"

Alan inquired, "Did you drive across the pond on a snowmobile?"

I reply, "Yes, we both took turns on separate snowmobiles like a Russian roulette game with snowmobiles over a frozen watery tundra hoping that the pond is frozen enough. Finally we stopped when we got tired and nobody lost."

Alan inquires, "Did you have sex?"

I reply, "No."

Alan and I suddenly began looking at rings in Atlanta, suddenly he wanted to get me the biggest and best round solitaire diamond engagement ring that he could locate in the mall and afford. In the back of my mind though, I wondered why he did not want to go back to that moment in Lafayette Square and re-introduce that lost in time gold band, with diamonds and rubies? It was the ending I wanted. Alan claimed I wanted it all in this lifetime, he was going to see to it I had it all.

Alan and I often would go to a place we revered as our sanctuary, northern Georgia, the end of the great Appalachian Mountains. This also happens to be where Alan proposes to me for a third time, and I refuse. We'd often go white water rafting, eat B.B.Q. chicken and corn on the cob outside on a patio lodged next to the rafting place. I loved the sounds of the birds in the forest, the sound of the flowing river as we felt the warm rays of sunshine streak through the tall tree branches above us. We both were lovers of nature, we loved to engulf the sounds of the forest. Listen to what the birds and sounds of the forest were trying to say to us, as if the heavens could communicate with us on earth through nature, we'd often remark.

Sometimes we'd spend a weekend in northern Georgia at a hotel along a river that flows through Helen, Georgia. Sometimes Alan would lead me down a trail hand in hand in the humid yet cool Georgia afternoons in northern Georgia. Alan would lead me down his path he'd create, just off the beaten path, thick in the woods, and put my back up to a big tree trunk. He'd unzip my pants, slide his hand inside, having me continue to stand still, my legs slightly like a book open, as he would stand in front of me. He'd tell me to remain as still as possible and describe in a whisper into his ear what I was feeling with his touch.

His strong shoulder pressed against mine as he takes his stance with his fingers as the paint brush. He would make me color the canvas of the feeling, the moment for me, for his mind, with bold and unique descriptions of what he could not see or feel as an artist as he painted. As if he was blind to what a woman feels when a man touches her. Alan's other hand just as strong with twitching muscles in his forearm was in motion on me as well, next to his other hand holding open the book. I would best describe to you the reader as, "He would move in an uninterrupted glide across a smooth moist surface, a dependence spot of raw emotions that needed the basking stroke of his touch, the book slightly open, like in late spring, that magnolia bloom....it really is more like a rose bud Alan." I whispered and kissed his ear.

"Talk out loud Lori, in my ear, no one is listening, come on talk." Alan requested with a controlling pinch of punishment as he felt he waited too long for an answer, a description desired, urging me to speak, for he was in control.

I agreed at his commands……..

"You're touching me Alan, in a place of my feminine flower, the bud feels totally engaged with electricity of a rare kind as you touch me Alan. The roots of that bud are coming alive with a need for more, inside me now. I'm totally dependent upon what you can do to me. I'm not like some woman you've been with, whom do not need all that you can and are able to deliver. I am very dependent, I cannot see underneath me. You're touching a place that shows great dependence for you, just like you remember in heaven. I realize I'm not built with just a high flat piece of skin protruding outward. I'm built like a flower of a rare kind, when aroused, like a blossoming bloom, a pink bud so rare, very dependent upon you…..just like in heaven." I kissed Alan's ear as I continued in my needy speech of wanting more, begging to lay down as the feeling he is producing demands more relaxation than standing. Begging to sit on him for a final relief inside of me, but he kept me standing as he reached between the book cover. Under that flower moving me to new heights of awareness that I could feel of what he was doing as the artist in the woods, unaware of his next move.

Alan remained in continuous contact with my flower, pinching tremendously on my pink rose bud if I stopped speaking in his ear with descriptions……"O.k., o.k., I'll talk… it's like experiencing an ecstasy of friction on a very slippery low slope as I cross over into another dimension of time and space where the goal matters most, as one crosses to the other side. You're carrying me over that intense hill, you're in full control of my feminine attributes Alan. It feels climatic, emotionally and physically, a must, tangled and lost in an abyss of just feeling your sexual power control mine. Making me dependent and addicted on what you give and deliver to me."

"I know, I can see that, feel that about you." Alan commented as he whispered and kissed lightly on my ear for me to continue talking……

"That's it Lori, keep talking, keep describing to me what I cannot feel, but you can at this moment." Alan said as he breathed upon me slowly. Pressing his cheek to my face, his fingers pressed under me as I whispered on and on in his ear. Describing all I could without receiving another surprise yet terrifying pinch from Alan as a form of punishment for saying a lame description, or ever using a cliché. He held my pleasure, and I also knew the punishment pinch I could feel at any moment.

I began to sweat in a very unusual place with the tension of extreme pleasure mounting against the fear. The relentless anxiety of punishment which could also be instigated at any moment was so intense. It was a lesson in the woods, a lesson we would repeat in the future of me learning all I can about not using clichés and boring, non- original descriptions. He taught me, rather he stressed to me the importance of becoming an original author, one that brings the readers onboard a ship to helps them to the other side of an existence, a reality unknown by some.

I did remind him though, "That heaven does exist, it is a real place, and what I can feel at this moment is just a few minutes of utopia with a relaxing destination ahead."

And then he continued, and pressed on, and would not let up, as if heaven could be felt on earth too, in this lifetime, and always, I would yearn for his pleasing touch of knowledge. And I again told him, reassured him, "That heaven, elements of heaven, can be felt on earth." Alan made me beg for his touch to reach a climatic plot in the woods, "Between the book, and all you hold and punish, Alan."

Alan pulled back then reached for me again and again. The afternoon felt like I was placed in his hands of detonating pleasure of the exotic senses, as Alan demanded. "I want to give you another, another chapter, another story, another plot I want to hear you describe in my ear. I must know more about what is between your open book that others cannot feel in intensity, as you can feel. You must talk on, and I will press on, keep going with me on this adventure Ms. Jones……I'll give you water, food, ice cream, whatever you want or need. Do not ever give me a cliché of what you are feeling as I touch you. I pinch hard. Your description is a need, a need that I must and shall have, or there is a painful pinch, and I pinch hard. I love how you are standing, and I want to give as well." Alan spoke with his mouth pressed against my ear firmly and tightly. I felt as if I was about to be punished as I spoke on and on, the best I could describe.

If my description of what I was experiencing from him sounded too much of a cliché of a description of the sensation he was giving me, he would pinch me as he held me in a pinching position, before he would continue with the pleasure part of the lesson. Demanding with his grip, his intense pinching, until I came up with more of an original distinctive meaning to what sensation he was giving me against that tree holding up my back….. "It feels like an underlying essential purpose Alan, what you are doing to me, like a tide, like the waves are now edging closer onto shore. The idiomatic rhythm of pleasure you are delivering feels as good as the anticipation of the ocean crashing a tidal wave of fierce momentous pleasure any moment now…..I am so dependent on you Alan, I am so close to shore." I was very dependent upon Alan for my next destination, and he knew it.

Afterwards, after the poetic many literature lesson in the woods, Alan would have me beg, at least that is how my knees felt over the green and sunset colored leaves. Alan always was trying to get his point across in the most unusual of places. Sometimes he'd have me kneel in a praying position over a rock, then he'd ask me to stand up. As I did stand upon his request Alan could feel I'd struggle a bit with difficulty with his power of persuasions in full control inside my voluptuous body as I stood up. Then was asked to then sit back as Alan took full control of the ship with what felt like an anchor inside of me as I moved to stand. Struggling to stand upright with him inside me, as he relentlessly was demanding, whispering, caressing. Then I would be asked by him to sit down on his lap again, backwards. This time he was on the rock like Santa Clause, and I was giving him his favorite toy for Christmas. He loved that reversal of asking and begging, giving and receiving, as he held onto my hips. As if he controlled every movement, the band of my lace thigh high stockings almost itched away at him in the movement of Alan gaining pleasure and control of me as he held onto my hips.

Alan loved how I was built, very dependent upon him, dependent on him to see, touch and know all things about me, and all I could not see. For my pleasure that he controlled, because he could see more, more than what I could even see of myself. Sex was his domain, I was a prodigy.

I remember one particular time in northern Georgia Alan bought me an ice cream cone. When I was in my early twenties I did not have much of an appetite though. I licked the dripping butter pecan ice cream all the way back to the hotel room overlooking the river in that quaint town of Helen. We entered the hotel room, but I felt so full, and had no place to put a melting ice cream cone that would only attract ants if I placed it in the bathroom trash can.

So I had this idea, I asked Alan to get fully unclothed and lay on the bed. Licking the ice cream melting off the cone, I asked Alan to undress me slightly, or as much as he liked. I licked the ice cream. Alan took his two free hands and began undressing me, revealing my dark slate blue lingerie underneath my clothes as he opened up my flannel tan shirt. He commented how he liked the contrast of pink hidden behind dark blue lace, and how he liked the contrast of my red hair hidden behind darker lace. I reached over him, brushing his face with fullness hidden behind a slate blue lace bra as I reached for the nightstand drawer. I began taking massage oils from the drawer next to the bed, one by one, and used one hand at my best attempt in mimicking a massage technician at the end of many of dates in our past. Commenting "It's been a long hard day." As Alan would say often after dinner with me.

But because I seem to like to incorporate food and lovemaking, I took the ice cream cone and tipped it upside down, over his head. Covering "his favorite part," the brains of his life, the part he wants me to get to first, I'll leave for last, I thought. So the sugar cone rested like a witch hat on Halloween in that hotel room along the river. The sticky humidity in the atmosphere pouring into the room from the window, melting the ice cream quickly as I began licking fervently along the sides of the cone. I could feel the electricity building up inside of me as well as I then began eating the top of the sugar cone point until it revealed a hole. I kept eating, and eating, until the cone was gone and I went for my last bite…..Alan begged for me to stop with the biting and pleasure teasing routine of his moment. I then whispered this in Alan's ear, as I began giving him butter pecan kisses, nibbling on his ear lobe and as I removed my lace coverings, I whispered this, "May you always remember that between the icy coldness of this relationship, inside it is always warm for you. I know I will always be your home. I know you are my greatest love, my greatest teacher, I know I am your greatest comfort. I know your heart and I know this journey of love will be one to remember and write down for the ages. A love saga of learning all I can about you and from you, as I had learned before this lifetime, and in the afterworld."

Alan grabbed ahold of the curvature of my hips, his hands resting a firm grip as he pulled downwards, I knew I was not going anywhere. I felt warm molten ice cream topping, garnishing, filling my void like a flood of wanting to know everything about all he could possibly teach me, within minutes of him entering his sanctuary within. I then whispered as my response to the hot lava explosion…. "I do love you Alan, I do."

Alan pulled me closer, then commented to me in a whisper that only he knew how to fill that void within me.

I commented back to him, "When you and I write that gothic novel, will the words I type be like the current old and new testament Bible for Christians? Where the people go to read what pertains and penetrates to their interest, their lives, or will our books be like an evenly worn-out mattress?"

"Only time will tell. Only time will tell." Commented Alan as he laid back to rest under the covers.

He was refined yet rugged, passionate and intelligent, and never bored with exploring the dimensions of love and the divestible power of being alone with me. He was bold yet tender. His thrown was irresistible, his touch smooth yet unyielding, aggressive in how he could deliver a message of passion and purpose of the moment to me, at any moment, in the most unusual of places. Often followed by the apologizing tone in his voice as he spoke these charming words to me….. "Brilliant Lilly, that was brilliant, won't you marry me?"

Alan sighed as he slumped down under the covers. I kissed his forehead. For now I was just happy being content like him, relaxed. Marriage for me was something I wanted to push off into the distance. I wanted **this** to just last for as long as it could. Our love, our passion, was like a volcano that could not be stopped. Moments, to hours later together, inevitably always led to the sensation of mother nature delivering her hot lava onboard, whether in convenient of places or not, it just was, that is how nature was between us, man to woman, or woman to man, it just was. Stimulatingly explosive in reaction to the other's touch that evoked within us an insatiable need, no matter where our location, this need of his to open his favorite book, move to the middle, and lift down a white lace veil before him. I was like a book, always ready to be opened and read by him. We had the duality between a man and a woman, the way it was meant to be and experienced on earth.

On many long Saturday afternoons back in Atlanta, Alan would sit on his sofa watching sports. He'd give me some cash to go buy groceries, then I'd come back and spend time in the kitchen preparing salads, homemade bread and soups, casseroles. He always liked the smell of freshly prepared meals going on in the kitchen while he watched sports for hours. I made everything gourmet. I would take fresh raspberries or strawberries and grind them in a blender, add a slight amount of red wine vinegar and sugar, creating my own dressings for our salads. I would finely chop and dice black olives and Georgia pecans for our salads. Adding in sliced sweet red onions which is a natural stimulant. Cook eggs, and spread my homemade dressing in a bowl, drenching the green leaves. There wasn't a sauce or a meal that was not prepared from scratch. A homemade delineate of something warm and good, always. Just as I was a silhouette of dessert for him to divulge between the lines. My bread was from scratch, and many of my creations I simply just added ingredients to what I thought would taste well, and prepared the dishes.

Alan loved for me to have dinner ready for him on the wooden antique table in his dining room. His house was old and when I looked up or around I wondered if there were any former residents, now residing as ghosts, just lingering around the table, watching us as a couple. Alan loved to hold me from behind, wrapping his arms around me while we sat or laid on the sofa after we left the wooden antique table. Sometimes I would sit on his lap and he'd embrace me, he'd love to stand behind me and hold onto me as well. He did love me, but part of me just did not want to be owned and married, that is how I saw how our love might turn into, an ownership of sorts.

During his afternoon of sports watching, I would take the remote and flip around the stations. I could predict within fifteen minutes who was going to win, which team that is. After a while, Alan began listening to me, placing bets where I called the shots. I have this innate ability to spot the winning team, the winning play. Sure enough, Alan won many gambling bets in sports with my keen sense of seeing what it takes to win, and spot the winning moves in the first half.

Alan often would say to me, "You could write a book on how to get to a man's heart through cooking, baking, your refined manners, your sense of humor, your intelligence. Let's not forget how you wear lingerie so well, and you never get jealous when in public places. You truly are one of a kind. But I need to know you love me through and through….. and then it will be our wedding night in Lafayette square, or a nearby bed and breakfast inn."

In 1993, Cindy called me up, it is always unexpected when Cindy calls and interrupts my life as I am about to be engaged and married. Cindy announced suddenly she was licensed in Georgia as a nurse now and was coming down to Georgia to visit, to stay with me in one week, then locate her own place. What turned into a visit, was a one year stay. Cindy never asked if she could live with me, she just told me she was going to stay for a while at my apartment. I mostly would stay at Alan's when I could. Cindy never paid rent or utilities, ever at my apartment. She asked for money which I was earning at The Gold Club, then laid the money out on an end table near the window in her furnished room that I furnished. Cindy said the money smelled like smoke and a bar, and she was purifying the money I handed her before she would spend it on herself or her bills. I kept wondering how could this woman claim to be a mother? My mother? She used me for money, a place to live for free, she located a big church nearby and always went to church on Sundays. She never asked me to go to church, she never helped with the bills, or helped me locate another job, ever. She liked the money I was making, she was the saint, and I was a whore. It was her perfect painting for Christ. It was just as she wanted to keep it, less Alan around me. He spoiled me, and wanted to marry me. She was not happy that I might have what she did not have in her own life. Having or wishing for a true mother in Cindy, to just be happy for me, just was not possible with Cindy. Once again, it was her theory over my happiness. Her theory was: What can you do for me? Cindy liked money. Cindy liked the money I was earning at The Gold Club.

I thought I was going to run off and get married to Alan in the same year Cindy arrived to live with me in Lithia Springs, Georgia. I never thought during this wonderful independent early twenties life of mine that Cindy would actually pack up and leave her Michigan condo to my brother Dave, rent free to Dave, and move in with me, and expect to live off me, but Christians will always surprise ya.'

Alan once said to me, "Your mother should pay half the rent while staying with you Lori, you can't allow her to just live off from you."

I responded to Alan's suggestion by saying, "No, I have asked her, she gets mad and slams the door behind herself and cries in the bedroom, just feeling sorry for herself. Cindy creates a delusion in her mind or mine, that "NO! She, Cindy is the victim. As I work, I go to college, as I pay all the bills. I cannot be insistent that she contribute financially or she goes ballistic with me, Alan."

I never will forget when Alan first met Cindy earlier, his face went white, and after the brief introduction to Cindy. Alan said to me in private, "Your mother is a monster. She is going to try and kill you, she will create a silent way, or accidental way to do so, she has the eyes of a killer Lori, you need to watch out. I think Cindy has killed before." I ignored Alan, how could a person be a monster? A true monster? I thought to myself. Although, people say first impressions can be very accurate.

The months began moving into years. It was maybe now 1994? One night while at The Gold Club, I forgot what song was playing by the D.J. Steve in the booth. I was being brought to the stage in an oriental rug, placed between two Roman pillars right after the five exotic belly dancers dressed up like Egyptian belly dancers performed first for me on stage. Something weird happened that night as the fog machine blew clouds of smoke onto that black stage floor. The neon lights blurred my vision. The spotlight can be a bit blinding on stage as one looks outward. I unravel from the rug and began taking off my black cropped wig before undressing on stage to the song being played. My auburn hair is up, styled in a bun on top of my head. I reach to pull my hair down and shake the auburn curls to rest on my shoulders. I look up while lying across the stage front………………to see so many government federal men.

I cannot believe my eyes. I went to rub my eyes and clear my vision….oh, boy, this is getting weird…. I thought to myself, the crowd is coming to life in a very unique way, a sense of humor almost……. as I stared at the neon lights revealing that the crowd was **now** coming alive so to speak….I looked straight on.

Oh, God…..I need to get a new job, as I look towards the blinding spotlights, my job is getting too weird……the crowd is now playing tricks on me and coming to life while I am on stage……I just stared blankly ahead, still trying to focus on the reality that may lay ahead of me. I took his hand from sheer peer pressure from the three hundred and fifty men clapping in the audience and proceeded down the stage steps and through an aisle in the crowd.

I wore purple, with green lingerie underneath, which I never took off that night, I never even disrobed the purple Egyptian antique style dress I wore, really. I had gold snake bracelets on my arms, and a bold necklace of turquoise and gold. I left my black cropped wig on stage, and just walked out hand in hand with this man, he looked familiar. A limousine was parked by the front valet booth…..

He asked next, "You're not going to sit on my lap?"

"Who are you?" I asked.

Odd, how during my lifetime, even at The Gold Club, I really was not in search of a date, or to take that next step in life and become someone's mistress or someone's wife like the other girls. I really analyzed the situations of all the stupid yet bizarrely strange, yet so vivid epiphanies that rattled and stirred in my pretty little head. It was never what I was handed, or could have, it was what I never got over, or ever had. I wanted a real loving mom and dad, a mom and dad alive and who loved each other and me, that family unit. I knew that all the other girls around me at The Gold Club were on that chapter of their life in their early or mid- twenties. Yet, for me, oddly enough, with all this, or should I say "opportunities offered" I felt inside like a fish out of water for a stripper.

Inside I had a void. Not that my personality was shallow. I had a void. So deep was that void, so detrimental. I just was stuck, my life on pause, verses living and moving on to other chapters that the other girls so graciously could move to without being stuck like I was in life. At times I felt like a butterfly or bird in search of the perfect pollen unable to land. I was missing such a big piece of my puzzle in life, but the pollen that I was in search of was not a date. My vague stare must have been mesmerizing to most, but behind the dazzle of being in my twenties, the longing I wanted most of all that needed fulfillment was to have a mother who was normal and a father who was alive. My puzzle, my life seemed like a scrambled mess. What I really wanted was to put together this perfect puzzle, but I had two pieces missing in my life, or perhaps one puzzle piece missing and the other, my mother, just was not a good fit for my puzzle of completion? I mentally could not move forward and be this normal twenty-four year old girl that I look like I am supposed to be in life now. I was a record on skip. I was that pizza less the toppings, I was a root beer float without ice cream. What I wanted most was parents. Alive and loving, really cool parents. What I wanted most of all in life, was something I was too old for, yet I felt too young at this time too, to give up that dream, or ignore that desire. But I'm too old to make a wish for parents or need parents? I'm past that point as I looked down at the way I was dressed in that limo. I'm all grown up now. I'm supposed to like the way I look, I'm a real knock out I'm told. I'm grown up. Perfectly curvy, perfectly seductive in appearance. I'm the sexy girl next door, a rare Bavarian beauty, all grown up right now, perfect. I felt hungry, hungry for something, but it wasn't on the menu. I went my whole life waiting to grow up, and here I was finally, grown up. Yet the music that I yearned for were soft lullabies to be played. I felt so unready to grow up and reach out from out of that rug to the audience. I wanted to pass on the adult champagne, I wanted back in that rug, and back into a baby blanket. I know that is not what my thoughts are supposed to be, but they were, as inconsistent to sexy as one could be.

The next day I received a brown box at my Waterford Place apartment in Lithia Springs, Georgia. Inside was a stuffed animal {which I still do have}, and a box of chocolate. When I opened the heart shaped box, it felt too light I thought. Inside were no chocolates! Just a note that said, "Meet me for lunch we'll talk later kid."

I did drive downtown and met with the distinguished white haired gentlemen for lunch. He was very charming. We talked, and laughed, he felt like family, like the family I never had, no arguing over the dinner table, just talk. And then he said this…."You really are shaped and built like a young Jane Fonda."

"Oh, I said. Thank-you, but I am not blonde."

"I know." Was his response.

One month later I went to my mailbox by the water fountain, near the pool at The Waterford Place Apartments. There were toads everywhere, the birds were singing. For the moment everything seemed relatively normal in Georgia that sultry afternoon near the mailbox gazebo. It felt like a nice spring day, but when I opened my mailbox, I sunk…. as I opened a white envelope addressed from Alan. Inside was a letter, with one question asked…… "Is this all about seduction?" Signed, Alan.

Not "Love, Alan." Or anything like a real letter, just a question? A statement question of weirdness, with, "Signed, Alan." Strange, a bit cold, I thought.

I called Alan's house he did not answer the phone. I just let it go for a week or so, him not responding back to my phone calls. I was a bit perturbed as well, he was not the only one mad. Alan must have followed me to that downtown meeting, just a lunch, he must have been spying on me. I was mad, I thought.

After two weeks I went to knock on his door in Virginia Highlands. I noticed a real estate sign out front. Alan was not home. I then called the number on the sign and left a message for the realtor lady, trying to reach Alan perhaps through her connection, obviously he was not picking up his phone. I had no such luck.

A month and a half went past, then I knocked on his door in Virginia Highlands, to try again, I thought he was being a little extreme. When the door opened…. A lady answered, she said she had just purchased the house and had no idea where Alan was, she thought he moved back to Michigan or Chicago. She thought he had mentioned those States at the closing.

Alan was gone, really gone, I was twenty-four and a half. I never felt that gold band with rubies and diamonds on my finger, as if I thought it would just be inevitable to receive that ring from Alan in this lifetime now, I never did. Our relationship, our romance was like a masterpiece painting left unfinished. I called Emory University, they acted like they had no idea who Alan was, it was a dead end to get answers or to possibly locate him.

Months passed. I remember looking out into the audience at The Gold Club and hoping to see Alan's face. The music kept playing on and on, those three song stage sets. The music trends and what was once popular to dance to changed too. I no longer wanted to do any mermaid green sequence skits, or my Cleopatra pull off my black wig skits……I just wanted Alan back, before too much changed in the world. Before our favorite songs we'd listen to just weren't popular anymore……….

I missed Alan, but was willing to settle, I had to settle. I was too young to be this alone in a world passing by too quickly. So, for the sake of not being lonely in Georgia, well, remember that Jewish guy, "Pig Pin," with the down to earth family? The Jewish family from Poland, that thought I was a trip? His last name in Polish he told me means "pike."

Steve and I went to all the old hang out taverns, not luxury massage parlors and high end spas that Alan and I frequented after a lunch date at times. No fancy romantic evenings in front of a fireplace at Alan's place. Alan made me always feel like such a woman. Now I was just single and lonely with a friend in Jesus? No, a friend in Steve. That is correct. Life was not a cliché of a happy ending? Or was it? Who knows, I can't predict. I simply live and experience life.

Steve who was a friend of mine, now was becoming my boyfriend, like me kissing a toad with no prince surprise afterwards. We'd hang out in taverns, playing pool at The Famous Pub on North Druid Hills for hours. I would play music from the juke box of songs that Alan and I would often listen to, make love to, and then I would just go back to playing pool with Steve. As Steve repeated all his old jokes over and over, just hoping that someone would laugh and think he was charming, and not just a guy revered as the one guy in North Druid Hills with great pot on hand, always.

My life was a shuffle, a very incomplete puzzle…..just like that juke box, shuffling, and shuffling a tune.

I do remember the first time I saw Steve undressed after a night out on the town, he is short, only 5'5 with his Doc Martins on. About 195 pounds, dark hair, covered in dark hair really, like a monkey. I said this as Steve stood in front of me in his bedroom at his parent's house where Steve lived, "I now believe in evolution, you Steve are the missing link." Then I laughed at my joke and commented in a helpful way, "Hey Steve, that is a great joke I made, you can use it sometime, maybe people will laugh and think you are funny! Really like you, not just for having great pot on hand all the time!"

"Eh, eh….very funny." Steve commented….. then he twirled around, wiggled his butt like a slow tick tock back and forth of a musical rhythm scale and pointed at me in a gay slang tone of voice and said…… "I'm your tiny dancer."

I clapped and laughed hysterically from his stupidly funny performance and the concoction of being totally baked, stoned. My own laughter echoed in my head as I laid my head on his bed pillows. I somehow felt relieved of loneliness for the night, Steve was a great anecdote for getting over Alan.

I might have appeared more like Eve naked, or perhaps the red apple depicted in a long ago Biblical story. Steve and I were very different in appearances, however we would become very inseparable for a period in my twenties.

Steve began scratching himself under his arms and said this to me, "I'm baked and horny, if you're just as bored as me, why don't you get naked too."

So I got naked in his bedroom, I'm twenty- something. He was born in 1968, I was born in 1970 on American paperwork, we actually share the same birthday of February 28th. Steve was well into his twenties and had never lived outside his parents' Jacob and Lucy's 1950's tri-level ranch home in Briarwood Estates.

Steve had a cluttered messy bed, old plates with dried food stuck to the plates like a Madame Tussaud's wax museum of food displayed on his bedroom floor for all eternity. Steve says this to me, "You really do look better naked than dressed. Most people look better dressed, but you're the opposite, you look better naked. Redheads are either a zero or they are a ten, you are a ten. You have what German women are notoriously known for, a perfectly shaped and responsive pink clitoris like your pink nipples, sometimes it grows big. Some woman have a lot of hooding, extra skin, not you. You can see more of the bud with you and it's not a nasty dark color like Jewish women have."

Steve had the most unusual perception and bold comments to make to me, he was a strange duck. He would often comment when we drove in his car how I looked like the silhouette girl on the semi-truck rubber mud flaps of redneck truck drivers. He would always comment about me in strange ways, not romantic talk. Just off the wall quirky comments in what he revered as a compliment. Such as telling me he liked how my shoulders were the same width as my hips. "German women have shoulders and hips that are the same width which gives them their hour glass figure, that's why they are always featured in Playboy Magazine. Jewish women are built like upside down lightbulbs, not you though."

We laid on his waterbed, his sheets and blankets I doubt have ever been washed since his mother first made his bed and arranged his boyhood furniture twenty plus years earlier. His room was covered in dusty high school trophies and posters of sexy girls staring back at us from all four corners of his basement bedroom walls. The ceiling, made me feel like I am at a dentist office staring at dorky, strange, smiley posters on the ceiling. He'd look up and around as he held me, Steve talked in a weird creepy romancing reminiscing way as he glanced at his bedroom walls, as he tells me what he liked in each girl poster. Or what about the posters he admired in a trophy way as we stayed hidden in his parent's "orthodox Jewish" house on that evening, or any particular evening that he snuck me inside his parent's house after dark. In some ways it was like retreating back to adolescence hanging out with Steve who lived with his parents. He made me feel that it is o.k. to be stuck in life and not want to progress. He was a never ending storybook of high school, my age would change each year, as his age changed, but he never evolved, grew-up. I felt warped in a time slot with him, which was at least fun and comfortable.

"Oh my God, I love you Alan, I love you so much Alan," I murmured as this hairy ape buddy of a guy (Steve) went down on me one night.

"What are you saying?" He'd ask.

"What are you doing?" I squirmed and inquired….. "Just try something else, read a book about the subject before going down on me."

"Steve, you have hair covering almost eighty percent of your body, you even have little black hairs on your back and arms, growing all by themselves, not in a patch like the rest of your black hair Indian mounds." I commented as I cringed in his attempts at pleasuring a real live girl, which would be me, for the first time.

Steve responded with a smile and a quick wit as he took a deep breath and gasp of oxygen from the base of his waterbed, as he alone was creating the waves as I commented, "Do you have to move around so much?"

He just then blurts out an answer, "Those dark lonely hairs are pioneers." He laughed because we both spoke at the same time. Then he commented in a joke of a way wearing his emotion and sex on his arm…… "If you and I grow old together, we'd be that married couple driving around in a red convertible, top down, wind blowing, I can't hear you, you can't hear me, but we'd both be talking at the same time." Then he leans back and smiles this big contentment smile as if I just made his day.

"Steve, you are well into your twenties, you have never lived outside your parent's home. Nor do you have a desire to move out and have a place of your own. That in itself, is weird. The Latin slogan, "Carpe Diem," should be on your license plate Steve. We're not going to get married, we are just fooling around, we're both bored. After this night you are taking me to Northlake mall tomorrow afternoon, remember? We're experimenting, remember?"

"Are you my business expense tax write off? Just explain to me again, which line on my income tax form on April 15th, where do I write your name again? Or….. would that be your stage name? Or you legal name?" Steve said, again wearing his sarcastic emotions on his sleeve at this moment.

"Steve, we are friends." I remarked playfully.

Steve responded, "I spent thirty thousand on you last year, that was before all of this experimenting. I can't afford to move out of my parent's house. I'd have lawn and garden furniture for my living room pad."

"Do you have to talk like that Steve?" I remarked as I began to think quietly……resting. His bed pillows smelled like Fritos chips, him, and mildew…..and somehow, I actually found that comforting this evening. Steve had his original ways. He thought everything living, should have a name. He named my monthly periods….. "Kirby." I have no idea why? I had no idea why, how, when, he would say something odd and unexpected.

Now, some people, many people actually would comment, "Boy, you two, what is your relationship? You two are kinda like twins, but you look so different, and he is a little more strange than you." We heard that for about the whole six years we were "Best Friends in Atlanta."

Regressing to a mild level of high school is more comfortable than the young blossoming lady I was or had become. I did not purchase one item of clothing unless it was black. I now feel as if I am stuck in life with Steve from sheer boredom and loneness on my part. I had reason to mourn. I reminisced for a flash of a moment as I laid in his waterbed. I remember I entered this club contest where Steve worked when I was twenty-one, kind of like a bathing suit contest, less the bathing suit. I won first prize, $550.00. I collected the cash to pay my rent that month, and then went up to the bar for a drink from the bartender. The night was still early, I was twenty-one at the time. This short, pudgy guy with a big nose and dark curly hair looked at me, he was the bartender and tried to impress me with his wit, and quick sense of humor. I laughed a little, I liked his face because he resembled my father's face growing up in Jenison. Steve asked me how old I was, I showed him my driver's license. Steve said, "You and I share the same birthday, February 28th."

"What a good line to say to someone at a bar, but I don't believe you. It's kind of like, every time I meet a musician they say they are going to write a song about me, you have your line as a bartender, they have theirs I suppose, you say that to any girl you are hitting on I bet." I remarked with a smile and a twinkle in my eyes as I shook my head at Steve in his bartender tuxedo outfit. He was bartending with another guy who slouched, noticeably very senior, who appeared to be on his tenth career since he retired from the Navy. It might have also been on his agenda, just like Steve's bar career plan, to be able to hit on us young girls who got naked for a living. But that old bartender next to Steve looked as if he had a hard time hearing a drink order and moving a glass. I noticed the waitresses would have to write down the drink order after giving up on communicating the old fashion way of just shouting in a loud repeated manner, the drink call. It was an interesting mix of people at the bar I noticed. I liked that about this time in my life, all the very interesting people I was meeting, and how people naturally just took to my smile and bubbly personality. Life seemed to be so nice at age twenty-one, as I reminisced in Steve's bedroom in Briarwood Estates that night remembering how we first met.

The plot I wanted, the friction, and climax, to gather and absorb experiences as a free flowing moon jellyfish. As I recalled as I first met Steve in 1991, before Alan and I broke up. I was supposed to end up with Alan, and have three or four kids, raise our family in the south…….take honeymoon vacations to Savannah. Now I would just daydream about how things were supposed to be, never understanding why these days, things were the way they were.

Back to 1991, Steve proceeded to pull out his driver's license and show everyone at the bar that sure enough, we do share the same birthday. He is born two years earlier though. We did start a friendship at that club, it was almost February, and on our shared birthdays we went out for two lunches and two slices of free cake, each year on our shared birth date. It became a tradition of ours while I lived in Georgia. We did become friends, but I always knew Steve was not a leading man type, just a buddy to laugh with and spend time with, we had similar hobbies and interests and such. We liked to get stoned and play pool, not watch the time, no restrictions, just enjoy life. He was very laid back and unconventional in his outlook in life, we seemed always together, everywhere together. Not a stuffy two hour to four hour date in a controlled hourly means of getting to know someone.

Despite the setback of losing Alan, my mother announced she was moving back to Michigan, it had been about a year, for that I was happy. She left a cool-whip plastic container of homemade broccoli cheese soup in the empty refrigerator for me. We said good-bye and Cindy drove away, it was 1994ish (?). The next night I heated up the bowl of cheese broccoli soup in the microwave and gulped it down after a long day of hardly consuming and digesting any food.

The irony in the next story within my life is <u>why</u> Cindy decided to just up and leave Georgia for Michigan. I was paying all the bills as Cindy worked in a hospital as she pocketed all of her money with the acceptation Cindy would purchase groceries and cook. Cindy looked worried and elated, manic, hyper in the eyes with her expression she gave me as I walked into my apartment in Lithia Springs, Georgia one day. Cindy said in a panic "The police think I have been murdering patients." Cindy was packed and headed for the Michigan border within two days of making that most alarming statement to me in my apartment. And then I did not think the statement was so alarming as time passed on that week, Cindy was a demon, a real monster.

Within twenty minutes of consuming the homemade broccoli cheese soup that Cindy had made and left in my empty refrigerator I laid down in the living room floor, passed out, with severe stomach pains. Hours later I awoke to a dark apartment except for the kitchen light that I had left on. The living room spun as my eyes could not seem to adjust, the room grew darker, and then I felt like I was going blind. I reached for the phone cord and yanked the phone down. Everything took so much energy to accomplish a simple task such as that one, I noticed my vision was beyond blurry. My heart felt heavy and I began to pass out. I felt around like a blind person going stupid, I then punched buttons on the phone, but I could not make out the numbers I was dialing, it all appeared fuzzy and dark. The numbers blended, it looked so fuzzy. I passed out for five hours? I regained consciousness and then focused hard on the phone pad of numbers when I regained consciousness, I needed 9-1-1. Yet it was such a task to get those numbers located and pressed. I finally heard a knock on my front door. It was a group of emergency staff bringing me to the hospital in Lithia Springs area. At the hospital I had tubes forced down my throat, and black charcoal mud like substance was forced into me. Tubes shoved down my throat were unbearably painful to save and combat whatever was in my system. The medical staff thought maybe perhaps I was trying to commit suicide? But I had not, nor was I trying to do such a thing.

By Georgia law, someone who is committing suicide or had attempted to kill themselves has to be then transported to a mental hospital. Which I was then transported after a three day hospital stay to a state mental hospital for mental evaluation. It was determined within the initial first hour there at the mental hospital that I had not tried to commit suicide, nor did I have any mental illness. I was released within that same afternoon, Steve picked me up. Thank-God I did not have to stay in that place. Thank God I at least had Steve to come pick me up from the hospital asylum, what a whirling three days Cindy put me through! Hospital records last forever. The hospital was close to Lithia Springs where I lived, the hospital drive was not far. This all happened within twenty-four hours of Cindy leaving her Georgia station as a LPN nurse and driving herself back to Michigan. I believe before Cindy even made it to the Michigan border I was passed out on my living room floor. But it was supposed to look like a suicide? Like I was trying to kill myself? But I wasn't. The dates can be coordinated for any future attempts of getting rid of me by Cindy and her Central Intelligence Agency staff. Cindy did not know what to do with me, I was a victim of her sexually abusing me as a child, and trying to make money off me. The CIA and her always were between what they could do to me, and what she needed to do to me, or get from me, income wise. My life was evidence of who Cindy was, she needed to get rid of the evidence of who she was? At times she would stare at me and wish she could paint a sunset. I knew what she was thinking, after a while, a child just does. Sad how I ate the soup, and therefore there was no evidence of leftover chemicals to test in a crime lab. Hospital records last forever though, just like in Michigan, October 28th 1982, but I kept my mouth shut. I was afraid of Cindy, and understandably so.

Growing up my friends would all say, "I don't think your mom loves you like most moms love their children, like we are loved." That was a common statement made to me by friends from Unity Christian High.

I do understand I was always receiving wake-up calls in my life to this fact. But for some reason I would ignore my actual reality of who Cindy is, it was a reality I did not want to face. I wanted to at least have a mother, and not be without a mother and a father, right? It was better than nothing, I would have a bigger void, right? I would turn the other cheek to Cindy's abuse and go skipping along my way. And then there would be another incident by monster Cindy, then another, and another, and I would keep ignoring who and what she was inside. Just keep skipping, and skipping along so I would not have a bigger wider void of nothingness.

I told Steve what happened, he could hardly believe that soup put me in the hospital fighting for my life for three days with tubes of charcoal substance being shoved down my nostrils with no pain killers. I had consumed the entire bowl, and there was no proof otherwise to show what had transpired. I stayed away from Cindy. When Cindy informed me that she was dating a man in Michigan, Jerry Honderd. I was relieved, Cindy could focus her attention elsewhere, and not on me.

When alone with Steve now, after Alan, I then became the teacher, I dreaded teaching. I like my man to know all. I knew my world had ended. And somewhere I thought, I must get Alan back. I must locate him and begin this novel of my life on a continued note, not this ending note…..I do love Alan, this is so unfair.

I mumbled, "I will find my leading man, I must, as I stared at the walls."

Steve said this, "My parents are asleep, don't make too much noise in my waterbed, my parents don't like it when I have girls stay overnight." Steve had to sneak into his parents kitchen to locate a bag of chips and two cokes, then tip toe back into his room without making a sound as to wake up his parents. He gave me strict orders not to open his bedroom door if anyone knocked. This relationship lasted until he broke up with me in 1995, and yes, he still lived at home when we broke up. Can you believe it? Steve in 1995 broke up with me, I was stunned too! However, our relationship was not totally over we then still continued to see each other until 1996, due to boredom in both of our lives. He stated that he loved me, but his parents insisted he should and will marry a Jewish girl, and sent him on a blind date with a Jewish girl named Susanne.

I asked Steve once, "Well, do you love her?"

Steve replied, "Not like you, but it is the right thing to do. I have to carry on my Jewish legacy, and have Jewish children, I cannot have that with you. What do you think our kids would look like?"

I kept repeating, "You're breaking up with me?" "For real now?"….. "You're breaking up with me?" Then I commented, "Our kids? What would they look like? How would I know? Dark hair, dark features, I think are dominate genes, I heard that in like 8th grade science class."

Then I asked Steve again just to be sure, "You're breaking up with me?"

Steve acted exasperated when he answered me back, "Yes. Yes we are now officially broken up." Then Steve pushes the break-up guilt back onto me with asking me in an angry voice, "Do you want me to fade out?"

I inquired meekly and a bit bewildered, "Fade out?"

Steve responded talking slow and loud as if I am now stupid and he is superior in intelligence, "Do you want me to fade out my blood line?"

And before I could answer that question Steve adds, "If I do not marry Jewish and have children with another Jew than the Jewish pool is diminishing in the sea."

I remark too late, "Maybe I can convert to Judaism?"

Steve stormed, "That won't count! Why would you even say such a thing? Jews need to stick with Jews. We have no tolerance for anything that is not Jewish! Someday we will populate the earth and there will be no more gentiles like you! Don't you get it? We can't be together."

Steve looked exhausted and frustrated as he had just blurted out his point.

I just stared at twenty-seven year old Steve as I thought quietly to myself at that moment at his house in Briarwood, Steve still lived with his parents Jacob and Lucy, I thought I was better than him. I can't believe what I am hearing from Steve.

Then I responded, "Yes. I do understand Steve."

Steve looked at me as if he was already starting to reminisce about me or "us," before the break-up was even completed and I left. He looked at me with bubble glow eyes and remarked sincerely, and passionately as someone who wears their feelings on their sleeve always and says…….. "I am going to miss you. Suzanne doesn't have your personality…she's not as curvy as you either….I'll miss the Playboy bunny in my waterbed…..and your personality, you do say the wittiest things, odd, original things like me."

I then repeated again, "You're breaking up with me?" I was dumbfounded to say the least. I really never saw that coming, I thought Steve needed me! Steve was someone I just took for granted, a choice in life I always took for granted. I never in five or six years that we knew each other even tried to impress him. And now I feel like I need to defend myself, impress him suddenly, or something like that. I thought Steve needed me! He acted like he needed me.

Steve then remarks, "There is an exception within the Jewish community that would allow for me to marry you?"

I ask Steve, "What?"

Steve looks as if he has the upper hand in life, break-ups, and romance for my life and says smugly, "The exception rule for the Jewish community to allow for me to marry you would be that I and the Jewish community would benefit monetarily or politically from our marriage union, I don't see how that is possible with you, and there for my parents want me to break up with you."

I look at Steve in livid disgust, "Why didn't you just say that in the beginning of us hanging out together? I wasted way too many weekends and time with you over the years! What about my life? You took the good years of my life!"

Steve looked at me with smugness as if he just won at the gambling table and I lost everything to him. Steve then comments, "Lori, you like wasting time."

Then Steve feels an apparent emerging need to soothe my emotions and remedy the situation by remarking to me, "By the way Lori, the Jewish community is correct, we would be fighting all the time if an outsider such as yourself could not provide me with a financial boost, or a step-up politically for my people."

I was stunned Steve broke up with me. Nevertheless, I thought I am the one who needs to get on with my life. I need to start to think about me, and what I want to do with my life. During this time, people were giving me advice, such as, "You would do well with your personality in the booming mortgage or real estate sales field. You do not need a college degree, just ambition, a real estate license and be hard working and friendly like you are." I seemed to hear that a lot in Georgia and decided to sign up for real estate classes near Galleria Mall. Even though the money is good at The Gold Club, I hated the late evening shift of 8pm to 4am. I wanted a day job, a real career, I wanted to wear fancy suits, be thought of as a smart woman that I am. Really do something with my life. Stop smoking pot. Get up early, and be one of those 9 to 5er's! Be like the rest of the world, "normal." And maybe, just maybe, if I am "normal," I will be happy."

Cindy married Jerry Honderd in January of 1996. Within a two or three year period of returning to Michigan from living in Georgia off me, she was married. I now felt free to move on with my life too. I thought Jerry was an angel sent from God marrying Cindy, she now had a new target to occupy her life. I felt a relief, it was like the sun looked brighter, better. I could dare to dream about what I want to do with my life and not Cindy's money demands of my life! Cindy had a man to take care of her now which made me feel free.

One day I was "working my rounds" so to speak in the upper level of The Gold Club with my tray of Jell-O shots and cigars. I was taking a break from dancing. I thought keeping my clothes on would make me feel normal. Remember I am in search of "normal" = "happy" math formula. My work associate friend of mine Melanie was also a "candy stripe girl," meaning we sold cigars and alcoholic shots to the patrons.

A man about forty or so, dressed in causal yet dressy attire was sitting in the last V.I.P. room to the right. I asked if he would like a Jell-O shot. He said yes, and so I served him a shot. When I sat in his lap, put the little Jell-O cup mixed with alcohol and cool lime between my cleavage, and pulled his head down to lick or slurp the Jell-O from the small white cup held in my black lace bustier, grabbing his silky dark hair. I felt a jolt from underneath me, this guy was instantly, full-fledged aroused within one minute, maybe thirty seconds of me resting on his lap, just his legs. As he powerfully edged me closer to him, he was not letting go, it was a struggle, he had my hips gripped. Then he pulled me up and closer in his lap in a super aggressive approach. This was going to be a game of cat or mouse in order to get off him. "Oh, my God," I thought. This really never happens at The Gold Club with an army of bouncer men in every corner of the club, the distinguished patrons actually do not get out of control.

The Gold Club is a very upscale club, and the women are in control, and men never get out of control, hardly ever. This man grabbed my hips and was not letting go of this situation or opportunity? I could not get up, off his lap. I struggled, as I struggled, he leaned forward and reached for more of me, all of me to just stay on him, with him, at that moment. It was as if he was embarrassed that he instantly got so… "aroused." Then he was just determined to not let go of me. You wanna hear what happened next? You won't believe this one. I saw a desert, the night was dark, he had cut marks from swords or fighting, his clothes torn, like at the end of a battle. There are other men in the background, as he approaches me. I am Cleopatra. He, that man, was or is Marc Antony. I then keep trying to pull away, and am mentally just quite shaken up by what is transpiring in the present. I cannot keep his hands off me, I am now in a struggle of sorts, in the here and now moment at The Gold Club. I'm stunned. I am also wondering as he touches me, is he having a past life regression too? Does he know who I am, inside, from our past life? Does he, is he aware of who he is? Does he have that ability to touch another and know who that other person is or was? I don't know…….

His red haired lawyer friend who looks just like that Grandville attorney, Mr. Rick Bolhouse actually stands up in V.I.P., moves from his warm spot on the black couch and tries to intercept this dark haired man attacking me. As if to take a stance to his apparent client to back off a bit from the grabbing. His red haired lawyer friend, Rick {which he introduced himself later to me}, said to me as I struggled in this dark haired man's lap, "Excuse my friend, he just got a divorce, he does not know what it is like to have an aggressive young woman feeding him Jell-O from a cup sitting on his lap like that."

"Me? Aggressive? He's the aggressive one." I remarked politely and poignantly.

"You sat in his lap first, you grabbed his head and shoved it into your chest. You are the aggressor, and he, my client is the aggresse victim. You are a whore, little girl. I know your mother Cindy, she told me all about you." Spoke Rick Bolhouse.

"Then why did you get up, to stop him, your friend?" I inquired to the jerk of an attorney, the same attorney my ill-will mother Cindy has been quoting all her life to me.

"Get a law degree, and we'll talk." The scoundrel redheaded, dorky Dutch attorney snapped off as some kinda important advice to me.

The dark haired man, kind of cute, but way too aggressive and ill-mannered in my book. He said this to me….. "You remind me of my girlfriend, well, fiancée, do you know who I am?"

I whispered back as I began sitting up from his very full and unavoidable firm lap…… "I do. I think I know who you are. You know Marc Antony, it is not nice to point at me like this, shame on you for your bad manners tonight." I left feeling overwhelmed at how brave that man was in that V.I.P. room with me. But I did not care for Cindy's attorney from Grandville….two laps over.

The aggressive dark haired man from Michigan that traveled with his attorney Mr. Rick Bolhouse, he one with dark hair, I swear is Marc Antony, the real Marc Antony.

Like bees swarming towards honey just minutes later as I step down from the V.I.P. upper loft area and head down the black barred staircase, the office manager Norbie of The Gold Club asked me a question as he pulled me aside to fill another tray of forty Jell-O shots on the black tray that I would carry around. Norbie asked this, "Do you ever feel like you are getting raped while serving those shots?"

I answered "No, not really."

Norbie then went onto say this, "We have it on video, in the office, Steve just radioed me, he saw what happened." Norbie pointed up to the last V.I.P. room on the left corner, the same V.I.P. room I had just stepped out of, a bit jolted from a patron being so bold.

"Video?" I inquired.

Nobie answered, "For your protection, to make sure nothing illegal goes on in those V.I.P. rooms. We have the evidence."

I responded back to Norbie, "Marc Antony is rumored to be CIA, he'll find a way to get the evidence back and you may not like his tactics."

Within thirty or so minutes, Melanie came down from the V.I.P room awhile later while I was serving more shots from table to table in the main arena area, the audience area on the main floor. Melanie said to me, "That man up there wants you to come back, he keeps asking all these questions about you, like who you are dating, where do you live, where are you from, he thinks you are Cleopatra, and the both of you have unfinished business. I told him you are dating some guy named Steve, or were dating some guy named Steve, and that you are from Michigan. He thinks that you are dating Steve Kaplan, the owner of The Gold Club. This man seems to know quite a bit about Steve Kaplan. And he somehow thinks that is **the** Steve you are dating. Are you Lori?" Melanie asked.

No, not at all." I responded.

Melanie responded and remarked, "I didn't think so."

Melanie then asked me, "When you were little growing up in Michigan did you have a snowmobile?"

I looked at Melanie with a strong stare wondering, what next will she say.

Melanie then went onto say, "That man upstairs is from Michigan too, and thinks you are Cleopatra and ran off with some guy after a war lost in a previous lifetime. He has a really big dick and is paying me to give him a hand job behind a pillow, he keeps stating that you look like his fiancée. He really wants you to come up there though and asked me to come down and get you…..would you go to a hotel room with him for $1,500.00?" Asked Melanie boldly, yet seriously.

"No." I said.

Melanie asked again, "You would not go to a hotel room with him for $1,500.00? He is worth like six million dollars, he's got money and he is cute. Come on Lori, he wanted me to come down and get you, he wants you back up in that VIP room. Come on, you should take him up on the offer."

I was beyond turned off with offering me money. I am not some act, I am not what he thinks I am, a whore to be bought simply because of where I work. I like to be spoiled, but not paid for an act. I knew he was not for me when Melanie said he wants to pay me or her. However, I did comment over my shoulder as Melanie headed back up the black metal staircase, "Maybe he can send me three million in a belated birthday card."

There were many FBI and CIA agents that would fill up the patron seating next to the round tables, in their attempts to loosen the starch within their collars around their neck, I suppose. Some FBI would stand against the walled mirrors or bar area in the necessity to feel more comfortable. When I asked questions after the table dance, such as, "What do you do for a living?" The usual response from FBI was, "I work for the government." The FBI demeanors was always stoic, serious, contemplative in nature. It's as if they were all produced on the same planet assembly line, then systematically released to earth. Perhaps they all thought that of us showgirls too? Who knows, their cash was as green and usable as the next patron, so no need to be prejudice on how they produce their income. It's as if we were all on the same playing field, them, and me, all the girls in the club.

One evening as I made my rounds in VIP as a showgirl, a man in about his mid-forties? About 5'8, sandy brown hair, Dutch looking, holding his beverage with a serious grip, moved towards me in the crowded isle. He introduced himself as General David Petraeus. I had met him several times before in The Gold Club. I could always easily scale his height at 5'8 and look him straight in the eyes with my five inch heels. He spoke to me as if he wanted me to always remember his name and him. He then leaned into my neck area, looked towards my eyes with intent, and said, "I had feelings for you when you were young."

Creepy, I thought silently to myself. My response you are wondering? My eyes grew big with bewilderment, and I walked away from creepiness. Oh my God, that must be one of Cindy's CIA associates. Cindy could always get the drugs from the hospital where she worked, and the CIA always knew how to erase my memories when they wanted to when I was young, a child.

I remember something else bizarre that General David Petraeus said to me at The Gold Club, early 1990's. He stated to me while I danced for him in V.I.P., "Cindy your adopted mother looks like the Roman emperor Nero in your Bethany adoption file."

I table danced for another U.S. government worker, Leon Penetta in V.I.P, it must have been around 1993. He again had that same demeanor that spelled, I know more about you than you think, as I danced for him. And sure enough, by the end of the song as I preceded to get dressed back into a sequence bathing suit outfit, Leon Panetta had something important to say to me. Mr. Penetta says this to me, "Your biological mother is not Diane of Dexter, Michigan. Your real mother lives in the Netherlands. I'm with the U.S. government and I have viewed your adoption file from Grand Rapids, Michigan. The CIA has a copy of your elaborate ancestry papers that Bethany Christian Services has on file. I know there is an organization selling you on paper to wealthy Russians and Arabs, I'm investigating that organization with a committee. I do not think it is a good occupation for you to be a dancer in this club. Your real mother is Queen Beatrix of the Netherlands and your real father is Claus Von Amsberg. Your mother is Dutch and German, your father is

German. There are many wealthy men in Saudi Arabia that paid money to the CIA and the CIA's associates for you to be brought to Saudi soil, this is a dangerous occupation for you. You might consider another field."

Leon Panetta was not the only man stopping me and asking me for a table dance, and then afterwards announcing to me that they know who my biological mother is. I would always then respond with a "Yes, I know, Diane Marie Bomers Umstead of Dexter, Michigan is my real mother." The patrons sitting down would shake their head "no." Then the patron would say to me, "Diane is not the name of your real mother. I know who your real mother is." I would walk away perplexed by the whole situation.

I would always wonder in confusion, why would Bethany Christian Services in Grand Rapids, Michigan introduce to me to my biological mother as Diane Marie Bomers Umstead and my biological father is Denny Garner? If in reality Denny and Diane are not my biological mother and father who gave me up for adoption, siting the reason as because they did not wed, what is the truth, and how did that lie arrive in a file? And can an adoption agency legally lie like that to me or anyone? I think not. I am just left bewildered, that's too big of a lie for an adoption agency to legally indorse. However, there is another oddity that does not make sense; Diane lived in Muskegon, Michigan during her supposed entire pregnancy with me. However, my birth certificate states I was born at Blodgett Hospital in Grand Rapids, Michigan on February 28, 1970. Why would a very pregnant woman drive or have her parents drive her all the way to Grand Rapids, Michigan during ice and snow storms and not just deliver me in Muskegon, Michigan? Grand Rapids, Michigan is a good one and a half hours drive in clear driving conditions with no road hazards of ice and snow to contend with. Diane's OBGYN doctor that she saw during her entire pregnancy would also have to be connected to Blodgett Hospital in Grand Rapids, Michigan for her to deliver me at Blodgett Hospital. Which would mean that Diane Marie would have to travel one and a half to almost two and a half hours ONE WAY just to have her monthly, and then weekly OBGYN appointments prior to giving birth to me. And then drive nearly one and a half hours to two and a half hours back home to her parent's house in Muskegon,

Michigan where she supposedly lived during the entire pregnancy of me. And then as always I would place the mysterious questions I was left with on a back burner stove within my mind, never thinking I will need to someday turn the burner on or move the pan to the front, ever, who wants to be confused. The CIA and FBI were coming into The Gold Club more than ever now, only those agents can answer the questions that will arise with the publication of my American memoirs.

Steve Kaplan bought The Gold Club in 1992-1993, I was twenty-two or twenty-three years old then. There were only eighteen of us girls working at the club at the time he bought The Gold Club in Atlanta, Georgia for 6.2 million, some patron told me it was in the Atlanta newspaper. Steve was a stereotypical Jew. Not at all like suave, attractive, and intellectually penetrating Jewish Alan. Steve was short, fat, and all about money. Steve instantly began making financial changes within the club. Such as the gold bucks us girls turned in at the end of the shift, he wanted more than ten percent to the house. At the end of the night shift, he wanted thirty percent now. So for every ten dollars, Steve Kaplan took three dollars. For every one thousand dollars of gold bucks we would receive individually, Steve took three hundred dollars at the end of the shift. Plus he was charging more on the patron side as well. I knew he was going to eventually piss off the elite clientele that visited The Gold Club with his money schemes. I would learn later from patrons coming inside The Gold Club that Steve Kaplan was just a front man for the CIA and any paperwork Steve's attorney needed to file or show to authorities would always protect the true owner of The Gold Club. What do I think? I was just there to make a living, I had adult bills to pay. I was not a girl who lived with my parents.

Steve had a northern attitude, brassy, and all about the money, a real carpetbagger type. Too opportunistic like, all the while operating a southern establishment of the south. I knew his attitude was like unwanted sandpaper on a fine, shiny, preserved pink and turquoise heirloom. Steve was abrasive, and all about the money, the profit the nightclub could bring in for him, what the girls could and would do for him. Verses, how the patrons, the elite who visited the nightclub saw the role of The Gold Club as simply tradition for southern gentlemen with substantial wealth and influences. Men with major alliances, Hollywood connections, whom did not take well to Steve's financially progressive shift of wanting power in their sphere of influences in the south, his flamboyant Yankee take over style. I knew a war in the south over The Gold Club would eventually erupt and follow suit, you could just sense the tension….the inevitable prediction.

Steve would appear as raw, blind, and abrasive in wonderment of that silent unyielding war, as when he first arrived to look around and then buy The Gold Club in the early 1990's. Steve took over Atlanta nightlife like a yelling, bullying, damn Yankee carpetbagger that he appeared to be in person or in print. Steve was either too loud and too mad about something, or contemplating and reserved in nature like a volcano that hasn't erupted for over thousand years or so. The descriptive words of handsome or refined seem to elude him in description, and probably always would.

His friend in 1994 once told me that Steve has this psychic, a real genuine psychic that can predict the future and she is never wrong, a real amazing psychic named "Sharon." The psychic told Steve while in New York that he just had to buy this strip club in the south. His friends, the managers, and Steve's sidekick named Ziggy informed me of what his psychic predicted. That "This girl would someday be the world's blue star and bring him a lot of money if he bought the club in Atlanta, Georgia."

The Gold Club printed their own money, paper money called "gold bucks." A patron could buy the money on his credit card with additional fees attached. Never was a guy, a patron, allowed to touch a girl, the showgirls would dance fully nude. For stage sets, the first song with the outfit on, second song with the top off and after the third song fully nude, a three song set on stage. Then we were free to sit at cocktail tables and dance an arm lengths away from the patron. Table dances were cheap, only ten dollars. Usually though, a man would give you money to just sit at his table and talk, laugh, have a witty amusing conversation, just sitting there at the cocktail table wearing a sequence looking skimpy bathing suit ensemble.

Musicians, professional athletes, sport team owners, celebrities, just about every anchorman from CNN, Wolf Blitzer was a regular, many successful businessmen, CIA, FBI, average joe's blowing the grocery money would all make up the usual crowds that filtered into The Gold Club in Buckhead. However, did I mention royalty from around the world would filter into The Gold Club? Especially European royalty made an appearance or two at The Gold Club. One day in the early 1990's in VIP I was stopped by a blonde haired boy. I say boy because he was no older than me, the young guys always made me nervous because I know I should not be a stripper, I should be studying for a college exam, right? The blonde hair, blue eyed, very thin young man had a young man next to him, a translator. The translator in English asked me to table dance, so I did. I really never thought much about it until the translator say, "He thinks you look like his mother's side of the family, no you look like his father's side of the family." The translator asked who my parents are, where I am from.

I stated I am from Michigan and I am adopted. Then the translator asked where I was adopted from. I answered, "Bethany Christian Services." Just as I finished saying where I was adopted from the blonde haired, blue eyed young patron's face goes flush white as if he saw a ghost and he goes almost into shock. I knew something I just said resonated like a ghost from the past he could not believe. I could tell by his shock and expression he had or was having a life altering experience within seconds, immediately after I answered where I was adopted from in Michigan. His older brother was motioned by the translator to come over. His older brother is now the King of the Netherlands. The father Claus Von Amsberg came over walking a bit hutched over on a cane. The father looked like the shorter version of the actor that played in A Sound Of Music, that was my impression. They all seemed ecstatic. I was confused, clue me into what you are all saying, was what I was thinking. The father kept rambling on ecstatic and growing visibly angry as he spoke in a foreign language. I was not sure what the commotion or situation was all about, until finally the translator spoke. This is what the translator said to me, "This is your father Claus Von Amsberg."

I just stared at them all, staring at me.

Then the translator spoke up again, "Your real father. This is your real father."

I looked bewildered and felt very bewildered.

The translator spoke up again to me as he gestured towards Claus Von Amsberg, "Lori you mentioned that you are adopted. Claus is your real biological father."

I looked perplexed. I looked at the older and very tired Claus Von Amsberg who was clearly frustrated that I did not believe he was my father. I remember looking at him with pity. I know it seems ironic, here I am as a stripper feeling sorry for a man married to Dutch Royalty with a grand life. However, if you were there in VIP and saw his exhaustion, his tiredness from trying to convince me that I am his long lost daughter, you would have felt pity on him too. He clearly one hundred percent thought I was his long lost daughter.

I spoke up, "I already met my biological mother and father, their names are Denny and Diane. I met them at Bethany Christian Services. I already met my real parents. Why would an adoption agency introduce me to my wrong biological parents? It does not make any logical sense to me. I am sorry for your confusion." The Dutch royals could not seemingly convince me, I truly felt sorry for Claus Von Amsberg. That must have been awful to think someone is your long lost daughter and they are not. They left The Gold Club unable to convince me that I am their long lost relative, a family member of theirs. It would not be until many years later when Greg, Diane Bomer Umstead's husband informed me that Diane plays the role of mother for a government salary to many Dutch and German children that were adopted out through the CIA's secret program that I began to realize what the truth might be, the truth in my past. I began searching and looking at photos online of the Dutch royals once my son Eddie, born in 2004, turned about eight and then ten that I noticed he had the same two front teeth and smile as Queen Beatrix of the Netherlands when she was about his age. I then saw with my own eyes how I noticeably resembled both Claus Von Amsberg and Queen Beatrix of the Netherlands from the Dutch royal online collection of photographs in comparison to me. Claus Von Amsberg died the same month and year I married my husband Ed. And then my mind flashes to my childhood and little tid bits of information given to me, which again does not correlate with Bethany Christian Services version.

One Central Intelligence Agent named John Brennan stopped me again in VIP for me to do a table dance for him. He acted as if he had seen me before at the club and wanted to let me know he could be a dick. Essentially, he acted as verbally powerful as he could be for a man of authority within the guidelines of a "dick hand book," he personally wrote, but was unpublished. And would always remain unpublished to save his other face he showed in the world of politics. As I danced for him in VIP, his back was to the wall of mirrors. He seriously looked into my eyes, very sternly and said, "I am going to execute a big demonstration of what the CIA can do to be noticed and appreciated, you and your FBI friends over there will not be able to stop the CIA. The Arabs are my brothers, the money is already overseas, and you can't stop the Geha organization from sales on American soil of woman just like you, we're too powerful and vast in numbers. The FBI are comprised of stupid men, why do you even talk with them?"

Then as I proceeded to make my way through VIP I bumped into another creep that asked me for a table dance, his name, CIA David Petraeus. "Do you know who I am?" He asked me.

I responded, "Yes. You are the man that comes into The Gold Club and always ask me, 'Do you know who I am?'"

CIA David Petraeus shifts his feet as if adjusting his height and uncomfortableness that I would make a slight joke at his expense. Then he clears his throat and remarks to my face as I remaining dancing, "You should not bother with finishing college. At the CIA we can provide you with a degree or multiple degrees without finishing college."

I inquire, "What?"

CIA David Petraeus speaks as if he is a source of important knowledge for me and my plight in life as he says, "Yes, come work for the CIA and I can land you a job in a school district as a principal or assistant superintendent. You'll earn an income through the school district and from me. You'll need to do just as I ask with no questions as part of the CIA's job placement policy."

I responded with a smile, "That does not sound like it's for me. I do not want a fake college degree."

CIA David Petraeus comments, "You can't dance in heels forever Lori, you need to think of your future down the road."

As I made my way to the girls locker room on the upper level I was once again stopped by CIA John Brennan who boldly grabbed my arm. John informed me, or rather warned me that CIA David Petraeus as a method of operation utilizes police like his soldiers to get what he wants.

Many musicians, celebrities, sports stars, and such would fly into Atlanta and party for a week if they were in the south on business. They'd stop into The Gold Club as if crashing an instant elaborate ongoing party where there might be fifty or so young and good looking girls with perfect tan lines, perfect curves, ranging in age from nineteen to twenty-eight, some younger. I worked at the Gold Club from ages nineteen to twenty-six and a half. We smelled of expensive perfume, most of us were in college and therefore could also hold an intelligent conversation, even while sipping on champagne. We liked to have fun. We were the cream of the crop so to speak of beautiful and charming showgirls in Atlanta, that drank with you, smiled, laughed, and oh, by the way, at your command, got naked and danced a song or two in front of you. And well, for everyone attending that party in the sky, so to speak, I am sure, well I know, it was a logical place to stop in and meet someone that might also accompany you later to your hotel. But quite honestly, I made enough money there working the 8pm to 4am night shift that I never did accept such an invitation. Ask anyone. Patrons would describe me as looking like, "Jessica Rabbit," a drawn yet very real description of a beautiful and curvy Playboy bunny, with that perfect Playboy, girl next door face. Who also so happened to be a "Playboy Book of Lingerie" model.

Like bubbles gathering in a champagne bottle, I had fans, my fans were the musicians, celebrities, and sports stars, business tycoons.

Nothing can be slanderous, or possibly ruin a reputation, because I never slept with any of the musicians, celebrities, sports stars, or regular local business men. I just didn't. And I do not know of any girls who did. We were like "American geishas." Most of us were in college, never paid a bill late, never were on welfare, never asked for a government tuition grant. And never needed college financial aid, although The Gold Club was sort of like a pool of money, a river of college tuition really, nice clothes, nice car, lots of spending money, and we earned it!

I remember one evening, a casually dressed, dark eyed, yet lighter appearing hair, sort of feathered hair, hair parted down the middle, casual guy, not too tall. This gentlemen locked eyes with me in the upper level of The Gold Club as I wore a light teal bathing suit style costume with five inch heels, which made me appear 5'8 in height. As though his eyes grew bigger as I approached him, he could not believe I was suddenly in front of him saying "Hello." Our introduction to each other was in the beginning of the night, amidst the smell of the lower main stage smoke machine blowing upward and onward and cigar smoking patrons. He commented to me, "I like the Chanel No. 5 on you." He asked if I wanted to locate a table there in VIP and sit down and have a drink. He kept staring intensely at me, I knew by the way he looked at me I was going to stay and talk with him for a while. He asked me my name, my real name, not a showgirl name. He needed to know my real name. He commented after I danced for him that I looked English. I commented that is a refreshing statement compared to what some Jewish men call me when they come into this establishment. He asked what my nationality is, and I said, American.

He, Gerry Beckley stated, "I don't see the German side, you look very English to me. You would look very nice in fine Scottish plaid spread out on hay, perhaps for your next photo shoot for Playboy?"

I smiled, I laughed as I sipped on my electric lemonade drink at his cocktail table. I adjusted the wide bands of my satin teal outfit that seemed to reach tight and deep between my tan lines, yet hardly covered my curves spilling out of my costume. I sat still and listened to Gerry, smiling at my prospects of yet another interesting late night school evening at The Gold Club.

Then from out of the blue I felt a hand slide across my bare shoulder as I took another sip privately, spilling my cocktail in the non- secluded V.I.P. cocktail table area as I felt a slight caress. I looked up to see whose hand felt as if it belonged on my shoulder. But before I could comment too abruptly to the chill, the intrusive brown haired patron whispered in my ear. I moved around in my seat from where he had just bumped me, causing me to spill the sticky lemonade drink. He said to me as his hands shook a bit, his lips quivering as if nervous tonight, "Do you feel like you are living in a dream?" He then takes a whiff of my perfume as if licking with his senses the scent off my neck as he comments back to his friend behind him…. "I think I smell sex and candy here…."

Then he looks to me and lowers his chin, pressing tightly against my cheek as he examines my slightly spilled drink of the sticky electric lemonade cocktail, as he says, "It's kind of like disco lemonade night here tonight, don't you think dear? I hear everything you are discussing at this table. I'll show you dear." He then pulled away from my ear in a smug stare back at me.

I knew the guy, he always acted like he had a regular seat in VIP, yet his name was not on the table, or a red velvet rope over his high top chair. I honestly was a bit startled, I did not know he was in town. He acted like he was on drugs tonight, geeked on something. I motioned for him to come closer so I could give him a piece of my witty mind. I whispered as his chin lowered and brushed against me, "John, why not channel all that creative energy that's bottled up inside you and write a song, that's what successful artists do, successful musicians and such, have you ever heard of channeling your creativity into a positive release?" I smiled as I finished that witty statement to him, John, the brown haired patron. As I gave him one last piece of advice….. "You know John, you should really lay off that caffeine substance……it may cause you an anxiety attack in life someday if I ever write about this moment in my memoirs."

Gerry Beckley gave the guy a quick hearty smile. The brown haired patron wanna be a famous musician guy smiled back, a bit cocky. Or perhaps wasted, as if it was opening night in a packed theater, or amphitheater for that matter, and he thought he was on stage in V.I.P. That cocky, I'll show you kinda gloating, was in John's attitude, maybe that is just how young guys act.

Just then the V.I.P. manager Greek George came over and whispered politely in my naive little ear…… "You are surrounded by America. I thought you should know that fact. In case you were unaware of that reality."

Gerry instantly ignored the most recent rude interruption. I looked at Gerry and then he looked back at me. Gerry went on to comment as if not noticing I spilled my lemonade drink a little on my lap that he thought I was very mesmerizing, "I like the way you are built." We talked about astrology, he commented he was a Virgo, born on September 12th.

I laughed, and asked, "Really? My best friend in Michigan is born on September 12th. I am your winter and you are my summer." I laughed as I commented further, "or vice versa. She knows I like men, and music, artsy philosophical men, how ironic. You are practical, just like her, yet you make your living in the music world, unconventional. I like that. My income is unconventional, this is not a mall minimum wage kinda place you know."

Gerry remarked, "Oh, eh, let me give you some money for sitting with me."

Gerry asked me, "So what is it that you really want to do with your life? You're young, beautiful, fairly intelligent, what is it you really want to do with your life?"

"Write. I met Jerry Seinfeld you know, I was star struck and could not talk in 1992…..1993 when I met him. Can you believe it? I could not talk? I want to write a screenplay where Jerry gets his girl, I feel bad I could not talk."

"Jerry? How about me?" Inquired Gerry.

"Oh you'll get me, I just need to experience life a little more." I commented.

Then he looked very serious.

I then whispered something to Gerry, and he whispered back to me as well.

And then Gerry said, "Do you remember heaven before this lifetime?"

I stopped laughing, sipped on my cocktail straw, and looked up, paused, and then asked, "Do you?"

Gerry responded a bit tipsy, "I think all musicians remember heaven before earth."

I looked at him and seriously spoke up, "Do me a favor, if you and I do meet up, perhaps at a book signing in the future, will you also donate the royalties of another song you wrote and sang with your band?"

Gerry asked inquisitively with a twinkle, "What song is that Lori?"

I responded, "She Can Do Magic. Donate that song and royalties to my best friend in Michigan, Carmen Van Noord."

"Why?" Asked Gerry.

"Carmen deserves at least that for her extraordinary contribution back in the 1860's. And then you and I will go out for a drink and laugh some more just like this charming evening in the south that we are sharing now." I said.

"How will I know it is you, that you wrote a book finally? How will we really meet again?" Gerry asked.

"How would I possibly know?" I responded.

Gerry whispered seriously in my ear......"America is going to be obsessed with you."

I whispered seriously and a bit tipsy myself, "O.k."

Just when I thought the brown haired patron had left the V.I.P. area, I felt a stare and looked around, as if stares could possess powers, and there he was, John. Not just any John though, a regular guy, a fixture almost, "the brown haired patron." He motioned for me to approach him, so I did, as always. I knew I was going to be in for some unusual conversation with him just by the way he was twitching and restless, and a bit tipsy, I suppose. Who knows what he is going to say, he's a bit wacky sometimes, I thought as I walked towards him.

"I hear everything you were discussing in conversation with your practical musician Virgo new best friend." John smiled smugly as if to say with his look, what do you think about that dear?

John from the Midwest looks at me seriously, "As if a Virgo man could really iron out your bohemian personality. You need discipline. Structure. Not this box of a nightclub structure, you need real structure and discipline."

"What? What can you hear?" I inquired from him as he held my light teal satin costume, then swung the outfit over his shoulder as he held his beer bottle, watching as he then takes a another swig of beer.

"Talking about astrology as if you are a real expert. How's this for a revelation……" John takes another sip from his beer bottle, and comments, "Saturn does conjunct Venus, I know all about your indulgences……sex and sweets up here in V.I.P……. You want to write a screenplay for Seinfeld?"……. John smiled cocky and assertively as he then announced, "The waitress works for tips too." John smiled big at his latest revelation to me.

"Yeah, so?" I said as I talked and danced in a swaying motion.

"O.k., here is a line, a real funny line to add in the end of the screenplay………..you're so funny, you….." John whispered in my ear, that comical line.

I'll give you a hint what he said……..when something is so funny you laugh so hard, it makes you pee a little. For instance, when you hear a joke so funny while you've had so much to drink that night, the old cliché John spoke to me? Well, I was told never to speak in clichés by Alan. Every artist or great writer is an original, if you are original, people will comment, "Hey I like that." That's what Alan told me anyways. So I cannot reveal the line John whispered in my ear, for it was a cliché of what a person says when something is so funny. John is an artist too, ya' know, we laughed many of nights. I was paid to be charming.

John leaned forward and whispered…. "I'm goinna write a song, I feel inspired to do so…..you're goinna feel like me, like I can't believe I took this trip, and met this person." John takes another swig of beer just as the song ended.

"What are you up to?" I inquired.

John began rambling on as the disco lights swirled against my naked tan lines and another song began playing……."Fate. You have sun square moon on your chart. Which means you like the opposite of your exterior shell. You like someone very much unlike me. You always comment to me when I ask you out that you think I look like I could be your brother or something. But you need to see, we will be together. You and I are alike. We are artists. We are communicators of inner dimensions, we transform the world onto our platform. We do. Don't laugh, sober up Lori. Those electric lemonade drinks have too much sugar for you. This is fate baby…..we change the world….us….the artists…..wake up, Lilly."

John leans forward and whispers….."Lilly…..wake up in there."

I looked at John and said as I slipped my teal satin and sequence bathing suit on over my tan lines…. "Write the song, when I hear it on the radio, or see you in a music video……I'll wake up, that's a deal John." I laughed and proceeded to walk away as John had one last statement to make.

John looked at me very seriously and said, "Your mother is bad news. It's as if you're living in a dream not realizing how bad she is. You posing for Playboy's Book of Lingerie was not a good idea, your mother and her questionable business associates are up to know good. They send men into this club, they are selling you on paper behind your back and you have no idea, or do?"

This is all too weird, why is he saying this to me? I just want a normal life. Why can't achieving normal be easy? John was making no sense. Maybe I am drunk. Later John wrote a song in the mid to late 1990's. The title of the song is, Sex and Candy by the band he formed called Marcy's Playhouse.

Throughout the charmed college career of entertaining for dollars and larger bills from 1989/90 to September 1996, The Gold Club, for the most part for owner Steve Kaplan, was all about the money. How much he could vacuum up in one night, one week, one month. He'd brainstorm about all the possible ways to sell more gold bucks, earn more money, and stuff his wallet, vault, and accounts.

Then Steve installed vending machines in the girls locker rooms, every corner of the club had a contraption of where Steve Kaplan could make more money. He added more VIP rooms, raised the price per hour to rent out the VIP rooms for private dances. Champagne jumped in price and we were all ordered to select the finest brands in the house. He added showers with glowing green Pert shampoo for the girls to make money in front of the paying patrons and of course line his pockets too. Steve was maybe five foot five, maybe. He was rounded, mousey brown hair, not an attractive man, perhaps just a wizard at how to squeeze more money out of The Gold Club and its staff and the patrons. He was constantly changing the features of The Gold Club, remodeling and such. His best friend, who really had no title, other than he was Steve Kaplan's best friend and buddy, Mr. Thomas "Ziggy" Sicignano. Always known as "Ziggy" in the club, wore a baseball cap always, tilted slightly, with the price tag left on, he always had a fast comment.

Ziggy was loud and charismatic as Steve Kaplan was quiet and contemplating in his presence. Ziggy was a wise cracking, adult punk. However, for some reason or another Ziggy would have some of the girls come up to me, such as Debbie, or Banks, or Melanie, from about 1994 to 1996 and say to me, "Steve Kaplan's psychic said this……" Or one of them would ask me a question, when I would ask, "What is this about?" They would comment…. "Steve Kaplan's psychic said this to Ziggy, she is never wrong."

I just brushed off the information given to me as complete nonsense.

Maybe the music was too loud, or I was too busy serving 350 Jell-O shots from my black lace bustier in a seven hour shift to really pay attention to what the girls and Ziggy were trying to inform me of in future events to transpire in Michigan. But later my mind would connect the dots, as to who Steve Kaplan's psychic is, I would meet her later in Michigan, in very unassuming surroundings, under very normal circumstances. What she would say to my face as warnings would be anything but normal.

Some nights I danced. On one particular night as I recall, flipping through the pages of recalling my early twenties of earning more than minimum wage without a college degree, in the early 1990's……

Lots of Russian patrons seemed to be filling the seats of that big box arena called The Gold Club. They would always ask me if I've ever been to Russia. I responded truthfully, "No. I've seen photographs of Russia in books. It looks like the buildings have dripping candy on top of them, like the game Candyland. Or when I was younger I would build gingerbread houses and use candy as decorations. I could never resist the temptation of not sucking on the gingerbread house when I passed by, I would suck on the candy when no one was looking. The candy would form its own unique mold and appear to drip dry in a unique melted candy shape. Russia looks like that in photos, but no, I have never been there."

I met Adam Duritz again, and again at The Gold Club, you know the Jewish kid that spent the summers in Jenison, Michigan during my childhood. Adam a musician and a singer now was on the brink of stardom with his band The Counting Crows. I was dancing at The Gold Club in Atlanta during the early years of the 1990's. Adam and his band would often fly to Atlanta for I can only assume, "big business and more pleasure from it."

I danced for him, Adam, and then I would always walk away, and then the yo-yo effect of him getting a band member to call me back to his table would always occur. I liked how he looked on the outside, no complaints. But…. I…..I am a great reader of people's aura. There was something about him that I disagreed with perhaps? Something inside him, what he was inside, made me not want to be around him. But quite the contrary was what he saw in me, or about me. I never told one bouncer in that club, not one thing, the bouncers just saw with their own watchful eyes of what Adam would try and get away with, what he'd try to do to me. As much as Adam wanted me to go out with him, just insistent with me, and bold by telling me he wants to have sex with me. Persistent to have me at least sit with him, date him once, talk, have sex with him, I would decline politely. He asked if I wanted to be in a video. I said no. He asked if I could sing. I laughed and said no. He never asked if I could write though. And I never did write a song, ever, for anyone.

His aura as I read Adam, when I was dancing for him, he would grab at me by moving his bent knees forward, then squeeze me with his knees and try to real me in. Like a child who knew the club rules, the ever imposing boundaries, he was somehow trying to create a compromise with wanting to touch me. The bouncers would always step in to intercept Adam Duritz's boundary issue display.

As forward and direct with me as he, Adam was with me, I would step back and just walk away. His aura said to me, "I want to sleep with as many Dutch, German, Swedish looking girls in my prime before finally settling down with a Jewish girl. I want to use, abuse, "get a piece" of as much of those Scandinavian girl types. Bavarian poster girl types. That was his aura, what I could read about him anyways. He was very captivated by me, and also frustrated with me, a very dangerous concoction. I did not like Adam Duritz harassing me, touching me, when he did touch me I could see world war II Germany and Nazi soldiers marching in the streets of Germany. Adam would always look at me as if he knew I could see into past lives and would say to me, "Don't be afraid." But I was afraid.

I then left Adam Duritz's table and responded to a motion, a wave from a dark haired guy, not too old sitting with a group of younger guys. The group? Pearl Jam. I danced a few table dances for them and then headed to do a stage set when my name was called. After my stage set I walked past Adam Duritz which was the only way to exit the stage. Adam grabbed my arm and squeezed my upper arm with intensity as he said in a low hush scolding tone in my ear, "You are making me jealous." The girl in front of him was greatly offended at his behavior as I was caught off guard by Adam too. She demanded he let go of my arm immediately as he just kept squeezing adding more pain. She then abruptly got dressed and exited his table with me.

One band member approached me later and warned me that Adam hates my social butterfly ways in VIP. He explained that Adam "wants me," and there would be serious consequences to pay if I do not go back to Adam's table. In many ways when Adam brushed up against me, I saw a son I had from 2000 years ago in Egypt, before the big battle with Rome. One of my sons I had with Marc Antony, jealous of my younger son I had with Octavia. He was raised by Jews in Egypt, for the most part, then taken to tribes, sponsor Jewish families after his father and I lost the war against Rome. I am six years younger than Adam Duritz in this lifetime of ours. I felt awkward, like Cleopatra dancing in this lifetime for Adam, whom I swear was one of my older sons 2000 years ago. A son I had with Marc Antony. The other son I had with Marc Antony? If I told you Adolf Hitler would you believe me? The answer: Only a mother knows her children. Could Adolf Hitler's anger and mistrust towards Jews have stemmed from an empire lost 2000 years ago? Marc Antony raped me on more than one occasion during Biblical times just over 2000 years ago. Marc Antony was no saint, he was a warrior, greedy for what the wealth of Egypt could bring to his war campaigns, he was a rapist to get his way with what he wanted. The souls of the children, his heirs, our heirs, would cast what he was and what I was made of, do you not agree? Demons do not produce saints. However, I am not a demon.

It felt uncomfortable how Adam looked at me, as if he wasn't supposed to look at me that way. I looked young, but my soul felt old, much older than his youthful soul in my presence. I also instantly felt as if my son spotted me in an establishment that he shouldn't have seen me in, that feeling was instantaneous for me. I felt like running for cover, and I was twenty-one? Twenty-two at the most when he first spotted me at The Gold Club as an adult. I also knew then at the club he was able to have that same gift that I possess, like when I touch someone or someone touches me, they know things, who that person is or was in a past lifetime. Sometimes for me, I can just look through a person, and they also have that ability. I can sense it, know it, but certainly cannot prove it, I suppose.

I just smiled back. I was the Bavarian poster girl, a true original, not a blonde dye job. I was on his mental list of must haves of Scandinavian looking beauties before settling down and starting a family with a Jewish girl in this lifetime. But I am not a dime a dozen. I'm a person with a soul, just like any girl. I am a remarkable soul, I deserve respect, even if the clothed people thought differently. Adam is six years older, and looks older. But inside, my soul, I am so much wiser, more mature. I find it ironic, 2000 years ago I surrounded myself with Jewish people. In my castle he was raised by Jewish people that coveted everything I did or had. If I wore a wig, the trend began that the Jews would where a wig. They were like family in my Egyptian castle, and there he is now, very Jewish looking now. I remember smiling, it just seemed so ironic, not in a racist way, just ironic. And the Jewish servants 2000 years ago thought I had a border line personality disorder with neighboring Rome. Marc Antony might have agreed with them.

I had no idea if Adam Duritz knew who I was 2000 years ago when we had touched in this lifetime, whether it be during my childhood or at The Gold Club. But to see my son, one of my oldest, who in this lifetime is six years older, and very much a grown man from a mothers perspective…..the connection of attraction from Adam towards me felt uncomfortable. Adam was mad I was not going to go out with him, or sit at his cocktail table, he'd get mad, explosive. If he saw me he'd ask me to dance for him. He would calmly ask, then when I got dressed and began to turn away from his tall cocktail table or bar stool to re-enter V.I.P upstairs, away, he'd turn explosive. Sometimes if I walked away he'd grab and pinch my arm until I felt punished for walking away from him. He would transcend his hands quickly over me, as much of me as he could before a bouncer spotted him or I walked away, which ever would occur first.

Those scenes happened on more than one occasion until I avoided his requests for a dance by me all together. I had met a dangerous man in Adam in this lifetime, so I thought at that moment. When he touched me, I saw things. I just saw my son, a Ptolemy that had a Greek warrior womanizing father. As if my son was in a strip club for the first time, like a teenage boy drawn to me he was, and he couldn't break the bond or attraction. He could not figure out his stirring and startling emotions, or why he felt a connection to me in my past?

Adam was very Jewish on the outside, his shell, but inside, he really did not like the way he looked, being Jewish. I could see that about him, within his aura. If my father growing up who raised me, who played both the role of a mother and father to me, had not had the face of a Jew, I too might feel like Adam inside. I wanted to ask him…… "Do you feel like you are at the wrong place at the wrong time, do you always feel that way? Or perhaps in the wrong shell? For how you feel about the world, or perhaps circumstances?" But I never asked Adam that question.

I could tell inside Adam was a restless soul about being born into a Jewish shell. Not just any Jewish shell, but a very, very, looking Jewish shell. Except for his nose. I never took Adam Duritz up on going out with him. He asked me where I go on my nights off from The Gold Club. I mentioned to Adam, "I like to play pool at The Famous Pub on North Druid Hills area with my ex-best friend Steve. He's Jewish too, he looks a lot like you, just shorter. Not really musical, not an artist type really, just a buddy, not really a boyfriend, we sort of grew on one another….It's not that I like fungus, but it's like I am a tree and he is the fungus. We are just accustomed to each other, that is the best way to explain it to you."

"He's your ex-best friend?" Adam asked.

"Yeah, we got into another fight yesterday, but if he doesn't get stoned tonight and leave me twenty messages on my answering machine, he'll be calling tomorrow for sure. We'll probably be at The Famous Pub tomorrow." I commented with a smirk.

"Do you sleep with him?" Adam asked seriously.

"You mean, do we have sleepovers? Yeah, sometimes he crashes over at my place."

"No, do you sleep with him?" Adam asked seriously like a principal talks and questions a student in a possible detention at his desk.

"Oh, eh, sometimes if we both get stoned, and then we both get, eh, bored, and he is too stoned to drive home, or complains that he feels uncomfortable jacking off in my guest bathroom. Well then… he usually goes down on me. If it's really good and satisfying, then I do the same for him. But no, to answer your question, we do not have sex. We're like guy and girl best friends, but right now we're in a fight, so today he is my ex-best friend."

"But why not date him? Why not say he is your boyfriend?" Asked Adam.

"Why would I date him? That makes no sense. We're always together, and I am not Jewish, his family is a bit…orthodox….they're from Poland, he was born there. I think to Steve I symbolize or represent everything American, you know, to a boy, a guy. And besides he's not tall enough, he's not leading man enough for me, 5'10 to 6 feet tall is a good height for a leading man. He's been at DeKalb community college for four years now and does not even have a college associate degree. We're just really comfortable with each other, stuck I suppose, stuck like fungus on a tree, and vice versa. Comfortable in being stuck and not moving in life, when he is not busy, and I am not here or there, I suppose."

"I never knew that pushing 'pause' was better than playing that song?" Adam commented.

"It's weird, but somehow for Steve and I, 'pause' is comfortable, 'pause' is not failing, or progressing, it's just comfortable, fun….when he is not mad about something."

"Mad? What would he get mad about?" The principal named Adam inquired.

"He's mad, gets mad. I don't know, he gets huffy and puffy and storms out of my life, my apartment. It's like he has a spontaneous combustive personality disorder." I remarked very matter of fact.

"My mother thinks you are the real deal, the real Cleopatra, and are going to, your purpose in this lifetime is to dispel a Biblical notion." Stated Adam, looking right through me.

I asked, "What notion Adam? What are you implying?" I then began a table dance for him as his band buddies stared at me.

If Adam saw me moving through in a crowd at The Gold Club, he would grab my arm. Pull and squeeze down on my arm as he pulled me next to him, even if he had a girl table dancing for him, as I tried to walk right on past him. He'd often whisper in a mad dictatorial tone in my ear as he squeezed my arm, "You are making me mad." He wanted what he couldn't have, sex from me. At The Gold Club he'd pinch with his hand on my forearm as hard as he could and say in a very authority driven tone, "I'm jealous. You working here, I don't like it. You are making me mad."

Adam would get out of control with me, just unable to handle his emotions of jealousy. It's like he wanted to discipline me, or something?

But who is he to discipline me? I prefer comfort and love, not a power hungry guy.

Inevitably the bouncers would escort Adam Duritz out of the club. Then come up to me and ask me, "What's up with that guy? Did you date him? Why does he come into the club and act like that towards you? Are you sure you are not dating him?"

I would respond honestly, "I don't know. I never dated him."

"Are you sure? He acts mad and jealous." The bouncer would comment.

"You've never dated him, ever?" The bouncer would ask.

"No. I have never dated him, ever." I stated firmly.

One time after I danced for a local real estate agent, not knowing Adam was right there sitting at the bar watching like "a crow," a V.I.P. manager said to me, "That man over there wants a dance."

I could not see who the manager was pointing to by the bar, I just followed the manager. It so happened to be Adam Duritz again who had requested me to dance for him. I just smiled and thought, one dance. Although Adam seemed very calm and prepared for what he was about to say next to me, he anticipated what he was going to say to me. Adam announced to me in a haughty tone of voice as he sipped on his cocktail straw slowly sipping on some whiskey blend in a small oval shaped glass while I danced for him….. "Your mother Diane is German, isn't she?"

"Yes. My biological mother is German-American. Why?"

He sneered, stared me down, then back up again as he nursed his straw from his whiskey cocktail in a cocky sneer as I danced for him. He then pauses from drinking, leans over and whispers slow and deliberately in my ear, "Greg, is not whom he claims to be Lori. I wrote about him in a song. The detective and I are musical geniuses.

"What?" I asked. "So what?"

"Have you had too much to drink?" Adam asked as he seemed so in control of what he wanted to say next to me.

As Adam sneered on, he then comments, "Greg is my favorite color. Do you understand, Grey."

"Eh, what?" I responded. The music was loud, I felt queasy. "Why would you bring up about my biological mother? Greg is my favorite color?" I thought quietly, what does that all mean? I look bewildered.

"Your real name if your biological German mother kept you was going to be Elizabeth Marie. The detective told me that, the detective I hired. Your bloodline goes all the way back to Prussia."

"What?" I asked.

"Greg. The detective told me about him, he likes to come into this establishment too, doesn't he? Diane's supposed husband, fiancée of twenty years. You got Nazi blood in you." Remarked the serious tone of Adam's voice as his eyes traveled over my tan nude body, very white tan lines, very pink young nipples, yet very full large breasts. Long, layered, auburn red hair. My blue eyes twinkled for him, I felt bewildered though by what he was saying.

"What?" I asked. Then I preceded to ask…..

"Nazi blood? I was born in 1970. I am not a prejudice person. I don't hate anyone. I've dated lots of Jewish guys, it's always them breaking up with me.

"Papers"…….. He sneered as he tipped his chin up in a proud stance of having something over me within his mind of filed conclusions. He looked at me with resentment and deep repressed sexual yearning. As if he wanted to bang me and beat me up all in one explosive moment that he himself was creating in V.I.P. There was tension. There was confusion. Lots of tension.

Who is this pompous creep with black dread locks? I thought to myself.

"What?" He sneered, as he looked down, then up again, as I swayed and danced naked by the bar in VIP.

"What?" I asked of him. "What is it that you are talking about?" I was mad.

"Are you deaf and dumb Ms. Jones from Playboy? Someday I'll come through loud and clear. You don't have a clue to who I am do you?" Adam spoke with a spike of cockiness filling his voice.

"I know who you are, you're a musician, acting like you're God of the universe. I hear.... Adam, I make all the real powerful men feel as if they are God on earth. I have that effect with men. Woman hate me for it. But you are not who you desire the world to view you as.... Adam. I know who you are inside." I said firmly, sexy and nude. I did want him too. But I knew I couldn't. Just then, I felt something drip, I danced, it must be sweat, from dancing? I rubbed my thighs, pressed them together as I danced on. Adam noticed, he stared downward on me and then our eyes met...... It was tension and heat. Extreme arousal. I know girls don't show, as much arousal as a man would or does, but somehow, pink showed, like pink whipped frosting....between two layers of cake. I looked down, I was embarrassed. Adam looked down and saw too. He was dumbfounded, alarmed for me, in a sensual erotic way hooked like a fish that had swallowed a hook at that moment.

I didn't know which way to turn in the boat, at that moment, so to speak in VIP......

The tension of meanness subsided with Adam..... "I like your pink clitoris, you look really aroused. Come here." Adam said as his voice changed to a nice soothing tone, verses haughty, like before. As he stood forward and leaned into me he lifted up his shirt slowly and discretely, he was totally aroused. His black jean pants tight, he lifted up his loose shirt slightly, just enough for me to see how he was also feeling too. He took his hand and thumb and rubbed it along his outline, upward. He leaned forward and sweetly and softly whispered in my ear, "I want you."

The song ended, I began putting on my blue sequence bathing suit style costume, as just then Adam leaned over further, gently brushing his entire body against me as I scrambled to put my skimpy wrap around and over myself, quickly......

"Put your knee up here." Adam said to me with a motion to where to place my leg on the base of the bar stool.

"I'm afraid of big dicks, really, I am." I said flustered.

"Put your knee up, right here, come on, now." Adam said.

"What?" I asked.

"Put your knee right here. Now!" Adam said with strong intent for me to understand his demand immediately. Like a dictator he spoke as if I am just a stupid Bavarian puppet trying to get dressed for him in a scramble.

Again he asked, as he insisted I put my shoe on the base of his chair. I thought to myself, he is going to just slide the money in my garter from the table dance as I put my foot up, right?

Oh, No, he looked at me, up and down, and in one fluid motion of staring me down, then up again, he reached under and between the lines, moved his body next to mine as I was trying to get dressed. Then placed the folded money in my garter as he then slid his hands further toward his intended target, his fingers slid in a place he shouldn't have. He went between the lines, totally feeling every area he could feel, reaching, searching, trying to quickly locate and push against my g-spot. Pushing upwards first with one finger, then two, scoping, pressing slightly on the pink outside exterior, yes, you name it, he felt and explored as he announced softly, "I knew it, I knew you were wet." As I pulled away as much as I could, he stood up and crouched over me again as he took on an authority tone commenting directly in my ear as he remained in constant contact with me, "Are you wet because you danced for me? Or are you wet because you danced for him, over there? You stupid German slut who won't go out with me. You got me excited. Don't you understand? You got me excited. I want to lay you down. Do you understand? I want to lay you down now. I want this over." Adam talked in my ear in a low hush, mad, seductive and very dictator like in tone. As he is doing this to me, I am trying to get his hand from underneath me, I am in total shock. He crouches over me, leans into me, he is literally shoulders and head taller than me, as if that can protect and conceal what almost took place in the crowded V.I.P……

"We can't." I said, I insisted.

I managed to put my skimpy too tight blue sequence bathing suit one piece wrap of an outfit on and around my midriff area. Just then Adam's two moist fingers I had managed to pull out of me, he then slides over the bottom part of my costume and went in again, between the lines. The front part of my costume remained slightly on and slightly off underneath, the costume bottom portion brushed up against his hand movements inside me. My outfit covering tight and skimpy gave a squeezing and pulling sensation on my low pink clitoris totally engorged, which squeezed into the front part of my bathing suit skimpy one piece. As Adam reaches inward pressing against my g-spot I felt like I was going to pee, and scream from sheer excitement, I almost collapsed. I know moisture ran down the side of my inner thigh…..it smelled like sex……in V.I.P.

Just then…Bavarian looking John from the Midwest arrives on the scene who always wanted to be either Superman or a rock star as his only plausible career positions in life. Whom just happened to dye his hair a funky auburn color and then appeared to have used hot curlers tonight on his out on the town hairdo, approaches us as we are standing. I can only guess, just before or after consuming too much white caffeine or some kind of psychoactive stimulant. John decides to walk over and hands me a bag of candy circus peanuts (which I love) and says…. "Nice playhouse…..you got going here. Eh, remember what you said to me….your older brother's favorite wife…..what was her name again? Oh, yeah, Marcy…that's it….Yeah, sometimes a guy's first love, his first serious love…..is that one woman that he can't forget, his first serious love….and who is he (John points to Adam), to cast such a devious stare at me now? That's my bar seat. That's what I wanna know…..can someone here in this bar establishment answer that question for me?"

I spoke up in the tension of wanting to pee and just finish the eroticism of the moment as I looked up and remarked to them both, "Can I just get a pair of ruby red slippers over here so I can click my heels together, and just be back home, I just wanna be back home…." I murmured in my silence of just wanting to sober up, and disappear instantly.

The big dirty blonde haired bouncer acted as if Superman was not on call tonight, and the E.R. was very, very, busy with emergencies, woman having massive heart attacks, or something in that order. And here was "Mr. Big" consuming no less than 3500 mgs. of over the counter steroids daily, compared to my intake of 4500 mgs. of German protein, under the counter from him, daily? I can only imagine that "Mr. Big" must have seen ironically what Jewish Adam was doing, or trying to do, or said to me.

Adam who only looked like Jesus having an open affair with Mary Magdalene in VIP had broken the club policy of no touching, Adam was then again escorted out of The Gold Club. I was told Adam received an electric shock outside. I have no way of knowing. I did not see him for a long time after that incident in V.I.P. in the corner. By the corner bar just in front of the fogged up mirrors.

Adam's band members would come in after that incident, and say things to me, about what Adam would like to do to me. It scared me. It was not long before I decided to hang up the dancing costume and five inch heels for good and take on a less risky adventure within that club. It was just getting to be too dangerous. That is how I became a full- time "Jell-O shooter girl," rather, decided to become a Jell-O shooter girl, until I moved back to Michigan in 1996.

Another girl, Melanie, asked me one day, maybe even a year later, if I knew a guy named Adam? I said "No." Never really thought about it, Adam who? Then Melanie asked me next, "Have you ever met Steve Kaplan's psychic? Her name is Sharon. The psychic Sharon knows some guy Adam, who supposedly you got caught making out with up here in VIP?"

I responded, "No. I never made it with some guy named Adam. I have no idea who Sharon is either." And brushed off what I thought was just nonsense questions amidst the thousands of people we'd meet briefly in a week. Quite irrelevant, really to the bustle of my busy moments at work. It was not until years later, I put two and two together.

There were many movie stars, many musicians, celebrities, sports stars, flooding into The Gold Club, even before Steve Kaplan owned The Gold Club, and after Steve took over ownership in 1993. All of which those celebrities never acted like a belligerent and condescending prowler as Adam Duritz, not one! In one night you might bump into, sit on, rub elbows or talk to several high profile gentlemen. Bob Seger. Kid Rock. Pearl Jam were regulars. Who was that singer that is or was married to Whitney Houston, yeah, he was in once or twice. Rap, R&B

stars. Lots of British bands, and American based bands. Not to mention, royalty from around the world would visit The Gold Club. It was "normal" and very routine to see movie or sitcom celebrities, Robert De Niro, that guy Jack from The Shining, sports stars, and musical artists. For a college student like myself, it made my part-time job at The Gold Club, for the most part, at least interesting, if not also lucrative, as if I was paid to just party. It sure was better than minimum wage at the mall for a college girl in her early twenties like myself.

It was always the other local patrons, or Midwest traveling businessmen that would comment to me, "That's so and so....I can't believe he is here, and you just sat in his lap, he owns blah blah team and he licked up Jell-O like there is no end to cherry filled Jell-O cups.....right here, I saw it."

I would always comment, "I know."

What happens in Vegas, stays in Atlanta? You understand. I want that past behind me too. After all, I would hate to ruin or tarnish my reputation. Isn't that something George Constanza from Seinfeld would comment about this subject matter? Probably, in a funny screenplay script.

By the way I met Jerry Seinfeld in Atlanta, it was 1992, maybe 1993? Eh....let's just say at McDonalds in Buckhead, that's the story I am sticking with, really Jerry. I think I was ordering apple dippers? Or did that joke come out on the menu later on? I don't know. I don't know much of anything.......some people think I am naturally blonde. However, I do remember Jerry Seinfeld does not drink alcohol, he ordered a diet Coke. I was not the waitress, I was the dancer in the VIP room with Jerry Seinfeld just before New Yorker Steve Kaplan purchased The Gold Club for 6.2 million dollars.

The local patrons that bustled into the club were always the most amazed at the celebrity clientele. The hype of the club and the popularity grew like an entity with its own reputation and apparent heartbeat, a real pulse all its own.

I noticed at the front desk in the foyer there were a lot of men signing into the club ledger from places I knew well, close to home, such as from Hudsonville, Michigan, Grandville. Places I never thought would visit The Gold Club, were in fact buying gold bucks left and right. I saw their drivers licenses on the front counter. It made me shutter, I thought I was a long way from home.

One day though was different for me, it was 1996, I had been contemplating whether or not to move back to Michigan and possibly begin real estate school there in Michigan. I was almost twenty-six now, and still wanted a mom and dad family unit of sorts this entire existence of mine, searching, longing, verses just getting married by twenty-six. I know it seems odd. In my mind, I saw this empty well, in my heart I could feel this well. At other times I was in the empty well, lonely, crying out in the echoes of that well inside me, and very aware no one could hear me, not crazy....so I just became quiet. A quiet type.

Then at times I would look into the empty well, and stare back at the darkness, the coldness. Like in a cave the watery vapor would condensate like drops of loneliness. And then I would want to shout and scream at that empty well, mad my voice would just echo inside of me. And again, it just appeared quiet on the outside of me. A quiet type, trying to understand why I alone cannot fix me inside. I can't seem to fill that hole, that empty well, and it's too damn big for me to fill in, scoop by scoop. I feel lonely and overwhelmed by the task. And then I would just stare blankly ahead at all the mirrors. I had hope. Hope inside. I'm young, my void can be filled. I am young enough to still fill this void inside, this empty well, I hope.

As I recall I thought about becoming licensed in real estate in Michigan, as a licensed sales agent ever since my mom married Jerry on January 12, 1996.

One day like any evening, one would wonder who you're going to meet. As I began my shift, a Gold Club waitress walked up to me as I was serving Jell-O from lap to lap she and said, "There is a guy by the name of Alan up there in that VIP room, he wanted me to bring you this present." I took the gift as she handed it to me all wrapped up, it was on or around February 28, 1996, my birthday. I had just turned twenty-six years old. Alan brought in a pretty wrapped box of Coco Chanel perfume for me. The waitress pointed up and commented to me that a guy by the name of Alan was sitting upstairs in a VIP.

The waitress went onto say, "Hey, the manager wants you up there, that guy Alan, you know him? He's got several major stars with him, they called ahead and requested your company." I finished wiping slobber and cherry Jell-O mixture off my cleavage and headed upstairs to VIP. I was honestly just thinking that The Wallflowers, Soul Asylum, Pearl Jam, Matchbox Twenty, and that song Live- Lightning Crashes would soon all be off the radio by the time Alan and I reunited. It was a relief that Alan wants to see me and a relief those bands are not off the radio waves with a romance and era gone by before I reached that destination that Alan had so spoken about to me.

I always wondered why the advertisers for Jell-O never called on me for a commercial, a girl like me is never featured in their T.V. commercials. Even though I sold more Jell-O in one night than ten blocks of suburban house mothers would serve in a year!

I headed up the metal black barred staircase to the VIP room, there was Alan, I could not believe it. He noticed me at the entrance of the VIP room and began to loosen his yellow and blue striped silk tie around his neck. He motioned for me to come closer, I did. I stood before him, and thanked him for the very thoughtful birthday gift.

Alan responded, "I know that's your favorite scent, it's mine too." Alan went onto say this as he leaned forward to give me a kiss on my cheek, "I have two pieces of paper, on each one there is a different message." Alan pulled me closer to him by holding my hands. I stood between his legs as he remained seated. Then he gave me a squeeze with his knees, I smiled in approval. He took his silk tie and wrapped the tie around my forehead covering my eye sight. The silk tie smelled like him, it was very stimulating just to smell him again. A flood of memories poured into my aching heart in that moment of reproach.

He put one paper in each of my palms, then he asked me to select one of the papers to unfold and open. I choose the folded paper in my right hand that I held up for him. "Open it up, let's see what it says." He requested rather enthusiastically. The message was intended for me to understand later in life, I suppose. The message read, "For everything there is a frame."

"What does this one say?" I asked as I tried to unfold it as well.

"Oh, no, we'll save that one." Alan responded as he folded the paper into his pocket.

"What do you mean? For everything there is a frame?" I asked, just baffled.

Alan pulled me down on his lap, and held me, kind of like he had in the German deli near Stone Mountain, our first date in Georgia in this lifetime.

Alan proceeded to wish me happy birthday as the music blared on at The Gold Club. I did not feel prepared for what he would whisper next after he whispered, "Happy Birthday." He smiled real big, he was happy to see me, to touch me, he held me close to him in his lap as he remained seated. The sexual chemistry between us never died, nor did my love for him, what was evident was the time we had spent apart. It made me miss him, appreciate him.

The music was loud in that nightclub establishment, a real Babylon kind of metropolis of international commerce and intellect mixing among the loud music overhead and around us.

But for a moment it was as if I could not hear the music. My world went still and quiet for a moment. Alan went on to inform me that he did get married. Alan was married now, not to me, not while he dated me married, just married now. I was shocked actually. I just did not think he was going to say that in my ear.

I was just twenty-six years old, unmarried, and wondering what I was doing with my life, what am I doing here in this nightclub?

Floods of regrets surfaced. I thought I was going to vomit up "regret" if there is such a thing one could cough up.

I pulled Alan close, his face clutched in my two hands. I missed touching his ear lobes, I missed being his girl. I said this to Alan, I whispered this in his ear like old times, I just couldn't let go of him yet…… "I am polished rounded crimson, devolved like the earth, against the pear in a crystal encrusted prism bowl, resting on a wooden table."

We began kissing. I pulled away for a moment in the heat of melting lust and anger. Then I flooded him with sour questions, "I thought we were only broken up? Mad about something, some place, this place perhaps? I did not think you were going to run off and get married? Why?"

Alan responded as he looked deep into my eyes, the pain evident for both of us, I was confused, left in the dark…….

Alan responded, "I was ready to marry, you were not."

"So you just ran off and married someone, just pulled her out of a hat like some stupid rabbit trick?" I inquired with a storm of emotion.

Alan did not answer my question, he just made another philosophical statement of truth for me to ponder. "People in love do not always marry." He had tears in his eyes, just as I did too. The moment felt so confusing. I thought quietly now guarding my own heart, how can you still feel for me, and be married to someone else?

I gave him a confused look as if to say, this is not how love is supposed to be.

Alan inched me closer in his lap. He grabbed my hands, and squeezed, hugged me tight as he whispered directly, warmly, "Beginning in late spring and towards the end of the hot summer months when the magnolia blossoms cover the south here in Georgia, I will always think of you, our romance in the 1860's and 1990's. I believe in reincarnation. I know we have a history together, a long history, well over two thousand years ago history, not just in the south. Someday the world will plant magnolia blossom trees to remind all us how God works in our lives. Mysteriously. I will think of you, and our love like the bloom of a magnolia tree, which comes undoubtedly each year, constant, a late bloomer in the spring and summer. I will always be reminded each and every year in thought and vision of you and us, always, consistently……."

I began kissing Alan's neck and ear lobe, as he whispered and kept on holding me……. "I can see in your eyes you do love me, you can really feel as I do, finally. I'll take the time to smell the late blooms, yet very fragrant blossoms. I'll stop my car and walk through a park, down a sidewalk, if I see a magnolia tree in fullest bloom. I always know you do love me, in the end, as I know now. Love does not die when a relationship does. Someday, you'll hear the music again."

"Hear the music again?" How did he just know that the music, as loud as the music is in that club, was in that club, I couldn't hear for five minutes or so? I was so wrapped up into what he had to say, was saying to me, I could not hear the music. I thought many baffling thoughts and questions to myself in silent desperation to make sense of my phobias, or the power I give to those around me, and the power I give to those who have already exited my life. But the VIP room at The Gold Club had gone silent, the music had stopped, as he spoke to me in my longing of a better reality. The music, I could not hear it. He knew it.

Many questions about my life I began to ask of myself now, examine, how can I make my life better? At a time when I was just starting to feel free in my life with my mother recently married and financially taken care of thanks in part to her marrying Jerry Honderd in January 1996. I began to realize with Alan visiting me at The Gold Club on my twenty-sixth birthday, I realized just how trapped my life had become, I did not feel free at all.

I had not graduated from college yet, I had little skills to land me an ideal good paying job, a real career. I needed to pull myself out of this hole, this cage of an existence, this trapped jar feeling, and begin the next chapter in my life. Everyone around me had begun new chapters in their lives, now it's my turn. It took me seconds to come to that conclusion as I sat on Alan's lap. However, it took months to pull myself together in trying to make a difference, a positive stride within my own life now. A positive step forward with a new career move and a new existence as I reached for the jar lid to get out. As a child I felt trapped. I never thought that when I reached adulthood I would ever experience feeling trapped with no freedom. I was an adult, twenty-six years old and I was burdened, trapped by my emotions I so wanted to escape from, free myself right then and there, and I couldn't.

I remember as I sat in Alan's lap as he is telling me "he got married," the words just echoed through my hollow mind, and here I am still in love with him. Sitting in his lap like old times, and he's married now. I could not even pose myself to ask, "So do you have any kids yet? Any babies on the way?" For me to ask that question would have been like pouring vinegar onto the fresh wound of my cut heart. For him to answer such a question would have been the same profound toxic result to my heart. I wish I could have just reached in and pulled out my alive, beating heart before he said those words to me that "he got married." But there was no warning to his words spoken and penetrated. I just could not believe the shock, he was my one true love, how many one true loves come along in a lifetime? How would I know.

I remember crying for periods of time in 1996, just lost in my direction to reach the top of that jar, unscrew the lid, and breathe in life, my goals in life, where were they?

I want to be normal. I want to be happy. Be in a loving relationship and get married this time around, start a family. Have two parents that were alive and loved me. Have a career worth liking, have it all. And there was Alan, who had it all in life. I seemingly had only one imminent goal now, to get out of this caged existence, and make strides towards my goals, not goals that other people have or want for me. It's my life. I am twenty-six years old. This is my life, I need to start thinking about me and my direction that I want to go in. I can reach the top and spit out the sea water that is drowning me inside, clouding my view to the top as I stared blankly ahead in the mirror at myself, my silvery-blue eyes looked as if they were melting tears from upon my face.

I hated the car I was driving for the longest time, but just kept driving it anyways. Finally one weekend I went with Melanie Smith and looked at BMW's. I bought a white BMW with tan leather interior that spring weekend in 1996. I loved the car, I loved how it drove, it was a totally different experience, better.

I was all about having better experiences. I changed my hairstyle, changed my auburn red long wavy hairstyle, to blonde, a short trendy bob style. I began speaking up to people who were rude or demanding. I began a transformation to never be in a cage again. I vowed to myself to never be on the bottom looking up, trapped. I never want to look up and around again, and think to myself, stop the music, how and the hell did I get here? How the hell do I get out?

Then I thought to myself, when I do get out of feeling so caged, I'll never be in a jar again! So I thought.

I realized that fears and phobias were not my friends. Fears and phobias were not keeping me from imposing danger, they <u>were</u> the dangers! Keeping me from what I wanted most in life, love and happiness. Marriage deep down I really did want with Alan, but was afraid.

I applied for real estate school immediately in the spring of 1996 in Georgia, I was on my way to becoming licensed as a real estate agent. I did not need to graduate from college to have a professional real estate sales agent career. Moving towards getting licensed as a real estate agent was my move to the lid, opening a new world for myself outside the cage of my existence here. No one could get me out of this jar, but me. I was going to make something much better of myself with the light inside of me, I began to push forward.

I was all about wanting a new world for myself as I pushed onward. However, what I got instead, was more experiences and observations to write within the body of this book. It would take years to finally put the pen to the paper canvas and begin that brush stroke. Like any great artist painting a masterpiece, boldly goes my soul, my hopes in 1996 in creating and "finding normal." To locate that really normal existence for me in this world as I so desired. I was going to move back to west Michigan, live among the Dutch Calvinists, reconnect to my old school friends from childhood.

Have a mom and dad figure with Jerry and Cindy. Scoops of dirt began to fill my void, that empty well inside my soul, so it seemed in 1996. Life was going to get better.

Alan represents to me the god of literature and philosophy. He helped me differentiate between the words of truth and conformity.

What I would encounter in west Michigan in the preceding years entering a real estate career in Michigan selling new construction and existing homes for Smith-Diamond Realty in Grandville, Michigan would not be a move not noticed by the CIA, it was a move they encouraged behind the scenes, with no regard for ramifications towards me.

Before any war, like also in one's lifetime, one rule remains so poignantly true, also written in chapter one of another lifetime lived; I have learned that those close to one will become your greatest strength, or your fateful demise.

The Great Octopus……A Bully Union.
CHAPTER TWELVE

Ancients believed that natal planet positions in conjunction with the timing of an eclipse has irrefutably dire consequences on natal planets touched by an eclipse, for families, empires, kingdoms, and nations. An eclipse is a time of rapid change in power positions, as if fate of the theme of the eclipse transpires to reality.

I would learn from multipole sources that Jerry Honderd agreed through the aid and assistance of the CIA and their counterparts in action, boots on the ground, that Jerry married Cindy in 1996 for one reason only; Money. Money would mean Jerry Honderd could have the type of retirement he so longed for after his recently ailing sick first wife had just passed away. The hospital bills took a huge slice of pie out of his retirement, basically the hospital and doctor bills piled up and consumed his entire retirement. Jerry and Cindy were engaged within six months of Jerry's first wife passing away, shocking even his adult children at how quickly they got hitched. How much money did the CIA pay Jerry Honderd to marry Cindy and move me out of The

Gold Club and back to Michigan in 1996? Hundreds upon hundreds of thousands of dollars placed into a Living Trust. A Living Trust is one of the sources that the CIA will join with ordinary citizens to unit a certain amount. Once the amount has been dispersed or laundered elsewhere the Living Trust is dissolved, legally by the busy attorneys. Rarely if ever do authorities even question the business of attorneys or well-educated people in general. Therefore allowing a protection, a naturally assumed societal barrier of what goes on behind the walls of well-educated people such as non- aggressive estate planning attorneys at law. How did the CIA earn that amount or any relevant amount? Through selling me on paper behind my back. Jerry disclosed that he met with the CIA in 1995-1996 in Byron Center, Michigan before marrying Cindy my adopted mother in January 1996.

Where would I work in real estate in January 1997 freshly licensed in real estate in Michigan? Smith-Diamond Realty in Grandville, Michigan. I thought I landed my dream job in real estate. The small residential development firm had just about ten plus residential new construction developments where real estate agents are assigned to market a particular plat and sell vacant lots and new builds and existing homes. I had no idea that the entire thing, moving me to Michigan, Smith-Diamond Realty, and the model house where I would live in the new construction plats in Wayland, Michigan was actually a set-up by the CIA. Until my attorney I hired named Genie Eardly clued me into the details of the horror I was about to embark upon in the presiding chapters.

In the late 1990's I began to wake-up to what Cindy was doing to my life and the money the CIA was raking in behind my back with sales of me. It would not be until March 3, 2009 when I learned through the Okemos police that the CIA had already printed my State of Michigan death certificate that I fully woke-up and began to type my memoir titled; I Remember Heaven Before Earth.

My story, this chapter of moving back to the sleepy suburbs of the Calvinist Christians of Grand Rapids, Michigan, begins here, September 1996. In the winter of 1996 my mother Cindy married Jerry Honderd of Grandville, Michigan. I was very happy for her. Cindy announced in the spring of 1996 that I should move back to Michigan and be surrounded by family and friends. I believed her, because I wanted a mother and father, I would be able to reconnect to my old friends from Unity Christian High and get back to basic living. I saw no red flags, none, I only saw potential happiness.

I often would feel so lonely throughout my life, my family is not a close knit family by any standards. I have no sisters, and have three older brothers that have one or two things in common with me, my mother Cindy, and we are from Michigan, that is about it really. Cindy promised me that if I moved back to Michigan that things would be different this time around. I would have birthday parties and Christmas gatherings to go to, family life would be better this time around. I believed her. I suppose I believed her because I wanted those nice things in my life, everything missing, never had, I still always wanted. A nice family, family dinners and parties. I looked forward to all she promised of a better life ahead for me. Cindy was so preoccupied with Jerry her new husband that she was not obsessively evil with me, Cindy seemed normal. Cindy being normal, acting normal, was indeed inviting.

I did move back to Michigan over Labor Day weekend in 1996. I remember the scenic travel from Georgia, through Tennessee, up through Kentucky, I just love the south. As I traveled through the flat and long state of Indiana, up to the Michigan border, I did miss the south instantly. I was sad to leave the south, but happy in a sense to have the positive notion of a new family. Now that my mother Cindy was married to Jerry, who also had four grown children and grandchildren a large family was created, or so I thought. Jerry seemed friendly and likeable, he seemed like he could be a real father figure. He was well respected in the Dutch community of Grandville, Michigan. At the time, it seemed like a good idea to move back to Michigan.

It was a sunny warm day after Labor Day weekend, my very first day living back in Michigan after living in Georgia for the past seven years. I pulled into the Jenison Meijer's parking lot store in my white BMW. I was there to buy a few things, it was maybe 10am on Tuesday. I open my car door and hear a guy walk past my car and say, "Hey look, a Georgia license plate, my dad lives in Georgia."

I recognized the voice and the guy talking. I slouch down against my tan leather car seat, turn my face, and say to myself, oh my God, that is Jamie. Literally, seven years ago to the day he was the one who took me down to Georgia. We had lived with his dad in Marietta, Georgia. If life truly contains seven year cycles, I was not sure where this new cycle would lead me. It was ironic. The first person I see back in Michigan, is Jamie. But he did not recognize me, my hair was different and I drove a BMW. He never bothered to even see that I was slouched in the front seat hoping to not have to make uncomfortable polite conversation with him, he just kept walking with his friend towards Meijer's. I stayed crouched down as Jamie Smith walked towards Meijer's with his friend. I remember thinking, God, he looks gay, I hope I did not do that to him?

In the early fall of 1996 I was looking forward to getting my real estate license in Michigan and very eager to begin pursuing a career I have always wanted, a normal career, I was thrilled. I was ambitious, full of energy, ready to learn and work hard. My outlook? I was completely thrilled about entering a booming world of real estate in 1996. I began shopping to buy a few nice wardrobe pieces for my new career in real estate at Woodland mall. I looked very polished and professional. No one would ever dare guess by looking at me that I ever worked at The Gold Club at one time. I looked conservative, yet classy. I began interviewing at several real estate companies. I also reflected back to that first week of returning home to Michigan……

I instantly began to feel lonely, like how the damp wet oak leaves smelled and seemed to carry a stench of loneliness in their scent for my return. I looked back to how my life had been so fun, interesting and relaxing in Atlanta, Georgia from 1989/90 to 1996. I missed that warm balmy southern breeze on my face. I missed the southern culture of just accepting people for who they are, a very non-judgmental culture, a fun culture. I missed lunches on the outside patio restaurants in Buckhead. I became very cautious in how I presented myself now. I always presented myself in a professional poised appearance. Wearing the nicest two piece suits I could afford, the nicest shoes, a conservative bobbed blonde hairdo now, just a little make-up. I drove a white BMW, with a vanity plate that read, "Lori VA."

I noticed right off the bat as we pulled into Jerry's driveway, Jerry's house, and later met his children Mick & Sheri and Greg & Libby, that they wanted nothing to do with my mother's side of the family, my mother's children which includes my three brothers and myself. Jerry's oldest son, Jack and wife Betsy who live in Atlanta, Georgia were always so friendly and invited me over for dinner with Steve. They also invited me over for Thanksgiving dinner while I lived in Georgia. Which did not surprise me, that's just the thing people do in the south. But here in the north, the culture was different. And now I was beginning to wonder where I belonged. I would try and make conversation with Sheri and Libby, be friends, or at least talk. They both looked at me like I came from a different planet, for moving away for seven, or eight years, to then move back to their subculture. It was weird hostile social manners and perception of me on their part to say the least about their hostility. If I did not attend their church or socially connected to them from church or church functions, they wanted nothing to do with me or you, or anybody. I was getting a crash course on what it is like to leave a cult, and then return back home to that same cult. I began thinking, Georgia felt so much more like home. But I now have a mother and father unit here now in Michigan, so I am going to stay. Jerry seems normal, my mother Cindy acts normal enough lately, and I have a normal career now on the way, as a real estate sales agent. My life has turned a page in becoming "very normal," or so I thought, or wished.

I remember a phone conversation I had with Betsy Honderd who lives in Atlanta, she stated to me that Libby Honderd and Sheri Honderd would call down south to Atlanta and say insultingly with a smile unfolding on the phone to Jack or Betsy Honderd, "We hope you move back, you're in our church and personal family prayers that you will return to God and the Christian faith."

If you leave the Calvinist area. In their mind you have also left the faith. Then the locals in Michigan place you on a prayer line, whether you know it, or like that dose of a reality from the Calvinists, you just do, that is their culture. Part of them believing their God sees their religion as supreme, so they have been brainwashed to believe from their minister, and the minister before him. Sort of a generational transference of what is superior on earth and what is not, I suppose, through the ages.

What religion are Jack & Betsy Honderd of Atlanta? They have many Jewish friends, but decided on being Quakers. Jack is retired now, he is a self-made millionaire. He graduated first in his college class of Architecture School from Michigan State University. Then moved to Atlanta, bought up acres of rundown neighborhoods in what he considered prime Atlanta city real estate. Then he built up high end five story contemporary style very modern homes. Jack was always in the Atlanta magazines, and Better Homes and Gardens magazines as their top residential developer of that city, Atlanta. Jack was a thinker, a doer, not a dependent source on Jerry's Living Trust as were Mick and Greg, stuck like glue like the ink itself on the paperwork.

I would learn years later that the American government, the Central Intelligence Agency paid Jerry Honderd "hundreds of thousands of dollars" to marry Cindy and move me back up to Michigan. What? That is exactly my response of an expression when I learned that fact in Michigan. Jerry was so grateful at how generous the American government was with him, that his meager little social security check of a mere five hundred dollars, totaling six thousand dollars a year, he sent back to the U.S. Social Security office as a mark of his gratitude for the C.I.A. being so generous to him in 1995? 1996? Jerry explained to me, that there was indeed a big federal government plan to get me to come back to Michigan and out of The Gold Club. Jerry also indicated that he had no idea what the government had in their deceitful bag of goodies in the preceding years to come. Jerry told me that he accepted the money and placed it into a Living Trust in 1995-1996 just as the CIA ordered, he did exactly what he was told.

I would best describe Mick & Sheri Honderd and Greg & Libby Honderd of Hudsonville as cold, uncaring and very selfish in their attitude towards my brothers and myself. Jerry's Michigan side of the family, literally gave me the chills. They were that cold to what they deem of outsiders.

I felt sorry for my brothers as well, it was such a non-Christian thing to exclude us from Thanksgiving and Christmas dinners and parties from 1996 to this very day! Jerry fully backed up his adult children's decisions to exclude us, boldly stating only my mother Cindy would go to the Christmas and Thanksgiving parties. My mother agreed with them, and would say to me each and every Christmas Day, "I do not know what you are going to do on Christmas Day."

My response to Cindy's holiday comment? I would wonder as I looked at her Christian wristband on her wrist that had the popular slogan of that time, "What would Jesus do?" I would scratch my head at her decisions rendered around the holiday season. I do understand Cindy and Jerry's family in Michigan, the wristband was only for show. The overstated philosophical drum beat in Christianity is all about presentation, as presentation of values was a deliberate shield to what goes on behind religious people's doors. An invisible wall, a scared regarded wall of daily proportions built. Trust me when I say that I do not promote any religion, as I so often explain why. You may not agree with me on my stance of earth bound religions. However, I do think you understand.

Cindy and Jerry made it very clear in the fall of 1996, there was not going to be a family for me, and that Jerry has an apartment for me to live in for a discounted rental rate if I managed the small apartment building in Hudsonville.

The snow began falling, it was going to be an early blizzard that winter. I had forgotten just how cold it could become in Michigan. It is a place that lacks warmth in many, many categories. Christmas was just around the corner.

Jerry and Cindy dropped off a bag of groceries, and announced "This food is your staples, to get you by until you pass the real estate exam and become licensed as a real estate agent."

I dropped nearly fifteen pounds in thirty days that cold holiday season back in Michigan. I called The Gold Club in December of 1996, I asked Norbie if I could come back, I needed money to survive. He said "Yes." But after I hung up I did not want to fail at a normal career. I wanted normal. So I stuck it out in Michigan, to be normal.

Although the snow was beginning to pile up outside, I decided to go outside. I put on boots and began walking door to door asking if anyone in Grandville needed to sell their home or wanted to sell their home.

That night I had a dream, in my dream Alan took my hand and we flew over the roof tops of Grandville, it was January 1997. He pointed below to a house that I would list, it would be my "first sale" he said in the dream. The next morning I was up early as usual, and out that apartment door by 7:30am. I went to the office of Smith-Diamond Realty as usual. I talked with a few people, then stated I was going to go knock on a few doors to see if anyone wanted to sell their house. I drove through the quaint Grandville historic early 1940's style of houses, and stopped in a driveway. This house looks very familiar, I looked up and around, it looked like in my dream last night, although I had been looking down through the clouds. I stepped out of my BMW and placed a real estate flyer in the front door. That night at about 5pm as I stood staring out the desolate windows of Smith-Diamond Realty watching the snow fall as most realtors had gone home to eat dinner with their families, the phone suddenly rang in the office with an echoing ring within the front foyer. I gave a polite Smith-Diamond Realty greeting, the woman on the phone stated to me, "You put a flyer in our front door, how did you know we want to sell?" She asked.

I responded to the caller, "Well I am looking for listings, this Grandville office receives a lot of buyer calls, and we need more listings." She invited me over that night for a 6:30pm listing appointment. I grabbed an empty listing package from the filing cabinet, and went to her house. Even though I had no idea how to fill out a complete listing package, I needed the listing. Regardless of the lack of training I received, I met her husband and her, filled out the five page listing contract the best I knew how, and put my first Smith-Diamond Realty sign in the snowy yard. I looked up and around as I eerily realized I just had seen this house in my dreams the night before.

On Tuesday morning at the regular sales meeting everybody kept asking me, "How did you get this listing Lori?" Others chimed in with comments, "Yeah, you are new, how could you get a listing your first week of work, your first week of being licensed?" The office sales agents asked me over and over, one by one during that regular Tuesday morning meeting at Jerry's Country Inn Restaurant in Grandville, Michigan.

I told Laura V.H. my dream story, she looked at me like I was a freak. A nutcase. Then said to me, "You should go to church and stop dreaming about flying over roof tops at night, how ridiculous." Laura V.H. whose been married four times by age thirty-one is giving me the holy run down on my ridiculous dream and how dreams are not how one gets listings around this Christian place!

One thing is for sure, I got my first listing and really began putting my foot in the world of real estate. A real normal career. A wholesome career. In fact, I sold the house in three weeks and hosted open houses each week and gained more listings and buyers as the season moved from winter into spring of 1997.

I had no debts, no children, no boyfriend, and my money went pretty far in supporting myself. I would drown myself in my new normal career. The pay checks were huge for the amount of work that was required as a real estate agent. For the most part, the more I worked and produced sales, the happier I was, really. I kept buying expensive well-tailored dress suits, shoes, purses. I loved it! I had my normal dream career at last. Gazing at myself with admiration in full length mirrors at the mall wearing the most tailored and beautiful two piece suits I realized just how far I came to be normal. Realizing how many years I seemingly had wasted at The Gold Club when I could have been selling real estate this entire time. I wish I had more direction earlier when I had turned eighteen, or twenty-one, I could have had this real estate career all along.

But there are twists and turns in everyone's life. As much as I wanted to just concentrate on real estate and putting sales on the chalkboard, the predominate male run office that seemed to work less than me, or not be so enthusiastic about real estate the way I was, saw me, well, as a threat. The men saw me differently, as a career competitor, a woman making over hundred thousand a year in their built world. The men who hovered around that front desk of Nancy Vanden Berg were very jealous towards me. I walked in every morning, I greeted everyone politely, but the men were jealous of my real estate paychecks, including her Nancy Vanden Berg. My best friend in Michigan Carmen Van Noord was also growing very jealous as her husband Doug kept remarking to Carmen, "Why can't you make money like Lori?" Cindy Honderd was growing jealous too. My high school friends seemed jealous of my success in real estate.

Most of the men at Smith-Diamond Realty were married and saw me as some kind of rare office opportunity to explore when away from their married little nest, with the look they gave me. Whether I was into excavating boredom out of the world or not, they were like Indiana Jones and I was going to get raided. Although, I was very unaware of the raid plans…..at the real estate model house.

When I look back on how I decided on which real estate office to work at, how I had arrived at Smith-Diamond Realty. I decided on Smith-Diamond Realty in Grandville because an old real estate associate of my fathers, he advised me that Smith-Diamond Realty was a great company. "A new construction residential gold mine," Al Reitberg commented to me. That with my background with my father being a builder, I would do well in this field. Al Reitberg had sold real estate for my dad for over twenty years. My dad {now deceased was a builder, he listed everything through Al Reitberg for many years. I trusted Mr. Reitberg's advice. I knew he was giving me his sound and best advice as if he were a young and ambitious real estate agent looking to make it big in real estate. That part was not a set-up, it was his solid and honest advice as if he were to start over and needed a base as a realtor in new construction sales.

I was hired in the fall of 1996 by office broker Dave Smith and office manager Steve Zinger. Dave Smith was the broker at Smith-Diamond Realty. Steve Zinger was a pencil pushing office manager, timid and insecure kind of guy shoved into a front office like a sardine. Mr. Zinger's office always appeared too small for his large size. He had just enough room for him, a desk, and a chair.

Mr. David P. Smith had a rather loud personality. He ate a powdered donut in front of me the very first time we met in the conference room for my interview. Mr. Dave Smith's face was covered in donut crumbs and white powdered sugar as he talked on and on, funny story after another story he told. He'd laugh with his mouth full of food. He'd laugh at his own jokes like a mule coughing up a bone, donut and white spattered sugar all over his face. It's as if his first impressions were of little importance to him in the world of real estate. After all, in these parts he owned the world of real estate, what people thought of him was not as important as what Dave Smith wanted in life.

I could see all the way down his throat, and his grin caked with sugar dust. I just stared at his mouth with digesting flour and white sugar over and around his mouth and his particularly wide spaced front teeth, no orthodontist growing up I suppose? None that his cheap father would pay anyways. And no apparent mirror behind me so he could see what he looked like talking to me. His personality was very polarizing. You either liked his no nonsense approach and loud verbal outlook in "his world," or he would offend you tremendously by his staunch humor of sorts. He was pushy, loud, a bit funny, polite on the surface of things. Deep down, he really could absolutely care less what anyone else really thought. Deep down he was ruthless, I could see that fact about him. He was on this planet for one thing only, to get whatever the hell David Paul Smith wanted. That wasn't so clear at first to most people, but would become clear as time progressed in that slow moving environment called Grandville. He always managed to appear to the Grandville society as a pillar, "as one of them." I knew his type well, due to the fact I had Cindy for a parent.

Dave Smith joined church functions and became a deacon in his church, year after year, a real good ol' boy pillar in the community. He liked being accepted in Rome. He really did. He was well established, his conservative father before him had started the family run real estate company.

Dave Smith saw me as ambitious, young, and a fish out of the water in these parts of Rome.

Always commenting to me and others within the office setting that I was very hard working, "More so than most women would even want to work in this lifetime. Most woman do not have your drive and ambition to succeed. If I put you in charge of an army, you'd come back a hero, you do what you're told, and you work twelve hours a day. If I tell you to get a listing, write an offer, you do. Most people don't, or can't, or are too stupid, but not you."

Dave was all about his power, clout, and people in his immediate environment accepting him, thinking he was cool for an older guy. Although he could care less what other people held as important decisions. Really, he thought no one else had an important thought, but him. His world was small and well controlled in his state of reasoning. To Dave Smith he had a big and powerful world that he controlled. He liked to keep the lid on his politics. On the other end of the token, Dave would go to extremes in what he thought was "acceptable behavior." He had no inner moral guide or compass that at all resembled "Christian." He looked identical to wicked, demented, and deceased Aleister Crowley of England. Whom also believed in theory, a man is his own compass, and man should never deny himself of what he wants in this lifetime, only fools deny themselves. Also, so I would learn was Dave Smith's core motivating motto in his life as well, that libido.

When reflecting back on my years at Smith-Diamond Realty from 1996 to 2000. I can only come to realize that there must be a connection in this lifetime from past lifetimes once lived. I may not have met Dave Smith in a previous life lived, but whatever attitudes and moral compass Dave Smith had in a previous life lived, he also came into this world with perhaps a similar disposition. It is as if he hatched from a different egg than most folks. I had met his father when he was alive, his mother and his father were very different than him. I noticed that when they would visit the office. They were quiet, conservative, and valued money more so than loose reigns Dave Smith with the pocketbook. And let's face it, Dave Smith was probably one of the loudest individuals I have ever come to know. Most people in town, or in that office would very much agree with my description of him. Quite frankly would not be surprised to have described our personalities and lives colliding as fate. As an accident that would not only happen, but in their conservative judgment of calculating his personality and wits, just a matter of time before that accident occurred on this planet.

One thing that Dave said in the summer of 1997 in the foyer of Smith-Diamond Realty, in front of Chuck Felder, Nancy V.B., and many sales agents bustling around the office, Mr. Dave Smith said to me, "Lori, with your hair up in that bun you sure do look like Cleopatra." And then he winked, winced and smiled a really big grin of sorts at me, very boldly in the foyer.

I responded calmly, "What…..? What did you just say?"

Chuck Helder the other broker and best friend to Dave Smith, and Steve Zinger (the office manager) just stood by the front foyer desk staring at me like someone spilled hot coffee on both of them, so was their expression. They both looked as if they wanted to throw hot coffee on Dave so he'd shut up. Dave on the other hand was being bold, loud, funny, I suppose. Dave appeared as having a very humorous moment, improv as only he laughed on and on like a loud hen cackling in a barnyard toward another. But Steve Zinger and Chuck Helder were not amused at Dave's blurting and rants. And then my mind jogs backwards…..back in time….to The Gold Club….and convention season. There was always a big Association of Realtors convention in Atlanta. We, us showgirls had a list posted and highlighted of the major business or sports conventions. I'm feeling delirious now, the two worlds I never wanted to collide were, or had, somehow, accidently collided. I wanted to just cover-up, how we first met, or were introduced to one another as I remember stepping up on his table, and Steve Zinger was there too, at The Gold Club.

If I act like I don't recall what he is talking about, there is no proof. Accept one piece of evidence……my credit report that Dave Smith ordered Steve Zinger to pull up. Where I worked during my college years, was on my credit report, The Gold Club. I thought nothing of it, and Steve Zinger never commented as he held my credit report on his desk while he interviewed me.

Dave Smith then shouts loudly as he cackles, "Your profile, with your hair up in a bun, you look just like Cleopatra. Your profile! Your profile!" Dave just stands with a big wide grin. He had this ugly big gap between his upper teeth, his face turns slightly pink from his sheer enthusiasm of his smile so big across his face.

I keep thinking about the evidence, my credit report. They all know, the brokers and office manager are aware, with proof that I worked at The Gold Club in Atlanta. I remember Steve Zinger telling me that he had to pull up my credit report in order for him to determine whether or not to hire me. Steve Zinger told me that a good credit report, was a sign, a positive sign that I had good moral character because I paid my bills on time. I always pay my bills on time. Sure I had agreed, pull up my credit report. I had a great high score credit report. And then he shook my hand and congratulated me, welcomed me aboard……

Chuck Helder is not smiling or amused, and says to bold Dave Smith just grinning away with his elbow prompted on Nancy's tall foyer desk of oak cabinetry and blue glazed laminate, Chuck Helder says to Dave, "I can't believe you just said that Dave."

Then Mr. Helder says to me, "Why *is* your hair up today?" As if it is a big deal, I thought to myself to his question just asked.

Nancy the office secretary chimes in, "I think it looks nice, it looks like you had your hair done for a special occasion Lori. Like a wedding or something."

I answered firmly, "I was running late today and just decided to put my hair up in a bun, I did not realize it would be such a big deal today."

I wore a white blouse, a light blue medium length skirt, nylons and black high heels. I did not look like I just stepped off a stage as a stripper. I looked very much like a professional real estate woman. Polished. Young. Conservative. I also was working seventy hours a week, listing for sale by owners, and selling real estate left and right. I was twenty-seven, young, ambitious and very hard working, and flourishing in sales due to my diligent open houses and calling potential buyers back. I was not married and had no children. I seemed to live for myself, my clients, my real estate career. By no means did I ever say anything at all sexually suggestive to anyone in that office, or my clients, or "the Goodale family." I was 100%, unequivocally, just a hard working real estate sales agent.

The summer of 1997 was a busy selling and listing season for all those real estate agents who were in on the booming real estate market. The older agents seemed to just sit back in padded blue office chairs in the foyer area and not even realize that interest rates were actually low and the market conditions had picked up from ten years ago. Making it ideal for both listing a house quickly and selling a house. I was double dipping the 7% commission percentage left and right, it was the easiest five to eight thousand dollar checks paid out to me weekly, sometimes daily, I ever even knew existed to earn. I should have been doing this all along I thought. My clients, the sellers, praised me at my ability to sell their homes at top dollar. I was just thrilled to work so hard and get such great returns for my hard working ethics. No one in that office fed me leads, handed me leads. I generated my own real estate leads, clients, referrals, just like the top men in that company. I was competitive and ambitious.

On the flip side of being young, successful in Dave Smith's world of real estate, the negative side to the local fame, I did endure some harassingly rude statements from Dave Smith and the other men in the office. Scott Chandler explained to me that Steve Zinger pulled up my credit report and learned I worked at The Gold Club at one time, and that is why the male office staff and male agents are harassing me and making comments when I walk through that front foyer at Smith-Diamond Realty (daily now).

I just felt crushed. I needed my job as a licensed sales agent. I did not want to go back to The Gold Club, or any strip club. I liked my normal career. I needed the real estate listings that I had acquired from knocking on doors of for sale by owners, or clients I was now working with from calls coming into the office, or leads I generated from open houses. It was a snowball real estate effect of success right now,

I worked so hard to get to this normal career point. I was earning such good money. No completed college. I really, really needed this real estate career. If I left now it was warned and made very understood by everyone that my listings would stay with the office, under the office title. I could not take the listings with me. Nancy Vanden Berg and the brokers made it very clear to me that if any clients call me that I generated, those clients would be told I do not exist if I leave Smith-Diamond Realty.

I could not just pack up and leave my normal career because I am being harassed by the male agents, I rationalized quietly by myself. I would have been harassed anywhere in west Michigan. I was now beginning to realize in the world of west Michigan, that Dave Smith governed a lot of territory in these parts of west Michigan.

I was single, I needed to financially support myself. I probably would have been harassed anywhere I went in Grandville, if the boss pulled up my credit report and saw I worked at "The World Famous Gold Club" in Atlanta, Georgia. I would have been harassed anywhere in west Michigan. I was beginning to understand that very poignant fact about something I knew might not be so accepted here, so therefore I never talked about my life before. I kept striving forward, onward, despite the male opposition in the heavily male dominated family run real estate office of Grandville politics as usual.

My continued efforts of trying to make something of myself in Grandville was something of a goal I rather set for myself. Everybody expected me not to work hard, family led gossip led by Cindy and friends, and also led by Carmen that is, not to generate my own real estate leads. I was out to prove that I could be successful in real estate, generate my own leads, and close deals. I would learn all I could about negotiations, "the art of the deal." And ignore harsh criticism from many, my family, friends, co-workers, and extended family and business associate's hostile and negative remarks and overtures to my face and behind my back. Just ignore them all, keep forging ahead, was my motto in survival.

I did happen to make a few friends in the office, people I would talk with when not working so much. Scott Chandler was about my age, he had a very practical, down to earth approach to life, very methodical in his everyday life at the office. He seemed to think I came from a different planet. He was always asking me, "Where are you from?" "Where did you say you were from again?"

I would always respond in a very inquisitive manner, "Why do you keep asking me that question Scott?" "I am from this area, born in Grand Rapids, Michigan, raised in Hudsonville, and Jenison, I graduated from Unity Christian High."

Scott would go back to work, and a week later ask that same stupid question, "Where did you say you are from again?"

"Scott, why do you keep asking that question, where am I from?" I asked.

Scott responded, "You just do not seem like you are from this area, you say whatever is on your mind, you go around pissing off people in the office cause you just say whatever is on your mind, no mental filter. You are like that George character on that Seinfeld show….but a girl, and a bit better looking, I suppose… "sexy George" could be your nickname. You work hard, you probably never collected unemployment, am I right?"

I responded by saying, "Yes. I have never collected unemployment, never been on welfare or food stamps. I do have distinctive qualities about my personality I suppose, I am a bit quirky I guess. But honestly it sure beats being normal around here." I went on to disclose to Scott, "I met Jerry Seinfeld once. At McDonalds in Atlanta. I could not seem to talk though, I don't know why, I suppose you just call it star struck."

Scott inquired, "You met Jerry Seinfeld, and **you** could not talk, **your** tongue was tied?"

I responded, "Yep. I could hear voices speaking inside my head…like, "say your name Lori," "order a drink Lori." But I could not talk, so after he stared at me for ten minutes with his eyes bugging outward as if he tried to engulf what he saw too quickly, as if his eyes were going to choke, and I stared at him for ten minutes just unable to talk because I am star struck…….well I just walked away. I thought his eyes looked red, maybe jet leg, or from opening his eyes up in the deep end of the ocean perhaps? You know how salt water can turn one's eyes red when swimming deep in the sea."

Scott asked, "What?" "When was this?"

I responded, "I was 22 or 23 years old. So in 1992, or 1993, while I lived in Atlanta, Georgia, I met him with two of his agents, he drinks diet Coke. I am assuming the two older gentlemen were agents. We met at a trendy McDonalds in Atlanta called Buckhead." I smiled back at Scott.

Scott asked, "What were you wearing?"

I responded, "Royal blue, a light, <u>light</u> blue outfit."

Scott asked seriously, "Did you meet lots of famous people in Atlanta?"

I responded with a smile, "A few. But none that made me go star struck like when I met Jerry Seinfeld."

Scott said, "I bet if you were able to talk and did order that drink, you two would hit it off. You're like a sexy George kind of personality, and Jerry Seinfeld is very level headed, practical, that is exactly what you need. Sometimes you act as if not from this planet. Someone like Jerry Seinfeld would be a calming effect to your quirky high energy personality. You would balance each other out. You see things oddly, objectively, not like the norm, just like that George Constanza character, but a woman. If you were to apply for a job outside of real estate, you would probably want to be a talk show host, or something very unconventional, and people would say, "I can't stanza." Just like that annoying George Constanza television character. I do not think you can do many things, you just go around pissing off people with the oddest questions and statements that you make or ask. People see you coming near their office door and they just shut the door. They don't want you asking them strange philosophical questions about life, or their life………. Everyone around here liked it better before you were hired to sell real estate. I am the only one besides Laura Hayden that can actually tolerate you. And you taking Jewish classes at some synagogue in Grand Rapids, well, is very over the top. Why would you do that?"

Scott was right. You either liked me or hated me, some people in this world have very polarizing personalities, qualities, I suppose. I have to admit, my polarizing personality seemed to swing more to the later in west Michigan. Making it difficult for me to be accepted by people who felt fitting into this Dutch subculture was a far better goal. I was just starting to accept that my role in life, maybe, is all about not being accepted by the status quo in these parts.

I did make another acquaintance friend during the summer of 1997, her name is Laura Hayden. She is one year younger than me, but acts and looks at least five or ten years my senior, she is very mature. I knew we'd be friends right off the bat. Real estate was and still is her world. Real estate back then in 1996 to 2000 was my world too, my driving career I just loved to be in. I loved wheeling and dealing, negotiating contracts and making things happen for other people, their success was my success as well. My many real estate sales commission checks were also my reward.

I just loved writing another sale on the board, having one up on the men in the office, I was their competition in that office. I was earning what my two brokers were earning, and by far earning more in commissions than pencil pushing Steve Zinger. Way more than jealous Nancy Vanden Berg who just sat there catering to the men in the office, answering phones and setting up haircut appointments for the men. Steve Zinger could make a living out of warming a chair in the office lobby listening to Dave Smith cackle. I had ambition and career drive. I loved real estate. I was different. I don't want to be their idea of "normal." I wanna be my own normal.

No one handed me leads, I had to do it all on my own, and I did prove myself as a success in real estate. I still have a file cabinet to this very day stuffed full of each and every real estate transaction I ever completed for Smith-Diamond Realty, as do they hold the proof as well. I produced well over fifty real estate transactions per year while my license hung on their wall. There is not one person I worked with during those years that did not think and know I was a professional, very hard working, tenacious real estate sales agent. My real estate hours were no less than seventy hours per week in my quest to get both listings and sell homes. I had integrity, good work ethics, and loved my job.

I stepped into Scott's office one morning, "You know Scott, my biological mother and my biological father both have their masters degrees.

I should have my PhD or something verses being just a wheeling and dealing sales agent in real estate."

Scott responded, "You're adopted? Well, that explains why you don't act like everybody else."

"What do you mean Scott?" I asked.

"You don't go to church, you say what's on your mind, no one wants to hear your opinion about their life or what they value, but you give it anyways. You make strange remarks about religion, 'stating that religion has adopted and molded their idea of God, but God has not created religion.' You do not have Christian music playing in your office like everyone else. You don't belong to Bible studies, you stick out like an outsider who does not care to join us in our conservative community. Your shoes are too expensive looking. Where did you buy those shoes, Jacobsons? They are too high and flashy. And you wear too much Chanel perfume, it stinks up the office. It smells like the mall makeup counter when I get near you by the company fax machine. I have to open my office window when you leave. No one wears layers of pink lip gloss, but you. You just look....well....too made up, and you're so bossy and opinionated. Yet… yet, every once in a while you say something profound and people turn around to listen and stare at you for a moment, freeze for a moment, then they go back to their offices and close the door. They go back to being normal and you go back to just being you. You act like you own this place when you walk through the front door and you've been here less than six months. Now, you are ambitious, and you get real estate listings and your clients adore you for being successful for them, I'll give you credit there. But around here, you just go around pissing off office people that have been trying to sell real estate and be successful for over ten years and still have not been successful. You need to not have such, well, just try and not be yourself, you'll do fine here if you do not act like yourself." Scott lectured one early afternoon day.

I responded to Scott with a smirk as I clicked my high heels together, "It does feel good to breathe in planetary air, I feel so grounded when I work at this normal place Scott." (wink, wink.) And I left his office…..

as Scott dramatically lifts open the base of his window as he slides his desk chair in one fluid motion towards the window.

The next day I opened up Scott's office door slowly as I peered in and said this, "I know I am a very un-networked Christian around here, but that does not give people the right to harass me from the office, don't you agree Scott?"

"Guys will be guys, there are more men in the office than you. You can always quit!" Scott barked that remark as I left his office.

"Shut my door!" Screamed Scott at me as I headed down a flight of stairs to the foyer.

Maybe the documentary film director Michael Moore could take on the project of interviewing everyone I have mentioned in my memoirs. The documentary film could be based in west Michigan exposing real answers to his probing questions to be asked, titled, Calvinism, A Love Story.

In August of 1997 I was twenty-seven and a half. Knowledgeable in real estate, yet naïve to men and their motives perhaps in real estate, just a bit too trusting on my part when placed in social situations that the men orchestrate, such as work parties. I am thinking to myself, it is just "a work party." Nancy Vanden Berg, the office secretary places flyers in everyone's mailbox, there are about 25 or 30 agent mailboxes in the fax room. Most of us full time agents decided to go to Florentines restaurant in Grandville. It so happened to be Dave Smith's watering hole, where he liked to hang out and have a beer. There were about ten of us that showed up. Dave announced that the office would pick up the tab, and he was buying dinners and drinks for everyone. Sounds fun, right?

A party at a restaurant of course was not odd. Dave was a jolly guy that needed everyone to like him within his immediate environment. I am more like a two drink minimum kind of girl at a party or at home for that matter. Two drinks relax me, maybe a slight buzz. I am a control freak of sorts and never, ever, "get wasted," or "drunk," that would feel out of control.

The night progressed like any other small work party in that bar. About eleven o'clock everyone decided it was getting late, it was a Thursday late evening and most of us planned on working tomorrow, Friday. Dave Smith kept begging Laura Hayden and I to stay a bit longer and talk about business. I could tell he was slurring his words. I was looking at the clock just ready to go home by myself to my apartment. Dave became very insistent that Laura Hayden drive my car back to the office. He then threw my BMW keys at her, just insisting she drive my car back to the office. Dave said he wanted to talk a bit longer with me and then he would drive back to the office parking lot, taking me back to the parking lot.

I insisted "No" over and over. "No, I want to drive my car home, I do not want anyone driving my BMW." The more I protested to Dave's idea, the angrier Dave Smith became, he got really angry. Angry that I was not going along with his plan, and angry that Laura Hayden was not budging from the table either. Finally after his firm and angry tone began to flare more intensely and she feared getting fired, she left with my keys and my car. I was then left with Dave Smith. He then paid the bar bill with company money and we set off for the parking lot. I offered to drive his car, I could tell he had way more to drink than I had consumed. On the less than half of a mile back to the Grandville office, Dave Smith grabs my upper thigh, and squeezes my left thigh. I remember thinking; this guy, this boss of mine, was that a move? I felt uncomfortable. Was that just a drunk inappropriate grab to just overlook?

He is not an attractive guy, I like his personality a bit because it is different than the average person in this town. But I instinctively knew I did not want to have an affair or a one night stand with this guy. Dave Smith was my boss, and I depended on my real estate career that I had built up for myself in the last half and of year in 1997, almost eight months now of success in my new real estate career. I liked my job as a realtor and I wanted nothing to come in between my normal career and the good income my career was bringing in 1997.

When we arrived back at the Smith-Diamond Realty parking lot, Dave Smith made a move on me. This hillbilly of a grey haired, pudgy, silver back gorilla of a man is insisting I kiss him. I laughed, the entire situation in his vehicle was making me nervous and uncomfortable. He asked again, he begged almost as he repeated himself, this time in a more aggressive tone. I laughed again, and said, "I'm going now." I proceeded to open his passenger side door of his vehicle, I looked beneath my feet, in between his car and the door cracked open. I can see the pavement move beneath me in fast motion as Dave cranks his vehicle in reverse and tells me, "You're going home with me."

"What? What….I want to go to my car." I said firmly, very sober as his vehicle speeds backwards in reverse.

"My wife is up north at the trailer, I got the whole long weekend to be free." Spoke Dave just staring straight ahead out the front of his vehicle, oblivious to what I was feeling.

"I just want to go back to my car, it's almost midnight Dave!" I said back to Dave in a mad and fearful voice that I am not in control of my fate.

I just looked at him in shock. I can't believe I am going further away from my car, down Wilson Drive in Grandville. Dave is showing no signs of remorse, no alarm bell ringing in his head that this is not at all what I want, or what he should not be doing. It is as if his conscious is dormant within his soul. As the lights of his sports utility vehicle flash over his metal mailbox, the numbers 666 are on his mailbox, his address on Wilson Drive in Grandville, 666. Right on the outskirts of town surrounded by undeveloped remote land at that time. His driveway winds back at least a quarter of a mile. I can hear the crunch of small stone pebbles under the tire wheels of his gravel driveway. I am wondering what am I doing here? And how am I going to get back to my car? If I ran, there was not a neighbor in sight, it was pitch black. I am also embarrassed that I am in an awkward criminal scene with my boss, I am the victim of what no one can see. If I screamed, the noise would not be heard, but lost in the midnight sky above us. I was stuck and needed to get out of this situation. My cell phone was back in my BMW.

"We're here, let's get out and go inside. Lori, you look so worried. Don't worry my wife is up north, it's too late for her to call or come home." Dave said as if trying to reassure me that everything is going to be fine.

I remain in shock, frozen in shock. I am now wondering if I scream at the latest developments, would Dave Smith then fire me? I can't scream, that is not the best option, he might fire me and also not drive me back to my car.

Dave tries to relax my look of being completely in shock within this integrated maladjusted idea of fun for him. "Come on, come on, just get out, I'll take you back to your car in a little while." Dave said to me. I was not reassured.

I am stubborn. I wanted to go back to my car, not be alone with Dave Smith at midnight, my boss, are you kidding me? I am thinking. Oh my God, I thought as I got out. My thoughts are screaming in my head, racing, as my rational mind is just trying to cope with this beast of a boss before me now as the pages are being turned very quickly in my life. Stop this chapter of my life! I don't want to read what comes next! I get a headache from my panic.

When we went into the dirty house, smoke filed air. Just a cluttered mess of a large ranch style house in filthy ruins with cheap dark paneled walls. Dave Smith demanded I sit down by the kitchen table. I did. He then went and unplugged each phone with a cigarette butt dangling, hanging from his mouth, as he comments, warns me, if I tried to run or call the cops, he plays poker with the police. The chief of police will make a report that looked like nothing took place and that I made the whole story up.

"What story?" I am wondering in quiet seclusion.

Dave then reassures me like an appropriate neighborhood bully would, "You don't fuck with the Michigan State Police, I've got aces you don't even know exist Lori."

I knew I was doomed, because of how doomed I felt right then and there. Dave was embedded with power in Michigan, or maybe that was just an idle scare? I was just a sales agent at his company. It was still unclear as to his full intentions of me here in his house now. It's late, I just want to get back to my car in that deserted office parking lot in Grandville. If there is a God in heaven, why is he not saving me at this moment? It's as if the umbilical cord began to loosen in heaven, I was beginning to see the angels were not going to tread were they dare not walk as I feel the abandonment from my earthly location. I am just absorbing this whole other side to Dave Smith that I never comprehended in the office environment when I would laugh at his jokes, or give him a compliment. I was nice and outgoing to many people, I have charm. But I never flirted with the guy, ever. I had no idea he read anything above and behind my charming personality. I did not know that there was even anything to read? Perhaps he had not read anything from my behavior or words, perhaps this was all about Dave Smith getting what he wanted. I am in shock. I am shaking at the table, uncontrollably shaking at the table. Dave Smith is a deacon at his church in Grandville, trusted, respected. I am just a girl who moved back to Michigan after working at The Gold Club in Atlanta. He has no conscious morals for how he is making me feel, incredibly uncomfortable. Even my teeth are chattering from uncontrollable fear. He thus goes and gets a blanket off the sofa, and comments, "Why didn't you just say you were cold."

"Dave, I am freaked out, I am not cold, I am freaked out. And want to go back to my car. It's late, I have to be on floor call duty tomorrow at 8am."

Dave went into a rage, slammed down a dining room chair, I heard a crack, a splinter. Then he boldly comes up behind me, takes his hand and reaches in my suit coat and begins grabbing me. Not in a romantic way, a scary way, a very much unwanted touch. I was shaking so bad my teeth were chattering together, I thought I was going to pass out from surging fear. How could Dave Smith go to church, live in this Christian community and get away with this? He absorbed nothing in his fifty plus years of going to church each and every Sunday. Accept keeping up a perception to the community, it seemingly was a well-guarded secret, a code within that subculture, **perception** matters most to that community.

I was perceived as an outsider for being away for eight years, now only trying to fit in. Dave was trusted, respected, almost counted as a pillar that held up Grandville……

I was not thought of that way. The only thing I had to look forward to is more fear, and then how quickly I could forget the fear or memory created. I wanted a savior, and I had none.

Dave comments to taunt me emotionally, psychologically, "If your dad was alive, or if you had a boyfriend, or husband, you know I would never do this to you. Most girls your age are married by now."

Tears rushed to my eyes. I never should have left Atlanta. I stared ahead hardly able to breath from the sheer anxiety. My mind flips backward. I should have just accepted a date at The Gold Club. I should have run off and married one of the many prospects who viewed me, well, as possible marriage material. I should have taken a chance with one of those men who asked me out on many of occasions, the many men who proposed to me at The Gold Club. I should have, I had no idea so much would again happen to me in Michigan, bad things, the velocity of my mind twirls. I really had no idea this next chapter was going to be in my existence, no idea whatsoever. No one warned me about Dave Smith.

Dave Smith asked me to stand up and take my shoes off. I was wearing a very nice high end tailored light blue suit coat and skirt, nylons and high heel. He stood on my feet, I weighed at that time maybe 122 pounds, or less. Dave Smith weighed no less than 220 pounds and is about 5'9. He was a man, but looked nine months pregnant. He stood on the front part of my feet and began undressing me. He ripped my nylons off and demanded that I go lay down in his bedroom. He pointed and directed which direction was his bedroom, and then he took off his shirt. What does Elmer Fud look like without a shirt? I never even wanted to know that answer. I am now stuck in a really scary situation with my real estate boss who is friends with all the cops in town. Even though I have blue eyes, fair skin, I can't help but feel like I am being treated like a black woman in the 1800's or even the 1950's. Somewhere in a rural southern town, where good ol' boy politics rule over people's rights, women's rights.

My mind flashes to Bessy in the 1860's, I realize she had sinister intentions with that spell, that voodoo. Because right now, I feel like a black woman right now, like Bessy, with no apparent help or salvation from what is about to take place next. Not only that, there would be no justice, just another crime against me, towards me, and no justice. As if

I am a black woman in rural Alabama, before anybody heard of Martin Luther King, or cared. I never was so aware that outside of Cindy was a whole festering southern twisted territory here in Michigan that treated me like a black woman slave with no rights, no legal recourse, no police, no judge, or no prosecutor that would ever care for my rights. Dave Smith was correct, he was not fabricating, he played poker with the cops monthly, the first Thursday of every month, the local law.

I never should have trusted Bessy in giving her my locket. My life born in 1970 was like a tunnel of horror with no escape. Yet I always just kept persevering and let hope remain in me.

If I say the word rape, would his attorneys Rick Bolhouse or Don Visser of Grandville sue me for slander? It was rape. I finally just gave in verses putting up more of a battle of escalating violence with this deviant person I never knew existed upon what I thought was a harmless, yet loud, bolstering personality boss of a man. I gave in, I did. The other alternative would have been the backlash of a more violent situation transpiring before me and on me. I was smart. Really. If you were there. You as the jury, would have said, "I agree, she got smart Mr. Judge. It took her a little while. But she got smart…..towards the end."

The next morning he made me shower, washing away evidence, he peered into the shower to make sure, giving me instructions in how to wash. Dave Smith made it perfectly clear that he owned this town and all that walked into this town, "Cops, Judges and Prosecutors can all be bought off Lori, it's been done before." He laughed at his power. He was bold and scary, just like Cindy. Victims like me in west Michigan always are the lesser victors. Victims are not even counted in the population as people who matter, not to the pillars that structure the Calvinist religious subculture that Dave Smith belonged to, just like Cindy. I received yet another demonstration of crime on why their membership to church is so important to them and people, criminals just like them.

Dave Smith made me feel like there was no way out of him ever not getting his way with me again. I now feared a man I used to just laugh with at the office. His character was warped. No matter how funny or pleasant he seemed on the surface, he was a different animal to know privately. A knowing, I never wanted to know. Dave drove me back at 6:00am, the streets were quiet and dim in Grandville.

The next day, or today rather, I had to arrive at 8am back to the same parking lot where he just dropped me off. To work and to take the incoming real estate calls from the advertising booth of being on-call. Laura Hayden called to see if Dave Smith made a move on me, I told her everything over the phone.

Laura Hayden thought maybe he'd make a move on me, but was very surprised he took me back to his house and raped me.

"I am surprised too." I commented.

I asked Laura Hayden, "Dave mentioned that he owned this town, Cops, Judges, Prosecutors alike. Do you believe him?"

Laura said, "I've heard that before, but I have never had Dave Smith do that to me, or try something on me. I have a husband, and that's probably why Dave never forced me back to his house like he did you. Get a husband and I bet Dave will leave you alone."

I responded, "I just can't believe what happened to me last night. I was not drunk, but Dave Smith would not let me go. I just gave in so I could possibly be driven back to my car Laura. You never should have left me with him." I was a bit mad.

That afternoon in August of 1997 I went to Carmen's house in Hudsonville. I told her I was raped by my boss, Dave Smith. Her eyes got big and angry and she said this to me, "He better watch it or I'll give him a piece of my mind." Carmen was furious with Dave Smith. Furious.

Although within one week, maybe two weeks, Carmen changed her tune. I found it odd too. She told me every time I would bring up the horrors of that evening with Dave Smith, she would comment, "Well Lori, that is Dave Smith's company he can act any which way he wants to. If you do not like the way he acts, then you need to get another job, go elsewhere." Carmen spoke very matter of fact, no warmth of emotion in her voice, very stoic. I was stumped into what must be going through her head now? Carmen had such a different attitude now than a week or two ago. Carmen began showing me a rather cool side to her warm personality now. I did not understand why she had such a different tune. I was just left now in shock with her new attitude towards the rape that occurred to me at Dave Smith's house.

I kept more and more to myself at Smith-Diamond Realty. I just worked harder on selling more houses, being more successful. I avoided the office more I noticed. Dave Smith pulled me aside outside one August afternoon in 1997 and said this without mention the rape at his house, "I'm really sorry, I don't know what came over me."

Dave did apologize. Ironically enough though, he'd turn around and say something an hour later, loud and boldly in the office foyer, "Lori should not go to the real estate golf tournament, her boobs would get in the way." Dave would laugh and cackle. Chuck Helder and Steve Zinger would stare at Dave saying such a harassingly open comment loudly in the open foyer in front of office receptionist Nancy, in front of the other sales agents, mostly men. As they all shook their heads in amazement at his bold comments as they all laughed. That was one of many comments Dave Smith made openly and behind closed doors at the office. I felt trapped in my real estate career, for just being a woman. I had no faith in west Michigan. I was treated very unfairly, I was outnumbered by the bully union army. Should I move? Where to? Back to Georgia? I just did not have a ready and good answer for myself. I felt in a daze. I felt stuck. I was starting to feel less ambitious. I felt beaten down, down trodden, as daily I just tried to keep my chin up and smile like I used to when I entered the office in Grandville.

But within the Dutch Calvinists society blending in matters most, go to church on Sunday, have a family, mow your lawn (but not on Sunday), and get involved with Bible studies and church functions so that people in the religious club community can see you, see that you are one of them, reflections do matter! I was walking in Rome, and doomed because I did not want to be one of them.

At the end of August 1997 Dave Smith decided to add me to two new construction plats in Wayland, as a way to remove me from the office I suppose. "Superior Estates and Galaxy Estates, these two slow sales plats needed someone with ambition and drive," Dave commented to me as all the sales agents looked at me.

"Success in selling, and putting sales on the board, that's you." That is what Dave told me two weeks after kidnapping me and forcing sex on me back at his house. His idea seemed to spring out of nowhere, just to add me all of a sudden to two plats within two weeks of Dave Smith basically kidnapping me and bringing me back to his desolate ranch and raping me. I had bruises on the front of my feet for weeks from him stepping on me prior to the forced rape. I wore darker colored nylons to hide the deep bruises on the front of my feet.

Dave Smith always made it to church, he smiled and shook everyone's hands. People liked him, he greeted people that really had no idea what he was up to at work, or behind closed doors. Dave Smith knew "the drill" in being a Christian, a Calvinist in the Grand Rapids society. Dave was on the Grand Rapids Association of Realtors, "ethics committee," for years. He was the one who yelled and threw the book at people. You know, the wrongdoers in his world of real estate in west Michigan. Dave knew each cop by name in Grandville, and warned me to not even attempt to speak up in the office or report him to the police. "No one will take your complaint seriously, I've got the Goodale family backing me up on whatever I do in this town, that's real guns. Any lawyer you think about hiring and suing me for sexual harassment will be paid off by the Goodale family's attorney, we own this town. You don't like it, well, you just find your own place of employment. It will be you that will leave this town broke and beaten, not me." Dave Smith spoke those words in a voice that was commanding.

Who is the Goodale family? I wondered. Why does that name sound so familiar? I never see them, and Dave Smith talks about them like a Dynasty family on television all of a sudden. Who are these people that own part of Smith-Diamond Realty, but we never see them? I wondered. "How can one family just pay off people and get away with it?" I asked Dave.

Dave grinned big, like a howdy dowdy backwoods cowboy and said as he gleamed power in his eyes, looked at me like I was cattle to be rounded up, grinning wide at me, "You just try it, just sue me and your lawyer will drop the case, it won't go anywhere, even if you had a video or a witness watching us. Lawyers can be paid off, Judges are owned in Michigan. Rick Bolhouse will always ask for a trial by a Judge, never by a Jury. This kind of thing happens all the time in Grandville. Do you know how many businesses Jack Goodale owns? Any lawsuit goes to a Judge, not a Jury around here, and goes nowhere, sometimes I wonder if the toilet ain't big enough to flush the amount of lawsuits and paperwork down it, but my God, it is. Jack's power amazes me. Don't fool yourself, this town is full of buried treasures by no other than the American CIA. We'll run you out of town, it's been done before, enemies are run out of town in these parts. You best not ever go against us." Dave laughed and went on to convince me as he shook his finger at me, "Not one business gets shut down, and not one business has any bullshit manual on sexual harassment either." Laughed the mad Dave Smith spitting fire in my face at my obvious obstinacy about where I was now living, the north. Some place on earth where angels refused to visit.

I wanted to call the Governor, the President, and let them know that the bully union army has never been dismantled! But Dave Smith was correct, as I looked around the office, Dave was right, it would be a very useless call out for help. Dave kept grinning at my shocked expression of horror at how I am stuck selling real estate in a town owned by corruption, and I actually thought I had rights as a woman, I was wrong. Really wrong in this town about a woman's rights that I just took for granted in Georgia.

I asked Dave Smith, "Do I look like a black woman and this is the 1940's in rural Alabama and the rest of the world's rules and laws just don't mean jack shit in this part of the country?"

Dave answered with a smartass remark, "Don't get cocky with me, I might fire you, you'll never sell real estate in this town. You better just kiss up to me, or I or the Goodale family staff of attorney's over there in that granite building will destroy your young and precious life, it's been done before! I know just how to run this company with no problems. Dave points down the road to the granite bank building on the corner of Wilson and Chicago Drive. Dave Smith's expression went from grinning a cocky smile to spitting fire with his eyes within thirty seconds flat of his statement of facts and power in my presence. Dave Smith was never shy about bringing me up to speed on Grandville politics as usual.

Scott was a bit mad over Dave adding me to the new construction plats in Wayland, and so was Chuck Helder. Associate broker Helder and Chandler did not want me to advance in real estate commissions for the year, or in that office. It was a hostile war just to be treated fairly as a woman. What was so shocking to me as I looked at this situation detached from the men, is the large amount of support from both the men and the woman in the office environment and community that supported treating me unfairly. I was outnumbered in believing I had rights in that small town, the Calvinists' cult.

Now Scott Chandler and Chuck Helder were seeing me as a direct threat to Scott's plats, his financial accomplishments thus far for the company, his projects. Another layered war, really. And again it was me, just me that made up my army of rights….imagined rights…..imagined army on earth…….I began daydreaming, it was a happy escape.

Accepting to go to Wayland to live and work out of a model home was a pivotal point in my young real estate career at Smith-Diamond Realty. Do I walk away with nothing? Or do I stick it out and move forward and just shrug off the rape and constant harassment from Dave Smith? Do I make lemonade from lemons? I was just trying to stay afloat in a world that wanted to drown me. I did not go to church, in fact, I saw church as their alibi for crimes they would commit Monday through Saturday at the office. I was beginning to see the Christians of Grandville, Michigan as "monster Christians." I was truly scared and shaking in my boots at these so-called Calvinists.

I would just smile behind the fear I felt. I decided the very best thing for my survival was to shrug off the rape. After all, Dave Smith warned me that the Goodale family was on his side, and they owned the town. Moving from my step-fathers apartment building to live in Wayland at the new construction house, the model home, seemed like a way to make lemonade out of a lemon situation. I may not have liked the cards that were being dealt on the table, but I played my hand the best I could, with what I was dealt at age twenty-seven and single.

Financially dependent on paying my bills and having my real estate career stay afloat no matter how turbulent the storm grew in the north sea here. I just had to keep forging ahead. When I met new people in real estate I felt like I was holding in a world of hurt and anxiety underneath my smile. But I kept smiling.

Honestly, I thought this place is one scary town, Grandville, like growing up under Cindy's roof. Powerless over what people thought they could do with my life and what they could camouflage themselves as, law abiding citizens, if they all just stayed together I suppose. What I would learn and experience in Wayland later would turn my world upside down. What I thought was a step up being added to Galaxy Estates and the plat Superior Estates was another cage situation I was entering, another locked lid jar of good ol' Bessy. What seemed on the surface like a smooth transition from a bad office situation was actually an orchestrated set-up in the model home. One conspiracy I did not see on the map before me as I drove to Wayland to set up my signs in Superior and Galaxy Estates. What I thought was just another situation of me making lemonade from lemons, was a trifling layered plot against my life by both conspirators, the American Central Intelligence Agency and a small real estate company, Smith-Diamond Realty. However, in 1997-1998, I did not know it.

I moved to Wayland, Michigan from my step-father's apartment building in Hudsonville that he owned. I moved into Superior Estates in Wayland first, then Galaxy Estate's model home. Dave Smith asked me to meet him at Talsma's Furniture in Hudsonville in September 1997 to buy me five thousand dollars' worth of model home furniture and a computer and fax machine that I would need in Wayland. He suggested that I work more home hours, and do at least twelve hours per week of model home hours, selling vacant lots and new construction within two plats from the Wayland model home. Scott Chandler, not a dumb person, began raising his eyebrow to this latest and new development he was learning about, how I suddenly was added to his two plats that he already was assigned to market and sell. We all had to sign a contract in September of 1997 adding me to the lot list side of commissions, and the whole splitting of real estate commissions for those two plats. All seemed well in September 1997 for the most part of just making lemonade out of a lemon situation. But I was naïve, totally powerless, a terrible concoction.

I went to work right away, creating and placing real estate ad's in the Wayland Pennasee Globe. I made sure each lot had a for sale or sold sign as needed. I created real estate brochures, answered numerous calls, wrote and negotiated deal after deal. I stayed focused on real estate sales and my real estate career. I kept my mind off what Dave Smith did to me. I mostly avoided Grandville accept for the numerous real estate closings I was required to oversee and attend for the new construction and lot sales I had generated for the Wayland plats.

One thing though, Chuck Helder and Dave Smith were refusing to pay me any of the list side commissions for two years as I lived and worked in Wayland!

Finally they both coughed up a check for the eighteen lot list side commissions they had paid themselves during those two years, and never paid me a single check on the listing side! Dave said it was Chuck Helder who is the office accountant and the one refusing to cut me the listing side commission checks. Then both Dave Smith and Chuck Helder informed me that CIA John Brennan ordered for them not to pay me rightfully owned commission checks. In essence, it was all just a power play to show me who has control over me, my finances, and my real estate career that I was very dependent upon to financially support myself. Those in power kept reminding me who was in power, in those parts. I truly felt like a black woman in the wrong part of Alabama, it was before any civil rights movement ever existed. At times I was tempted to drive to the borders of Michigan to see the welcome to Michigan sign, where was I? I would often wonder. In fact, any attorney I spoke with in Grand Rapids knew the very reputable Smith-Diamond Realty and would not file a lawsuit against them on my behalf. Any out of town lawyer stated it would be too much trouble to abandon his or her own law practice and other clients, to drive to Grand Rapids for long drives and court appointments. You have no idea of the pain and exhaustion of dealing with the Calvinists alone that I had to deal with as they now saw me as an outsider to their cult, their ways. Grandville and Hudsonville is the heart of that religious sect, the pulse of the cult, and the well camouflaged Grand Rapids CIA with their attorneys busy at work at the old granite State bank building.

Life was not getting easier with these Christians, it was like walking in quick sand and trying to stay afloat. I did not know how much longer I would tread.

I was learning through experiencing life among them, that many, many people were just like Cindy, the woman who adopted me. Everyone seemed to know the drill, but me. What was the drill in Michigan? Be a very networked Christian with the CIA and you'll survive and be successful.

I want to say at least 90% of these Calvinist, simply used church as their alibi, and their pristine conservative appearances to fool even the slightest criminal sniffing detective that *maybe* could not be paid off by the Smiths or by Mr. Rick Bolhouse or the CIA.

In the fall of 1997 Doug, my best friend's husband began buying a lot or two in Wayland from me. He would say after I wrote up the deal and he'd sign the vacant lot purchase agreement, "O.k. what do I get now Lori?" I would say in my shocked response, "Well Doug, I will make sure to sell that spec house once it is constructed."

Doug was always harassing me these days, but why? He'd say, "You posed for Playboy and took off your shirt for Playboy, wore those lingerie outfits for Playboy, what are you going to do for me?"

I would respond, "I am not going to do anything for you Doug other than sell you a vacant lot for you to build a house on or list a house that you build. Your income I help produce from the spec house selling is your profit, but I am not going to take my top off for you."

There were a couple of times Doug would just lunge at me, grabbing me and trying to get his hands in my clothes, underneath. I always pushed him away. He was not my type, he was Carmen's husband, he literally stunk as he lunged for me, had a bad order. I am not into sleeping with my best friend's husband. I did bring up this very alarming harassment fact to Carmen in the fall of 1997.

Carmen in my shock and dismay said to me, "Well Lori, Doug wants to bring in another woman into our bedroom. I suggested you." In her supportive tone of voice of her husband's harassment of me, Carmen actually seemed proud like. Weird Carmen.

I responded, "Well don't, don't make those kind of suggestions. That's not my cup of tea. I'm not into that kind of thing Carmen." I just looked at her and kept shaking my head wondering who Carmen really is inside.

Carmen responded, "Oh, you're acting like a baby about the adult world of sex Lori."

Oh, my God, I thought to myself. Do I even really know Carmen? I thought. Has Doug warped her mind on acceptable behavior in this Christian cult? I do not want to be harassed.

Carmen restated what Doug had said, "You posed for Playboy, worked at The Gold Club, what is the big deal Lori? You are not a saint, nor viewed as a saint in these parts, what do ya expect Lori?" Carmen spoke so eloquently, as if she had so much unyielding power and I did not. I was not a saint. But I did not deserve the unwarranted sexual harassment. It was annoying. Carmen's attitude was very alarming and annoying as a supposed friend.

"What is the big deal?"............I blurted, "The big deal is that I do not want to be harassed every time I sell a lot to your husband. Do not encourage him to harass me. I like selling real estate. I do not like all the sexual harassment, but I like my real estate career. I think I am really cut out for it. Why you have changed your tune on what your original opinion on what Dave Smith did to me, is bizarre. I'll get to the bottom of why you suddenly changed your opinion." I said with stature as I stood up to her in anger, speaking up to Carmen.

"Well, Dave Smith bought you all that model home furniture, that is an affair." Carmen said, still speaking so eloquently.

"An affair? Are you kidding me, Dave Smith is trying to cover his tracks. It is not an affair." I said, just fuming at how ignorant Carmen could be. All of a sudden I am looking at her, talking with her, and now wondering who is this warped delusional Christian I claimed was my best friend for twenty years or so?

But there would be many delusional and shocking Christians to encounter in the upcoming years as I made my way through the spooky woods.

Within that same time period during one of my many model hours in Wayland in 1997, a woman enters through the door. I greet her, she says "Hello," we begin slight chit chat. She introduced herself as "Sharon." She looks familiar, I've seen her before but I cannot place where as we make small talk. She stated she is a psychic for a living, living with her daughter in the basement and was looking to purchase a home of her own, something affordable and new. She looked so familiar, but I just could not place where I have heard her voice, where did I know her from? The Gold Club perhaps? Her voice, I've heard her voice before…..

I then asked her, "What do you mean exactly? A psychic for a living?" Sharon went onto explain she could predict the future, and she reads tarot cards. Interesting I thought, in Atlanta often hanging out for lunch in little five points or Virginia Highland I would pay money to have my fortune told. It was fun, some psychics can really predict the future. I thought it was a refreshing antidote to have a psychic show up at the boring model home in rural Wayland, Michigan. I was all game. I had never met her before, I briefly thought, or have I, something about her was so familiar. I really thought nothing was odd or off about meeting her in Wayland. I really thought it was a random honest meeting. As a real estate agent, one is always meeting new people, constantly, from all walks of life. However, my mind still seems to be clicking through an assortment of mental files as I look at Sharon and observe. The rational side of my mind believes this is the very first time I have met her.

I respond to Sharon, "I've had my cards read before, it is always interesting to hear what psychics have to say." I was polite, and never really thought much about meeting her was odd, really. I met strangers all the time that look familiar, passing through the model hours that I hosted. It was my job to meet and greet and pass out brochures, sell a vacant lot, custom build-job or a builder spec house for sale. All the while making polite conversation, trying to connect to that person, that stranger, that potential real estate customer. Greeting new people, strangers for that matter is part of my job.

Sharon gave me her first name only and phone pager number on a piece of paper, she asked me to call her some time for a tarot card reading.

I later called her pager number, in the dullness of my life one day I located space to fill. I was bored one day during the late afternoon when most were eating dinner with their families. I was interested in my future, curious I suppose. Sharon returned my phone call at Smith-Diamond Realty in Grandville, Sharon had a very mono tone voice on the phone I noticed. She agreed to meet me after work, after 6pm at Smith-Diamond Realty. She stated she read tarot cards for many of the people at Smith-Diamond Realty. Sharon went on to say she held Dave Smith's watch and told him of his future. Anyways, she asked for sixty dollars cash, no checks, and began laying down worn tarot cards on the main floor conference table in Grandville. No one was left in the office after that particular work day, I was hoping no one would pull up and see a bunch of tarot cards spread out on the office conference room table. It was sometime in the early autumn months of 1997.

Sharon stated next summer I would buy my first rental home. Sharon described people coming into my life, and basically gave descriptions, time frames, etc. She even brought up about a friend's husband harassing the hell out of me, and stated I better watch my back and be careful what I drink. "Do not drink any open cartons of milk, soda, wine, etc." I heeded Sharon's warnings. Sharon went on to say that an attorney in Grandville was playing a game of world domination for a elite group of wealthy Arab men. She said his name was Mike or Mick, something like that. She stated he worked for an Arab-Russian organization and they had me under surveillance, as did the American Central Intelligence Agency. She explained that I had been sold more than once on paper to foreigners in the Middle East. She explained that the model house was a set-up by the American CIA. Sharon warned me that I might be taken out and brought overseas.

My response was stunned silence to all Sharon had told me, coupled with the unknown of what the hell was this psychic talking about. Nothing made any immediate sense whatsoever. I quietly thought perhaps there is some kind of residue on the tarot cards from another appointment? Residue and reveal from another person's reading or something.

Then Sharon sharply lifted her head as if another entity was inside Sharon as her voice mouthed these words directly to me, "No Lori, this is your reading, not another person's reading."

I was creeped out. Something inside Sharon was now reading my mind. Then I heard a crashing sound of something falling, something heavy fell on the second story level of the office. I thought I was alone. There were no cars in the parking lot. My next thought? Maybe Sharon's bizarre second spirit of sorts is now residing in Smith-Diamond Realty and taking the place over like a haunting of sorts. Then I am suddenly left thinking I do not even want to know my future and all this weird stuff.

Mary Kay McCleave another real estate agent, about twelve years older than me, oddly, also said that to me during this same time period as Sharon warned me about getting poisoned at work or in a work environment, or a party.

Sharon stated she saw me attending holiday parties, searching for "the one," but my true love would come later in life.

In the fall of 1997 I called up a Grand Rapids synagogue, I signed up for some classes being offered. A Jewish woman teacher invited me over for a Friday dinner. She reminded me of Dr. Terri Ann, short, pudgy, round, with a warm personality. I was hoping to meet someone like Alan here in the north, would it ever happen I wondered? I did not know, but I did know one thing, I was not a Dutch Christian Reformed cackling hen type who wanted to just fit into the subculture and systems. I could tell I was just different from the average Calvinist. Perhaps I spoke my mind too much, and my heels were too high, and

I wore to many layers of pink lip gloss. Scott was right about me not fitting into this Dutch subculture. I just wanted to be myself in a town that wanted to crush me, but why did the Calvinists want to crush me and not befriend me? Just because I did not want to follow their very two-faced duality's of existence of hiding crimes and sins? The real life behind closed doors where anything goes, and their surreal life, the perception the Calvinists would impose to the world outside. I wanted to expose them for all they were. They wanted to repress me, rebuke me, and remind me that I am not saved because I am not like them, normal like the church goers, the Bible study people. My history I remember from 2000 years ago was not told or studied within their many Bible studies. I was viewed as trouble because I did not believe exactly the way the Romans narrated Biblical history recorded. My history I remember is not something I cannot believe, my history is part of my soul, part of who I am as a person. If my history, my truths, my sagas were not narrated by ancient Romans recording history 2000 years ago, would my truths, my history, my sagas then not be true and valid in 1970? 1978? 2012? Do you understand my point about history?

I decided after about a year after moving back to Michigan. Normal was not what I wanted to be, it was for a long time though. But I do not want to be them, their normal, what they classify as normal.

In December of 1997 I decide to go to a Jewish singles Hanukah party at a Grand Rapids synagogue. The party was mostly comprised of overweight Jewish guys in their mid-thirties to fifties with no personality and sex appeal. I was searching for Alan, an Alan type, a replacement of Alan and the dream we had at one time.

I could sense instantly upon entering the Jewish Hanukah party that no matter how many parties were thrown in behalf of these single men now before me, these men would never meet their mate and marry, that was my impression of them. And in walks me, looking for my next Alan, my G.Q. Jewish man, a chic professor kind of guy to have incredible sex on a desk, great philosophical conversations with on or off a wooden table or off a beaten path in the woods...... and of course say the word's "I love you," in unison. This time around marry, have children, live in a fabulous house, and of course move away from Grand Rapids. Perhaps to a southern location, maybe even move back to the State I miss so much, Georgia.

Through the twirling anxiety of hope and anticipation I hung my coat up and proceeded into the meeting area room of the synagogue……

Oh my goodness I thought as I walked through the doors of the synagogue that connected to a gathering room where the party was hosted. I can't just leave now, I just walked in and all the dorky men are just roaming around the beverage and food table, double dipping chips as they look up at me. As if wondering how to get to me from behind the chip and dip table where they stood slouching and munching.

Just then a skinny young guy, maybe around my age so I thought, begins a conversation with me. I am a hand person, and instantly look at a man's hands. He had the skinniest fingers with skinny narrow small little nail beds, very unattractive, as if he bites his nails. He would not leave me alone. He introduced himself as "Michael Risko." I left after thirty minutes of the lame party. I went to my car and he followed me out towards the dark and windy Grand Rapids synagogue parking lot. I thought he was leaving because there was no one else for him to talk with at the lame party.

The evening is dark as I set out down on highway 131 south to Wayland, back to my now residence of the model home at 405 Discovery Drive in Wayland. As I drive south on 131 I notice a large older style car following me, close behind me, I feel a little creeped out. I keep looking in the rearview mirror on my front dash. The car that is following me then moves to the right side of me, the right lane on 131 headed south. I look and make eye contact with that same skinny young guy from the synagogue party driving along side of me now. He keeps staring at me as he drives parallel to my car for about ten minutes. Then he pulls behind my car again. I am really freaked out, he is following me home to Wayland. I pull into the real estate model home's snowdrift driveway and open my garage door automatically. I shut my garage door but he gets out before the garage door closes.

"What are you doing here? Why did you follow me home?" I ask totally taken back by the latest circumstances derived from the synagogue party.

"I wanted to come over. I want to go inside." Michael states, very insistent.

"I don't think so." I said as I opened my door to get away from him.

He puts his hand on the door and allows himself inside my residence. I am thinking oh my God, I need to get this guy out of my house. We had a brief argument at the base of my spilt staircase of the spilt bi-level ranch model house. I sighed and said "O.k., you can stay for ten minutes." I felt like I had to appease this guy so that he would eventually leave, and soon I hoped. What a skinny dork of a guy I thought, bordering on a description more befitting such as "a creep."

Mike Risko followed me up the bi-level stairs to my living room, dining room area. He sat on my sofa and stated that a psychic told him that he would meet his dream girl at a Jewish dance in Grand Rapids in December of 1997. I thought to myself, I have gone to psychics before in Georgia and met one here in Michigan. But at this point in my life, my naïve existence in the model home, I never thought that the psychic Sharon, was also perhaps **his** psychic? It was not until I saw this man in court years later in Allegan that I began to put two and two together as I tell my story of my life back in west Michigan, to you the reader.

He looked about my age, dark hair, olive complexion, but he did not look Jewish really. His nose was not Jewish, his face did not look Jewish. He had dark features, maybe Italian? Maybe Arabic? He looked like a runt, the runt of the litter, I thought to myself.

Making lemonade from a lemon situation, I sat next to him on the sofa, I asked him if I could read his palms at the table. He then moved to the table, where we would talk. He stated that he worked "as a cameraman for Fox news," he repeated that statement over and over, and then glanced at my expression as he said that last statement to me. "Odd guy" I thought. He went on to say he had free-lanced in college for the Fatman Detective agency in Grand Rapids, that they had many locations. He then informed me that he was Lebanese, and an Arab government sent him to west Michigan. I just kept looking at him as if to say, why with my expression worn.

He stated he was from Detroit and did a lot of work on the east side of the state for the Fatman Detective agency while in college.

I responded with an loaf, "Oh."

I looked at his palms and then felt very queasy to the point of vomiting almost. I looked at his eyes, they gave me the creeps, as did his palms. I knew he was pure evil. His life line was a complete mess, his emotional line was that of a serial killer. My "now" impression of him, was matching the scary reveal on his palms as well.

I knew I was dealing with not just a young pushy man who followed me home tonight. I knew I had to escort this man out immediately, his hand read "psychopath," "Jack the ripper." I have read well over ten books on palm reading and read well over hundreds of palms. I am very knowledgeable in the field of palm reading.

I said to Michael as I laughed nervously, "Your life is messed up, I don't like what I am reading on your palms, you are a psychopath, and you must go." I said with a smirk, but I was serious. I led him to the door, shut and locked my door. He begged me to have him stay when we got to the front door. I said, "No way, you need to leave," and he did.

I remember the last thing he said to me as I closed and locked the door……

"You like world domination, you wanted it 2000 years ago. I am like a really good game you might enjoy, the game of Risk."

I looked over my shoulder for weeks to come but never came across that man until I entered a court room in Allegan county years later and saw the new attorney that Rick Bolhouse hired in Grandville from the law office of Visser & Bolhouse, "Michael P. Risko."

Mike Risko grew a goatee on his chin, wore a green suit, gained maybe five pounds by the time I re-met him in out of all places, a courtroom defending three men, two of his clients had raped me. The CIA sealed the case in Allegan according to CIA John Brennan and CIA

David Petraeus, really sealed the case meaning that no one can read the court transcripts and know the details of the case in Michigan.

Mike Risko in the Allegan courthouse tried to act very lawyer like, very professional in attitude and manners. When I saw him in court years from the date of December 1997 (which was our first meeting), he immediately flipped his hands over in court so I could not recognize his palms that I had once read. His eyes spelled fire, as if I knew who he was as his eyes and mine met head on in court. We both knew at that instant, that glance of recognition, when we first *really* met, that night in December of 1997 at a synagogue. I saw his hands again in court, his fingers, and knew that was the same pushy "Michael" that was in my residence of the Smith-Diamond Realty model home at 405 Discovery Drive in Wayland. The same "Michael" that followed me back to the model house after the synagogue party, but I never invited him over.

Late December 1997 rolls around, the snow begins to drift and winter is upon us once again. Carmen called me up and said she was throwing an annual Christmas party at their house for their friends and that I was invited. I did accept to go, Carmen asked that if I wanted to, I could come earlier than 7pm. She stated that Doug and her were going to order Chinese take-out.

I drove in from Wayland, about a thirty-five minute commute to their house in Hudsonville. I arrived at 6pm, Carmen stated that her in-laws were going to watch her children. Carmen asked me if I wanted white wine or red wine? I stated "Merlot, the red wine."

Carmen then said rather loudly, "O.K. I'll have the white wine then."

I am thinking, whatever, why are you talking so loud from the kitchen where you are pouring wine into glasses Carmen. Carmen poured the glasses of wine in her kitchen, a blocked view from the great room where I sat on a sofa. Carmen then proceeds to then hand me the glass of red wine. I began sipping on the red wine, at first I felt a little buzzed, then from zero to sixty seconds my head began to spin. I felt out of control in the sense that I could not stand, needing to grab onto another piece of furniture to stand upright or just sit for a moment. I sat by the kitchen table as the guests began arriving and pouring into their house.

Carmen insisted that I go to a back bedroom if I am too drunk, "Just go lie down Lori in the back bedroom. You are wasted Lori."

"I had one glass of red wine Carmen……" I barely could get out that sentence.

My head spun, and kept spinning. My eyesight was diminishing, I lost my peripheral vision. I remained at the table. I had only tunnel vision left, and even that vision was starting to cloud in and get darker. Lynda Poele Devries walked in and said to me by the table, "Gosh Lori, you're loaded already?" I could not respond verbally, I kept shaking my head, no, no. I wanted to call out for help, but I could not speak. I knew I had to do something drastic because my body senses were shutting down. I had a locked in feeling, and soon all would go blank, I thought. I headed for the bathroom to vomit whatever I had in my system that was causing this break down of my senses. I was not drunk, I was drugged. On the way to the bathroom Carmen's neighbor who is a pharmacist, states as I walk by him, "She's been drugged." He actually sounded alarmed, as he was referring to me being drugged.

Carmen is very good friends with the neighborhood pharmacist's wife. I proceeded to the bathroom and vomited. I stuck my finger down my throat and forced myself to vomit in order to save myself from whatever was in my system. Placed in my system against my will, and my intentions of just going to a Christmas party in Hudsonville.

I then stepped outside to the garage, the garage door was open. I could breathe in a fresh gulp of icy fresh wintery air. My face was red, I still felt sick from whatever was still in my system. Doug followed me outside and kept verbally harassing me to lift up my shirt, just insisting. I refused, and just left in my car, the party had been underway for maybe one hour. I would forgive Carmen, and just assume it was all Doug's idea to drug me. Lately, forgiveness was a solution to just survive and have a few Christian friends and associates in west Michigan.

It was a long cold winter, I would rent movies during the long model hours, just watching the snow go past my big living room window in

Wayland. Sometimes I'd cook in the kitchen of the model home, listen to music and just remember those times I had just let slip from my fingers in Georgia.

I thought, I really should have married in Georgia. I never should have come back to Michigan to the shock of my life the way these Calvinists treated me simply because I am not a cookie cutter version of them. The winter months produced one or two real estate sales, very slow is the selling season in Michigan during the very bleak cold months. Not many people want to move in the winter months.

As sales were slow and traffic through the plats were slow I got bored and paged that psychic Sharon, it must have been winter going into spring of 1998. This would become my third reading from Sharon in Michigan. I never knew her outside of Michigan, I thought, but she did look so familiar……

In February 1998 us real estate agents had to sign up for continuing education for real estate agents, a required six hours of real estate continuing education by the State of Michigan. The required real estate class was to be held at Jerry's Country Inn and Restaurant hall conference room in Grandville. I had to drive from Wayland to Grandville, a bit of a drive in the snow. I slept in a bit and wore my hair up in a bun, I quickly got dressed. My back hurt, I almost did not go to the continuing education for real estate agents due to my sudden severe back pain. I arrived late in Grandville and noticed upon opening the large conference door that there was one seat in the back of the room. I sat down next to a guy, never really thought much about it really. He handed me a pen as I scooted up in my chair. Steve Zinger was sitting next to him, and Dave Smith was sitting in the row in front of me.

At the ten o'clock break, Steve Zinger addresses the dark haired man dressed in jeans and a flannel shirt next to me as "Patrick Goodale." I looked at him, and thought quietly, oh, that is who Dave talks about, one of the Goodale family guys whom own everything in town. I was able to get a better look at Patrick Goodale during the morning break, he was rather attractive. I asked Pat, "What do you do for a living?" "Do you sell real estate? I have never seen you before at a meeting." I inquired as we sat next to each other in that back row. He responded back to me in a pleasant voice, "My dad is Jack Goodale." Pat looked very familiar. I could not place where I knew him as I roller decked through my mind of faint and familiar places, people, and things. I spoke up again, inquisitive about him......

"Yeah, but what do you do? For a living, what do you do?" I inquired as I sat there thinking that was an odd answer to my question of, What do you do? And he just states who his father is, Jack Goodale.

I asked him another question, "What do you do for fun?" He stated he liked to go snowmobiling in the upper peninsula of Michigan, sometimes for eight hours at a time.

"You snowmobile for eight hours straight?" I asked. My mind begins to have a flash, like a camera clicking in reverse motion. I was five? Six? Seven? My dad's cousin on my father's lived in this big sprawling ranch house on Second Street in Caledonia, Michigan. My dad's second cousin would throw extravagant parties, helicopter rides, snowmobiles, sunken in bar and classic Hugh Hefner set up in the basement. Anyways, my father had a drinking problem, and so did his cousin who lived on Second Street in this magnificent ten thousand square feet home. Ever since childhood, this particular uncle of mine (my dad's first cousin), were close. He was a high roller, drinking, king David type. Every guy could relate to him, my dad's cousin. Needless to say, he had been married a few times, bankrupt a few times, then back living the high life, lots of ups and downs, but mostly a high roller, successful. Nevertheless, just like my dad, his cousin was not so embedded into the community like a dorky Christian, the rest of them. He was more in motto, Here I am, accept me the way I am, or screw you. Laugh loud, and throw you a beer, in his attempts to get to know you.

So anyways, being that my dad's cousin was a high roller in those parts, west Michigan, the apparent other high rollers, "the Jack Goodale clan," knew my dad's cousin. The man sitting next to me in 1997 during real estate continuing education, is the same man who "accidently" killed my dog Pepper when I was four or five years old. I screamed for a week. He also liked to attend the high rolling parties that my dad's second cousin hosted, and the snowmobile bashes, challenging me to take the snowmobile over icy ponds as a dare. I was young, adventuresome, and lacked adult supervision most of the time. I did every Russian roulette trick he asked. Then he asked my age? I did not want to tell him, because, well, I did not even have a developed chest, I knew I wasn't the age I wanted to be, and so I never told him. He developed a crush on me nevertheless, and I developed a crush on him. He never, ever touched me as a child, that I recall. He commented when I was five? Six? Seven? Right in that age, he said, "Cleopatra, when you get older, we will have sex." I remember wondering as a elementary age girl, what sex was? And he acted as if I knew that term. We had a big age gap one could say, but we connected, we had a crush on each other, but he did know better. He was very good looking, and very dangerous, adventurous, that was my very first impression of him in the 1970's and now in 1997.

"Yeah I do, it's what I like to do." I looked at his face when he talked to me, he did have a nice face. He had dark hair, blue eyes, maybe about 5'11 or or 6'1, tall, broad shoulders, strong knees and legs. Very handsome, great sex appeal. I thought to myself, this guy Pat has some strange answers to my questions but he is exactly my physical type of a drawn description of my ideal man. If I was to draw an ideal man on a paper canvas. I know him……..

I did not notice him so much when I first sat down. But when I looked at him now, I did take notice once I sat down after break, and I liked his steady voice. He seemed stable and practical in his appearance and tone of voice. I do well with earthy grounded people, I thought. Like him…..perhaps.

I then put my head down and noticed he was falling asleep in his chair as the real estate speaker babbled on and on, Patrick had his eyes closed. As the teacher in class kept rambling on about stuff we were supposed to write down, I put my head down, to relax too, or maybe daydream a little. I pulled my folded arms to the edge of the table then peaked at his lap, his legs, his jeans, his strong knees, then quickly back towards his face to see if he could see what I was looking at, thinking about in such. I glanced quickly at his closed eyes to make sure he was still dozing off. I felt "weird" inside, like my abdomen area inside felt electric and anxious. I suddenly wanted to sit in his lap and have nothing to do with the boring lecture. I wanted to touch his jeans and see what his jeans felt like next to me, my hand perhaps? I couldn't sit in his lap, in a real way, we were in class of course. But I fantasized about what if we weren't in class. What if..........

I kept my head down and just brought my folded arms next to the edge of the table, which disguised the fact of what I am looking at, which was this guy's lap and thighs under the table. My lower stomach area inside me felt "weird." After the hours were up and we both stood up in class, I said to him, "Maybe you can come to another meeting that Smith-Diamond Realty holds." He looked down at me, his broad shoulders slumped forward slightly, his chiseled cheekbones, his face looked down at me as if I had something important to say to him. He made me feel woken up for a moment as I thought to myself, he reminds me of Morgan my father from the 1860's, another lifetime. His eyes looked a bit glassy, very blue like mine. He had silky dark hair, the kind that falls just right after being just toweled dried. I began to stumble over saying the words goodbye, "Talk to you later sometime," as my mind refocused. That man, he looks identical to my father Morgan in my past life. I felt a bit guilty for staring at his lap that afternoon. However, I thought about him secretly that night, I then began to wonder in a bizarre way if we had telepathy that afternoon, ESP? Germans often possess ESP, sonar, like how sharks signal each other under water, which is not obvious to other living creatures. Germans can radiate and transmit information. You would not know this unless you had a large amount of German DNA, or at least the unmistakable German sonar gene.

He looks so familiar, his name, I've heard his name before?

Within a week of meeting Patrick Goodale he began coming into Smith-Diamond Realty in Grandville, dressed in flannel shirts and jeans, just my type. He had the build of Alan in the days when Alan went to the gym, and often Alan would wear jeans and flannels as we hiked in northern Georgia. He looked like a sufficient enough replacement for Alan, even though he was not Jewish. I felt he was an easy compromise. I need a husband so I am not harassed in this town……. I thought. Instantly, without an ounce of hesitation of thought, he would do just fine to be my husband. I am twenty-eight, he is recently divorced, has too teenage boys. I would probably be looked at as the sexy stepmom, verses what I was in Jerry's family, the redheaded stepchild. I instantly felt grown-up and ready for marriage in his presence. Was it my age? Was it him? It did not matter I thought, but oh, am I ready……..

Pat would be an arm's length away, ten feet away, and I felt like I was going to tip over from some kind of climatic lava rush of a rare volcano inside me erupting. I felt dizzy. I told Carmen how I felt inside when Pat would stare at me, step into the same room as me. "I'd feel climatic, he would not even be touching me. I can see he is thinking the same thing, but I won't let him near me."

Carmen told me, "That's chemistry, Lori. Keep playing hard to get, guys like a girl who is hard to get."

I commented back to Carmen, "It's like we were astrologically hatched for one another. A real man, woman thing going on between us."

Somehow though I got this feeling I would be the educating teacher when it came to literature or philosophy, or writing a novel, or war, substantial debate or intellectual intrigue discussions of any kind with Pat. I don't believe he ever went to college or inspired to be anything outside of being known as wealthy Jack Goodale's son. He was kind of cute, and I did wonder in the back of my mind…….if I cooked dinner for him, would he allow me to serve him dinner while sitting on his lap? Feeding him? I remembered his lap, how his lap looked, how his lap appealed to me. Thoughts like that began to swirl in my young and exuberant mind, creep in almost. I realized he was having the same thoughts as me…..as we glanced at each other in the foyer of Smith-Diamond Realty, telepathy. I felt embarrassed. He looked both intrigued and mesmerized by me. Dave Smith walked in once and noticed too, Dave then made a loud cackling nervous joke. We did not laugh, or notice Dave. It made Dave mad, and made Dave speak louder to get noticed at that moment.

Patrick Goodale would often now stop in at the front desk these days. Sometimes I was in the real estate call answering area that had a big window, or standing next to Nancy by her desk. Pat would grin big, almost embarrassed at what he was thinking, perhaps he thought I could read his thoughts? He'd look at me as he entered the office as if he just finished fantasying about me in his truck and then decided to stop by the realty office to solidify his next day dream at 4pm tomorrow.....or 4am tonight, early morning? Like looking at me was some kind of lock and seal fantasy he was harboring for later on when he was finished putting in a day's work.

I was embarrassed at how he looked me up and down and simply just stared at me, taken back a bit I suppose at his forwardness in his eyes, verses trying to make conversation with me. No matter who was talking to him, he just stared at me, a target, his immediate target. Just trying to engulf what he saw before him, examining me during his many unexpected visits to the office now. After he left, Nancy would stand up and eye me up and down mimicking his expressions. Nancy commenting with a nervous laughter, "Pat has never been here so much in the last ten years as he has been in this office in the last three weeks combined." Then Nancy asked, "Do you think he is going to ask you out Lori?"

I responded, "I'm getting the feeling that cerebral interaction is not his core attraction at this point. I don't even know if he knows how to make or create educated conversations and stimulate my mind."

Scott walks in laughing, "I hear he does not want to stimulate your mind Lori!"

"What? What are you talking about?" I asked.

I was actually kind of taken back by Pat's stares, it made me feel nervous. Where at the restaurant I felt he seemed like a very in control kind of guy. Now Pat was making me nervous with how he gazed at me now. The pupils of his eyes radiated a red ray of light, he was either into the occult, or had a spell on him that was my first impression of his red eye syndrome when he stepped out of Dave Smith's office with one hand up in a gesture to wave at me. Something seemed amiss, as if he could not control his attraction to me, something, some power was inside his body. His eyes radiated red beams of light from his pupils, I told this to Carmen too. He was truly checking me out, zooming in, and seemed to have one thing on his mind verses asking me out. As if something he could not control within himself. The way Pat looked at me was starting to make me nervous. I remember once he came out of Dave Smith's office, raised his hand in a gesture to say "Hi" to me, and his stare scared me so much. I was so taken back by the intensity of his red stare I opened the first office door I could locate to the left by the fax machine and jumped behind the door to now escape his captivated stares. And again, his eyes radiated out a red beam of actual red light, and that was scaring me. Like I just turned on, sexually turned on some kinda monster, and he or it was not going away. I was his target, and there was not going to be any polite conversation, I could sense it.

Kyle shouted, "Get out!" Kyle was talking with two clients near his desk. "Get out Lori!"

I said, "I can't, I can't. Pat's out there. He's staring at me." I felt panicky now. My gut instinct lately was to run from Pat, and I could not explain why, or control wanting to run from this guy now. My hair on the back of my head would sweat when he was around me. I was embarrassed that every time Pat walked into the foyer, I just wanted to run as I felt sweaty and doomed in his presence. I could not logically explain why I suddenly felt this way now, or explain my fear rationally, that jump of a message inside me that was now saying, Run! Run!

I started rationalizing to myself while trying to overcome my fear instincts of him lately. If I date Patrick Goodale I will not get harassed by Dave Smith. I'll get my lot commissions, no withholding of what I am due from each closing. I might actually get respect around here. Chuck Helder and Dave Smith started in 1997 to withhold lot commissions from me, as a power kick over me, wanting a power kick over me? Dating Patrick Goodale would mean that I would be able to have my real estate career and not be harassed. It was all starting to look like a very logical solution to Dave Smith harassing me. A philosophical, politically correct career move. I would be raised up a notch in power status within this male dominated world of real estate new construction in west Michigan if Patrick Goodale and I date or marry. I guess I can just overcome my anxiety when Pat looked me up and down. I guess, I thought. Some woman might think that Patrick Goodale would be a ticket to no longer having to work or have a career, just have a life of ease. But actually I like creating my own wealth, I like having a career. I hate to sleep in, I like not being financially dependent upon a guy, I hate to ask for money. I just can't stand to be financially dependent upon a man for every dollar I spend. I am a big spender, money flows like water through my fingers, but so what if it's mine, who really cares, if I earn it, I can spend it, no argument to make. Pat would be my power card against those within my real estate world that wanted to control me. Dave Smith and Chuck Helder, Scott Chandler would all have to bow to me. There would be no power plays left over me if I dated Patrick Goodale, right?

I would have power, substantial power, and it appeared like I might be in for one of those steamy war escapades. I had a sneaky spurious feeling, I would be getting undressed be him. The tension was intense. It was like walking on a tight rope in a circus. Or like watching the weather change from sunny to stormy in his eyes, in his presence these days at work if he could not touch me, his very intended subject.

I thought Patrick Goodale was attractive, his voice seemed nice, very practical and calm are his manners for the most part, I liked that fact. His gazing right through me though, was making me nervous, I would sweat instantly now upon him entering the office as he gazed around the room to locate me, his target. It was as if he too was trying to focus on when he really had first met me too and I was trying to just recall when I first really just met him. His lap looked familiar, I had encountered him <u>before</u>, but where?

I have a photographic memory, if I meet a person once, I never forget a person. It is great in business.

Scott Chandler began making odd insidious comments to me, right in front of Nancy Vanden Berg the receptionist. Such as, "Do you think Patrick Goodale wants to rape you Lori? Is that why you keep running from him Lori? Maybe you should get a bb gun and keep it at the model house."

Nancy took offense to Scott's outburst, and she would comment, "Guy Scott, why do you say those things?"

I would respond to Scott's comments shaking my head, "Why would Pat rape me? Why would anyone rape me Scott?" I was just baffled at Scott making such bold and crude comments in the office too.

"That's creepy Scott." I said as I shuttered with my shoulders in a playful way, joking as I said, "Why would a wealthy, good looking guy like Pat rape me? It makes no sense Scott. Don't be stupid and say that."

Now days Scott would bite his lip and give me a serious warning look as if he knew something but was warned not to discuss the matters with me, warned by the brokers? I found Scott's comments odd, off the wall, I felt his comments had no real relevancy at all, really, to take seriously.

I thought Scott was shooting his young mouth off, maybe to make me feel uncomfortable because I had now basically taken over Superior and Galaxy Estate lot and new house sales, the plats. And everyone in the office was giving Scott a hard time, saying how I was showing him up and he was the veteran real estate agent. I was new and was really showing Scott up so to speak with my sales on the board in 1998. One power play was very true and evident by the men, I was <u>not</u> getting paid for all my sales. All the guys in the office such as Kurt and Kyle, even Dave Smith were now teasing Scott that a woman (me) was showing him up on the sales board. I love winning, I am very competitive. I won't jump in the water unless I call a race to the other side. But I do not roll the dice first, ever.

I do remember mentioning to Carmen about Patrick Goodale's eyes, "It's as if his eyes illuminated a red cast, a red ray from his pupils when he looked at me. Cigarette smoke from Dave Smith's office swirled and twirled through the smoke rising vertically through the red beams of red light coming horizontally several feet from Pat's red beam eyes towards me in the office hallway by Dave Smith's office. It scared me, I thought it was an unusual zoning in on me, it made me uncomfortable."

I wanted to make sense of things, and so I called upon that psychic Sharon one day, to confirm our reading, it would be the last. It had been about three weeks since I made the appointment with Sharon, placed her on my calendar. I was anxiously awaiting what she could or would predict, it was an exciting time in my life being twenty-eight and all.

Now Scott had warned me not to call upon Sharon, a psychic that read cards for Scott and others within that office. Scott stated in the office in front of Chuck Helder, that Patrick Goodale was gathering any and all information through a detective at The Fatman Detective agency on me, including having her locate proof I was in Playboy. Scott told me that the psychic Sharon was also a detective, I just did not know it. Scott Helder also explained that Sharon was CIA and that I was in over my head with moving back to Michigan from Georgia in what the CIA has planned for my life. Honestly why would I believe Scott? Why would a detective be sniffing around Smith-Diamond Realty anyway? Unless someone from my past sent her? But why? It just was not logical. It made no sense to me.

Scott blurts out in the office, "Lori, someone from your past wants Pat Goodale to rape you. You must have made enemies with someone."

"Patrick Goodale just met me, why would he pay any psychic or detective to locate information on me, if he can just ask me? Just call me and ask me! Or ask the information in person, through conversation with me." I remarked to Scott. It made no sense to me to heed Scott's warning. Why pay for information to learn of me, when you can ask for the same information from me? That was my rationale. I did not listen to Scott, or connect the dots at this young seedling point in time.

As winter turned into spring of 1998 I paged Sharon the psychic to confirm our appointment. I actually kind of had a serious crush on Patrick now, but I could not really explain why, but I did. Yet when Patrick arrived at the office, I was always running from him now and his stares which were making me nervous.

Chuck Helder mentioned he knew that I just wanted to jump Patrick's bones. That is an expression, to mean you are interested in a person's sex appeal only.

Chuck also reiterated what Scott had already told me, as he sits in his office, as I stood by his desk, Chuck says, "Patrick had his astrology chart read in relation to yours and he thinks you are going to take all his money, that's what the astrology chart shows. That's what he told me at least. Some lady by the name of Sharon, read his tarot cards too, he thinks you're gonna run off with all of his money." Chuck Helder smiles as he gives me that information.

"Sharon is always right, she has read our cards and astrology charts for quite some time now, she can graph and predict. She reads Dave's cards, she can hold a watch, clothing item, pen, and tell you all about yourself, or anyone you want to know about, she is amazing with accuracy." States Chuck Helder.

I responded, "I don't want his money. I want power so I don't get sexually harassed around here. Maybe I'll have clout and people will leave me alone and give me some respect for my hard work in putting up sales on the board, instead of constantly getting teased and harassed for being an ambitious woman around here bringing large commission checks in, the same as a man."

I walked away thinking quietly, in work, duty and career, I'll give a man a run for his money. In the bedroom, I actually like the man to have all the experience, knowledge and sexual control for the both of us.

Chuck Helder responded back to me like eyes of a wolf, "You better lock your doors, and watch your back. I think he thinks you're his type, but he's not going to marry and divorce again. Your astrology chart shows you take all his money, and he eats hand to mouth for the rest of his life. He's been watching you grow up since you were a wise cracking little girl, now you are in his domain. Have fun trying to get out of the spider web Lori."

"What? I'm not going to take anybody's money!" I stated firmly.

Chuck Helder said as Scott stood close by wanting to chime into the conversation, "Lori, he hired this Fatman Detective agency to locate some old Playboy books you were in. Is that true? Because if it is, he will dig it up, he will locate those magazines and store them at some ladies house near Ann Arbor." I ignored Scott's comments and Chuck Helders as they both now looked me up and down, truly wondering when I landed on planet earth in Grandville, Michigan, or worse, fell into some rabbit hole of the CIA's doing.

"I don't want his money, and I don't believe in divorce. I want to marry Mr. Right, that's why I am not married and divorced over and over, I've never been married before." I added, "If he calls maybe we'll hit it off."

Scott chimed in again, "I don't think it is conversation Lori that he wants to make, this Fatman Detective Agency told him you worked at The Gold Club. He thinks you're a whore or something, even if you're not, that Sharon tells people you are, people around here Lori. Steve Zinger pulled up your credit report for Patrick, as requested by Pat for confirmation that you have turned into a whore. Steve Zinger showed him what Pat's been wondering. The Gold Club is on your credit report Lori."

"I'm not a whore, I'm going to save myself for when I am married. I am hard to get, really. Ask anyone!" I said.

"How old are you?" Mr. Helder asked.

"I will be twenty-eight years old on February 28th." I said.

I paged the psychic Sharon that afternoon from the office. Sharon is a genuine psychic, and why would she go around telling people I am a whore? I hardly even know her! And if she dug up dirt on me, she would not locate a whore!

Sharon called me back on my cell phone and agreed to meet me at the model home in Wayland, 405 Discovery Drive. She drove a sporty red Ford Probe. I let her inside and asked if she wanted a diet coke or something to drink.

She stated "No...well, yes I'll take a diet Coke."

Sharon's hair was different, from color, to style, she gained a lot of weight too. She wore Levi jeans. She looked pale. Her nose and profile looked "Romanesque," which I loathe by the way. Cindy and her, I just noticed, look a lot alike. And then my mind jogs back to growing up, age eight, my mother Cindy's best friend……Kim Livermore. Sharon….is Kim Livermore….and is also Steve Kaplan's psychic…..is everybody's psychic. As I lead Sharon in, I say "Sharon" because that is the name she wants to go by…..I remember her now. The Gold Club. Steve Kaplan's office was up front, behind the shark fish tanks, behind the front desk where the men would pay their twenty dollar cover charge. Sharon….I saw her being escorted into Steve Kaplan's office in the 1990's. Weird. I am just going to keep my mouth shut. Why is she up here in rural Wayland, Michigan…. from New York? New Jersey? To Atlanta, Georgia? To Wayland, Michigan? It makes no sense. I am confused, because it just makes no sense.

"Would you like to have a seat? By the table?" I asked, inquired in a poised manner.

Oh, my God…..I lead Sharon in….I just stare at her for a moment…. not wanting to blow her cover of what Sharon is trying to pretend she is….. the psychic….. I keep my mouth shut, and play stupid, and a nice hostess. Ironically, I just so happened to be wearing a rainbow colored dress.

What is going on? What really is this all about? I wonder in silence.

Sharon pulled out a stack of tarot cards from her purse as she eyed me up and down. Sharon looked nervous about what she wanted to say and relay to me. Sharon gave me a sharp glance and a sharp glance around the walls as she shuffled the tarot card deck. As if hoping and praying I do not remember her from The Gold Club, or just now realizing that I recognize her as one of Cindy's many friends and associates. The cards were very worn, I knew she probably really did this for a living, as a cover. I never asked her last name, or asked to see her driver's license. I always felt it is rude to ask more than what a person is willing to tell you. I always let a person talk and what they are willing to give as information, well, that is all they want me to know. I also want nothing to do with her. Looking back with meeting with Sharron on a total of three times where she read my tarot cards three times, I should have asked more information about her. I learned later from Robin, a high school friend of mine that Sharon works as a detective for Fatman Detective Agency.

Apparently Sharon is both a detective, astrologer, and a psychic, that is now the third or fourth person who has told me that, but so what if she is both a psychic and a detective like everyone tells me, so what. Robin gave me confirmation on what Scott warned me about as well, that Patrick was collecting information on me through Sharon, but who cares. I have nothing to hide. Sharon looks so much like Cindy's friend Kim Livermore.

Sharon's eyes were very piercing, her pupils like tiny pins, she scared me a bit as I led her to my dining room at the model home in Wayland.

She had man hands, she was not overly feminine, and she looked like the lady who played the "mom" on the hit show, **Home Improvement, which ironically was filmed in Michigan**. Same build, similar face, medium brown hair or bleached hair now, slight perm. No make-up, no lip gloss or nail polish. However Sharon is not that lady from Home Improvement. She stared right through me, something was odd about this woman, as if the heavens were trying to also funnel, channel information, a warning to me, as I sat at the table with her at 405 Discovery Drive in Wayland.

Sharon began speaking fast, and then she began to speak in verses, as if in a rehearsed manic state prophecy. I found it amusing and odd at first. It was nothing like a card reading in the past from her. She seemed a bit manic as she proceeded, obsessed in her glare at me, then the cards. I felt uncomfortable with her mannerisms, her speech within ten minutes of the cards being spread on the table by her. Sharon noticed I felt uncomfortable. I was trying to conceal my knowledge that I know who she is and the people she knows as well.

"Sharon, I noticed that you are not looking at the tarot cards as you give me this reading? Why are you just looking at me, and not the cards? How can you predict the future that way?" I diligently inquired.

Sharon looked at me in a serious and sober expression, "I don't have to look at the cards to tell you what is going to happen in your future, the American CIA told me what to say to you."

"What?" I asked.

Sharon responded, "John Brennan."

Sharon preceded to tell me about a multitude of rapes that would be occurring to me in the wee hours of the morning here at the model house. She warned me I was going to be drugged, raped, and some of the assailants would be F.B.I. agents that saw me at The Gold Club, that know how to get away with this kind of thing. She warned me that a brick or stone would be used to bash in my face and scare me from talking. "Undoubtedly, the same way your nose was injured in California. And in Georgia when your mother Cindy moved in with you for a year. There is a man and woman in business to make a lot of money off you. They are selling you on paper to foreigners by U.S. government employees. I see a male wearing a purple turbine. The couple is involved with the cement business or cement projects in the area. Somewhere close to Wayland."

"Why?" I asked. She ignores my question, flips more cards over, and rambles on with the weirdest predictions. Eerie. She predicted at my table in Wayland, in 1998 that Steve Kaplan was going to jail for two to five years for tax evasion in the future. But why tell me that? How does that relate to me? It really made no sense, why was Steve Kaplan's never wrong psychic sitting at my table? In rural Wayland, Michigan? Why is she going around Grandville giving members of Smith-Diamond Realty psychic readings? I just cannot connect why. Someone step forward after reading this book and explain this all to me! Please!!! She went on to say that Steve Kaplan has VIP videos and is going to make a ton of money from them, black mailing people.

Most of all, I just did not believe her predictions, any of what she said to me in "that hour of terror" tarot card reading. The predictions were too far out, really strange odd predictions that made no sense, not to me at least, not at that moment, that afternoon. I felt offended. I did not believe her. I rationalized silently as I mentally digested what she was saying at my table. I thought someone just wants me out of real estate, out of these two lucrative new construction plats and sent Sharon to freak me out, scare me into moving out of the plats and from the model house where I lived rent free.

She also predicted I would have two lines, two wrinkles forming on my forehead, "The rapist is like a man from the Middle East with many woman in his life, although, he is white, dark hair. You sat in his lap at

The Gold Club…..black hair against spiced praline….is his favorite. He leaves his snowmobile ski mask at the front door, he wants you to see him, but not remember everything about the rapes." Sharon looks right through me. I am now pale as a ghost. "He is connected to Hollywood. I see pink candles being burned, this has to do with a spell that you did in Georgia. I also see a black woman and jars of water from the civil war era, she took care of you back then. I see into the windows of the past, present, and future. I see you being sacrificed on a bed. You are being sacrificed, and this dark haired man, is named Patrick. Patrick is going to teach you a lesson you will never forget about loyalty, this is about the past. This dark haired man has arrived at a conclusion that he will sacrifice you in this manner, it's very sexual what he does to you. It's as if your body is a temple, and he goes to church twice, although he enters through two distinct doors." Sharon spoke in odd phrases, odd analogies. I have not written in this book all of what she predicted, it was so far out, strange really. Very scary.

Sharon is also a big, big threat to national American security based on what she said to me of future warnings that afternoon in 1998. But I did not believe her, it was too weird. Just too far out. Not believable. Not rational. Sharon also mentioned in 1998, "When the airplanes crash into the buildings in New York, you will understand just how psychic I am."

"What?" I've never even been to New York, what is this lady saying? All of which in 1998 made absolutely no sense, none. I did not believe it.

I just could not possibly fathom all she was saying and predicting, or had rehearsed prior, to then be a messenger at the table at that model home at 405 Discovery Drive at that time, until the future events began to occur. She even went on to predict that a decade or so later, I would write a best seller book, and that many, many movies and television mini-series would be created from my literary success. Musicians. The songs. The dedications. The foundations. Everything. But why? I make over $100,000 a year in real estate, why change anything? I thought. It just did not go with my plan of a normal life. Everything was better than ever in my life, why would I want to end my real estate career as Sharon had predicted I would.

What are my thoughts? What do I say to at this moment to Sharon? "I've lost my interest in writing, I like real estate, I want to just stay in real estate and give up writing. I like putting deals together, negotiating on behalf of a client. I have found my niche, I am really good at listing and selling real estate, working with buyers and sellers. My life is normal. I like my normal career. I am making really good money, even with Smith-Diamond Realty withholding back some commission checks that I have rightfully earned. I would have to disagree again with you about my future." I wholeheartedly was offended and argued in 1998 with her predictions as I sat across from Sharon, just shaking my head at every new and weird revelation she had to say to me. It was too far out and strange to be believed. I thought, this is Wayland, Michigan for God's sake Sharon, how could all that stuff possible happen.

I responded positively, "Sharon, I believe we navigate our own lives."

"Your life is not going to end in the manner you believe, such as old age, I am here to tell you, you are getting raped, more than once, drugged and raped in this very house and soon. Your life is not going to be what you have planned, your life is framed. Your life is not normal. This is astrological, you have been warned!" Sharon said firmly and seriously as I just shook my head in complete disbelief at anymore tarot card horror that could possibly be bestowed upon me in the future at my table in 1998. "The system is going to let you down, you need to pay heed to what I am saying Lori!"

I thought Patrick certainly did not look like a rapist! Why would a man like him rape? It did not make logical sense, no matter how uncomfortable his stares grew towards me, I honestly did not believe he was a rapist. He was a good looking guy, with family money, why would he rape? Risk going to jail?

Pat does not need to rape to get sex, I disagreed with Sharon wholeheartedly. You could have sent ten messengers to warn me, I never would have believed one of them. Patrick just did not look like a rapist of the worst kind, and absolutely did not fit into a criminal profile of a rapist, why a man rapes. I just 100% did not believe Sharon. I thought she and Diane Marie, were just playing some mind trip game, saying things to scare me, or scaring me to move out of a new construction plat, in the heart of my real estate success. I 100% thought, those two are jealous and are trying to scare me out of my success and position in real estate, jealous types conniving together. I just was not going to be scared, bullied out of my real estate career and move and locate a different career.

Sharon proceeds by saying, "The man that reaches for your chest area, places his hands on you first before Patrick, while you are feeling drugged, is the one who set up your rapes. There is talk, serious talk and planning, you need to get out of this house! I do not think you are going to make it out alive…….I think you are brought to the hospital to get revived. I see an ambulance."

"What?" I said in disgust now.

Then Sharon got mad.

"Patrick reads your journals, when you are away selling real estate, he comes in here. You are going to write a best seller novel, that's what he tells me, and he wants to be your leading man, Alan. Patrick has his own way that he wants to enter into your mind subconsciously, he wants to be part of your future. I am just the oracle. I see a series of books and movies in your future, and he wants to be your leading man."

I respond in complete disbelief, "What? You are making no sense. I am a real estate agent, I make good money. Why would I just quit real estate because you are trying to scare and bully me away from this area, why, what is the real reason?"

Sharon went onto to say a whole load of information. I just was wondering about a dark haired man, Patrick, and if it was in the cards that we would date, was he the one, Mr. Right? Mr. Normal to make my life more normal? That was the purpose of me calling Sharon for what seemed like just pure curiosity of me about Patrick Goodale and my future, after all, I am twenty-eight and still single.

She then states, as I was just thinking about Patrick, curious about the possibilities of him and I, Sharon looks up at me with evil eyes and says to me, "Curiosity kills the cat."

Sharon was creeping me out, really. I thought she looked almost possessed during her tarot card reading to me, and was also trying to freak me out, scaring me. I thought she was a nutcase. I just wanted her to leave 405 Discovery Drive.

Sharon went on to say, "Well, here is the dark haired king card, he is upright, but he will make a mistake, he will color inside the lines." This tarot card reading was like no other she had given me, she acted manic, erratic, she talked fast, and was full of predictions, just one after another. She stated, "Hollywood is going to come to west Michigan and make a documentary of your life, many movies are going to be made of your life, many songs, which has to do with past lives and what you come forward and tell and write."

"What?" I said. "What are you saying to me?" I asked totally bewildered.

Sharon went on and on, "You are going to get raped, it will be brutal, and he stays in you, and his friend that stands next to him, he will intimidate you until you quit real estate all together, you will be banished from west Michigan by the year 2000. This is about his revenge from 2000 years ago. This is about loyalty."

I gasped in horror. I was getting scared now. "My life is normal. I like it that way." I said to Sharon.

Sharon spoke further, "I see your face is bloody after the rape, he will sodomize you, and you won't know what the hell happened to you because he drugs you. Or what hit you, you'll go crazy from the fear. You will be out of it, drugged and beaten, and they will get away with murder. They will feed you too much of the drugs through your arm. Although at first you will breathe in a substance to knock you out before he begins. He knows of Octavia, and this man is Marc Antony that will brutally rape you, you both have unfinished business, residue from a past life, a war lost, he raped you 2000 years ago too, in the desert before the Roman guards took you to Octavia. Marc Antony is jealous and wants to get to your subconscious mind in this lifetime and destroy you, push you over the edge…….there is a war, now, in this lifetime, he wants to be Alan."

"Why?" I said seriously.

"Because of all the men." Stated Sharron point blank, matter of fact.

"Men? I am not a whore." I insisted.

"You look like a whore. You are going to become a very famous whore in the eyes of General David Petraeus." Sharon stated in a cold tone of voice in that model home in 1998 in rural Wayland, Michigan.

"What?" I asked.

"The story, your novel you have been working on, he wants you to write that story about you and him. He wants to leap off the pages and become your famous teacher, 'Alan,' but first he needs to get to you……"

Sharon paused, then looked around the room before continuing her tarot card reading. She suddenly appeared a tinge bit frightful of any possible hidden camera lens recording video and such.

"He is going to break into here through your front door, or back slider. He will inevitably cause a lot of emotional and mental problems as you enter a post-traumatic stress period from the rapes in about two years. The police will treat this whole rape incident as if a flying saucer landed in your backyard, ridiculous as ordered by the CIA. The Central Intelligence Agency will be in touch with the local police before the rape even takes place. His intention may not be what you want, but in the end you come together and write a story, the love story is sad on many levels, but he astrologically does not care about your feelings, he just is not able to, he is very objectionable. The cops, the Judge, any attorney you call, and the prosecutors will think you are crazy and will insist that you say you made up the whole story. Treating you no different than as if an alien lands in your backyard and rapes you! But more so than that, you will realize which family owns this town. It will be a brutal lesson, but I am warning you stay away from the cops, it will only get worse if you push for DNA evidence testing. If you try and testify, it will not be in your favor. I am warning you now, lock your doors, move out, move away to not experience what he is planning with the CIA, FBI and local cops. I see him paying off detectives, some guy named David. The police, the prosecution. I am here to warn you and you need to listen to me. He will enter this house when you least expect to see him and it will happen more than once in the evenings, early mornings after he has partied, he has many connections to get away with what he does."

"What? I do not believe you!" I stated firmly.

"You are not his first victim, and you will not be his last. He does take a liking to what he will do to you, like you become his addiction. He can get whatever kind of drug substance he wants from the hospital and from a Kent and Denise Smith of Wyoming, or some Kent company? This Patrick guy poses as the son of a wealthy man, and during the day he strategizes which town he will visit next. He will call you a whore to the police, his lawyers will call you a whore, and convince the police you are a crazy slut. And you will know him as a past husband of sorts, you had a past together. He knows inside you have the soul of Cleopatra, and your last meeting in the desert did not end well. He found out about an affair, an illegitimate son you bore 2000 years ago, and that younger son was not his child, and the contract you signed in Rome. This is about the past, left over residue between Octavia and Marc Antony, and a war that went wrong, a war in which you will again lose everything." Sharon stated with such seriousness.

I just gasped.

"I don't want to be Cleopatra. I do not like that life. I lost everything in that lifetime, everything I believed in, I went to war over, I lost." I exclaimed.

Sharon looked at me as she shook her head and said, "Ever since you were a little girl you would tell your father about these dreams on a chariot, about a kingdom you ruled over, and the strategies you had to win more land. Your father told a friend of the family."

Sharon grabbed the back of her hair and said this startling true fact, "When you think you are losing, in your dreams, that battle from 2000 years ago, your hair feels hot, damp, sticky as you travel back to the city, you have lost all that is dear to you."

I gasped at her.

"When you think you've lost the war your hair gets hot and sweaty, as if you are riding back to a city on a chariot in defeat, all sweaty, you lost everything, you will lose everything again in this lifetime, history will repeat itself and soon." Sharon kept repeating herself as she stared right through me.

I gasped, but said nothing. I stared at Sharon like she was some kind of mind trip.

"You'll be lucky to make it out alive, he wants you dead, he is like an assassin to your astrological chart, he needs you dead because you will open your eyes and regain some consciousness during one of the first rapes. You will remember too much, you recall and see too much he fears and he will plot against your life after that because of who you are able to recognize in the bedroom. The FBI can get into hospitals and they will, the FBI are solders in his personal war against you in this lifetime. When you bear your first child, a son, a husband from a previous lifetime will send the CIA to be in the room to see to it that you get stabbed with a knife when you least expect it during natural labor. He will see to it the doctor gets paid to make you bleed and suffer with an unnecessary episiotomy. Begging for your life. Do you understand? He wants to lay you down in green pastures. Do you understand?

He will rape you hear at 405 Discovery Drive and then he will develop a war campaign against you. You will want you the rape victim destroyed. He will taunt you by saying spiteful things to a dark haired real estate agent, about his age, a female. She will relay that information to you in their attempts together to emotionally push you over the edge, trying to get you to commit suicide for remembering too much………He will rape you more than once here in his attempts to get you to commit suicide. You'll be out of it by the drugs he puts into your system, on more than one occasion you will be sedated each time. You really should leave." Stated Sharon. Then Sharon pulled out a card that had a lion and a naked girl on the back of the lion. "This is the Aleister Crowley ninth card, The Lust Card."

I looked closely at the card…….

Sharon held the card up and said, "This is you, this is him. He knows your dreams. Your first time Lori."

I gasped, my eyes wide, this woman was a mind trip.

Sharon stated that in December of 1998 I was going to have a leg or ankle injury involving a fall off a horse, due to a magazine. Bizarre prediction, and reason. Sharon grabbed her ankle as she looked down to the cards and spoke of that prediction. She also stated she saw me moving out of the model house eventually, but I would still be in danger. "Patrick, known here as the dark haired king, he's going to stalk you, after he rapes you and gets away with murder, well, it's like murder."

My heart is racing, this woman is a freak, she is a stalker to dig up my birth certificate. I thought to myself quietly. But why? She told me, or gave me the strangest tarot card reading I have ever had in my life, ever. She was a mind trip.

"I see dead people…..a cemetery…..a statue of a lion and a lamb……." Sharon stated.

"What? You see dead people in a cemetery?" I asked just flabbergasted. This lady is weird, I thought, really far out. I looked away just wondering how can I politely ask her to leave, I wondered quietly.

Sharon read my thoughts as I turned away from the table, my table. "You need to pay attention!" A voice within Sharon exclaims as Sharon pounds her hand on my table, "You need to get out of this house."

I sighed.

Sharon went on to say, "Patrick wants to pour cement down your throat, that is his intention, he wants you dead, in the grave. He is an assassin who will leave his mask at the door, he thinks about keeping it on, but doesn't. I see you in a cemetery. You may survive the mental, emotional and physical torture, maybe. But parts of you do not survive, parts of your soul Lori. But most people would not be able to endure such hardships. It's as if you write from the grave, your novel. He knows from researching you through our firm that you have had a tragic life. He feels that he can get you over the edge with just a little more pushing, and into that grave. Cindy your mother is going to help him."

"What?" I gasped. I stopped Sharon there. I just want to hear normal things. Normal predictions. I am angry at what she is saying to me at my table, offended. But before I can tell her to stop talking. She continues, Sharon is not letting up on information. Such information I don't even care to hear anymore. It was all so scary.

Sharon went on to say, "I see a cemetery, I see your gravesite. Your best friend in Hudsonville has put a spell on you, a voodoo curse from a past life, some know her as the Virgin Mary. Patrick will think you are the virgin. But when he touches you, your skin, he realizes you are in fact Cleopatra, and he has made serious mistakes in the past, his past. But he cannot turn back time and undo history with what he has done with his decisions."

I responded, "Why would a man like Patrick Goodale rape me? It makes no sense, why not just ask me out? Why come into my house unannounced? Why rape me?

Sharon answered, "This is not all entirely about rape, it is about pushing you over the edge in life. Raping you was his idea, how to get you over the edge in life. Your life is framed by many, and I am here to tell you that fact. God framed your life before you were ever born on earth."

Sharon was really scaring me. Well maybe that is just her intention. I just need to ask her to leave.

"Please just leave." I asked politely.

Sharon continues, "Your life is not going to turn out like you have hoped for, your astrological frame. Patrick is just that, you change religion together, you're part of a movement that started before this lifetime. You are not aware of the movement here on earth, of the meetings that go on behind your back. There are people who have been following you since you were a baby. Patrick was brought on board years ago, to the group, you met at The Gold Club. Don't you remember? You wore a black bustier, black tights, you sat in his lap, and he gave you a big surprise, a really big surprise, his lawyer was in the room and blamed you. Then you abruptly left the room, he was mad, is mad that you left the VIP room. He has intentions to teach you, beyond what you can see, he hides his motives from the police. If you go to the police after the rape, guaranteed the police of Wayland will treat the rape as if a green alien landed in your backyard and walked through the back slider door. As if this is Roswell with what the CIA have already ordered done to the future rape and assault case."

I gasped and asked Sharon again to leave at this point. I never saw her after that meeting. I did page her later, I had questions to ask her. But weeks later her pager was disconnected, which was the only way I knew how to get a hold of her, by the only number she gave me. I called the agency she free-lances for, Fatman Detective Agency. The owner answered and said he never heard of a "Sharon." I got the impression she did not want to be located. Fatman Detective Agency would forever protect her identity, the male owner more or less just acted like he did not know of her and I was crazy for asking for Sharon.

Inside I really just wanted to wipe away the very awful things she said and predicted would happen, it sounded like a horror story really. I totally did not see that coming, the ending. I thought my life was normal now. I have a normal career now, I live in a small rural country town, Wayland, Michigan.

I remember the last thing Sharon said to me as she exited my residence, the model house marketed by the company I worked for, Smith-Diamond Realty, the real estate model house in Galaxy Estates, "The next time you see me, my eyes will look different."

Sharon shook the interior of my house's front door knob, shook the door knob as she spoke her last warning, "Make sure to lock your doors." She smiled.

I followed her outside, said "Goodbye." I remember Sharon drove a 1990's red two door Ford Probe. That was the last I saw of her in person. I was glad she left.

And then a sequence of events began happening in my life……..

Paper Dolls
CHAPTER THIRTEEN

Within maybe weeks of that psychic meeting, "terror tarot card reading," whatever total nonsense that Sharon spoke of an her urgent, yet very non-persuasive argument of sorts, urging me to move out of 405 Discovery Drive. Strange warnings by tarot cards and she feared I was going to get raped by Patrick, I was raped by him.

I wake up, I am startled and waking up as I feel as if I am going into surgery or waking up from surgery. I was experiencing that kind of lethargic feeling one has as they wake up from surgery. It is beyond evening, it is sometime in the middle of the night, I was fast asleep. I see my body is being touched in a sexual way, caressing, fondling. I am being dragged to the center of my bed by a dark haired man who is already fully nude…… it looks like Patrick as my eyes focus, I cannot believe it. He had my body in the center of my bed, a pillow he is placing under the area he is concentrating on, adjusting the pillow underneath my bottom. As he rests on his knees alongside the pillow, he is fully nude. His glassed over gaze is looking down to my body as he is positioning me in the center of my bed at the Galaxy Estates model home, my residence. He bends my knees and tucks my calves of my lower legs under my thighs. He begins a series of ointments, applying ointments, "preparing the petals."

His chest is kind of bare, no chest hair, he works out, he is really kind of attractive, he has dark brown hair almost blackish it looks. His eyes are blue, watery, as if glassed over. I remember that feature of his eyes as I look upwards, unable to move, get out of bed. His shoulders are well formed, muscular. His face looks concerned for me, he is in no rush or sense of panic at what he is doing to me. He just keeps rubbing and kneading the pink frosting area on either side of what he has opened, what is open before him. He has a stern look, an expression of concern as he looks up from "preparing the petals." He is seconds from sexually entering my body fully. He is fully aroused, he continues with spreading and layering ointments on me that he brought with him. He positions himself with using one hand, he keeps raising my conscious points of sensations. He looks into my eyes, I feel I am waking up from a drug and having an orgasm all at the same time. I try desperately to reach for my consciousness to fully understand this moment as it is occurring. My eyes focus, we connect in eyesight just as he moves forward into me full force, I have an orgasm. The kind of orgasm that Alan would deliver unto me as he would often do upon entering me. I think Patrick read my journals under the sofa? Why was he obsessed with my story, my novel, my manuscript? Just as Sharon predicted. I am dumbfounded. I just cannot believe it.

Patrick is staring down to me while holding his position inside of me as he rests on his knees and my bent legs. He remains in me, he stops for just a moment, wondering why I am not totally knocked out by the drugs? His expression is of an inquisitive concerned look worn on his face, bewilderment, a tangle of confusion. I have a pillow under my derriere, he has my legs spread and my knees bent and my calves folded under. As if I can kick? So I do not kick? I can hardly move from the drug given to me from a substance brushed over my nose from a wash cloth. I can hardly comprehend this moment. I do not understand why he is in my bedroom. I cannot even fathom why. Why this? Why does he want to do this to me? I just can't move, I can't talk, I'm immobile, that's how it feels. I don't understand. It was rape. I never invited him over. He drugged me and had sex with me. It's rape. I am completely in shock, and about to go further into a deeper state of the drug induced that he administered on me…….

I feel dazed and frozen in place almost. My long white Victoria Secrets nightgown is pushed over my chest and gathered at my neck line, my body is nude. I cannot pull my nightgown down, I cannot stop him. He has no condom on himself, I am not on birth control. Nor am I active sexually. I am twenty-eight years old. Chuck Helder is to the right of me, standing, watching Patrick have sex with me. And then Chuck Helder comments, "She looks like a virgin."

Patrick then pulls outward, almost all the way. Meanwhile I feel totally dazed and sick and immobile. Patrick fiercely and sternly is applying all kinds of ointments again on my private parts and then reaches upward, now circling my nipples with ointments. Why? Why is he circling my nipples with Vaseline? Why is all of this happening to me? And why did Sharon not stop him raping me? I am locked in my own body, unable to talk, to speak my thoughts out loud.

Patrick leans over and whispers, "In the future, you will understand the scars, Sharon wanted me to relay that to you." As he applies ointments on my nipples, I look to the side and notice Chuck Helder standing between the bed and a dresser where a yellow bulb light is on. Chuck Helder the broker/accountant of Smith-Diamond Realty is standing to the right of me as Chuck Helder reaches down to touch my chest. The dark haired Patrick having sex with me pushes away Chuck Helder's arms and hand reaching upon me. Chuck Helder remains quiet as if holding his breath and intently observing the scene before him. I look downward now too, still resting on my back unable to move, sit up. Patrick begins "preparing the petals and the bud" more and more, not letting up on the pleasure, yet I am drugged, unable to move. He looks up to my face, our eyes lock for a moment, he re-enters again half-way, it feels like more than what I can handle, he is stopping half way again. My body remains on the bed, and it is as if my soul is rising upward to the corner of the ceiling as I leave my body. The drugs begin to take on a deeper level, at first I felt frozen and only could absorb what was going on around me, see, but not able to move. Now, I feel totally powerless as my body transcends upward, I am leaving my body, having an out of body experience. Everything is going blank, and I am leaving that scene in the bedroom. Simply blank in memories for a moment, or hours, I do not know what happens next to me, I am unconscious.

In the beginning, from all I could recall of this incident, it was as if Patrick and Alan, well, read from the same manual on how to make love to a woman, as my body tries to regain consciousness, but cannot. It just goes blank in my world again, blank, not heaven or hell, just blank for a while, a blank slate. My mind would flash to bits and pieces of the rape event, and that is probably his intentions, Pat's intention for me to not remember a full story to tell in a police report. I would sound crazy of not sound mind if I cannot recall all the events and sequences of the rape. I am now just as he planned, a non-credible witness, to my own rape. The evolution of lust gone mad. Why? Why did he rape me? Control? Hate? I don't know. That is a big mystery, the motivation of him?

I am not sure if hours pass, or minutes, or it is a new scene, a new night…

He then holds that position inside of me as I glance down to my body, and takes a pink wash cloth and brushes the dry washcloth over my face for about five minutes. It smelled like furniture stain remover on the pink cloth. I am starting to fade out of consciousness now and again, and begin to rise upward again and I don't know what happens next. I can feel my body slightly, as if I am being totally entered now, in a tight and painful way. But I am feeling as if I am going totally unconscious. I can't feel all the pain, it is a bit numb, almost instantaneously as he had rubbed a wash cloth under my nose again for me to breathe in, I just can't feel anymore. Yet before he entered me a second or third time, he made sure I was aroused as he pushed inward, causing a sexual climax that I could not stop. I began to wonder too if he was on drugs, a different kind of drug than the sedation drug he was giving me during this catastrophe at age twenty-eight. Or could not stop what he was doing to my body because he was on drugs?

I recalled seeing a shadowy female figure moving around my bathroom attached to the bedroom, close to where I was desperately trying to fight the sedation. I remember brief, fleeting scenes only. The commotion within the room, then it all goes blank.

Then bits and pieces of my rape scene remerge…….like a slide show of horror stuck forever in my brain...for many years to come. I recall later it was more than just one rape at 405 Discovery Drive in Wayland, Michigan.

The next scene I can remember; Patrick then begins to inflicted pain after the pleasure, especially on my arms. All of which I am not able to control or fight back. I remember only bits and pieces of that sequence of events of that evening like a puzzle scattered in my mind's memories. It was like being in the hospital, unable to move and he is some kind of sexual doctor and sadist all at once. I know he sodomized me, maybe even more than once at 405 Discovery Drive. I have no idea if I was raped by other men that night, or any night for that matter. Only perhaps "Sharon" and Patrick Goodale and Chuck Helder would know. It hurt to go to the bathroom for at least a week after that rape. My tender pink inner lips were cut, bleeding, not from a period, but from tissue cut skin inside me, but I do not know how he cut me? I don't remember. And that's the sad part of this ordeal, I would sound stupid if I went to the police with only bits and pieces of remembering what occurred to me. It was as if that was his perfect storm, his agenda, but why? I just don't understand.

When I woke up one morning it was sometime between 6am and 7am, the morning light of the new day was filtering through my bedroom window at the model home at 405 Discovery Drive. My sheets were in disarray. My white nightgown was still pushed up over my chest. I looked up, and to the slight right of me by the door frame there he was, Patrick leaning against my bedroom door frame, his arms folded. He appeared calm, focused, sober, he looked full of regrets, but would not speak as our eyes locked. I have no idea how many times he raped me. Or who all raped me that night, or any night at the model home. I desired a normal life. I did not want to think anything was a set up and not normal within my life. I glanced downward. I had something written in my pink lipstick color, on my chest, between my cleavage. I felt groggy as I proceeded to get up out of bed. Patrick unfolded his arms in slow motion and hiked out, ran out, before I was even able to slowly stand up and look around the room, my house, the phone cord was unattached. I reattached it. I had no intentions of calling 9-1-1. Or even calling a rape crisis hotline. Hell no, not after I had been examined with scopes in such at a hospital in Riverside, California. Never again. The numbers 666 were written on my chest cleavage area with pink lipstick, my pick lipstick, but I did not write those numbers.

My crisis in 1998, I knew I would eventually get over what happened. But I did not want to create a more uncomfortable situation, or a more painful situation for myself. I was in total shock. To this day, as I write about this, I have no idea how many times I was raped at 405 Discovery Drive in Wayland, Michigan. Why did Patrick rape me to have sex? Did he think I would say no to sex? I just don't even slightly know why, and why he took Chuck Helder to watch? I literally have more questions, than answers. So I suppose when I die for a second time I will have to bring that question and all my many unanswered questions up to God. Asking God, "Why again was I raped, so brutally by Patrick, who honestly is Marc Antony, the real Marc Antony?"

I stared at myself in the mirror the next morning. As I opened my mouth I took a toothbrush and scraped blood off the top of the back of my mouth and throat the next morning. The left side of my nose was painful to the touch, very swollen, but no bruises on my nose. I could not blow my nose, too painful. I had three red pin marks on my inner left arm, with bruising rings, many finger print bruise marks on my both upper arms, the middle of my arms. Which made no sense, because I did not remember struggling. I was out of it. And what I do remember, I was immobile. I could not move hardly, because of the drugs administered to me. I do not know if they or he put bruise marks on my arm to mess with my head? It was very mentally scary, an uneasy feeling that my world was contained in what I thought was a safe neighborhood, model house, in the rural country farmland of Wayland, Michigan. I always lock my doors and basement windows. I could not make sense of this. I just couldn't. Oh, the real estate lock box attached to the front door!

The last thing about that night or early this morning, what I can remember last, is Pat is standing in the doorway looking into my bedroom as my lifeless body remains still. The time is near dawn, about 6am? 7am? His arms were folded as he stands in the doorway of my master bedroom as he leans against the hallway doorway. As I regain consciousness, or wake- up, open my eyes, what have you, he unfolds his arms slowly and walks out. The back slider is left open as I try and catch up five minutes later, to figure out what is going on.

I go back to my bedroom now, just dumbfounded at last nights unexpected events. I did not make that wet spot nor do I know what or who caused that wet spot on the carpet floor near my bed and night stand. My sheets in a disarray. A huge wet patch by the bed floor, by the night stand. And a now soaking wet pink wash cloth next to that wet spot. I am in shock. It is a very surreal scene in my house. And I think the best thing is to just hope and pray I get my period on time, and this will all just go away, just as quickly as I possibly can forget this ever happened. As rational as that sounds, what I was very unaware of, is the extreme shock of the rapes. What my mind absorbed subconsciously, unconsciously, would cause me later, in about a year or so, to begin to just spiral out of control. Not intentionally wanting to spiral out of control, not a choice, but in a very unrehearsed way, my mind would spit out fragments of trying to cope with what he took from me. Number one, mental security, stability, feeling safe, would be mental ingredients to replenish. Very, very important. But at this young and surreal infant stage of trying to cope and be wise, I had no idea about the trauma in the headlights that would stare me down. As much as I wanted to stop, squelch the breaks in defense, my mind would crash right into that deer about the year 2000 as I have a mental breakdown suffering from Post-Traumatic Stress Syndrome.

And when I tell you of what happens in the Allegan hospital in December 2000, you won't even believe me. You won't. If it did not happen to me, to personally experience, I just would not believe it, ever.

When he walked out of Galaxy Estates, he took with him my sense of safety for years to come. My sense of peace, my sense of optimism that I am safe in the model home or any home for that matter. The rapes were more damaging to the lasting effects of my sense of safety, sanity, just stripped away. For years to come when I would enter my home after work I would have panic attacks that logic could not dispel. I began slipping into a state of confusion, that thin line between sane and not knowing if I am safe. I now would feel an overwhelming emotion of traumatic shock, more so than anger. I can honestly say, anger was not until later. For now I am in complete traumatic shock, panic-stricken almost. I shake, and I don't know why I am shaking. I don't want to feel panicky, but it was not an emotion I could control, and that made me mad. The rape sunk into that vast space called my unconsciousness, a lost file for now in 1998.

I really had felt when I met him, or shortly thereafter at Jerry's Country Inn Restaurant in January 1998, I really just loved him. I was bewildered why he would do this to me. Just bewildered and scared and wanting answers. My mind also flips back to The Gold Club, and a VIP room….. and Melanie Smith…..it was all clicking in place, but a horror. Patrick Goodale and that Rick Bolhouse, now I remember when we first met as adults……..1996 in Atlanta, Georgia. I felt creeped out and scared, he doesn't look like a criminal who does these kinds of things to women. He, Patrick, I've known since I was five, from the parties on 2nd street in Caledonia, Michigan.

In this next phase of my life, I then began sleeping on the sofa with one eye open as I would now leave the television on to remind me that I am not alone. I would try not to fully fall asleep, because I was afraid to sleep, for fear I would be drugged and raped and sodomized. This fear went on in the preceding days, weeks and years, and rightly so. Like a rare portrait, so would begin the next chapter of my life on this paper canvas reveal. Burrrr. It seemed so unfair that he did that to me, it disturbed my sleep patterns. I was afraid all the time. My sense that everything is going to be o.k. in my life, in my real estate career, gone, vanished. The feeling I had now was that of shock, dismay, I just could not believe he took so much from inside, my sense of safety stripped away inside, mentally just gone. I remained frozen in panic for years to come. I thought Patrick went to church, was a good person, a normal guy. I was fearful to talk about what happened, because I was made to be made fearful of them, Patrick Goodale and Chuck Helder saw to it that I was made to fear them and I did.

Within the same week of being raped in 1998, the next time I was in Grandville getting my work mail from the company slot boxes at Smith-Diamond Realty, Scott comments, "Having any bad dreams about Chuck and Pat lately Lori?" Scott smirks as I painstakingly do not have a comment or an expression. Scott Chandler goes on to say, "Maybe you should get a bb gun.......you know that you have a tin of kerosene under your sink." He winked, and walked away from the fax machine room. I realized I was not in charge of my own existence, my own life, these monster Christians all around me dealt the cards.

I was horrified at the rapes, and now have to deal with taunting from several office staff of sales agents. Scott went on to describe what I looked like during the rapes. He said the room was not as empty as I thought, or perceived the room to be just Pat in the room. But Scott went to church, and so does Chuck Helder, and Kurt, and Kyle, and Joel. What seemed like a prank to joke about, was my real reality, my reality of horrors, shaking inside at my fear of Christians now more than ever. The more they talked, the more they joked and taunted me over the rapes, it was like a plate of reality being shoved in my face. I did not want to take another spoonful of the dreaded reality of what I endured from Smith-Diamond Realty. I longed to just be wrapped up in my comforter and this time buried somewhere in a comfortable place, just wrapped up in my comforter.

My mind, my emotions, felt like I had been placed in a jar and shook up by monster Christians as I could visibly see my emotions in that jar but could not put my life and emotions back inside me. If I screamed to stop, no one would stop. That is what I can best describe my fragile mental state of trying to just hold on to my real estate career that I had worked so hard for, just to remain strong for myself, within my place in residential new construction, within this community of west Michigan.

I thought I might just vomit up emotionally, vomit up psychologically, and lose my place, my place I had worked so hard for, and needed to keep in order to keep financially supporting myself. I felt so robbed inside, and I could not point out to the police if I wanted to, those stolen parts of me, taken and gone. The parts you cannot see or touch, yet vital in sustaining life, my life. If at that moment you took a picture of my life, framed my life, it would appear just white with a frame, it was that empty inside of me at that moment in time.

I wanted my soul intact, all of me, not just some of myself left in my physical body. What I wanted in this west Michigan community of Calvinists was not what I was going to have. It was my life they taunted and tortured because they could. I was just a low ranking solider and they were the General in full commando of my life, destroying my life.

Mary Kay McCleave had become my supposed friend ever since Patrick Goodale sat next to me in Continuing Education for Realtors at Jerry's Country Inn in Grandville in the winter of January 1998. Mary Kay noticed that Pat was suddenly now in the office, more and more. Mary Kay took me out for lunch, it was very usual for us to go out for lunch and talk, especially since Pat was giving me so much attention in the office and she was the one with a crush on him first. As we sat in her car, just her and I, she looked at my face, "What happened to your nose? It looks swollen. This psychic lady that reads cards for the office staff, Sharon, well, her and Chuck Helder go out now and then. Well, she predicted you were going to get beat up or something, she told Chuck Helder about a month ago at his last reading. What happened? Chuck Helder wanted me to ask you if you are o.k.? Who is Steve? And what is this about a video Chuck fears?"

I looked at Mary Kay, what I was feeling inside could not be expressed, nor talked about. I lacked the immense descriptions of the words. I could not form words to explain my shock and horror trapped inside of me now, and that scared me further. I wanted to go back in time and be normal inside. Not a frozen, frazzled, dying emotional and mental state of what I once was. It's as if I could not get enough oxygen to breathe in while living among these Christians, just trying to have a successful real estate career and support myself financially. The harassment, the torture, it was more than I could bare or understand. I closed real estate deals left and right, sold homes, bought up rentals, but I was dying inside. I was terrified that I was dying emotionally and mentally from how the Christians acted towards me. I had no family to fall back on, no family parties at the holiday times, no birthday parties like Cindy had promised. No support system that did not support Smith-Diamond Realty in some tying business agreement of sorts. Smith-Diamond Realty had its tentacles attached to everything in that town and that region in west Michigan.

I did not want to call the cops, I did not want to even admit what happened to me. Let alone answer any questions or reply back in a smart ass comment back to the taunting staff at Smith-Diamond Realty as so many men at that office taunted and teased me about the rapes.

Even Nancy the office secretary would chime in with her two cents about what she knew concerning my rapes. She was an over the hill secretary with a space between her teeth, albino eyes, she looked inbred. Nancy Vanden Berg now enjoyed taunting me as if it was a new habit fix from weaning herself off moonshine. As if her new habit was enjoying the men's power kick over destroying my life, for all she was not in this lifetime.

It was like all my power and sense of safety was stripped away, and now the taunting would just eat away at my soul like an encore of pain. I could not control their behavior, nor could I regain a sense of fully breathing to just simply survive in real estate. I was just dying inside, eventually I would have to come to terms with that death and just touch that headstone, to verify my own murder.

I began to feel less focused, I felt confused, and terribly scared, just frightful, and I could not regain a sense of control over my mental and emotional losses slipping away like a sinking ship in the middle of the darkest ocean. Nobody was around to lift me out of that sinking boat abyss or explain my emotions to me. It did not matter if the sun was out or not, my life felt dark and scared inside, trapped, and I could not get away from being scared inside. I could not run or flee for the fear, it was trapped inside my subconscious. For now, I could not pull out the fear.

I tried paging Sharon the next week or two after my initial rapes by Pat, her pager number was disconnected. I tried again months later, still the same thing. I had no way of contacting her, I did not even know her last name, or her real name from the folder at the CIA. I had a feeling she gave me more than a psychic reading, I think she was involved with my rapes, but I alone could never prove it. Others would have to step forward and compromise their life in doing so from what the CIA wants shut and closed, sealed, stamped "classified."

A few months later I was talking with an old high school acquaintance of mine, Robin, we went out for drinks downtown. She stated that she had met a Sharon who worked at The Fatman Detective agency with a Kent and Denise Smith, husband and wife detective team that worked with Sharon, that was related to Sharon somehow. Robin stated that they helped Robin who is also adopted to locate her biological mother. She said that Sharon had given her a tarot card reading in the past as well and she also can read astrology natal charts. Robin had first met her at a book club in Grand Rapids, Cascade area. Robin went unto say, somethings did come true, somethings did not come true.

I called the Fatman Detective agency in 1998 and the owner Theodore G., he said he had never heard of Sharon, Kim Livermore or a Kent Smith, or Denise Smith. My mother Cindy, claims she had not seen Kim Livermore since Atlanta.

I was at a lost to drawing and piecing together what Sharon knew, or wanted to encourage me to know about my own rape and murder.

Time passed slowly, I remember one night, feeling drugged again, unable to move off the sofa that I was now sleeping on, due to the fact the rapes took place in my bed at 405 Discovery Drive in Wayland. I remember a dark haired man going down on me, lifting up my nightgown and licking on me slowly, sticking his finger in me. It was Patrick again. But I could not move or get up from the sofa. The next morning I thought, God, am I having some strange nightmares that are making me second guess reality? This small rural town of Wayland, a town that looks like a Norman Rockwell painting of innocence was actually a well formulated CIA set-up for the CIA committing crimes with no CIA getting arrested. What is going on? I ask myself. I woke up that next morning and I have underwear on and I have a tampon inside me. Odd, I never wear tampons since I turned twenty-five. Nor do I wear underwear to bed. I do not even own a box of tampons in my possession for fear of toxic shock syndrome. Then………

That next day Mary Kay, a woman about twelve years older than me, who suddenly wants to be my lunch buddy all the time, asked me to lunch in the spring of 1998. She asks me, "Do you wear tampons?"

"What Mary Kay, what did you just ask me?" I inquire.

Instead of answering my question, Mary Kay proceeds with another strange question, "Does your nose hurt? It looks different somehow." Mary Kay said with a smirk of a smile. I felt just sick inside. Like a trapped bug in a jar on a warm hot day, shaken a bit too in her car.

I just looked at her in disbelief. I gave her a stern look as if you better tell me who told you to ask me that question.

Mary Kay stumbled over her next sentence and said this, "Pat paid me some cash to get some information from you. I don't know why, we all wondered when he was going to ask you out at the office. He called me up this morning and asked me to ask you those questions. Why doesn't he just ask you out? Steve Zinger and the guys all want to know that question."

"What else does Pat ask for you to say to me?" I asked in a serious tone of voice.

"Well, he wanted me to say this, Wouldn't it be awful if you were dating a guy and some other guy raped you and you got pregnant." Mary Kay said to me as a sentence, a statement that Pat paid her to say to me as she claimed. She often now would say very rude and mean things to me, as if to mentally and emotionally stain me. Oddly enough, Sharon had predicted this all as well, about a month ago!

"Is there anything else Mary Kay?" I asked.

"Did you ever work at The Gold Club?" Mary Kay asked. "Pat thinks you worked at The Gold Club, and Steve Zinger confirmed it by opening up your credit report." Mary Kay wore a smirk, a high and mighty smile, as if to say, Smith-Diamond Realty knows a lot about your life……

Mary Kay re-phased the question again, "What's The Gold Club?"

I looked at her soberly and said, "A nightclub in Atlanta, Georgia."

"What? I cannot believe you are saying this too me. Do you think Pat has a devious second personality that the rest of the community just does not know about Lori?" Mary Kay stated, as she then comments, "I'm freaked out. Whatever you do, don't talk with Chuck Helder about all this. It needs to stay quiet."

Mary Kay went unto say this from Patrick, "He thinks you were sold on paper through Visser & Bolhouse, behind your back, to someone in the Middle East, and he's got the proof."

There was silence in the car as she drove.

"I do not even want to think about that as a reality about my life Mary Kay. Please understand I cannot control the American Central Intelligence Agency. I never could. Sometimes life is a roller coaster. When I am in charge of my life, my fate, everything is fine."

Mary Kay then went on to warn me not to drink any of the open containers in my refrigerator. She looked worried now and changed her tune as she drove. Her chin down, she floored her car pedal down harder now, she just looked piercingly ahead as she drove.

I asked Mary Kay, "What are you talking about?"

"Just don't drink any of the red wine. Do you have an open container of red wine?" Mary Kay asked.

I responded, "Yes. What is going on here Mary Kay? What do you know that you are not telling me?"

Mary Kay responded, "You were raped by him, but I know if you go to the police, they will do nothing. I know you have to support yourself financially, solely support yourself. I know there were payouts, even before he entered that model home. Trust me, you don't want to go to the police, it will be messy, a sloppy police report is what Chuck

Helder stated. You'll ruin your real estate career if this all goes public. Chuck Helder wanted me to warn you not to drink any red wine that might be in your refrigerator now, or in the future." Mary Kay shook her head in disgust of the seriousness of the situation as she said that last sentence.

I responded to Mary Kay, "I do not want to go to the police. I just want this all to go away. I want my life back, before I was raped and now made to be scared all the time. I can't stand it. They cannot possibly have power over the police!"

Mary Kay responded, "Well, just don't go to the police." She said this as she shook her head firmly, her eyes big like wide saucers with no place to rest as she drove along the countryside.

I responded back, "I was raped in college before, and I thought the hospital exam was just as bad. I do not want to experience any of what occurred to me again. I want an apology from Patrick Goodale and Chuck Helder! I want an apology, you tell them that! I really do not want to go to the police. This is not about money or filing a sexual harassment lawsuit in court, or going to the police. I just want them to know they did wrong, they did me wrong and they are sorry. I do not want my name smeared in real estate or the press, I have to solely support myself financially. I can't afford a lawsuit to ruin my name, I know the Goodale family will say I am a whore because I worked at The Gold Club. I know all that Mary Kay, I am not stupid."

"Well, you will never get an apology from either one of them. The Goodale family owns this town and the attorneys, not just Grandville. You're right, they will call you a whore in court. Maybe you should not wear such high heels." Mary Kay said as she busted out laughing, as if laughing at this moment or the subject matter could take away the tension within our heated conversation concerning my life and circumstances involved in my own death in Wayland, Michigan.

I was just hurt, wounded by these so called Christians. I kept telling myself.

Within months Mary Kay kept asking me if I was pregnant. As was Nancy Vander Berg the office receptionist asking that question. I always responded back with the same reply, "How could I be pregnant? I am not dating anyone!!"

"You look pregnant." Was their response always.

I was not pregnant. I did gain weight in 1998. But I was not pregnant as Sharon predicted I would become after the rapes. I know she did more than predict, I know she helped orchestrate my rapes and druggings I endured at 405 Discovery Drive with all she told me, and then her pager is disconnected. How convenient of a conspiracy act on her part, Sharon's part!

Because I was asleep when the "occurrences" began happening, then drugged to be unconscious, only remembering some scenes of my rapes here and there, like some stupid person's mind. I thus, just mentally began just repressing the rapes and abuse for now. I did not want to confront the devastation caused again by the Calvinist society. So I intentionally just tried to forget as a forgiveness antidote and move on with my real estate career, a career I needed. I did not want to be destroyed. What these Christians were doing to me was no less than unwarranted harassment, abuse, and bombings on my young life.

I was not going to receive apologies. To give an apology you need to have a reason to apologize. These Christians were not sorry what they had done, or sorry for what they would continue to do, it was simply their bully lifestyle clashing with my innate values in west Michigan.

Joel Pounders a real estate agent who once worked at Smith-Diamond Realty in Grandville said to me suddenly in front of Laura Hayden in 1998, "Boy Lori, you have a heart of gold to forgive those guys for what they did to you, I couldn't, you got a bigger heart than me." Then he shut Laura Hayden's office door smiling at me, holding his hand over his heart, shaking his head back and forth, "I don't know how you forgive, I couldn't." He stated as he looked back at me, smiled, shaking his head, and closed the door behind him. Laura Hayden just ignored him as if it was none of her business what he just said.

In June of 1998 I went to a funeral home for Daryl, a former part owner of Smith-Diamond Realty and a friend of Jerry Honderd my step-dad.

After going through the visitation line my mother Cindy, step-dad Jerry and I headed outside. I had driven separately, and to my horror there was Patrick Goodale and Chuck Helder with their feet up on the back bumper of my white BMW, smiling and looking at me as I approached the parking lot of the Grandville funeral home. I felt an urge to run, I ran to my step dad's mini-van and rode home with them and went back to my car later that evening. Sharon warned me that Pat was going to rape me, taunt me through Smith-Diamond Realty, his lawyers, then try and date me, and then begin stalking me after I refuse to date the dangerous guy. I was sweating with horror as I entered the parking lot, it was as if the cards in life were being dealt so unfairly. I'm twenty-eight, this is supposed to be a wonderful time. The town of Grandville was like a cardboard village and only I knew what was behind the façade.

The cards were being dealt very fast, none were in my favor. I continued to keep up my appearances by still booking real estate showings, working. I was purposely gaining weight as a method of not getting raped ever again in my young adult life. I dressed sharp, my appearance was very polished and professional, just heavier as each month passed. I had no idea how to create boundaries that these evil Christians would respect and ward off the abuse.

In July of 1998 Chuck Helder pulled me into the work conference room and yelled at me in front of Nancy Vanden Berg that if I ever repeated what occurred to me at 405 Discovery Drive that I would have my real estate career destroyed. Especially if I ever went to the police. He kept saying as he screamed in a fuming manner, "You don't know what I can do to you." He was red in the face, just fuming mad as he made his very intimidating verbal bullet points of his power with the CIA. He kept saying, "If you go to the police, you'll hurt my friend." I kept wondering, is he referring to Dave Smith or Patrick Goodale?

I finally inquired, "Which friend?"

He stated, "Don't make me tell you!" I seriously was wondering, is he referring to Patrick Goodale or Dave Smith? He went on to warn me that I would never put up a real estate sign in this town again or ever get hired at a real estate office in Michigan if I ever told what happened. This entire time Chuck Helder is yelling at me, Nancy is just sitting there smiling, her face is blushed as if she is embarrassed, as Chuck Helder just continues to yell at me. This was just "normal" everyday politics to yell at the rape victim at Smith-Diamond Realty? I did not really know what was going on, really, he was yelling but being very vague about what exactly he was mad about, and which friend. He kept yelling that I had too much to drink. But I don't drink. Nor was I at a party. I was left confused, really.

Not only was I getting yelled at, my career in real estate threatened by Chuck Helder, he was also the office accountant who was also refusing to pay me lot commissions on the list side of Superior and Galaxy Estates. Scott Chandler, Dave Smith, and Chuck Helder were all were paid on time when a lot sold. I was under the very same contract to get paid, but was not getting paid.

Due to a power kick Chuck Helder wanted over me? The two brokers claimed it was the CIA that wanted real estate commission checks withheld from me. This continued in the upcoming years, the withholding of lot list side commissions, even when I also was the selling agent on many of those lots too! If I contacted an attorney that would make them mad and the situation worse for me.

One thing was sure, when I contacted Carmen and confided in her about all that had transpired at 405 Discovery Drive, Carmen did not want me to move out of the model home that Smith-Diamond Realty had set me up in to live rent free. I know what you the reader is thinking. I too wonder now in hindsight why would I ever take heed to any advice given by Carmen. If I was to be on a bridge with Carmen holding a camera, at this trusting stage within our relationship, if Carmen asked me to take two steps backwards I would have only assumed it was for a better picture, a better photograph.

I left for Colorado in July of 1998, a family vacation for a week. Cindy was playing this role that she cares about her family, I went along with it, because I too, wanted to believe. I had Mary Kay hold model hours for me in my place of Galaxy Estates while I was on vacation. When

I returned Mary Kay stated that Chuck Helder and Pat Goodale were at the model home rummaging through my items, my drawers, poking through lingerie, and such. Going through my trash, wondering if I had been getting my period. I was very shocked by Smith-Diamond Realty, but also was outnumbered in the amount of people who would ever side with me that the Goodale family and the Smiths cannot get away with what they want in a town they seemingly owned with the American CIA. I was beginning to feel, sense, and believe now too, that I was not in charge of my own life, they all were. I was beginning to feel a level of being brainwashed almost, powerless since the rapes, I do not know how else to explain it.

I noticed when I returned from Colorado, half my lingerie was gone, bras, panties all from Victoria Secrets, and a Gold Club large t-shirt was missing from my dresser drawers. Mary Kay and I headed to the mall, to Victoria Secrets to replace what was taken from my drawers while I was gone on vacation.

In the fall of 1998, I felt just totally devastated by the sequence of tragic events, unable to truly capture my breath of coming back to the living like I once had felt or hoped so I sought out legal counsel in Grand Rapids. In my attempt to regain consciousness over all that I have endured from the Dutch Calvinists, I felt I needed to talk to a lawyer to stop all the laws that were broken at my expense lately. I began flipping through the attorney pages of the phone book, in an attempt to get answers of my rights, resolve what I feel is missing, what has been already taken from me during the rapes. Unable to still sleep in a bed, even though I now just moved from 405 Discovery to another model home in the same plat due to a sale, I was still in the plat, just at a different model home, I would not sleep in my bed. I called up a Grand Rapids attorney by the name of Chuck Rominger. We met after work in the evening at his office, just down from a Heritage Hills 9-unit I was in the process of buying, 106 Prospect.

Mr. Rominger and a Jewish looking woman, a female attorney within his firm with an east coast accent met with me to discuss my rights. We sat in a historic living room setting within his mansion turned law firm in Heritage Hills. I told them everything.

The both of them wanted to go to the police with me, be there to help me fill out a police report with an officer taking down the report. Then they wanted to sue Smith-Diamond Realty for sexual harassment in a civil lawsuit filed by them representing me. They stated the police case initiated by them would more than likely just turn into a sexual harassment lawsuit or settlement. I stated at the end of our two hour late meeting in November 1998, "I do not want this to go public. I have a real estate career that I have worked hard for and would like not to have any more parts of my life destroyed by all this."

Chuck Rominger and the east coast accented Jewish lady looked at each other, nodded slightly, as Mr. Rominger said, "We can't control what the Grand Rapids Press prints. This all could go public."

I responded, "I'm just not ready to give up my career, I've lost enough from this ordeal."

The Jewish attorney lady watched me exit as I am leaving the appointment in late fall as enveloping darkness had fallen over the back-yard parking lot, rusty dry leaves swirled like mini tornadoes all around me as I opened the door of my white BMW. The Jewish attorney lady says, "You are repressing, eventually you'll be ready to go to the police and file a lawsuit. You want us there to make sure the police do their jobs, the police can be very sloppy with reports. You need us."

I left that law firm with many questions answered. Yet, feeling unnerved by this whole sequence of catastrophes in my life, when all I wanted to do, or be, is normal. The rain was blowing a storm, wet oak leaves hurled in the air, sweeping the driveway of that law firm in a late November fall storm of 1998. My emotions felt like that storm. Convinced that I should just move on with my life and forget, that would be the best solution I thought, I wished.

Eventually I will not be scared and intimated. But how much more could I absorb? It was all so much to take in, and just accept. The Dutch Christian Reformers (the Calvinists) had no sense of accountability for their actions upon me or another. Absolutely they felt as a group, an office, a church, as a society, an empire for that matter, no remorse for any ill action towards another in this civilization they created in west

Michigan. After all, Jesus is on their side, and "he forgives instantly" was their motto. I was starting to see what was killed inside me, part of me, my essence, gone now.

I wanted a wonderful life, I had repressed so many traumas in my life verses dealing head on with the trauma of rape or any trauma I had encountered thus far. I was a sponge just absorbing traumas and a demented religious culture all around me. A very dangerous emotional and mental accident was about to occur in the next year as my mind repressed more and more, "forgive and forget" they say in west Michigan. Time would only be ticking like a time bomb when I would mentally crash into that deer in the headlights of my traumas repressed thus far. Hitting straight on, memories so devastating that I could only have begun to write down or speak of the horrors of living within the large Calvinist's society which had many sticky tentacles on my young life.

I truly felt just like a confederate daughter in the middle of a storm, a war, as I realized I truly was now in the north, home of……**A Bully Union**. I wanted to move out of the model home in the fall of 1998, out of the Galaxy Estates plat forever. I wanted to move in with my mom and step-dad, but they refused. It was always a feeling in this lifetime, thus far, that I have no family. I was scared and wanted a roommate, a family, something protective, I did not want to be alone.

I ended up buying a house, a three thousand square foot new construction home at 2030 Winding Oak Drive in Dorr from Glen and Michelle Kuperus. Glen was a local builder. Glen stated to me that Patrick Goodale was stalking me and was offering them money to give him information. Such as, Pat would stop by and chat with him, ask about me. I thought Glen was not a person to take seriously, he seemed to be quite the jokester. I never paid heed to his many lured comments of Pat stalking me, and them raking in dough to do so for the Goodale family. I just filed away that nonsense Glen said and moved about my business, so to speak. Just staying focused on my real estate career and ignoring just about anything I considered strange, weird, or harassing in nature towards me. Why? Because I longed for a normal life.

In the fall of 1998 I was shopping around for a horse to buy. I had been taking lessons at The Silver Dollar ranch in Wayland and wanted my own horse. In December of 1998 Carmen gave me the name and number of a friend of theirs in Jamestown that had a horse for sale, Carmen was a hairdresser by trade and knew of the girl through a salon in Grandville that was selling a horse. Carmen mentioned that the horses name is "Dodger Playboy." The horse was saddled up with two straps attached to the bridle area. The stirrups were too small, Carmen's friend put children's stirrups on the saddle. I did not know this until I fell off as the horse was bucking me off, my boot got caught in the stirrup, my ankle was severely broken. Not from the fall, but in the air my bone broke as my ankle in my boot cracked to release itself from the tight hold mid-air. I had emergency surgery. I have a metal hinge and seven metal orthopedic screws in my ankle still to this day from that horse bucking me off. Strange, Sharon predicted that horse accident, even down to the month, December 1998, and she grabbed her ankle, and it so happened to be my right ankle that broke. How can she predict such events? How could she predict a horses behavior to the month? A horse acting erratic and not responding to my commands at the reins? The horse just kept backing up, and then bucked me off. How could Sharon predict a horse's behavior? I had been looking for three months that fall of 1998 for a horse, I "test drove" several. And suddenly this one particular horse bucks me off, and cracks my right ankle? I just am stunned at her prediction. I don't understand?

I remember back when I first met Diane Marie, my biological mother, the very first thing she said to me at age nineteen was, "Don't ever pose for Playboy or work in a high end strip club, my husband and his twin brother frequent those kind of bordellos." The horses name was, "Dodger Playboy." I remember asking the owner of the horse for sale, what a strange name for the horse. Why Dodger Playboy? For a name? For a horse? She stated that was on his papers, his nose was a significant sign he was from that line.

After my surgery in east Grand Rapids and hospital stay on or around December 8th, 1998, I also closed on a nine unit apartment style old fashioned mansion in Heritage Hills in Grand Rapids.

I opened up a P.O. box for the renters to mail me rent checks. I was acquiring rentals, staying busy, and moving on with just trying to be a strong woman inside. Keep the focus on business verses personal and emotional devastations exploding everywhere in my young life, with no one being really helpful in picking up the pieces of my life and putting everything back. I felt like I could not control my unannounced panic attacks that I was now suffering from. I did feel more panicky these days, and often would have panic attacks where I would find myself checking my new home in Dorr, Michigan for possible unlocked doors and windows in the middle of the afternoon. I vowed to buy a smaller house for my time consuming habits these days. I gained weight. I felt scared. And I couldn't control the panic.

I did not feel happy inside, more than feeling sad, I felt "panicky." Looking over my shoulders all the time. I found myself collapsing, needing sleep suddenly at odd hours of the day, I would crash sleep. I wanted to close out any personal contact in my life, other than the real estate calls I had to force myself to return. I forced myself to keep the real estate showings and listing appointments. The bare minimal of real estate to keep the commission checks coming in, I had certainly lost my zeal and ambition for real estate. I could not mentally focus.

There were no shoulders to cry on, there were no Christmas parties to be a part of, there would be no personal happiness, other than real estate success that I created and controlled. And eventually, I would give that up as my last connection to that awful place called Grand Rapids, Michigan, the John Calvin headquarters, which was my destination truth while in the north. I would tell the truth on paper and to the police….. and telling the truth, well, I would be thrown in jail and called a liar and a whore. Fiction could never be so strange in this damn Yankee territory. My very philosophical life was a real life power struggle against all the evil that remained hidden within the bully union. They say the south can be prejudice, but look at how the Calvinists treat me, someone who is not their dreamed mold of exactness of them! They hate outsiders, and those who leave the cult, and then come back to west Michigan, are in fact "outsiders." The Calvinist get suspicious and taunting. Believe me, I now know, oh, so well.

My relationship with my mother Cindy seemed to be a one way street of improvement. I was becoming a better daughter, but she was still Cindy. My mother Cindy was always bragging about my real estate success these days to her church friends. Did she ever take me out for my birthday? Buy me a birthday cake? Bake me a cake? No. I have had maybe three total birthday parties from Cindy. She never would ask how I was doing? Did she care about anything other than money? Success? Appearances to the Calvinists? Answer: Not really.

If we drove past a real estate sign that did not have my name upon it, she would ask, "Why did you not get that listing?" Cindy never became a warm person, a warm mother, she never even ever took my three brothers out on their birthday either. Cindy on the other hand will call or write a list of what she wants for her birthday or Christmas. I am shocked, really, at how she is so undeniably self-centered. I have never met a more self-centered person in my life.

When I look back to Pat raping me at 405 Discovery Drive, I remember his glassed over eyes. He did not look drunk, or on drugs, his eyes looked fixated, glassy. I remember Bessy of the 1860's telling me that a person with a spell on him or her, has glassy eyes. "That's how yous can tell dear Lilly, glassy eyed peoples, theys have a spell on them."

I recall back in 1995 while still living in Georgia at the time. I was dating Steve at the time. He was not a leading man type, but more like a best friend, someone you're comfortable with and spend a lot of time with I suppose. During that time, I remember going with Melanie Smith in 1995 to Little Five Points, a section in Atlanta that seemed to attract gypsy types of people, college kinds of kids with unusual attitudes, from the shops to the cafes. The place attracted a lot of strange punk style people, some gypsy types and new age types. Next to a Caribbean style outside café that I often ate at, was a candle shop of sorts, they sold tarot cards, crystals, you know that kind of new age store. In the back room you could go through the purple string beads of a door and have your cards read. I did one afternoon, it was not Sharon who did the reading, it was a heavyset, dark haired women known as a root doctor. Whatever that is, I thought. The owner of the store commented as I paid for the appointment that "She is very good, she has one opening this afternoon."

So I took that appointment. She asked me in the back room with scents of sage burning, many candles lit, "Do you want a reading on career? Love? What brings you here today?"

I pause.

"What do you want to know dear, in the cards?" She asked me again.

"Well, I really want a man in my life back, or someone just like him, a real leading man kind of guy. Tall, dark hair, sexually experienced." I said as I silently thought….. Forcefully seductive.

My mind wandered as she mumbled and moved things on the tablecloth… Intimating in the woods, making me want and beg to be able to sit on him for the sheer build-up of the sexual electricity sparks between us. I want incredible sex like I had with Alan. I want intensity…….I want moments I would die for………passion and electricity, a man who is in control when we are together….

Then I looked up and smiled as I said, " I would give up sweets for good sex again. I would." I said boldly to the strange gypsy lady. I looked at her with big puppy eyes, slightly rosy chubby cheeks. As if to say help me please, if you can, with my most important venue of wants and desires… please…..if you can root doctor lady. That was 1995, Little Five Points in Atlanta.

She responded by explaining the phases of the moon. "You need to wait until the moon is full, you need to prepare, buy candles in the color that are symbolic of your love, your binding. Gather music that was once considered yours, together. An eclipse would add a heavy dose to the antidote of love." Spoke the heavyset gypsy lady.

Her gypsy demeanor made me think this was her life's work, knowing about spells and such, surely she is a guru in this department. And soon, I will have all I can handle and more with a man just like Alan.

Thoughts began swirling and twirling in my head, I'll buy pink candles, play, ***Pearl Jam….Marcy's Playhouse…The Black Crows…Horse With No Name song by America….Lonely People…..every vintage southern rootsy music from the 1800's….that Missionary Man song…R.E.M… U2….Reggae…Fragile by Sting…..***

"Now listen to me dear, it is important that it is just before the full moon or at the fullest point, not after a waning moon period. Your wishes won't be effective on a waning moon, a waning moon takes away. Burn candles in the color that is symbolic to you and your love interest. Let the candles burn through the night, do not blow them out, the spell will be intense if you let them burn out by themselves naturally. By midnight have the dolls created of fabric or paper. Create one doll that represents you, one that represents him, be detailed, color, draw, sew, use yarn if needed. Place the dolls together in a position that you want. Do you want him on top? You on top? The one on top will hold the power within the relationship. Stay up through the night, channel his spirit back to you. Then in the morning place the dolls in a hollowed spot, bury them in the earth, then place the dripping hot wax of the burned out or burning candles over the dolls positioned ever so carefully. Bury the candles with the dolls, cover with the earths soil, and repeat, over and over, "Come back to me, come back to me Alan."

"Repeat his name, channel his spirit as you cover the site, a site that is special and unique to your relationship." Spoke the guru gypsy. "If Alan does not return to your side within time, someone like him or his likeness will enter your life and love will bloom."

A flash of a magnolia blossom tree in full bloom captured an idea, a flash of an idea. Stone Mountain…..the magnolia tree we once……

I talked it over with Melanie while having lunch and one of those electric lemonade drinks back in Little Five Points again. I said to her, "I think I am going to do a love spell, and get Alan back."

Melanie just laughed, "You think that can really work?"

"Yeah, I'm going to try it, what do I have to lose?" I said.

"You know what that lady said to me?" Remarked Melanie.

"No, what?" I asked.

"She said I am going to get raped. I'm going to get a dog, a fierce dog." Spoke Melanie.

"She said that? That is creepy. Do you believe her?" I asked.

"I do not know, but I am going to take any and all precautions so that does not happen." Spoke Melanie, a bit nervous now as we walked along briskly to my car.

It was 1995, I was twenty-five years old when Melanie and I had our tarot cards read and the advice given to us by that heavyset gypsy lady in Little Five Points at that crystal book place. Men, Myth, & Majik?

I drove to several Walgreen and Rite-Aid drugstores, buying and stocking up on dollar light pink candles, I bought nearly thirty of them. I bought smooth white paper with no lines and began drawing the image of him and I, then used marker to color our hair and such. I cut us out. I pinned us together.

I started playing Pearl Jam, and popular songs while we were dating in the early 1990's, I also played old music from the 1800's era, I played hip-hop music, anything and everything we listened to together, danced to, had sex while the song played. I played that evening in my bedroom…...Fragile…..over and over by British Sting. I locked myself in my room so that my nerdy roommate would not know what I was up to that night in 1995. I placed the pink candles on my dressers, my nightstand, I placed books as shelves on my bedspread. Then placed lit burning pink candles surrounding my body as I stared upwards from my bed, channeling Alan's spirit to come back to me. I could also channel someone most like him, for that person to enter my life, and soon I hoped. I began to go into and out of a trance like state. Some candles burned through the night until early morning, some pink candles burned out sooner than others. In the wee morning about 6am or so, tired and a bit dazed from staying up throughout the evening, I slowly and deliberately placed the hot candle wax still enclosed by the small glass frames into a shoe box or two. I then placed the wavering spellbound wax within the protective shoe box carrying cases on the floor of my car ever so carefully and sneaky…..I tip toed out carrying my boxes of passion spell enterprise of getting a guy back into my life like Alan.……..

I drove to the base of Stone Mountain, I believe I must been the first one here today, I thought as I parked my car. It had been a full moon night, the fullest of the month's end. A large Harvest Moon had loomed overhead all night. Then I carried the shoe boxes and two pinned together paper dolls. I switched out the position at the last moment, of Alan on top, and placed me on top instead. I forgot the root doctor's warning about a waning moon, and not to change or do any spells on a waning full moon period, "disaster could strike the spell cast."

She had warned me. But I thought, this time around, I want the power and control as seen with a position of on top symbolically within a relationship. Then I dug a hole under that saucer magnolia tree. I carefully took the very fragrant full and fainting petals from pink roses that could resemble the fullest magnolia blossoms ever and placed the pink petals under the pinned together paper dolls. I looked at papier-mâché Alan staring back at me, and decided, I should go first, then lay him down next to me. It's not so much the power in the relationship, it's just that I want him next to me, alongside me.

Then I took jar by jar of that hot molten pink candle wax that early spring of 1995 and bled the pink wax over the paper dolls, it was cooling as the wax hit the dolls. "Come back to me, come back to me, be my everything, I will embrace your love, I promise. I will be just as fragile inside as you feel this time around Alan." I closed up the earthly pit, all candle jars enclosed, shovel by shovel I covered my secret up. "It is finished, the spell is cast." I said out loud. I could feel electricity in the air. It would happen. I felt tingly.

I did just as the root doctor suggested for what I thought would bring Alan back to me. What position did I first place those dolls? The same position Patrick was positioned into in 1998, just as Alan would take with me. Yet Pat had a look of glassed over eyes in the bedroom located at 405 Discovery Drive in Wayland. He kind of looked like handsome attractive Alan when naked, yet with glassed over eyes, and a different nose. But then I reversed the dolls position at the last minute in 1995, so that I would be on top, the power position, in my love spell, then placed the two paper dolls next to each other in the grave I dug...... As I recall now, remembering the bedroom incident in 1998, I did float upward at 405 Discovery Drive in Wayland, to the top of the ceiling like a raising, that's what doctors call a near death experience, "a raising."

As my memories scan through the years, in timing with meeting Patrick in 1996 at The Gold Club, in the upper level, the VIP area, and Alan coming back to me at The Gold Club in 1996 in the upper level, the VIP area. What did I in 1995 invoke? A powerful spell over me? A powerful man over me? Or I over him? I began adding numbers, such as one does in numerology. The beast 666? Or 6+6+6=18, =1+8= 9. Then there is 405 Discovery Drive, 4+0+5= 9. Was there a numbers connection? The number 9 in numerology means attainment and knowledge. Sharon said in 1998, "When Patrick touches your skin, he realizes something. You are Cleopatra. And he had made a terrible mistake with his life choices." 1+9+9+8= 27, =2+7=9. Sharron gave me a reading, information, like no other reading before.......999.....equals lots of attainment and knowledge with that tarot card reading. Yet, the cards faced one way to me, and one way to her? We sat opposite from each other at my table. I am just trying to decode, solve a mystery........ "Is it cooperation and responsibility 666?" Or is it "attainment and knowledge 999?"

Can what happened to me in 1998 at 405 Discovery Drive in Wayland be blamed on me not knowing what the hell I was doing in creating a spell of love for Alan to return to me in 1995? After all, I am not a love spell guru to have love return. Did Patrick see himself, feel himself to be a Jewish man out to change the course of Calvinism? Christianity to be viewed by the world by pushing me over the edge in my life of trying to be normal in 1998, search for a normal existence? Could this all be blamed on paper dolls under a magnolia tree in a full yet waning moon at Stone Mountain in 1995?

Or is there a much more sinister evil blowing and howling in the wind in west Michigan, more powerful than my one love spell cast in Georgia in 1995? Had Bessy's much more powerful of a spell cast over a hundred years ago, lasting through the decades, from the south, created such a sinister horror in my life now?.......Bessy's sinister spell of the 1860's, cast out towards jealousy of a young and beautiful white girl, me, Lilly. A spell that has haunted me in this lifetime? In the north? In the south? I can only wonder as I write, decode, decipher the mysteries. As I unravel truth upon truth on a paper canvas.

To this day I sleep ever since 1998 with a pillow over the side of my face that received such a painful blow after those rapes. I could not fight back, or remember all the details of the rapes, for I had been drugged during the rapes, or drugged prior.

I will never forget that extreme pain and the strange bitter taste of blood going down my throat as I laid in a vegetated state. To this day, I cannot fall asleep without a pillow covering and protecting my face. I just can't. Ever since 1998 and what occurred in the bedroom of 405 Discovery Drive in Wayland. Those brutal series of rapes at 405 Discovery Drive from members of Smith-Diamond Realty and the American CIA. Ironically, hate did not emerge as an instant emotion. I did not feel an instant urge to call 911. I felt shock, the surreal emotion of shock, not hate. I felt overwhelming emotions of shock, dismay, and being totally freaked out and scared. Scared of Sharon, scared of Patrick Goodale and Chuck Helder. Those were my immediate emerging emotions. I was afraid to talk about what happened to me, I was made to be afraid of them. And I was.

Donna Vander Ark my now former sister-in-law pulled me aside one day in Wayland and explained to me that she had a conversation with Jerry Honderd, Cindy Honderd's husband, my step-dad in Michigan. Donna Vander Ark explained to me that when she told Jerry Honderd what had happened to me at 405 Discovery Drive in Wayland he said to her, "Oh no, it was a set-up."

Donna Vander Ark inquired further to Jerry Honderd to explain what he meant by a "set-up." Jerry Honderd looked in disbelief after Donna told him what had happened as he elaborated with "It was all a set-up by the CIA. I was paid hundreds upon hundreds of dollars to marry Cindy and move Lori up here to work for Smith-Diamond Realty. The amount of money was foolish to pass up. I did not know this was going to happen to Lori. I feel so bad. Does Cindy know?"

Eventually I went to the police, the Michigan State Police post in Wayland, Michigan. Then again to re-open my rape cold case in 2004 with proof of $30,000 shut-up offerings from the rapist attorneys Mike Risko and Rick Bolhouse, and brought those items to the Wayland City Police in Wayland, Michigan. The police report is case file #211-04. Contact the FOIA coordinator at city hall in Wayland. FOIA stands for Freedom of Information Act. Request a copy of all audio tapes (15 or so), all police reports (2) and documents from the earlier investigation of the Michigan State Police in Wayland report (first investigated by Detective Ziggy David Guiteriuz. Then the second investigation by the Wayland City Police report. Gather a copy of the polygraph test that I was 100% telling the truth conducted by the Michigan State Police, and proof on the legal letterhead of the March 2001 pre-settlement offer of $30,000 from Visser & Bolhouse attorneys. All those items are located in Wayland, Michigan in case no. #211-04.

2002- Patrick Boyd from the Michigan State Police headquarters in Lansing, Michigan (A relative to Judge Thomas Boyd) conducted an internal investigation into the misconduct and mishandling of the first investigation by the Michigan State Police. Which upset a lot of authority in Wayland, like stirring up a bee's nest, sooner or later, that beehive would calm down and strategize revenge on the victim, me. The American Central Intelligence Agency would be "the first to arrive on that scene" to give orders on how to shut me up, legally, the American way, through the judicial system they could control from behind the scenes.

In 2001- Mike Risko from Visser & Bolhouse attorney law firm in Grandville, explained out of court that indeed what occurred in 1998 at the model house was an actual attempt of drugging me and removing me to another country, with help from the Central Intelligence Agency employees and the Geha Organization. He explained to me that a secret order within the CIA dressed me up during the rapes as Queen Beatrix, because certain high profile Africans in Washington despise whites and colonization in the world. He explained that the Arab world and Blacks have a plan to take over the western world and destroy the American dollar, a game of Risk.

"Paper dolls," Arab Risko explained that I was sold on paper to a foreigner in Saudi. Apparently the American government employees who sold me overseas on paper were feeling the heat to deliver the goods, me. The American government was getting leery of a backlash from the Middle East, that is why there was an elaborate hoax to get me up here to Michigan.

Mike Risko also known as Arab Risko because he is not Italian added, "Your relatives on Cindy's side and the Vander Ark side and your high school friends knew what was going to happen to you in Michigan once you arrived, they were supportive according to Cindy." He warned me, "Watch your back, watch your drinks, the FBI is assisting the CIA's covert mission to deliver you to Saudi royals."

"Why is this happening to me?" I asked.

"Money. It all comes down to money, and what the government can make off you. A lot goes on behind the scenes Lori." Mike Risko was serious.

After the rapes in 1998 at 405 Discovery Drive, realtor Scott Chandler began calling me "Queenie." Mike Risko explained why Scott Chandler would call me Queenie, it was how the CIA dressed me and photographed during the rapes at 405 Discovery Drive in Wayland, Michigan.

Tentacles

CHAPTER FOURTEEN

I learned in college that "social conditioning" is a gradual training process, each society and subculture within that civilization has a method of conditioning and controlling. Influencing the way people or animals behave or think by using a gradual training process, thus termed, "social conditioning." How one reacts or acts within a subculture or society, has been their social conditioning of what is acceptable, and furthermore is the conditioning program. The micro-matrix of how a person reacts in a trauma situation, a job interview, how one acts within religion, etc. Take a person from one culture, place them in another, and vice versa, you will have two different social reactions given to the same stimulus. I was raised in a society, a home, and a Calvinistic religious subculture that instilled fear in victims by those in power or control, or from those who were guilty. The victim was always treated like the problem within the Christian faith of the Calvinistic subculture of west Michigan. A victim knows that the elite members in the churches alike would ignore rumors of a perpetrator, rather than confront the truth. Which has always been viewed by those in charge, them, as volatile, "too unpredictable." For a victim to tell anyone in this religious west Michigan community would risk the truth coming to the surface, without protection from the enemy, the bully or perpetrator. For a victim to come forward in the Calvinist community is also too receive harsh punishments by the entire tentacles of what holds that society together which is deeply bonded and crushed upon the victim for creating a perception other than the one told by the Calvinists. I observed that the American government works that same way. Any type of totalitarian society does not like to give power to the victim, or want to hear from a victim. If you become a victim, it is simply your loss.

I remember listening in on a conversation growing up. The CIA scientist said to my mother, "Africans are the destroyers, give an African child anything, and that child will destroy. Adult Africans will destroy properties, systems, trust from others, just about anything they can get ahold of, they like to innately destroy. The parasites to any host system, are Arabic countries and Arab people. They innately like to attach themselves to whatever they can. If Africans destroy, the parasitical people move in, and take over, pushing whatever is left, out. Parasitical people, need destroyers, they are co-dependent upon one another."

I did not believe a word of what was spoken at the table on Curwood, Lamplight Estates in Jenison, Michigan during the late 1970's. Looking back, I think some children believe what they believe, no matter how many adults in charge tell them this, that, or the other thing. Yet, some children grow up believing what they were told and never question an adult. But I never trusted adults, and so growing up, I questioned everything, even if it was silent questioning in my mind. I wanted to see and test everything. If Cindy told me the stove top burner is not hot, I would place my right hand on the burner and find out.

Deep down, I knew that was wrong of the Calvinists. I remembered heaven before earth and instinctively brought with me to earth, elevated values, a higher conscious on how to treat people fairly. A unique prism in which I saw the world around me, how I could see through people….. But I was not sure how to change the world or how to change all their misconceptions and twisted levels of power. You know, what people term and explain as validation to hate another. I wanted to know if there were behavioral differences in people, like there are in dogs and other species.

Take for granted that the dark ages you believe have long passed, but in some parts of the world, such as west Michigan, the dark ages exist and the civil rights movement never even took place yet, for many white people, white victims. If one tries to write and contact the Michigan Attorney General's office, you would find that the real job duty of importance is whether or not Walmart or Walgreens drugstores are correctly placing matching price labels on the merchandise boxes that also match the correct sticker label posted on the shelf of the item. What happened to me, is my problem, not a general population concern for the greater good. Locate all the information I have provided to any and all State agencies in Michigan. I truly felt like a black woman among a group of whites that felt as if I had no rights, that is how the State of Michigan made me feel. If I screamed, they laughed. The layers within Michigan, the bodies that govern Michigan, they also agreed with west Michigan principals of values. It was my private burial, not a greater concern. But I am now becoming determined, my memoirs will become peregrinate around the globe.

I realized that it was not I that could change the world instantly, miraculously one day, but rather it would be a transition, from words to a reader, from one world to another. It is you the reader that could actually change and be part of a world that holds my elevated values that create harmony and balance, which does not include, ***harassment, abuse of power, lying, the list goes on and on***.

One day like most days, I thought to myself, I just cannot take anymore harassment from Smith-Diamond Realty, it was the year 2000. But this day was different, I am going to confront my abusers and stand up for my rights. I had so many real estate commission checks withheld by Dave Smith and Chuck Helder. I was mad I was sleeping on my sofa now for two years, afraid to fall asleep. I was afraid to date, I was afraid of sex. I was fifty pounds overweight because I thought that would ward off any future sexual harassment and taunting from within the real estate world of that Calvinistic society. I felt murdered inside as I stared at people in the office and community that appeared mad I was still breathing. I did not smile anymore, it was force on my part to smile or laugh or listen anymore. I felt confused, distracted, and very unaware of the dangers that still loomed ahead for me, in this life path better to be termed as the road less traveled. Nothing could have prepared me well, because, in this case, the tentacles of the great octopus had already touched upon the police, just as Sharon the psychic "had predicted" back in 1998.

In the winter going into spring of 2000 I was fed up with the continued harassment from Dave Smith, stopping by my home office at 2030 Winding Oak Drive in Dorr, Michigan. Dave would stop in, pound on my front door to harass me and show me who is boss over my life. I was not even in a work related office situation and I was still being harassed by my boss, my broker. I was harassed in the home that I paid a mortgage on monthly, it was unbelievable how he thought so little of women he wanted to harass and boss. He would apologize for his bad behavior. Acknowledge his bad behavior by saying it was not fair to me, then wait a month or so, and harass me again, and again. He would threaten, take, then apologize. It was a bizarre cycle of events, but nevertheless, was a normal fixture within my young real estate career that I was made to feel by the Calvinist society to just deal with. I was still, after two years of proving myself to be successful and a very competent real estate sales agent, I was still not getting paid by Chuck Helder the broker and accountant for Smith-Diamond Realty for the list side lots in Superior and Galaxy Estates in Wayland. I was missing from them well over eighteen list side lots in the last two years now. All the while, the men paid themselves for two years straight, ignoring my name on the plat contracts. Yet all the while, Scott Chandler, Chuck Helder, Dave Smith, all were paying themselves on time. Even if on paper I was to be an equal as the real estate plat contract stated, I was not getting paid according to contract, no enforcement of equal rights. I still was far from equal on the chain of evolution, light years away in their established circles in west Michigan.

According to the plat contract I was to be paid as well, beginning when I was added to the new construction plat to market and sell lots, way back in the beginning of August of 1997. Now over two years later I realize that proving I am an equal, does not matter. It's on paper to pay me my equal portion, but paper contracts mean nothing to a dominator, nothing. I would have to beg for my other commissions checks over the years. I generated all my own leads through model hours, real estate ad's I wrote, placed, and paid for myself, open houses, referrals, etc. To have my career was exhausting, to deal with them, the Calvinists, was unbearable at times, even when I was not around them. It was a dark cloud that no one cared about. Or cared if I proved there indeed was a dark cloud. I still could not figure out why Carmen Van Noord wanted me to stay living at that model home in Galaxy Estates. I shiver now thinking about her advice then.

It was as if I was placed in a jar by the harassing men and jealous women of the office of Smith-Diamond Realty. As I looked up and around my world the fresh oxygen had evaporated in my world. I was left to squeeze off the lid, to just survive, if I could survive.

If indeed I could survive their mental torture, and physical imprinting of torture upon me. The energy it would take these days for me to believe for just a moment, that yes, I do have power, I do not have to take this anymore. They saw me as something else, someone else, as if they were all unitizing collaborating Romans and I was not part of their massive empire. You know, that empire I loathe, well, 2000 years ago I did. I want to be treated like an equal, I want to be treated fairly with respect and common courtesy. Just as I am constantly always doing for them and my real estate clients, it's always about others. Another analogy, how the Calvinists made me feel, I felt like a black person in the south surrounded by governing whites. Sure you can vote, but your vote goes into this trash can, and won't actually be counted, but sure you have "the <u>right</u> to vote." We have not taken that <u>right</u> from you, so hurry along now, go on, carry on about your business now. Seemingly was my destination of discovery here in the north, their bully politics.

One day I erupted, I just don't want to feel this way anymore. I marched up to Chuck Helder in the office and demanded that he, "Pay me those back commission checks that I am rightfully due, or I will go to the police, and tell them everything. It was unfair what you did to me, emotionally, mentally, physically and financially, simply unjust! That model home was a set-up! I now am aware of that, I was so gullible!" As my words echoed inside my head I could not believe that I even had enough energy and power left within me to stand up for my rights, where did that hidden energy come from? I was exhausted from what I endured with my experiences at Smith-Diamond Realty in Grandville. I was exhausted with my persistent notion that I can make lemonade from lemons, and all will just work out and be fine. It was not fine.

What was Chuck Helder's response?….. very laid back. I did not rattle him a bit. I felt rattled inside. I thought I lit a real firecracker under his seat with my bold words, but he did not even move, or twitch.

Chuck Helder mouths, "Go ahead, call the police, they will do nothing, it was Pat's idea to hold back your real estate commission checks after that party. It is Patrick's idea, he is the real guy that wants a power kick over you, I feel sorry for you. But there is nothing you or I can do. Pat believes that somehow astrologically you are going to take his wealth, his inheritance, that is what Sharon informed him of in 1997. He's got you played like a chess match already won, go tell the police everything, just try it. The CIA will shut-up up the police and close the case. Your own mother Cindy is willing to testify it was an affair." He calmly spoke his no-nonsense advice like a belligerent animal as he sat shuffling stacks of papers and files on his desk that he could care less about. Just muttering to himself at that side corner office, just inches from the check machine. He could care less about printing off the past due commission checks to me, why should he? Was his response. He was sure the Goodale family had covered all bases to insure a homerun for his winning team, his stupid Roman Empire of a world in which he simply just played a stubborn guard.

"What party? What party are you talking about? I never had a party at my house." I remarked inquisitively back to Chuck Helder.

He looked at me dead on, point blank and said in a slow, firm voice, as if he was able to instantly sober up and speak on cue, "The party. You obviously were not too with it, you had something, or too much to drink, you were so out of it."

I turned and walked out, not knowing what he was talking about.

I called up Dave Smith in March or April of 2000. "I know that you have blamed Chuck Helder and CIA John Brennan for withholding my earned real estate checks over the years. I will go to the police Dave Smith, and tell them everything! Everything! What is this all about, Pat Goodale has Wayland in his back pocket or something? That is what Chuck Helder indicated to me yesterday."

Dave Smith responded in a startled panicked tone of voice, "Don't do that, we can talk about this tomorrow, I'll go to the office tomorrow and sit down with Scott and Chuck. Just give us a day to go through the old Superior and Galaxy Estates files, just cool your jets. I'll talk with Chuck tomorrow. I can't do anything today, I'm at a birthday party for my granddaughter. I don't know nothing about Pat or Chuck and the police. But that Sharon lady, she has my watch. She gave me a phone reading two months ago and predicted you'd crack and go to the cops on us in the spring. This ain't good, we can figure this out tomorrow, I'll talk with Chuck Helder. We'll get this worked out, I promise. Just take it easy, take a deep breath, cool your jets."

The next day I received a fax from Dave Smith, it was a Sunday in April of 2000, around 12noon. The fax outlined in his handwriting when lots were sold in Wayland, how many, to whom, and the amount I would finally get paid. There was a note on the bottom, when Deppe builders pays us for the land contract on 8 lots, we will pay you then. I did get paid for 18 past due lots in the spring of 2000, finally, after Smith-Diamond Realty withheld commissions from me for over two years! I am still missing payment on the last 8 Deppe lots as I write my memoirs. Smith-Diamond Realty in Grandville has no honor. None.

Despite the nightmare I was about to leave, there was no peace as I began to enter upon another nightmare around the bend in 2000. I just know that through revealing can come positive change. I certainly cannot fold the entire world's civilization, and sprout out a perfect world. But I can write, reveal, and hope you see your reflection within my book and see what can change within your depths. Octopuses can be located anywhere in the sea, there are many subcultures just like the Calvinists. Many parallels…..tentacles sticking to everything like organized crime, hidden from common sight, until this book washed up on shore? Landed on earth? To each their own conclusion. Each reader has their angle of interpretation?

In the spring of 1999 I had moved into a new house, 2030 Winding Oak Drive in Dorr, Michigan. I bought the new construction home from a local small town builder named, Glen Kuperus. He called me up to list his new construction home he was building, I decided to buy the home and move out of the model home in Wayland, Galaxy Estates. Upon making final finishing touches, decisions about flooring, and hickory cabinets, finishing the basement in such. Glen looked at me from his clipboard of scribing and jotting down notes as we walked through the new build.

He said this, "You know, Pat, that son of Jack Goodale approached me and my wife Michelle four months ago, asking us if we'd be willing to eavesdrop on you when you move in. Listen in on your phone conversations, give him the up and up of who you're dating these days. I told my wife Michelle, we can't do that, she's goina be our neighbor. But I gotta tell you, he offered us b-i-g bucks. Michelle thinks you're goina retire us and we should do it, but I disagree. It's a bad plan for retirement."

I ignored what Glen said, even if Pat Goodale approached him and his wife, my new neighbors to be in Dorr. I knew Glen was a better character to not involve himself in any illegal spying and eavesdropping. It just did not seem like his style, he was a small town guy with integrity, a local builder. Despite what my other neighbor warned me to the right, Ms. Lindsay, I ignored the foolish talk.

I quit Smith-Diamond Realty in the spring of 2000 just after moving into 2030 Winding Oak Drive in Dorr. I also picked up the phone and called the Michigan State Police at the Wayland Post, Allegan County. I began pouring out my story as if the police could be therapists. I just told everything I knew about Smith-Diamond Realty and how office harassment transpired into serious crimes committed against me at the model house.

The first thing the two police officers wanted to know was, how did the men from Smith-Diamond Realty get into the house, the model house?

I responded, "The Grandville office had a combo box on the front door, the combo number would have been in a file at the office, they had a key to get inside. In fact, Mary Kay told me often Chuck Helder and Pat Goodale and Scott Chandler would visit the model home when I was not there. Mary Kay McCleave knew lots of my Victoria Secrets underwear and bras, a Gold Club t-shirt was missing. I had to buy more Victoria Secrets lingerie, nearly spending five hundred dollars from what they stole, Mary Kay is aware of this."

One officer spoke up, "Wait a minute, you worked at The Gold Club? This will go nowhere on Margie's desk, she'll never prosecute these guys." Officer Dromny smirked as he glanced back at young Officer Theaker.

The young officer turned to him and asked, "What's…. The Gold Club?"

"Who is Marge Bakker?" I asked.

"She is the lead prosecutor in any and all rape cases in Allegan county, she writes the warrants for rapes. She will not like you as a rape witness, or rape victim because she will think the defense will call you a whore and it will be a big waste of her time to prosecute the case. Just a big waste of tax dollars spent to have someone like you testify against established business professionals, land owners." Spoke Officer Dromny in a very polite advice tone of voice to me.

"Well, maybe we should not go any further." I said.

"Oh, no, please tell us all that happened to you." Said one officer flipping over his pad of notepaper by my table.

"This is a people crime, not just property, we take people crime seriously." Said trooper Orville Theaker.

"Where is Smith-Diamond Realty located?" Asked trooper Orville Theaker.

"Grandville and Caledonia Michigan." I answered. And so I began telling those two officers everything.

"Do you go to church around here?" Asked Officer Dromny.

"No." I kept talking and telling, it was a surreal moment, to finally talk, open up about what had been kept bottled up, my horrors. I finally began telling of my horrors. I thought that I would be freed of my nightmares by telling the cops of the horror that seemingly was forced to stay lodged in my mind. The imprint of my rapes, sedations, pain, all imprinted will leave my mind now I thought, if I just keep talking. It sure felt good to talk. For so long I had remained silent and scared. I did not even want to admit anything bad had happened to me, afraid my real estate career would be scarred like I was.

What I was pulling out of my file cabinet in that great mental abyss would lead me mentally and emotionally down a rabbit hole. It was as if I had engulfed too much pain mentally, endured too much misery, and now was underground in a dark maze, and somehow that was my fault. Or perhaps to better explain it to you the reader who has never experienced Post Traumatic Stress Syndrome, I was on a water slide too high, too fast, too scary, and too late to stop the fall as I inevitably headed down that emotional and mentally high and steep slide. I was falling, had fell, sliding head first into very deep waters of that deep blue abyss, plunging head first into the lost files of my subconscious mind. What I would experience in the upcoming years was the lid opening up on Post-Traumatic Stress Syndrome. As much as I wanted the horror stricken imprinting to just vanish, just escape that big splash into the great unknown, the memories clung to me, unable to leave. Like powerful tentacles attached on my mind, my emotional state of being. I did not know how to escape what the rapes did to me, inside my mind. I had moved out of 405 Discovery, where the rapes took place. But honestly, I was just as scared in my new home, as if I had never left the scene of the crimes that took place on me, in me, destroying me.

The Michigan State Police case file in 2000 was handed over to a State detective, Detective David "Ziggy" Guiteriuz. State trooper Orville Theaker was moved to nights, and the daytime detective was assigned the case, to investigate all that I had reported about my rapes, including the harassment from Smith-Diamond Realty.

"Just call me Ziggy," spoke the Hispanic Michigan State Police detective with sleeked black greasy hair, wearing shiny leather Italian loafers. I remember his eyes and his shoes, as what stood out the most in my impression of him. His eyes were that of a cold blooded murderer, I shivered. His shoes looked as if he was a detective in a shady part of Sicily. He stood out in appearance as different than the other cops. He tells me he mostly works on murder cases, cold cases, but on occasion a rape case.

He asked me a few questions, not really an in-depth interview. He asked me to handwrite down my statement, details and such. I did, and turned it into the front desk the following week, which did make it into the rape file he prepared for Margaret Bakker, the Allegan County Prosecutor.

"Ziggy," as he wanted to be called, calls me back to his office months later to tell me a few facts. Such as, "I am not going to dig up all these supposed witnesses at Smith-Diamond Realty that you listed on paper. There are too many laws on hearsay that would and could be used against me in court. Dave Smith and his friends have a well-established business in Grandville. I can't take that away from him by siding with you. No one else is coming forward with a similar complaint of rape by these men or willing to talk about what they know. Rick Bolhouse, the attorney for Smith & Goodale calls me on a daily basis. Every time I check my cell phone messages, my work answering machine, he is calling me, acting like he is my best friend or something. Asking if there is a warrant for Chuck Helder, Patrick Goodale, and Dave Smith…..Stressing me out. Reminding me that these men are outstanding members within the community, that have no prior arrests, no prior criminal history, and for me to not destroy their lives based on your testimony alone. Not to mention, you got quite the reputation in VIP at The Gold Club, according to Rick Bolhouse." The south of the border speaking Michigan State Police detective smirked, as if I was the criminal in this matter, and some kinda criminal joke at that.

I looked at him, my eyes grew big in disbelief, this "Ziggy" is some kind of nut of a State detective, I think. Then he literally reads my mind, as I am about to ask……..

Ziggy speaks up quickly, "No you cannot have a new detective on this case. I am the only one you got to investigate. There are plenty of cops, but just one State detective in these parts. I am the one assigned to the case and I will do my best." Spoke the slick haired Mexican detective with crooked teeth, cold blooded pupils and bright green perfectly polished alligator skin loafers.

He took the question right out of my mind that I was about to ask, he was correct, I was just thinking, "Can I have a new detective assigned to the case?" He was treating me like a was the daughter of a confederate soldier and he was a bully union general with absolute power in this part of the country, the law in these parts. Bringing me up to speed as if briefing me on power and status, the law in these parts. The cause Ziggy saw I was fighting for? The truth to be known. I finally came forward with what happened, what occurred at 405 Discovery Drive, to only be beheaded by a nut of a State detective. "Ziggy" did not want the truth to be known. He acted like me telling the truth was a rebellious act, rude for a woman to speak the truth of what happened, the truth he wanted to dump into a bottomless pit, along with me. The man terrified me, in such a way, I was in disbelief for a moment in how could such a nut gain such power within the Michigan State Police system? What an abuse of position and power on his part, on the part of the police system at large in Michigan.

His whole attitude could be summed up in two very distinct words, "*gross negligence*" towards a female rape victim. I agree with conservatives that hate big State budgets that create deficits for the unaccountable spending of other people's money through the underground railroad of crimes called high northern taxes. I do not care how much money was filtered this year, last year, or the decade before last into the State of Michigan's budget for police. No matter how much money is or was spent, large amounts of tax dollars, the result is the same as if no money was spent on the State budget for the State police. The result was, and would have been the same. Detective David "Ziggy" Gutierrez still would have been the State detective in these parts, west Michigan, working for the State. And I would have had the same results on a police report, a very, very "gross negligence" sloppy police report. Topped off with laws not enabling me to sue him or the State of Michigan. He knew that, schooling and education for State detectives and police was not a big budget item of priority. Police budgets were spent on cars, or uniforms, or golf outings, or high tech state of the art buildings. The

State lawmakers knew that very prevent fact before I was even raped, and drew up law protecting paperwork, had it signed into a law to protect the State, the police, from victims like me, from suing the police and State, for what occurred (get the report). The lawmakers also understand how very, very difficult it is for a civilian to sue a police officer or police unit. The laws favor the pillars for the State, "the police and those who work for the State." Not me, a stupid looking victim who thought I had rights as a woman in this State, this great State of Michigan.

"I read through your handwritten account, I can hardly read your messy handwriting. It sounds to me like a civil case of sexual harassment. Not a criminal matter to investigate. I'll type up a report and turn this tape over to Marge Bakker, the prosecutor in any and all rape cases in Allegan county. But honestly, I do not think she will write out warrants for the three men, there just is not much to go on. She's goina need more evidence. It cost money to prosecute." Spoke the calm disposition of the Michigan State Police detective, David "Ziggy" Gutierrez. I felt stupid, crushed, and beyond belief abused by what happened to me at 405 Discovery Drive, and that is precisely what he wanted, his point, in wasting his time.

"Eh…uh…" I started to speak up….. "What about the two tapes, the confession of Dave Smith? He admitted on tape he raped me, made me feel uncomfortable, took me back to his house." I stated to the State detective as I pleaded in tone for my case not to be dropped like a sack of trash out a pick-up truck's window.

The State detective paused, became quiet, as if to give me bad news.

I spoke up before the detective could talk and provide me again with what I did not want to hear, "Trooper Orville Theaker, he gave his phone recording device so that when Dave Smith called, to harass me, to talk with me, I got a confession out of him!"

The Mexican-American slick State detective said this as he settled and squirmed in his seat from impatience brewing, he put his finger over his mouth, leaned forward as if to give me some potent wisdom that he alone held, "You can't tape a confession, or use a confession on tape that the other person, Dave Smith in this case, does not know he is being taped at the time of the confession. Since he raped you, admitted he raped you, there have been many incidences where his harassing you led to you giving in to his sexual demands. That is called 'sexual harassment,' not criminal sexual misconduct in the State of Michigan……..seen and viewed as a crime. Rick Bolhouse his attorney listened to the two tapes and will never allow those tapes of his client to be admitted into court, never. This is an uphill battle for you, I can't help you. There is no evidence, no DNA. You have a big case of hearsay. This is a sexual harassment case, at best. But I am not a lawyer, I am a State detective for the State of Michigan."

This whole entire ordeal, from the harassment to the rapes, to coming forward and talking to the police, telling them the truth, made me feel like I had been drowning at sea. To only finally make it to land, only to discover the island is sinking into the sea as well, and what I had hoped as survival, was just a fleeting glimpse of hope. Drowning and dying at sea or on the shore was my impractical but real reality.

In August of 2000 when David "Ziggy" Gutierrez sent me a letter to my residence at 2030 Winding Oak Drive in Dorr, stating in writing that the State has closed its investigation into my rapes at 405 Discovery Drive in Wayland, Michigan and that no warrants will be issued. I then walked inside my home, picked up the phone to request a copy of the police report prepared by the Michigan State Police in 2000. It was a joke. It looked like a fourth grader prepared and typed the police report. Much of what I reported, incidences to investigate, witnesses to talk with, what they told me they knew in such, the men bragged afterwards is the impression I got from many members of Smith-Diamond Realty in the taunting words spoken to my face, was not of course documented in the police report. The police report had a statement from Carmen, my best friend in Michigan, that if I had been going to church that I would not have been raped. The Calvinist society wanted me under the bus, so did the CIA, the State detective was the tool to do so, or so I read in the police report.

Scott Chandler had pulled me aside in the office in Grandville and told me all he saw, what I looked like naked, flaunting in my face, he now knows what I look like naked. So much was not on the MSP report of 2000. If I was a teacher, and a grade school kid prepared that police report, I would have flunked the student. But to my horror, this was the incompetence of adults, professionals paid by the State of Michigan that I would be faced "to just accept." In fact, usually a police report will keep the name of the rape victim off the report, to protect the victim. In this case, they had my name on the report and blasted my social security on the report, Lori Vander Ark, and left off the names on the 2000 Michigan State Police report of Dave Smith, Patrick Goodale, and Chuck Helder, who are the perpetrators (alleged perpetrators).

I'll be honest, I thought if a German was in charge of the investigation and police report the outcome would have been different. I was left to simply realize that some people on the planet do not possess competence within their DNA to thoroughly do anything well within the duties of their job position. Examine how a German does things. Then examine how a slick Mexican-American does things. It is o.k. to be observant and not complacent, correct? At some point you will also realize that people that cannot do their job, brings down the whole system. Is it the system? Or is it the people running the system? Ask yourselves.

The August of 2000 letter from State detective David "Ziggy" Gutierrez, stated that Marge Bakker will not be issuing any warrants, and the case is officially closed against the men I alleged, Patrick Goodale, Dave Smith, and Chuck Helder. At times I would stare at myself in the mirror, and just look at myself, and ask, do I look black? Why am I being treated like this in west Michigan?

In 2000 I began receiving rape counseling for my Post Traumatic Stress Syndrome. I hired a personal trainer at the Michigan Athletic Club in East Grand Rapids and began dropping the fifty pounds I had gained. I knew I was in yet another jar, trapped again this time in a jar of lard. I could see the outside world through the inverting glass window of my own eyes but I could not be part of the outside world. I was locked in a trauma state of being scared and frightened mentally all the time now. I was also now trapped in layers of fat. I would have panic attacks at 3pm in the afternoon, consumed with fear. I would go around and check each window and door, not knowing why. I could not prove why I was so scared all of the time. I could not point to my fear or identify my fear, why I was afraid or freaking out. However, fear was real. Fear was instilled into my mind during the rapes, and I could not escape. I began to realize there would be seven jars? Seven lids to open? Seven hurdles to overcome before being able to write this book and have it published.

I began traveling in the summer of 2000, up north to Petoskey, it was a favorite childhood vacation spot of mine. I gave Donna Vander Ark my sister-in-law at the time my house keys to keep my plants watered and collect my mail, I really did not think twice about it, really. I just wanted to get away from everything brewing in lower Michigan. I was beginning to be viewed as a drama queen with a big mouth now that I finally called the police and told them everything, opening a big can of worms. I just wanted peace, I was in search of peace. If peace could be found, located, I was in. I spent my days working out at a gym in Petoskey now and laying out by the sandy beautiful shores of Charlevoix by Lake Michigan.

The sounds of the waves crashing unto shore, then trickling backwards into the watery haven of pure blue, was calming, for hours, calming. A sign on the beach posted the words "peace" written in four different languages. I thought, I am here, I just want peace in my life. I listened to music and blissfully kissed the days away on the beach. I would spend weeks at a time in northern Michigan, it really is the perfect summer place in the whole wide world. After a few weeks I then traveled back to lower Michigan. To the village of Dorr where I had this beautiful new construction house I owned, 3000 square feet, finished just the way I wanted it. But really, I was happier camping in a tent at Petoskey State Park. Just soaking up the hearty woodsy scents of the forest in the evening as I rested in my flannel sleeping bag. Verses being in a nice house in lower Michigan receiving harassing phone calls from the bully Visser & Bolhouse law firm. Along with the many harassing volunteers sent to my doorstep by members of "team Smith-Diamond Realty," such as many Kuperus' sons and another male neighbor now.

My sister-in-law Donna calls my house and brings up the name "Sharon" during the summer of 2000. Donna Vander Ark, my sister-in-law at that time in 2000, states that a Sharon, a detective and a psychic approached her at the hospital where Donna worked in Grand Rapids and asked a few questions. Sharon stated to Donna that she wanted to meet with me again. I had not seen or spoken to Sharon since the spring of 1998, weeks, if not days before the rapes at 405 Discovery Drive in Wayland, Michigan. Donna kept encouraging me to meet again with "Sharon," I refused. Donna was insistent, I refused every angle of Donna's persistent arguing. Donna went onto tell me that a Denise Smith, a friend or relative of Sharon is willing to dress up like me and hangout at Florentines Restaurant to see if Dave Smith or Patrick Goodale will come on to her and eventually rape her.

I remarked to Donna, "That is the most ludicrous idea I had ever heard of, I want no part in any of your ridiculous ideas of investigating what happened to me! Or trying to compensate for a sloppy Michigan State Police report by getting some other girl involved with a sloppy police investigation!"

Mary Kay called me during the summer of 2000…….and asked me, "What is it that you want? From all this? Just name it Lori! Money?"

I responded to Mary Kay, "I want apologies, heartfelt apologies Mary Kay. I want my life back to normal. I want to feel normal again, before I moved to 405 Discovery Drive, I can't forget Mary Kay. It was more than just harassment, you know that!"

"Well, you won't get an apology from Chuck Helder, Dave says he is sorry and is willing to get counseling or treatment. Patrick Goodale won't talk about it, he is denying he had anything to do with the rapes. Lori, he says you two just were hanging out at the model home, and he never had sex with you. You really opened a can of worms Lori by going to the police! This is not good." Said Mary Kay.

My friendship with Mary Kay ended very abruptly, seemingly over the phone.

In 2000 I began to sell off rental properties that I owned as a source of creating cash. Sometimes I would buy a fixer upper, remodel, and sell it for a profit. I had my feet in real estate. However, not dependent upon real estate sales as my license was no longer hanging on the wall of Smith-Diamond Realty anymore. I contacted a Grand Rapids mortgage company to refinance my nine unit apartment building in Heritage Hills which held a lot of equity that I needed right then and there. Three days later I called the mortgage lender to see how quickly we could refinance and pull out some cash equity to take care of the bills piling up. She stated to me that I had many "credit inquiries" on my credit report and that was hurting my credit score and ability to receive a loan.

"What? I have not been applying for credit cards. What do you mean?" I asked.

The lender replied, "Your credit score, you have all these hits on your credit report, it's affecting your credit score. Have you been applying for furniture leases? Office equipment recently? Because that is what is showing up on your credit report."

"What? I want a copy! I want proof of what you are saying. I have not applied for any credit recently in the last six months or longer." I said. I was disgusted, and at a loss for words…. "I'll be at your office later on today. I want to see my credit report!"

The lender replied, "I'm not supposed to hand out copies of a person's credit report."

I responded loudly, boldly, "It's my credit report! It belongs to me. I am going to call any and all people or companies on that credit report of mine and get to the bottom of this!" I remarked totally flabbergasted at the lender almost denying me the right to see my own credit report. "It's mine!" I screamed.

I got a hold of my credit report, reviewed the inquires. I called New Equipment Leasing, Inc. I spoke to the young ditsy secretary on the other end of the phone, and asked her, "Why is the company New Equipment Leasing, Inc. on my credit report, and often? I am not trying to buy or lease office furniture." I asked firmly.

I waited and waited, she just paused in confusion. I asked the bewildered secretary a series of questions again. Trying desperately to figure out why the Grand Rapids company was all over my credit report of inquiries.

She finally said in her frustration of not knowing either, why the company was on my credit report under recent inquiries…..

"I don't know, maybe you can call our company attorney's to figure this out." She said, just as bewildered as I was, as to how the company she worked for was suddenly on my credit report. In her bewilderment and at a loss to explain, she added, "Call Rick Bolhouse & Mike Risko in Grandville, they represent our company, they are our attorneys at law."

"What?!?!" I said loud and strong in the phone…. "Rick Bolhouse, from Visser & Bolhouse they are the defense attorney's for the men that raped me!"

Rick Bolhouse and all his too active attorneys had also now seriously crossed the line of privacy with me. Seriously now affecting my credit score! And my ability to refinance my nine unit which had substantial equity just sitting there that I needed to tap into now that I am not selling real estate for Smith-Diamond Realty, working on plats in such. I could not change my credit score. I wrote to the three big credit agencies from advice given from the lender, and wrote what happened. Needless to say, nothing happened to improve my credit score, it was damaged, and damaged from the men's attorneys, how ruthless, it was serious financial crossing I thought! I do not want to be a victim. I never asked to be a victim. And I can't stop them from victimizing me and destroying my life, I thought, as I felt so broken inside. I'm too shattered to glue the pieces of my life together and make things whole again.

If they could not drown me personally, or get to me and rape me and cause me more damage, they would do the next best thing to damaging my ability to just stay afloat financially and move on with my life. All the while, Don Visser, Rick Bolhouse and Mike Risko all made it on time to church, dressed in a two piece business suit, and lived in upscale white neighborhoods surrounded by Dutch Calvinists who would never ever call them what they are, "Criminals!" The FBI in Grand Rapids, Michigan would all refuse to investigate.

Although criminals behind closed business doors those three were, and yet to the unsuspecting general public in conservative Grandville, their reflections fit in very well within the Dutch Christian Reformed community of mirrors matter most, sacred reflections and all. The victim role I really do not want to play. I want to be the victor, but I mistakenly was not the victor. I had serious hopes, wishes and dreams to be the victor, rise above the rest of them! But honestly, that is not how I was viewed by them or anyone in that Calvinist's community. I was a misfit, a victim, seen and treated like a rebellious woman in west Michigan, because I thought I had rights. But I was mistaken. I was tired, exhausted, and mistaken. I did not want to be in a war. I just wanted to live, be happy, and assume that all Christians would treat me fairly and with respect and kindness in their community. But I was mistaken. I was tired from fighting for my rights, which were written down somewhere in their law book in invisible ink. It was truly like pointing out laws, rights, that I had, or thought I had, and they all shook their heads "no" in church, in their Bible studies, on their prayer lines.

Then, that same week, the summer of 2000, I learn from Carmen that her husband Doug met with Mike Risko and Dave Smith at Florentines Restaurant in Grandville. Doug sold for money any and all Playboy magazines they had stored in their bedroom closet shelf, editions I had been featured in, sold them right into the hands of my enemies. To make me look like a whore to the police, the prosecution, the men, to all my enemies, by their demising of me. Keeping any future rape cold case investigations at bay in Allegan County with evidence to provide to the nutcase detective "Ziggy," that I somehow deserved the rapes, or that I encouraged the rapes.

Rick Bolhouse was cunning, ruthless, and obviously knew what the court wanted, he knew how to get a hold of what they wanted to win, to keep the warrants from being signed. Why did Carmen even tell me that bit of information? I wondered and finally asked her.

"I thought you should know, eventually you might learn that fact and I wanted you to hear it from me" Carmen said. Please do note, Carmen and Doug Van Noord made it to church every Sunday, usually twice on Sunday. They lived in Hudsonville, a conservative religious farming town, just like Byron Center where they live now. I was pinned "the whore" in the police case, and everyone else was a saint in that pristine Dutch Calvinistic subculture who just wanted to keep their society glued together and away from the misfit spotlight I was now placed under. I was viewed as "chaos," a real annoyance to say anything different than what that closed door subculture wanted the world to believe of them, or know of them. The only thing I had to show for myself these days was exasperation.

I lived out in the rural countryside, the village of Dorr. I was thirty now, still unmarried, scared to date, scared to sleep in my own bed. I was afraid in my own house in which I paid a monthly mortgage payment. I was afraid to go to church, I was afraid of the non-accountable Christians, just terrified of them. I slept with the television on, I slept on the sofa. I remained inside of my house for days at a time with the security system on, just paranoid, frozen in time, unable to move the pages, the chapters of my life forward now, to flip yet another page, I just froze. I did not want to commit suicide, I did not want to be frozen in fear, paralyzed in life and career. I remained in shock, frozen at how my life had turned out by age thirty, and how everyone in the Dutch subculture reacted when I did come forth and tell the truth. Truth in their eyes was evil, it was as if me telling the truth about what happened to me in their subculture, and by whom, was going to collapse their world? Was it their perception to the outside world that mattered most? One thing is for sure, they did not want to hear the truth. They wanted their lives to continue on a horizontal line, as if I no longer existed and was already buried six feet under them. I was put on a back burner, then pushed off the stove by that Dutch Calvinistic community, as if I had tainted their perfect farming community, "with the truth."

Holidays such as Valentine's Day, Christmas, my birthday, Easter, Fourth of July, Thanksgiving, were just holidays on an empty calendar. Memories of how I celebrated those days in Georgia. Such as the smell of colorful roses brought to me, or my favorite perfume, or clothes given to me, the clinging and clamor of wine glasses at my favorite restaurant in Atlanta, how I looked on a date with Alan. Were almost like nostalgia stains almost too painful to recognize now, here in the north, sentimental reminiscing was painful. I did not want to look back and cry at my decisions made in Georgia. I was afraid to move forward, afraid at what opportunities life was going to bring me next. It seemed that my life's opportunities had been so disguised, it seemed so unfair really. The memories of climbing Stone Mountain in Georgia. The sultry humidity in the air, or how my laughter would carry and echo in the southern air on those still humid nights in Georgia as Alan and I would hike down the side of that steep rock of a mountain all sweaty before heading to his house.

Those pleasant memories were painfully dear, close and real in my mind, but so real was the close horror of this reality now as well in the north. Locked in the horrors instilled by a Dutch Calvinistic society, as a subculture made up of many, or one individual, all could care less about the truth, or helping the victim, me.

To reach back in time for me, was painful, to reach forward in my hopes, my future, was scary. I did not want to live in the present either, I wanted to leave the present, I wanted to escape the present, go up north, feel peaceful. I did not want to die, I wanted to escape feeling murdered. To finally feel peace finally and rest.

Seemingly unable to get out of this jar, I could not even see the lid most of the time. I was just buried alive with overwhelming Post Traumatic Stress Syndrome. My darkest hours, were now days, weeks, months, and now years long, so I feared. My mind was playing tricks on me, the ice maker made me jump at two a.m. in the morning, that noise alone would force me to keep myself up in fear and paranoia. I was a mess. Afraid of sleep now, I became delusional during the daytime hours from the sheer lack of sleep. I was afraid to leave my house to show any homes in real estate. I wore no smile, I looked panicky, I was sweating all the time. I did not want to even admit during my therapy sessions what happened to me for fear of facing that reality and then having to talk about my life and the experiences I was trying to run from inside.

I had this locked in feeling of total powerlessness, I was starting to get angry, and hopeless. I had undoubtedly lost my identity as a strong, intelligent, powerful woman that I once felt inside. In hindsight, as I look back to 1998, I realize that was the plan of the men, Dave Smith, Patrick Goodale and Chuck Helder. My counselor at Pine Rest told me that rape is about control, power, and hate. Rape really is not about the sex, the feeling of sex is not the motivating factor in why a man rapes, so I was informed. It was a lot for me to comprehend, but the real question of hindrance was, "When am I going to stop feeling like I have been murdered inside?" When do I get to feel bubbly, warm, vivacious again, alive, like my old self? Wherever is my old self? The person I was? The person I loved? I wondered for days, months, and years to come. It was the year 2000 going on the year 2001. If you could shape and mold a part of me, to represent that part of me torn, taken, lost, kidnapped, never to be returned to me again…….I would say it represents a lamb. A lamb slaughtered, murdered, gone, a lamb that could not take any more from the Calvinist's society and what the American CIA was dishing out. It felt as if I was moving with only a portion of my soul intact, a paraplegic soul is what I am now. I am on earth, part of my soul alive still, but not all of me is still here. I live as if like a paraplegic soul now. Someday I will be reunited with the part of me lost, stolen, gone, murdered by the Dutch Calvinists………. in heaven.

For now I can breathe, but barely, life is different now for me, I have to acknowledge that fact. I would escape the painful memories created in lower Michigan by going up north to Charlevoix. There was a sense of peace on that sandy Lake Michigan beach. I was alone, but I liked the sound of the waves, the seagulls, they seemed happy and busy.

I listened to music endless on my musical headsets as I laid out on the beach in the afternoons. I covered my face to avoid wrinkles and a sunburn. I had lost a lot of weight, I was down to 122 pounds again. Working out in the gym in the mornings in Petoskey helped me burn off my frustration. Men, wealthy types from Chicago, strangers on the beach would come up to my beach blanket, ask me out, almost daily. I would look up from the towel covering my face, and say, "What?" "What?" I'd have tears flowing down my face from manic crying episodes I could not explain.

Strange men would ask, "Why? Why are you crying?" They would look concern. But I could not explain my situation inside of me to the outside world. To them at least, let alone understand it all myself. I was in a glass jar looking outward. I could press my face and hands against the glass jar, but I was locked in, at least for the time being, so it felt. The men vacationing would be maybe five feet away, and yet, I felt so distant as a human being. I think it was in part to the fact of how the Dutch Christian Reformers treated me, all their members, I felt less than human. I felt distant. Cold. Yearning. Simply unable to connect to people from fear of disconnecting from the disillusioned world I was creating in my mind of safety. Where the seagulls, waves, sand and sun, were all that was left? I gave up on people, in a big way. I thought people were very scary. And I had enough of being scared. So now, when people would approach me, try and make conversation with me, I felt startled, jolted almost. I had begun just to block people out of my painful jar. I had music as my friend now, the beach sand to rest on, the crashing waves to soothe me. Lake Michigan to cool me if the sun was or became too intense in the late afternoon hour.

In the Afternoon, daily now, I was asked out, some single men with kids, some without their kids, or simply just had no kids yet, men asking me out left and right. I looked up from the blanket, crying, and again, children, men, would inquire with concern……. "Why are you crying? What is troubling you?" I don't know if it appeared to them on the outside, as if I was in a glass jar simply unable to talk or to be heard. But I felt I was in a glass jar, and it would be useless to even begin to explain why, or how, I just didn't even know why I was crying. And quite honestly, I do not remember when I began crying either. I didn't know.

"I don't know, I don't know why I was crying, it was just a sad song, I suppose." I would reply as I took my headsets off my head.

I never accepted a date in Charlevoix, I was too scared of being alone with a man, even in a public place like a restaurant. I'd go to quaint restaurants in Charlevoix, order take out to take back to the beach to eat by a picnic table. Often the owner of the restaurant, a male, would ask me out as he approached his cashier ringing my order up, noticing I was alone, and wore no wedding band. I always declined, I felt bad, I was not trying to be rude or unsocial. It's just I was afraid of life's opportunities, I was scared of any intimate situation, any type of closeness. I built a fortress around me, an invisible barrier. I was afraid of what had happened to me in the past, events in the past, and from that fear stemmed this isolation of being scared to move forward in society. But I still had, hopes, wishes, desires. I still liked myself. I was just afraid of the world.

Cindy would often call during these very difficult times in the year 2000, she would call me often, it was as if her sadistic addiction fed off my pain. Cindy called not to help me, or guide me, but to really believe and hear how my life had turned out this way. It's as if she gained pleasure from my distance to society. I tried not to pick up the cell phone when she called, it gave her pleasure to hear of my problematic fears, too much pleasure in how my life had turned out thus far, talking about my problems. I noticed she just relished listen to my horrors, loving it I was thirty years old with a destroyed real estate career in west Michigan and unmarried. A real misfit woman in the standards of the Dutch Calvinistic society, that great and powerful octopus. Cindy would remind me I was on the church pray lines in lower Michigan, and that she was praying for me, as I could hear her voice gleam. I could not actually see Cindy's eyes and facial expression gleaming, but I could hear it in her voice.

I was mentally, emotionally, just helpless, dead of the person I once was. I was thirty, still beautiful, I lost so much weight, I was tan, my hair auburn, long layered. I was at my best again. I was too young to feel dead inside. But where was my soul? Inside, it's as if it's gone. I have felt frozen in fear for too long, years now. This is not just some deep unthawing I need to go through now. My soul, part of me is gone. I just feel too empty, for too long.

Cindy never helped me out other than putting me on a church gossip prayer line, and on occasion would lend me money, which is still unpaid, someday I'll repay her. I felt stupid and dependent. When I wanted to feel powerful, smart, have comfort and love right now. When I look back to the year Cindy lived with me in Georgia I realize the similarities in Cindy's guidance as a mother now, more like lack of guidance to assist me in locating a new job, a new career.

I knew better than to ever expect a real genuine Christian out of Cindy, or expect her at this point to act like a mother, or act how a mother should act and be. The horrors that transpired from September 1996 and 2000, just in four years times those Calvinists killed me. Inside, my soul, part of me had vanished.

Cindy never helped me locate a new job, go back to college, find a nice church, or find a nice guy to marry, never, at any point in my life, ever. I simply remained on west Michigan church pray lines by Cindy's requests and guidance of those church prayer lines so Cindy could let others gossip in the church, see me destroyed, and Cindy remains elevated as the saint, her intention all along in my life. I remember when she came and lived with me in Georgia in the early 1990's, she never asked me to go to her church with her in Georgia, she never insisted that I quit The Gold Club, locate a more saintly job in Georgia. Never. I was a misfit, a whore. And she was a saint. I was inside a painting, I never even wanted to be in! I wanted to be in charge of how everything is and was painted, it's my life, my mural! But sadly, I was not in charge of my life, my life so unraveled, out of control by the Dutch Christian Reformers attacks of my life and me personally. "Roman Calvinists," how could I ever pick up the pieces and create any beauty and reward out of my life?

Cindy had me near a plank, and in her deliriously evil mind I would walk that plank if she could just push harder. It is as if she kept in contact, to be close to the source of what she deemed she could visualize as a final failure, she could paint the sunset finally. I felt murdered inside, but I could not prove the murder. I did not feel like killing the rest of me. I was always wandering around, wondering when I would feel normal, like myself again? I did want to laugh again, I wanted to marry someday, have a family. I wanted these imprinted phobias and fears to just evaporate inside of me. But for now I was just frozen scared, parallelized. This was not how I wanted my life to be or end. I was just stuck. Thirty years old and stuck. Cindy is not going to win. The Calvinists are not going to win! I screamed in my head. But it seemed they had won. Cause look at them, and then look at my life, and that is somehow all my fault?

Donna Vander Ark called, she is now my ex-sister-in-law, but back in 2000 she was still married to my brother Dave. She wanted me to meet with Sharon from the Fatman Detective Agency and a husband and wife detective team, Kent and Denise Smith. Donna was persistent for about a year with this matter that I wanted nothing to do with, it was too ridiculous.

"Why? Why Donna do you want me to meet with those three? I told you that in 1998 I received a psychic tarot card reading from Sharon, and she predicted a brutal series of rapes at 405 Discovery Drive, brutal, she predicted the police would do nothing, she predicted the police would be paid in advance from Patrick Goodale and the CIA. Then suddenly two weeks later Patrick rapes me with Chuck Helder watching, just as Sharon had predicted! She predicted I would be drugged, feel as if I am floating upward, and maybe, <u>maybe</u> live to tell the story. Then I try paging her, after the rapes in 1998, and her pager is no longer in use. I paged her for a year, and her pager never was on again. Now she wants to make contact with me? She located you at work in a Grand Rapids hospital? I think Donna, she is trying to set you up. And that Denise Smith, she's bad news according to what Sharon said in 1998. You said Denise Smith works in a hospital? Sharon said in 1998 'that a Smith that lives in Wyoming and works in a hospital, and free-lances for a detective agency is how Patrick gets his knockout drugs.' Are you kidding me, I am absolutely not going to meet with them! Stay away from them Donna. They approached you at work, and they have this idea to be my friend now through you? Or act like your friend? That's crazy! I want no part of Denise Smith dressing up like me, hanging out at Florentines and waiting for Dave Smith or Patrick Goodale to rape her, so she can be some kind of additional complaint to file on a police report. To show a consistent criminal out of Patrick Goodale or Dave Smith. A pattern, is this your idea? Her idea you said, it's ludicrous!" I hung up my cell phone, I was in Charlevoix, Michigan, it was the summer of 2000.

Donna was mad, just furious I would not give money or support her espionage gig of proving Patrick Goodale or Dave Smith is a rapist. It was an utterly ridiculous plan. Supposedly conjured up by Denise Smith according to Nancy Drew Donna.

Donna told me she was going along with Denise Smith's plan, and was going to pay her $35.00 an hour. I wanted no part in it.

Donna kept trying to get me to file a legal suit on Patrick Goodale, Dave Smith, and Chuck Helder in 2000. A civil lawsuit. I wanted peace, I wanted my life to be normal. I did not want a civil suit, court appearances, I wanted my life back to a sense of normal. I wanted that great real estate career I once had.

I never took Donna's advice and hung up the phone while on the beach at Charlevoix. The sunset was spectacular, a kaleidoscope of warm colors.

I just wanted to be on a normal track, not a tossed up chaotic destruction of my young life, thrown disgusting paint colors, and told that's the mural, that's your life, so what if it sucks. I also did not want to roll the dice in a civil lawsuit and hear Rick Bolhouse call me a whore in the court room. I wanted "normal."

I listed my nine unit in Heritage Hills in lower Michigan with Laura Hayden, within two months she sold it and I received a cash equity payment of $60,000. I never refinanced the property thanks in part to Rick Bolhouse and Mike Risko putting hits on my credit report like Woody woodpecker to a tree. I was able to sell the nine unit in Heritage Hills, for profit in my pocket. I used a great portion of the money to pay down the many debts that were piling up. I was not earning money in real estate commissions like my good ol' days. Smith-Diamond Realty refused to cooperate and give me a good referral from all the resumes that I circulated around, just trying to get a job. I was selling off my rental properties in lower Michigan to create an income, at least for now.

Summer turned to Indian summer, early fall, it's a warm and colorful time in northern Michigan, but soon the snow would begin to fall. I rented out a Harbor Springs, Michigan condo in October and November of 2000. I remember looking around the condo, the interior, it was just as Sharon had prophesied. From the front door, the stairways going up, she talked about an old movie theater condo. I learned later it was an old movie theater converted to a condo upstairs and retail below. The white picket fence headboard above the bed I choose to sleep in, I felt like I was Alice in Wonderland as I looked around the condo. How could she predict in 1998, the 2000 interior of this condo in Harbor Springs? I choose the bedroom with the green walls and white picket fence headboard, just as Sharon described in 1998. I choose that particular bedroom because of the window, the light, the other bedroom which was the old movie projector headquarters, had no window. It was the first time I had seen this condo, as I headed up the stairs, it was like a reel playing, Sharon's words to what I saw around me now, as I looked around that condo. Minute details, it was strange, at a time when I wanted the strangeness of my existence to turn to a simmer. All the bizarre predictions she had made to me in 1998, I wanted to just go on simmer for a while. Yet the reality was, all that she predicted I was seeing more and more of, all around me, like a 3D movie of strange sequences, which also freaked me out mentally. It was like stepping into a dream world of Alice and Wonderland, really. I never want to go to a psychic again! This is just too weird.

I continued to exercise at a Petoskey gym. I was lonely, but did not know how to connect to people, I was scared of people. I wanted to be held by a guy, rocked, (that is my favorite) but I was terrified of what that could lead to, inevitably. How can I in my mind, desire and want sex, yet I am 100% freaked out about the idea? It makes no sense, I do agree. Men would come up to me in the gym and ask me out, I must have given them a scared and paranoid look, that's also how I felt inside, and quickly said, "No…no thanks." What people had done to my life scared me. I was disappointed in my friends, it was as if my friends, family I had, all my former associates sided with Smith-Diamond Realty, even the police, the attorneys for the sake of belonging and keeping peace in their world, they shove out the victims. For the sake of clinging to that octopus of power, themselves. Just like Sharon predicted in 1998 would happen. Why she wanted to meet with me now in 2000 seemed inexcusable in my mind. She claimed that CIA agent John Brennan had sent her to the model home in 1998 to warn me to get out of that real estate plat. I know she was involved with my rapes at 405 Discovery, based on all I know as well at this point. I was very unable to pardon her for what she put Patrick Goodale up to, and what he did. Why does he obey her? Why is he connected to her? Why? And why is Cindy, my adopted mother connected to Sharon the psychic since I was about seven or eight years old? Although, Sharon, around my mother Cindy, always went by the name Kim Livermore, the young Bethany Christian Services social worker. Totally and completely undetected by the State system with a private adoption agency.

At age thirty I could not still believe that I was still in search of "normal," not only in my life, but in life in general in Michigan. Wherever normal was or would be, I would someday have it, I could only hope, like some kinda wish upon a star tonight happening. I closed my eyes, I was so exhausted.

Weeks later just after the warm and wonderful Indian summer autumn, I decided to go back to lower Michigan, pay some bills, put my Jeep up for sale, keep my BMW. I decided to take a trip out west, avoid the snow expected to fall soon in Michigan. The wind was picking up, and as anyone knows in Michigan, autumn turns to winter, almost overnight.

So I decided to travel southwest to warm summer like weather, extend the summer that made me feel a sense of peace. I was gone maybe three weeks out west to Colorado and Arizona. I felt like I was being followed, I don't know how to explain it, but wherever I went these men with dark sunglasses, real straight laced looking guys, would be behind me, to the right of me while driving, alongside of me and stare into my car as I drove. I thought it must just be a coincidence that Sharon predicted in 1998 I would be followed. Sharon even had given me dates and time frames. In 1998 I thought that along with everything she said was so ridiculous, so the opposite of normal which was my aim in life, I totally disregarded her strange prophecies. Strange was in understatement of real facts now. Normal as I looked all around, was strange. Why me? Why is this all happening to me? But now paranoia was setting in, her strange prophecies seemed all around me. I could not control the paranoia, I could not control the fear inside me. I was in shock how my life had turned out at age thirty, so spun out of control, by Cindy, Patrick, something larger, bigger? I don't even know. I liked how peaceful I felt this past summer, I linked the nice summer weather with peace. I wanted the summer to continue as I traveled onward to warmer climate out west. But I was being followed by straight laced dressed suits, wearing dark sunglasses, short haircut style men, driving conservative cars. Just as Sharon predicted. Was she playing some kind of joke on me? Yet, I cannot step out of this weird dream called my reality. But why? Why are they following me? Why?

While I was away, out west, I had placed my Jeep at my brother Mike's house in Wayland. My Jeep sold, but no one called me on my cell phone. Instead of keeping the check for five thousand from the sale of my Jeep until I returned, handing me the check for five thousand when I returned. Mike obeyed Cindy and gave Cindy, our mother the check for five thousand. It was her demand that she would take the check and pay some of my bills. I never, ever gave him or her permission to take that $5,000.00 from my Jeep sale and do whatever. Donna Vander Ark had my key to my house at 2030 Winding Oak Drive, and collected my mail while I was away out west for a few weeks as I extended my summer. Donna and Cindy took over my life, although I was unaware of it.

My Jeep sold. My brother Mike sold the Jeep for me. Cindy stepped forward, and said I'll take the bills? The mail? My mail! I suppose that is what she said, and took over paying my incoming bills from the proceeds of the five thousand dollar Jeep sale. I still owned three rental properties at this time in the fall of 2000. Cindy took the liberty, without my knowledge or consent, and spent the five thousand dollar Jeep proceeds on mostly winter taxes for my rentals, nothing towards my own house. In December of 2000 my private residence went into foreclosure. The proceeds from the Jeep sale would have gone a long way in paying my mortgage payments on my primary home. I just could not believe it. The rental homes were for sale, and I have by law three years to pay the property taxes on those rental homes, it certainly was not first and foremost on my list of most important obligations, especially because those rentals were listed, on the market now. My plan was to pay the rental property taxes at the time of closing when the rentals sold and closed. I needed the money from my Jeep sale to pay my mortgage on 2030 Winding Oak Drive in Dorr to avoid foreclosure. Cindy was now back to treating me like a child with no rights. She saw me as a person the Calvinist society had thrown away and she jumped in like a hungry ravishing member of that cult, just ready to devour what she could of my leftover stability and financial flow of money coming in.

Cindy insisted that I give her power of attorney for all my remaining real estate properties. Cindy demanded that at age thirty I should have a will prepared, commenting that it was irresponsible of me at age thirty not to have a will. I ignored her wishes, I considered the source. What I need is a support system, friends, a great family, a new job, a new career, I had nothing. But I was not suicidal like Cindy kept hoping and assuming, praying and wishing. It was as if she could not understand the facts, my reality. I was in rape trauma counseling for my panic attacks, nightmares, my frozen existence in the world.

Essentially, I did want to find a nice guy, get married, have children. Yet Cindy was just insistent that I was suicidal. Why? I never talked about being suicidal. I mentioned I felt murdered inside. There is a difference. But to Cindy, she hears what she wants based on her personal agenda I suppose.

One evening about nine o'clock or so, I am on the sofa watching television at my residence which so happen to be in recent foreclosure in December 2000. I hear a loud bang on my door. I jump up startled. I had just returned from out west, I was not even unpacked yet. I was just lounging around, flipping through the T.V. channels, trying to locate something funny to watch on T.V. to make me laugh. I go to the door, and there is a female officer and a male police officer at my front door.

"Can I help you?" I ask as I open the front door to the brisk winter wind blowing into my house.

The female officer states, "We have a petition, you need to come with us for a mental health evaluation."

I ask, "What, you have a warrant or something for my arrest?"

She responds, "No, a petition."

I ask, "What is a petition?"

The male heavyset officer, chimes in, "The Judge thinks you are going to hurt yourself. There are people who have signed a petition to have you evaluated."

"What?" I inquired.

"Mental evaluation, we have to take you for a mental evaluation." Spoke up officer Rollins.

"Can we come in?" Inquires the female officer.

I respond by asking, "Why?"

The male officer states, "We need to take you to Allegan General Hospital to have you looked at by a staff of mental health professionals."

"You do?" I say, I inquire.

"Yes, can we come in?" The female officer asks again.

"No, I'll be right out, I'm going to get my purse." I stated quickly and within five minutes proceeded back to my front door and followed the female officer to her police car. I am thinking, well, I have to go. I am bewildered, but o.k., whatever, is what I am thinking. They handcuff me, place me in the back of the police car.

The female officer states, "I am driving you to Allegan General Hospital."

"Then what?" I ask while in the back of the police car. The police officer has a female friend with her in the front seat, and comments, "Oh, this is my friend Sherry, she is a loan officer at Independent Bank. She's just along for the ride, to keep me company tonight."

"Can I have some fresh air? Can you crack my window?" I ask from the back seat of her patrol car.

"Well, you will be evaluated, someone is going to talk with you there, to see if you need medication." The female officer states.

The date of all this transpires on or around December 15, 2000.

I arrive and go to a large brown brick hospital. I am led to the main floor large room to the left, then led to a white and light sea foam green room on the main floor, with pastel Easter yellow and teal square floor tiles like elementary school.

But this situation is not kindergarten. I am not on drugs, yet. My life feels like an edited scene from Alice and Wonderland before the edits. And I am told, more than likely, I may need medication.

Later a social worker type of person interviews me while I sit on a hospital bed. Within minutes she states that I am bi-polar.

"What is bi-polar?" I ask bewildered, it was surreal. I had no idea.....I think quietly to myself.......I was just on my sofa watching television. Now, within thirty minutes I am in a hospital with a female police officer and a social worker. It was surreal. I ask, "How long am I here for?" I glanced to the sterile yellow wall, there was the outline of a ship, drawn with pink lipstick, hidden slightly by a drawn curtain. I wanted to instantly walk over to that hospital bed, and fling back the rest of that curtain, and see who was there, if anyone at all. And then examine that pink lipstick drawing of a ship. I felt like a marble inside a maze. You cannot remove yourself, you just move forward and keep following that maze pattern, right? You have to. It looked like what this trip felt like, a dream........but real.

"Well, by law we can keep you for three days, your mother Cindy pleaded with an Allegan Judge that you need to be rescued from your suicidal thoughts and got the Judge to sign her petition that she started," Spoke the social worker.

"But I am not suicidal. I just spoke to my mother Cindy yesterday, she never mentioned this whatsoever." I stated, mad that my mother is such a cunning and devious person behind my back, and that an intelligent well educated Judge in Allegan county actually believes her, she is dangerous, to put me here. There is nothing I can do. They make a copy of my driver's license, my medical insurance card and then lead me to move upstairs for an extended three day vacation all covered by my health insurance, Priority Health of Grand Rapids.

There was maybe about eight patients there, mostly all woman. I did not sleep a wink the very first night. I just stared at the ceiling. I could not believe I was sleeping tonight in a mental ward, I was just watching T.V. thirty minutes ago, I think I left my T.V. on? But I was not anywhere near my remote, my house, my own bed.

The next day Cindy and Jerry Honderd arrive. The first thing Cindy blurts out with a grinning smile, "I feel sorry for you. Are you homeless yet?"

"Homeless yet?" I said with a wince of anger. But I could not yell at her. I am afraid of her and her unyielding power among the Calvinists elite.

"Yes, you have financial difficulties, that is why you are suicidal, that is what Mike Risko and Rick Bolhouse have told us and the Allegan Judge. We just all feel so sorry for you in Grandville. We are all praying for your mental recovery." Spoke the manic and elated Cindy at the very sheer sight of me locked in a mental ward as she glances around the lime green room with accomplished eyes. "Cindy," the one who is technically by law my mother on paper, my only parent left. I remember looking at Cindy in a new light in that mental ward she put me in, standing there next to my hospital bed. I distinctively remember the shine of the commercial grade interior design of my mental ward hospital room, it was such a sterile environment. Void of key elements of love and a voice for human needs, it's as if she matched the cold commercial feel of that hospital mental ward. I always loathed Cindy, I never bonded with her. I was now completely fearing her, and her new found power in Mike Risko, the new attorney at the Grandville granite old State bank building.

I looked at Cindy in this shiny of places and saw how she resembled all that is acceptably fake in that subculture of west Michigan. I was actually really scared of her, what she could do to my life, the power she held over my life with her title of "mother." The acting, her mother acting of being all concern was twisted. My mouth was a bit dry as I spoke, a combination of the medication and the sheer, very real, non-delusional fear of what Cindy can do to me and my life…..if she supposedly wants. My life since 1996 moving back home to Michigan is a complete nightmare. It has only been four, going on five years since I left Georgia. I looked down and around to my unfamiliar surroundings, this was so surreal.

"I brought you some clothes, perfume, shampoo, curling iron, things you might need from your house." Stated Cindy as she began arranging and pouring out items on my hospital bed. I wanted to be powerful as I stood in her presence, but I just stared at her in stunned silence, humility, my throat parched.

Then I spoke up, mumbled, just dazed, "I feel like a builder…….like dad. Defeated. Set-up by you to look like a failure, when I am not, it is just a label they or you want on me. Because you think you can, you can do this to a victim. It's wrong." As much as I wanted to stand up and speak there was someone in that subculture that wanted me to shut up. Wanted this moment of defeat for me, but why?

Jerry responds, "A builder? You're not a builder, your dad? You need help, you are not a builder. You are not your dad." Jerry shakes his head back in forth in disbelief at what I had commented as a philosophical analogy of how I felt right then and there. I just stared at Cindy, she is evil. I can't prove it, but she is evil. I looked at Jerry, no matter what I say, he will deem it as crazy now. And hey, look at my surroundings, I guess I am crazy, legally. Cindy has me where she wants me. Nothing I say will be believed. I am in a jar made of genuine thick hospital glass, screaming, but the lid is so tightly sealed by the four inch thick glass no one can hear me scream if I wanted to scream in this nightmare. I could not seemingly, frantically wake from this nightmare as the back of my neck and hair began to sweat. Just like a dream, a bad nightmare, like when I was young. A flashback of when I was eight, tormenting nightmares, watching myself drive a chariot back to a city after a lost war against Octavia and Marcus Agripa of Rome. I feel doomed.

"That one lady there is friendly, she talked to us for about ten minutes." States Cindy, referring to this heavyset lady in the mental ward, a patient. Jerry was quiet for a moment, and then looked shocked at the latest turn of events by Cindy too, or perhaps shocked in discovering the real Cindy, what had he married? He must be thinking Cindy is devious and somehow I also ended up crazy, was a bit freaky for him. He must have thought Cindy is very devious to control those she thinks she can manipulate. It was a thought also shared by me, also in shock at the latest turn of events as Christmas 2000 loomed around the corner. Cindy though was not shocked, she acted like she was in church and the minister just finished his sermon and she was meeting and greeting all she could in that hospital mental ward. It was a well anticipated social event for her, she appeared happy, elated. Cindy acted like she had waited a long time for this party, in her mind, in her visions, this was actually a very happy moment for her and the American CIA to finally label me crazy. I remained stunned. They had a plan I just realized now, to make me look crazy, or go crazy. Why would the United States government do that to a citizen? Me? Because I knew too much about what they were up to, as if they couldn't get those pills shoved down my throat fast enough, and make me bang into walls. Then point at me, "Oh, that witness, over there?"

I shove aside my dignity, my terror I feel inside at my situation I was placed in, and speak with relative calm. "I'll be in here for three days total. Please make sure the lights and television are off in my house." I really did not have much to say to elated Cindy at this obvious moment of joy for her.

I also found it odd that during my Post Traumatic Stress period of 2000, the memories that would surface. When I vomit my memories in 2000 up, the rapes at 405 Discovery of 1998, how I was drugged and beaten, harassed and taunted by the Calvinists, when I began addressing the deer in the headlights, so to speak. I also began coughing up other lost issues, matters that Dr. Terri Ann estimated in her psychoanalysis in 1986 when I was just sixteen that I would eventually question what really happened to my father Charles Vander Ark. Questions within me such as, did my mother have something to do with my father's death? Somehow that was an issue I was now wondering about in 2000, and talking about, and recently had questioned Cindy about! I also brought up many issues I had as a child, just repressed at the time of the trauma occurrences, such as 1982, when I had surgery to remove swollen cysts from my body due to a significant beating from Cindy and her CIA male consorts. Whatever I repressed, I was now coughing up in 2000. I did not know why, I could not control the mental vomit of past situations, as if I could not hold it in any longer. In 2000 the files were being spit out of my head like a malfunctioning computer that Cindy needed to shut up, close up. Get rid of, for her fear of me talking and people believing the truth, unless I am labeled crazy. Not just labeled crazy by church gossip lines and the community, but truly labeled crazy as in classified professional documents on hospital psychiatric letterhead paper labeling me crazy with a definite legal term.

There were many truths Cindy wanted thrown away forever. If she could take my traumas she inflicted upon me all my life and shove them in a back drawer somewhere, slam the drawer shut, lock it, she would. She would go to extremes to never have her image tarnished, or the CIA. How very loyal of Cindy! To never extenuate her true essence of her soul. And sure enough, here I was in a mental ward, take a picture Cindy, no one will believe any past abuse now.

Image is everything in the Dutch Christian Reformed religion and U.S. government. Everything is in your reflection to the outside world to them, not what is behind the watery reflection. That whole society is a glue of reflections on a paper canvas. Even at their Dutch Calvinist funerals of their dearly departed they would cut and paste the picture of that person all over a cardboard poster, as being very representative of their existence. Memories in such of their wonderful cardboard life among them.

Carmen called me up at the mental ward one afternoon. As if to call to confirm a rumor now circulating around town, she needed the truth, she needed to know if I was actually in a mental ward locked up. I took the phone call. But I could not change my situation that I was literally locked into, another jar, with no way to the lid, no way out of the thick metal mesh of glass windows to the outside world.... another jar I am in. This one I can actually see and feel, it is not just in my head. I am not laughing or amused. Carmen asks me if I ever met any celebrities at The Gold Club? I answer "Yes." Then Carmen methodically asks me if I ever met any CIA agents at The Gold Club? I answer "Yes."

Carmen then says, "It's a good thing you are in a mental hospital getting the help you need."

The conversation was brief with Carmen. Her voice as warm as ever, her demeanor and logic very chilly on the other end of the phone receiver.

I met with several social workers in the hospital. I was placed on something, a drug to help slow down my electrons in my brain. I was categorized as being in a mania stage of bi-polar, so I was told, so I was diagnosed by the professionals. I was told that I talked too fast, my thoughts were racing, so I was told. And I did have trouble sleeping. They would know, because I was videotaped every night. A video camera set up in my room at the hospital. I remember looking out the big commercial size windows at the hospital. The snow looked so pretty falling down. I touched the cold glass but I could not get out and touch the snowflakes transcending on the ground and large pine trees. But somehow this place was going to help me forget the past, so I was told.

I met on a daily basis with an Italian psychiatrist for three days. He was very tall, lanky, dark hair, with a sympathetic disposition, he looked like an Italian Jesus. He was not bold and dashing, he was non-aggressive in his aura, very reflective and contemplating in demeanor. His office however was oddly decorated like an Egyptian tomb. I remember looking around for the first time in his office, just weirded out by the sheer number of Egyptian artifacts piled on top of cabinets. Egyptian artifacts decorated the other furniture and walls in his office. I felt nervous, and laughed, "Is this where I have come to die?" I asked as I walked into his office.

"What?" He asked quietly as he absorbed me in his thoughts, his mind for a moment, as he looked at me, he was trying to soak in my being? To figure out how my mind works?

"Why is your office decorated and adorned with everything Egyptian? It's like the pyramid cavities ran out of room." I asked.

"Oh, we have a doctor who works part-time in the hospital, I share this office with him, he is from Egypt." He remained seated, contemplating in nature, his hand resting on his face, holding his head up, gazing ahead at me.

"Interesting. Can I meet him?" I asked.

"Oh no, he works part-time and is off this weekend." The Italian doctor stated.

I looked around as I left that office, as one patient slumped to his office door as I was trying to open the door to leave. I looked around the hall at the zombies. I said to the Italian psychiatrist, "Do you know what these people really need?"

He responded, "What?"

"They really need love. The balance and harmony that love can bring them." I said as I looked over my shoulder. I knew what I was missing in my life. I knew that the human elements of balance and harmony and love are needed for human stability. Yet I could not bring in what was not in my life when I needed those elements for stability. Somethings are just not controllable, or as I was discovering, not attainable, like simple comfort after traumas.

His eyes perked up, "You are really insightful." He wore a surprised twinkle in his eyes. As if I knew something that the rest of the general public knew nothing about inside Allegan General Hospital's mental ward, fourth floor.

I had stumbled upon a possible cure for mental instability, mental and emotional trauma. Love is not a doctor's prescription. Sometimes the mind wants to search deeper for a cure. Religious scholars can have that same effect of deciphering God, and salvation to the masses. The other end of the spectrum is the de-caffeinated instant forgiveness of the Calvinists, so to speak, who just select and choose which one verse in the Bible that pertains to them and their eternal relationship with Jesus. Yet, it is a fact Jesus never even wrote that very memorized "Christian verse of salvation." Please note, for those zealous fire Christians, in heaven, one does not speak in tongues, to enter heaven. For now, it appeared to me that the world was lonely, the world was so misguided, yet, I was stuck here, for now. Not as a philosopher, but a patient, petitioned by no other than Cindy and the courts. I spent time thinking, plenty of time to think while in a mental ward about religion, society, and how systems and status quos were always trying to mold me to be like them. It was December 2000, there was a lot of media hype about "the world ending," yet there were no news broadcast about my world ending, none whatsoever. It was my own private hell created by the Calvinists, Calvinist Cindy put me here with her petition that I am crazy, a misfit. I felt so alone.

And then about 24-hours into my vacation, "trip of sorts," I got a knock on my hospital door that was open, but a knock nevertheless. It was not Halloween, it was Christmas 2000, but this person was dressed up in a lion suit, furry, fuzzy, large and ostentatious lion costume. I shook my head a few times as he approached me with a black doctors bag. He walked in, approached my bed, and took the head of his costume off. He looked so familiar, he immediately asked me to be quiet by a gesture he made….. "shisssh." He said, "I'm Greg." He asked me not to tell anyone what took place between us. I agreed, it was a concoction of purse size vodka dosages and hospital drugs prescribed by nurse Ratchet in the hallway, I agreed. It was so good what he did to me between the sheets, it certainly was worth keeping quiet about, I rationalized. I did wonder, if it was caught on tape? If it would ever turn up? The video? I was not sure if this was a CIA scandal kept secret in the making.

It appeared that it was a man secretly obsessed with me and would do anything to please me before stepping back behind the hospital curtain, back behind the scenes. I wanted an encore, but he said I would have to wait. I remember he brought with him, testosterone cream, smeared it, massaged it, and stated to me as I remained quiet and still, "I looked at your medical records, your blood work shows you have very little testosterone, and a high level of estrogen, more than most woman. I will help you recover. I know I was rough at first with you, but I will be part of your sexual healing process. I will prepare you well before entering you. I know it is difficult for you to get aroused because of your rape traumas in 1998. I will lead you through to the other side, the rainbow, the colors, you will begin to see in your life once again Lilly.

I will let you know what I am doing and when and why I am touching you a certain way. You will build trust with me and not be scared anymore. I want you dependent upon me, I need you dependent and trusting……….I have great hope that you will heal, and I will be the man you depend on to lead you.

Then he added…. "We'll practice some more tomorrow, I'll have my two assistant nurses wash you and help clean up this mess you and I made on each other." He told me to be quiet. I did as he said, and remained still as the two young yet heavyset nurses that he came in with, the nurses who watched, also now cleaned us. I felt like I had wet my pants, but I hadn't, the hospital blanket was wet…..but I couldn't control it either. I was also very aware that I was not in control. I am now left wondering, is that what all this is about? Control by the CIA to make me go crazy? Or at least make me sound crazy if I talk about things? We practiced a total of three times in the hospital room, of me giving him full control. He looked identical to Patrick Goodale, same features and all. He never fully undressed. I could not see his chest and shoulders. The other two times in the hospital he was dressed like a doctor in a white long jacket. He opened his fly area only. He said the weirdest thing well he was in me. He turned to the two nurses and stated just as he was fully in me and there was no way for me to move. He remarked, "Black hair against spiced auburn praline like this moment is my favorite." He would pull out of me at times, have the two nurses remove his condom, be very hands on like, groping his part. Not that he had a difficult time keeping it up. But he liked the attention, how the women would fuss over putting on a new condom. Washing and stroking, and commenting, and then helping him insert…….This "attention withdrawal syndrome" of his happened about five or six times during the sex sessions. We were not between the white sheets, but somewhere on white paper sheets the red ink was drying on the stamped word of "Classified."

O.k., that wasn't so bad, what's next? I was released after three days. I never knew that so many worlds within a world, this world, ever existed, but I was learning through experience I suppose. I agreed that week to my mother Cindy that I would make out a will and to give her power of attorney over my real estate deeds, and name her as the beneficiary of my will, I gave her a copy as requested. I walked around in a daze, it could have been from the medication prescribed to me. The hospital charged up my insurance card like a credit card, a shopping spree of five thousand dollars charged for an unexpected trip. I knew I was not in control of my life. But honestly, I did not know how to get my life back, and to regain control of my life. I felt beaten down emotionally and mentally, but I wanted to heal.

During the winter of 2001 I began a three week outpatient treatment from 9am to 4pm in group and individual therapy at Pine Rest. The male intake social worker asked me what I thought the cause of my mental breakdown, or mania episodes were caused by.

"My mother? My rapes at a real estate model home in Wayland? What I endure by the Calvinist's subculture daily? My whole life? What I have to endure from this world? I don't know. The American Central Intelligence Agency? You tell me. You're the expert."

I explained to him about the rapes of 1998, he stopped me and said, "You breathed in some substance on a washcloth placed under your nose? That was probably ether, a chemical that is used to knock out a person before surgery." He spoke so matter of fact about the subject of my rapes at 405 Discovery Drive. Odd, because as I reflect upon the feeling I felt as I was raped in 405 Discovery Drive, it did feel as if I was coming out of a surgery, that same drowsy feeling one has after surgery.

To me, lately, I was in such a daze, confused why my life was turning out in this manner. It was as if I had fallen in a rabbit hole, entered into a passage of a maze, backed into a corner, how do I get out? How do I get back to being the powerful, self-confident, happy, a bubbly person that I used to be? The police were supposed to help me, not side with the powerful CIA and their devious plans! I was just stunned as I looked out the windows of his office, I was turning thirty-one soon, in a few weeks. He shuffled around paperwork in the chaos of his own very busy schedule at Pine Rest, scribbled down his notes, his evaluation of me.

I wanted to grab his arm and scream, <u>Look</u>, I had a life, I don't know where it is, but I had a life once. I am more than a stack of paperwork. Life, my life cannot be measured by a description, notes, my life meant so much more than that to me. This paperwork does not measure my life's worth or my problems!

But I kept my mouth shut as I stared straight ahead in a daze, drugged, weak, powerless to becoming the standard I once was inside. I was only thirty, almost thirty-one, but inside as I looked outward to him, to the world, my surroundings, I felt like how an elderly person feels like inside as they slump around on a cane towards the end of their life. Somehow unable to get back what was lost in my ability to live a quality life. Although physically I looked so healthy, I looked beautiful on the outside. But inside I could relate much easier to an elderly person or vice versa, in how the world viewed me now. How the world views seniors as throwaways in America, especially the Dutch culture here. I felt as if I was a toss away of the same society, the Dutch Calvinists who made me feel this way, it was unfair, I could never prove it though. And how I saw the world, there, existing, but just passing me by, unable to smell the roses in my state of being, was not by choice, I was stuck. I wanted to smell the roses. The sun was out, but I could not feel it's warmth. I snapped out of my daze to answer, to respond to another question asked of me……

I responded slowly, "That's how I felt, as if waking up from surgery or going into surgery." I went on to ask him, "So what am I?"

"What are you?" He responded quickly, sharply as he looked at me.

"Eh, my diagnosis? What you just wrote down there on the paper." I asked.

"You're bi-polar, that's what Allegan General diagnosed you as, I would have to agree with them. I need a copy of your driver's license and health insurance card." He asked and stated to me as he shut his folder rather briskly.

"That's what is wrong with me? I am bi-polar? That is why I feel this way inside, murdered? Breathing, but murdered inside? How do I get myself back?"

There was a pause, a moment of silence…….then he spoke up.

He sighed, looked at me like I appeared not as a patient but a professor of mental health for a spilt second, I startled him with what I had just said. He looked me up and down as if to size my intelligence up of that moment of truth in his office, "Yep, you're bi-polar."

I met many people at Pine Rest during my three week outpatient treatment that all had a different story of trauma. Whether it be a divorce, loss of a career, accident, or just a plain old mental break down. As we all sat in a group I noticed some were very forth coming about their trauma or traumas and the people they blamed for their mental break down. Others just sat paralyzed staring at the floor, almost angry. One thing was for sure, what we had in common was we had our lives folded by others and we were like zombies. It made me feel uncomfortable to be like a zombie, a daytime sleep walker in life now.

Most of them in the circle complained about a person in their life, whether it be a boyfriend, soon to be ex-spouse, mother, etc. A significant portion of their complaint, what they could not forget or get over involved another person, a person they deeply regretted knowing and giving control of their life to for a span in their history. That person however, was not present. Everyone had some trauma that they could not fully understand, comprehend, and get over in their life. It was as if we all hit a deer in the road and could not figure out how the deer got there, or why we could not stop or swerve to avoid the poor deer in the road as we obviously all collided into a mental file from out of nowhere as we sat in a circle and shared our stories. Some people could not seem to open up, they remained hostile to the group, but somehow benefited from listening for hours to our misery and discomforted realties. Listening to our unsuccessful broken lives at that moment in time they connected to, you could see it in their silent appeasing expression they wore. Our deep subconscious abyss seemingly spit out old tossed out files, our lost mental trauma files, lost in that deep abyss of our minds that we never dealt with at the time of our traumas. I just kept going to the group therapy meetings, and individual one on one counseling. I kept searching for what I lost in my mind, I lost myself, part of myself. I determined I lost myself, and I was mad. I was determined to find what I lost, I wanted all of me back, back inside my body. I was told that if I talked about it, my issues, that I would recover.

Recover? I just felt tired. Yet ironically, I could not fall asleep well at night. I still just stared at the television screen as some last source of positive personal interaction to comfort me as I laid awake scared each night. I was overwhelmed at the reality I had so unexpectedly discovered in thirty-one years of knowing the Calvinist's subculture. Everything they portrayed to the world around them, it was a lie, a cover. It was a society lacking in moral conscious for one another, an instant dose of forgiveness culture that adopted Jesus. A society that hated victims, the Calvinist society appeared powerful and united, and hated outsiders who did not fit into their mold of normal among them. I was at the bottom of the pit they dug for me, but I did not want to be the victim. I obviously could never prove who held the shovel, and who dumped the dirt over me. I realized that truth, I could taste the dirt, spit it out if I wanted to, but it was my fault I was looking upward to fading light in my world. I was aware of where I was, who put me there, many, many members of the Dutch Calvinist society. However, I could never prove my murder among them. And that subculture, knew it, as do the many victims, misfits labeled by them. The Dutch Calvinist is a large octopus with many tentacles, many powerful attachments, I now know that fact, I experienced and had endured that fact.

I met with a Dr. Gary at Pine Rest he was my assigned psychiatrist during my three week outpatient therapy, he would become my psychiatrist for the upcoming year as well. In the spring of 2001, Dr. Gary said to me, "You mentioned you worked at The Gold Club, it is under investigation, the owner Steve Kaplan is being investigated for tax evasion and racketeering, it's all over the news." He said one morning or afternoon.

"What?" I asked. My head began to spin, this was a surreal moment for me.

Sharon had predicted in 1998, while sitting at my table in 1998 at that real estate model home in Wayland, Michigan, 405 Discovery Drive, that Steve Kaplan was going to jail for tax evasion in the future. I begin to flip the pages of time back, Steve's friends would come up to me in the years of 1994-1996 at The Gold Club and say, "Steve's psychic said this in his last reading….." all of which were bizarrely being played out now in of all places, Pine Rest. It was surreal. I began thinking back to many things she predicted that I chalked up as bizarre. I also recalled a phone message I received one year ago, spring-summer of 2000. I came home to my house in Dorr in 2000 and played a blinking red message from a woman on my answering machine. It stated that Patrick Goodale had paid an enormous amount of money to have The Gold Club investigated for money laundering, racketeering and shut down with no investigation of the CIA's human trafficking ties to Middle Eastern foreign countries.

The stranger with a monotone female voice went unto say, "Patrick Goodale needed The Gold Club shut down because you cracked and went to the cops about getting raped, he had to get rid of other victims from that nightclub. You were not supposed to go to the cops. You have been warned." I played the message over and over in 2000. Just trying to place the voice, it did not sound like Sharon, as I remembered her voice though. Who was it? On my caller I.D., it just read, "out of area," with no number to call that person back.

It was baffling in 2000 to hear that message on my answering machine. Now in 2001 I am just trying to place the pieces of this jigsaw puzzle, all of which Sharon predicted in 1998 to my face, is now strangely occurring. I very much felt as if I was sucked into a situation that was a bigger picture than what I could comprehend at the time in 2000, or ever prove. I brought up to Donna in 2000 what that lady said on my answering machine, I even played the message for Donna. She thought it was Sharon's voice, but I only spoke to Sharon during three tarot card readings. I only slightly remember her voice, I do remember what I remember of her, what she looked like. What she predicted. One day I came home and my answering machine messages were erased, even the saved messages.

I remember Sharon telling me in 1998 that Hollywood was going to come to Grandville and roll back the clouds and create a movie about my life years from now, many movies would be made of my life. I scratched my head, and asked why? I remember Sharon telling me many things I could not fathom, let alone believe…..

"A documentary, a motion picture, many television mini-series are going to be made of your major life memoirs, still unwritten, but will be written." Sharon said in her 1998 predictions of my life.

I remember firmly telling her in 1998, "I do not want to write a novel, not now, I like real estate, it's my niche. I want to put off writing, and just have my normal real estate career, I am earning six figures in real estate."

It is now 2001, three years after she made that prediction. I could hardly take another breath here on the sofa. I felt so exhausted from these people, the Calvinists. I had no family, my mother controlled my three brothers and Jerry's side of the family, his kids she controlled. Carmen told everyone that I went to school with that I went off the deep end of the ocean, complete with a hospital stay in a mental ward. Warning everyone to stay away from me in the community, I am contaminated with not being like them, a perfect façade, a perfect label of normal.

My house at 2030 Winding Oak Drive was now in foreclosure since December of 2000. Winter 2000-2001 was now breaking into spring of 2001, the snow was beginning to melt like an iceberg in and around Michigan. I felt like a shut-in within my own home. I was too young to feel like an old shut-in, I thought as the ice sickles dripped water off my roof. If I talked about anything, it seemed to unreal, and I was labeled crazy. I could hardly sleep, barely concentrate, I did feel crazy, drugged now, what have you. But I used to not be like this mentally and emotionally. I needed to pull myself together, I don't know where to begin though I thought in quiet desperation. I want restitution for all that I lost. I want an apology from the three men. I want an apology from their bully set of attorneys and associates. I placed several calls to a few Grand Rapids attorneys. I honestly forgot all about attorney Chuck Rominger, he would have been helpful at this junction in my life. He was the first attorney I sought out help and legal advice from in the fall of 1998 over this very matter of feeling murdered. But for some unknown reason, I just opened up the phone book and began calling around, down the list of Yellow Pages attorneys posted.

I talked with an attorney named, Lee Silver. I met with him at his office and told him everything, and then looked up from his polished conference table with many scribbled pages on a pad of paper. I looked at the Picasso painting on his wall before me. I thought to myself, that Picasso painting is my life, beautiful to some, yet a fragmented painting, very controversial in it's rare beauty, yet worth so much if I could just write away, on and on write about my life.

I glanced away at the Picasso painting on his wall, and I asked Lee Silver, "Now you know what happened, what I endured, where do I begin? Where do you begin? How can you help me now? The Michigan Police Post in Wayland treated this case like something they wanted to discard, like I am some kind of confederate daughter with no value on northern territory, lost or something."

Lee Silver paused, he then states, "I read the Michigan State Police report. I don't like the police report prepared by Detective Gutierrez, it's sloppy, it does not favor you, or collaborate anything that you have said at this table. Policemen and police detectives are not attorneys. Details matter little to them in the scope of paperwork or getting paid with a pension. Frankly, eighty percent of the time I read a police report, it is sloppy. Always an attorneys nightmare of the worse paperwork typed and prepared, always. The police are too busy, underpaid, under educated, and frankly they just don't care. If I filed in civil court, a formal lawsuit against Smith & Goodale it would turn into a he said she said case. Jurors are very conservative in Grand Rapids. Not in Detroit, but here, they hate victims, and they hate plaintiff attorneys. You would never get an apology you want or deserve from those men. Let's face it, you deserve at least an apology, you deserve to have your career put back in place. But let's face it, they destroyed your career, basically firing you, by raping you. They knew you would not stay in real estate if they raped you. Perhaps they raped you because they wanted you out of the area. They feared your presence in their world, their real estate world. They owe you money for pain and suffering, but you will never get an adequate amount, the amount you should be awarded with a west Michigan jury box, never. What I am willing to do for you is put together a pre-settlement letter. Basically explain in length what you went through and put it on paper, details caused by them, and demand that they give you restitution."

I responded, "A pre-settlement letter?"

Attorney Lee Silver responds, "Yeah, it is what us attorneys do prior to filing a lawsuit. But I am not going to file a lawsuit, it is an uphill battle with that sloppy police report. The police report favors them, they will have their attorneys pull the police report out in court, if indeed the whole case is not dismissed prior to the big day. Pulling out the police report like a magic trick, a rabbit out of a hat that favors them. Juries place a lot of weight on police reports, they just do. I can scare the men of a lawsuit, a very public lawsuit, scare them with interviewing the people you mentioned that supposedly know so much. But I will only scare them into believing I would actually file one. I'll bluff, they'll believe I am serious though. I wrote down and documented everything you just said here at the table. I will type this and fax you by Friday. I'll need for you to initial each page as correct information on paper, something the police should have had you do as well. But that's another case, that's just how police are. I need your fax number, sign this ten percent agreement of attorney fees. Notice I have highlighted that I will not be filing a lawsuit if you do not accept whatever they offer as a pre-settlement. There is no guarantee that they will offer any money in restitution, no guarantee, but I will try for you. I have a reputation in town, and I know their attorneys will want to settle verses going to court against me." (See the multi-page pre-settlement letter prepared by Lee Silver in the spring of 2001 in Wayland City Police case file #211-04, Wayland City Hall in Michigan. Along with my polygraph test results that I am 100% telling the truth.)

The attorney Rick Bolhouse for the three men addressed in Lee Silver's pre-settlement letter, Patrick Goodale, Dave Smith, Chuck Helder, offered in their response that the three men are willing to pay $30,000 cash. If I did not accept the cash amount by the specified date in March of 2001, Rick Bolhouse threatened verbally to Lee Silver that his associate attorney, Michael P. Risko would file a slander suit against me. In their written response on letterhead, cunning and devious Rick Bolhouse then writes in, We are not willing to pay $100,000.

I thought as I read Rick Bolhouse's response, what an odd response. I never said $100,000 would correct taking my real estate career away. I never mentioned any amount to Lee Silver, ever. Lee Silver never mentioned that amount or any amount other than the $30,000 offered on the table by their attorney. So where did attorney in crime Rick Bolhouse ever come up with the amount of $100,000 would not be paid? Seriously.

I rejected the amount. I was mad more than anything. I wanted to be treated fairly, I wanted my real estate career back before I had been raped. I wanted apologies. I wanted these men to know how much they damaged me. I made an average of $89,000 in real estate from sale commissions, listing and selling homes. In 1999 I earned $163,000. What made me the most mad, is being treated like a black woman run out of a white town by Cindy and the rest of the Calvinists in on the crimes against me. What those men took was my livelihood, how I supported myself financially. I liked my normal real estate career, less the sexual harassment and torture by those in power. In 1999 I was twenty-nine years old earning $163,000 that year. If you took my average yearly income in real estate and times that amount of $89,000 over the next thirty years, the lifespan of my real estate career from ages twenty- eight to fifty-eight. I just am not coming up with any number close to $30,000 or $100,000. I was told in the spring of 2000 when I left Smith-Diamond Realty that any and all past clients, referrals would never reach me again. I was told by Chuck Helder, Dave Smith, and Nancy Vanden Berg that any and all phone calls that came into Smith-Diamond Realty for me now, into their office, would turn into a sale for their agents. They would never forward on those past clients that I had built, and pass them rightly to me. Everything I had built in my real estate career, the Calvinists at Smith-Diamond Realty would and could take, and did. Just another power play on how they controlled the world of real estate in those parts. But I am not black, why the hell are these people treating me like this? I wanted to scream, and if I screamed, they would also call me "irrational," laugh at me. All nod with one another that they are correct over my life. But they are wrong.

Wrong to treat me like this. Wrong to go to church, and act like God loves them. Wrong.

Then there is the legal matter of pain and suffering, I am not even close to the happy bubbly person I was before 1997. I sleep on the sofa with the television on. I put my security alarm system on by the afternoon hour. I am scared out of my mind. I sleep with a pillow covering my face because I can't fall asleep now without feeling a need for a sense of protection, to avoid a painful blow to my face that I received at 405 Discovery Drive in Wayland. How does one measure the worth of safety? Feeling safe? A sense of peace and security lost?

I have no idea when I'll be back to my old self, that is a mystery still unresolved, unsolved, I thought.

About a week after rejecting the amount of $30,000 in the spring of 2001, cash to wipe this all away, "shut-up money," swipe my life aside, my career loses, my pain under the rug for $30,000, the doorbell rings. It's about 9pm in the evening, the sky is dark with no apparent sparkling stars, it's pitch black. I'm already in my pajamas, my hair pulled back in a ponytail. I proceed to the front door to see through the glass panes, a women. An older woman about seventy years or older. She was not too tall, not really heavy, maybe slightly stocky. Her hair in a short stacked hairdo, her hair grey, eyes cold blue. She wore shorts and drove a silver Jeep Cherokee parked in my driveway just inches from my garage door. She begins pounding, "Let me in, let me in."

I gasp, I am just taken back by how forward and bossy this senior citizen stranger is at my door. I glance at my security system, thank God it is activated. I stood by my dining room bay window, she could see me, but she remained focused on my front door for some reason. My house is three thousand square feet, and I am at the center of not knowing which way to run or hide. And I can't get away from this bully of a woman, I'm blocked in, she's in my driveway.

She wanted that front door open, she kept knocking, and knocking, and saying repeatedly, "Let me in!" I could tell by her insistence and demeanor that she was one old lady that is accustomed to getting her way. I talked with her through the glass, the bay window area, she finally after ten minutes or so said to me "You're not going to let me in?"

I responded, "I don't even know who you are. No." I felt my throat get dry from sheer fear of this sudden disturbance, this unannounced stranger at my front door, wanting to come inside my house. I was scared of this woman, she comes unannounced, and demands that I let her in my house late one evening. I am wondering, who is waiting in the dark if I let her in? Shut off my security system? My heart is racing, pounding, this is so bad for my recovery of my fear and phobias. I thought quietly as my startled heart raced on and on by the glass window.

"Let me in, let me in this door I said." She kept repeating that over and over.

I asked through the glass, "Who are you? Are you an attorney?"

She pauses, not wanting to tell me who she is outside that door. And says slowly, "No...... I am not an attorney."

I ask, "Well who are you? What do you want?" I am terrified at this strange woman who wants in my house. I thought, she just bought me ten sessions with my therapist to discuss feelings of being paranoid, therapy of healing from being scared and paranoid. This strange lady is not helping my therapy, my road to recovery.

"I am Pat's mother, I want to talk with you, we can all work this out. I do not want this to go any further. Then the senior citizen threatens me by saying, "Or we'll tape a lawsuit on your door here next week."

Now I am totally frightened of her. I respond, "I am not going to let you in."

She left, she was actually shocked I did not let her in my house, shocked. But why would I let an unannounced strange woman in my house at 9pm, while I am in my pajamas? What was she going to do to me? I was freaked out. If I disarmed my alarm system to let her in, who knows who would have popped out of the bushes or her car. It was scary how the Goodale family conducted themselves in a town they made others believe they owned. Everyone bought into their clout and allowed for their misbehavior in west Michigan. I was scared, I'll admit that very prevalent fact. But I am not going to bow to them.

Two weeks later as I came home from the gym I approach my garage door as I drive up. I notice there is a large yellow envelope duck taped to my garage door. I open up the envelope, inside is a proclamation of a lawsuit filed in Allegan county courts. Attached to filed case no. 10-28818NZ is proof that it is a sealed case. I cannot believe that the men I refused $30,000 from, have **now** actually filed a slander suit against me, for telling the police what they did to me. They consider it slander **now** because they were not arrested at the end of the police investigation? Unbelievable!

Coupled with this is blackmail on their part for me refusing to accept $30,000 from them, simply blackmail on their part! Just as Lee Silver had warned they would do to me in retaliation, in a world of power and battles they wanted to control all. My mind skips back, flashes back to Sharon the "oracle psychic" sitting at my dining room kitchen table in 1998 at the Wayland model house……..

"There will be seven lawsuit seals broken open, a Hollywood producer locates the seven seals in court and opens up what has been hidden from society concerning the CIA." Sharon stated in 1998. I was bewildered, I had no idea what she was talking about then, so puzzled back then. How a lawsuit would relate to me in the future, back then? It made no sense in 1998. But what made no sense in 1998, was now in 2001, making clearer sense as my veil covering was lifting, of what was transpiring now. This sealed slander suit, I was one of seven hidden and sealed lawsuits by my perpetrators, just as Sharon had predicted. This was so out of my control and comprehension of controlling.

I rushed inside and called Lee Silver. He gave me a list of five attorneys that could possibly defend such a case of slander and file a countersuit of sexual harassment, attorneys that dealt with that area of law. I met with several of them, one really wanted the case. A female attorney who just filed a very public in the news media lawsuit of sexual harassment against the Grand Rapids Police Department, her clients, female officers of the same force.

I met with her at her home office in Rockford, Michigan. Her husband was an attorney too, also located in the basement wing of her attorney law firm. She had cats everywhere, a nanny upstairs taking care of her newborn baby girl. She was an odd, quirky attorney who really wanted my case and wanted to go after these bully men, so she claimed. She immediately filed a countersuit of sexual harassment, as expected what would come from a slander suit filed first against me, the rape victim, the sexually harassed victim. I think filing that slander suit and declaring war on the victim, me, was insanely preposterous in a winning move from Rick Bolhouse's law office. Genie Eardley disagreed, she stated, she felt a move of making me on the defendant side of the war line was a smart move. Genie adds, "You're now on the defensive side, having to prove this all happened as they make you look guilty, a liar to the police and the jury. It's a uphill battle as the defendant now, you, to look like the victim. They are smart."

I saw her point, but disagreed strongly. I was now involved with a war that I never wanted, the cake of disaster was an over indulgent blend, quite the concoction, rotten confection layered up I might add.

I sold off my pool table at 2030 Winding Oak Drive in Dorr, my stainless steel appliances, and proceeded to write Genie Eardely a check for five thousand as was her demand for an attorney retainer fee, after all, I am now "the defendant." It was May 20, 2001, Laura Hayden wrote up a real estate offer for my house in foreclosure and helped me sell off my real estate. My mother Cindy? Well, I took the power of attorney away from her. I was determined to take control of my life and not keep being placed inside of a jar I could not escape from.

Why is it those close to me, those who pretend to be my friend, or a close confident, really want the worse for me? Why? I just did not understand.

In July 2001 I moved up north to Petoskey, I rented a home on Bear River road. I gave Genie Eardely my cell phone number, time passed, I never heard about my case she had filed as a countersuit. Then one day in August 2001 I receive a certified package from her office. I am thinking it is the interrogatories? No, instead my attorney Genie Eardely mails me back a copy of my filed countersuit, dismisses herself in writing from the case and representing me, box marked, "Due to attorney-client breakdown in communication."

"What?" I said out loud. I call her office, I get her secretary, and Genie refuses to come to the phone, refuses my phone calls, I am bewildered.

Within two weeks I receive a motion hearing notice from Michael P. Risko announcing a motion hearing to dismiss my countersuit of sexual harassment with prejudice. I called several Grand Rapids attorneys and Harbor Springs attorneys, no one is willing to accept an orphan lawsuit filed by some attorney in Grand Rapids who removed herself from the case. I was fucked, again, and not in a good way.

I also for the last six months was trying to locate employment up north. On my resume I had to list Smith-Diamond Realty as a place of employment from 1996-2000. I could not get employed anywhere, based on a future employer checking my references. It was an employment seeking and applying nightmare after leaving Smith-Diamond Realty and seeking new employment. I had mice at night eating what groceries I had in the house I was renting in Petoskey. I had to borrow money from Jerry and Cindy for food and rent. I hated the financial dependency created. I had no one up north, no one. No employment, I was begging Jerry and Cindy for money just to survive. I was truly at my lowest point, and I had thought last year was, or the year before last was my lowest point. I was totally ostracized from the Calvinist's society at large in lower Michigan for blowing the whistle on Smith-Diamond Realty.

Was it my choice to move to northern Michigan? Yes. Was I in search of peace? Yes. Was I pushed out of the real estate world run by those in power over my real estate career? Yes. Was I banished from my high school friends because of Carmen? Yes. I was told by "the girls" that Carmen was their friend and if she asked them not to talk with me, based on her reasons, well then, they would not communicate with me, or include me in any of their outings. Cheri stood by Carmen, anything Carmen said, like water pulled to shore, but why? Why is the rape victim the one who is banished, pushed away for telling the truth? From a Christian standpoint it made no sense either! Carmen and Cheri, all "the girls" that graduated from Unity Christian High, wanted nothing to do with me. I was labeled "crazy woman," and tossed out of the community. Carmen announced that she said that she and Cheri would see to it that no future class reunions would ever take place. From a moral standpoint it made no sense either. Why was Carmen and the others acting this way towards me? Does it have something to do with DNA? Then I remembered Rick Bolhouse, Cheri Hulst is married to Rick Bolhouse's illegitimate son, Shawn Hulst. Perhaps Rick Bolhouse's law office and the CIA, as Visser & Bolhouse is connected through legalities and representations to the CIA, perhaps they are a greater presence at work in lower Michigan. I know too much, and that is why I am ostracized by a greater presence in Michigan? Many questions, and very few answers.

After a while, trying to make sense of everything I endured, made no sense. I found it difficult to fall asleep at night, my life felt scary and unreal. The behavior of the Christians in lower Michigan was undeniably unfair treatment towards me. Unwarranted behavior from them to me. The hate they had for me coming forward about the truth, what happened behind closed doors, many incidences within that Dutch Calvinist subculture was just over the top, absurd distaste toward me, but why? Only a camera crew and a well prepared director could ask those probing questions to them all, those philosophical quest interviews for the truth behind the reflections.

In November 2001 I went through many sleepless nights. I finally called Cindy and Jerry and said, "I just can't take living alone. I want to move in with you both so I can sleep at night. Being alone, being scared all the time, I don't know what approach to take to get a good night sleep. I need people around me, I need a roommate."

Cindy was not my favorite person. But sleeping under her roof while she is married to Jerry, I did not think harm would come to me. I was alone, desperate to feel not so alone so I could fall asleep at night. Cindy hung in as a confidant when no one else would talk with me. My horrors gave her pleasure, yet I had no one, I was desperate.

I slept with the television on, I sipped and gulped cough syrup nighttime relief in my many attempts to finally get a good night sleep.

Nothing was working, no remedy could pull fear out of me. I was anxious and weak, tired yet manic to most observers. I called Cindy in lower Michigan one evening, just unable to fall asleep once again. Cindy and Jerry decided to drive to upper Michigan to bring me back to lower Michigan. I pack my bag and got into their car. It was late, maybe midnight by the time they arrived in Petoskey at the house I was renting. I thought we were going to their house in Grandville, instead we passed their exit and headed further south on 131. Instead of pulling into their driveway, Cindy brings me to the south entrance of Pine Rest. I don't have a choice. Cindy insists in that parking lot that I just need more medication to sleep. "You just need to up your meds," as Cindy puts it bluntly. Jerry stayed in the car, and Cindy escorted me into the south side of Pine Rest. She checks me in and tells the nurse I am suicidal. But I clarify, "No, I am not suicidal!" Why would you say such a thing? I wondered. "I feel murdered inside, but not suicidal. There is a difference I begged. There is a difference!" I had no car in lower Michigan. I am stuck.

Cindy and the Pine Rest intake nurse looked at me and said, "Everything will be all right."

I don't believe for a minute that everything will be all right. I go willingly, reserved, yet many questions spin in my mind. Why can't I just stay at Cindy and Jerry's house? Being alone is scary. So Cindy's cunning idea is to have me dropped off at Pine Rest, labeled and then processed inside Pine Rest as suicidal? Why that label Cindy? Questions and no answers.

The next day I meet with the psychiatrist onboard. I was expecting to see Dr. Gary Rich who is my treating psychiatrist at Pine Rest. I was greeted by a short half oriental, half-white looking doctor barely reaching the height of five foot two inches.

"Dr. Gary Rich is off this weekend." Responds the short, suspiciously odd half oriental, half white staff psychiatrist. He opens his locked office and asked me to sit down. He asked me a series of questions, some seem to pertain to my mental health evaluation, other questions are really off the wall. But to a psychiatrist, all questions hold relevancy I suppose. He then asked me to stand up. I do, he asked me to put my arms out, I do like an umbrella, or a cross. Bizarre.

Then he asks me to sit back down, I do. He then leans forward, stops looking at his paperwork inside his folder, puts down his pen. And says this, "Sharon wanted me to tell you something, the State detective, 'Ziggy,' I believe that is his name, wanted you to read a book on manners. That is the message from Sharon."

"What?" I ask, just dumbfounded….. "What?"

"A book on manners. Sharon wants you to read a book on how to be polite, a book on good manners." He states seriously, while in his office.

"What? A book on manners? What are you talking about?" I asked just simply bewildered.

"Sharon, you know a Sharon don't you?" He asked so matter of fact.

"Yes, in 1998, she is a psychic, detective lady." I answer.

He prescribed well over ten different pill concoctions. He scribbled quickly in his folder as if making a joke on paper with a signature. Within fifteen minutes or so he ushered me out of his office very quickly and abruptly. As we leave his office and he locks the office door I hear his keys rattling as he does so and then he whispers in my ear, "Cindy and the CIA are afraid you are going to talk about the dates in the file."

I pull back and create space, personal space as I inquire to him "What are you talking about?"

His eyes dart to the left and then the right as he scans my face and states, "The dates. Cindy told you four dates. One of which was 9/11. If you don't keep your mouth shut this institution will see to it that you can't talk. Do you understand me?"

I was fearful and replied, "Yes. I understand." I had to say that, I would think later, long and hard about what he actually was communicating to me in his warnings. How could Cindy and her CIA friends such as CIA Barney Fife David Petraeus control Pine Rest from behind walls? From behind doctors? I need to get out of here were my thoughts. I never should have moved back to Michigan from Georgia, I should have stayed in Georgia, bought a house there.

That evening at Pine Rest, the south wing, two male nurses were giving out Dixie cups of everyone's different mixture prescriptions. My cup was the fullest. The male nurse looked into the Dixie cup, then poured out the pills on the ledge of the counter where they were stationed during a shift. He then says to the other male nurse, "Why would he prescribe this pill with this pill?"

"I don't know, let me see that chart." He observed my chart and was beginning to question the mixture of prescribed pills by the doctor as well.

"You don't have to take these pills. By law, you don't have to take these pills. In fact, studies have shown that these two pills together will cause permanent twitching condition, damage to your brain." Spoke up the male nurse from behind the counter.

The other male nurse standing next to me agreed and was confused as to why the doctor prescribed that mixture for me. I was bewildered and locked in, just helpless.

I was in Pine Rest for a week. My mother convinced all she could that I was suicidal. Cindy even called my insurance card and told Priority Health Insurance I am crazy and suicidal (that was according to the lady at Priority Health who disclosed that fact to me). But I was not crazy or suicidal. I was afraid to fall asleep at night, I was alone, I had no support system, no love, and I was freaked out by how people were treating me in Michigan. Finally after five days, I begged to be released from that insane asylum wing of Pine Rest. It was November 2001, Cindy arrived with one of her church friends. Why would a mother bring someone else to see me in this locked mental ward? What kind of mother does that? I don't want people to see me in here! Cindy evidently wanted a witness, a church witness, that indeed I am crazy. Not just Cindy gossiping at church, it really was true and everyone in church should believe Cindy over me. It was bizarre how Cindy thought, she had no shame, she had no motherly instincts, none. I was just a pawn in her schemes, she to be viewed as a saint of a mother, stuck with a daughter that was crazy, and for everyone to believe her, and feel sorry for Cindy.

If I could have shouted and screamed, or even remarked politely in a whisper, "Stop this awful play!" I would have. But this was not a play I could pull away from, step aside, hand the part to another, this was my real life saga. A real nightmare, I was determined to get out of, alive.

I decided to move from Petoskey, Michigan in November 2001. I stayed at Jerry and Cindy's house on Parsons Street in Grandville for a few weeks while I searched for a roommate and a real estate office to hold my real estate license. I told Cindy I was taking the pills prescribed, I think Dr. Gary Rich had me on Depocote that week. Every time I took the pills, I felt drugged, incapacitated, when I walked I bumped into the wall and chairs. That lasted for three days, a week tops, and then I decided I needed to get my life back together.

Pills, despite all the advice, was not the answers to stabilizing my life. I joined Calvary church, located a roommate, and had my real estate license placed at ReMax in Grand Rapids. I stopped taking the strong pills and kept up with the anti-seizure pills that Dr. Gary Rich had first prescribed to me a year ago to control the mania, manic episodes as I talked and worked through my issues and trauma's slowly. My electrons in my brain were moving too rapidly because of the induced many traumas from the Calvinists. In a case or cases of trauma, your electrons can speed up. It is the bodies reaction to the induced trauma, whether it be a physical trauma or mental trauma, so I was told.

I knew the Calvinists were very dangerous people, but I could never prove it, never. They had me drugged, looking stupid, I even slurred my words and had many fleeting thoughts of relevancy, which made no sense, so I was told.

Sleeping at Jerry and Cindy's house in November-December 2001 made me feel safe in the fact that I was not falling asleep in an empty house scared out of my mind. I did clearly see in Cindy's facial expression how Cindy just relished in labeling me crazy, having the doctors on her side, thinking I am nuts.

It all played so well into her persona as she wanted to perceive to Jerry's older kids, Mick and Sheri, Greg and Libby that she is a saint with a burden of a daughter. Whatever I warned them about in 1997-1998 about my mother, warning Sheri Honderd that I saw bath photographs of her three daughters ages 8 through 12 on Cindy's desk by the phone in those years. Well, all that concern I gave to Sheri, well I was now labeled "the nut," playing right into all that Cindy thought she could control, those valued and needed character opinions of others. For me *not* to be believed by others, my voice never to be as big as the sea and what I see as bad values in Cindy's behavior. Cindy needed me crazy, Patrick Goodale and the CIA needed and still does need me crazy or criminal. Those who wronged me, needed or need me "crazy," or criminal, and therefore "not believed," and put away as not being relevant or coherent. As much as I understood those facts about my life, I could not control or stop others from damning my life.

Cindy would insist to those who were around her (family, friends, church people), "Well, Lori just got back from a mental institution, let's all just pray for her, let's get her on the church prayer line." Well, you get the picture, how Cindy manipulates, controls opinions of others in the Dutch Calvinists society. I had no one that believed me in what was going on in my life, or wanted to even care to believe me.

I knew that subculture was not genuinely of God. It was the worst of hell. And I was out to prove it, and they did not like that fact. They were out to shut me up or lock me up if I talked about their closed door society, the Calvinists. I knew I had to get from under Cindy's control of me and my mind, my life. I knew I needed to get married, and soon. Just to be under the control of someone other than destructive Cindy would be a step up in my survival. When I had spent a week in Pine Rest in November 2001. I literally called up a dating service on a pay phone in the hall, and asked about joining. I needed to get married to create a block, a road barrier against Sharon and Cindy and that whole CIA mob of organized criminals, and now Patrick Goodale. I was in a jar, Cindy noticed how she could keep tightening that lid if she so desired and eventually there would be no more air to breath. And boy, she had a will to do destructive things. I knew that of her as I gasped for just a little air to speak.

I remember the dating service lady in November 2001 asked me on the other end of the phone receiver, "Where are you? Where are you calling from?"

I paused, "I'm…..I'm…. in Pine Rest."

"You're in Pine Rest?" She asked in a quick manner, shocked but polite. I noticed how clear and crisp her voice was on the other line. I envied how her voice sounded compared to mine. I sounded weak and tired. I so wanted to just sound happy and cheery, and quick minded like her.

"Yeah, I need to date." I said out loud. There was a pause on the other line. I waited in quietness, hoping she did not think I was truly crazy. I needed someone to believe me, or my mother would take control of what is left of my life. Throw away the key for bringing up past incidences she had done to me, along with her CIA associates. I knew too much about CIA classified information of the most destructive kind possible. Information the trusting general public would find of interest if I was believed.

I spoke up in the still silence on the other end, "I need to date."

I thought to myself…..I must have sounded crazy, but I clearly knew the problem and the solution. I needed to marry, first I need to date, then quickly marry to get from under Cindy's control of destroying my life and my big mouth of what I knew she was involved in, was it all in my mind? I knew it was not, but I could never prove it. But I needed to survive, at least survive this whole ordeal.

"Well, when was the last time you went on a date?" The lady asked trying not to sound prejudice of my situation.

"Well, it's been at least five years." I said.

"How old did you say you were?" She asked in a startled quick voice.

"I'm thirty-one. I need to date, I need to start going out. My mother is going to destroy me, you have to understand." I begged in a pleading voice for her not to hang up on me, but to understand all that I am trying to relay to her.

"Call our service when you get out of Pine Rest." She said firmly as she hung up.

So I did. In December of 2001 I joined a Grand Rapids dating service, Match Makers located in Kentwood, Michigan.

I had recently moved back to Grandville, I located a roommate I met at Calvary church. She was single, never married and in her forties. My bedroom was below her bedroom at 4242 Redbush Court in Grandville, Michigan. I asked her one day, "I hear you get up in the middle of the night, you sound restless at night, why?" I stated.

"I am going through my change, I have hot flashes, cold sweats." Phyllis said.

I realized the person I did not want to become, her. I did want to marry and have a family before I am not able to have children. I did not want to lose out in life because of fears and phobias which held me from moving forward. But the fears and phobias were justified. That I could agree on, just as you the reader can now understand. But I needed solutions. I knew my hurdles, I needed to get married, have a family, continue with my quest for "a normal life." I saw my goals, but I needed more solutions to arrive at my goals. I talked around, and learned of a therapist in Grand Rapids that had a progressive approach to healing trauma stuck in a person's mind. Her name is Irene Suk.

I met with her in the beginning of 2002. She was all about going through my past traumas, from childhood to now, everything she wanted to know. She stood up suddenly, looked shocked one day during one of our initial sessions, as if she spilled hot coffee on herself or something.

"What? What is it?" I asked Irene Suk.

"You talk about these horrid shocking traumas, but you don't cry, your voice doesn't even change an octave. You just tell what happened to you, but you don't cry or show natural emotions attached to the trauma, you are so matter of fact. In fact, you have mentally detached your emotion as a victim, from the traumas. You just act and tell a story as if you were talking about what you ate for lunch. Which is displaying an antisocial element. This is not good. You have a new issue to work through, not just traumas replaying in your head, like a record stuck, paralyzing you from moving forward in life. You have other issues, due to your childhood traumas induced from your mother."

"I do? I do not want other issues. This is not fair. It is not fair that I am like this, I just want to be normal! Make me normal, like before I was born, before all this shit happened to me. This is not fair of the Calvinists!" I remarked in a sulking kind of way, both bewildered, and frustrated. "Why I can't I just snap back to being like I was?" I asked.

Irene answered, "You mentioned that your mother who adopted you, Cindy, abused you as much as she could, and you had surgery at age twelve from a severe beating. She also broke your leg by your knee and refused to bring you to a doctor, and so your knee has a bump just below from where the bone was cracked. You mentioned that those Playboy executives would have to crop out your knee in photos due to a large bump under your knee. Your mother Cindy was frustrated in her marriage, and she took it out on you."

"Yeah, so what is your point?" I asked.

"This is not good, this is not healthy, this tells me that you are so conditioned to pain, infliction of pain from others, that you are now so jaded in emotion. You cannot even attach that right emotion, the correct emotion which would be to cry. You don't attach the right emotion to the story, you are so matter of fact, too cold. Why were you raised this way?" Spoke Irene Suk so eloquently.

"Well....these are facts about my life you asked about, I am telling you. I know these facts about my life, because they are a part of my memories, they have become facts, just facts. But why do I need to cry when I tell the story?" I inquired.

"This lack of emotion from you in relation to the story you are telling me of your childhood, tells a deeper secret, a deeper problem." Irene stated.

"What? What are you talking about?" I asked the shocked therapist.

"You seem to be antisocial a condition in which a victim of childhood abuse is so conditioned to abusive, unmoral circumstances, unreal pain inflicted upon you from abuse from your mother that your social programming is cold. Rather your emotions are cold. You have become so accustomed to your abuse, from those who have abused you, that your mind has been conditioned not to react in a proper way when you discuss the abuse." Spoke Irene Suk so eloquently.

"So what?" I said.

Irene pleaded, "It is unhealthy to not have the right human emotion attached to a painful situation. You have been conditioned to be cold. How a person reacts to trauma tells a story. Emotions play an important part in who we are, you need to feel. Your antisocial nature was created by your mother, your mother has deep rooted tentacles like an octopus. She has a hold of your mind, just as the men who raped you, it's time for you to put those traumas into a mental glass jar and seal the lid, so you can cry. This greater issue, it stems from how you would endure your childhood, it was an emotional detachment that you used as a child, but as an adult, this could be dangerous." Spoke Irene in a convincing, soothing voice.

"What? What are you talking about? Why did you just say octopus?" I asked unable to simply change to a level of warmth or crying that she was looking for like a director-actor improvising a role direction. I just remained myself, still and unmoved by what I had to say.

Irene Suk sighs and then remarks, "Lori, you mentioned to me that this guy Scott that you worked with in real estate began calling you Queenie after you were raped. You explained to me that Scott mentioned that a black guy from the past hates colonization of India and Africa and wanted harm to the Dutch people and that is why your nose was bashed and why you were brutalized during the rape or rapes at that real estate model home. How does that make you feel?"

I looked at Irene Suk in her office and replied, "I feel nothing now." I knew that was not the answer she wanted, but I did not know what else to say.

Irene seemed exhausted as she lectured on in her office, "O.k., let's just take it from here. What I can do is talk about your most recent traumas. The traumas that are resting on the edge of your subconscious, without digging deeper, and getting into uncharted waters that actually might be difficult and very chaotic in healing. What we will do as an exercise to help you heal and feel powerful, like the woman you were before the rapes by those real estate men. We are going to say the words that empower you as I swing a pen from side to side. Let's try it Lori."

Irene went unto say these words, these statements as she swung a pen like a tennis match as my eyes followed the pen from side to side as the words she spoke resonated as the words traveled deep within my subconscious mind......

Say with me now, "I am powerful, I feel powerful." I stared at the pen and kept repeating that statement over and over. These therapy sessions went on for eight months in 2002.

I said to Irene Suk one day in a cheery voice, "I used to want to become a philosopher, a writer perhaps, although my first inspiration was to be an oceanographer." I felt like I had hope inside me again, as if I am inspired to be something other than the zombie I was from 2000 through 2002. I had insight, beyond and above, before all this occurred to me.

Wisdom was resonating as I fought back for my life in 2002. I was thirty-two years old. I was pulling my body out of a grave, pushing that dirt and sand aside as I regained strength within me again to be what I am supposed to be in this world.

Irene Suk, one session just looked at me very dumbfounded and said, "Have you seen that movie, A Beautiful Mind? You are not a college professor experiencing his mental health issues, but it is like you have this beautiful mind, with a breakdown, Post-Traumatic Stress Syndrome and antisocial behavior issues."

I responded, "No, I have not seen that movie. I don't know if I would want to, the previews do not look appealing to me."

During this period in time, the spring of 2002, I began receiving "pink slips" from a dating service called Match Makers. Sometimes twice a week I would receive these pink slips. I do not party, I do not go to bars to pick up a guy, a date. So the traditional way in meeting a guy, would never happen. They did match me up with a lot of college educated professionals. Most had been married, actually, I believe all had been married before, had three children, or more, and were not compatible with my wish to have children of my own. They all seemed to want a nanny type, a new wife to pick up where the old one had left off, dirty laundry and all. Not really romantic, I just was not getting swept off my feet or being placed with a match that wanted children, more children.

I did feel that the progressive, radical mental treatment performed by Irene Suk did in fact make me feel more empowered. Empowered to live, flip the page to the next chapter of what is my life story.

I still was seeing my psychiatrist at Pine Rest, at least once a month now, Dr. Gary Rich. He said one day in the spring of 2002, "You do not seem to define the parameters of bi-polar." He announced as he looked up from his paperwork one day while sitting at his desk.

"I am not bi-polar?" I asked him.

Dr. Gary Rich explained one day in his office, "Bi-polar is a mood disorder caused by a brain chemical imbalance. Causing one to have extreme highs, followed by extreme lows, or vice versa. It is a lifelong condition, monitored by medication to allow for a stable existence. You have thus far in one year or so only displayed the mania part, the high. You could in fact, not be bi-polar, but you went insane, manic for a brief period in time, due to the trauma of rape. Coupled by the other traumas in your lifetime, you went clinically insane for a brief period in time. Such trauma, severe trauma, can cause a reaction in your brain, such as pushing one over the edge, causing insanity, known as mania. No one can predict how a person's mind reacts to trauma, you can't control your reaction to trauma, the brain reacts, the brain is in control, not the person."

"I never felt suicidal. I never felt like I slept too much. I felt murdered inside, but not suicidal. Why do people think I am bi-polar? Why does my mother Cindy keep telling people I am bi-polar and suicidal?" I asked.

He looked up and appeared startled. "I cannot speak for other therapists or your mother Cindy. I did meet Cindy, she seems very supportive of you as you work through this difficult time in your life."

I left his office, amazed at how quickly people in the past wanted to label me, charge up my good health insurance coverage and continue in their everyday system of treating "the mentally ill." I did have trouble sleeping, I had nightmares still, I wasn't myself. I stayed on the medication that Dr. Rich prescribed to slow down my electrons in my brain that were speeded up from trauma induced from a series of rapes at the model house in Wayland. I was on a steady course to recovery. How long this mental recovery would take, I could only wonder each day as I glanced at the sunshine, but did not feel happy and bubbly.

One day I called up that Grand Rapids dating service and said, "You know I really prefer Greek, Jewish, Italian, that is my preference. I like older, wiser types. I like a man to be well traveled and cultured, to think big, not really someone from this dorky Dutch Calvinist community. I do not like dorky blonde haired men. German is o.k., but not dorky Dutch guys. I like a refined man that I can look up to, as if he is smarter somehow, has an edge in life, has a stable career. I would even be willing to travel out of state."

"Well, we'll do our best. Your six month membership is almost up, but we are short of girls that are young, and fit the criteria of what the guys are looking for, we can give you another six months free, on the house, if you'd like." Spoke the female on the other end of the phone.

"O.k., that sounds good." I replied with enthusiasm. I did realize I was what the men were looking for, yet most men turned me off with their search for a new wife, just a replacement fixture in their house, like changing out a sofa.

In the spring of 2002 I was so disgusted with the power that Michael P. Risko and Rick Bolhouse held over my credit report with their relentless constant credit checking, I then located a social security attorney, Phil Rogers is his name. He had actually gone to high school in Grandville with Patrick Goodale. Mr. Rogers filed a federal lawsuit against Rick Bolhouse and Michael P. Risko, the attorneys in Grandville immediately on my behalf in U.S. District Court. The case no. 1:02-cv-00348-RHB is filed in the federal building in downtown Grand Rapids.

Ironically, the once dormant lawsuit of slander filed in retaliation in the spring of 2001 by the three men and their attorneys, well, still rested sealed, dusty, but alive nevertheless in Allegan County. Judge Beech was the presiding Judge in that civil case of slander, filed and sealed in Allegan County. But in the federal arena of battles, a far greater threat loomed over the head of Rick Bolhouse, Michael P. Risko, and Don Visser, the chapter of discovery. Judge Bell was insisting that the three Grandville attorneys turn over to federal court, each and every file at the granite building they worked out of and release to the federal courts how many other victims are in fact out there, that have been victimized by Visser & Bolhouse attorneys at law.

My social security fraud attorney, Mr. Phil Rogers had asked Judge Bell of federal court, that the law office of Rick Bolhouse empty out their files and show the Federal Judge how many times Visser & Bolhouse indeed misused, illegally obtained a person's social security number in the community, and used it unfairly to their advantage to gain access of information for the CIA on many, many clients of those they did not represent. Essentially spying on opponents to their clients, those on enemy lines of their clients.

This was more than a threat to Rick Bolhouse's conservative well-established law office in the church belt community of Grandville, Michigan. It was a discovery request made by my attorney Mr. Phil Rogers and request to Judge Bell, who honored that request of discovery. If the law office of Rick Bolhouse did not comply with the discovery motion granted they would be in deep water with Judge Bell. If they did comply, but lied about how many times they illegally pulled up their client's opponents social security number in the past, on many cases, on several occasions over decades possibly, they would be held in contempt of court, federal court. Very serious business with my attorney Mr. Phil Rogers also able to turn over the files to a criminal court and they would face federal indictments. Don Visser & Rick Bolhouse were sweating this one, and for good reason. A civil case that could turn into a federal criminal case for violating federal law, and they were all in serious trouble. But what I would learn in my young naïve battle is that when the enemy sweats, well, that can cause a bigger larger battle, and the outcome is not always pleasing for the one who makes the other sweat. I was making Visser & Bolhouse attorneys at law to sweat. The rumor was that my federal filed lawsuit in federal court was causing an earthquake within the law firm of Visser & Bolhouse. My federal lawsuit would cause Don Visser and Rick Bolhouse to part ways, legally ending Visser & Bolhouse for good, forever.

Mr. Phil Rogers tells me optimistically one day, "We gottem Lori, and we gottem good!" I agreed with Mr. Phil Rogers and thought we had them. But every attorney is a warrior in his mind, I suppose, strategy and defense are conjured and scrutinized at their polished cherry desks? Their library in Grandville? Making the enemy sweat, is not always a good plan, a good defense, so I would learn the hard way. I just did not know it yet, but would soon learn………

Within two weeks I received from Mike Risko a motion hearing on the sleeping slander suit to rattle me. The once dormant lawsuit of slander filed in the spring of 2001, that slander retaliation suit, had new meaning for Mike Risko and the attorneys sweating in Grandville over the recently filed federal lawsuit.

In June of 2002 I attended my first motion hearing of the once dormant slander suit for a year collecting dust on the appointment books of the county court clerk. But evidently a very alive slander suit filed by Mr. Risko in Allegan County, on behalf of Dave Smith, Chuck Helder, and Patrick Goodale. It was Mike Risko's rabbit out of his hat trick, every lawyer has a rabbit and a hat, so I was learning. The more rabbit's one can pull out magically in court, well, you get the picture, the big picture.

Judge Harry Beech presided over the sleeping slander case in rural backwoods country called Allegan County. He was a heavyset Judge, a few blonde hairs left on the sides of his head, mostly bald though. His skin was alabaster white and he had blue eyes. The Judge spoke in southern cliché styles of statements that most do not hear on the everyday playing field of life outside his courtroom. Such as referring to me not as "crazy" or "mentally and emotional imbalanced or challenged," as Mike Risko had referred to me in the closed door courtroom that day. Rather, Judge Harry Beech looked at Mike Risko, read his motion hearing request, could care less what I had to say in Allegan court, in fact he hardly looked at me at all. After all, the case was sealed, he said directly and loudly in the echoes of that courtroom, "I think she's seeing spooks in the closet."

I don't know for sure what Judge Harry Beech meant, but it was derogatory, unfair in tone, and I believe it referred to me as being crazy in his terms or phrases of sorts? In agreement with Mike Risko that I am nuts? I had no attorney, no money to pay an attorney for the defense of that filed slander suit in Allegan County. I know what you are thinking, what about attorney Phil Rogers?

Attorney Phil Rogers stated that he was not going to represent me in an ongoing yet dormant slander suit in Allegan County. "That's not my expertise, my practice of law, I practice social security fraud law only," Mr. Rogers informed me in June of 2002. I had to endure motion hearing, after motion hearing filed by Mike Risko that summer of 2002.

I went from law office to law office in Allegan county, no attorney would take the case, to represent me as a defendant. I felt black, but I was white. But did I look black in that Norman Rockwell town. I do not know, it was discouraging, I am sure that was the intention of Mike Risko, better known as Arab Risko to make me feel like a misfit, or labeled a misfit for his gain. I never will forget his expression when he noticed that I recognized him in court. Not from television, not from a past life, not from any other source, but my memory of December 1997 at the model house, my mind jogs back.......

December 1997, the guy who followed me home from that Grand Rapids Jewish Hanukah party held at the synagogue. But he did not look Jewish ever. He was five pounds heavier now in 2002, to a man who had a skeleton shape, he had no weight then or now, he looked hungry to say the least. He wore a green suit as I approached him sitting down in court and then he flipped his hands over, concealing his palms from me. He looked up, and had a calm demeanor in court, but his eyes spelled fear in what I clearly recognized. The same "Michael" that I had asked to leave my residence at the model home in December 1997, at 405 Discover Drive in Wayland. He mentioned the psychic had predicted he would meet his dream girl at that Jewish dance. I am now connecting more pieces of the puzzle, how big is this jigsaw puzzle of astrological disaster of my young and innocent life?

Attorney Mike Risko filed motion hearing after motion hearing in the summer of 2002, he laid on the legal heat, his eyes spelled fire. He acted connected with the Judge in Allegan county circuit court on a cerebral level of unity, which I was not a part of, so I endured that summer of 2002.

The refreshing element to the saga of my life, I was going to marry. I was meeting guy after guy in 2002 and had a feeling the right guy was right around the corner. Anybody, someone, who would not treat me like a new piece of furniture in their house, was going to be Mr. Right for me. Love was not a requirement for me. I just wanted to be treated well, feel normal and have the same goals for the future within our lives. Marriage also meant that Cindy could no longer control or destroy my life. If I was married, my husband would be her obstacle, and an obstacle I could hide behind in her sabotaging of my young and innocent life. If I was married perhaps I would not be bullied by the Dutch Calvinist's subculture cult who were out to dagger me to death, their attorneys and all that the great octopus clung to in power, the great CIA.

I was thirty two in a half now. I wanted to marry and have a family, I wanted what others did not want for me…..happiness. I told myself the next man that proposes marriage to me, a man that is acceptable, I will cross that bridge to the next chapter of my life and journey over the rainbow. To win on earth you need power. To win in west Michigan, one needs more than power, you need a strong will to survive as your foundation in a battle, so I was learning, or did learn.

Nearing August of 2002, Mike Risko during a motion hearing (or prior) had convinced himself and Judge Beech that I should receive 90 days in county lock-up if I did not sign his "three letters of retraction." That is what Mike Risko termed the written documentation that I shall and must sign, and that he, Mike Risko would prepare. I listened in court as Judge Harry Beech agreed with him wholeheartedly, without a doubt. I listened to the Judge, as the Judge threatened me with 90 days in county lock up if I did not comply with signing three retraction letters that Patrick Goodale, David P. Smith, and Charles Helder did any wrong to me whatsoever.

If I was in county lock-up for 90 days for not signing three retraction letters in a sealed Allegan County court I would thus ruin my plans to fly to Vegas and marry Ed DeBartolo (Dr. Edward DeBartolo) on Labor Day weekend 2002. There was going to be no trial in the dormant yet alive slander lawsuit against me, just this motion hearing, a very legal maneuver in these parts, Allegan County, Michigan. I wanted to scream and cry, "But I am not black, look at me! I am the poster child for the Bavarian race, why do you treat me this way in Allegan County?" However I remained hushed and stunned. I must have appeared well behaved in my silence over the slander lawsuit matter in court.

I remember in the summer of 2002 looking around the empty closed door courtroom in Allegan County. The sealed lawsuit transcripts being diligently typed by the clerk who soaked up that mornings motion hearing like a very committed soap opera fan not wanting to miss one scene or episode. I thought quietly to myself, can this really be said by a Judge? Can this really be legal of them both?

Then Judge Harry Beech wakes me of my philosophical silence and orders for me in his condescending and commanding tone of voice that blares through the empty courtroom, "To get smart like your sister- in- law Donna Vander Ark, and settle with Michael P. Risko now! I'll throw you in county lock-up for 90 days if you don't." He snarled. I shuttered. I felt like a black woman, and any minute the white law was goina beat me. I just stood still. Scared to move. It was the summer of 2002.

Donna had been sued for slander, why? Even she does not know. I was baffled as to why as well too. She had mentioned that Michael P. Risko, the attorney filed a lawsuit of slander that would keep her from going to the media with tapes she had taped? Or had? Or so he feared she would go to the media with tapes in her possession, so she explained what her defense attorney had explained to her. The whole situation was like trying to grab onto a slippery wet ice cube of the truth before it fell into the sink drain to be lost, or melted. Or cards being played too fast at the poker table after too many beers and shots of vodka consumed. It was odd, I could not wrap my mind around all that was going on, it seemed surreal, what that Judge ordered....... Judge Harry Beech, ordered that I sign the retraction letters and agree to end the federal lawsuit or I spend 90 days in county lock-up which would then ruin my plans to get married Labor Day weekend 2002.

I had additional real life issues of trying to regain my personal power and mental and emotional stability over my rapes I endured, by the very men who held powerful alliances in Allegan County. As if they were the tentacles of that law society, the ones that held all the power over my life too.

On August 12, 2002 I signed Mike Risko's prepared documents of "retraction letters" for Dave Smith, Patrick Goodale, and Chuck Helder. After that fiasco of threatened jail time requested by Mike Risko and threatened by Judge Harry Beech towards me I knew I wanted to stay out of court with Mike Risko as my opponent, especially in Allegan County. I was about to get married, he knew that fact and boldly took control of the sealed slander lawsuit, and waved around keys to a county jail cell, astonishingly so, as Judge Beech agreed with Mike Risko, so dishonorably. My eyes were open to politics in Allegan County. Me? I felt like a black woman trying to have justice over rapes in a world before the civil rights movement ever took place. Or perhaps a Jew in a Nazi concentration camp? I was wrapped up in a case of "hate" but I could not prove it, like a phantom motive, I could not prove it.

I ended my lawsuit in federal court in a Grand Rapids courthouse without a fight to avoid the threat of 90-days in county lock up by Judge Harry Beech in Allegan. Rick Bolhouse and Michael Risko gave my attorney Phil Rogers a measly $3,000.00 (three thousand) to spilt between me and my attorney Phil Rogers, to get rid of their social security illegal activity headache in federal court.

"It was such a good case!" Exclaimed Phil Rogers, "We gottem Lori, don't give up now, don't sign anything in Allegan." He pleaded with me in August of 2002, for me to desperately see his point.

I did see Mr. Phil Roger's point, but I also wanted to avoid Allegan County jail before my August 2002 plans to elope in Vegas. I am thirty-two years old, I do not want my chances of having children to be like my roommate Phyllis.

I had to give up the federal fight, just as Mike Risko and Judge Harry Beech joined alliances and had angled their swift march for me to surrender or else go to Allegan County lock-up. I was afraid Mike Risko and Judge Harry Beech. I could see them, I also wondered if someone was behind courtroom walls pulling strings on courtroom puppets that would do anything to destroy my chances for happiness before I reached Labor Day weekend 2002. Mike Risko and Judge Harry Beech were ruthless, part of the octopus, I was not.

I did marry on August 29, 2002. I gave up the court battles to avoid the brute force of the alliance Mike Risko had built in Allegan County's legal arena, where my rights did not matter, my legal rights were not even enforced.

I married Dr. Edward John DeBartolo of East Lansing, Michigan. I would not describe our marriage in the beginning or now as passionate. I would describe our marriage, our relationship as "comfortable." When sitting at his residence, a condo in East Lansing, Michigan I saw the outline of my father Chuck Vander Ark in Ed while Ed sat in the living room keeping me company as I flipped through the T.V. channels, somehow that was in my world, "comforting."

I moved to East Lansing, Michigan. I told my mother Cindy after I married, eloped, after the fact, so she too could not put me in a mental hospital before crossing that rainbow to have what others have in this world, marriage. Cindy thinks she controls everyone's pot of gold and if you allow her that kind of domain within your life, she will take and take. Take like a Kansas tornado in late August, destroying, wrecking, selfishly taking, like a force some have never come across in their lifetime. Rick Bolhouse & Mike Risko were like that too, they work well together, as if all are from Rome, the place I loathe.

Tentacles- "Something far-reaching; Something that gradually insinuates its influence or control (literary)." (Quote from definition #3, Windows dictionary)

Harvest Moon
CHAPTER FIFTEEN

I looked up to the late September 2002 full moon appearing low in the sky as I walked with my new husband Ed. This would be my first marriage and his first marriage. The season in early autumn in East Lansing, Michigan is one to savor before the weather grows bitterly cold in Michigan. By mid-November Michigan will be hit with blizzard after blizzard endlessly as is typical of Michigan's long hard winters. For now the orange-yellow moon looked like traditional harvest colors as the moon appeared extra-large in the sky. As if the moon was going to drop out of the atmosphere and roll on us as we walked along on the sidewalk and worn footpaths through the woods by the lakes. The loaming large moon so close a bird could have landed on it, or so it appeared to us.

"The harvest moon is the moon at or about the period of fullness that is nearest to the autumnal equinox. The harvest moon is often mistaken for the modern day hunter's moon. The harvest moon is simply the full moon closest to the autumnal equinox. Often the harvest moon seems to be bigger or brighter or more colorful than other full moons. Hence, all celestial bodies look reddish when they are low in the sky. Not just an ordinary full autumn moon. The apparent larger size is because the brain perceives a low-hanging moon to be larger than one that's high in the sky. This is known as a moon illusion and it can be seen with any full moon. It can also be seen with constellations; in other words, a constellation viewed low in the sky will appear bigger than when it is high in the sky." (Information source: Wikipedia, the free encyclopedia online, concerning, "Harvest Moon")

The harvest moon is special tonight. It is when farmers, Indians for that matter, government, family, society, are reminded to reap what is sown in the fertile soil within one's life, one's own crop. It is the time to reap one's benefits, one's crops in life. Ed has no children, I have no children, never even been pregnant before. This was a clean slate, someone who wants a family of his own with me.

In astrological terminology, the moon in a person's natal chart represents women, mother, wife, female boss, etc. The moon also represents emotions, and instincts, how you come across to another emotionally, and to the world at large. And in astrological terminology, the sun represents power, authority, and also men in one's life.

The astrological symbol II, the twin towers, represents in astrological symbolism; the duality between a man and a woman and patience.

According to Revelations 21:1, "the sea will be no more." I disagree, I know the sea will remain, the sea will never dry up. How could the sea actually dry up on earth? The earth is mostly ocean!

Dinosaurs existing and roaming on planet earth are not mentioned in the Bible. However what is <u>not</u> mentioned in the Bible may in fact be very true. What is also written in the Bible may in fact <u>not</u> be true. My history written here, may in fact be written very differently by someone other than me, with different words and facts, a completely different perspective than my words written. Written history works that way.

Setting up roots in metropolitan East Lansing-Okemos area with my established husband who has lived in Lansing, Michigan his whole life, felt normal. And normal felt good for a change of pace from Grand Rapids, Michigan. Away from the Calvinists and Cindy the Calvinist Christian, better known as the church lady from that Saturday Night Live skit.

The distance from my new residence in Meridian Township, Michigan was a good one and a half hours to Grandville, Michigan. The distance felt like a good barrier to the busy Calvinists region in Grand Rapids, Michigan. My new residence, a condo, was not my vision of my ideal residence. However, the condo was large and backed up to woods and lakes and was situated within a quiet cul-de-sac just minutes from the Meridian Mall, parks, and every restaurant imaginable. The location was great. The condo was paid in full, no mortgage, and no fighting over bills and debts with my lifestyle in East Lansing with conservative with the finances husband Ed. Most couples fight over money and bills, high mortgage payments, I could see we would not. I thought East Lansing had more charm and character than downtown Grand Rapids. Many restaurants in East Lansing had large patio seating open in the warm months and shade like many Buckhead restaurants in Atlanta, Georgia.

In September 2002 while Ed was at work I decided to look through the Yellow Pages. I came across a page, I noticed that the Michigan State Police headquarters was located near Michigan State University and minutes from my new residence. I began wondering if my voice as a victim would forever be silenced in the Wayland rape cold case, or if justice would ever be served? I placed a call to the MSP headquarters to make an appointment with internal affairs department of the MSP to investigate that David "Ziggy" Gutierrez nutcase of a MSP State Detective for the Michigan State Police Post in Wayland. I thought let's start here, let's get an investigation going, turn over a new leaf, a new angle, yeah. I located a box of mine in the basement in a storage area of my new residence and located proof of the $30,000 cash pre-settlement offer. I also was willing to take a polygraph test conducted by the Michigan State Police that I was 100% telling the truth about the breaking and entering and rapes, assaults, so that the MSP would know they were not wasting time investigating real crimes that took place.

And so there I went, I headed down to the Michigan State Police post which at the time was located near the campus of Michigan State University. I met with the lead detective in the MSP internal affairs department, Mr. Patrick Boyd and an older, senior looking man next to him. When I arrived we took an elevator to a different floor, then we sat at a table to discuss my case that I wanted brought up and investigated properly, thoroughly. Patrick Boyd pulled out a file, he had the handwritten statement of my account of what occurred in 1998, all pages, which the Wayland MSP Post had forwarded to him. Patrick Boyd also had the fourth grade style police report prepared by David "Ziggy" Gutierrez from 2000 that missed so many details of the crimes. It appeared that Patrick Boyd spoke with Mike Risko. Apparently Mike Risko had went on and on to him about how I am crazy and spent time in a mental ward and that I should not be believed by anyone, and that he had proof that I was lying about the rapes and that he would immediately fax over three retraction letters signed to prove I am a liar. So in other words, when I arrived at the meeting that I called only one week prior, Patrick Boyd had already done his homework on the case in the last few days. Patrick Boyd simply wanted to talk with me in person and get a recorded on tape account of what I went through, my testimony to conclude or open the case as I had so hoped.

Patrick Boyd looked at me serious and slow as he held my handwritten very detailed account of the crimes that occurred at 405 Discovery Drive in Wayland. Then held next to my multi-page victim statement, the fourth grade style report prepared by David "Ziggy" Gutierrez. Patrick Boyd then states, "These accounts of what occurred are different. However, I did have a chance to read the lengthy pre-settlement letter prepared by Lee Silver that you faxed my office recently, thank-you, and your handwritten account that you did provide to detective Gutierrez is identical in details as Lee Silver's pre-settlement letter of 2001. I believe you are telling the truth. I believe you were raped. I don't know what was going through detective David Gutierrez's mind when he prepared the police report. I cannot speak for him. However, I am going to get to the bottom of this and find out why the MSP police report does not match your account of what occurred, which is also an exact replica of Lee Silver's pre-settlement letter."

I just looked at Patrick Boyd as if waiting for him to tell me more, tell me what he can do for me, the victim in all of this. And then he spoke up again, "This is what I do, internal affairs, I am going to have a conversation with Det. David Gutierrez. I will tell him not to call you, that I am going to handle this case from here on out."

I inquire with a positive glow in my face, "Is he going to get fired?"

Patrick Boyd responds, "I don't know, but after you leave I am going to set up an appointment to confront him."

I inquire, "Will the men get arrested, the men that raped me?"

Patrick Boyd stands up as if to announce the meeting is over and he has other appointments. He says to me as we are headed towards the elevator, "Marge Bakker is not one of my favorite prosecutors. I do not think she will prosecute this case. I'll mention to her that I am reopening the case, but I do not think she will go after the men who raped you at the real estate model house in 1998, the case is old."

I never heard back from Patrick Boyd.

In the spring of 2003, April 6th to be exact, Ed and I adopted a puppy, George. He was born on January 21, 2003, he was a few weeks old. He was like our first child, the way we would treat him, and how George saw himself. He was Lhasa Apso and half Cocker Spaniel, mostly black fluffy fur with white markings and big brown eyes. We definitely humanized George by how we treated him, socialization is the commonly used term. I think sometimes he was confused whether he was a dog or a human child. He would look at other dogs as if they were stupid dogs and he was an intelligent furry little human.

During the spring of 2003 Ed and I decided to have wedding photos taken of us. The very best way to have wedding photos is to have a wedding reception, a renewal of vows. I set up the date of June 21, 2003 at Fredrick Meijer Gardens in Grand Rapids. We had about one hundred guests. It seemed to rain about every day leading up to June 21st, and then the clouds opened up and it was a perfectly sunny summer day in Michigan. Most of our photos were photographed outside in the lush and ornate gardens and waterfalls. After our luncheon in the ballroom all of our guests could visit the entire Frederick Meijer Gardens that day. Which was a great benefit to see the immense landscape designs covering so many acres, waterfalls, wandering the beautiful grounds inside and out on such a perfect summer day on June 21, 2003.

We had already taken so many vacations we decided not to vacation directly following the June 21st reception and renewal of vows. Instead we headed up north to enjoy Michigan in the summertime, staying at hotels or camping in a tent with George. One such trip up north we decided to look at vacation homes. Ed was only working four days a week in dentistry and so the weekends were wide open. We did purchase a vacation home near Petoskey, near Walloon Lake area. Ed got a mortgage and had the vacation home paid off in just five years. Later we would sell the vacation home and use that bundle of savings towards a less conservative main residence someday.

In the Fall of 2003 while Ed was at work I decided to contact Patrick Boyd. I learned that he had been transferred elsewhere and was no longer the head of the internal affairs investigative department at the Michigan State Police headquarters.

I also decided to have rhinoplasty surgery to correct my once broken nose that then created a crooked nose at the base on the left side of my nose between my nose and my eye. Mr. Rick Smith performed the surgery and I could not be more pleased with the results. Without changing the shape or size of my nose which I like, he only corrected one slight bone that had been bashed in during a visit from Greg Umstead to my college dorm room at California Baptist College. Ed paid for the surgery that was done in East Lansing, Michigan. Ed a dentist, had me set up an appointment to fill a few cavities that I had. During the appointment Ed commented that since my teeth are numb on one side of my mouth he would like to shave down that one crooked tooth on the upper right front where orthodontist Dr. DeVries had taken and twisted that tooth after my braces were off back in 1984. My husband Ed shaved that one tooth on the side and filled it, shaped and molded half of that tooth with some type of dental material. The result is perfect, my smile back to perfect like when my braces first came off in 1984 and I smiled in a mirror for the first time.

I was making improvements with myself and my life which infuriated the watchful eye of the CIA that had purposely done things to me, committed crimes against me for their reasons alone. The CIA's fury with what I changed would be seen. Just around the corner in life I would once again be reminded of their power and fury in my life. When a bully government department such as the CIA decides to cause chaotic in one's life because they can, one does not have the ability to push on the brakes and stop their abuse, so I know, so I have experienced and endured. The CIA had intended for my nose to remain crooked looking, deformed, making my California headshots not desirable to talent agents in Hollywood. The CIA does not want me noticed, and most certainly does not ever want me to become famous.

Then the matter of dental records the CIA controlled, like the tooth they had Dr. DeVries twist to make my dental records matching to Diane Umstead. The CIA had intended for my physical changes to remain permanent. To the CIA everyone is a lamb, and the CIA is the lion.

In February 2004 I thought the next best thing to do is to head to Wayland's Michigan State Police Post and see if the State police are willing to open my rape cold case of 405 Discovery Drive. I brought my Michigan State Police polygraph test results that I was 100% telling the truth. I brought with me the seven page or so pre-settlement letter prepared by Lee Silver in 2001 and proof the men offered me a cash settlement offer of $30,000 in 2001, and headed to Wayland one late morning. Upon arriving at the Wayland Michigan State Police Post and opening the front door to the smallest foyer ever, I received a not so warm of a welcome. The male police officer working the front area, on call, on duty, waved his hands for me to leave the building as he hastily shouts at me, "Get out of here! Internal affairs was all over us, get out of here, we are not going to take any case you report or open any case of yours."

And so I left. Then I headed down the street and turned on Main Street in Wayland, as I did so I noticed a sign, Wayland City Police. Oh, I should stop in there and maybe they can re-open my rape cold case, I thought as I turned my steering wheel into the parking lot. I was not ready to drive all the way back to East Lansing, Michigan without seeing if I could turn possibly another leaf over in my saga in obtaining justice for what happened to me at 405 Discovery Drive. And so I walked in and spoke with the receptionist, a female, who called to a policeman in the back room. The heavyset officer Rollins arrives to the front, the same officer Rollins who had at one time been at my former residence of 2030 Winding Oak when Cindy placed me in a mental ward at Allegan General Hospital. I instantly recognized him. I do not believe he recognized me.

Officer Rollins wanted to know why I would want to report a rape case of 1998 to his office when the Michigan State Police had initiated the investigation and police report. I remark with knowledge, "I just came from the Michigan State Police Post hoping they would re-open my rape cold case of 1998. The State police guy on duty asked me to leave." I informed officer Rollins that I had about a year or so ago contacted the Michigan State Police headquarters to launch an internal investigation into the detective in charge of my rape case, David "Ziggy" Gutierrez. Just as I finished saying the syllables of Gutierrez, officer Rollins turns to the receptionist and remarks, "That makes sense why you are here now."

I respond, "What makes sense?"

Officer Rollins and the receptionist recall and repeat what they remember from a few months ago. Then officer Rollins finally adds to my awaiting curiosity on the subject, "That detective was asked to resign. That's why the Michigan State Police Post would not re-open your cold case and asked you to leave."

The female receptionist remarks to me, "You should sue them."

Officer Rollins remarks to me, "Oh, you can't do that. But I can take down your story of events and create a new report and begin a new investigation. I can't do it today, but if you set up an appointment I can take down a new report and begin there."

And so that is what I did. The next week in late winter, early spring 2004 I drove back to Wayland and met with a officer Rollin whom seemed willing to re-open my rape case. The file number is 211-04. I provided to him my polygraph test results that I was 100% telling the truth. Officer Rollins informed me that any polygraph test results would never be admissible into a court of law and are used primarily as a tool among police and detectives to uncover who is telling the truth and who is not. I also provided officer Rollins with a copy of Lee Silver's pre-settlement letter and proof the men offered me $30,000 cash from their attorneys Visser & Bolhouse in Grandville. Officer Rollin's stops me there and inquires, "Did you take the money offered, the $30,000?"

I remark startled, "No, why?"

The others listening at the table began reciting extortion comments, commenting law to one another.

I ask again, "Why? Why do you ask if I took the settlement money?"

Officer Rollins remarks from across the table, "Well…..if you took the money….the men could come back and try and charge you with extortion since they were never arrested on assault charges."

I wince at officer Rollins, "What? I am the victim here."

Officer Rollins remarks, "I'm just saying……go on…tell us what happened."

And so I did. The following weeks I heard nothing from officer Rollins. Then he called me at home in East Lansing, out of the blue and informed me that he spoke with Pat Goodale, Dave Smith and Chuck Helder and a few others from Smith-Diamond Realty. He explained that he was able to get some information but their attorneys are very protective and stop just about anything coming out of their mouths.

I inquire over the phone, "Do you have their investigative interviews taped?"

Officer Rollins inquires, "Yes, I do."

I ask, "Are they going to get arrested?"

Officer Rollins responds a bit perturbed and I could not tell why, "I'm going to turn my report and taped interviews over to Marge Bakker but I do not know if she will sign warrants for their arrest, she has to make that call, not me."

That was the spring of 2004, I also learned I was pregnant with Eddie, my first and only child. My due date was in November 2004. I was thirty-four years old when I conceived, was pregnant with Eddie and delivered him.

My aunt Thelma on my adopted father Charles Vander Ark's side called me one day and announced she would like to throw me a baby shower. Out of all the Saturdays I was pregnant with Eddie, aunt Thelma Vander Ark-Battjes and Cindy Honderd select Saturday 9/11 2004 to host my baby shower. What am I supposed to say, no?

While I was pregnant with Eddie I had shown Ed's mother Roma DeBartolo my ultrasound photos, revealing a baby boy was on the way!

During the preceding weeks and months to come my mother-in-law Roma kept claiming that Cindy Honderd keeps calling them announcing that I am crazy and that I need to get back on my medication. Roma would remark to Ed, "What mother would say that if it was not true? I would not say that."

Ed would remark, "Oh mom, that's just Cindy. She can say not so nice of things about Lori, just ignore her, that's how we handle Cindy, ignore her mom."

Roma responds flabbergasted, "Ignore her? Cindy, Lori's mom and your sister Nancy (DeBartolo-Vander Laan) talk just about every day. I'm warning you Ed, they are up to no good with that Visser & Bolhouse attorneys in Grandville. I think they are going to snatch up your little boy before he is even born. They are devious and are cooking up something. Lori better watch her back. Al and Nancy have no male grandsons and Nancy wants to get ahold of yours, they're making arrangements and Cindy is in the middle of helping them accomplish their end goal Ed. Why does Cindy act like this Ed?"

Ed remarks, "Oh Nancy and Cindy are two peas in a pod. They can't take our baby away, even if the corroborate to do so, they can't get away with snatching our baby on the way."

Roma looked alarmed that Ed was not alarmed and remarked, "Ed, they are going to try."

I am so accustomed to Cindy that I also was not even alarmed. Cindy's evil behind the scenes behavior and bold sabotaging was so common place to me now by age thirty-four, that nothing shocked or alarmed me about Cindy. Like a dog barking, or a turtle crawling slowly, the sun coming up in the morning each day, so exact was Cindy's behavior to expect, never a surprise, not to me. And Ed was getting used to her ways after being married to me, common, and his sister Nancy was just like Cindy. Therefore he understood Cindy and Nancy's evil side not revealed to most in the community of Dutch Calvinists.

On Saturday November 20th, 2004 I was so uncomfortable that I could not fall asleep. The pain of being pregnant was increasing and I could not escape the pain as I tried to fall asleep one night. I did not know what to do so Ed suggested we go to the hospital as my due date was a week ago. So we headed to Ingham Regional Hospital in Lansing, Michigan. Upon arriving to the hospital I learned that I was in labor and was dilating. The labor lasted seventeen hours, I had a natural child birth verses a C-section.

During the last minutes of natural child birth, if not seconds, Dr. Mazer stabs me with an ultra-sharp knife just as my son Eddie is being born. I learned later the medical term is called an episiotomy. Just as the doctor is pulling out Eddie and I can hear Eddie, my body is going into convulsions and I begin to shake uncontrollably, the room was ice cold all of a sudden. In my mind I was wondering if someone had cranked up the air conditioning as my body felt so cold I could not stop shaking. I open my mouth to speak and I cannot speak I can only see the doctor and nurses scrambling and talking around me but I am not able to speak to them. Like a weird freak nightmare scenario I can't talk, but I want to talk and communicate. Then a nurse leans over me and explains, "You lost so much blood that's why you can't talk and are shaking, don't close your eyes. I know things look blurry in the room. Stay with us, we are going to give you an emergency blood transfusion, someone just went to get a bag of blood."

And so I received a lifesaving blood transfusion by the nurses demands in the room, not the doctor's demands or orders, the nurses demands to the doctor, and then the nurses demands to each other, when he refused.

Eddie was born at 4:59pm on Sunday November 21, 2004. People will often ask me, "Why only one child? Why not have more, you can, can't you?"

Do you know why I only have one child? I just explained why.

The other odd thing I remember about my pregnancy. I was not too happy about the care I was receiving in Okemos at my OBGYN so I decided at five months to see another OBGYN in the Lansing area. I called my insurance company Blue Cross/ Blue Shield located in upstate New York to find out why my health insurance was only being accepted at the OBGYN in Okemos and not anywhere else? Which narrowed my choices to only have my baby delivered by Dr. Mazer at the only hospital he delivers babies, Ingham Regional Hospital. Blue Cross/ Blue Shield explained that at five months along I was too far along to switch to another OBGYN doctor and therefore I could not switch OBGYN doctors.

Dr. Mazer would say things to me during my monthly appointments that only CIA agents would say to me at The Gold Club. Word for word statements. It creeped me out, made me feel so uncomfortable and made me feel unsafe. That was why I was seeking out another OBGYN doctor, I could see red flags, and sadly could not stop the crime against me once again.

About three months after Eddie was born I hear a loud knock on the front door of my residence in East Lansing, Michigan. I have Eddie in my arms and was in the process of feeding Eddie. I look out the front window to see who is knocking so loud and fervently on my front door. To my surprise there is a Meridian Township Police Department officer at my front door. What was my very first thought? I thought maybe someone had a break-in within the neighborhood and the police officer was going door to door to ask if anybody witnessed anything, that was my immediate thought. I had no idea he was at my front door to arrest me and charge me with three counts of felony fraud false police reports. One count for Dave Smith, one count for Chuck Helder, and one count for Patrick Goodale, all because way back when in the summer of 2002 I had been forced by Judge Harry Beech to sign Mike Risko's three prepared retraction letters. I had no idea. I had no way of knowing. I was just as shocked in February 2005 as you probably are reading this right now.

The MTPD officer inquires if I am Lori Vander Ark DeBartolo. I respond "Yes." He then opens the front door wider and steps inside my residence as he brushes against me holding my newborn son. My dog George is alarmed and begins barking at the police officer who just entered our residence. The MTPD officer requests for me to put my baby upstairs. I am wondering what is this all about? It was a scary and very unnerving scene.

The MTPD officer responds to my many questions as he side tracks and also speaks into a radio device, "You have three felony counts against you. Mike Risko made sure a warrant was signed for you, that was three months ago. We learned you were pregnant and let you deliver your baby before arresting you. Each felony count is up to four years in prison. You are looking at a possible twelve years in jail. I have the phone number of some lady, some relative of yours in Byron Center, Michigan, some Nancy Vander Laan. She mentioned she would be willing to drive to East Lansing and take care of your baby. Is she a relative of yours?"

I looked at the officer just stunned as I slowly am able to say, "Yes, she is my husband's sister, older sister."

I reach for the phone, ignoring the phone number the police officer is handing me on the counter and I dial my husband's dental office in Brighton, Michigan where he is employed which is about a forty minute drive away. Then the doorbell rings and a female officer arrives. I take Eddie upstairs and lay him in his crib. The female officer instructs me to change my clothes. The entire experience was nothing shy of a kidnapping feeling of me and the unsettling unknown for baby Eddie.

Ed finally arrives home. He says to me, Cindy and Nancy are up to no good. I'll hire an attorney and we will get this all situated. Ed was starting to shake in fear at how our lives were changing at such a rapid speed of horror that we could not change at the moment, if ever. I remember thinking right then and there that Cindy and Nancy and their CIA connections can make anything possible, my fear of them rose to an alarming level that morning around 10:30am. I stood in fear right then and there in my own residence with those two cops staring at me as they kept repeating, "Well, you must have done something in Allegan County, prosecutors don't sign warrants for nothing. We have to arrest you and then Allegan will pick you up in Mason."

I inquire in horror and shock, "Mason? What is in Mason?"

The male officer responds as he handcuffs me from behind and clinches the key tightly and tighter behind my back, "Jail. That's where the jail is, they will keep you in a holding cell until an arriving officer from Allegan takes you to their jail."

The female officer comments in relief, "Well, he is here now I can go." Referring to my husband Ed pulling up in the garage.

As I enter the patrol car backseat I comment to the arresting MTPD officer "This is so unfair. It's sad." My dog George stayed barking by the front door at the strange police cars and bullies that invaded our home as I stared at my residence through the glass of the back windshield of his police car. I could not push on the brakes or stop where the male police officer was taking me. I simply watched my world disappear from the backseat in handcuffs with no possible way out accept through the system that would be in front of me now. Within a minute I could no longer see my world as I was brought against my will for a thirty minute fast ride through the country side as I slid around on the slippery cold backseat of that police car in handcuffs as the handcuffs tightened behind me with every corner he turned. We traveled against my will, but willingly without a choice to a set of cold experiences awaiting for me just ahead in the book, my life.

My very first thoughts upon entering the jail in Mason, Michigan was noticing all the painted cement block walls painted in Easter colors and the high wattage lighting system in the jail. How strange and ultra-bright the place looked compared to my comfortable residence. My next thoughts, how long will I be in here? And what is Ed doing to get me out of here? I missed my dog George and newborn son Eddie tremendously, beginning with the car ride to the jail. Now I am stuck in a cement walk-in closet in Mason, Michigan, no windows to the world outside the jail, unable to move normally, only allowed to move a few feet within the cell. I was in horror. I have heard the word jail,

I was aware of the vocabulary words "jail" or "prison." Those words do not come close to describing the essence of jail, the experience and cold atmosphere of jail and all that jail takes away that is normal in one's life. Cement walls, floors and ceilings, extremely bright lights that hurt one's eyesight and offer no rest or peace. No windows to the outdoors, no sights and smells of the outdoors. One is in a cement cell the size of a walk-in closet, extreme lighting with a rubbery plastic cot on the floor. Everything has four walls with no furniture, no scenery other than brick walls like a basement cellar painted brightly, with no escape. No choices one can make while in there, one simply sits. One can constantly hear metal, metal doors, metal keys and a buzzing sound. There is no furniture or television, or rooms to go to, no way to walk to another room or leave or go outside or grab one's car keys to drive away or do errands. I just so happened to finally after three months with no period, get my period in that jail cell. I had to bang on the glass and wired glass at that, to get a feminine pad so I would not bleed all over myself and my outfit. Anything needed, such as aspirin for a headache is not available. The only thing available is the mistreatment of mistreating me and others in the most inhuman way possible by the State of Michigan, or government, and all those who are employed to do this to another. Whether a person is guilty or innocent, it does not matter inside there, not when they put you in a cage or cell. Someone has a lot of power over my life and I do not believe it is me. Then I rationalized in my silence, maybe Marge Bakker the Allegan County Prosecutor is ruling me out as a liar of the rapes in Wayland and this is her algebra problem worked backwards to get the correct conclusion, the desired correct answer that I am not a lair. I never lied about the rapes.

I waited hours in Mason, the local government kidnapping of me and separating me from my newborn was yet another saga and experience in which I would honestly wonder, what the hell is everybody thinking by doing this to me? What is the point? What I would learn about the very established and bustling American legal system is that one does not need to have broken the law or committed a crime, if local government puts you in jail, there is no walking away in a cement closet. Jails are simply resources and real estate.

Finally Allegan, Wayland City Police show up, and it's officer Rollins! He is here to transport me to Allegan County so that Marge Bakker can prosecute me for what she believes or officer Rollins believes is that I lied about the rapes and who raped me. Unbelievable mistreatment of the rape victim, me! Someone obviously wanted to flex their power in my naive little life that they have power and I do not. If someone could create a company motto of the American government, modeled after my experiences what would that motto be? Create one. Who in their right mind would do this? Seriously, is the DNA so screwed up in America that everyone in power, everyone in government acts crazy like this to me? To others? This is insanity by the State of Michigan. Everyone in the system doing this to me is insane. I looked around at my surroundings in disbelief of the American government.

I was handcuffed and led to a large sport utility vehicle in the extra-large garage of the jail. I stepped up to the backseat and was told to brace myself for a long ride back to Allegan.

"Then what? What happens next?" I ask.

Officer Rollins spoke up, "We will book you, process you and you'll stay in the Allegan jail, the Allegan jail is not as modern as this facility here, the Allegan jail is a bit more primitive. The Judge has not set a bond yet. I think your husband is working on getting an attorney for you. Just sit back, it's a long drive."

I inquire, "Primitive? What do you mean by primitive?"

Officer Rollins looks up at me from the interior rearview mirror and remarks, "Oh you'll see." The female cop laughs next to him in the front.

And so I sat back, I could finally see the outdoors. It seemed strange that someone could take so much away from me all under the umbrella of power and authority in America, Michigan for that matter. It is February 2005, I thought officer Rollins had just been busy with other cases in the last year that held more importance to him than my rape cold case of Wayland and Smith-Diamond Realty since I tried to re-open my rape case. I just assumed my rape case was just collecting dust in a metal file cabinet. I could not have been more surprised that he arrested the rape victim, me! I said to officer Rollins, "There was more evidence, even if it was circumstantial evidence, that the men I accused of committing crimes, rape, had committed crimes against me than evidence I am a liar about the rapes!"

I noticed that officer Rollins was not jolted emotionally like I was when he calmly answered, "Now don't go blaming me for your arrest. Marge Bakker is the prosecutor who signed a warrant for your arrest. I simply gave her the police report and interview tapes, I did not sign the warrant for three counts of felony false police reports."

Silence resumed amidst the atmosphere in the police vehicle. I stared out my window as I slumped my back against the tight handcuffs. I watched the tree line zooming by me and realized how far away he was taken me from my newborn. I can feel breast milk sticking to my bra as I stare out the vehicle back and side windows unable grab the steering wheel to turn back and go home. I feel kidnapped, but somehow this is legal in America for police and prosecution, it seemed surreal to me.

I can feel my stomach turning in knots, I have to get back home. I do not want to be handcuffed, driven away like this and brought to Allegan. I have to speak up, "What evidence do you have that I lied about the rapes?"

Officer Rollins pauses as if re-thinking what he should tell me. Then he speaks up, "John Brennan wanted you arrested while you were pregnant. I told him I could not do that."

I wait, I assume he will tell me more. Then I ask, "Why would John Brennan from the CIA want me arrested? That makes no sense."

Officer Rollins looks at the heavyset female officer next to him in the front as he looks back in his rearview mirror and remarks, "John Brennan wanted you arrested and charged while you were pregnant because you would not look like a rape victim that Goodale would touch and he could get you prosecuted by a jury. I told him I did not think it would work, I said wait until she delivers and has baby weight on her, then we'll prosecute."

I am handcuffed, I can feel the sharp metal handcuffs scrapping against my skin, poking me. I cannot take off the handcuffs or grab the steering wheel to turn back. I am in the back of a police sport utility Ford vehicle. I have watched so many trees wiz past me at such high velocity for some time now that I know I am a long way from my baby, from my home. I could not tell you where I was, only that he is bringing me to Allegan, I assume in horror and panic as I try and remain calm to ask more questions. I need more answers to my questions as my frantic mind is racing as fast as the trees alongside the meadows. The woods in the distance behind the empty cornfields, alongside the vehicle, seem to wiz passed us as he races in the frozen tundra of west Michigan towards a primitive dungeon unseen.

I swallow and calmly ask, "What evidence does Marge Bakker have that I lied about the rapes?"

Officer Rollins responds, "Well, she has three retraction letters that Mike Risko provided my office, that I forwarded to her."

I ask, "And what evidence did I provide to you that I was 100% telling the truth? Why would the men even offer $30,000 to make this all go away if they are innocent?"

Officer Rollins settles in his seat and remarks, "It does not matter what evidence you provided. If the men stated they did not rape you, I believe them."

I remark, "I had to sign those three retraction letters prepared by their attorney Risko or Judge Harry Beech threatened in court to throw me in county lock-up for 90 days. I had no choice."

Officer Rollins remarks, "Oh, you had a choice."

When I arrived at the jail in Allegan, right next to the large court in downtown Allegan I stepped into something primitive, dark and dismal. I had no idea something actually so primitive existed in the modern world. The large cage holding cell had several men in it, everything open, even the urinal. I could hear the men pee, I could smell the urine. I could hear their talking just a few feet from where I was being booked into the jail and fingerprinted next to the open cage with metal bars from the 1800's. Just one large cage holding cell in the dungeon of a jail. I can hear a woman whaling and banging against a door somewhere in the back of the dungeon to get out, as a female officer shouts for her to stop banging.

I do not have a choice to leave this situation, just like these people. My mind begins to go blank. I can faintly hear condensation dripping from the interior gloomy cold stone of the dungeon walls or ceiling corners. I could breathe in the musky damp cold air, only space heaters existed in that place. My mind begins to go blank, I cannot even absorb anymore experiences of this day. I begin to go numb, a white canvas, I cannot paint what happens next. Then my luck turns around for the better. I am told my husband located an attorney to represent me, and I am out!

It was late afternoon, the sun was starting to set as I could finally breathe in snowy cold air, fresh crisp wintery air into my lungs as an attorney leads me down the sidewalk in Allegan County towards his law firm across from the courts in Allegan. As soon as I could finally breathe in that fresh wintery air and smell the ice in snowflakes, I could hear the crunch of the sidewalk ice and snow beneath my shoes I soon forgot how exhausted I was as I could now feel and see freedom all around me, I was finally outside. I noticed how the outdoors has so many dimensional layers unlike the one layer of just a wall or walls. In the outdoors or in a normal setting freedom surrounded me in peaceful bliss with many layered dimensions that I had never contrasted before to the one dimension of a wall or walls. We walked into the creaky old house converted into a small law firm resting against a big drop to a big river. He explained that my husband had hired him and he explained that my husband was on his way to pick me up. He explained this was all some confusion and family saga of Ed's older sister Nancy wanting to get her hands on my newborn baby boy. He explained that all of this legal stuff will soon be over and my husband would stand by my side and not watch his sister do this to me. The Allegan Judge stated that my jail bond be zero dollars. My attorney Steve Kastran reassured me that all was rosy.

One or two weeks later Marge Bakker dropped the charges of three felony false police reports down to one count of a misdemeanor charge. I requested to my attorney to have all charges dropped, even the one misdemeanor false police report. I exclaimed to my attorney, "I did nothing wrong, I did not break the law!"

He responds back, "I know that. Marge Bakker knows that, but she is afraid you will file a civil suit against her office for a false arrest. She needs to protect herself legally and therefore she is only offering one option for you to take."

I ask, "What?"

Steve Kastran replies, "One misdemeanor count false police report, no jail time, six months of probation. A $500.00 fine which is customary for a misdemeanor fine. This does not go on your criminal record, and she drops the three felony charges of false police report/felony fraud that you made up the rape stories. You know each felony charge is up to four years in jail per count, that's twelve years Lori that she is willing to drop! Take it. You have a son to raise. Don't fight it. I'll quit as your attorney if you fight it. I am telling you this is a good plea deal."

I stubbornly respond, "I did not lie about the rapes. I do not want any charges, not even a misdemeanor charge!"

Steve Kastran looks at me like I am the most frustrating client he has ever had to deal with and remarks, "Take it! You have to take it!"

I look at him, "I'll talk to my husband, see what he says."

I turn to Steve Kastran as I am leaving his office, "Will the men get arrested, the three men?"

Steve Kastran responds much calmer now, "No. The men will not be arrested."

I inquire, "Why?"

Steve Kastran replies very logically, "Because, my only job as your attorney is to see to it that I get the charges against you dropped. My job is to dismiss any allegations towards you."

And so I took the plea deal. I felt I had no choice. Then I filed a complaint against the Michigan Attorney Grievance Commission against Steve Kastran and Marge Bakker. Both were licensed and practicing attorneys in Michigan acting unethical. Like any complaint I have filed and brought to the attention of the State of Michigan, nothing became of my rights.

Cindy returned from vacationing one day and I inquired to her about a rumor that she and Nancy corroborated to throw me in jail for all eternity to snatch Eddie from me. Cindy laughed and said she knew nothing about such a plan.

I inquire, "So you are not trying to sabotage me and my son?"

Cindy remarks, "No. Why would I do such a thing?"

I have to admit, Cindy married to Jerry Honderd made her strive to be more normal. I actually trusted her to even babysit Eddie as he turned two as I would be remodeling the up north home with projects here and there. I needed her to watch him a weekend here and there during the summer months. Ed and I had no babysitter for Eddie. However, me wanting a mother also made me overlook facts about Cindy in the past. I wanted to believe it was the distant past.

One day Cindy had arrived back from a ten day Mediterranean cruise that she and Jerry went on. Cindy actually said something that contradicts Calvinism, I was shocked. Cindy informed me that when she stepped off the cruise ship and placed her foot on soil near Rome she felt dizzy and began having a past life regression. Cindy remembered a past life in Rome, not just any past life, but a past life as a notorious leader, a crowned leader of ancient Roman times.

Then my mind traces back to The Gold Club when I danced for CIA David Petraeus he remarked as I danced, "I had feelings for you when you were young. Your mother Cindy resembles the Roman Emperor Nero in your adoption file photo at Bethany."

Despite my earlier distrust and hate for Cindy, I have to admit that while Cindy was married to Jerry Honderd she displayed the most normal behavioral side of her personality that I have ever witnessed or known from her. I actually began to trust her. When she wanted to take Eddie for a weekend and give me a little break as Ed and I never had a babysitter, I let Cindy babysit Eddie while he was out of the baby stage and two years to ages four or five. I wanted a mother and Cindy was acting normal, or so I perceived her to be acting normal for once in my life.

However, Cindy's bad habits, criminal habits are very interrogated into her personality. So well interrogated are Cindy's bad habits, criminal habits, that Cindy knows how to conceal and mask what goes on behind closed doors.

The Carson family lived next door for a year or so as they had inherited their mother's condo in East Lansing after their mother died of cancer. Cory Carson was a sheriff in a different county than Ingham County. He informed me as the 2008-2009 school year rolled around late in August for me to reconsider not enrolling Eddie in Okemos Public Schools. I informed him that Okemos had excellent testing scores from the State of Michigan which I researched online. I had only heard good things about Okemos schools. I planned on enrolling Eddie the next day to begin September pre-school for the 2008-2009 school year. He informed me that he was going to enroll his three girls in Haslett Public Schools, school of choice, even though our addresses belonged to the Okemos school district.

He barked, he warned, "Okemos' Wardcliff Elementary has just closed many elementary schools in Okemos, at least three Okemos elementary schools are shutting down. No one wants to put their young kids in Okemos schools. I'm telling you, you do not want to have Eddie in the Okemos school district. White women and elementary age young boys and girls are being targeted by a well-structured group of criminals."

I stopped him there and inquired further, "Targeted? What do you mean by saying targeted?"

Cory Carson responds with more warnings meant to scare me, "I'm a sheriff, I know things. People from Okemos get killed, the bodies are not discarded in Okemos, the bodies are dumped in another county if the group has too much difficulty transporting the sold person to the buyer. We get those calls of a body dumped in another county, the county I work for is the dumping ground. And that's not all, the organized criminals target real estate, they try and get a woman to sign over real estate she owns after she is kidnapped, they steal her credit cards. Usually within the first three days of abducting a woman she is raped financially first."

I remarked with a smile not even wanting to process what he just warned as a reality, "I checked the Okemos test scores. The State of Michigan has favorable ratings for the test scores of students at Okemos. I am going to enroll Eddie in Okemos." And up until the year 2010,

Okemos did have excellent test scores based on State testing of students, the MEAP scores.

Sheriff Cory Carson just shook his head, unable to get through to me with his many warnings about the Okemos school district. I paid no heed to what he had just said to me. Certainly no media in the Lansing area was giving the Okemos school district a cloud of suspicion to any illegal activities. I blissfully thought Cory Carson was perhaps too wrapped up in his job, but not reality.

Then one day Cindy was sitting at my table in East Lansing and remarks, "Eddie thinks my pubic hair looks like grass."

I am at a loss for words. I do not have a response for Cindy because I am utterly shocked at what I just heard her say so nonchalantly sitting at my kitchen dining room table as I reached into the refrigerator to politely pull out a drink for her, my guest. Eddie had just arrived back home from a weekend at Cindy's condo in Grandville. His small suitcase was resting by the table. I am stunned. I have no response for Cindy as I hand her a refreshing drink. I simply make a mental note placed in a mental file cabinet within my head that Cindy will never watch Eddie at her house or mine ever again. Only supervised visits from here on out, I mentally jot down. Quite frankly as long as I feel that I am going to vomit when I hear those words of Cindy in my head, I frankly do not even want to see her again or have Eddie in her presence.

Later Ed told Cindy that I wanted nothing to do with her. Cindy began sending letters and packages and making annoying phone calls to Ed's work when I would not pick up the home phone. To cease the harassment of Cindy towards us we retained an attorney for the fee of five hundred dollars to have attorney Meri Ann Stowe send Cindy a Cease and Desist Letter. The Cease and Desist Letter referenced Cindy's harassing behavior towards us and requested for Cindy Honderd to immediately stop her unwanted behavior. Okemos attorney Meri Ann Stowe prepared the December 10, 2010 Cease and Desist Letter and mailed it to Cindy Honderd.

Cindy's behavior changed, only now she would camp out in my neighborhood, a good one and a half hours drive from Grandville, Michigan. She would always drive a different vehicle than the one I knew her to own. When I would spot her she would leave. Uncle Warren Stob her brother who also lives in Grandville would do this same activity in my neighborhood and startle me by his presence in a vehicle parked close to my mailbox. Or parked somewhere in my neighborhood when I walked my dog George, there he would be or Cindy, always on different days, different times, different vehicles, with the same consistent behavior towards me. Behavior to let me know that I cannot stop them, no one can, not the law, not an attorney. I called the police, the police asked if they were doing anything illegal? "Well, no, they are in my neighborhood where they do not belong."

The harvest moon reminds us all, great and small of the time to reap what we have sown, that goes for the State of Michigan as well. Democratic Michigan Governor Jennifer Granholm and Republican Michigan Governor Rick Snyder are both very aware of case #211-04 in Wayland, Michigan and all that has transpired. However, both of their Attorney Generals and them do not believe questioning CIA illegal activity within the State of Michigan is within their governorship duties. I disagree, just as you the reader might also disagree.

My mind jogs back to a conversation I had with attorney and future FBI Director James Comey concerning the CIA and election ballots. Information about the CIA, real information, not the information that only the media will broadcast, but real news. Real information about the CIA would resonate questions within me now, who is running America? And why are they running America into the ground? What is America's debt at right now? Does it take the correct formulated DNA to solve tough problems? Problems others could not solve. Pertinent questions were beginning to really resonate within me now. James Comey in the 1990's had told me that the CIA has a very powerful shadow government presence in America.

"Medium Coeli"
CHAPTER SIXTEEN

A theory, a fact, a notion, a reality, have one thing in common; If your mind rejects a notion, rejects a story, rejects facts of a crime scene, that does not mean something is not true. What remains evident, is simply that your mind cannot fathom and process the truth as presented perhaps. For instance, as everything you view as "real" in this world, presented as real and true, may in fact not be true and real. Such as corruption in American government, can result in Cognitive Dissonance, which is what I experienced. Typically I have experienced the opposite of what government is designed to do in America, which is to provide help. Just as you can read and research all I have revealed of my kaleidoscope of knowing many truths.

What is real and true may in fact not be politically correct. And what is deemed politically correct or politically incorrect now, may in fact have been deemed politically correct or politically incorrect in a different time period. For example, if I was to exclaim the world is round and not flat and boldly write that down in a book, depending on the time period, would also indicate whether I was labeled crazy or correct by the critics and general population of people.

Let me give you an example of being politically incorrect for the year 2017: If you were to section off Detroit and give the inhabitants of that section a fair market value for their residences and then move into that same Detroit section authentic Dutch, or German or Norwegian, or Swedish people with the same level of education and the same amount of money of financial worth of the recently former inhabitants in Detroit, would you also get the same crime rate year after year, or something different in results? Would residential housing improve? Would economics improve in that section? Would jobs be created and economic opportunities, businesses be created? Would the quality of one's life and one's family blossom? The experiment, the study has never been done before. So how would you, or the American government, or the world know the outcome? However, the answer to keep pouring money into Detroit is the only politically correct solution accepted in this time period that I complete volume one, third edition of my memoir collection. If you want to receive positive results to any problem you also have to be willing to examine the problem thoroughly to come to successful conclusions that produce positive results, or you are insane, you keep doing the same thing over and over with no positive results. In this time period that we live in many groups of people that know themselves too well might not like the truth and repress the truth. The CIA works that way, so do certain religious organizations and ethnic groups, people can work that way. Repressing the truth is not what this book is about.

"Resilience" is a word many people would use to describe me. "I can't believe she is still alive" is a sentence often spoken about me. I cannot count on my fingers how many structured assignation and kidnapping attempts I have lived through. I cannot count the attempts on my hands because the attempts on my life outnumber the amount of fingers I have on my hands.

To understand peace, one must understand what creates conflicts. To have good in the world, you would need to also have evil? Or at least understand the nature of evil? Everything is the same. Or everything has a polarizing opposite. To understand anything, any subject, is a step away from blissful ignorance.

The Latin words "Medium Coeli" means in translation "Middle of the Heavens". When you are unable to leave this earth and move on due to unfinished business, residue from a previous life lived, it is said that your soul rests in mid-heaven.

Yes, I would have to say that "Medium Coeli" is something I could clearly see and address in my own existence, or what is left of my existence. This entire book could be summed up by the Latin words "Medium Coeli". However, in this chapter I am only going to highlight a portion of issues and not repeat the entire book at hand.

I enrolled Eddie at age four, almost five years old into Okemos Public School's pre-school for the 2008-2009 school year. Mrs. Fields was Eddie's pre-school teacher. I could not have been more pleased with his pre-school teacher.

I was also mad at Cindy. I wish Ed and I had never purchased that up north home and taken on all the remodeling projects. Right around 2008 the real estate market began to come to a halt, a real estate crash. I decided to not work as a realtor, a real estate agent part-time. I became full-time, just a stay at home mom. Also, right around 2008 we listed the up north home, the house did not sell until 2011, that's how bad the real estate market was in Michigan.

I refused to go to any family functions in west Michigan that would involve Cindy, which were all the family functions. I could not get those words and feeling of horror to leave me, "looks like grass" as Cindy announced what Eddie had remarked about her private area in the shower. Why would a grandma take a shower with her four year old grandson? Why? I don't get, I don't understand, I can't take anymore inappropriateness from Cindy, I will avoid her always.

"Medium Coeli," Middle of the Heavens; I had a lot of unfinished business when it comes to Cindy. Another issue, the older I became the more I would wonder if Cindy had done my father in, killed him. The more interaction I had with Cindy, dealing with Cindy since my father Chuck's death in 1986, the more I grew to understand Cindy had killed my father. I went from wondering, to accepting the other reality not marked on his death certificate, which is I believe she did murder him. One day I got the nerve to request an autopsy of my father Chuck Vander Ark. I called the Grand Rapids Coroner's Office and was able to speak to the coroner that had performed the partial autopsy on my father Charles Vander Ark. The partial autopsy performed made the coroner arrive at a professional opinion on the cause of death, the coroner whom gave my father Chuck Vander Ark a written cause of death on his Michigan death certificate. I learned that the coroner had only been on the job for a few months, precisely around the time period when I turned sixteen on February 28, 1986. Cindy divorced my father through Visser & Bolhouse attorneys at law, March of 1986. Then my father suddenly passed away, died in June or July 1986. I thought the timing of my father's death seemed suspicious, in light of the sequence of events in 1986. The coroner made it very clear to me on the phone that he did not want my father's body exhumed from the grave.

I started asking questions to the coroner on the phone. "Why did you not do a full and complete autopsy?" "Why did you not check for drugs other than alcohol?" The coroner stated the detective in charge from the Grand Rapids Police Department that had arrived to my father's house in 1986 in a bad section of Grand Rapids did not want an autopsy performed, did not think it was necessary. I was informed from the coroner that the only time an autopsy is performed is if the detective suspects foul play. The coroner informed me that the detective did not suspect foul play. I asked, "Why did the police not talk with me his daughter in 1986?" His response was that again was the detective's direction and considered it a closed case. I requested to the coroner on the phone that my father's body be exhumed. The coroner stated that would be expensive and only the Grand Rapids Police could make that call. I hung up the phone and called the Grand Rapids Police and made an appointment to meet with a detective from the Grand Rapids Police. The meeting was very brief. The detective stated to me that he spoke with Cindy and that Cindy is a fine woman who probably hated my father due to an unhappy marriage, but she did not kill my father and that the case is closed. Then the detective said to me that the coroner suspects foul play by me because I questioned whether or not my father had been tested for any other drugs than alcohol. The detective stated that if I was to pay five thousand dollars to have my deceased father's grave exhumed I better also retain an expense attorney because the focus is not on Cindy, it would be on me if I did not consider this a closed case. I was shocked and creeped out by the detective's tone, all because I wanted to open the case up. The fact that the coroner told the detective he suspected me, blamed me, all because I had serious questions as to why he did not do a full autopsy led me to a stronger feeling towards a conclusion of foul play and a cover-up by the coroner and the Grand Rapids Police. I cannot change corruption, and I realized they are in the position to punish anyone such as myself for questioning "their work." I left the Grand Rapids Police Department shocked. I remember looking at the detective at the end of the meeting, a meeting that I had called and wanted, just wondering why he wanted to have me leave my father's death alone, and not raise any questions or concerns now about my father's death in 1986.

Driving home to East Lansing, Michigan I realized my father was probably done in, murdered, and Cindy had people in place to cover-up the murder of my father. If someone does not do what Cindy wants or what the CIA wants done or accomplished, the word "no" is not an option or conclusion to their problems. The word "yes" and solutions to their problems are the only acceptable conclusions in their overt and very understated handbook in how they conduct their lives. The older I became, the more questions that were resonating within me now. I wanted to know for sure, with scientific proof if Cindy had murdered my father. I also wondered if the reason that rookie coroner in 1986 was hired in 1986 was due to the fact that perhaps another coroner would not write on an official State of Michigan death certificate the cause of death as requested, directed, as instructed by a corrupt person or entity. My father is found dead by his former spouse (Cindy) that hated him and never visited him. I was not allowed to visit him and I could not drive a car. There never was child support payments or visitations from the time they legally separated in 1984 to the time they divorced in March of 1986. I was instructed by Cindy in 1984 through 1986 to write off my father as if he did not exist, I was ages fourteen to sixteen. Cindy controlled the law, the Judge and so much more with the CIA. I do not think she even saw my father Chuck Vander Ark for at least a year or longer before his death as she would always mail off any of his bills directly to his house in Grand Rapids that arrived at her residence in Jenison, Michigan. She would mail off his bills in a large yellow envelope mailed to his Grand Rapids residence. Perhaps Cindy had paid him a visit before he died? Cindy out of the blue paid him a visit and found him dead in 1986, what prompted her to pay him a visit? The mail. And then she found him dead, a real answer to all of her prayers! Why would she bring his mail to him in person after two years of only mailing off his mail in a big yellow envelope? There were a few nights Cindy was out to midnight during the week, and on days she had to work early the next morning, only a few that I recall in May and June 1986. Cindy hated him, she loathed him. Cindy moved on with her life and wanted nothing to do with him. Cindy hated it when people from the church would question her about being a divorcee, commenting derogatory statements after their questions about her divorce after the Hilcrest church services we attended each and every Sunday. In 1986 Cindy was being pushed out of the Dutch Calvinist community that she loved, that she needed. She was happy he was dead. Then she immediately joined the Hilcrest Christian Reformed Church widows group. What would Cindy have to say to a church widows group that she suddenly joined? I remember asking Cindy in 1986, "Why would you join a widows group? You and dad were divorced."

Cindy remarked with a jolly smile, "Well, I was married to him for twenty-seven years. I was married to him longer than I was divorced from him."

Nothing Cindy did or said in 1986 made sense to me. However, I do not think in 1986 I was looking at her in the correct light of the situation, as I do now. I began to look at people through a three dimensional lens that seemed to develop naturally within me the older and wiser I became of people. I could seemingly look beyond the cover and into the pages of people's minds. Far and beyond what they wanted to show, what they wanted revealed as a safe cover of their pretenses.

Cindy would not be the only person I would believe was a murderer, a monster that I would encounter within a highly moral atmosphere such as the Dutch Calvinists in Michigan.

Around the year 2005-2006 Ed and I received a phone call from Dave Page informing us that something terrible had happened to Carol Geer in the hospital. Carol Sharp Geer is the wife of Rich Geer. Rich Geer is a good friend of my husband Ed DeBartolo and a good friend of Dave Page. Ed tried to get as many details as possible before hanging up the phone with Dave Page. We headed to Sparrow Hospital in Lansing, Michigan. Upon arriving we entered a waiting room filled with family of both Rich Geer and Carol's side of the family. Ed and I sat and waited, no one was talking. Finally Rich Geer arrived to the hospital waiting room, we sat up and walked into the hospital hallway to talk, to ask Rich Geer questions about what is going on, what happened to Carol.

Rich Geer was not crying, he was not sad, shocked, or distraught. However, by what Dave Page had informed us of, something terrible had happened to Carol and she was not waking up from a surgery or something like that is what Dave Page had told us prior to talking with Rich Geer. Rich Geer was elated, excited, happy, fearless in how he was handling the whole situation of his wife not waking up from surgery.

Ed inquires to excited and elated Rich Geer, "What happened Rich, we heard that Carol is not waking up from surgery? What's going on Rich, is she awake now?"

Rich Geer exclaims in a happy, loud, excited tone, "She never even had the surgery! The doctor never performed the surgery! The doctor stated this has never happened before!"

Rich Geer could not calm down, like he had too much caffeine or was on some kind of adrenaline rush of sorts. Rich Geer's emotions were not going along with the somber group of people waiting in the hospital room for Carol's recovery. Ed and I were confused at Rich Geer, why was he so happy and elated when the news he is telling us is horrific. Carol must be better we thought.

Ed asked again and again, "But she's awake now, right Rich?" Ed began repetitive asking if Carol is o.k., as if Ed was trying to match the correct happy emotion that Rich Geer was displaying to something happy, but to no avail was the news good. We were standing there talking to Rich, a bit confused. So why is Rich Geer so excited and happy, almost manic, we stood and wondered in the hallway just watching Rich Geer talking manic with big elated saucer eyes.

I began getting chill bumps on my arms as Rich Geer exclaims in a zealous manner and tone, "She won't wake up! She never even had the surgery! The anesthesiologist does not even know what happened to her! She never was even wheeled into the surgery room. The anesthesiologist had come running from Carol's pre-op room saying this has never happened before in his career, that something is terribly wrong and called for medical help."

Ed inquires and keeps inquiring to wildly excited happy Rich Geer, "Well what happened Rich?"

Rich Geer was not angry. He was not yelling at anyone in the hospital, all the while his wife is laying in a vegetative coma down the hall. Rich Geer was not even in shock! I just stood there looking at Rich Geer as I tried desperately to mentally process how his emotional state of being did not correlate to the information he was telling us. I was in shock as I watched Ed ask questions as I watched Rich Geer acting in behavior, mood, and tone as if Rich Geer is one or two days away from a much anticipated Hawaiian vacation where he is unable to hold his excitement down to a simmer and talk and answer questions. I got goosebumps. I felt sick almost, nauseated as I stared at Rich Geer talking on and on in such an elated tone. Then I had an epiphany. I have seen this behavior before, his mood. I stare ahead at Rich Geer as a mental file cabinet within my head fervently searches for the correct file......... Ah! 1986. Cindy. Cindy acted just like this the very day I saw her for the very first time after her parents Martin and Teresa Stob pushed open my front door in Jenison and announced my father is dead. Cindy had that same zeal and uncontained excitement in her eyes when she talked about how Chuck is dead and how she now can move on with her life in 1986. Cindy would spin around like she was on cloud nine, happy and excited when she first told me of when she found my father Chuck

Vander Ark dead. Cindy's behavior in 1986, mood, tone, was an exact match to Rich Geer directly following a tragedy, a time of what most would term and feel as sad and shocking. I looked at Rich Geer differently from that point on at Sparrow Hospital. Baby Eddie was still in a stroller and was teething at the time this tragedy suddenly happens to Carol Geer during the summer of 2005.

The focus of my compounded stories is for all readers, everyone on the planet to take the time each week and examine ideologies. In this time period, my lifetime, my opinion and what I learn would cause me to think Cindy Honderd is scum and Rich Geer is scum, each for various and different reasons. However, in today's times and current ideologies, society and individuals have not relayed negative opinions of either Cindy or Rich, based on what is accepted ideologies of this time period that I live in.

Ed keeps asking questions and Rich Geer keeps talking. The more Rich Geer talks, the more I see Cindy in his answers, to his elation over a tragedy.

Ed inquires, "When do the doctors think she will come out of the coma?"

Rich Geer responds as happy as ever, "I don't know! None of the doctors know, this has never happened before! They don't know what happened to Carol! She stopped breathing in the pre-op room when the anesthesiologist gave her too much of the knock out drugs, that's all we know so far."

Ed inquires, "Is she going to be alright Rich? What do the doctors say about her condition?" Ed kept asking questions, Rich kept bouncing like a ball off the wall.

Rich exclaims, "I don't know. I was one month away from filing bankruptcy, but I don't think I'll need to now. Hal gave me a number of an attorney in Detroit that handles this kind of thing. Hal thinks I'm going to get fifty million! We can go and see her, she's in a coma."

Rich Geer acted at Sparrow Hospital as if the hospital had done him a favor. It was only the beginning for me to understand the grasp Rich Geer had on my husband and how jealous Rich Geer was that Ed married and now has a wife and child. It would be revealed in the coming years to me just how jealous and obsessed Rich Geer was that Ed married and the extent of external forces that would be bestowed upon me because Rich Geer could never get over the fact that Ed married and has a child now. Ed being married now with a wife and baby was way more unsettling to Rich Geer than Carol Geer's condition.

Rich Geer leads us down the hospital corridor to a room where Carol was hooked up to a breathing tube recently cut into her throat. The size of the tube was slightly small in diameter to a household vacuum cleaner hose, it was a horrific sight. I was horrified at the sight of seeing Carol in a coma with that large tube going into the center of her throat like that. I just stared at her, I had no words for anyone next to me. She seemed asleep but was in a coma.

Carol and Rich Geer looked so happy at Frederick Meijer Gardens when Ed and I had our renewal of vows on June 21, 2003. She had such a big smile, it was a sunny day, and so much fun outside wandering the acres and acres of beautiful gardens, and now she cannot talk, she cannot breath if it was not for a recently cut and inserted breathing tube (hose) into her neck. I remember looking at her, then quickly looking away. I was not prepared to see such an awful sight of her sudden condition. I looked at Rich, he was talking non-stop, excited as if he could not reach everybody at once at the party to talk to and mingle with at his party he threw, was his attitude.

I turn to Rich Geer and ask, "When did this happen to Carol?"

Rich answers very matter of fact, "Just this morning Lori. I brought Carol here this morning to the hospital and waited with her in the pre-op room before the surgery, which the surgery never took place."

I inquire to Rich, "She never had surgery? How did she arrive at this condition of not waking up from surgery?"

Rich Geer exclaims, "Yeah, she never had surgery, the anesthesiologist must have given her too much of the knock-out drugs prior to the surgery that never happened, it is the strangest thing." As Rich Geer ends his statement he smiles jovially.

I just stared at Rich Geer dumbfounded at his joyful overt happiness and no obvious signs of shock or anger over this recent and most horrific circumstance and scene concerning Carol Geer. And then he shocked me again with more bizarre behavior for me to process that day at Sparrow Hospital.

Rich grabs Ed's hand and they lay hands on Carol talking in some demonic sounding mumble jumble. When they finished, I inquire, "What was that?"

Rich answers, "That was speaking in tongues Lori. If you do not speak in tongues you will not go to heaven, that is what the master has told us." Just then I looked Rich Geer straight in the eyes in complete horror at what I saw in him right then and there. I felt as if a demon was afraid that I would call the demon out of Rich Geer at that very moment. As if something demonic was attached to Rich Geer's soul that knew that I knew that was a demon attached to Rich Geer's soul. The demon almost seemed afraid of me as I stared through to Rich Geer's soul right then and there as he stood by Carol's bedside as Carol laid in a coma.

I ask, "Why do you talk in tongues Rich? I have never heard you talk in tongues before today?"

Rich Geer responds cheerfully, "Lori, I've been talking in tongues ever since the 1980's. Ever since I joined the master's house in downtown Lansing."

I remark with a scowl of disgust, "Master's house? What is the master's house?"

Rich Geer respond's, "The master's house is an old run-down dilapidated house in downtown Lansing near the Michigan Historical Museum where I met Hal. If it wasn't for Hal I would not have my job as an artist for the State of Michigan at the Michigan Historical Museum. I was an unemployed used car salesmen with no college education, not a degree anyways. Hal turned my life around by giving me things, sort of like a sugar daddy."

I respond, "Unemployed used car salesmen?"

Rich replies just as chipper as ever as we step out of that hospital room where Carol remained in a recent coma, "Yeah, I was fired. I sold used cars and I was fired. I had to move my family into the basement of the master's house. I had red sheets separating the rooms in the basement. The rent was free, Hal became my best friend. We still go out of town on vacations all the time, Hal pays for everything from airplane tickets, to hotel rooms, to food, everything. Come to think of it, Carol and I will not be arguing about me taking off with Hal anymore. Now that Carol cannot talk, we can't argue about what I do with Hal."

I got chills as he spoke, answering my questions. Just like Cindy, Rich Geer was reminding me of Cindy. The times I do ask Cindy questions, her answers give me chills, as do the answers to my questions that I am asking of Rich Geer. I feel I may not even be prepared emotionally or mentally to ask Rich Geer any further questions because his answers simply give me chills. His answers are painful to process, just like Cindy's answers to my questions.

Rich Geer continues as if on a caffeine high, adrenaline rush, "Yeah, Hal gave me the phone number of an attorney so I can sue the hospital for millions." Then Rich Geer jerks his arm and elbow dramatically backwards and forwards like a punch and shouts "Yes" in the hospital hallway as if the team he was rooting for scored a goal. However, there was no T.V. on, or game being played.

I inquired further, and very unaware and unprepared for the answers from Rich Geer. "Rich, what goes on at the master's house? Is that where Hal lives too? Is the master's house his house, his property he owns?"

I would learn through Rich Geer that Hal lives in Eaton Rapids on a track of land with a swimming pool. I would learn through Rich Geer that Hal is married but gay on the side and Rich and him take many vacations out of town together, to remain private from the rest of the world. I would not learn who owns the master's house, but that Rich Geer claims it is a real place. I would learn through Rich Geer that many people that go to the master's house to worship were married but gay on the side, or simply single and homosexual. I would learn through Rich Geer that mostly men made up the group, but some women too. I would learn through Rich Geer that Hal was very connected to Washington D.C. and would travel to Washington D.C. quite often. I would learn through Rich Geer that Hal would entertain a lot of CIA agents at his house in Eaton Rapids, Michigan, which apparently is quite the house.

What is the master's house in Lansing, Michigan? Have you ever heard the song Hotel California by the Eagles? The song sums up the description and activities of the master's house as described by Rich Geer answering my questions. Inside my head I am screaming as Rich is telling me this. However, my demeanor is calm, as I am interested in learning what the hell happened to Carol.

I asked Ed as we left Sparrow Hospital if he had ever gone to the master's house. Ed claims he has not, but he has met Hal through Rich Geer. Ed mentioned that he has been to Hal's sprawling ranch house before in Eaton Rapids, Michigan. I asked Ed, "Why was Rich Geer so elated, hyper and happy at the hospital when his wife is in a coma from some surgery that never even took place?"

Ed remarks as if protective of Rich Geer's odd behavior at the hospital, "Oh, that's just Rich, that's how he acts. He is always talkative and hyper, he acts like a kid, a big kid."

I state back to Ed loudly, "His wife had a breathing tube stuck into her throat so she could breath, she's in a coma! When she arrived to the hospital this morning she was fine. How could Rich Geer be so happy?"

Ed remarks somberly, "I don't know, that's just how he acts."

I directly point out to Ed as I state, "Ed, he was not even shocked what happened to Carol at the hospital! He was not even slightly mad or distraught at the doctors, or staff or anesthesiologist at Carol's condition! He blamed no one by yelling or screaming at anyone. He was not even slightly agitated! She was fine when he brought her to the hospital for the surgery this morning."

Carol Sharp Geer remained in the hospital for months, then she was released to Rich Geer to place into a nursing home. He selected a nursing home in Eaton Rapids, we visited her there. Carol eventually pulled out of the coma, only to remain in bed in a vegetative state of being. Carol could not talk, only a moaning sound she can make. Carol's arms and hands became rigid, Carol was only forty-nine when this happened to her at Sparrow Hospital. I had only met Carol once or twice before this tragedy at Sparrow Hospital. I was horrified, just thinking, what if that was me? What if that happened to me? Like the worst nightmare ever. However, Rich Geer had a completely different outlook on Carol's sudden condition of being bedridden indefinitely. Carol unable to talk, only moan, and remaining in a vegetative state after the coma from the surgery she never had.

Rich boasted and bragged, "Don't feel sorry for me Lori. Hal's got me connected to a good law firm in Detroit, everything is going to be o.k. Carol and I never fight any more about Hal. I can come and go as I please with Hal, or anyone now. She did not want our son Dan to go and work for Hal and now he can with no argument. I was ready to file bankruptcy before all this happened to Carol, I was in a financial pinch. I am no good with money and credit cards Lori. I still might file bankruptcy though, I don't want the debt collectors calling me now to take my millions coming my way to build my dream home out in the country. Carol liked East Lansing city life at 2785 Still Valley, but I want to live more like Hal, have a sprawling ranch house on some land, that's me." Rich just stood there smiling as if to pleasantly reassure me that everything in his life was o.k. with him.

I inquire, "What about Carol? Are you going to keep her at the nursing home in Eaton Rapids?"

Rich remarks, "For now, I do not know what else to do with her."

Rich Geer was like Cindy, answering my questions gave me chills. How could he be so cold? Then again, Cindy was so cold too. I would learn from Rich Geer that he is the oldest out of nine or ten brothers and sisters and that his mother never had any time for him, she was too busy with the other siblings. He had zero respect for women in how he would talk about women or his mother whom he claims had so many children to keep his overworked dad around through her female manipulations of having so many children. I noticed that Rich Geer preferred to have male attention on him and the focus of male attention while he spoke. Male attention mattered most, women were not clearly understood by him and he avoided conversations and eye contact with females if he could in fact talk with a male instead. Rich Geer informed me that he has a minister license with the State of Michigan and was now interested in starting a church and have followers of his own. He exclaimed that he has no need for the master's house or what goes on there anymore.

I would describe Rich Geer as a person who desires to be charismatic, that's his whole heartily intentions. However, he lacks charm and many other qualities. He is only about five feet tall. He has grey hair with an ugly physical form and terrible social graces, manners. He relies solely on his socially domineering personality to intentionally captivate and hold a sense of power in the room. Rich Geer likes the spotlight, especially in a room or group mostly made up of men paying attention to anything interesting that he might have to say. He works diligently to soak up worldly information, odd facts about movies or actors, U.S. Presidents, geography, music, anyone or anything ionic. Becoming an expert of information on just about any subject that might be entertaining to the social norm. Contributing motivation of his need to be viewed as a guru. If you took Rich Geer on a tour of a historic home or a cave, Rich Geer would speak at the tour guide. Then he would speak at the group as if Rich Geer knows more about the subject of the tour than the tour guide, that's Rich's instinct, he is annoying to some. He is a guru of information from books to movies to actors to religions to politics to animals to scientific nature facts like bizarre mating rituals of bugs. "A guru of bottomless knowledge" is how he would like you to view him, an interesting knowledgeable guru of sorts with a wide vocabulary to impress all who listen to him. Rich Geer will always come across in a social setting as an expert on any topic of conversation discussed, whether light conversation or in-depth topics. If you ever interrupt him mid-sentence with a fact that contradicts what he is speaking about, his face goes beet red and his crooked teeth glow yellow, I learned that one day.

Rich Geer was once explaining to my son Eddie and I "that through human evolution humans now all have flat heads in the back of the head verses ancient Nordic shaped heads which were at one time rounded in the back of the skull with a Nordic nodular shape to them." I looked at Rich as I felt the back of my head and my son's head and corrected Rich Geer on his preaching of what has gone extinct in humankind. That is when he got mad as he realized he was wrong on a subject he initiated. Rich Geer's face turned beet red and his crooked teeth glowed yellow showing off his poor upbringing in his sudden anger at being corrected on a topic of conversation that he had initiated. After a few moments he then remarked as he felt the back of my head and Eddie's head, "Oh, I guess that's not an extinct feature in humans." Rich Geer's libido in life is for you and everyone to like him, think of him as cool, hip, and of course knowledgeable about any subject. Rich Geer has no college degree and could care less what others have to say about a subject. He will also portray himself to know more about any college subject than any college professor on any subject as he incisively talks on and on endlessly.

If you ever have Rich Geer stay over at your house in the guest bedroom he will create a nest. He will structure around the bed a nest consisting of a circling crumbled comforter, wet towels, dirty and clean clothes, and accumulated items like straw woven and sticking out of a large bird's nest. He will stay up late and sleep in, claiming he has odd sleeping patterns. In fact, the State of Michigan allows for Rich Geer to clock in and out of his artist post at any time of the day or night at the Michigan Historical Museum, understanding that artist people can be a bit whimsical with their mind and time. There is no Governor Cam on Rich Geer on wasteful government spending by the State of Michigan, only catering to the "whimsical."

If you are ever not captivated by whatever Rich Geer is saying in a group or individually, he will then enter your personal space. He will enter that invisible boundary that everybody relishes and he will talk right in your face like a drill commander. Talking non-stop about an array of topics demanding in tone and mood that you listen to him, whether you want to or not, he is difficult to escape from in conversation.

Rich Geer is always the loudest. You will always be able to hear him before you see him. Rich Geer also does not like to pay for anything. If you are in line to order food he will get in line, order his food holding back no expense, step aside and make conversation with a hungry stranger next to him and expect you to pay. Rich Geer refuses to pay for his meals, always. Rich will create excuses, saying he left his wallet at home or in the car. He does this at Red Lobster, he does this when in line to pay for anything such as amusement parks tickets and food, beverages, museums, etc. He explained to me that he is a girl in a man's body, or at least that is what his friend Hal told him and Rich believes Hal. I do not think there is a girl inside Rich Geer. I think there is a clever and sinister demon inside Rich Geer, attached to his soul. I have noticed that if you or anyone do not treat him like a special woman, his face goes beet red and his crooked teeth glow yellow. I would notice from 2005, for years and years how Rich Geer would clinch his teeth into my marriage with Ed like a snarling Pit Bull not wanting to let go of a bone. I could never quite understand why. I encourage you to become his friend. I feel as if I have described Rich Geer well enough that if you were in his presence, you might even smirk a bit when he begins acting like a guru of sorts. Even if it is subject territory he really knows nothing about, he will always try and convince you he does know lots of things about everything and therefore you should listen to him. Rich Geer loves the spotlight in social settings.

The situation with Carol was not improving in the two years that Rich Geer filed a lawsuit against Sparrow Hospital and the anesthesiologist. Carol remained in a vegetative state unable to walk or talk. She remained in a nursing home bed void of her normal life that she had before Rich Geer checked her into Sparrow Hospital during the summer of 2005 for a surgery that never took place. Rich Geer was not receiving the financial news he had hoped for from his hired attorney in Detroit. I learned through Rich Geer that the lawsuit attorney could not prove medicine shock or the wrong dosages in medication given by Sparrow Hospital's anesthesiologist. Rich Geer after two years of Carol being in a vegetative state and no hospital pay-out in hand, Carol stuck in a nursing home, Rich was only now actually showing the very first signs of discouragement. Rich Geer appeared to mope a bit, discouraged in his quest to make millions off Carol his wife was not going as planned. He never cried, he just began moping with listless apathy abounding in him.

Then Rich Geer exclaimed one day while we sat at a picnic table, "I want to build my dream home in the country like Hal. The hospital is not settling and my attorney does not want to take this to court because he cannot find or prove the hospital did anything wrong. I am going to be stuck on Still Valley forever! I want to embrace and entertain important CIA men like Hal does!"

In my head I am screaming by what I am hearing from Rich Geer. I realized I am once again just a bystander absorbing information in a mental file that is not even a relevant file or an existing file for the FBI or any investigative agency or department. I do not know where to even go to get an investigation going on Rich Geer or any other person that provided me with shocking information, other than reporting the valid information to the FBI or police. I would go to the FBI in Grand Rapids and Lansing while I lived in East Lansing, Michigan on multiple occasions and provided them all the details to launch investigations. I would also learn that the FBI could care less about crimes I report or have information on. The FBI seemed to be an all-male agency, an all-male club, women and women reporting of crimes are not accepted as valid claims a crime took place.

Another year passes and then Rich Geer informs me that he is buying thirteen acres in Meridian Township just outside Okemos going towards Williamston on Grand River Ave. Rich Geer begins the construction of his custom house. Rich Geer purchased land and built his dream home in which to entertain and embrace CIA men that he had met at the master's house. Rich Geer begins construction on his custom home in the country like he has always dreamed by getting jumbo loans, several jumbo mortgages. Rich Geer built his sprawling new construction ranch to rival Hal's sprawling ranch house in Eaton

Rapids. Rich Geer custom selected pink cultured stone around the mid-point of the exterior of his new house. The pink granite matched in color to the large pink granite countertop on the kitchen island and kitchen countertops, all in gleaming pink granite. Then he had a white glass stone two-way Liberace inspired gas fireplace installed. He had a pond dug in the front with intentions of a sprouting water head with colored lights to be installed later. He built Carol's room and bathroom in the same wing as his. Everything looked grand to his homosexual standards at his new property, an estate at 283 West Grand River, Okemos, Michigan.

I asked him, "How are you going to pay for all this Rich? You make twenty dollars an hour for the State of Michigan as an artist?"

Rich Geer exclaims, "Don't worry Lori, Hal has hooked me up with an accountant that is also employed with the State of Michigan. I provide him a list of Carol's medical needs, he prepares billing statements to the various insurance companies and then overbills the insurance companies, it's a cool set-up."

I inquire, "What? He overbills the insurance companies?"

Rich says with a smile, a gleam in his eyes, "Yeah, he over bills the insurance companies so that I can afford my mortgage payments and new lifestyle."

I ask, "Mortgage payments? I thought you were going to get millions from suing Sparrow Hospital?"

Rich remarks, "I thought so too. My plans to sue Sparrow Hospital did not go as planned. I have now had to acclimate to plan B."

I stop Rich there and inquire, "Plan B?"

Rich Geer speaks with confidence as he informs me, "Instead of winning millions through Sparrow, I have Hal helping me through this accountant guy of his. I still have a mortgage on my old house on Still Valley, I might just rent it out. I have two mortgages on this place. As long Carol is out of the nursing home and I am her legal guardian I can collect extra money through the accountant from Hal's devices of overbilling insurance companies through Carol's medical needs. It was Hal's idea to shut up Carol in the first place. To hush my sister Tish up I am giving her full reigns to Carol's social security monthly benefits."

I stop him there and ask, "Carol's social security benefits you are giving to your sister Tish, why Rich?"

Rich Geer looks at me with an elated smirk on his face as his eyes beam with joy just like Cindy, "I'm not such a saint Lori."

I inquire, "You're not such a saint, what do you mean Rich?"

Rich says with a worn smirk still smiling, "In the hospital, with Carol, I am not such a saint."

I inquire further with a million questions going through my mind right then and there, "What does Hal do for a living Rich? Why did you and Carol fight about your son going to work for Hal?"

Rich remarks, "I can't tell you what Hal does, it's covert, his exact position in government I do not discuss with anyone. I can tell you that he is involved with school districts and he gets a portion of what is collected. Monies that the CIA is shipping to Afghanistan and Russia, at least that is what Hal has told me. Hal is pretty high up in government and secret projects. He knows how to skim off the top. Russia is going to destroy America, it's in the Book of Revelations."

I remark with a question, "Secret projects?"

Rich Geer comments, "Yeah, how money is collected."

I inquire, "What makes you think Russia is going to destroy America? And where did you read that in the Book of Revelations?"

Rich Geer looks at me as if he is perturbed that I am a female and perturbed at my intelligence that I have not located in any Bible that Russia is going to destroy America.

Rich Geer begins babbling on and on about stuff that is supposedly in the Book of Revelations. As he talks he acts as if I am stupid, maybe just stupid because I am a female or stupid because I went to Christian schools and churches in my formative years and Rich Geer attended Lansing Public Schools and he has some upper hand knowledge of the end of times.

My mind remembers another strange coincidence. ATM Al, that's what I call Allen Vander Laan behind his back. Ed and I were at Al & Nancy's very modest house for Christmas festivities in Kentwood, Michigan where Al & Nancy raised their three children Jeff, Sarah and Matt Vander Laan to adulthood. All three kids entered college and went into the workforce and married while Al & Nancy lived in that very modest two-story home that backed up to a commercial property near a busy run-down street in Kentwood, Michigan. A place I would never even live. They could hardly afford to replace the carpet, and then selected the cheapest, that goes for their refrigerator too. Al & Nancy were always fighting about money, as were my husband's parent's Bruno & Roma DeBartolo that were in their eighties and still had a mortgage on a small condominium just around the corner from Al & Nancy Vander Laan in Kentwood, Michigan. ATM AL was continually spitting out money like an ATM machine for his grown adult kids. ATM Al seemed very frustrated that his grown kids could not earn and save for things the way he had to budget when he was their age. Then his youngest son Matt takes home "a Geha". A Geha is well known in Michigan and other parts of America as a gypsy Arab from Saudi Arabia that was once Muslim in Saudi and in America converted to Christianity, the whole clan, to fit into American culture to swindle American companies. Especially swindling with insurance fraud schemes and human trafficking networks that partner with corrupt authority for transaction purposes. A well-known news anchor for channel 8 news in Grand Rapids was let go right after 9/11 happened. "A Geha" is often involved with money laundering, insurance fraud of all kinds. Including but not limited to senior citizens fraud, human trafficking of German and Dutch children and woman to bring to Saudi Arabia, selling of German or Dutch women on paper, so ATM Al informed me during a crowded festive gathering over the Christmas holidays in Kentwood. Then in 2004, the year my son Eddie was born and around the time his son Matt had dated "a Geha" for some time, ATM AL's fortune began to change. ATM Al bought a vacant residential lot in prestigious Railside Estates in Bryon Center, Michigan from Smith-Diamond Realty. He joined the Railside country club and built a million dollar sprawling ranch house to rival the homes of all his new neighbors. ATM Al and his wife Nancy, now empty nesters move from a run-down section in Kentwood to expensive

Byron Center. ATM Al hires the best home designer and builder to build and design the million dollar house in Byron Center, ATM Al hires a relative of my grandma Kate De Haan Vander Ark.

In 2008 I learned from ATM Al Vander Laan of Byron Center, Michigan and his sons Jeff and Matt Vander Laan that they became involved with an Arab family (the Geha family) out of Detroit involved with human trafficking and money laundering and insurance fraud to pay for the million dollar home. The Geha family became Christian to disguise themselves from Saudi Arabian origins. The Geha clan becoming Christian would help them disguise their illegal activities in America from the victims the Gypsy Geha's would prey upon in America. Activities such as insurance fraud, human trafficking and money laundering. In 2008 I learned that Al & Nancy Vander Laan became involved with a money laundering scheme involving Bruno & Roma DeBartolo as the named people on a Living Trust that would be controlled by Al & Nancy Vander Laan as the ones holding Power of Attorney on the senior citizen Living Trust that the FBI or IRS would never audit or investigate as to where that money originated before being placed in a Living Trust in west Michigan. The Novi, Michigan Geha mother showed Al & Nancy the importance of using elderly people for Living Trust paperwork and bank accounts. As apparently elderly people are seldom selected by the IRS for audits, and non-flashy estate planner attorneys are rarely under the microscope of the FBI for illegal activity. Apparently "Hal" is also involved with Kent Cement Companies not going belly up in 2008. Apparently Hal assisted for a fee in changing the tune of how money is generated and filtered into Kent Cement Companies in Michigan and Texas as a savings mechanism, a financial tool to keep Kent Companies afloat during dry financial times. According to Rich Geer many companies were saved by CIA Hal in America for a fee, in very illegal maneuvers, backed by a system paying out to FBI and police to keep structures and systems in place and whistle-blowers silenced. The criminals involved are not criminally prosecuted, and according to Rich Geer, he too was protected from prosecution in Michigan for what he did to Carol his wife. As well as protection from criminal investigations and prosecutions through Hal's resources for the overbilling of insurance companies in their continuous fraud schemes taking place. Rich Geer and Hal had it all worked out, like so many, until I wrote this book. However, my next hurdle will be publishing. My hurdle after that will be getting government people to do their job and investigate. It is not the author of the book that has the final say in a matter, it is literary agents to publishers that have the final say in a matter, and how it is said or written. The CIA watches everything I do since I was a baby. So I am not sure how far my information will reach in the world of publication and exposure of crimes, and what the CIA vultures will add or subtract in content to protect them and their ongoing unscrupulous businesses currently not under the microscope.

For instance in the spring of 2010 someone provided Citizens Bank in Okemos, Michigan a fake but legitimate Michigan Death Certificate of me as a test run of the paper document. Then the criminal person or entity against me moved my bank account funds to the State of Michigan as a test run, I learned this in June of 2010. I contacted the Meridian Township Police, David Hall the chief of police informed me that he would investigate. He later called me back and stated that he learned someone was after my book royalties through Infinity Publishers in Pennsylvania and that someone had created a fraudulent Michigan Death Certificate and forged my signature on Power of Attorney paperwork. He explained that "the someone" lived in the Grand Rapids area and the "the someone" was not working or collecting money alone. He advised me to go to the State of Michigan's website for unclaimed money to get my bank account money back. I had to then provide evidence to the State of Michigan that I was alive and not dead and waited six months to have the State send me back my money. Chief of police David Hall informed me over the phone that the CIA would make his life hell if he prosecuted or disclosed who that person was that created fraudulent documents to make money off me.

The extreme unheard of harassment and major criminal activity towards me does not end there. Nor is it subject to just me, soon my young son will receive unwarranted treatment from "an entity." In the beginning of the 2009-2010 Okemos school year I began receiving truancy letters from Dr. Catherine Ash in the fall of 2009. Dr. Catherine Ash is the superintendent of Okemos Public Schools. The truancy letter stated that my son Eddie had been tardy twenty-two times since school began in September 2009. I thought that could not be because I take Eddie to and from school, I am his primary caregiver as Ed works. I solely take Eddie to and from school and take care of Eddie.

I decide to call the head of Okemos Public Schools and have a meeting about the received yet false truancy letter. I walk into the office of Dr. Catherine Ash for the scheduled meeting to discuss the relevancy of receiving a false truancy letter and to put an end to the unwarranted harassment from the school district. My very first impression of her standing so short in stature barely reaching four foot nine inches, and her teeth, she had prominent fangs like a snake that one could only see when she smiled, I thought she was a demon. Not all demons occupying human bodies are short, Marc Antony was tall just like Patrick Goodale is tall. Dr. Catherine Ash appeared to be of Irish ethnicity as I put aside my very first impression of her as she welcomed me into her office to sit at a small round table. The very first thing I notice in her office is a wall of college degrees. When I say a wall of college degrees I mean from top to bottom of that wall, and spread out all in rows, many rows of college degrees. It almost appeared as wallpaper of college degrees on one wall, from a Ph.D. of mathematics to a Ph.D. in philosophy, to a degree in finance, you name it, she had a degree in it, with her name of the college certificate. A comedian probably would have busted out laughing at the wallpapered wall of college degrees, each degree a separate piece of paper with Catherine Ash's name on it. However, I was not laughing. I realized that no one could hold that many earned college degrees. I realized that I walked into a meeting, a situation where the head of the school district is not very forthcoming in what she is involved with. I am now more than ever very curious as to why so many mothers were not re-enrolling their child or children in Okemos Public Schools.

I sit down by the small round table, as Dr. Catherine Ash talks, questions begin fluttering inside my head like snowflakes. As I begin to ask very relevant questions to the head of the Okemos school district, my very first impression of her becomes very pronounced as a demon emerges within her eyes to greet me at the table. I know now that my very first impression of Dr. Catherine Ash is the correct impression.

Dr. Catherine Ash explained during the meeting that her computers never make a mistake. At the end of the brief meeting I stood up and walked to her wall of college degrees. Each degree had her name on it, the wallpaper wall of college degrees of Dr. Catherine Ash. I tapped the wall, looked at her as I remarked, "I'm going to get to the bottom of all this and you are not going to like the end result." I was bold and brazen in 2009 to let her know that I knew something was terribly wrong with Okemos schools and I was not accepting harassment and crimes.

Dr. Catherine Ash was bold and brazen when she then informed me that any crime that happens to me or my son Eddie on school grounds would never be prosecuted by Stuart Dunnings (the Ingham County Prosecutor) or the FBI in Michigan. Her exact words were "Any police report concerning a crime committed against you or your child in Meridian Township would be at best an irrefutable gross negligence report and would never be prosecuted by Stuart Dunning's office or the Michigan FBI departments." I thought Dr. Catherine Ash was full of herself to make such a wild remark to a parent such as myself. I would learn the truth of her statement the hard way.

After the meeting with Dr. Catherine Ash I decide to place a much needed phone call on the way home. I called the Meridian Township Police Department (MTPD) to investigate the validity of the wall of college degrees containing Dr. Catherine Ash's name on the multitude of college degrees. The female officer I spoke with over the phone informed me that the Meridian Township Police does not investigate suspected fake college degrees and certainly would not be investigating the college degrees of Dr. Catherine Ash. The female MTPD officer ended the conversation with me by remarking over the phone, "That's just not something we investigate."

Without hesitation and without direction or advice from the Meridian Township Police I contacted the FBI in writing to investigate. I listed many things in 2009 for the Lansing FBI to investigate.

What happened next? The fall of 2009 was just the beginning of the harassment I would receive from the joining forces against me and my questions. My concerns were viewed as a nuisance by local authority and the school system in Okemos, Michigan. The Meridian Township Police Department and the Okemos School District head and elementary principal at Bennett Woods Elementary would join forces and harass and allow for crimes committed against my son Eddie and I. To the point that on May 8, 2012 I ended his schooling in Okemos by letting principal Noelle Palasty know I was moving Eddie to a new school district. I felt and knew that would be the best for Eddie and myself. I thought I created a win-win situation by no longer having my son or I be affiliated with Okemos school district. I had enough. My son had enough. My son learned absolutely nothing from Okemos schools in kindergarten and first grade! I was done with it. Okemos school district would not have to hear or read any more complaints or suggestions from me, an overly concerned parent of an only child. I could take no more abuse and crimes against me and my son from a school district. I enrolled him in school of choice in June of 2012 and moved him to Bath Elementary School in Michigan, just fourteen minutes from our residence. During second grade and third grade at Bath Elementary School Eddie earned and received all A's on his report cards, he learned how to read and write which he was not learning at Bennett Woods Elementary. Eddie at Bath Elementary had zero tardy days with no truancy letters, zero absent days. No harassment experienced whatsoever from the head of Bath schools or the school principal at Bath, or anyone at Bath schools, what a difference! Great peace of mind and school security at Bath Elementary. If we still lived in Michigan Eddie would still be in Bath schools. Bath Elementary was such a different, such a better experience than Okemos school district and each school district was the same drive time from our east Lansing condo.

I hated the treatment of my son in the Okemos school district and the terrible school security and the crimes we had to endure that are still unprosecuted in 2017 as I write and complete volume one, third edition of this manuscript. My son Eddie attended Bath Elementary School and had wonderful school years, great school security. No crimes against him or me on school grounds while he attended Bath Elementary School for two years in Michigan. However, during his years after he left the Okemos School District for peace in a new school district at Bath Elementary, the Meridian Township Police patrol cars would constantly follow behind me, harassing me. We finally listed our condo in East Lansing, Michigan in the summer going into the fall of 2013. Why would the State of Michigan allow such bad behavior, daily, from the Meridian Township Police towards me? Because the State of Michigan does not intervene with districts in Michigan, some districts capitalize on that fact boldly and brashly towards victims. Before I pull Eddie out of Okemos schools for good on May 8, 2012, and before we list and sell our condo and move away as a family from all that we endured, let's re-cap what led up to Eddie getting pulled out of Okemos schools by me…

2012, The End of What?
CHAPTER SEVENTEEN

During the 2010-2011 school year Eddie was in kindergarten at Okemos Public Schools, Bennett Woods Elementary. Mrs. Price was his kindergarten teacher and was also a neighbor in our cul-de-sac on North Wild Blossom Court. Mrs. Price kept to herself and unlike me never ventured out to walk or bike on the many sidewalks and bike paths that the area offered.

I noticed that Eddie was not learning how to read or write in kindergarten. I was not sure at what age children learn how to read and write as Eddie was my one and only child. I would read age appropriate books to Eddie and he would simply memorize the words and each simple sentence per page. Then if I introduced a new book that was also age appropriate he seemed lost in how to read. His report cards during his kindergarten year were always good. The parent-teacher conferences were always good. Red flags of his Okemos school progress were certainly not flying or disturbing in kindergarten of what he should be learning, after all I thought, it's just kindergarten. When I spoke with other mothers from Bennett

Woods they informed me that their child also did not know how to read or write.

Soon after the 2011-2012 Okemos school year began Eddie came home frustrated that he did not know how to read or write and other children in his first grade did. The first grade teacher at Bennett Woods Elementary was expecting that each student write in his or her journal about what they did over the weekend. Eddie complained to me that he could not write down anything because he did not know how to write. During a meeting that I called with the head of Okemos schools, Dr. Catherine Ash, I was once again horrified by that school district. Dr. Catherine Ash explained in September of 2011 "that the State of Michigan does not require Michigan Public Schools to teach a child to write because when that child grows up he or she will only need to know how to use a computer keyboard to type." Dr. Catherine Ash reminded me to not worry and to stop overreacting. Pacifying me that she hires the teachers and she believes that Eddie is getting a fine education. I angrily reminded Dr. Catherine Ash of the amount of money per student that Okemos Public Schools receives, something like $8,500.00 or slightly more from allocated State and federal school funds, and that I expect the school to be teaching my son to read and write. Dr. Catherine Ash ended the meeting with a sigh, by telling me that if it is so important for my son Eddie to read or write then I should be teaching him how to read and write at home.

I looked at Dr. Catherine Ash as she spoke so coldly about education and saw her in her true light. I saw an older homosexual women in a hidden position as the head of Okemos Public Schools with absolutely no real concern for children or their education under her rule and educational direction in the school system.

The school year had just began and school of choice would not open up until June of 2012, for a span of three weeks next June to local area school districts bordering Meridian Township. I was stuck. Eddie was stuck. I began emailing and phone calling into the school to the elementary school principal Noelle Palasty and to Dr. Catherine Ash at Okemos school headquarters, many suggestions on matters of curriculum. I had all kinds of suggestions to make Okemos Public Schools a better school system. My intentions were good. However, I was in a school district that did not want to listen or read any of my good suggestions to improve education. They instantly saw me as a nuisance, an annoying mother.

During the beginning of the school year in the months of September 2011 through the beginning of November 2011 my husband's twin brother Mike calls and warns me and warns Ed that Al & Nancy Vander Laan are up to no good and to watch my back. Mike DeBartolo informed us that Nancy had Al hire a private eye to spy on me, get some dirt on me to take Eddie away from us.

The private eye hired by Al & Nancy Vander Laan was a man by the name of James Southworth. I do not know if that is his real name or a fictitious name. I would learn what Mike DeBartolo was warning us, was a correct and real worry to fear, not that the private eye would locate any dirt on me or photograph me being a bad mom of Eddie. I would learn the hard way again, on why to fear Al & Nancy Vander Laan and their connections to public corruption people and entities and the power people have over others.

On Friday 11/11/11 I traveled the short distance from Meridian mall where I had my nails done. From the mall I then traveled a few miles to pick up Eddie from Bennett Woods Elementary. Just one week prior to Veterans Day, November 11, 2011 I had requested by writing to Dr. Catherine Ash of Okemos schools to fire principal Noelle Palasty. Just one week prior I also had a meeting with the city manager of Meridian Township because I had learned he was the overseer of Okemos school superintendent Dr. Catherine Ash and the Meridian Township Police whom seemed to be at the root of many problems. I clearly indicated that I do not believe Dr. Catherine Ash was hired for her position because she cared about children or education. I spoke that Dr. Catherine Ash does not care about children or whether they could read or write, and that opinion based on my experience goes for Noelle Palasty too. I would learn later through Meridian Township's Rich Geer the vital role Okemos School District plays in relation to his friend Hal's finances and income and a whole network of other people involved with criminal activity, both ordinary citizens and government. I would learn that I could not stop or expose what was going on behind the façade. What I would experience is nothing shy of almost drowning me by so many individuals and entities involved with public corruption in America and American systems in place.

I pulled into the long carline to pick up Eddie on 11/11/11, Veterans Day 2011, Eddie is six years old, almost seven years old. I noticed nothing odd or peculiar about that day. Boy, was I in for a surprise and shock of my life. Apparently I was being stalked for quite some time by a man hired by Al & Nancy Vander Laan, at this moment I did not know it though. I pull into the long single lane of cars moving somewhat quickly through the Bennett Woods Elementary after school pick-up carline. Finally it is my turn, principal Noelle Palasty opens the passenger side back door as Eddie is about to climb in and sit in his car seat. Just as see principal Palasty open my car door, I notice in my interior rearview BMW car mirror suddenly an old tall man running towards all the young elementary children that are standing and waiting, at least fifty or so children. As he nears the children standing, groups of young kids, he is running full force. I just assumed at that moment that he might be picking up a grandchild and maybe he thought he was late so he panicked and ran towards the school and groups of children outside near the school entrance. That's what I thought when I noticed an old man running towards the group of school children just as Eddie is about to get into my BMW with principal Palasty holding the backdoor of my BMW open for Eddie. Just as Eddie climbs into the backseat and makes his way towards his car seat behind my driver's seat that old man running enters my backseat and plows down Eddie! Holding Eddie down by laying on Eddie's back and head as the old man slugs the right side of my cheek as papers fall out of his hand, the old man angrily says inside my vehicle, "The CIA director selected this date to correlate with your hospital room, no one is getting prosecuted Lori." 11+11+11= Ingham Regional Hospital room 222? Is that what he meant to say? I screamed, the man got off from Eddie, principal Palasty shuts my car door and does not look bothered at all. The school principal does not call for help or appear alarmed and rattled as my son and I am! Principal Palasty just motions for the next car in line "Next."

I shout to Eddie very shaken by what just happened, "Hold on Eddie I have a camera in my purse here I am not letting him get away with what he just did!" Every parent in the carline just froze in shock and allowed for me to snap photographs from behind my steering wheel as I approached where that strange assaulting man parked his vehicle. Kids were screaming in horror and pointing to the old man running for his car parked close to the school entrance in visitor's parking. I push on my gas pedal and zoom my camera lens to snap photos as I am the only moving car in that school parking lot and carline as parents freeze so I can snap photos of that old man, his vehicle and license plate. His Michigan license plate CFC-1266, pasted on the car a decoy that reads Hyundai of Jackson (Jackson, Michigan) with an orange tag in the upper right corner of the plates. He drove a light silver 4-door Hyundai Elantra. How do I know this? I snapped the photos and I am looking at the photographs as I type this manuscript. Next I drive off locating a space towards the parking lot exit to see what he had dumped paper wise in my lap. I immediately looked down and saw he had given me three PPO's (Personal Protection Orders) signed by a Kent County Judge to legally stay away from Al & Nancy Vander Laan, Matt Vander Laan, and Jeff Vander Laan. Highlighted boldly was to stay away from their residences, places of employment, and school. What? What is this for? I have not even been to the Grand Rapids area to visit or see the Vander Laan side of my husband's sister Nancy in two years! Why would they even consider giving me very unwarranted and not needed PPO"s to stay away from them all? It made no sense to me, I do not even talk or see that side of my husband's sister Nancy for at least two now! I grab my cell phone and dial the number to information based on the paperwork that was dropped in my lap from the 17th Judicial Circuit Court Kent County at 180 Ottawa Avenue NW Suite 1500, Grand Rapids, Michigan 49503, 11-10702-PH, 11-10703-PH, 11-10704-PH. I speak with a Judge's secretary late Friday afternoon and I explain that a process server climbed over my son in my backseat while I was picking up my son after school in the school carline and shoved paperwork for three PPO's in my face as he said something strange about my hospital delivery room number. The lady on the other end in Kent County was shocked and dismayed, absolutely shocked that a process server would deliver PPO's in that manner as she exclaimed to me, "That's not how a process server is supposed to serve court paperwork!"

I responded, "He did. He just did. I want to know his name and I am going to file a complaint against him with the police in the jurisdiction where this crime just occurred at Bennett Woods Elementary School!"

The Kent County lady responds, "Fill out a Freedom Of Information Act form, call (616) 632-7570 for the form. I do not know what the name of the process server, he has not filed proof of service, once he does his name is on the paperwork, proof of service PPO's, one proof of service per PPO served. I called the Meridian Township Police Department. I was told that the chief of police, David Hall was off duty today as it was a federal holiday. I immediately developed the photos at Target store and typed my account of what just happened. Then I dropped off the information at the police department, my information and request for a police investigation into what happened, the unwarranted and criminal behavior of the process server that criminally trespassed at Bennett Woods Elementary carline on Friday 11/11/11 Veterans Day 2011. I filled out the Michigan Freedom of Information Act request and sent my FOIA request to the County of Kent FOIA Coordinator. When the PPO Proof Of Service paperwork came back to me, my copies requested, I learned the process server's name is James Southworth. The Meridian Township Police Department assigned the police report for the Bennett Woods Elementary School altercation of 11/11/11 to be #11-05364 MTPD police report. The African-American Mr. Stuart Dunnings III working as the Ingham County Prosecutor for many years did not prosecute James Southworth as requested by me and requested by the police department. Rather Mr. Stuart Dunnings III went along with the request NOT to prosecute James Southworth the process server and to consider me a mental case through the sources of the two people who did not want James Southworth the process server prosecuted.

The two people who did not want James Southworth prosecuted: elementary school principal Noelle Palasty and Okemos school superintendent Dr. Catherine Ash. Can this happen in America? OMG it just did in 2011! There is a very fitting cliché, "Only in America."

The Veterans Day weekend of 11/11/1 my six year old son Eddie began having real nightmares at night of what had just shockingly occurred to him as he had climbed into my backseat after school after waiting for me in the carline. What is supposed to be a place and scene of security, was not. The people that are in charge of school security absolutely did not want James Southworth prosecuted for trespassing and simple battery assault charges!

On Saturday, November 12, 2011 Eddie drew pictures, a sketch drawing in pencil of him aiming a gun at the assailant James Southworth. Eddie showed me the drawing when he completed the drawing and said "Mom, this is what I would like to do to that man who laid on me at Bennett Woods yesterday." Eddie then began to get more and more interested in violent action movies where guns are used to kill the bad guys. The next summer of 2012 Eddie would insist upon carrying a large water gun at the MAC pool (Michigan Athletic Club). Eddie was changed after that criminal altercation by James Southworth and his criminal supporters. The nightmares continued. The cops and the courts were not going after the bad guys, the criminals that had committed crimes against us.

On November 11, 2011 I told my husband Ed what had just happened at Bennett Woods Elementary School in the parking lot as I picked up Eddie through the carline. Ed immediately called his brother in California, Mike DeBartolo, and said, "Mike, you won't believe what just happened today." Ed told his brother Mike what had happened to Eddie and I at Bennett Woods and then I heard Ed say, "really." Mike DeBartolo explained that Al & Nancy wanted to somehow gain custody of Eddie because they did not have a male grandson. Mike explained that Nancy and Cindy hated me and wanted me dead, in a mental institution or in jail. Separated from Eddie so that Nancy and Cindy could get their criminal hands on Eddie. Mike explained that Al was paying off Judges and police to make this all happen according to their devious plans behind the scenes that we could not see. Mike explained that Al hired a private eye named James Southworth to follow me for months, leading up to the assault on school grounds. The PPO's were a plan when I made no mistakes with caring for my son Eddie, Al needed another means to get Eddie for Nancy and Cindy. Mike DeBartolo informed Ed that Al was concocting ways in which to make that all happen and that the PPO's were served in such a way that I was supposed to wig out and make the mistake of calling Al & Nancy Vander Laan to tell them off after the Kent County Judge had just signed the Personal Protection Orders. Causing the PPO orders to go into effect and then the police would throw me in jail for disobeying the Kent County Judge's order. Mike informed Ed that between Okemos and Grand Rapids I would have been shot in the head by the police before entering the boundaries of Kent County. That was ATM Al's plan to please his wife Nancy with her sidekick Cindy Honderd, to get those two off his back. Mike DeBartolo informed Ed that Bruno & Roma DeBartolo had Al's blessing to do so to me.

Two years previous to 11/11/11 I told off Al & Nancy Vander Laan and called them evil. I wanted nothing to do with them. I allowed Ed to take Eddie to Kentwood to visit with his parents Bruno & Roma DeBartolo. I personally wanted nothing to do with his side of the family, his sister Nancy or her extended clan, or my extended family that included Cindy Honderd or people that liked her.

My horrors and my son Eddie's horrors with Okemos School District were growing worse and more frequent. I knew at the end of the school year 2011-2012 when school of choice would be made available in June of 2012, Eddie and I were out of a corrupt school district (Okemos) that held strings to a very tainted Ingham County Prosecutor. Mr. Stuart Dunnings III would only jump as high and as needed for Dr. Catherine Ash and the Michigan district she controlled. It would not be until March of 2016 before Mr. Stuart Dunnings III would be arrested and charged with multiple felonies and misdemeanors for human trafficking all around Michigan and America. Finally Stuart Dunnings III was removed in March of 2016 from the position as the Ingham County Prosecutor for his wide and extensive involvement with crimes with a pattern of crimes on innocent white children as reported by The Lansing State Journal and USA Today in March of 2016.

One week after Friday 11/11/11 on Friday 11/18/11 at 10:30am I hear a rapid loud knocking at my front door. I look down and see a man with a dark knit cap on his head dressed in a Meridian Township Police Department uniform. I look at the man from an upstairs window pounding loudly on my front door. As I look at him I recognize him, he was a Gold Club bouncer. I immediately then call 911 to see why the police have sent him dressed like one of them to my front door. The male 911 intake caller informed me that he could not tell me why. The male 911 intake caller stated that he had no idea why officer Diebolt was at my front door. I stared at officer Diebolt to see if and when he will give up knocking and either leave or break down my front door. I know one thing, I am not going to the front door or the main floor.

Finally he leaves. And then the commotion starts up again. At around 12noon MTPD officer Kristi Lisik joins MTPD officer Diebolt with once again attempting to contact me via my front door. This time they pull up together in a police patrol car, jump out in a rage of adrenaline and pound together on my front door. I open an upstairs bedroom window near and over the front door and speak to MTPD Kristi Lysik whom is standing next to officer Diebolt. She then informs me that I have a PPO on me from Al Vander Laan, Matt Vander Laan, and Jeff Vander Laan and for me to not make contact with them. I stated "I know. I was served those PPO's last week at Bennett Woods Elementary. I have not seen or spoken to those people in Grand Rapids for at least two years. I have no intention of contacting them, I do not even know why they would place PPO"s on me, it makes no sense." Then I ask officer Kristi Lisik, "The people that have PPO's on me, they did not lie and then say I have been contacting them, they did not say that right?"

Officer Lysik responds, "No. Officer Diebolt and I are here to remind you that the Kent County Circuit Court Judge has signed these Personal Protection Orders."

I then responded, "I know. I have already been served those PPO papers."

Officer Kristi Lysik and officer Diebolt leave.

I then call the Meridian Township Police Department and through the FOIA department received duplicate copies of the PPO proof of service that Meridian Township Police served the same Kent County 17th Circuit Court Personal Protection Orders of the Vander Laans to me at my residence of 2374 North Wild Blossom Ct. in East Lansing, Michigan. Why serve me twice? To cover the tracks of what James Southworth did to Eddie and I on school grounds at Bennett Woods Elementary? Serve me twice to erase what James Southworth did to my son and I at Bennett Woods where James Southworth does not belong?

When I say you have no idea of the ordeals that would transpire in Meridian Township, Ingham County, Okemos School District, East Lansing, Michigan, I mean you have no idea! During the 2011-2012 school year at Okemos when I would bring my son Eddie to school or pick-up Eddie from school on many occasions as I drove slowly into the school parking lot and waited in my BMW in the carline I would notice every once in a while the actually men that raped me in California! They men were never in the same vehicle, always separate, and backed into a parking space so that their license plate was not visible for me to photograph as evidence of who they were. This would happen from time to time only in the Bennett Woods Elementary parking lot, odd and scary, unsettling.

The Meridian Township Police began parking in my cul-de-sac in East Lansing and as I pulled out of my residence, a condo in East Lansing, Meridian Township. The police patrol car would follow me around Okemos, stalking me as I did errands. Stalking me as I brought my child Eddie to school and from Bennett Woods Elementary, Eddie noticed every time. The Meridian police sometimes even parked a patrol car behind my condo, parking on a public bike-way where vehicles are not allowed. Many nights and days a helicopter would fly at roof level behind my condo over the bike path and then hover by the back condo windows. The harassment out of the Meridian Township Police and Okemos School District was constant and relentless. My son Eddie would be pulled out of class and yelled at in the principal's office by principal Palasty for a mother that called the FBI on the police and school district! I complained about the school security. I complained about the fact my son was not learning anything in school in Okemos. I complained about principal Palasty and Dr. Ash not wanting James Southworth arrested and charged with criminal trespassing and simple battery assault charges on school grounds.

We listed our residence because of the constant harassment we received as a backlash from Okemos schools and police. The real estate market was slow at the time and our condo did not sell right away. What we needed was a real plan to get away from the harassment by public corruption officials and the people and entities that seemingly directly and indirectly controlled the chaos we were experiencing in our lives. I wanted out of Michigan and back to Georgia. I began seeking out information online on how to have my husband licensed by credentials in the State of Georgia. I was seeking out managed care employers with chain dental companies whereas Ed would not need the financial worries or headaches of owning his own dental company. I was at my breaking point of how much harassment I could take, I wanted out of Michigan! We began taking every step necessary for us to move, and Ed the bread winner to have full-time dental employment in the State of Georgia. As escape measures that became a frequent hobby of mine when Eddie was at school I would go on Realtor.com and search for a Georgia home I would rather live in, with a community far, far away from East Lansing, Michigan. I would then go to the mailbox in hopes to see if my royalty checks were rolling in yet from my new literary career.

I could not fully understand why I was being harassed by Okemos schools and police. I could not stop the harassment by Okemos schools and police by going to the Lansing FBI on all I knew. In fact, the harassment just became worse from sources towards us, many sources. Dr. Catherine Ash called Animal Control on me over three times and stated that I was not taking good care of my dog George. After so many false alarms called in by Dr. Catherine Ash, Animal Control finally took a picture of my dog George to put into the file that he is not emancipated like Dr. Catherine Ash had reported to Animal Control. I would be left wondering, how did she even know I had a dog?

Then Dr. Catherine Ash kept calling CPS (Child Protective Services) in Ingham County to inform them that I am a bad mother and that I am crazy and they need to remove Eddie from my home. The CPS social worker after the third or fourth time coming out and looking for a case to open, explained to me that Dr. Catherine Ash always does this to mothers in my area, never the mothers that live in super expensive homes does she pick on. The CPS workers explained that because Dr. Catherine Ash has the prestigious title and position as the Okemos School Superintendent, CPS is always required to investigate and take the call. OMG! Case closed. Oh no, Dr. Catherine Ash was not done torturing my life! Here is my overview formulated opinion based on my experiences endured; Dr. Catherine Ash is an older homosexual woman with no children of her own, true facts. I have a theory on why she participates, fully contributes more than likely with a human trafficking group targeting white mothers and white children in Michigan. Causing well over two thousand young children to leave Okemos Public Schools at the elementary level during her leadership, her years as school superintendent. Dr. Catherine Ash is fixated on hating attractive mothers with young children. Something about young attractive mothers with young children at the early elementary level was her mental fixation of who to target with resources she could use at her disposal day and night. Stay tuned! There is so much more!

During this time period in Okemos, Michigan and America, a prevailing ideology would also cause any investigator not being paid off by the school or not being paid off by the real organization of criminals controlling the school, police and judicial system to look the other way and not see a need for an investigation based on programed ideology of the media and culture that one instantly, unconsciously absorbs during a time period, this time period. For instance, in this time period there is a movement of Black Lives Matter. African and white Americans coming together to support a movement not of American lives matter, or all lives matter, but instead promoting only that Black Lives Matter, Black History Museums must open, Black History Month, the list goes on and on promoting Black this, and Black that. For years and decades now a cable television channel exist called BET, which stands for Black

Entertainment Television. Now if I started a channel called WET, standing for White Entertainment Television, every one of every color and nation including whites would term me as racist.

Ideologies are powerful in propagandas of what a certain group wants. What if you unconsciously bought into a propaganda of gay people and black people are always the victims? After all that is only what news executives will all air on mass media and printed news. What I endured and would continue to endure would be like trying to put a song on the radio that would never be heard with today's current status quo airwave ideologies controlled by who? At whose expense? The people that benefit are the criminals that get away with crimes based on ideologies at my expense, or at my son's expense.

First of all what is an ideology? Ideology as defined by Wikipedia; 1) A systematic body of concepts especially about human life or culture. 2) A manner or the content of thinking characteristic of an individual or group.

The last thing the Jews would want in the past, present or future is for anyone to examine what makes them Jewish, the basis of Judaism. If it was not for the Jewish anti-sematic and intolerant view of others, there would be no uniting of Jewish ideologies. The only way for the Jewish race to continue and exist on planet earth is for each Jew to continue hating others that are not Jewish and only love and marry Jews. Think about it. Think about Jewish ideology, what makes them Jewish. The core concept that makes a person Jewish, a couple Jewish, a family Jewish? Ask a Rabbi "What makes a person Jewish?" Ask many Rabbis and expand the questions to know something before reading this book.

Jews consider themselves to be "the chosen people of God." Yet not one of them remembers heaven before earth. When a Jewish literary agent asks me, "Why the title of your book, I Remember Heaven Before Earth?"

I always respond, "Because God <u>chose</u> me to remember. God chose me to remember heaven. I was selected by God to remember heaven before earth."

What is antisemitism? According to Wikipedia anti-Semitism is the hostility, prejudice or discrimination of another. Apparently the Jews and the homosexual people have convinced *most* cultures, religions, world-wide media and politics that it is others not like them that have displayed overt hostility, prejudice and discriminate against what is not gay or Black. If you tune into that ideology whether it be conscious or not, an ideology that was calculated, formulated, and exercised by the masses in this time period, crimes against me or my son would never be solved in my lifetime.

Dr. Catherine Ash is clearly a homosexual woman that harassed me and my son with every resource possible and the nightmare is not over yet with enduring her relentless abuse and abuse of resources at her disposal. My theory concludes that she probably has done to me and my son what she has also done to thousands of other white women and children because no one stops her behavior in today's ideologies of the times. In today's ideologies of the times no one in authority even questions the population drops that continues and the many Okemos elementary school closings in Okemos between 1998-2008. Key hidden figures who do not want this investigated and will stand with Dr. Catherine Ash to keep this information silent.

Questioning; It is so telling of our day and age when no person, no media, no politician, no investigative authority has even questioned Collin Powell on why he told President George W. Bush's cabinet and congress that weapons of mass destruction existed in Iraq, when in fact Collin Powell had no evidence of weapons of mass destruction. It was Collin Powell's word. Examine the facts and video footage of Collin Powell purposely lying to congress concerning the existence and fear of weapons of mass destruction. It is also a fact at that time and now that most U.S. soldiers are white, most are from southern states. It is also a fact that Saddam Hussein the leader of Iraq at the time of 9/11 had nothing to do with 9/11 and any terrorism against America or the Western World. Saddam Hussein had no terrorist groups in the country he governed, Iraq. After Collin Powell convinced congress and President George W. Bush to go to war against Iraq, sending U.S. air and ground troops and bombs to bomb Iraq, how many white soldiers were killed or maimed in battle?

I want you to step out of your box thinking that you were placed into by the status quo media and culture of today. Examine the NAACP. What does the initials of the NAACP stand for? These things exist in the world, in America and you are not examining them, you are not recognizing them. What are the similarities and differences of the Iraq war and the Vietnam war? One similarity is the amount of white soldiers that died. If I look at the sun am I not supposed to notice the sun is yellow? Do not stare at the color of Collin Powell's skin or any African or African-American, rather examine Collin Powell's DNA and others like him. Where is Collin Powell today for lying about weapons of mass destruction to the American people, congress and the President and causing an unnecessary war, unnecessary loss of life on a mass scale, huge American war debt, where is he today? If Americans were intelligent or cared about life or cared about debt the way Dutch people do, Collin Powell would be charged with what is appropriate. Instead, Americans let him collect a military pension off American tax dollars. Then when President Obama and Secretary of State Hillary Clinton, both who wine and dine at the Congressional Black Caucus's dinners and parties sign policies to send home the U.S. troops from Iraq. What happens next? Then the Middle-East terrorist groups against America and white western European countries cross into Iraq for oil profits and a land base to grow and develop unharmed.

I read online that the Congressional Black Caucus is an organization founded on March 30, 1971 representing the Black members of the United States Congress. While race and party affiliation are not explicit prerequisites for membership, all of its members have been African-American and most of them Democrats. Its chair is Representative Cedric Richmond of Louisiana.

Louisiana is also the capital of voodoo in America. If I was to pray to God to shake a black voodoo curse placed on me from the 1860's I would continue to point out the following facts about the current time period as I write this book:

It would be very unacceptable in my lifetime socially, culturally, and politically for me to point out that a Congressional White Caucus be established. White American's also see themselves as American, so the idea of separating politics based on one's color of skin does not make sense to most whites. However, is there a black group against white Americans, and if so, who are they? I would be called a racists by

Whites, Blacks, and the mass media based on today's ideologies of this time period if I even suggested founding a Congressional White Caucus. Anyone who founded a Congressional White Caucus would be termed a racist and the Caucus would be shut down in today's times. Keep in mind, the Congressional Black Caucus was founded in March of 1971, with absolutely no white people jumping on cars, starting fires and looting stores and burning the American flag in retaliation of the existence of a Congressional Black Caucus. The ideology of today's times only allows for acceptance to allow Blacks to do whatever it is that they want to do.

Another example of what I am pointing out as facts about today's ideologies. This past weekend I was at the newer Kroger in Cartersville, Georgia. I was pushing my grocery cart down the aisle of either skincare or shampoo, one of those aisles. I notice a Black woman in her thirties with her look alike teenage daughter that resembled her, almost identical to her but younger. The mother and daughter were picking out items, no cart, just standing and selecting items. I move my grocery cart over as much as possible to not bump into them or bother them or have to ask them to move. I keep to my business and shopping list and push my cart against the shelving away from them as much as possible. My cart accidently brushed up against the daughters oversized purse. I say excuse me and continue down the aisle shopping just as the Black mother flips out on me and screams at me with psycho hate in her eyes, "You stupid Ass!" is what she screams at me.

My response? I am in shock at her unwarranted words shouted at me. My heart racing, I am utterly offended, I remain silent and just stare at them as I move to the end of the shopping aisle. I continue pushing my cart and go into a different aisle and avoid them and anymore hateful unwarranted shouting at me. The question remains, will I shop at the new Kroger in Cartersville? I do not want to. Then I think to myself, is that how areas that were once completely White, turn suddenly all Black, because areas do, look at the facts, is that how it happens? Is that how it works? Because honestly I just want to locate a new grocery store to shop at, I, like so many other Whites do not like confrontation, I like peace. In today's times the ideology in the deep south and America has changed so much that I cannot help being shocked as I notice how Blacks act after freedom of slavery in the south. I am left wondering, is there something in the DNA of people that makes one act a certain way innately? Is peaceful behavior located within a person's DNA?

I read online that the NAACP was founded on February 12, 1909. I read online that the initials for the NAACP stand for the words; National Association of Advancement of Colored People. The NAACP is an African-American civil rights organization in the United States formed in 1909 by Moorfield Storey, Mary White Ovington, W.E.B. Du Bois, William English Walling, Oswald Garrison Villard, and Henry Moskowitz. The headquarters for the NAACP is Baltimore, Maryland which also so happens to be the birthplace of Adam Duritz, that teenage boy I mentioned earlier that would grow up and form the musical band The Counting Crows. The mission of the NAACP is to ensure the political, educational, social, and economic equality of the rights for black people. Since the founding year of 1909, has the NAACP ever helped a white American that has had violated civil rights? Has the NAACP ever filed a lawsuit to ensure the equal protection of a white American's civil rights or any rights? Not in today's ideological times, the time I am born and alive. How does one change today's ideology? Even though in today's ideology, I deep down do feel as if I should have protected civil rights. Even if today's current White, Black and Carmel population has suppressed my rights as being valid.

What are your exact thoughts when I say that someone should found the NAAWP, just like the NAACP except; National Association of Advancement of White People. Your thoughts in this time period that I live in would be that I am a racist for suggesting the NAAWP. Potential founders would be labeled a racist based on the accepted ideologies of the day which conclude that only colored people should receive an organization that assists in the advancement of colored people. Since 1909 not one American politician has viewed the NAACP as racist, or a divider of the United States, that is how accepting damaging ideologies are in the political and social arenas of life. If I was Black I would already have been given leverage of many attorneys before even writing this book to shed light on wrongs. Those attorneys might have been Black or White and they would have filed many lawsuits on my behalf. Color does not matter, the ideologies do matter. However, I am White and therefore no attorney or American government department would file upon my request and on my behalf and see it through, one or many lawsuits for all I endured so unjustly from others. Just think of the Civil Rights and U.S. Constitutional violations I endured and suffered, and all the other crimes endured by me. Then the severe retaliation by the police and CIA for going to the FBI and blowing the whistle on crimes!

Your attitude, your resilience, in combination with opportunities that life offers one, is who you are and who you become. An ideology is a powerful tool, a useful tool that makes another agree to a point of view of another.

Everyone knows that if you accept bad behavior, you will relentless see that bad behavior again and again from the perpetrators. Another example, every inner city such as Detroit does not enforce housing and lawn violations, obviously. Just imagine, dare to dream of a better and more beautiful Detroit, the way it used to be if a task force was created to enforce housing and lawn violations with stiff penalties and jail time for the violators that have vandalized the inner city dwellings that have created a destruction of American cities. Why should I or anyone have to be scared out of any area? The true race to the finish line, the winner, is the race(s) of people that are intelligent and innovative that will be and become civilizations greatest asset. Why then do so many people want to be a detriment to society? Because they can be, they are allowed through ideologies of law and culture of the time period, and because they innately want to be. What makes a grey wolf naturally howl without being told or taught to do so? What makes a newborn sea turtle naturally crawl to the ocean when they are hatched without being told or taught? What makes a wasp naturally sting without being taught or told to do so? What makes one breed of dogs act in general very different from another breed of dogs? Black bears are more likely to climb trees than brown bears, but they are both bears. Is a bear a bear, or are there noticeable differences? Without studying DNA you and I can see it through observation very easily. It is through science we learn about hard-wired behavior and instincts located in the fabric of the DNA that define innately driven behavior in all of us. Predictable behavior, I can only assume that not all races of people want their DNA linked behavior studied and posted on the internet, why? Ideologies govern what is permissible to post on the internet and what is not, what is socially acceptable for the media to broadcast and report. Ideologies govern what is socially and politically acceptable for literary agents to represent and publishing companies to print, keeping all in a black box. The dark ages of freedom of speech until I can finally push through into the atmosphere of awareness and say "Wait a minute, I have something relevant to say."

For example, currently for many decades in this time period there has been an all colored people cable station called BET which stands for Black Entertainment Television, purposely excluding white people, even if the white person is American. The bold theme of BET cable channel is to keep the whites out and off the airwaves, unite all blacks, not unite all Americans, or not to unite the world, every race of people. Why then is BET legal and accepted? Answer: Ideologies.

Why does someone in America not start WET? Standing for White Entertainment Television? Well, based on today's ideologies the person or group would be called "racist," and receive scorning publicity from the outraged media. The NAACP would file a formal complaint and rev-up a revolt in the inner cities of America. Civil rights attorneys would file lawsuits all working pro bono to stop WET.

Another example, African-American actresses and actors have in the past and probably will again in the future boycott Hollywood's Oscars when the working Blacks in Hollywood decided that not enough or any Blacks were or are nominated for an Oscar. For example, in 2016 Black actress Jada Pinkett Smith announced her boycott campaign to boycott the 89th Academy Awards. Creating a revolt campaign for the Academy's failure to yield a single Black nominee to be nominated for an Oscar. How do Blacks display how they when in life? They demand to win. Because the rest of us all know how Blacks behavior when life and career do not go as planned, as they would want, we give in as a society to let them win to avoid their known Black bad behavior. You know what I am referring to, bad Black behavior that CNN and Fox News covers. Behavioral instincts, behavioral demonstrations such as but not limited to when a court trial does not go favorably for a Black or Blacks can easily result in the following accepted uproar behavior of blacks in America; Boycotting, hissy fits, burning down properties. Jumping on cars, looting stores and destroying neighborhoods and cities and other destructive innate behavior. The bad destructive behavior is tolerated in America when African-Americans do not get their way. Bad behavior displays publicly have driven fear into other Americans to give the Blacks whatever they want. A two-year old child that behaves destructively or throws a temper tantrum (hissy fit) goes into a crib. Again, ideologies drive behavior, and reactions. Ideologies mold and shape the mind, for better or for worse. Think about it. It is o.k. to think on your own, give it a try, think outside the black box.

I am going to ask a very daring and pertinent question, daring because the question has never been asked or printed before. A question that deserves an answer: Are American inner cities safer today than before the American civil war? I like to get to the core of any matter.

Let me put the question in perspective; If I placed a child in a fenced area with 100 Pit Bulls I would be charged with child endangerment by the law. However, if I placed that same child with different variables in the same fenced area such as placed with 100 Golden Retrievers, or 100 Beagles, would I be charged with child endangerment? Species; a group of plants, animals or individuals such as people that are similar. There are similar qualities in a grizzly bear and a panda bear, and then there are distinct innate behavioral differences too. If I gave a gun to each person in a group of 100 authentic Dutch people and to be fair and equal I also gave a gun to each individual in a group comprised of African-Americans, where do you think I would feel the most safe and protected? More importantly which group of 100 would you feel the safest and most protected? In today's accepted ideologies what is "politically correct" may not be the truth, and the truth is not an aim of ideologies in today's times. Get out of the black box!

I think the NAACP and BET are very dangerous for America, and fundamentally very un-American. The NAACP and BET are rooted in a divider ideology, not a united ideology. However, you the reader have never heard such an opinion from anyone, and therefore my voice, my message is not the status quo of this time period.

If one was to examine the crime rate, neighborhoods, housing structures in Detroit and Grand Rapids Michigan, Chicago Illinois, Baltimore Maryland from the onset of the foundational grounds of the NAACP in 1909 to now, what would be discovered? Discover and study through historical crime rate statistics and post your findings on the internet. Discovered and studied with before and after photographs of the exact home, exact neighborhood, and the exact change, and changes that take place year after year, decade after decade. Please create a professional, truthful and accurate account timeline website of postings like an HGTV style of information showing the before and after photographs of the exact homes, yards and gardens, exact neighborhoods, exact schools in contrast and comparison from 1909 to now. There is an old cliché, pictures are like a thousand words. Gather the evidence of Atlanta schools before, during and after the ratios increased with African-Americans in attendance and running the school. Post evidence of any school heads with photos of the convicted school heads in Atlanta in administrative positions that helped school children cheat on the State of Georgia testing exams at every grade level to improve Atlanta school's State test scores. Those school administrators were caught! Post all news of the Judicial intervention to then save the Atlanta schools after the scandal.

I recently watched The History Channel, The Haunted History of Halloween narrated by Harry Smith of CBS's The Early Show. In the video rented at the library the historical Halloween video shows what goes on in Detroit, Michigan chronologically through the ages. In Detroit on Halloween many houses set on fire. An epic crime rate of over one thousand house windows vandalized one year in Detroit and epic proportions of crime on Halloween in Detroit, where local African-Americans refer to October 31st as "The Devil's night." Harry Smith reporting of crime in Detroit does not follow mainstream media for the most part.

In today's ideologies the mass media seemingly only decides to select to air and broadcast crimes of Whites to Blacks or White crime on White crime, yet statistics show that the most crimes committed are Black against Black. However, Black crimes against Black is not aired on the mass media even though in today's times Black against Black is the highest crime rate. Today's ideologies, not statistics, actually govern what is acceptable politically, socially, and culturally to air in America. Why? Because at some point Americans unconsciously decided to not think for themselves and would rather just let the status quo think for them. The status quo is the ruler, what is accepted to air and what is not, what is accepted as the best picture for an Oscar, or what is not. We live in an age not of supply and demand, but rather demand and accept.

The ACLU of Michigan, known as American Civil Liberties Union of Michigan located at 2966 Woodward Ave. in Detroit, Michigan made it very evident to me when I contacted them in 2012 that the crimes mentioned here to the end of the chapter never would have taken place if I was gay or Black. The ACLU of Michigan, along with Governor Rick Snyder made it very clear to me that because I am straight and White these crimes are allowed to occur towards me in the State of Michigan.

Biology; Breed: 1) Distinct animal, plant or people; a strain of an animal, plant or people with identifiable characteristics that distinguish it from other members of it's species. 2) Somebody or something of particular type: a particular type of thing or person, especially one that can be easily distinguished from other similar things or people.

I have noticed from the news media, many various media video footage that Blacks riot and Whites protest. I have noticed many distinct behavioral differences in many various breeds of people, so have you.

However, in today's dark ages it is termed "politically incorrect" to even notice and remark about the obvious behavioral differences between the breeds of people on the planet. With today's ideology mentality we are all supposed to socially, politically, and economically accept the venting of Black rage on American people and American infrastructures, buildings, houses, vehicles, looting and robbing of stores in the moment of Black rage against America. What if we don't want that Black rage venting and destroying of America? What if I don't want it, and you don't want it, and we don't want it? Then what? Then we have just begun a new page in rebuilding America by establishing what we will not accept in bad behavior, no matter your skin color.

Get out of your black box mentality of always accepting bad behavior. I want to see "American Museums." I want to see "American History Month." I do not want to tolerate or see Black Museums or Black History Month. I refuse to be brainwashed in today's ideologies to believe and accept what the Blacks can have in society, but the rest of us cannot have in society.

Look at America, it is a melting pot of races. Why would a society even allow for a Black Museum and Black History Month in America? Why not have Mexican History Month or Asian History Month or White History Month in America? I know the answer to the question I asked. You are afraid to say no to Black History Month and you are afraid to say no to Black Museums being built and attained through American tax dollars, so you give in to avoid something being destroyed by Black rage venting. You are afraid of another store being looted and robbed from, you are afraid your house might burn down by Black rage venting because you said no.

When you say "no" to a two year old child and that child reacts badly by "acting up," you then place that child in a crib.

Different breeds, different survival techniques. Blacks will demand, demand, riot, campaign, demand and then accept the Oscar award. We are not living in an era of supply and demand. Rather we live in a black box era of demand and accept. The demand and accept of the Oscar award, the food, the money, the word "yes." And then the endless cycle repeats itself until all is depleted from others on the planet. It's exhausting to see this happening time and again on this planet. If you do not believe me, go visit America's inner cities today and <u>fine them for what they have done and taken. Create a legal task force and begin the clean-up.</u>

During the fall of 2011 my first edition of I Remember Heaven Before Earth is published through Infinity Publishers in Pennsylvania. On the evening of December 26, 2011, going into the wee hours of December 27, 2011 something odd and very unexpected happens. My dog begins barking, I am sound asleep, my husband Ed wakes me up and is questioning why our Dog George is barking in our bedroom in the still and silence of the night. I get up and check on Eddie, I notice he is asleep but tossing and turning about as if having another nightmare, which is frequent since the attack of 11/11/11 on school grounds.

George keeps barking a warning, then I hear a knocking sound. Is someone knocking at my front door at this late hour or early morning hour? Who would be knocking at my front door? I look out the upstairs bedroom window and notice a very quiet cul-de-sac, no movement, very dark as it is nighttime. Very quiet except for the occasional zap of an insect on the commercial lightning of the cul-de-sac and driveway lights. Then I glance down and notice a man dressed in a Meridian Township Police Department uniform holding a flashlight up to my front door. He did not drive up in a police vehicle, there are no parked police patrol cars. There is no one up in the cul-de-sac, just this strange policemen at my front door.

"Can I help you?" I ask as I peer down from the upstairs window. Eddie is still asleep, tossing and turning, but asleep.

The MTPD officer remarks, "I need you to come to your front door." The police officer keeps repeating that demand to me.

I am alarmed and startled among other unsettling feelings of dread at that moment. I call 911 to find out why a police officer is at my front door demanding I leave with him at this hour. A woman answers as the intake 911 dispatcher. I ask her if there is a warrant for my arrest. She says no. Then she instructs me to leave with the police officer, and clearly addresses him as a police officer. She also states that she does not know why he is at my front door. Odd, I think. I comment to my husband that George is barking because there is a strange man, a police officer at our front door knocking. My husband remarks, "A police officer!" Then Ed inquires to me "What should we do?"

I respond, "I want to know why he is here."

I go back to the window and ask him again, "Why are you here?"

He keeps repeating that he needs for me, and only me, to go to the front door. I am not opening that front door is what I am thinking. I asked him to come back during the day as it is very late. He remarks he cannot because he is off work tomorrow. I ask him what his name is, he remarks, "Officer Jurhs."

I then go back into my master bedroom and call 911 as my husband keeps asking me, "What is a police officer doing here this hour of the morning? It is nearly 1am in the morning!"

"I don't know, I don't know, I am going to call 911 again and find out." I then dial 911 and a female answers the dispatch call, a different female, but sounds the same age as the other female, older. This female dispatcher offers no information either as to why officer Jurhs is at my front door. She also states that he is a police officer and that I should leave with him.

I am baffled as to why this police officer needs me to come to the front door of my residence. I open the window back up and ask, "Can't you just come back tomorrow?"

The MTPD officer Jurhs responds, "No, I don't work tomorrow."

I say to him, "Just a minute." I go and put my robe on and tell my husband to tie up George, hold back George, I am going to the front door." I then head back to the window and look down, the MTPD officer is gone. Ed and I look from the upstairs windows in the front area and backyard of the condo. Ed exclaims, "He just vanished into thin air." The officer was gone, no one in our household saw him leave or saw how he left, he was just gone.

The next night or the following night, sometime that same week as evening approached and I was making dinner in the kitchen, Ed was not quite home yet from work, a Meridian Township police patrol car pulls up in my driveway. I go to the front door before he sets off my dog barking uncontrollably. The MTPD officer introduces himself as officer Jurhs by my front door and tells me he is investigating a vehicle vandalism that occurred on Burcham. I look at the police officer and remark, "You are not the same officer Jurhs that was here last night."

He looks at me and says, "Yes I am. I remember you would not come to your front door. That was me standing here."

I look at him and remark, "You are not the same man. You are bald, you are tall, but you are not the same officer Jurhs that was just here."

He remarks with a smirk as if ready to laugh but needs to remain serious for the moment and says to me, "Yes, it is me, I am officer Jurhs and I was here the other night knocking on your front door. You would not come to the door, you wanted me to come back during the day."

I sighed, I did not know why this MTPD officer wanted to be the same MTPD officer as the other night, but arguing about that point was useless, I could see that much.

I comment and inquire, "You are not the same officer Jurhs that was here the other night. Whatever. Why are you here?"

Officer Jurhs (the fake one) says to me, "There was a vehicle vandalized on Burchum. You are having problems with your neighbors at 2428/2426 Burchum, they don't like you walking your dog near their property. There was cat food that tapered out to your front steps, that is how we determined that you are the number one suspect in that car vandalism on Burchum."

I stare at the MTPD officer. I am just trying to absorb what I just heard. "What?"

The MTPD officer remarks as he is putting up the palm of his hand, "Whooa, don't get mad."

I respond calmly yet distraught, "I do not even have a cat. I have no cat food. Go locate someone that has a cat or cat food. Do you have photographs of this cat food tapering out to my front door? Do you have fingerprints of the vandalized vehicle that I am the suspect of?"

The officer Jurhs (the fake one) responds, "No."

I ask, "What is the police file number of this supposed police report that names me as a suspect to a vehicle vandalism?" He wrote on his card, MTPD #11-06254. I later received a copy through the Freedom Of Information Act known as FOIA. I was shocked. In today's era with all of the modern day technology trappings in how to catch a criminal, the Meridian Township Police Department known as MTPD, never bothered to take photographs of the crime scene, no fingerprints brought into evidence, no police evidence of cat food tapering out from the crime scene to my front door, just a report, a police report, naming me as the number one and only suspect.

I am freaked out to say the least. It's as if the police have made my world unsafe with their behavior towards me. Larger government does not entail the safety net for people within "the districts" to also receive a large microscope on police activity and administrative school activity. Concluding that larger government does not mean larger protection and a larger emphasis on safety for people. Larger government just means more money out of your household.

In January going on February 2012, just a month or so after this strange encounter with Meridian Township Police Department I am on the phone with Infinity Publishers, the female employee of Infinity Publishers on the other end informs me that there is a group of people that want me dead. She informed me that fraudulent Power of Attorney paperwork was created, along with a fake Death Certificate for me, all in order for a government group to make millions, and they need me dead, really dead.

What did I do? With my heart racing, like my mind now I ended my publishing relationship with Infinity Publishers and contacted the Lansing FBI, the Detroit Michigan headquarters of the FBI and the Washington D.C. FBI with evidence to investigate everything I have alleged. In 2012 I contacted Governor Rick Snyder and his Michigan Attorney General's office in Lansing, providing full details and evidence of what is occurring so unjustly to me. Later in 2012 and 2013 I would contact the Michigan ACLU. During this time in March of 2012 President Barack Obama appoints Judge Mile's son to be the U.S. Attorney General for Michigan. Judge Miles as in the Judge from the 1960's and 1970's that was allowing for fraudulent birth certificates to be produced in Michigan, such as my Michigan birth certificate. The son of Judge Miles would oversee legal activity in Michigan courts for very illegal purposes for President Obama and his CIA. Very powerful illegal things are about to occur in my life, stay tuned.

The harassment and harassment tactics and resources would not cease as Ed, Eddie and myself just tried to live peacefully in Meridian

Township, Michigan, a predominantly white area in Michigan. The school security at Bennett Woods Elementary was alarming and unsettling to say the least since 11/11/11. Dr. Catherine Ash, the Meridian Township Police, and principal Palasty herself verbalized to me that they would not be testifying against the trespasser and assailant on Okemos school grounds James Southworth, as the Okemos police and school all recommended for me to just "forget about it."

On May 8, 2012, just weeks before school of choice would begin enrollment, I pulled Eddie out of Okemos Public Schools after one too many phone and email messages from either Dr. Catherine Ash or principal Noelle Palasty harassing me or my son Eddie, or notifying me of bad things that were happening to Eddie on school grounds, during school hours. I thought the safest thing to do is to not have Eddie attend Okemos Public Schools anymore. I provided written notification to Principal Palasty only that Eddie DeBartolo would no longer be attending Okemos Public Schools, Bennett Woods Elementary. During the weeks leading up to my decision Cindy Honderd and her brother Warren Stob were frequently seen in separate vehicles parked, lurking in my neighborhood, or parked lurking near Eddie's Okemos elementary school on my route to take Eddie to and from school. I said nothing to Eddie because I did not want to alarm Eddie. Inside I was a frazzled human being just trying to hold it together from all the imposing danger around Eddie and I.

On Monday May 21, 2012 my husband Ed was home from work with a terrible cold and raspy voice. I have Ed watch Eddie for two hours while I go to the mall and have my nails done. While at the nail place a Meridian Township female office is staring me down. I am thinking to myself, the MTPD officer probably thinks that I left my seven year old son Eddie at home by himself and she does not realize or inquire out of her police incompetence of investigating to know that Ed is home with Eddie.

Within an hour or so of arriving back home in East Lansing, an unmarked police car and a Meridian Township Police patrol car pull up to my residence. A detective introduces himself as Detective Greg Harris with the Meridian Township Police, he informs me that Dr. Catherine Ash has ordered for me to be psychologically examined for mental illness for pulling Eddie out of school on May 8, 2012. Within minutes CPS, Child Protective Services arrives to my doorstep to interview Eddie with many questions. As much as I do not want to be psychologically examined, the detective demands that if I do not go to Ingham Community Health to be mentally examined then his officer, a cop, will handcuff me and put me in jail. Detective Greg Harris says by reassuring me that when the mental evaluation is over I will be able to go home this evening at the latest.

I had to go, what would you have done considering the choices? The police officer and detective lead me to the patrol car and insist I sit in the police car on my own free will or I will be handcuffed and forced to go.

I am then brought in a MTPD police car to Ingham Community Health to be evaluated. Ed and Eddie drive in Ed's car, separate from my mode of travel. Once there, Ed and Eddie and I join in a waiting room, lobby of sorts. We can clearly see Det. Greg Harris arguing with a healthcare worker. The female healthcare worker then leaves hastily and angrily out of that small glass conference room towards the front of the intake waiting room waving their hands, remarking, "I can't be bought to just write down any ol' thing for a detective."

Ed and I look at each other, as I say, "That Det. Greg Harris just pissed her off, he wanted her to write something on an evaluation form that she refused to write down."

Ed remarks, "I wonder if it was for your evaluation?"

Soon we would learn my fate. Det. Greg Harris located another healthcare worker in that same wing. This healthcare worker was clearly from India, bald, and male. The new healthcare worker seemed to know the drill of how the police control things in these parts, much more so than the frantic pissed off female healthcare worker. Time passes, about thirty minutes or so.

I was then asked to join the male healthcare worker for an evaluation of my mental health. What did he write down in the room? Whatever Det. Greg Harris asked him to write down on my evaluation. I realized by my observations of my situation that this was no time to begin a revolution or protest as the doctor of sorts is ordering my treatment plan. What was his treatment plan for me? Not to be able to go home as Det. Greg Harris had promised before I entered that patrol car in my driveway. Hours seemed like ages ago as I realize I really do not own my own life in America, not in these parts anyways. The doctor's treatment plan is for me to stay one week in Carson City Hospital's mental ward and be further evaluated and receive treatment up there, almost an hour away! I was asked to step up into the ambulance that was waiting for me in the parking lot there at Ingham Community Health. I asked the ambulance guy, "How long will I be at Carson City Hospital?"

He responded with a laugh, "At least a week."

The intake doctor at Carson City would not be able to mentally evaluate me until the next morning, or so I was told upon arrival to Carson City as the sun was setting. The intake nurse informed me that I was here in Carson City because the Meridian Township Police felt as if they were constantly harassed by me. I knew that was not true, but I was in no situation to argue or point out the facts to people, a hospital staff that only wanted in their career to dictate to me and others that passed through the locked heavy security doors of that hospital wing. Within minutes of arriving to Carson City Hospital I was asked to put out my arm, in went the pin prick, and out went vials of blood. I wanted to stay stop! But quite honestly, I went along with the program of what they wanted to do to me. I knew not going along with the program was not going to get me out, they would extend my stay if I asked too many questions or tried to put a stop to being there in a wing of the hospital I could not escape or even gently walk away from if I wanted to. The next morning another doctor from India mentally evaluated me. I asked him what my mental evaluation was, what did he conclude. He looked up from his clipboard and remarked, "The same as the doctor in Lansing."

"Oh," I said.

Ed and Eddie came to visit me a few times, and finally took me home after a week. I felt so bad for Eddie not having a mom for a week. I was alarmed when Eddie commented that Rich Geer was trying to be his mom while I was away. After one full week in the hospital

I am released. Ed and Eddie pick me up and drive me home, the day was sunny and warm, rare for Michigan.

About two weeks later I go to my mailbox and open a bill from Carson City Hospital. The amount of my seven day stay in a mental ward against my wishes and better judgement, a whopping six thousand, five hundred dollars and some change! I made a copy of the bill, retained the original. I typed a letter to the Chief of Police, David Hall in Meridian Township requesting that the police department pay the bill of $6,500.00 because it was the police, his police, that put me in a mental ward against my wishes, with his detective not even following Michigan's procedures of law to even place someone in a mental ward! I also remarked in the letter, if you do not pay the bill I will file a civil suit against his Meridian Township Police Department for illegally placing me in a mental ward. I also remarked with satirical awareness within the body of that letter, what is your department & associates going to do with all the blood you had drawn out of my arm? Throw my blood on a crime scene to frame me? I know your police department well enough to know that was a possible motive by your police to illegally place me in a mental ward.

The chief of police, David Hall, immediately paid the bill of $6,500 in full.

Just when I thought my luck was turning around for the better and I would not have to endure retaliation from any sources, my luck changed on a sour note. On or around June 15, 2012 I receive an envelope from the 55th District Court in Mason, Michigan. I have no speeding tickets, I have not been pulled over by the police lately, so as I open the envelope it is very vague to me what could possibly be inside. Do you know what it was? As out of the blue as possible, it was a notice that two counts of misdemeanor stalking charges was entered into the court computer system in Mason, Michigan at the 55th District Court, that's what the local government notice stated. One count misdemeanor charge for Noelle Palasty, one count misdemeanor charge for Catherine Ash. I could not have been more shocked myself. I never stalked them, so how could this be? I do not even accidently see them out in public. There has to be some kind of mistake with the court computer systems in Mason!

On Monday I go to my arrangement. The Magistrate just reads my charges as some morning formality of his job as Magistrate in Mason, Michigan. He sets my bail at zero, but $5,000 if I should make any contact with Noelle Palasty or Catherine Ash or the Ingham County Prosecutor. Afterwards I drive back to East Lansing, Eddie by my side, the first attorney law firm I see is The Abood Law Firm, I stop in. I am brought into a large conference room to discuss my case. I provide a $2,500 dollar retainer. I request that The Abood Law Firm provide to me what evidence if any that the Ingham County Prosecutor has in his possession that I stalked anyone, let alone Noelle Palasty and Dr. Catherine Ash. Mr. Abood (the son) goes to my first pre-trial conference to let the court know he is representing me and gather the evidence of why a warrant was signed for my arrest by the Ingham County Prosecutor so that Mr. Andrew Abood can plan a defense. No evidence was provided by the Ingham County Prosecutor and Judge Thomas Boyd overseeing the case.

I inquire to Andrew Abood who accepted money to represent me, and apparently is not, I ask, "Isn't evidence required to have a prosecutor sign a warrant? Isn't evidence required to prosecute a person?"

Do you know what my attorney Andrew Abood told me? He informed me that in America anything is possible. And that no, a prosecutor does not need evidence to prosecute a case in court against someone. Rather, it is up to the prosecutor who he believes, if the detective in charge convinced the prosecutor you are a stalker, than you are a stalker until proven otherwise in a court of law.

What was my response to Mr. Abood, "Stuart Dunnings the Ingham County Prosecutor has not even interviewed me to hear my side of events and all that I have endured by that school system in Okemos and the police in Okemos that those two women control! I have not stalked anyone, ever!"

What was his response? "It does not matter."

Help! OMG!

During the month of June 2012 I began receiving surprise visits from CIA John Brennan in East Lansing, Michigan. Surprise unannounced visits even at the tanning place I frequented. Why would a Black U.S.

President such as Barack Obama appoint CIA John Brennan to become the next CIA Director? Many questions were never asked by whom? You tell me! If the CIA is really so intelligent and not just a pasted company motto "Intelligence Gathering" for America, and if the American leaders are so intelligent, than you tell me!

CIA John Brennan seemed to know every place I referred to on my list of errands or where I liked to hang out. I was just as shocked as you might be reading this. I also knew that members of the CIA would also vouch for CIA agents and CIA sub-contractors whereabouts, especially if a crime or investigation was at stake. How do I know that fact? Many CIA agents at The Gold Club drank alcohol and bragged about that CIA rule. The CIA would go as far as to create fraudulent proof of whatever they need or needed covered up. In June of 2012 the CIA Director was General David Petraeus, hand selected and formally appointed by President Obama. In November of 2012, CIA Director General David Petraeus would step down as the CIA Director and John Brennan would replace him as the CIA Director, all under the leadership direction of appointees hand selected by President Barack Obama.

One day, like many days in the summertime when Eddie was young I would place him at the East Lansing MAC (Michigan Athletic Club) nursery, kids club. Sometimes I would workout, sometimes I would go by the pool, just have a little break.

Once again, there was CIA John Brennan at a place a frequented weekly, the MAC. He was sunbathing on the job? Covered in suntan oil like a greasy snake before lunch and laying out on a MAC lounge chair by the pool. When our eyes met, I knew he feared I knew too much about what is going on in Okemos, Michigan, illegal things going on with the CIA in the school district. He was here to shut me up and shake around his weight in a matter he was very confident would remain dormant, the court case, as if nothing was said.

What was said to me at the MAC from John Brennan? He reminded me of his power over Judges. He reminded me that bad things happen to informants telling on the school districts in Michigan laundering money for CIA projects. He informed me, he bragged rather, that there is not enough manpower and intelligence to solve a mass scale CIA covert operation and that I need to shut my mouth to the FBI, they could care less, I am just making a fool of myself. He boldly bragged that 9/11 purposely happened on the clock of a Republican Presidency by democrat CIA agents, and the FBI will always protect that fact from the American people. John Brennan warned me not to bring to the attention of authority the astrological II symbolism of the Twin Towers in New York that was destroyed and directed by an American mastermind. He bragged that the school district that gives the most to the CIA each year was the school district that selected the buildings II to target for 9/11, apparently more than one. Bragging for CIA John Brennan was an obvious way for him to vent his destructive power in a world that could care less about the truth concerning American authority, such as the CIA's rank in power over the people. Ironically, the police in Meridian Township, Rich Geer, ATM Al Vander Laan and CIA John Brennan all had at least one thing in common, they all mentioned to me that I would end up in a mental hospital, jail, or dead if I ever brought up the CIA's connection to the significance of why II was targeted and destroyed by an American mastermind and a certain very giving $ school district.

CIA John Brennan reminded me of how he can get away with murder, because the FBI has his back in any matter he selects, including any case that is filtered through the court system. Warning me he is going to have the Judge shut me up for good. He reminded me that the State of Michigan would make school audits make me look crazy for blowing the whistle with what I knew. He said both the FBI and State of Michigan would always look the other way with what Dr. Catherine Ash is up to with elementary kids in her school district. Reminding me that the CIA would shut me up if any media or investigator called Dr. Catherine Ash for an interview and asked questions, such as recently a reporter from The Lansing State Journal had.

CIA John Brennan boldly bragged that hot summer late morning in June of 2012 that he has ways to shut me up, as does President Obama, many resources. CIA John Brennan informed me that President Obama ordered me silenced through the courts for what I knew about the tie-in between school budgets and Yemen. CIA John Brennan gave me a look that he was up to no good on the account of President Obama's orders to the CIA and FBI to shut me up.

One problem I noticed facing America is how politicians along with local, State, and Federal authorities of law were connected to crimes making it almost impossible, an uphill battle to have the crimes solved and the voice of the victims heard. In my head I am screaming at all that CIA John Brennan warned me of in an informative way. However calm on the outside I appeared, inside I was falling apart with fear and trepidation. Was my voice about to be silenced?

Which could explain the motivation by American authority towards me with the newly filed charges of June 15, 2012 that I stalked Noelle Palasty and Dr. Catherine Ash. In July of 2012 I fired The Abood Law Firm when the law firm could not provide any evidence that I stalked or even explain legally why this was all happening to me. Evidence Andrew Abood requested and was denied apparently from the Ingham County prosecuting attorney in the case, Stuart Dunnings III.

Andrew Abood wanted another $5,000 from me, and he wanted thousands of dollars per month with no guarantee in writing that he could get evidence in the stalking case against me from Stuart Dunnings III, the Ingham County Prosecutor. In late July going into August 2012 I then met and hired East Lansing attorney Jacob Perone. He stated that he would get the evidence from Stuart Dunnings the Ingham County Prosecutor and represent me through the court trial for a lump sum of twenty-five hundred dollars. I signed his required client-attorney contract of representation. During the 55th District Court pre-trial and pre-trial conferences the Ingham County Prosecutor refused to provide any type of evidence that I stalked anyone, including evidence that I stalked who he alleges I stalked to get my information, Noelle Palasty and Dr. Catherine Ash.

I began to wonder if this was a case of retaliation by the Ingham County Prosecutor himself, Stuart Dunnings III. Back in March of 2012 I sent information to the FBI about what I discovered was going on in Meridian Township and requested an FBI investigation into a list of things. I also sent to the Michigan Attorney Grievance Commission a complaint against the Ingham County Prosecutor Stuart Dunnings III. A complaint against prosecutor Stuart Dunnings III for not prosecuting the 11/11/11 Veterans Day trespasser and assailant James Southworth. I never heard back from the FBI. I did receive in April of 2012 a letter from the Michigan Attorney Grievance Commission in Detroit. I noticed the head of the Grievance Committee and all the listed board members were Jewish, had Jewish last names as I read the letter of disappointment for me on their opinion in April 2012. The Michigan Attorney Grievance Commission decided that any crime committed against me or my son in Ingham County is at the discretion of the Ingham County Prosecutor to prosecute only. The letter stated that if I was not happy about the crime rate or crimes occurring within Ingham County that I could always move to a different county.

As I finished reading the disappointing April 2012 letter, I remember a conversation I had back in November-December 2010 with a Okemos attorney named Meri Ann Stowe. She informed me as she represented me by her sending Cindy Honderd a Cease and Desist Letter. Meri Ann Stowe informed me that many families, the whole family, not just the young child targeted, but entire families were being selected, targeted and harassed by the head of Okemos Public Schools through various sources. Meri Ann Stowe and her office space partner had represented such families that were harassed, targeted, then harassed by many sources within Meridian Township by Okemos school heads. Meri Ann Stowe stated that one thing the targeted and harassed families all had in common was an ancestor of direct descent from Germany. I remember commenting back in November-December 2010 to Meri Ann Stowe as she prepared the Cease and Desist Letter to hopefully stop harassment from Cindy Honderd towards Ed, Eddie and myself, I commented to Meri Ann Stowe, "Cindy is worse than the Okemos School District."

Now in the year 2012, I could not say that same sentence. I would honestly say that the Okemos school superintendent and school principal were more turbulent in my life than Cindy Honderd had been at times while I still lived in East Lansing, maybe equally as bad now, I thought.

I could not stop the hate. I knew I wanted to live back in the south, Georgia, where I never experienced any of this harassment and level of crimes against me. Well, once a Black man jumped out from behind my apartment complex when I lived briefly in Little Five Points in the early 1990's. The neighbors, the apartment complex people went to the windows and called 911. I am sure there is an Atlanta Police Report on the incident. I screamed and kept screaming as the big Black man told me to shut up, but I did not shut up as the Black man ordered repeatedly of me and therefore I saved myself. If I shut-up, then what?

Back to the stalking case where the Ingham County Prosecutor believed I had stalked Noelle Palasty and Dr. Catherine Ash. There were a total of four pre-trial conferences in 2012 in whereas my attorney(s) requested evidence from the Ingham County Prosecutor that I stalked as I was charged. And at each pre-trial the Black assistant prosecutor Mr. Cruz representing African-American soon to be arrested African-American Stuart Dunnings III for human trafficking just kept trying to have me take a plea deal of three months of probation, no jail time. None of this was making sense fully, even though I had attorney representation.

The trial at the 55Th District Court in Mason, Michigan was in early November 2012. The trial was all day Friday and resumed Monday morning. The trial consisted of chilly Dr. Catherine Ash taking the stand testifying that I am an annoying person, an overprotective mother that bothered both her and principal Noelle Palasty. They both admitted on the stand that none of my communication was threatening in nature. They testified in court that I never surprised either one of them at school, home, or anywhere, and all meetings were announced in advance. The only ones allowed to take the stand and testify at my stalking trial was Dr. Catherine Ash, Noelle Palasty, and MTPD Detective Greg Harris.

Then there was intermission, during the courtroom intermission my attorney Jacob Perone insisted that I take the plea deal offered by the Ingham County Prosecutor. My attorney Jacob Perone just insisting I take the plea deal of three months of probation, no jail time, if I took a no contest plea. I looked at my attorney Jacob Perone who is supposed to be representing me and realized he had not prepared for my stalking trial and now he was looking for a legal way out from representing me. There was no evidence going into the misdemeanor stalking trial, just Dr. Catherine Ash and Principal Palasty bashing me, roasting me on why they hate me and why the jury of six at the 55th District Court in case 12-01740 should also hate me and put me in jail. Hate, not that I broke one law, just hate towards me. Even the MTPD police report no. 12-02462, which is the basis of why a warrant was signed for my arrest in the alleged two counts of stalking of Dr. Ash and Principal Palasty was not at any time even brought up during the trial. The police report not even brought up at the trial! When Noelle Palasty testified against me by following a written timeline of hers in the notes she read from in front of her. I did not really think it was a big deal that there was no evidence during the whole court procedure from beginning to end. After all, I never stalked them or anyone for that matter. I just assumed the whole stalking case would be dropped for lack of evidence, after all I am innocent. I never pressed or questioned my attorney to create a defense for me, ever, other than a few phone calls to him between August 2012 to November 2012 requesting that he provide evidence on the case by gathering evidence from the Ingham County Prosecutor's office. Required case evidence that would be used against me at the trial in November 2012, to then possibly create a rebuttal of the evidence. Case evidence that was supposed to be turned over from the soon to be arrested Ingham County Prosecutor Stuart Dunnings III, was in fact never turned over to my attorney or at the pre-trials. There was no evidence to create a need for a defense, so I learned. I did not know what would be said at the trial. But I surely did not think the trial would not end in my favor either. Judge Thomas Boyd and my attorney Jacob Perone would also not let me testify, for my voice to be heard? This was my first rodeo so to speak, I was not in charge, and I did not want to disrupt the courtroom by raising my hand to ask questions that I had now at my trial. In hindsight I probably should have raised my hand. I felt I was led to the slaughter by people who hated me. I had not disobeyed the law. African-American, Ingham County Assistant Prosecutor Mr. Cruz had a loud and dramatic voice of hate towards me and wanted everyone to get onboard his hate ship towards me. I realized in court I had no legal floating device, I was left to sink. I could only assume Mr. Cruz's rage in the courtroom was because principal Noelle Palasty and school superintendent Dr. Catherine Ash hated me and fueled his fire to burn me at the cross, as was common place, so I learned towards the end. Mr. Cruz is a heavyset Black man that resembled the character Fat Albert from a cartoon I would watch as a child, however, as an adult female now, I was not amused by him or his tactics in court. Mr. Cruz ranted and raved at the jury of six, "How can you not put her in jail? Why would a school principal and a school superintendent call the police if they did not feel their lives were threatened!"

I just kept thinking to myself with assistant prosecutor Fat Albert's words echoing in my head, why would they call the police? Why would they fear for their lives? Why did Fat Albert Mr. Cruz say that in court? I did nothing threatening, other than I wanted them both fired and replaced by the city manager, whom stepped down from his post in the same time frame that these stalking charges were brought against me. I had way more questions circling inside my head, a frenzy of unanswered questions to this stalking case now than before this trial began. I could also clearly see that it was I going to the slaughter, which apparently was legal in these parts. With no evidence presented in court, the slaughterhouse, because I am hated, not that it was proven that I broke one law. I was hated by those controlling the court room trial of the day, clearly it was not me at the steering wheel in a legal battle of my fate.

I stayed inside my residence over the weekend, not court ordered seclusion. Rather I did not want to even accidently see Noelle Palasty and Dr. Catherine Ash in any type of public setting. I hate confrontations. Monday morning rolled around and as ordered by Judge Thomas Boyd on Friday, we were all ordered to come back on Monday morning to resume the trial, the slaughter of me, and possible hear the jury verdict.

On that Monday morning in early November 2012 my defense attorney Jacob Perone says to me in the lobby of the 55th District Court, "You'll know the Obama's administrations power in America when the jury of six come in wearing all black." And they did! The Judge enters the courtroom, we all stand, and the Judge says to both my attorney and the prosecuting attorney Mr. Cruz "The jury would like to see all the evidence on the disc, the complete voice-mails recorded and emails kept by the police."

I am thinking what disc? What is the Judge talking about? Then Mr. Cruz takes a disc from his laptop computer and hands the mystery disc of evidence to the Judge. WHAT! I tap at my attorney Jacob Perone and ask him, "What is on that disc? I want to see what is on that disc before it goes to the Jury!"

Jacob Perone turns to me and quietly scolds me by remarking to me, "You should know what is on that disc, you are the one that sent all those emails and phone calls which are on the disc."

WHAT? I have no idea what was on that disc then, or now. No idea. What if the people who hate me, the ones I wanted fired, Dr. Catherine Ash and Noelle Palasty, what if they erased my email messages and created something devious? Just to make me look bad or guilty? I feel panicky, but I know I have to remain calm or I will be called "irrational." Possibly even sanctioned if I question Judge Thomas Boyd's request to only have the jury of six see the evidence in private.

Judge Thomas Boyd then comments to us again that only the jury will see the disc in the jury room, the disc of evidence will not be seen in open court. Judge Boyd calmly reminds us in a procedural tone that once the jury has heard and seen all that is on the disc, the jury will reach a verdict. The Judge Boyd comments in court, for now, court is dismissed.

WHAT! My mind is unable to process what the Judge just said, yet I did hear it. I say to myself, I have to remain calm or I will appear like a disorderly woman and be punished. My attorney turns to me and states that I have to stay in the lobby of the court and he will be contacted when the jury has reached a verdict. Two hours, maybe just over an hour later, the jury reached a verdict. My attorney Jacob Perone steps back into the 55th District Court lobby and then ushers me into the courtroom. When the jury walked in wearing all black, I knew what the verdict was before the envelope was opened by the Judge, it was not going to be in my favor. Even though I had given $2,500 (twenty-five hundred dollars) for Jacob Perone to represent me, and I signed the client-attorney contract, obviously someone had given Jacob Perone more money to not represent me. I learned a painful reality that my attorney was not representing me, and the time to represent me was suddenly up, it was too late. Sure enough, Judge Thomas Boyd announced that the jury of six has found me guilty of two counts of stalking, one count for Noelle Palasty, one count for Dr. Catherine Ash. Then the Judge yells at me in the courtroom that I am a bad person. However, he put it more sophisticated than simply using the terminology "a bad person." Hate towards me was definitely radiating from the Judge's perch, making five foot and feeble Judge Thomas Boyd appear large and scary like that Mr. Toad's Wide Ride that was once at Disney. Then Judge Boyd orders for me to be psychologically examined, a mental evaluation before the sentencing date in December 2012. Judge Thomas Boyd court ordered for me to by psychologically examined by Dr. Douglas Ruben. The probation department then provided me with written court documentation that I have a court order to be psychologically examined within the next 24-hours by Dr. Douglas Ruben.

Directly following the early November 2012 trial of me in Mason, Michigan I type a request for a Summary Disposition to the Ingham County Prosecutor. I was very curious as to why police reports in whereas I and my son were the victims were not being prosecuted. Why is it that Eddie and I are not receiving justice for crimes committed against us? I think that is a relevant question to seek an answer to, however, Mr. Stuart Dunnings III hated the question asked in my Summary Disposition sent to him at his office. What happened next? Within days of mailing off that Summary Disposition a Meridian Township police car pulls up in my driveway. The female MTPD officer jumps out and heads towards me in my garage as she inquires if my name is Lori DeBartolo. I answer "yes."

The female MTPD officer informs me that I have a $100,000 (one hundred thousand dollar bond) and a warrant signed for my arrest for contacting the Ingham County Prosecutor's office with a written request for a Summary Disposition which violates Judge Thomas Boyd's court orders of my jail bond in my stalking case. I am handcuffed in my garage, my son Eddie is inside playing with his toys and has no idea that I just got arrested in the garage. Getting arrested is a feeling of being kidnapped by legal measures, if you want to call it legal. Ed steps out to the garage to see me sitting in the back of a police patrol car near the garage as the female officer shouts at him, "She's got a one hundred thousand dollar bond. She contacted the Ingham County Prosecutor's office with a Summary Disposition, which she is not allowed to do."

Ed screams in the doorway of the service door to the garage. Every word he says to me or the cop, he is screaming. The female officer tells him to calm down and pulls out of the driveway with me handcuffed in her backseat.

I do not even think she is going to take me to the jail. After all I have been through in the last two years, and all I know. I believe she is looking in the countryside for a safe place to put a bullet in my head. It's been thirty minutes of a rocky ride handcuffed and I do not see a jail in sight, or any building, I see acres, endless acres of cornfields. When we actually do pull up to the jail, I wonder if she had changed her mind, it was an hour ago that she had handcuffed me in my garage. Despite her possible change of mind, seeing the jail attached to the court in Mason meant to me we had arrived to the destination, I am still alive, my son still has a mother. I thought quietly to myself, I am actually happy and relieved to see the jail.

I was booked into the jail and led to a maximum security cement closet with no windows. Just like the one on the other end of this jail floor three months after I gave birth to Eddie, a few years ago. I realized sitting in that jail cell that someone was very pissed with me and wanted to demonstrate what they could do to my life as a warning of sorts. Sure enough, my bail was one hundred thousand. Jail bondsmen and jail employee staff in uniform were flocking to see if I wanted to sign over my condo residence in East Lansing which had no mortgage debt attached to the deed. Apparently the police or courts or someone had done their homework on me and knew the condo was paid in full, no mortgage, just like our up north home, paid in full, no mortgage. I refused to sign over real estate to the State of Michigan hustlers. For my punishment I would spend three days and three nights in the outfit I arrived in, unable to move more than a few feet in a cement closet. No toothbrush, no outdoors, Eddie had no mom while I was in there. I was just held captive by the State of Michigan and those misusing the title, State of Michigan verses Lori DeBartolo. I had no idea what time it was other than listening by a steel door of the shift changes that occurred or noticed it might be a certain time when meals were shoved through a mail slot opening to my cement closet. The bright annoying light remained on at all times, as did a camera recording everything. It just so happened to be Veteran's Day weekend 2012, which meant there would be no Judge on Monday, Veteran's Day to reduce my bond amount of one hundred thousand dollars bail. I would have to wait until Tuesday during the day to go before the Judge. No shower, no toothpaste, no clean outfit. Judge Thomas Boyd realized I was not going to sign over real estate to get out of jail and reduced my bond to a mere five hundred dollars on Tuesday, following Veteran's Day 2012 in November. I also learned that week from online pop-up news articles that CIA Director David Petraeus stepped down as the CIA Director following the very weekend I was shoved inside a cement jail closet in Mason, Michigan. I knew that the CIA had something to do with misusing jails and cement cells to hustle real estate in illegal, but legal maneuvers on paper, before this all happened to me. I learned that from sources in my neighborhood in East Lansing, before this all happened to me. I learned through conversations that the CIA was targeting young mothers with young children that owed no mortgage and had real estate or possessions. At the time, I did not believe the warnings and rumors. I feel stupid, and my back, my leg cramps, my entire body is killing me in pain from hardly any movement inside a cement closet for 24/7 too long. Who would do this to me? A bunch of hustlers that's who!

It was an elaborate CIA scheme behind the scenes that would gain little notice for an investigation by the FBI, State of Michigan, or media, that is just how powerful that real estate to money scheme proved to be by those in charge of investigating and reporting. I was just wondering if I would live longer enough to write and report. Would my voice be silenced?

At the December 12, 2012 sentencing date of me. My attorney Jacob Perone announces in court that he is resigning as my attorney. I did not fire him. I did not know that he was quitting the case as my attorney until I heard first hand in the empty courtroom on December 12, 2012, on my sentencing day. I am just learning as I listen in the open courtroom on my sentencing date of 12/12/12 that he was quitting as my representative and washing his hands of court case no. 12-01740. Quite honestly I do not remember if Jacob Perone announced his resignation before or after Judge Thomas Boyd informed me that I could choose between one year in jail or sixty months of probation for the two counts of misdemeanor stalking. I selected I would rather have sixty months of probation. I was given a long list of probation conditions, orders from the Judge. I had to go to drug and alcohol testing for two years, every week, randomly. I never failed a drug or alcohol test as they probably wished I had. I was ordered to go to counseling, see a therapist for my stalking behavior that the Judge and Jury claim I have. I was brought up to speed by Judge Thomas Boyd that I am a bad person in the sight of the State of Michigan.

It would not be until February 2013 that I would hear from someone, my therapist, that Dr. Douglas Ruben is not even a licensed Ph.D.! He was not licensed as a Ph.D. in November or December 2012 even though all of his court paperwork in my court file shows he is or was representing himself as a Ph.D. When in fact he was not licensed to do so. A huge ethics violation, a huge criminal violation, one in which the court would see to it that he is not charged! No warrant for his arrest for committing boldly crimes with the courts in Michigan. I would learn that the State of Michigan has sanctioned Douglas Ruben in the past, multiple times, for using letterhead and advertisement with Ph.D. and doctor stamps when in fact he is not licensed as a doctor, a Ph.D.

When I learned that Dr. Douglas Ruben is not a licensed Ph.D. from my therapist I immediately went to the State of Michigan website she pointed out, LARA. The L stands for Licensing. I then located Douglas Ruben's sanctioned license, he was not a licensed Ph.D. Just as she stated to me! I sent in a request for proof of his past sanctioned information from the State of Michigan licensing through FOIA. Once I received and reviewed the shocking information I immediately contacted the 55th District Court by phone and mail, mailing them the same exact copies I had received from the State of Michigan on Douglas Ruben through FOIA from LARA.

What happened next? I received a notice a week later from the 55th District Court that I had violated my probation conditions. The probation order not to contact my probation officer other than my required one meeting a month. I also violated another probation condition because I contacted the State of Michigan Licensing Board. I am not allowed in five years from December 12, 2012 to December 12, 2017 to contact any governmental entity. I received a hearing. I admitted to contacting the State of Michigan Licensing Board and I admitted to contacting my probation officer by phone and leaving her a message about what I had uncovered about unlicensed Ph.D. Douglas Ruben. The Judge and my probation officer sentenced me to one weekend in county jail. I served.

I had another probation violation when I contacted the Lansing FBI to look into my case as possible retaliation by the police for going to the Lansing FBI on the Meridian Township Police Department. I provided the Lansing FBI with MTPD police reports to investigate, reports that needed investigation. I had a hearing on my probation violation. The Lansing FBI suggested that I do forty hours of community service. I served and completed the forty hours by working at a Habitat for Humanity in Williamston, Michigan during school hours when my son Eddie was at Bath Elementary.

I had another probation violation when I wrote on social media that Chief of Police David Hall, his police force, and the Ingham County Prosecutor Stuart Dunnings III were involved with taking women out of their homes for human trafficking purposes. I received a notice in the mail that I violated my probation by saying or writing something derogatory about authority. I had a hearing. I argued I have Freedom of Speech rights, U.S. Constitutional rights! My probation officer and Judge Thomas Boyd informed me that because I am a convicted criminal, found guilty by a jury of my peers, that I do not have U.S. Constitutional rights like everybody else. I was given another forty hours of community service. I served and completed those hours of community service.

Ironically, in March of 2017, while I still remain on probation. The FBI in Michigan find and charge the Ingham County Prosecutor Stuart Dunnings III with human trafficking across Michigan and the U.S. I read online news articles from media outlets such as from The Lansing State Journal and USA Today captured the story of the long list of charges facing the Ingham County Prosecutor. Stuart Dunnings III was then removed from public office as the Ingham County Prosecutor based on many charges and much evidence against him. He currently is in jail. Oddly, no FBI or State of Michigan employee has taken the time, the next step and go through every case prosecuted by convicted Stuart Dunnings III. Therefore, my case would remain irrelevant, I would remain on probation with a muzzle over what I know. Silenced through my 55th District Court probation conditions until December 12, 2017 "to not say anything derogatory about authority," or I face up to one year in jail.

I know what you are thinking. Only in America. Perhaps there is much truth to that American cliché.

Another irony, another layer to my case 12-01740 collecting dust in a file at the 55th District Court in Mason, Michigan; the week I read online news articles about Stuart Dunnings arrest in March of 2016, I receive multiple emails from my own email address. How can this be possible, I wondered. I called Go Daddy on the phone and inquired as to how I can possibly receive an email from my own email address? Go Daddy informed me that someone must have hacked into my email account. Go Daddy then suggested for me to change my password on a regular basis. Go Daddy informed me that in 2012 when a pink bar was over my email site, that in fact my emails were hacked and my email address was hacked.

In March of 2016, I began to receive emails from my email address from a Sony Experia cell phone using my email address! I do not have a Sony Experia cell phone, I do not know of anyone who does. I have never owned a Sony Experia cell phone, nor do I know of anyone who does. I begin to panic and wonder if someone is now sending out emails from my account and I am going to jail for their hacking and message sending! This is so out of control! I cannot control my fate! What is that person or group writing from my email address and then sending to others? I am freaking out, and there is nothing I can do about it, just wonder what the hackers are doing to my account at my expense as they, he or she, taunt me of their actions! Shit, I could go to jail and have done nothing wrong! I was reminded of that harsh reality in my past!

I sent the evidence to the 55th District Court and the FBI headquarters in Washington. No one has contacted me about my case or why I am still on probation, the FBI, or the court. I have come to only one conclusion about Due Process in America; U.S. Constitutional Due Process is only a <u>concept</u> in America, not a requirement by the American court systems. I would always be left wondering, how many other innocent victims were slaughtered at the 55th District Court in Mason, Michigan? How many other victims were also told by the same people that do not follow Due Process Laws in the court system that they can spend tens of thousands of dollars to file an appeal and have the case overturned by another Judge in the American court system?

Eddie had spent second grade (school year 2012-2013) and third grade (school year 2013-2014) at Bath Elementary. I remained his primary parent. Eddie had zero absentness, zero tardiness, and straight A's at Bath Elementary School. Ed and I would remain married.

In 2013 we had listed our East Lansing residence. In June of 2014 we accepted a real estate offer for our condo and headed to Georgia to look at homes for a few days, we needed to purchase, there was no looking back. My husband Ed signed an employment contract with a dental chain in Georgia that offered him a thirty thousand dollar sign-on bonus, travel reimbursement to view Georgia real estate for one week, and free reimbursement of all moving expenses. He had never received such a good employment package from any dental chain in Michigan. Ed received several dental position offers from Georgia based dental companies. The southern economy in Georgia from businesses to real estate seemed so much better in Georgia, and boy was I correct! We moved to Georgia on August 12th & 13th, 2014. My only regrets as we left Michigan was that our condo and up north home took forever to sell in the Michigan market drowning me in crimes and harassment towards me and my son. I wished I had raised Eddie in the south all along, with no bad memories created by Okemos, Michigan. I realized then as I do now that we were just a White statistic moving out of Michigan. I made sure by writing to Governor Rick Snyder and his Michigan Attorney General, that they knew every detail of the horrors I experienced in Michigan. Providing police case reports to investigate all the public corruption in Michigan if in fact they investigate public corruption. I sent out the information to the State, even though Judge Thomas Boyd court ordered in my 60-month probation conditions "to not contact any governmental entity."

Moving To Georgia Again, August 2014.

CHAPTER EIGHTEEN

Our assigned Georgia real estate agent stated to us that she is originally from Langley, Virginia as we made introductions before house hunting that summer morning in June 2012. We all climbed into her large used looking white SUV and headed out on our house hunting adventure. Our realtor Ms. Smith drove us from Kennesaw, Georgia, north on Highway 75 to where the southern tips of the foothills of the Appalachian Mountain range could finally be seen. Many small mountains steeped with Georgia pine trees and not a trace of entrenching modernization. Ms. Teresa Smith our realtor drove us to a quaint old-fashioned town resting within a valley called Cartersville, Georgia. As the realtor drove us down Main Street and around town I notice Confederate civil war statues proudly displayed at municipal buildings, street signs with names like Lee and Stonewall Jackson. The summer of 2014 was also the summer of the 150th year anniversary of the American civil war.

I gaze in curiosity at the sights all around me now, realizing the south is a real destination not just a dream, a real place on the map, I reach for my camera. As my camera begins clicking photos I realize truths about the south never recorded in traditional history books in print. War stories and outcomes passed down from generation to generation in the south seemingly would not let history books override their pride and heritage of wars fought in this region of America. Life in the late 1800's in the south must have resumed with how the south would have liked their own soldiers history remembered. I notice as we drive around town it is as if the south had won the civil war, or at least never admitted losing the civil war. I think quietly to myself as I gaze out the realtor's passenger side of the SUV about how remote my new destination is in the unexplored south. The picturesque store fronts are that of a wild, wild, west town, the streets narrow and best suited for horse and buggy. As we drive further I notice large antebellum white column old mansions with enormous front lawns that stretch past a football field in length that remain undisturbed in size through the growth of the southern town all these years. Some old white vacated antebellum mansions had for sale signs staked in the tangled overgrown weeds and brush. Such places I would never dare step into with what appears to be trees, vines and shrubs growing and reaching through windows with no glass panes to stop the invasion from the yard. Vines horizontally creeping up onto vacant rocking chair front porches. Old vintage painted oak heavy front doors weathered and splintered just blowing open in the welcoming breeze of an abandoned homestead with no apparent buyers and settlers. Rusted antique door knobs that at one time experienced much hustle and bustle during many days gone by, seemingly now have no family left to clinch the front door knob and call the place home. I am not sure if some of those old southern mansions even have electricity or modern plumbing. Large magnolia trees planted long ago now provide much needed shade here in the sweltering south. I spot a large saucer magnolia tree on a southern lawn near the edge of a vast untamed forest. My favorite tree in which to meditate under and dream endlessly and never climb! A saucer magnolia tree in the south can appear slightly sinister, a bit eerie, hiding an abyss of ideas and images in my mind. Immeasurable infinite space that is not visible to most ordinary passersby or apparent to mindless readers prone to always selecting "comfortable and easy" subconscious brainwashing by unvarying leaders in the real world over actual original thoughts conceived by oneself. The untouched scenery since the civil war is boundless, as is my mind and thoughts this sunny morning. I gaze out the realtor's SUV windows, I can feel a channel open within me as I can almost physically feel a story about to emerge from the overgrown forest all around us now as I lean my face almost to the glass of the window. Something is trying to reach me here in the sweltering south as our real estate agent drives us along, I can feel it. There is a story in the woods perhaps, maybe a civil war soldier's ghost caught in the humidity unable to free himself from the south and days gone by.

I notice the reddish orange rich in iron Georgia southern soil along the way blowing a heap of copper colored dust past the realtor's tires. I keep my eyes open and alert for any poisonous snakes that might lurk right out into the open to spook us as we journey along the backroads of Georgia's untamed countryside. Swamps and vine overgrowth cascade the wide open plains that surround the outskirts of town that somehow seemingly remain undisturbed over all this time since the civil war blazed through Bartow County nearly one hundred and fifty years ago to the day! Some old homes not built from cotton wealth and slave labor appear more like rustic shacks barely standing. Humble home sites one after the other that had been abandoned when barreling battles must have disrupted their quiet humble way of life in these parts. Perhaps abandoned shacks from a sheer lack of work in the area from The Great Depression or something? Shacks still standing stayed barely built and tilted on an angle from which the howling wind blew the old frame structures with peek-a-boo dried wood boards. Ms. Smith our realtor informed us that the county seat in Bartow County was the town of Cass until General Sherman from the Union army set the city of Cass on fire, burning down Cass the county seat in Bartow County. Cartersville then became the county seat after the civil war. After burning so much in Bartow County General Sherman blazed a fire trail to Atlanta. Then onward for the Union troops to their victory March to the Sea reaching the port of Savannah to declare victory for the Union army and President Lincoln. Our realtor explained that Savannah was a southern port town where most slaves were imported and sold at auction in America prior to the civil war. As the ashes cooled to a simmer after the civil war the people in the county of Bartow got together to name Cartersville the county seat for Bartow County. Sherman somehow forgot to burn Cartersville in his long ago war strategies fought. Some folks have even rumored to say Sherman knew a lady in Cartersville back in the day that prevented Cartersville from Union army fire torches. Even the county "Bartow" is named for the very first Confederate soldier that died in this area during the civil war.

I comment from my seat, "Sherman, is that a German surname?"

Our realtor Ms. Smith shakes her head, "I don't know."

I comment, "Light red hair, blue eyes, I bet he was of German heritage. Some Germans are very competent, very intelligent and fierce, get the job done. They think outside the box and win while others are still stuck with box mentality."

"What's that up ahead?" I ask as I point to large smoke stacks blowing manufactured clouds into the atmosphere at a rapid uncontrolled pace right before us.

Ms. Smith replies, "Oh, that, that is a nuclear power plant."

I inquire, "What is a nuclear power plant?"

Ms. Smith replies, "Where large amounts of electricity is produced."

I respond, "Really? I never knew that before. I have never seen a nuclear power plant before."

We decide to turn back in our direction and weave our way back to a list of homes not seen by us yet. We cross over Highway 75 and head down Highway Twenty. As we pass through certain sections of the county in Cartersville I cannot help but notice that some parts of town look as if they need a government economic stimulus package. Many businesses just up and left town, many empty spaces for lease or rent. Finally we pull out of the run down section of town and reach our destination of several houses to view and walk through today. Out of the stack of ten or fifteen homes the realtor is showing us during our house hunting trip, the homes in Cartersville are less expensive than Acworth. These homes in Rowland Springs Estates are offering a lot of house for the money!

I roll down the realtor's SUV passenger side window as we enter Rowland Springs Estates. I undoubtedly hear the faint hum of Indian voices chanting to a methodical steady repeated drumbeat. So faint of sound, I stick my curious face slightly out the window to capture the faint Indian chanting explicitly before the mysterious rhythmic chanting faded in the wind. The gushing hot air from outside whirled my long auburn hair within the great furnace known as summertime in Georgia. As we drive up the long steep road leading into the new subdivision I turn to the others in the vehicle and ask, "Did you just hear that?"

My husband Ed comments to me from the backseat as the realtor simply ignores my alarming question just asked, "Yeah, it was like Indian chanting, or like Indians dancing around a campfire beating on a drum, the same sound just repeating itself over and over in the distance somewhere."

Businesslike Ms. Smith blurts out as she abruptly places the gear shift in park, "O.k., we are here!" Ms. Smith continues in a commanding babble, "This is the first house on the list in the subdivision that we will be viewing today. The house was built in 2012, never been lived in, 2400 square feet, two-story, large yard, 10,000 square feet of sod and professionally landscaped. The back of the house faces the woods with privacy, sidewalks a must. Master bedroom upstairs with the rest of the bedrooms. Tall ceilings, ten foot on the main floor if I am not mistaken, and priced under your budget limit of two hundred and seventy-five thousand. This house checks all of your boxes compared to some of the other homes. Let's go take a peek." Ms. Smith our relocation specialist seems to have dollar signs etched in her pupils before we even exit her vehicle to begin this journey of house hunting in hot June of 2014 in Georgia.

House hunting is a big deal, we saved, and saved, lived in a small condominium in Michigan and finally are ready to pay cash to buy that perfect house with the perfect floor plan. With the perfect yard, located in that perfect neighborhood with friendly southerners. However, our real estate agent doesn't see it that way. Rather, her overstated tone is for us to find a house quickly on the list of homes she is showing us today so she can move on to the next sale, the next clients. Ms. Smith looks rather old, as if she should be retired but opening up a realtor key box and walking potential buyers through a potential sale each day of her career is far too easy of money earned for her to give up, I can see that about her. I can see things about people that some people try hard to mask with words, I see it anyways. Maybe this place spooks her, or something about the neighborhood makes her on edge? I step out and gaze at the enveloping bluest sky above, soaking in the warmth of the clear blue radiating all around us on the top of the small mountain top as we head for the front door.

My Italian-American husband Ed is temperamental, and usually one sided about most subjects. Our nine year old son Eddie is catching up to my adult height, and probably will be taller than me by the time he turns fifteen. One of my hopes is that Eddie becomes his own man. I hope Eddie does not genetically exhibit the dreadful traits of his father, is it nature or nurture? We'll see, time will tell. I do work hard to insist Eddie to be different than his father, for Eddie's sake and mine of course too. However, Eddie likes to repeat just about anything Ed says, like an annoying echo.

Ed begins to thumb through the realtor sheets of all the homes we are going to view today as if he is already losing interest in the whole house hunting experience. Ed immediately decides to stop looking around at what this house has to offer us as we enter the home for sale at 10 Altar Rock Ct. Ed pulls out the realtor rap sheet on the house we are currently looking at and poignantly remarks in his discovery on paper, "This one is the least expensive one out of the homes Ms. Smith is going to show us."

I had a sinking feeling, an instant feeling from that comment he just made that this house could be the one. The clue of a verbal comment he just made was that I should start looking around to see if I even like the house and yard, because this house just might do in Ed's mind already made up. Ed and his side of the family are numbers people.

Price, money, and profits are looked at far and beyond and before aesthetic values, or any values for that matter. Someone peering into our marriage might even comment that Ed possesses only two mere moods, tyrant or silent.

"Eddie go see the bedrooms upstairs and see if there is one you like." I briskly motion and say with impatience to Eddie almost ten years old.

A few minutes later Eddie shouts down to us, "Mom, come check out the upstairs, you gotta see this huge bathroom, it has one of those big tubs."

Our real estate agent drove us around the subdivision called Rowland Springs Estates to show us ten more houses for sale in the subdivision. I noticed that not one child was playing outside and so many for sale signs. The entire subdivision was quieter than most public libraries. The frogs and insects created the most noticeable noise in the large neighborhood. I ask, "What is that loud rattling sound coming from the trees? I have never heard a group of insects or frogs so loud in my life."

Ms. Smith replies, "Oh, that noise? Those are cicada bugs. They can be loud, they are some kind of tree cricket. We don't hear them in the city."

Where is everyone? This is summer break, I thought to myself as the realtor shuffled us from house to house that day in Rowland Springs Estates. I notice the large yards, decent size houses. Mostly newer houses all nestled in the rolling foothills of the Appalachian Mountain range that extends down into northern Georgia. "Look up there!" I shout as I point to rows of an ancient rock formation displayed of one hundred or more altar rocks. I inquire, "How old is that formation?"

My husband Ed looks up with amazement at the geological find in plain sight at the top of the hill behind a sprawling ranch house at 28 Aaron Lane. Just then our realtor steps into the conversation to inform us about the newly built homes on ancient land. She remarks, "This subdivision began here in 2004."

Ed comments, "It looks like a nice subdivision."

Ms. Smith adds, "Well, this is Georgia. Five hundred years ago this region was called the Piedmont region by the native Etowah and

Cherokee tribes. If you take a look around you here you will notice the grapes and blackberries that still grow every season, woven into the now tree lines of backyards that were planted by the feet that set foot on this land before us. The Indians would plant these briars that have sharp thick thorns to ward off the black bears from eating the berries farmed here long ago. It's rumored that there is some kind of ancient aqueduct system buried behind the foliage of the mountains around here somewhere. No one has been able to locate the ancient aqueduct system with so much green canopy to my knowledge. Just over a hundred and eighty five years ago President Thomas Jefferson organized troops to lead out the native Indian tribes. Historically the plan was known as The 1830 Removal Act, commonly known as the trail of tears around these parts. Many Indian tribes ran further and deeper into the Appalachian Mountains to avoid the round up to migrate west against their wishes and upon President Jefferson's executive orders. It makes you look at a twenty dollar bill differently," Ms. Smith our realtor comments boldly.

We ended up buying the house at 10 Altar Rock Court in Cartersville, Georgia. Far away from 28 Aaron Lane with all the altar rocks, why our street is named, "Altar Rock Court" I may never know. We moved in mid-August 2014 into a new construction home with vintage flare. Just after moving down in August we learned that in Georgia the school year begins in August rather than in September. Eddie began school, and I began exploring the woods and undisturbed hilly mountain terrain behind our street with a metal detector. According to our real estate agent, famous civil war battles were fought just north of our property and just south of us. I went treasure hunting. As we became familiar with our surroundings we began to venture out and explore Georgia all around us now. Being that we are close to Highway 75 which was a dirt road 150 years ago when thousands of troops traveled and set up military camps around these parts, I knew my chances of locating something either of Indian nature or civil war would be great. The very first thing I noticed was an Indian tree near the community park and pool in the neighborhood. An Indian marked a spot for some reason by bending a young tree to grow as a permanent marker.

The very first civil war piece of history I located that was not buried too deep was a heavy metal part from a civil war cannon that connected to the rotation cylinder part that would allow the cannon to move in a certain direction, and then another part I found. I also noticed a stream sandwiched between the mountain we live on and the next mountain slope in front of me. When I stand on my back deck and face the mysterious woods I can feel balmy sea air when ocean storms brew close to the coast of Georgia. Of course one cannot see the stream with fish or the mound formations in the woods until one is deep in the remote forest behind my house. Where obviously modern man has not frequented the steep wood embankments and shallow valleys where the mountains and woods abound here. The terrain is never flat, and there is no path, except for an old two-track that stops at another limestone mountain slope that touches our deserted cul-de-sac. I would learn in the presiding years from residents of Rowland Springs Estates that they too have located artifacts not too far from their backyards and not deep in the soil, such as civil war guns, Indian arrowheads, and bones!

In August of 2014, shortly after moving in we had to enroll Eddie right away. Our address and subdivision has assigned county schools verses city schools of Cartersville, even though our address is Cartersville, Georgia. Eddie came home from school and complained the very first day of county school that the other 4th graders are very rural in nature and play games on the playground called "road kill."

I inquired to Eddie, "What is road kill?"

Eddie explained that one person runs between people swinging on the swing sets, if a swing hits or even taps the child running, the child is out, the swing set game is called "road kill." Eddie explained that the school has a solution to the obvious rural nature of the county kids by blaring classical music over the loudspeaker during lunchtime. He complained there is never enough table and chairs so many kids just stand and eat their lunch. He complained that the school lunch portions are so small, not like Bath schools. He complained that in the last three days of his new school in the south that he had not learned one thing in school and missed Bath Elementary. I reminded Eddie that we are not moving back to Michigan, now is not the time to look backwards, now is the time to enjoy living in the south.

During the day and early evenings I had been walking my dog George at least three or four times a day. As I walked George I would always stop and have a conversation or two with the friendly neighbors all around us now, the neighbors on the hill by us. One neighbor across the way told me that county schools have a lot of drugs and to move Eddie to city schools as soon as I can, before middle school. Another neighbor to the left, Cindy Hickom informed me that she knew many of the office staff at Cartersville Elementary in the City of Cartersville and that she would contact them and see if Eddie could enroll in city schools even though the enrollment time is done for this school year 2014-2015.

Sure enough, Cindy Hickom came to me and gave me an email print out from the registrar lady on what the city school will need to enroll Eddie. I brought Eddie's birth certificate, vaccination records, the past two school year report cards showing perfect attendance, zero tardiness, and straight A's earned by Eddie. No behavioral issues, no sanctions, just a perfect student with records to show!

Thank God I did not keep Eddie in Okemos schools! The next morning I was required to bring Eddie to the county health department in the city for a required routine examination before he could officially begin Cartersville City Schools. We arrived at the health department opening time of 8am and took a waiting ticket in the health lobby. Eddie was examined, I brought the excellent report to the front office of Cartersville City Schools. I signed him in by 9am and walked him down to the 4th grader wing of the school with the school secretary. Why the city schools marked him absent that day I do not know. But I was not going to complain, complaining got me in trouble before with a school system. During the 2014-2015 school year at Cartersville Elementary Eddie was only marked as having one day absent, zero tardiness, and straight A's, no detentions.

Eddie instantly felt that the city schools were much better. I could tell by the homework he was taking home and his tests and quizzes he was learning more parent-child expected academics than he would ever receive at county schools. Eddie told me that county schools are like Okemos.

School was going good for Eddie now and he was making friends at school. From what I could tell in our neighborhood thus far, there just were not a lot of kids for Eddie to play with and make friends. We had moved from a condo in East Lansing where no kids Eddie's age lived, to this Georgia neighborhood where the homes were not too small, not too big. It appeared to be a neighborhood that would have many kids, however none seemed to exist, or they just stayed inside away from the Georgia heatwaves, or something.

The very first night we slept at 10 Altar Rock Ct. the smoke alarms went off in the middle of the night startling us. We would always look around the house, no fire, no smoke, it was bizarre occurrences with no explanation. The smoke alarms would go off usually around midnight to 3am. This occurred so much in the beginning that I called the builder Mark Stevenson to locate why. He came over and checked all the smoke alarms and explained to me that perhaps dust from new construction blew past the smoke alarms while the air conditioning kicked on. The explanation seemed reasonable, however, other occurrences were happening inside this house too, that could not be explained away so logically. For example when we first moved in, that week, the phone in our master bedroom would ring three quick rings, one ring after the other, real fast like, not a normal ring of a phone. Ed would pick up the phone and no one would be on the other end. By the end of August, going into September 2014 he just unplugged the master bedroom phone by the bed, however, the phone would still ring.

Then at other times something would go and draw energy from our upstairs smoke alarms only. Trying to make them buzz as if the energy was too weak to fully make the smoke alarms go off completely, always enough to startle us in the wee hours though. Then one night I noticed while lying in bed a glow from the dresser lamp which is in direct view of the upstairs hallway. What I thought was the upstairs hallway light going on, then go off, then go on, then off, then on again, creating a reflection of a dim glow on the dresser lamp base, was in fact not the light coming from the hallway. I got up to see if Eddie was o.k. assuming he had turned the upstairs hallway light on many times, causing a logical light reflection off the lamp base on the master bedroom dresser. To my surprise he was sound asleep in his bed! I walk in the dark hallway and go back to bed laying on my side facing the dresser with my eyes wide open. Then it happens again! However, this time I notice it is the actually dresser lamp going on and off all by itself that had seemingly caused the glowing lamp base.

That's not all folks on the subject of the unexplainable. One night I was awoken by the music of Thomas the Tank Engine playing, in the wee hours of the night, waking me up as everyone else stays asleep. I get out of bed and in the dark of the night follow the musical melody down the moonlit darkened upstairs hallway and then turn into my son's bathroom to locate the music being played. I turn on the bathroom light and push the toothbrush button down to make the melody stop. Pushing the button on the toothbrush would always cause the song being played on the toothbrush to either stop or start. I keep pushing the toothbrush button to stop but the melody keeps playing, one song after the other. Ed and Eddie are still asleep, and quite honestly I do not want to wake them to this crazy toothbrush playing by itself or we will all get no sleep. I set down the toothbrush and stand there watching and waiting for the toothbrush to stop. After a few minutes the toothbrush Thomas the Tank Engine melody finally stops. I turn off the light and go back to sleep.

The next night I am in bed with the T.V. on, just as I begin falling asleep I am awoken by a tugging on my blankets and comforter. I remark half asleep, "Stop it Eddie, I am trying to sleep." I am alerted enough to wake up fully and notice Ed is in the master bathroom getting ready for bed and Eddie is not in our bedroom. I get out of bed completely awake now and in search of Eddie. I then locate Eddie sound asleep in his bed, my heart is racing for an explanation.

When the unplugged phone would ring in our master bedroom at odd hours of the early morning, sometimes Ed and I will just stare at the ceiling in being awoken by the unexplainable extra quick, extra short fast three rings of the master bedroom phone only. I would then notice that Eddie's phone that is still plugged in would never ring at these odd hours! Sometimes I break the silence by saying to Ed in anger, "Unplug the phone!" We already know by the rings as always, that if we pick it up this time, it is always no one on the other end. Sometimes I shout to Ed staring at the ceiling in disbelief himself at the strange occurrences, "This house is new construction! This house is not supposed to be haunted!" Ed always comments in a somber tone and mood, "I know."

The only strange occurrences I can recall at our former East Lansing residence was when I began typing my memoirs in 2008-2009. Anytime I typed about Bessy's voodoo during the 1860's in the beginning chapters of this book, my son's battery operated toys might also visible light up or make noise in the basement clothes baskets where we would store the toys when not in use by Eddie. At no other time would a toy just randomly be set off all by itself. At times I could push on the keyboard of the computer and then lift up testing the abilities of the correlation between those battery operated toys like a game of musical chairs to what I was typing, there was always a correlation in content to random toys going off.

All's I can say is that I had one jealous black mamme of me in the 1860's if you were to consider all that has happened to me.

Back in Georgia now, however the year is 2014. Eddie was making friends in school. The fourth grade wing consisted of twelve classrooms. For whatever reason, not by my request or direction or demands, Eddie was placed in a homeroom that the city school selected, not selected by me or Eddie or Ed, keep that in mind when I tell you of the next story. As the 2014-2015 school year is underway Eddie requests that a friend of his named Sam Ford come over to play and hang out with Eddie. I agree, and Sam Ford's mother brings him over a few Saturdays during the day. Upon meeting Sam Ford's mother I thought his mother looked familiar but I could not place where I knew her from. She was tall, thin, curly long brown hair. She spoke with a thick Alabama accent but looked rather Jewish if you asked me. She looked very different than her son Sam Ford whom resembled in coloring and facial features to the cartoon character MAD. His mother seemed polite as she introduced herself and commented that I had a nice house. The house is certainly not really my standards and definitely not the house of my dreams, but I commented anyways, "Oh, thank-you."

Sam Ford's mother introduced herself, and quite honestly I do not remember her name, even to this day. However, I never forget a person if I meet them, even if the music is too loud, I always remember a person. She informed me that she is a high school teacher at Cartersville High teaching advanced English. I would describe her as polite and normal, nothing seemed odd or off as a warning bell.

As Halloween 2014 approaches Eddie selects a Halloween costume and wants Sam Ford to come over for Halloween trick or treat and sleep over too. Halloween was on the weekend and so I agreed. Ed and I took the boys trick or treating and then Sam Ford slept over.

As November 21, 2014 was fast approaching Eddie wanted Sam Ford to sleep over and celebrate Eddie's 10th birthday. We just moved here from Michigan, I did not have a big party planned and I agreed that Sam Ford could come over and stay the night. I did of course have a fancy birthday cake from the bakery and ice cream. Sam Ford gave Eddie some nice Pokémon gifts that Eddie appreciated. I had gifts for Eddie too. The next day on Saturday Ed had to work and I took the boys to Stone Mountain for the day, we had fun all day. Sam Ford had never been to Stone Mountain before. The day was long, I allowed Sam Ford to play over once we got back from the park. By the time Sam Ford's mother arrived it was dark and late on Saturday evening. She pulled up in a large new SUV, different than her Audi sports car. A shorter and older than Sam Ford boy in the backseat got out to meet us as did a tall man from the front seat. The man had wavy short blonde hair, blue eyes. The man I instantly recognized as a regular from The Gold Club from the early 1990's. He looked the same, tall, about 6'1-6'3. Heavy through the middle, his torso area, yet his arms and legs are not fat. He had introduced himself as a CIA agent way back when at The Gold Club. I looked at Sam's mother, now I remember her and where I first met her! The Gold Club. She was the curly haired waitress at The Gold

Club back in the day when CIA John Brennan would have me dance for him, she was the waitress in VIP that would wait on John Brennan! Then I look back at Sam Ford, his mannerisms and coloring are just like John Brennan! Auagh! This is so awkward now that it is 2014 and I am a wife and mother in Georgia with a son that goes to school with her son. The other boy that climbed out of the backseat looks more like her face, and the other son of hers has no southern accent like his brother Sam Ford.

Honestly, from that day forward I suggested to Eddie that he make more friends, other friends besides just Sam Ford. I told Eddie I do not feel comfortable with him being friends with Sam Ford. In the following weeks of late November-December of 2014 Eddie would often tell me that Sam Ford wants him (Eddie) to come over to his house (Sam Ford's house) but that his mother and step-father do not want me (Eddie's mom) to know where they live.

"What?" I ask Eddie.

My son Eddie proceeds to tell me that Sam Ford would like for him (Eddie) to go home after school sometime with Sam Ford to Sam Ford's house and that Sam Ford would have the driver. "What?!?!?"

I respond to Eddie, "No way!"

Eddie answers back to my remark by telling me he will never ride home with Sam Ford, ever. Thank-God.

Then to my surprise and horror in January 2015 I see a CIA agent that I knew as a regular at The Gold Club in the 1990's, now in early 2014 just standing under the covered sidewalk area connected to the school as the elementary kids await to be picked up by their parents. I am of course there to pick up Eddie from school, the man by the school looking outward to all the cars in the carline is a different CIA agent than Sam Ford's step-father. What is that guy doing by the teachers, kids and school? Creepy!

When Eddie climbs in as I pick him up from school, I remind Eddie never to ever go home with anyone after school, there are some creeps out there!

Then one day my beloved dog George is doing what he instinctively is good at as he is part Lhasa Apso, he is alerted to something unusual on the main floor as I am upstairs calling for him to go to bed. As quiet as the night seems, not one strange noise to be heard, just General George telling me the fort is not safe. I cannot think of what the problem could be, it was around 9pm going on 10pm that evening. George won't stop barking at the silent front door in the dark of the evening on the main floor. We are all upstairs, he always follows us up.

Everything appears quiet except for George's excessive barking by the front door and he won't come upstairs to bed with us. I have no choice but to go downstairs and turn the lights on to see what he is obsessively barking about. Just as I silently turn the front porch light and hallway foyer light on, there is my neighbor Scott Hickom on my front porch trying to loosen my front door knob! I open the door and startle Scott Hickom who is wearing a helmet with a small bright direct flashlight built into his hat. Scott pulls away from my front door, my dog George still barking loudly, obsessively at the situation that startled me too! I look at Scott and ask, "What are you doing Scott?" He just keeps staring at me like a deer in the headlights without ever answering my question as he slowly steps backwards almost tripping backwards. No matter how many times I inquire and ask, "What are you doing here Scott?" He just stares at me with no answer for himself. Then out of the blue I catch movement in my peripheral vision, I turn and look only to be surprised more by a strange man that just emerged from a tall, thick full shrub alongside my front porch. As my eyes shock me by what I see, it's the CIA man from the Cartersville City School carline! How do these two even know one another? I keep asking questions to the two men wearing frozen expressions like two deer caught in the headlights as I stand in my doorway.

At this point Ed keeps shouting in the background from the master bedroom, "Who is at the front door?"

I slam the front door and shout to Ed upstairs, "We are moving! That creep Scott next door was going to break into our home with some other creep he had with him!"

Ed screams to me on the main floor from the bedroom, "We are not moving, we just moved in!"

I remark calmly as I still am rattled by the whole situation that just unfolded by my front door, "Come on George, let's go upstairs." George let's out a few more barks to let the world know he is General George, beware he is in charge and then we head upstairs. George's mood went from alert to disappointment that he could not get to them, bite them, and rip their paint legs into shreds.

What kind of dog is George? Half Lhasa Apso and half Cocker Spaniel, black fur with white markings on his chest, chin, and three paws, with brown eyes. I always find it strange in today's times how the internet will display known personality traits, behavioral traits, intelligence traits and physical traits of every species of dog known to man, but the internet does not display the same set of information about people. I can google to seek information on races of people, but the only information posted on the internet during my time period are physical traits only.

However, there was one website page that I read that stated you could point out a German by their personality sometimes more prevalent than a German's physical appearance and typical physical traits. Do Germans have a different personality than most? Leon Panetta once told me that Germans retain knowledge more than any other race of people. I asked Leon Panetta, who or what is his source of information? He replied, "The CIA."

In the spring of 2015 Cindy Hickom my neighbor to the left of me whom lives with Scott Hickom at 42 Roberson Drive begins setting down four rose bushes at the edge of her property and where my sideline begins. I notice this as I head out for a walk down the sidewalk past her house. We live on the corner of Altar Rock Ct. and Roberson Drive in a two-story. As my dog takes his time sniffing between her house and mine I wave and say hello and ask what is she doing. Cindy digs one rose bush in the ground and comments that a teacher she cleans house for wanted these four rose bushes planted between her house and mine. I am thinking and then I blurt out, "If someone gave me rose bushes, I would plant them wherever I wanted to plant them."

Cindy Hickom places her hands on her size 200 inch hips, looks at me in apparent physical exhaustion and remarks like a smart Alec,

"Scott and I do not get paid if we do not plant the rose bushes where the teacher wants us to plant them."

I was a bit taken back by her sudden rude tone that was completely unwarranted towards me.

I shout back at the top of my yard slope, "Who is really going to notice where you plant the rose bushes Cindy?"

Cindy still with her smart Alec tone of voice towards me says, "This one is for 9/11, the other dates have not happened yet. When a helicopter flies overhead they will be checking to see if I planted the rose bushes as directed. Once they are planted with proof, Scott and I will have certain bills paid by the teacher."

In my head I am screaming at what she just said to me. I could not hold back my expression of surprise. I just remarked, "Oh."

Then I muster up courage and inquire, "What does Scott your husband do for a living?"

Cindy Hickom shouts back as she digs a hole, "He sells paper and pencils for a living."

I remark with a questioning tone and with smartness in my tone now too, "Just on paper Cindy.....That's what he does just on paper?"

Cindy remarks mad, "What?" And keeps digging and planting the other three rose bushes.

I am completely disgusted and horrified by what she just disclosed about the rose bushes. I remark to sweaty Cindy, "How can you live in this neighborhood with you cleaning houses part-time and your husband selling paper and pencils?"

Cindy looks up and says very matter of fact, "He doesn't sell paper and pencils Lori, he works for the developer in the office two days a week."

I remark smartly and wittily, "Oh, Mark Stevenson the developer and builder, does he ever sell any lots or houses in this subdivision or is it just a front for illegal activity?"

Cindy does not take well to my smartness. Cindy remarks frivolously, trying to show me up, with a shovel in her hands, "Oh, I don't know, but I am sure you will find out, that's why your real estate agent sold you your house Lori."

At this point I realize the conversation is getting to dark for me and I turn my back and proceed to walk George down the hill. However, as I make my way back up the hill I am bound and determined to learn and gather more information about what my neighbors are up to with their vague careers. Most people are very forthright about what they do for a living, what their career is, where they attended college. Cindy Hickom was very forthright on many occasions when she told me things as I walked my dog and her dog Molly came towards us, or if I saw her, or she saw me walking. Cindy Hickom boldly disclosed when we first moved into 10 Altar Rock Ct. that Scott had no pension, no college degree, just like her, and they go out of town on jobs for the developer. Then her dog would pull her away, or my dog George would pull me in a direction, head down the sidewalk and I was not able to get any more details.

One day in the summer of 2015 Scott was out walking his beagle Molly and I was out walking George my dog. We got on the subject of "what do you do for a living?" The conversation evolved and Scott explained that he works for the real estate developer in accounting and finance a few days a week, he has since 2004. Scott informed me that the developer and the investors are really up to no good and require that he create loan applications in their Ponzi scheme to stay afloat from names and information provided to him from Bill & Nancy Terrill that live at 37 Roberson Drive. Bill & Nancy Terrill both work at H&R Block.

I ask, "Why not quit if your conscious is getting to you Scott?"

Scott says in his coy southern accent, "Oh, I could not do that. Quitting is not a financial option for me, Cindy and I could never pay the bills if I quit. We do what we can to get by. If Mark or the government needs me to do something, I just do it for them."

I looked at Scott and question, "American government?"

Scott says coy and almost convincingly patriotically, "Well the American government is involved with the investment group, I know, I work in the office you know."

I was just amazed at how Scott spun his job reality as if he had a normal legal job position in the American workforce of human capital. I inquire further, "How can Bill & Nancy legally give you information on peoples identities? How can they get away with that? How can you and the investors get away with that?"

Scott remarks with a smile, "I don't know, they just do."

The conversation evolved further from work related questions to people in the neighborhood related to his job. Scott Hickom warned me not to have my son Eddie play with Grayson Hollifield or Henry Smith in the neighborhood, warning me "that those kids like their parents are up to no good and they have orchestrated disappearances of young ladies and children in the past." Scott informed me that a group of investors that he works with gave Floyd Medical Pharmacist Jody Lee Smith (male) the 8100 square foot house with high end finishes, 12-foot ceilings at 28 Aaron Lane. "All for a low price of $187,000 in 2009 in exchange for unlimited prescription drugs that are used in kidnappings and the transportation of victims to hideouts built into wealthy homes in Arab countries." Scott explained that "when 28 Aaron Lane sold back in 2009 there was no real estate sign, just a bank deal between the developer and the pharmacist. The pharmacist is the Floyd Medical manager and only he can sneak quantities of drugs for the CIA off the hospital shelves with no one noticing. The real estate closing department at the attorney's office and the Bartow County Tax Assessor's office was not even required to disclose what bank did the deal on formality paperwork, thanks in part to the CIA. I got friends in high places Lori."

I sigh and wear a look of horror mixed with intrigue as I say, "What? CIA?" I want Scott to explain further about what he has said to me.

Scott remarks with a coy smile as he tugs on Molly's leash, "I told you the American government is involved with the group of investors I work for."

"Come on Molly" orders Scott towards his Beagle sniffing at the ground.

Then Scott Hickom looks at me, tilts his chin down and up as if he is a cowboy with a cowboy hat as he uncannily remarks directly to me, "The neighborhood is not what it seems to be." Then he raises his eyebrows and leaves the sidewalk.

Scott headed back to his green ranch house that looked as if another season of no touch-up paint would pass on by. Scott clearly felt some guilt and remorse about his means of making money and paying the bills. However, with his ideologies, as with so many other people's ideologies, money was the factor that kept him dishonest. Guilty feelings made him share information about dishonest bill paying and so much more about the secrets in the neighborhood.

In July of 2015 I awake in the middle of the night due to a very real and vivid dream of being visited by the deceased author of Gone With The Wind, Margaret Mitchell. I have never read the epic book, Gone With The Wind. However, I have seen the famous movie on Turner Classic Movies, the TCM cable channel. If you were to ask me what I envisioned Margaret Mitchell the author to look like before I had that dream, I would have told you I envisioned her to be like a southern belle. An old fashioned southern belle with a fancy long dress on and she probably wrote her tales by a fancy heirloom style desk in a large antebellum mansion resembling the female protagonist, Scarlet O'Hare. Probably writing in a graciously furnished oversized upstairs master bedroom with an open veranda blowing in southern breezes, a sophisticated cocktail mixture on her writing desk or near her on a dresser, with way too much time on her hands, maybe due to the combination of wealth and boredom.

O.k., that was how I envisioned author Margaret Mitchell to be and look like before my very real dream that woke me up in late June or early July 2015. In my dream Margaret Mitchell looked like a New York socialite in the roaring twenties, way too thin, frail almost, no curves, with bobbed dark hair and a long cigarette like a 1920's movie star. Very opposite of the southern belle days of fancy southern balls for the aristocrats as I had envisioned her before "the dream." She did not communicate with words to me, or introduce herself to me with words in my dream. Rather she stood by my bedside and walked around my room dressed like a roaring twenties flapper as she radiated her thoughts to me as I was asleep. She pointed towards the north and told me through radiating knowledge that seemed to transcend from her to me, encouraging me to write about all that is occurring in the neighborhood and that I would receive a New York literary agent to represent my work. She radiated that she would also visit the New York agent that she had in mind for me and together we would be saving women and children caught in slavery.

The next morning when I awoke in daylight of that summer's morning, I looked to the bluest of skies and said to my husband Ed, "We have to go visit the Margaret Mitchell House in downtown Atlanta this weekend. We have free tickets that we have never used yet." It had been at least a half of year since we joined the Atlanta History Center, we viewed the Swan House, but never made it around to traveling to the Margaret Mitchel House. Then I told my husband Ed about my dream. Eddie whined that he hates museums and touring old homes and did not want to go, stating that I was going to ruin his summer break with boringness. We went anyways and you bet I took Eddie. I had to go see and learn about the author that had just visited me in my dreams.

Upon arriving to the downtown Margaret Mitchel House I notice the old red brick structure sandwiched within the ever intrusive new and modern Atlanta skyline of buildings. Once we arrived we headed to the front door, we were greeted by employees of the Margaret Mitchell House in the bookstore gift store lobby of the old Atlanta apartments. We were very quickly brought up to speed that Margaret Mitchell did not write Gone With The Wind in an old Antebellum southern mansion in town or out of town. In fact, she wrote the epic story in apartment one which was a main floor almost studio apartment. The apartment building had all the vintage charm of her time period. At first I just could not get over how small of space she lived in for quite some time with her second husband. There was a small bedroom that was also used as their dining room with two chairs and a small table shoved against the bedroom wall. The bedroom and the tiny living room made up the total rooms in the apartment, unless you would count the small closet with a window as an actual room, set-up as a kitchen prep room as her kitchen to be the third room in the apartment. When I first stepped into the old small living room with vintage décor and small antiques I quickly notice the old typewriter. Although I believe she hand wrote many of the chapters that she later would store. Each chapter in large envelopes for separation and safe keeping. I then look at the window that was next to the small drawing desk where she wrote Gone With The Wind. The bottom of the window would have barely reached the top of her head, making a direct view to the outside almost impossible to see while sitting down and writing. The window near where she wrote was a high window to allow daylight into the room as she wrote. I instantly looked at that seat by the desk and felt a kindred spirit, a pioneer like myself, writing, exploring a world outside of one's exact existence. An escape from decisions rendered, an escape from the mundane, an escape from the living quarters, a safe place to escape to within the mind, just like me. When I stared at that desk in that small living room in Margaret Mitchell's old apartment, I was reminded of East Lansing, Michigan on North Wild Blossom Ct. and all that I was escaping in my trapped existence as I typed away on a small desk against a wall in a basement with daylight windows. The windows could not even reach the top of my head as I sat and wrote my first and second edition of I Remember Heaven Before Earth in East Lansing. I could see similarities in her writing room in Atlanta and my writing room in Michigan. My writing room now in Georgia at 10 Altar Rock Ct. is on the main floor with lots of light and mountain scenery from two windows, the temperature is pleasant as I type away at volume one, third edition of I Remember Heaven Before Earth.

 We were shown photographs of Margaret Mitchell. That's when I realized how real my dream was the summer of 2015 in Georgia. Seeing actual photographs of the young Margaret Mitchell gave validation of the visit within my dreams and all she spoke of to me by radiating the information to me in my dreams.

 When the tour guide informed us that most of the book royalties went to the Catholic Church in Atlanta by the direction of Margaret

Mitchell's brother after she passed with no will and childless. A small portion of book royalties are given back from the Catholic Church of Atlanta to the Margaret Mitchell House to run the operation of the gift store, minor maintenance of the quant building and grounds and pay the staff at the House. I could instantly feel sadness and dread from Margaret Mitchell in that drawing room as the tour guide spoke about where her book royalties were going and had gone all these years. I do not think she was fond of the Catholic Church and we learned the Catholic Church was not fond of her work with writing Gone With The Wind. The Catholic Church had condemned her book Gone With The Wind. A book that was not conventional or conservative for that time period when she wrote and published Gone With The Wind, just like my work that is not conventional or conservative. My work also is not a cookie cutter version of anything on the book market of what repressing ideologies lodged within today's society or organized religion would want me to write about either. My book is daring, just like what she felt inside, a daring escape to break out of the molds and constraints set in place by others.

When I was in her drawing room, her writing room, I could sense a message from her that she would rather have the Catholic Church to receive not a penny of book royalties for the book the Catholic Church condemned when she was alive. I could sense she wanted the staff at The Margaret Mitchell House to receive a raise and for a larger portion of her royalties to go towards the Margaret Mitchell House than what the Catholic Church currently tithes out of the pool of royalties to give to the Margaret Mitchell House.

I could tell you she would like to see her royalties go into a talent award fund set up and based with a committee that runs the Margaret Mitchell House. A fund and award similar to the Nobel Awards in Sweden, such as the Nobel prize in literature. I can tell you she would like many literature awards given in many different categories. I can feel it, sense it, and know it. However, I cannot change how currently her royalties are sent, which is against her wishes. Dead people can tell no tales, but they can still communicate.

The rest of summer 2015 proves to be pretty uneventful. Eddie enters 5th grade at Cartersville Elementary. Sam Ford is not in Eddie's class as I wrote an email to the 4th grade homeroom teacher to make sure Sam Ford is not in Eddie's 5th grade homeroom class next school year. I had learned in December of 2014 from Sam Ford's mother that Sam Ford is the biological illegitimate son of CIA John Brennan. Seriously, out of twelve classrooms in 4th grade, why was my son placed with Sam Ford's homeroom? Ask Cindy Hickom? She was the one that actually got my son into the good schools of the City of Cartersville.

In the neighborhood, on occasion Eddie plays with a boy named Grayson Hollifield. Grayson and his mom tell us he is the same age as Eddie. Now, keep in mind, Scott Hickom had warned me not to have Eddie play with the neighborhood kids Grayson Hollifield or Henry Smith. I paid no heed to what Scott Hickom had to say as warnings. I thought Scott was a criminal, uncaught criminal, nevertheless a criminal in my book. Therefore I paid no heed to what he had to say as valuable at this point. I thought his four hundred pound wife Cindy Hickom was crazy and up to no good, and he was up to no good. I placed very little value, very little worth out of anything she said to me these days, she likes to run her mouth, but how much of it is true? I have caught her in lies in the last year, during simple conversations.

In August 2015 going into September 2015 Scott Hickom had warned be briefly and more than once during this time that one of his co-workers at the office informed him that I was going to be kidnapped by a group already in place to do so. Scott informed me that a local sheriff has provided police uniforms as often police uniforms are used in conjunction with abductions by a group of people that his co-worker knows about. He explained that the Hollifields and Jody (male) and Heather Smith are involved with that abduction group. It made no sense to me, I paid no heed to his warnings, it was not what I wanted to believe perhaps.

November 2015 proved to be an exceptionally warm November in Georgia. Eddie played with Grayson Hollifield off and on during the one week off from school for Thanksgiving Break 2015. On Saturday November 28, 2015 Grayson called early wanting to hook a playdate with

Eddie. I agreed, Eddie wanted to go play with Grayson. I let Eddie walk down the hill to Grayson's house at 12 Aaron Lane. Later for lunch I picked the boys up and took them for lunch at Zaxby's and then brought them back to Grayson's house. The mother Melissa Hollifield asked if Eddie and I wanted to hike Pine Mountain with her and Grayson. I love the great outdoors, I love to hike, the day was sunny and a perfect seventy degree day in Georgia. I thought everything was perfect too, I had no idea what the Hollifields in combination with others, what was in store for Eddie and I at Pine Mountain. I had no way of knowing, unless for instance, Scott Hickom was correct and I was naïve to this neighborhood in Georgia.

At around 1:30pm I heated up lunch for Ed whom had to work that Saturday and would be coming home soon. I placed the meal on the table and as soon as Ed walked through the door just after 2pm I told him where Eddie and I were headed, Pine Mountain for a hike.

I had only been to Pine Mountain one other time, that was when we first moved down here in 2014. We walked as a family, we took George for a walk on the trails at the base around the mountain and not a direct hike up as we are doing today, November 28, 2015. Melissa Hollifield was very insistent that I drive my own vehicle just in case I get tired and need to head back and rest in my vehicle. She warned the hike to the top is steep, steeper than hiking up Kennesaw Mountain.

When we arrived to the base of the heavily wooded Pine Mountain the small parking lot is almost full with at least twenty or so vehicles parked there. Standing in the parking lot, Melissa Holifield calls someone to say we have arrived. I thought it was strange when I asked her if she wanted to put her cell phone in my crossover purse that she responded, "No, I would rather hold onto my phone."

I also thought it was unusual to constantly talk and text as Melissa Hollifield did on the hike up and down the mountain. About ten minutes into our hike up the mountain I notice a yellow and red helicopter hovering over the open area of what is the parking lot where no trees of course grow. Why would a helicopter just hover over a parking lot?

I thought. Then I comment "Maybe the helicopter is rescuing someone with a medical emergency?"

On our way down the mountain I felt eyes on me all of a sudden, so I look around, turn around, and to my surprise there is a man in his thirties that suddenly gives an expression that he is worried that I just spotted him behind me. He then moves forward and makes conversation with Melissa Hollifield in the lead. As we are rounding a bend in the trail and can finally see the parking lot I notice as does our small group, a man, that same strange man is now near my vehicle, a 2013 Ford Edge. He shouts and points to what appears to be a broken window on the passenger side window.

"Whose car is this?!" He shouts at us on the weaving trail down to the parking lot where he is standing.

Eddie and Grayson run towards the parking lot in a fast fury to investigate. Eddie shouts to the man, "That's my mom's vehicle!"

I also answer tired, "That's my vehicle!"

The creepy thirty-something year old man stays inches from my vehicle's broken passenger side window, not removing his eyes or distance off me or the newly discovered crime scene in the dirt parking lot. I begin to panic, then I remind myself to remain calm and assess the situation. I ask Melissa Hollifield if I can use her cell phone to call 911. Melissa Hollifield tells me "no." I ask her if I can use her cell phone to call my house and get a hold of my husband. Melissa Hollifield says "no."

I open my Ford Edge to check if anything is stolen as Melissa, Grayson, and Eddie, and the creepy guy next to my vehicle all encourage for me to check my vehicle to see if anything was taken. What I discovered in a hurry was that the entire vehicle was undisturbed except for my well-hidden wallet. My wallet was missing, stolen, and was the only thing gone, along with my passenger side window which was shattered into a million pieces of light green glass, a mess.

The creepy man sandwiching himself between my broken window and his vehicle driver side doors does not let his eyes off me as he points to his white van parked next to my vehicle. He insists that I need to get into his van and look around in the back of his van for my wallet to rule him out as a suspect.

I begin to feel panicky as I am assessing this current situation as getting creepy and scary. Melissa Hollifield yells back to Eddie as she and Grayson begin to walk away towards their vehicle, "Come on Eddie, you can ride with me."

Oh my God. This is not good, I need to get my son and I out of here and this impending danger lurking ever so close to us. I have no protection or phone. I am using my vehicle drivers side as protection for Eddie and I.

I am by the driver's side of my Ford Edge with Eddie near the backseat door on my side. I look in fear across towards the creepy man putting his head through my broken vehicle window on the front passenger side just staring at me directly on the opposite side of him as he seemingly will not remove himself from the crime scene. I quickly turn to Eddie alongside of me, "Get in Eddie, hurry."

I jump in my car just as my butt hits the seat my hand places the key in the ignition and I crank up my engine as I peel out of that parking lot, out of a second layered situation of harm. A second apparent crime scene of an attempted kidnapping of me, a separate crime from my stolen wallet and all that was in my wallet. Green glass was shattered everywhere, the wind blew loudly through the broken window as I sped home to safety. My stomach was in my mouth.

When I arrived home I ran inside with Eddie and screamed to Ed what had just happened. Ed screamed back to me in his frustration of my broken window and stolen wallet. He called 911, the intake 911 operator informed him that no police would be coming to the house to take a police report for something so minor. She instructed him that if I needed to make a report to drive down to the city of Cartersville. I was shocked that no police would come out and take photos and a report and find out who had done this to me. However frustrating the whole situation was, I was powerless to make someone do their job. Ed screamed at me to start calling my credit cards and cancel them. I told him I need to call the insurance company on the broken glass. He got on the phone and began calling my credit card companies and then would hand me the phone. For hours I was on the phone outside by the hood of my Ford Edge still in disbelief staring at my broken window on the passenger side. When I opened the vehicle door I could hear more and more glass, tiny fragments sliding in the door frame. I watched the sunset that Saturday by the hood of my vehicle as I used the hood of my vehicle to write down notes as my mind whirled about in constant conversation with my credit card companies. Every single credit card that I had in my wallet had been used by one set of perpatrators, even during the time frame I was hiking up the mountain side. It must have happened within minutes of me arriving to that dirt parking lot, right about the time we all saw that red and yellow helicopter hovering over the parking lot. Maybe someone had seen what happened, called 911, and that was a police helicopter? I don't know. I just know I am exhausted.

When I got back inside my house from standing on my driveway for hours, Eddie remarks a startling true fact. Eddie says out loud to Ed and I, "Yeah, Grayson and his mom were not shocked that our vehicle was broken into. Grayson's mom would not even allow us to call 911 or call you dad! I am never hanging out with him again. He is low class to do that to us! I hate him."

The next day on Sunday, November 29, 2015 we go to Cartersville City Police Station to make a report. That morning I typed and signed my account of what happened at Pine Mountain's parking lot. The blonde haired male officer took photographs of my vehicle and told us not to drive with a broken window. Informing us that the broken window has tiny pieces of glass that if blown into the eye will cause much damage, especially vulnerable would be the backseat as wind blows backwards into the vehicle.

I reminded the officer that I have Safelite coming to my house tomorrow to replace the glass.

As soon as we arrive back home that early Sunday afternoon on November 29, 2015 the phone rings, it's the police officer that just took our report at the city. He announced that a Bartow County Sheriff is on the way to take the report and to take over the investigation as it falls more in the jurisdiction of the county verses the city.

Within the hour a Bartow County Sheriff arrives, a male and a female officer. They took photos of the window and passed the information along to the detective back at the station in the county. Just as the police are leaving my driveway Jody Lee Smith (male) jogs up the hill, gives me a look of "Oh, shit" as he looks at me and the police. Smith then jogs in the back vacant real estate phase as he does about three times a week. Other than his expression, nothing seemed odd or off, he always jogs past our house to the back area of the undeveloped subdivision.

Around 3:30pm on Sunday November 29, 2015 we get a knock on the front door from Grayson Hollifield and John his Syrian sidekick friend. They both inform me that Henry's dad learned that the abduction at Pine Mountain did not go as planned. They both informed me that prescription drugs to drug and kidnap me were given by Henry's dad to the kidnappers. They both informed me that Henry Smith's dad fears I am going to photograph him and he fears he will be getting caught in the conspiracy of kidnapping and sent the boys to find out about why I was talking to two police officers with my husband and Eddie today.

One thing is for sure, Jody Lee Smith (the male pharmacist) never again has jogged past my house since Sunday, November 29, 2015. It is early March 2017 now as I complete volume one, third edition of I Remember Heaven Before Earth.

In hindsight, it all adds up. I remember Eddie playing at Henry Smith's house at 28 Aaron Lane in the fall months of 2015, after school, on the weekends. Henry Smith led me to his three stall garage. He showed me a pick-up truck, a Tacoma style, burgundy, shiny, there were over eighteen or twenty small bicycles, mostly purple and pink bikes stored in the pick-up bed. Henry told me that his dad gets paid money to get rid of the bikes, that the bikes belong to no one.

Henry's mother informed me that they do not have any formal trash pick-up, it is too expensive, and therefore her husband Jody Lee Smith just takes the trash bags to work and dumps their trash in the hospital dumpster.

I noticed in the garage clear glass mason jars lined up against the wall, inside bones. Chicken bones? I do not know. Then in larger containers of plastic Tupperware two-gallon pitchers were loaded full with larger bones. The bones had a yellow cast to them. I thought bones were supposed to be white? What do I know. I then inquire to Henry's mother as to where did those bones come from and she told me that Henry and the boys dug them up in the back, behind the yard.

I refused to let Eddie play with Henry Smith anymore. I also received information that I believe Henry's father is somehow connected to the disappearance of Jessica Herringa, a Dutch-American girl from west Michigan, still unsolved. Jessica Herringa's facial features look identical to Heather Smith, as they are eerily the same weight and height too. Jessica has blonde hair and blue eyes, Heather Smith has dark brown hair, but if you lightened Heather Smith's hair, you would have a good rendition of Jessica Herringa. The last vehicle to be seen at the crime scene disappearance of Jessica Herringa in west Michigan is the same vehicle description of the vehicle Heather Smith drives, and Jody Lee Smith owns with Georgia plates PBH-1414. Silver Honda Odyssey mini-van, year built 2003-2006.

After I had a close call of being abducted in Georgia, meeting my demise. I would pay more attention in the next days, weeks, months and years to come in what Scott Hickom disclosed to me as our dogs daily would sniff and say hello to each other. I would also begin gathering information on daily walks with my dog George from Nancy Terrill, a senior citizen whom lived with her husband Bill at 37 Roberson Drive until they sold their house in the neighborhood and moved away in late fall 2016. Bill & Nancy Terrill had made it well into their senior years without getting caught at what they do and to whom they victimized. What I could gather from them and clearly see with my own eyes, with age does not come wisdom, with age comes boldness to mention facts boldly as if getting caught by the law at their age was pointless and not a reality they seemingly ever really thought about in their senior years of living and never getting caught thus far. It was such a way of life for them to commit crimes with the group and not ever get arrested or even under the radar.

Both Scott and Nancy disclosed to me that "the group" was involved with human trafficking. The group had ties to the local police. The GBI would never investigate because the police would never request a GBI investigation into the many disappearances. What they informed me of was that the CIA would fly the medicated, drugged woman or child out of the country through the route of small airports. If the woman or child proved to be too difficult they would be killed and disposed of in a bog, swamp, or mountainous wooded area. Often near or on the Appalachian Mountains or out west in a unpopulated area with steep terrain. Dumped out of a helicopter that the CIA owned and operated through front companies and names, just like the airplanes, many of which are in Georgia. They both explained that many times a helicopter is on standby in the air playing watchdog with knowledge of when the law is near or not near at the time of an abduction by the group. Often the helicopter pilot has insider information on the whereabouts of the police. The kidnappings are premediated and very well-orchestrated, a level of trust is involved to coax the victim aside and get the victim into a getaway vehicle. Never are the kidnappings done alone.

As I daily walk George my dog and learn more and more about Rowland Springs Estates and what Scott & Nancy are telling me, I am getting chills. Chills to the parallels to the exact details of what Scott & Nancy are telling me in 2015 and 2016 and what CIA agents told me. Such as but not limited to; CIA David Petraeus and CIA John Brennan told me in the 1990's at The Gold Club. I wasn't drunk, and I could hear what was spoken, even if the music was loud.

Then I am flipping back the pages in my memory book as I often do as I receive new information that correlates somehow to my past, in my past, there is a connection. In 1989 Jamie Smith brought me to Georgia. Jamie's dad John Smith is a helicopter pilot, he learned his trade skill in Vietnam, that's what they told me. One day Jamie took me to Cartersville, Georgia to visit John Smith's mother, Jamie's grandmother. Cartersville was always on the map for John Smith. Six months later after moving down to Georgia, Jamie breaks up with me suddenly, and apparently ran off with some girl. However, they never married, they too broke up rather quickly. Jamie then moved back to Michigan the summer of 1990. Upon his returning back to Michigan Cindy my mother in Michigan lands Jamie Smith a job as a cook in a Nursing Home where she was working at the time.

The whole time I am in high school at Unity and the whole time I am in Georgia, Cindy keeps life insurance on me. She does not pay medical insurance for me or car insurance for me, those bills are my responsibility. Cindy all on her own keeps a life insurance policy on me that I cannot cancel or object to or point a finger to, just live in fear with my eyes wide open is my only option. After a while disgruntled Cindy could not take out life insurance policies on me because of my age and the fact I had not lived under her roof for quite some time. I would always wonder, even as an adult adoptee, why would a Christian adoption agency as Bethany Christian Services ever allow for Cindy & Chuck Vander Ark to adopt me? I do not think I have all the pieces of the puzzle to my life, but I sure do spend time working on fitting in all the puzzle pieces that do puzzle me.

In March of 2016 I turn on my computer and learn from the online internet pop-up articles that Mr. Stuart Dunnings III has been arrested on over twelve charges, some felony charges, some misdemeanor charges. He was then arrested and removed from office as the Ingham County Prosecutor. I read online news of his arrest and charges from news articles from USA Today and The Lansing State Journal. As you remember he was the prosecutor that trumped up stalking charges against me the whistle-blower. I read that the former Ingham County Prosecutor was arrested and removed as the Ingham County Prosecutor in March of 2016 and charged with multiple counts of human trafficking and sex related crimes involving minors under the age of eighteen. Another surprise was the very same week I read online about Stuart Dunnings III getting arrested by the FBI that investigated him in Michigan, I begin receiving that same week of his arrest, weird emails. The weird emails were somehow sent from my email address to my email address. How can that be? I wondered that too and contacted my email hosting company freaking out that someone has used my email address to email me, and if they can hack into my email account who knows where else that hacker will send messages using my email address! I was scared, and rightfully so. I am still on probation from the 55th District Court stalking case whereas the Meridian Township Police and Judge Thomas Boyd and the Ingham County Prosecutor the Jury of six all unanimous convicted me of sending too many emails and voicemails in a stalking harassment case against me. I immediately printed the weird emails of the hacker that got into my email account and wondered what is on that disc of evidence that Judge Thomas Boyd would not allow me to see at my own stalking trial in his courtroom in Mason, Michigan. I then sent the information about the convicted case #12-01740 to the Michigan FBI, the FBI headquarters, the 55th District Court Supervisor with my probation form, and to the Michigan Attorney General, all of whom are legally bound by duty to uphold the U.S. Constitution and federal laws on Due Process. It is now March 2017 and I have never heard anything about my case prosecuted by Stuart Dunnings III on trumped up charges to silence me. Take the time to legally review the evidence and probation conditions. I still mail in my monthly probation forms with restitution fines that I was assigned to pay to the 55th District Court each month until 12/12/12.

2016 was the year I decided I need to include more information about all of this within volume one of I Remember Heaven Before Earth. I have now included so much information in volume one, third edition, and hopefully this manuscript will be published in 2017 with a mainstream literary agent and a traditional publishing company, not self-published this time around.

Because of case #12-01740 stalking misdemeanor the State of Georgia refuses to issue me a State of Georgia real estate salesperson license. Even though I have never had a formal or informal complaint against my Michigan real estate license, ever. I even passed the Georgia real estate salesperson course here in Georgia, I passed the State of Georgia licensing exam for real estate professionals, I paid my licensing real estate fee to be licensed. Then I received a letter from the Georgia Real

Estate Commission that they are denying my real estate license due to a misdemeanor stalking conviction in Michigan, case no. 12-01740.

Now if I was Black I could call the NAACP and they would see to it that I properly receive the Georgia real estate license that I earned rightfully. However, I am White, and therefore I have no legal support.

Eddie began 6th grade at Cartersville Middle School. Eddie informed me that Sam Ford is in his Video Broadcasting class. Eddie refers to the class as "the YouTube class" because he and the groups they are assigned to create YouTube videos. Eddie's YouTube name is Eddie 101. His goal is to have one million subscribers.

I told Eddie to just stay away from Sam Ford, I do not think it is a good idea that he hangs around Sam Ford. He claims Sam Ford is very electronically knowledgeable and is not a bad kid. I decide then to not complain to the school and not to remove Eddie from the class. However, I have made it very clear to Eddie to not ever go home after school with anyone from school.

In the beginning of Eddie entering 6th grade at Cartersville Middle School in August 2016 I noticed a CIA agent working the carline directing cars. A CIA agent that had introduced himself as a CIA agent at The Gold Club during the 1990's in Georgia. I rolled down my window in the CMS carline and say with a big smile, "I recognize you, I don't know if all these other mothers recognize you, but I recognize you!" Then I laugh and roll up my window. I never saw that guy directing cars in the carline at CMS ever again. I can't figure out why. Maybe he is still there, but works only inside now? He is a different CIA agent from the past than the one at the Cartersville Elementary School and seen jumping out of my side porch area with Scott Hickom picking at my front door.

Looking back to the summer of 2014, what was the point of realtor Teresa Smith wanting us to buy 10 Altar Rock Ct.? I had pulled up other real estate listings in our price range, she would look at the sheet and comment, "Oh, that one sold." Over and over she would say that as I flashed listing sheet after listing sheet in front of her in the front seat of her SUV. Teresa Smith did not even call the listing real estate agent to inquire whether or not the listing was sold! Our condo had sold in Michigan, and after all I had been through in Michigan, I'll be damned if I stay living in Michigan. So we bought the most affordable home from the homes Teresa Smith showed us in 2014. I am always making lemonade from lemon situations. However, at some point one just cannot take any more brushing elbows with criminals in this neighborhood and truly still call this place home.

For one year 37 Roberson Drive was for sale, Bill & Nancy's place. Nancy informed me in the fall of 2016 that "the group" was starting forest fires to get rid of human remains from abductions that did not go as planned. On October 25, 2016 I was walking George my dog as Nancy Terrill was walking her dog. Nancy Terrill informed me that her husband Bill started fires near their Blairsville trailer lot due to the fact the GBI was asking too many questions to group members about disappearances of missing people. She informed me that her and Bill were going to go live in an RV so the State of Georgia cannot legally make them register as sex offenders. She told me that Mr. Hall (whom lives in the 4-sided all red brick ranch) started fires near Rome, Georgia for the same reasons her husband Bill started fires in northern Georgia.

I do remember stepping outside in the front yard in the late night hours and early morning hours with my dog George and seeing Mr. Hall come home at odd hours late at night or early in the wee hours. Such as midnight, 6am, and all the in between hours, on a few occasions only during the month of October 2016. Keep in mind, there are twelve months in a year, and for one year I have been stepping out of my house with George my dog so he can pee. George passed away January 24, 2017. George was fourteen years, three days old. In the last year of George's life Ed and I came up with the idea to shut the master bedroom door to keep George from going downstairs in the middle of the night and peeing on our floors. In the last year of George's life he would have to get me up by how he talks to us when he wants something and wake me up. I would then go downstairs put a leash on George and walk him in the front yard so that he could pee around our bushes. In twelve months of getting up at odd hours of the night after I had fallen to sleep to then bring George outside to pee, only the month of October 2016 did Mr. Hall in his white pick-up truck pull into his red brick ranch house driveway at odd hours, which never occurred before, that I noticed and witnessed. I then realized there must be some truth to what Nancy Terrill bragged about to me. Truly it was Nancy bragging, as often confident criminals do brag about crimes. One such confident criminal is Cindy Stob- Vander Ark- Honderd my mother. Cindy Honderd is eighty-two years old and not in jail, she bragged to me about crimes back in the 1970's! Now I know why Cindy Honderd is so confident! The police and FBI have built-up her confidence, just like they built-up senior citizen Nancy Terrill's confidence as a criminal to get away with crimes!

Why do uncaught criminals brag? I think uncaught criminals brag to me and probably others to assert who has power and who should fear them. Why do I write about criminals in my memoirs? To have power over the criminals.

Sometimes I still have nightmares that I am on the bottom of the sea near a sandstone ancient structure covered in water, as I am also covered in ocean water. I was never able to be vindicated by the Roman rumors of the day that I committed suicide by having a lethal snake smuggled into my quarters. I could not spit out the salty sea water for so many passing years and tell my story as I am now. I have no college degree in writing, my writing skills come from accumulated knowledge, including my formative years in west Michigan. I have a will to tell what happened to me and explain all that I lost, and how I lost. As I swim to the surface I could face sharks, I am not out of the water, and I am not out of danger.

Do you realize the glue that holds together religion, an audience, a government, societies ideologies? A common belief works to gel and unify people together.

What if the common core belief is wrong? I can only suggest to re-explore history for the truth.

Eddie in 6th grade recently told me that they are celebrating Black History Month in school with assemblies geared in theme to Black

History Month. Eddie told me recently that a kid in line asked the teacher, "Isn't it racist to have Black History Month and to celebrate at school with Black History assemblies?"

I asked Eddie, "Well, what did the teacher have to say to the kid?"

Eddie answers, "The teacher just laughed."

I responded to Eddie, "I agree with the kid, it is racist to have Black History Month and special assemblies at school celebrating and honoring just Blacks."

Do corrupt people believe I am a royal ass? Perhaps.

Why do I wear a red Calvin Klein coat in a photograph on my Amazon Author Page? Red is the color of the American Heart Association. When my story is read, I believe there could be some heart attacks.

The focus of my compounded stories is for everyone to examine ideologies. The premise is for readers to understand mysteries lost in time, but not forgotten by me.

Let me say in closing what I wrote in the beginning of this journey, "Sometimes we are lucky enough to know that our lives have been changed, to discard the old, embrace the new, and run headlong down an immutable course. It happened to me.....on that summer's day, when my eyes were opened to the sea."

~ Jacques Yves Cousteau ~
(a quote from TheSea.com)

THE END

www.ingramcontent.com/pod-product-compliance
Lightning Source LLC
Chambersburg PA
CBHW081751300426
44116CB00014B/2093